The Germania of Tacitus

A critical edition by
Rodney Potter Robinson

1991
Georg Olms Verlag
Hildesheim · Zürich · New York

Dem Nachdruck liegt das Exemplar der
Universitätsbibliothek Erlangen zugrunde.

Signatur: Phl. A-I-162 [5]

(Ursprünglich erschienen in:
Philological Monographs published by the American
Philological Association, V.)

Nachdruck der Ausgabe Middletown, Connecticut 1935
Printed in Germany
Alle Rechte vorbehalten
Herstellung: WS Druckerei Werner Schaubruch GmbH, Bodenheim
Auf säurefreiem Papier gedruckt
ISBN 3-487-09523-8

The Germania of Tacitus

A Critical Edition

BY

RODNEY POTTER ROBINSON
PROFESSOR OF CLASSICS AND FELLOW OF THE GRADUATE SCHOOL
IN
THE UNIVERSITY OF CINCINNATI

Published by the American Philological Association
Middletown, Connecticut
1935

TO
PROFESSOR WILLIAM ABBOTT OLDFATHER
THIS VOLUME
IS AFFECTIONATELY DEDICATED

PREFACE

My interest in the textual criticism of the *Germania* dates from almost twenty years ago (*grande mortalis aeui spatium*), and was coincident with my work upon the text of the *de Grammaticis et Rhetoribus* of Suetonius. Inasmuch as my examination and classification of the manuscripts of this Suetonius fragment yielded results which were of value for improving its text, I naturally began to wonder whether the manuscripts of the *Germania*, deriving as they do from the same archetype as the *de Grammaticis*, had yielded all their secrets. My doubts on the matter seemed all the more well-founded, when I learned that the standard texts of the *Germania* were based upon only five or six out of a total of nearly thirty manuscripts.

The actual preparation of the present edition has extended over a period of more than twelve years, with several interruptions, some of considerable length. Whether or not the results justify the large amount of time and labor expended must be for others to decide. Although I can lay no claim to having remade the text of the *Germania*, which has never been among the most corrupt, I do believe that my collation of all the extant manuscripts, my classification of these manuscripts with reference to the Hersfeld codex, their common archetype, my investigation of the manuscript evidence in the light of the information afforded by the extant fragment of the Hersfeld codex, and in particular my searching examination of the grossly neglected codex Vindobonensis 711, have all resulted in placing the text of the *Germania* on a much firmer manuscript foundation than has heretofore existed. I have convinced myself that in some places I have restored the text *pristino nitori*, that in other places I have with justification recalled to the text readings which had been banished because of a misconception of the manuscript relationship. In still other places, where previous editors have disagreed regarding the choice between two variants, I hope that I have shown conclusively which of the variants has the best claim to authenticity. Finally, I trust that I have established certain general principles which future textual critics of the *Germania* will not wish to ignore, and in addition I trust that my discussion of the codex Aesinas may prove of value to editors of the *Agricola*, and possibly to students of Latin textual criticism in general.

In establishing the text of the *Germania* I have preferred to err on the side of caution rather than of extravagance. My purpose throughout has been to restore as accurately as I could the text of the Hersfeld codex, and to depart from this text only where there seemed to be cogent reasons for so doing. To those familiar with *Germania* textual problems my critical apparatus will present an unfamiliar appearance. Many time-honored variants I have cast out, convinced as I am that the evidence proves them to be of fifteenth-century origin, while to other variants, which have received little or no consideration in the past, I have given the prominence which I am led to believe they merit. Having classified the manuscripts in the Introduction, with citations of readings copious enough, I trust, to satisfy the most exacting, I have aimed at conciseness in the critical apparatus, admitting as a rule only those readings which appear to offer something toward the restoration of the two lost apographs of the Hersfeld codex, **X** and **Y**. However, because of the importance of codex Vindobonensis 711, and because of the neglect from which it has suffered in the past, I have attempted to record all the variants of this manuscript with the following exceptions: orthographical details, errors made *currente calamo* and corrected by the scribe, corrections made by the second hand. For the orthographical details of the manuscripts the reader is referred to pages 235-260. Emendations proposed by various scholars I have quoted sparingly, using them chiefly as a means of calling attention to difficulties inherent in the manuscript tradition. In making my selection I have shown some partiality to emendations proposed within the last thirty-five or forty years, feeling that these more recent ones may not yet have received due consideration from students of the *Germania*.

One reviewer of my edition of the *de Grammaticis et Rhetoribus* expressed regret that my commentary was not more comprehensive, since it clearly reached beyond the bounds of a critical commentary. Some may feel that the commentary of the present edition is subject to the same criticism. In neither work was it my intention to go beyond the limits of a critical commentary, but the line of demarcation between a critical and an exegetical commentary is not always easy to define, since any consideration of a textual problem necessarily involves the interpretation of the passage in question.

The plan of this edition has demanded that numerous passages of the *Germania* be discussed in the Introduction rather than in the notes accompanying the text. I trust, however, that the cross-references will obviate any difficulty which the reader might otherwise experience. The Bibliography includes all works pertaining primarily to Tacitus which are cited anywhere in the course of the volume, and all works of whatsoever nature to which reference is made in the critical apparatus. For works not included in these two classifications bibliographical data are given at the first place of citation. My citations from ancient authors are made from the standard critical editions.

I was first enabled to begin my *Germania* studies through the kindness of Dean Louis Trenchard More of the Graduate School of Arts and Sciences of the University of Cincinnati, who allocated to me funds for the purchase of photostats of manuscripts, and I am glad to have this opportunity of expressing my gratitude to him. To Professor William Tunstall Semple, head of the department of classics in the University of Cincinnati, I offer my warm thanks for his constant encouragement, for relieving me of many routine duties which would have interfered with my study, and for placing at my disposal departmental funds for the services of a research assistant and for the purchase of books and photostats. To my colleagues in the department of classics, and to Professor Roy Kenneth Hack in particular, I acknowledge my indebtedness for friendly interest and for numerous helpful suggestions regarding textual matters. Great indeed is my obligation to my wife, Dr. Rachel Sargent Robinson, who for four years has been my most searching and most helpful critic, and who, to the neglect of her own special field of Greek economic life, has rendered me invaluable assistance in the arrangement and revision of the contents of this volume. To the library of the University of Cincinnati, and to the many libraries both in the United States and in Europe which have aided me in the preparation of this edition, I offer my thanks. The names of the libraries which so courteously permitted me to examine and to have photographed their manuscripts and rare volumes will be found in the Description of the manuscripts (79–90) and in the Bibliography. I am under special obligation to Sr. D. Pedro Longas y Bartibas of the Biblioteca Nacional of Madrid, who located for me the hitherto unnoticed Matritensis of the *Germania*, and to the Centro Germano-Español of Madrid for kindly providing me with photostats of the Toletanus. Finally, I wish to thank the American Philological Association for the publication of this volume, which I fear has proved both troublesome and costly, and the Editor of the Philological Monographs, Professor Joseph William Hewitt, for his utmost consideration and patience, and for correcting many errors which might otherwise have escaped my notice.

This volume is inscribed to my friend and former teacher, who has always manifested a keen and sympathetic interest in my scholarly endeavors, and under whose guidance I first became acquainted with the Hersfeld codex.

AMERICAN ACADEMY IN ROME,
November, 1935.

ADDENDA ET CORRIGENDA

Pages 13-14. An examination of the manuscripts of the *Dialogus* which, with the aid of two of my students, I have undertaken since writing these pages leads me to believe that codex Ottobonianus 1455 (O) descends from **Y**, *i.e.* from the same apograph of the Hersfeld codex as all the other manuscripts with the exception of Vindobonensis 711 (W). It was, however, copied from **Y** before this lost manuscript had received the numerous corrections and interpolations of fifteenth-century scholars which are to be found in its other descendants. I strongly suspect that a re-examination of the manuscript evidence of the *de Grammaticis et Rhetoribus* will show that the same situation obtains for this work as well.

Page 80. In codex **b** the text found in the lower margins of the pages of the *Germania* and on the verso of f. 42 is not that of a commentary on the *Germania*, as I was led to believe by the description in the Catalogue of the Harley manuscripts, but consists of excerpts from Solinus followed by a brief mediaeval or renaissance treatise on the geography of western Europe, which I have not identified.

Page 278, ch. 4, 2, *aliis aliarum nationum conubiis*. Gudeman (1928) aptly cites by way of comparison *Dial.* 10, 18 f., *ceteris aliarum artium studiis*, where, to be sure, the manuscript tradition is sometimes questioned.

Page 305, ch. 28, 15 f., *decumathes agros*. It was only after the present volume was in the hands of the printer that a second masterly work by E. Norden dealing with Germanic pre-history became available for my use: *Alt-Germanien, Völker- und Namengeschichtliche Untersuchungen*, Berlin and Leipzig, 1934. The third section of this work (137-190) bears the title, "*Decumates Agri* in Tacitus' Germania," and is devoted to a searching investigation of the meaning of *decumates*. I regret that Norden has not even mentioned the variant *decumathes*, which, I am persuaded, has the better manuscript authority. In view of the convincing evidence set forth by Norden that *decumates agri* originally designated a territory of ten divisions (*Zehenschaftslande, Zehenschaftsmarken*, "ten-canton lands"), some will probably feel that I have been rash to admit the spelling *decumathes* to my text, regardless of the manuscript tradition. Nevertheless, it is a fact that either form is ἅπαξ εἰρημένον. Norden, in agreement with Hesselmeyer, sees in *decumates* a latinized Gallic word, but may there not have been a step in the transfer of the word which they have failed to take into account? That is, may not the word have been introduced into Latin through Greek ethnographic literature, and might not such a descent have had a bearing on its spelling? Clearly, it is a matter for the comparative philologist to determine, and in the meantime I prefer to adhere to my general practice of allowing the better attested manuscript reading to make good the absence of inscriptional evidence.

Page 323, ch. 46, 1. Add to critical apparatus: finis *Puteolanus*, fines ω.

Pages 351–356. An article by C. W. Mendell, "Discovery of the minor works of Tacitus," *American Journal of Philology* LVI (1935), 113–130, appeared after this volume was in press. I fully agree with Mendell that Enoch of Ascoli did not bring the Hersfeld codex to Rome, but I remain unconvinced that two, or even three (p. 126), manuscripts of the *Germania* were brought from Germany to Rome in the fifteenth century. My examination of the internal evidence of the *Germania* manuscripts satisfies me that all are descended from the Hersfeld codex, with which I identify (again in agreement with Mendell) the manuscript described by Decembrio and the fragment of the *Agricola* now preserved in the codex Aesinas. To my mind, the simpler and more probable way of dealing with the difficulties which Mendell seeks to explain is to assume that the minor Tacitean works formed no part of the discoveries of Enoch of Ascoli.

CONTENTS

INTRODUCTION—THE MANUSCRIPT TRADITION OF THE *GERMANIA* 1–268

I. The Archetype of the Extant Manuscripts ... 1–78
   1. The Quest of the Hersfeld Codex 1–14
   2. The Codex Aesinas 14–30
   3. Variant Readings and Sources of Corruption in the Hersfeld *Agricola* 30–56
   4. The Ancestry of the Hersfeld Codex ... 57–78

II. The Extant Manuscripts of the *Germania* ... 79–268
   1. Description 79–90
   2. Classification 90–235
      a. The Division of the Manuscripts into the **X** and **Y** Families 91–153
      b. Codex Vindobonensis 711 153–157
      c. Codex Monacensis 5307 157–162
      d. Codex Hummelianus 162–177
      e. The α Group 177–190
      f. The β Group 190–211
      g. The φ Group 211–233
      h. Codex Stutgartiensis 233–235
   3. Orthography and Other Details 235–268
      Orthography 235–236
         Vowels 236–245
         Consonants 245–255
         Prefixes 255–260
      Traces of *scriptura continua* 260–261
      Separation of prefixes and enclitics 261–262
      Punctuation 262–264
      Paragraphing 264–268
      Capitalization 268

THE *GERMANIA* OF TACITUS................ 269–326
   Sigla.. 270
   Text, Critical Apparatus, and Critical Notes...... 271–326

APPENDICES................................ 327–359
   I. A Survey of the Textual History of the *Germania* 327–350
   II. Enoch of Ascoli and the Hersfeld Codex 351–356
   III. Abbreviations and Ligatures in the Hersfeld *Agricola*.................................. 357–358

BIBLIOGRAPHY.............................. 359–379

INDEX 380–388

PLATE—*Stemma Codicum*.................... *facing* 388

INTRODUCTION

The Manuscript Tradition of the Germania

I

THE ARCHETYPE OF THE EXTANT MANUSCRIPTS[1]

1. THE QUEST OF THE HERSFELD CODEX

All extant manuscripts of the *Germania* are of the fifteenth or early sixteenth century, and descend by varying degrees from an archetype containing the minor Tacitean works and the *de Grammaticis et Rhetoribus* of Suetonius, which was brought to Rome from the German monastery of Hersfeld between the years 1429 and 1455, but is now lost save for a portion of the *Agricola*. Our knowledge of this Hersfeld codex is derived from the correspondence of Italian humanists,

---

[1] The existence of a manuscript of the *Germania* in Fulda or its vicinity around the middle of the ninth century is indicated by the quotations of Rudolph of Fulda in his *Translatio Sancti Alexandri*, an account of the transfer of the bones of Saint Alexander from Rome to Saxony in 851 (cf. M. Manitius, *Geschichte der lateinischen Literatur des Mittelalters* I [Munich, 1911], 670–672). Without making the slightest acknowledgment of his source, Rudolph appropriates almost verbatim in his first chapter part of *Germ.* 4, and in his second chapter all *Germ.* 9–10 and part of 11 (see p. 278, pp. 285 f.). The existence in the same general region of Germany of a manuscript of the first part of the *Annals* is shown by a passage in the so-called *Annales Fuldenses* under the events of the year 852 (ed. Pertz, *MG SS* I, 368): *Igitur in loco qui appellatur Mimida, super amnem, quem Cornelius Tacitus, scriptor rerum a Romanis in ea gente gestarum, Visurgim* (*Ann.* I, 70, II, 11. 12. 16. 17), *moderni vero Wisaraha vocant.* . . . According to S. Hellmann, "Die Entstehung und Ueberlieferung der Annalen Fuldenses I," *Neues Archiv der Gesellschaft für ältere deutsche Geschichtskunde* XXXIII (1908), 697–742, whose conclusions are accepted by Manitius (*op. cit.* I, 674), the first part of the *Annales Fuldenses* (for the years 714–887) is the work of an anonymous author residing in Mainz, though it was formerly supposed that this work was compiled by Einhart, Rudolph, and Meigenhart, and that the reference to Tacitus came from Rudolph.

For such information as has been gleaned regarding the currency of the works of Tacitus in antiquity and in the Middle Ages see the accounts of Cornelius, Haverfield 1916, Massmann, Müllenhoff, Ramorino, Schanz (*Geschichte der römischen Litteratur* II, 2³ [Munich, 1913]).

chiefly letters of Poggio Bracciolini to Niccolò Niccoli, from an inventory of manuscripts prepared by Niccolò, and finally from a fragment of the codex itself embracing a part of the *Agricola* now preserved in MS. Lat. No. 8 of the private library of Count Balleani in Jesi.

Poggio and the Hersfeld Monk

The earliest mention of the Hersfeld codex is found in a letter of Poggio written in Rome on November 3, 1425, to the Florentine Niccolò Niccoli:[1] . . . Quidam monachus amicus meus ex quodam monasterio Germaniae, qui olim a nobis recessit, ad me misit litteras, quas nudius quartus accepi; per quas scribit se reperisse aliqua volumina de nostris, quae permutare vellet cum Novella Ioannis Andreae vel tum Speculo tum Additionibus, et nomina librorum mittit interclusa. . . . Inter ea volumina est Iulius Frontinus et aliqua opera Cornelii Taciti nobis ignota: videbis inventarium et quaeres illa volumina legalia, si reperiri poterunt commodo pretio. Libri ponentur in Nurimberga, quo et deferri debent Speculum et Additiones, et exinde magna est facultas libros advehendi. Vt videbis per inventarium, haec est particula quaedam, nam multi alii restant; scribit enim in hunc modum: "Sicuti mihi supplicastis de notando poetas, ut ex his eligeretis qui vobis placerent, inveni multos e quibus collegi aliquos, quos in cedula hac inclusa reperietis" . . . Romae die III novembris.

More detailed information regarding the discoveries mentioned by Poggio is given in a letter of Panormita (Antonio Beccadelli) to Guarino of Verona,[2] written in Bologna in

---

[1] *Poggii Epistolae*, ed. Tonelli (Florence, 1832) I, 168. Also printed by R. Sabbadini, *Storia e critica di testi latini* (Catania, 1914), 263, and "Notizie storico-critiche di alcuni codici latini," *Studi Italiani* VII (1899), 99–136 (119).

[2] Guarino had previously had an inkling of the discovery from his friend, the Bolognese Giovanni Lamola, as is gathered from his letter to Lamola dated January 26, 1426: . . . Quid nuntius renascentium virorum et in lucem prolatorum, quem mihi cum suavitate mirabili affers? O si Cornelium Tacitum ipsum, Plinii mei amicum socium collegam, spectare et coram affari detur! *Epistolario di Guarino Veronese*, ed. R. Sabbadini (Venice, 1915–1919), I. 503; also published by Sabbadini, *Stud. Ital.* VII, 120, *Stor. e crit.* 264.

April of the following year (1426):[1] . . . Compertus est Cor. Taciti de origine et situ Germanorum. Item eiusdem de vita Iulii Agricolae isque incipit: "Clarorum virorum facta" caeterave. Quinetiam Sex. Iulii Frontonis de aquaeductibus qui in urbem Romam inducuntur; et est litteris aureis transcriptus. Item eiusdem Frontonis liber alter, qui in hunc modum iniciatur: "Cum omnis res ab imperatore delegata mentionem exigat" et caetera. Et inventus est quidam dyalogus de oratore et est, ut coniectamus, Cor. Taciti, atque is ita incipit: "Saepe ex me requirunt" et caetera. Inter quos et liber Suetonii Tranquilli repertus de grammaticis et rhetoribus: huic inicium est: "Grammatica Romae." Hi et innumerabiles alii qui in manibus versantur, et praeterea alii fortasse qui in usu non sunt, uno in loco simul sunt; ii vero omnes, qui ob hominum ignaviam in desuetudinem abierant ibique sunt, cuidam mihi coniunctissimo dimittentur propediem, ab illo autem ad me proxime et de repente; tu secundo proximus eris, qui renatos sane illustrissimos habiturus sis. . . .

The next notice of our manuscript is in a letter written by Poggio to Niccolò on May 17, 1427, after the monk, who, as we now learn, came from Hersfeld, had paid a second visit to Rome, bringing with him another inventory of manuscripts, which greatly disappointed Poggio in his hopes of finding rare treasures:[2] Dixeram Cosmo nostro, quemadmodum scribis, monachum illum Hersfeldensem dixisse cuidam se attulisse inventarium, sicut ei scripseram, plurium voluminum secundum notam meam. Postmodum cum summa cura quaererem hunc hominem, venit ad me afferens inventarium plenum verbis, re vacuum. Vir ille bonus, expers studiorum nostrorum, quicquid reperit ignotum sibi id et apud nos incognitum putavit. Itaque refersit illud libris quos habemus, qui sunt iidem de quibus alias cognovisti. Mitto autem ad te nunc

[1] Published by Sabbadini, *Epist. di Guarino* I, 519; *Stud. Ital.* VII, 122; *Stor. e crit.* 267 ff. The letter is not dated. Here and elsewhere I follow the chronology of Sabbadini.

[2] *Epist.*, ed. Tonelli, I, 207 f.; Sabbadini, *Stud. Ital.* VII, 127; *Stor. e crit.* 272; Michaelis, *praef. ad Dialog.* xx.

partem inventarii sui, in quo describitur volumen illud Cornelii Taciti et aliorum quibus caremus; qui cum sint res quaedam parvulae, non satis magno sunt aestimandae. Decidi ex maxima spe quam conceperam ex verbis suis. Ea extitit causa propter quam non magnopere curavi hoc ad te scribere; nam si quid egregium fuisset aut dignum Minerva nostra, non solum scripsissem sed ipse advolassem ut significarem. Hic monachus eget pecunia; ingressus sum sermonem subveniendi sibi, dummodo Ammianus Marcellinus, prima decas Titi Livii et unum volumen orationum Tullii ex iis quae sunt apud nos communes et nonnulla alia opera, quae quamvis ea habeamus tamen non sunt negligenda, dentur mihi pro his pecuniis. Peto autem illa deferri eorum periculo usque Nurimbergam. Haec tracto, nescio quid concludam, omnia tamen a me scies postea. Romae xvi kal. iunii (1427).

Another letter of Poggio to Niccolò, written on May 31 of the same year (1427), shows that he had forgotten to send the monk's second inventory as he had promised, but was then enclosing it. Evidently Niccolò had taxed Poggio with indifference regarding the manuscript of Tacitus, but the latter now assures him that this is the one which he wants most of all, and that he had ordered the monk to bring it in person to Rome or to send it by another monk.[1]

In September of the same year Poggio was still awaiting a reply from the Hersfeld monk, as he plaintively writes to Niccolò:[2] De Cornelio Tacito qui est in Germania nil sentio; expecto responsum ab illo monacho. . . . Omisi hanc curam librorum absentium et ad eos qui adsunt nobis animum con-

[1] Optime suspicaris me cum obsignarem litteras oblitum esse illius inventarii, cuius mentionem feceram in litteris. Nunc illud ad te mitto. Id autem male accipis quia, cum procurem ut habeamus decadem Livii et reliqua volumina de quibus ad te scripsi, putes me omittere hoc volumen quo maxime indigemus. Id quidem imprimis est quod volo, quin mandavi isti monacho ut vel ipse secum deferret (nam credit se rediturum brevi) vel per alium monachum curaret deferendum; alios iussi Nurimbergam, hunc vero Romam proficisci recta via, et ita se facturum recepit. Romae pridie kal. Iun. (*1427*). *Epist.*, ed. Tonelli, I, 210 f.; Michaelis, *praef. ad Dialog.* xxi.

[2] *Epist.*, ed. Tonelli, I, 213; Michaelis, *ib.*

verti; nam nil audio praeter fabulas. After the lapse of a year, he again writes:[1] . . . Cornelius Tacitus silet inter Germanos neque quicquam exinde novi percepi de eius operibus.

The latest mention of the Hersfeld codex in the correspondence of Poggio is in a letter to Niccolò dated February 26, 1429. The Hersfeld monk had returned to Rome, but without the book![2] . . . Monachus Hersfeldensis venit absque libro multumque est a me increpatus ob eam causam. Asseveravit se cito rediturum (nam litigat nomine monasterii) et portaturum librum. Rogavit me multa: dixi me nil facturum nisi librum haberemus. Ideo spero et illum nos habituros, quia eget favore nostro.

With this the curtain falls on Poggio and his unfruitful dealings with the evasive monk. Or dare we suspect that Poggio had actually obtained possession of the book which he coveted, using the alleged perversity of the Hersfeld monk as a cloak to hide his newly found treasure from his too inquisitive friends?

The Inventory of Niccolò Niccoli

Even though Poggio may actually have given up hope of securing the elusive Hersfeld codex, his friend Niccolò Niccoli continued the search. Early in the year 1431 the latter took advantage of the departure of the two cardinals, Giuliano Cesarini and Niccolò Albergati, who were setting out as papal legates for Germany and France respectively,[3] giving each a copy of an inventory of books for which they were to search, as we learn from a letter of the Florentine monk, Ambrogio Traversari, written to Niccolò Niccoli on July 8, 1431:[4] Quod indicem dederis voluminum inquirendorum cum Iuliano nostro cardinali S. Angeli tum cardinali S. Crucis, Germaniam omnem omnemque Galliam diverso itinere peragraturis, fecisti tu studiose et ingenio tuo digne. Sed vereor ne cum occiduo

---

[1] *Epist.*, ed. Tonelli, I, 218; Michaelis, *ib.* The letter is dated Sept. 11, 1428.
[2] *Epist.*, ed. Tonelli, I, 268; Michaelis, xxii.
[3] See Sabbadini, *Stor. e crit.* 3.
[4] *Traversarii Epistolae*, ed. Petrus Cannetus, VIII, 2, 353; also Sabbadini, *Stor. e crit.* 2.

gelu eorum quoque refrigescat ardor: quamvis Lucius ille [1]
adolescens promptus atque excitus magna de se polliceri
videatur; vixque adduci possum illum non diligentissime hoc
munus impleturum.   Gustum illius cepi, brevem quidem; nam
transiens per nos me vidit atque adlocutus est tanta suavitate
atque copia, ut spem de illo conceperim maximam.   Thomas [2]
item noster, non ambigo geret votis tuis morem. . . .

By some good fortune a copy of Niccolò's inventory came
to light in 1913, at the end of a manuscript of some of the
philosophical works of Cicero.[3] The inventory bears the inscription, *COMMENTARIVM NICOLAI NICOLI IN PEREGRINATIONE GERMANIE.*

I quote here that part of the inventory which deals with
the Monastery of Hersfeld:

In Monasterio hispildensi [4] haud procul ab alpibus continentur
  haec opuscula. videlicet:
Julii Frontini De aquae ductis quae in urbem inducunt liber j.
  Incipit sic: PERSECVTVS ea quae de modulis dici fuit necessarium. Nunc ponam quemadmodum queque aqua ut principium commentariis comprehensum est usque ad nostram curam
  habere visa sit &c.   Continet hic liber xiij.
Item eiusdem frontini liber incipit sic: Cum omnis res ab imperatore
  delegata interiorem exigat & curam & me seu naturalis solicitudo
  seu fides sedula, non ad diligentiam modo, uerum ad morem
  commisse rei instigent, sitque mihi nunc ab nerua augusto,
  nescio diligentiore an amantiore rei .p. imperatore aquarum
  iniunctum officium & ad usum &c.   Continet .xi. folia.
Cornelii taciti de origine & situ germanorum liber incipit sic:
  Germania omnis a gallis [5] rhetiisque et pannoniis rheno & danubio

---

[1] Luigi da Spoleto, secretary to Cesarini.

[2] Tomasso Parentucelli, secretary of Albergati, and later Pope Nicholas V.

[3] The manuscript is now in New York in the Morgan Library. I have edited the *Commentarium* from photographs in *Class. Phil.* XVI (1921), 251-255. It was first published in the antiquarian catalogue of the Florentine dealers, T. de Marinis e Com. (1913), 14-16, and was reprinted from this catalogue by E. Jacobs in *Wochenschrift für klassische Philologie* XXX (1913), 701 f. See also Gudeman *ibid.* 929-933; W. Aly, *Rh. Mus.* LXVIII (1913), 636 f.; Sabbadini, *Stor. e crit.* 1-7.

[4] Read *hersfeldensi.*

[5] Corr. from *galiis.*

fluminibus a sarmatis datisque & mutuo metu a montibus
separatur etc. Continet autem xij folia. Item in eodem codice:
Cornelii taciti De uita Iulii agricole Incipit sic: Clarorum uirorum
facta moresque posteris tradere antiquitus usitatum, ne nostris
quidem temporibus, quamquam uniuersa suorum etas omisit.
Qui liber continet. xiiij. folia. Item in eodem codice:
Dialogus De oratoribus qui incipit sic: Sepe ex me requiris iuste
fabi, cur cum priora secula tot eminentium oratorum ingeniis,
gloria, floruerint: nostra potissimum etas deserta & laude elo-
quentiae orbata: qui liber continet xviij. folia. Item in eodem
codice continetur liber—
Suetonii Tranquilli De grammaticis & rhetoribus, qui incipit sic:
Grammatica romae ne in usu quidem olim nedum in honore ullo
&c. Continet hic liber folia vij.
Ammiani Marcellini rerum gestarum libri xviij. Qui peruenerunt
usque ad obitum Valentis imperatoris: qui est finis hystoriae.

There can be no reasonable doubt that this part of the
Commentarium of Niccolò was compiled from the two inven-
tories which Poggio had received from the Hersfeld monk, one
in October, 1425, the other in May of 1427.[1] The works
enumerated are the same as those mentioned in the letter of
Panormita quoted above,[2] with the exception of the Ammianus,
to which reference is first made in Poggio's letter of May 17,
1427, just after he had received the second inventory from the
monk. We may therefore assume that the earlier inventory,
upon which Panormita's account was based, contained no
mention of the Ammianus. The *Commentarium* and Panormita agree in treating the first and second books of Frontinus
as separate works and in listing them in reverse order, while
the reason for Panormita's doubt regarding the authorship of
the *Dialogus* is made clear by the *Commentarium*, which does
not give the name of the author.[3] It is true that Poggio in his
letter of May, 1427, mentions a volume of Cicero's orations
and the first decade of Livy, neither of which is listed in the
Commentarium, but Niccolò may purposely have omitted

[1] See p. 2, p. 3.
[2] See p. 3.
[3] See my discussion of this point on p. 12.

these items, since, as Poggio stated, the works were already known.

No word has come to us regarding the outcome of Niccolò's quest of the Hersfeld codex, but we may well suspect that the search bore no fruit, since there is no further mention of this manuscript for almost twenty-five years. Through whose agency the manuscript was brought to Rome we do not know,[1] but certain it is that it was there in 1455, for in this year it was seen by Pier Candido Decembrio.

The Note of Decembrio

A precious bit of evidence regarding the Hersfeld codex was brought to light in 1901 by R. Sabbadini in the form of an autograph note of the scholar and papal secretary, Pier Candido Decembrio. The text of the note is as follows:[2]

Cornelii taciti liber reperitur Rome uisus 1455 de Origine et situ Germanie. Incipit:

Germania omnis a Gallis retiisque et panoniis Rheno et danubio fluminibus a Sarmatis dacisque mutuo metu aut montibus seperatur. cetera occeanus ambit. Opus est foliorum xii in columnellis. Finit: Cetera iam fabulosa helusios et oxionas ora hominum uultusque corpora atque artus ferarum gerere. quod ego ut incompertum in medium relinquam. utitur autem cornelius hoc uocabulo inscientia non Inscitia.

Est alius liber eiusdem de uita Julii agricole soceri sui. in quo continetur descriptio Britanie Insule, nec non populorum mores et ritus. Incipit:

Clarorum uirorum facta moresque posteris tradere antiquitus usitatum, ne nostris quidem temporibus quamquam incuriosa suorum etas ommisit. Opus foliorum decem et quattuor in columnellis. finit: Nam multos ueluti inglorios et ignobiles obliuio obruet, Agricola posteritati narratus et traditus superstes erit.

[1] I do not subscribe to the commonly accepted view that the Hersfeld codex was brought to Rome in 1455 by Enoch of Ascoli. See appendix II.

[2] Published by Sabbadini from *cod. Ambros. R 88 sup.*, f. 112, in *Rivista di filologia classica* XXIX (1901), 262–264. The text of the note as I give it is reprinted from my work on the manuscripts of the *de Grammaticis* (Robinson 1922, 15 f.), where I edited it from a photostat kindly secured for my use by the University of Illinois. My text does not differ from that of Sabbadini except in matters of punctuation, capitalization, and paragraphing.

Cornelii taciti dialogus de oratoribus incipit: Sepe ex me requiris iuste fabi, cur cum priora secula tot eminentium oratorum ingeniis gloriaque floruerint, nostra potissimum etas deserta et laude eloquentie orbata vix nomen ipsum oratoris retineat.

Opus foliorum xiiii. in columnellis. post hec deficiunt sex folia. nam finit: quam ingentibus uerbis prosequuntur. Cum ad ueros iudices uentum. deinde sequitur: rem cogitare, nihil abiectum nihil humile. post hec sequuntur folia duo cum dimidio. et finit: Cum adrisissent [1] discessimus.

Suetonii tranquilli de grammaticis et rhetoribus liber. Incipit: Grammatica rome nec in usu quidem olim, nedum in honore ullo erat, rudis scilicet ac bellicosa etiam tum ciuitate necdum magnopere liberalibus disciplinis uacante.

Opus foliorum septem in columnellis. finit perprius. Et rursus in cognitione cedis mediolani apud lucium pisonem proconsulem defendens reum, cum cohiberent lictores nimias laudantium uoces, ita excanduisset, ut deplorato Italie statu quasi iterum in formam prouincie redigeretur .M. Insuper brutum cuius statua in conspectu erat inuocaret Regum ac libertatis auctorem ac uindicem. Vltimo Imperfecto columnello finit: diu ac more concionantis redditis, abstinuit cibo.

Videtur in illo opere Suetonius innuere omnes fere rhetores et Grammatice professores, desperatis fortunis finiuisse uitam.

A comparison of Decembrio's note with the *Commentarium* of Niccolò can leave no doubt that both are describing the same manuscript. The works listed are the same, they are given in the same order, and except for the *Dialogus* there is agreement as to the number of leaves occupied by the text of each.

Since these two important sources of information regarding the Hersfeld codex are sometimes at variance, it becomes necessary to test their respective validity by examining their points of difference in the light of evidence afforded by the extant manuscripts of the *Germania, Agricola, Dialogus,* and *de Grammaticis:*

---

[1] After *adrisissent* Decembrio first wrote *surrex*, but deleted it.

10 The Germania of Tacitus

		Commentarium Nicolai	*Decembrio*	*Codices*
Germania				
(i)		Inscr. Cornelii taciti de origine & situ germanorum ...	Cornelii taciti ... de Origine et situ Germanie ...	Cornelii Taciti de Origine et Situ Germanorum ...[1] Wm **ΔI** V b, ... Germanorum ... *etiam in* M LE s, C. Cornelii Taciti de origine et situ Germaniae ... **N**, ... Germaniae ... *etiam in* χ o π
(ii)		1, 2 & mutuo	mutuo	mutuo
(iii)		a montibus	aut montibus	aut montibus
(iv)		16, 6 * * *	utitur autem cornelius hoc uocabulo "inscientia" non "Inscitia"	inscitia
Agricola				
(v)		1, 3 uniuersa	incuriosa	incuriosa
(vi)		46, 21 * * *	multos	multos ueterum *cod. Hf.*[2]
(vii)		* * *	ueluti	uelud *cod. Hf.*
Dialogvs				
(viii)		Inscr. Dialogus De oratoribus ...	Cornelii taciti dialogus de oratoribus ...	Dialogus de Oratoribus W, Corneli Taciti Dialogus de Oratoribus ω [3]
(ix)		1, 2 gloria	gloriaque	gloriaque
(x)		35, 19 qui liber continet xviij. folia	opus foliorum xiiii. in columnellis. post hec deficiunt sex folia ... post hec sequuntur folia duo cum dimidio.	hic est defectus unius folii cum dimidio W, hic deest multum: in exemplari dicunt deesse sex paginas O, Hic desunt sex pagelle V, deerant in exemplari sex pagelle uetustate consumptę L, hic deficiunt quatuor parue pagellę M[4]

[1] For a detailed report of the manuscript evidence see *apparatus criticus*.

[2] For this and the following reading the text of Hf. is preserved in the partially erased f. 76ᵛ of the Aesinas (see p. 18).

[3] I cite from O N**ΔI** VL Mw, all of which agree in ascribing the *Dialogus* to Tacitus. O = cod. Ottobonianus 1455. The symbols for the other MSS. are the same as for the *Germania*. The citations are from my own collations.

[4] **ΔI** do not report the extent of the lacuna.

The Archetype of the Extant Manuscripts

(xi)   35, 20 * * *   nihil abiectum ni-   nihil humile nihil ab-
                             hil humile   iectum

de Grammaticis
(xii)   1, 1 ne in usu   nec in usu   ne (nec *B H*) in usu[1]

(xiii)   * * *   rudis scilicet   rudi scilicet (rudis,
                                                 om. scilicet **MKC**,
                                                 rudi, *om.* scilicet
                                                 BHU△Q)

(xiv)   32, 25 * * *   Regum   legum (Regum *U*)

In ii, iii, v, ix, the *Commentarium* is clearly in error. This is not surprising, for the extant copy may be several stages removed from the original.

In vi, vii, Decembrio is undoubtedly wrong, for he is contradicted by the Hersfeld codex itself. Likewise in xii we must distrust his evidence, for the *Commentarium* and all but two of the manuscripts of the *de Grammaticis* side against him. The two manuscripts which agree with Decembrio are corrupt, and their independent testimony is quite without value. Finally in i the agreement of the *Commentarium* with the most authoritative manuscripts of the *Germania* must be accepted as giving us the title of this work as recorded by Hf. It should be noted that while three of the manuscripts reading *Germanorum* correspond verbatim with the *Commentarium*, none of those reading *Germaniae* agrees exactly with Decembrio.

In iv, xi, xiii, xiv, I do not hesitate to accept the testimony of our manuscripts in preference to that of Decembrio.[2] The latter has no more value than would any other apograph of Hf., while for the *Germania* and *de Grammaticis*, and presumably for the *Dialogus*, our manuscripts are descended from two distinct apographs of Hf. So in cases of disagreement between Decembrio and the extant manuscripts the evidence is really two to one against the former. Decembrio's report

[1] On the MSS. of the *de Grammaticis* see my edition (1925).

[2] The reading in xiv of **U**, a hopelessly corrupt MS. many degrees removed from Hf., can hardly have significance.

of (iv) *inscientia* for *inscitia* in the *Germania* is curious. Apparently this notice belongs with the *Dialogus*, which is the only one of the Tacitean works to use *inscientia*. This circumstance may lead us to suspect that Decembrio did not have the Hersfeld codex before him when he composed the notice as it now stands, but that he compiled it from disorganized notes which he had previously made, perhaps rather hastily, when he saw the manuscript.

The situation in viii and x is more involved, and requires a detailed discussion. In both cases, codex Vindobonensis 711 (W), the only one of our manuscripts which has independent value, offers the clue to the solution of the problem.

viii. First we should notice that in the *Commentarium* the omission of Tacitus' name from the inscription of the *Dialogus* is not due to a copyist's oversight, for Panormita in his letter to Guarino expresses doubt as to the authorship.[1] W offers the following inscription for the *Dialogus: INCIPIT DIALOGVS DE ORATORIBVS*, while its subscription reads, *Cornelii taciti de oratoribus explicit*. I am convinced that herein is given an accurate reproduction of Hf. The Hersfeld monk sent the *incipit* to Poggio just as he found it, *i.e.* without the name of Tacitus, while Decembrio supplied the name of the author from the *explicit*.

x. The *Commentarium* states that the *Dialogus* occupied eighteen leaves, whereas the words of Decembrio imply that there were but seventeen—fourteen before the lacuna, and three following it. He really says that there were *two and a half* leaves after the lacuna, but can hardly mean that there was half of a leaf which had been cut in two. The logical supposition is that a "half leaf" means a leaf which has writing on but one side. But herein lies a significant point: Decembrio's numbering disregards the blank page. Is there then any reason why this empty page may not have been preceded by an entire leaf likewise devoid of writing? The total number

[1] Et inventus est quidam dyalogus de oratore et est, ut coniectamus, Cor. Taciti . . . (see p. 3).

of leaves would then be brought up to eighteen, which tallies with the *Commentarium*. In other words, I assume that at the point of the lacuna in the *Dialogus* there were one and a half blank leaves: the entire fifteenth leaf and the recto of the sixteenth. **W** again comes to our aid, and makes this assumption almost a certainty. This manuscript at the place of the lacuna has an entire leaf blank,[1] but at the foot of the verso offers the following subscription: *hic est defectus unius folii cum dimidio*.[2]

What of Decembrio's statement that there were *six* leaves missing? As Wissowa has seen,[3] this does not refer to the condition of Hf. itself, but to a notice written in Hf. regarding the state of some more remote manuscript. We may, I believe, assume with probability that the ratio of one to four represented by the blank leaf and a half in Hf. and the six lost leaves of its antecedent was intentional, especially since additional evidence will be forthcoming that a single leaf of Hf. held the contents of four leaves of one of its ancestors.[4]

Unfortunately, we are now facing a serious difficulty, for which I can at present offer no definite solution. It will be observed that with the exception of **W** all manuscripts of the *Dialogus* which report the extent of the lacuna read *sex pagelle* (*parue pagelle, paginae*),[5] not *sex folia*. Were *pagelle* (or *paginae*) found only in the **Y** family,[6] the difficulty would not be so

[1] Fol. 227. The recto has two lines of text at the beginning.

[2] An examination of this subscription both in a photograph and in the MS. itself leaves not the slightest doubt that it was written by the hand which copied the entire manuscript. Gudeman (1914) erroneously reports it as by the second hand.

[3] Wissowa, 1907, xiv.

[4] See pp. 73 ff.

[5] The reading *quatuor* instead of *sex* in **M** is probably due to a transposition of letters in the numeral *vi*.

[6] I am assuming that the MSS. of the *Dialogus*, like those of the *de Grammaticis*, divide themselves into two families, **X** consisting of **WO** (O = Ottobonianus *1455*), and **Y** comprising all other MSS., but this is a problem needing an independent treatment. The close relationship between **W** and **O** has been shown by F. Scheuer, "De Tacitei de Oratoribus Dialogi Codicum Nexu et Fide," *Breslauer philologische Abhandlungen* VI, 1 (1891).

serious, for we might suppose that the copyist of Y erroneously substituted *pagelle* for *folia*.[1] However, O, which is a twin of W,[2] reads, *in exemplari dicunt deesse sex paginas*. Can *pagella* or *pagina* mean "column"?[3] If so, the difficulty would be solved, for *sex pagellae* (= six columns) would describe the condition of the Hersfeld codex itself, but I can find no indication that *pagella* (*pagina*) was so used, though I may remark that in antiquity *pagina* denoted a column of writing in the roll. I can only suggest that in the *Dialogus* O has borrowed from some member of the Y family,[4] or that the copyist, evidently a scholar, adopted a hearsay report (note his use of *dicunt*).[5]

2. The Codex Aesinas
Discovery of the Manuscript and Its Description

In the fall of 1902 Professor Cesare Annibaldi made a discovery of the utmost importance for textual studies in the minor Tacitean works—a discovery such as is frequently the dream, but seldom the realization, of those who are fortunate enough to delve into the manuscript treasures of European libraries.[6] I refer to the discovery of MS. Lat. No. 8 in the

[1] Yet the use of the diminutive *pagella* would be strange.

[2] See p. 13, note 6.

[3] This is the explanation proposed by K. Barwick, *Rh. Mus.* LXVIII (1913), 283–285, but he gives no instance of such a usage of *pagella* or *pagina*.

[4] The readings shown by Scheuer, *op. cit.* 31, suggest a connection between O and L (designated as E and B by Scheuer).

[5] I was formerly inclined to discredit the statement of Decembrio (1922, 18), and to assume that he had written *folia* where he should have written *paginae*, but I now retract, for I am convinced that Hf. bore a definite ratio of one to four toward its archetype twice removed (see pp. 73 ff.).

[6] M. Vatasso, "Un codice antico e sconosciuto dell'Agricola di Tacito," *Bolletino di filologia classica* IX (1902), 107. C. Annibaldi, "Di un nuovo codice dell' Agricola et della Germania," *Atene e Roma* V (1902), 737. The find was announced to the historical Congress in Rome in 1903 (*Atti del Congresso internazionale* II, 227–232).

Description of the MS. with diplomatic text of the *Agricola*, collation of the *Bellum Troianum* and *Germania*, and five plates, by C. Annibaldi 1907. Diplomatic text of f. 76ᵛ (*Agricola*) and of the *Germania* by Annibaldi 1910. In my discussion of the Aesinas I have been obliged to depend upon these two works of Annibaldi.

private library of Count Aurelio Guglielmi Balleani in Jesi, now known as the codex Aesinas.[1] As now constituted, this manuscript contains the *Bellum Troianum* of Dictys Cretensis and the entire *Agricola* and *Germania* of Tacitus. The writing of the manuscript is of two widely separated periods, part being by a fifteenth-century hand which Annibaldi judges to be that of Stefano Guarnieri, and part in excellent Carolingian minuscule, which he assigns to the ninth or tenth century.

The character of the writing and the scope of the text found on the different leaves is as follows:

f. 1: Carolingian minuscule, apparently almost illegible owing to mutilation of the leaf. Text: *Bellum Troianum*, prologue and i, 1–2, 12 (*transmissa*).[2]

f. 2^r: Carolingian minuscule, erased, but without secondary writing. Original text: *Bellum Troianum*, end of book i and *incipit* of book ii.

f. 2^v: Palimpsest. Primary script: Carolingian minuscule, with text of *Bellum Troianum* ii, 1–2, 17 (*secundo*). Secondary script: 15th century, with prologue of *Bellum Troianum*.

Ff. 1–2, which form a single sheet, were originally the outer leaves (ff. 1 and 8) of the first quaternion of the old (Carolingian) manuscript. Because of their deteriorated condition, Guarnieri copied their contents on the leaves now numbered 3 and 10. Later, finding a manuscript which contained the letter of Septimius to Q. Rufinus, missing in his own exemplar, he erased the prologue which he had written on f. 3^r and inserted the letter in its place. The prologue he then transferred to f. 2^v, which had previously been erased.[3]

ff. 3–4: 15th century, Text: Letter of Septimius and *Bellum Troianum* i, 1–6, 15 (*parcius*).

ff. 5–8: Carolingian minuscule. Text: continuation of *Bellum Troianum* through i, 19, 8 (*vicariam*).

[1] So called from Aesium, the ancient name of Jesi.

[2] References are to the chapters and lines of Meister's edition of the *Bellum Troianum* (Leipzig, 1872).

[3] This is the account given by Annibaldi (1910), 9. His earlier account seems confused.

ff. 9–10, 15th century. Text: continuation of *Bellum Troianum* through II, 2, 17 (*secundo*).

ff. 11–50: Carolingian minuscule. Text: continuation of *Bellum Troianum* through VI, 14, 10 (*sanguinis*).

f. 51: 15th century. Text: end of *Bellum Troianum*.

ff. 52–55: 15th century. Text: *Agricola* through 13, 2 (*munia*).

ff. 56–63: Carolingian minuscule. Text: continuation of *Agricola* (13, 2 *munia*)[1] through 40, 7 (*ministeriis*).

ff. 64–65: 15th century. Text: continuation of *Agricola* to the end.

ff. 66–68: 15th century. Text: *Germania* through 14, 4 (*tueri*).

f. 69: Palimpsest. Primary script: Carolingian minuscule, continuing the text of the *Agricola* from the end of f. 63^v (40, 7) through 43, 15 (*testamento*). Secondary script: 15th century, continuing the text of the *Germania* from the preceding page.

ff. 70–75: 15th century.[2] Text: completion of the *Germania*.

f. 76: Carolingian minuscule, erased. The text was a continuation of the primary script of f. 69^v to the end of the *Agricola*. The leaf now serves as a *feuille de garde*. The erasure of the verso was so imperfectly done that Annibaldi has been able to decipher the entire page.[3]

The diagram on page 17 illustrates the disposition of the leaves. The Roman numerals indicate the gatherings, and the Arabic numerals the leaves. Arabic numerals in heavy type indicate intact leaves written in Carolingian minuscule. Arabic numerals in ordinary type, but connected by heavy lines, indicate leaves originally written in Carolingian minuscule, but erased or (in the case of f. 1) illegible through deterioration.

According to Annibaldi's description,[4] the leaves of the Aesinas measure mm. 220 x 273, the writing is in two columns to the page, each measuring mm. 60 x 203. The space between the columns is mm. 17 in width. In the older portions there are 30 lines to the column. In the humanistic portions

---

[1] F. 56 begins with *munia*. The same word ends f. 55^v, but has been deleted.

[2] In his later account (1910, 12) Annibaldi states that the sheet forming ff. 70 and 75 is palimpsest, but so radically erased that none of the earlier writing can be deciphered. Is there any trace of the older ruling with the hard point, as is the case with ff. 69 and 76?

[3] Annibaldi 1910, 21–24.

[4] Annibaldi 1907, 10 f.

The Archetype of the Extant Manuscripts 17

the number of lines varies from 26 to 33, although the columns are of the same dimensions as in the older parts. The ruling of the ancient parts is with the hard point, with punctures at the edge of the outer margin. Each sheet is ruled separately, convex fronting concave. The columns are bounded by perpendicular lines.

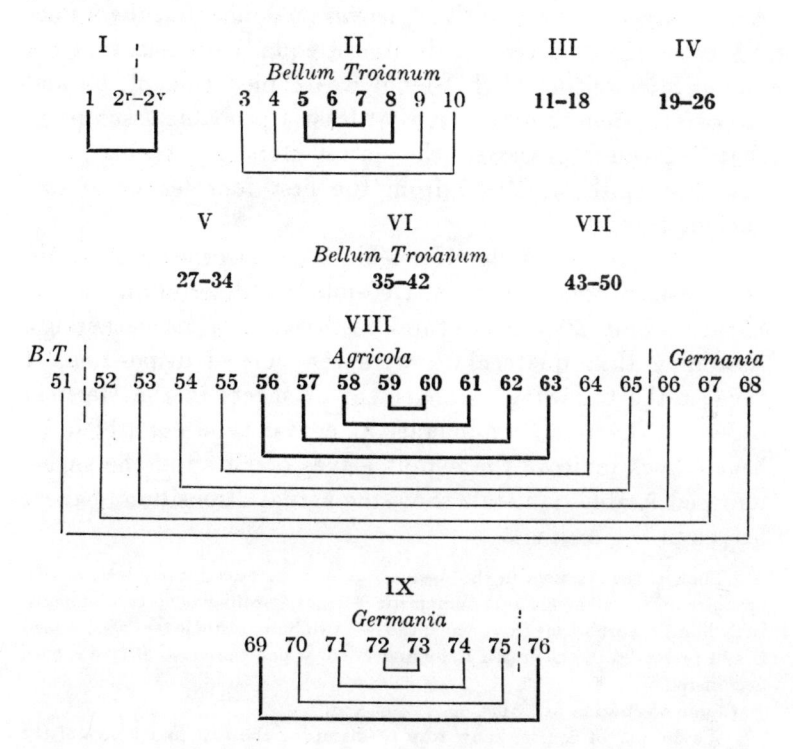

```
       I              II                III       IV
                 Bellum Troianum
      1  2r-2v   3  4  5  6  7  8  9  10   11-18    19-26


          V              VI               VII
                    Bellum Troianum
        27-34            35-42            43-50
                        VIII
   B.T. |             Agricola              |  Germania
    51 | 52 53 54 55 56 57 58 59 60 61 62 63 64 65 | 66 67 68


                         IX
                      Germania
              69  70  71  72  73  74  75 | 76
```

There can hardly be any question of the validity of Annibaldi's claim that ff. 56–63 of the Aesinas constitute a single quaternion of the lost Hersfeld codex, and that the palimpsest f. 69 and the erased f. 76 form a *unio* of the same manuscript, which immediately followed the quaternion. The identity of these portions of the Aesinas with the manuscript described by Decembrio[1] appears to be established by the disposition

[1] See pp. 8 f.

of the text into two columns to the page, and by the number of leaves occupied by the *Agricola*.[1]

It will be observed that for *Agricola* 45, 10 (*denotandis*) to the end the Aesinas offers the text in duplicate: (1) in the partially erased Carolingian minuscule of f. 76^v, and (2) in the humanistic writing at the very end of f. 65^r and on 65^v.[2] A comparison of f. 65^v with 76^v leaves no doubt that the former is a copy of the latter. It is almost equally obvious that the humanistic writing of ff. 64–65^r was copied from ff. 69 and 76^r before their erasure. It is at least a probable assumption that Guarnieri possessed the entire Hersfeld *Agricola*, and that he copied ff. 52–55 from the first four leaves of this ancient exemplar.[3]

The fragments of the Hersfeld codex incorporated within the Aesinas together with Decembrio's description of the former admit of a conjectural restoration of its gatherings. Assuming that quaternions were the normal disposition,[4] I suggest the following arrangement of sheets in the Hersfeld codex.[5] The Arabic numerals in heavy type connected by heavy lines indicate the extant leaves of Hf., and the superimposed Arabic numerals show the actual disposition of these leaves in the Aesinas.

[1] That is, the *Agricola* in the Aesinas, as was the case in the Hersfeldensis, occupies fourteen leaves: four humanistic + eight Carolingian + two humanistic, while the parchment from which the last two humanistic leaves were copied is still preserved in the erased ff. 69 and 76, of which the verso of 76 has been deciphered.

[2] Folio 65^v begins with *Agr.* 45, 11 *sufficeret*.

[3] We do not, of course, know why he discarded the first four leaves of the ancient MS. It may have been because of their deteriorated condition, or because of the difficulty of binding the four single sheets resulting from the separation of the *Agricola* from the rest of the Hersfeldensis (see the diagram given below).

[4] This is indicated both by the extant quaternion of the *Agricola* and by the use of quaternions for the ancient portion of the *Bellum Troianum*, which appears to be a product of the same scriptorium (see below).

[5] I find the restoration proposed by Wissowa 1907, xiv, unsatisfactory, since he allows but seventeen instead of eighteen leaves to the *Dialogus* (see pp. 12 f.).

The Archetype of the Extant Manuscripts

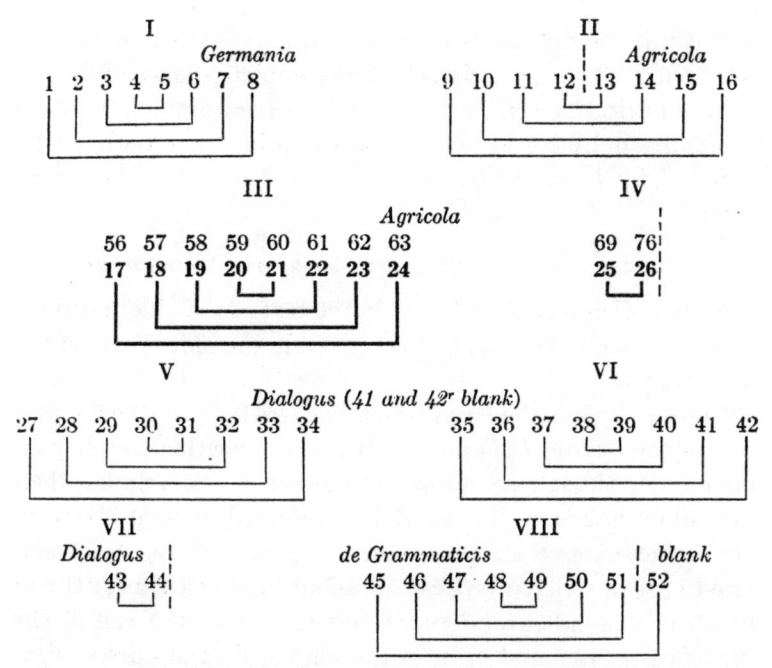

```
         I                              II
      Germania                       Agricola
1  2  3  4  5  6  7  8        9  10  11  12 | 13  14  15  16


        III                             IV
                 Agricola
   56 57 58 59 60 61 62 63        69 76
   17 18 19 20 21 22 23 24        25 26


         V                              VI
        Dialogus (41 and 42ʳ blank)
27 28 29 30 31 32 33 34       35 36 37 38 39 40 41 42


       VII                             VIII
    Dialogus         de Grammaticis            blank
     43 44         45 46 47 48 49 50 51 | 52
```

I quite agree with Annibaldi that the Carolingian portions of the *Bellum Troianum* and the *Agricola* are products of the same scriptorium.[1] The observance in both works of the same dimensions for the pages and columns of writing and the strict adherence to the norm of thirty lines to the column cannot be accidental. Furthermore, we may note the use of square capitals, with the shaft of *L* reaching well above the other letters, in lines alternating between red and black for the *incipit* and *explicit* of each book of the *Bellum Troianum* and for the *explicit* of the *Agricola*,[2] and the use in both works of similar capitals in the margin for the initial letters of the various chapters.[3] Additional evidence will, I believe, be

---

[1] Annibaldi 1907, 74.

[2] For the *Bel. Tro.* see Annibaldi 1907, 12; for the *Agricola*, *ibid*. 139. It is not expressly stated that the *explicit* of the *Agricola* is in square (rather than rustic) capitals.

[3] The first two lines of each book of the *Bel. Tro.* are in uncials. For the beginning of the *Agricola* we have only the fifteenth-century copy, which has the first line in capitals with an initial *C* three lines in height. The *incipit* is in square capitals, doubtless in imitation of the exemplar.

forthcoming in my discussion of the various hands found in the older portions of the Aesinas.[1] The complete silence of Panormita, Poggio, Niccolò, and Decembrio regarding the *Bellum Troianum* militates against the assumption that both works were originally in the same codex, but does not entirely preclude it.

Hands at Work in the Older Portions of the Aesinas

Annibaldi detects four hands in the text of the older portions of the *Bellum Troianum*, and two more in the older parts of the *Agricola*.[2]

Hand 1: This is the hand which has written the greater portion of the *Bellum Troianum*.[3] It is a well written Carolingian minuscule, though somewhat coarser and less regular than the other hands. The hand has retained several ligatures and other cursive elements: the *st* ligature is regularly employed; *re* is written in ligature about eighteen times; the *or* ligature is found several times, but always at the end of the line; final *nt* is found both in the majuscule and cursive ligatures; a curious ligature in the word *rex* is mentioned as occurring twice; open *a* is found some seventy times; *i-longa* is occasionally used, initially, for the consonant, and once in *deInde;* a hook is sometimes added to the bow of *e*, giving it a cursive appearance.[4] The shafts reaching above the line are frequently clubbed, the letter *s* is relatively high, and both bows of *g* are normally open. The use of capital *N* is frequent. Abbreviations are not frequent, and do not extend beyond those in common use in continental scriptoria in the ninth and tenth centuries.[5]

---

[1] See my discussion of hand III, p. 21.

[2] 1907, 24 f.; 74; 140.

[3] Facsimile of f. 47ʳ by Annibaldi 1907, Tav. i. My description is taken partly from Annibaldi 1907, pp. 16–24, and partly from an examination of Plate I.

[4] C. H. Beeson, *Lupus of Ferrières as scribe and text critic* (Cambridge, 1930), p. 10, mentions a similar practice on the part of Lupus, wherever the eye of the *e* has been filled with ink. Does the hook serve the same purpose in the Jesi Dictys?

[5] See Annibaldi's list of abbreviations, 1907, 21–24.

Hand II: This hand is found only on f. 20ᵛ, col. 1; 21, col. 2 in part; 23ᵛ, col. 1; 25ᵛ; and in some lines of f. 27, col. 2. Annibaldi does not give a facsimile. He describes the hand as "un unico tipo di lettere tondeggiante, tozze, tranquille."[1] Does the description suggest a type of Insular writing?

Hand III: This is found on ff. 27ᵛ, 28, and 29ʳ.[2] While this writing would probably qualify as Carolingian minuscule, I believe that it does show unmistakable signs of Insular influence. We may note the general fineness of the writing and the tendency toward height rather than breadth; the tall *e*; the tapering of the shafts of *m, n, r*, and of the shafts reaching below the line; and the angle with which the curve of *u* is joined to the second shaft. Other features of the hand, which are not particularly suggestive of Insular influence, are the peculiar ligature for *et*, in which the tongue of the high *e* is prolonged horizontally, while to its end is joined a hooked diagonal line reaching to the height of the bow; the relative height of *s*; *g* with its lower bow open; slight clubbing of the shafts; sparing use of ligatures[3] and abbreviations.

Unless I am greatly mistaken, hand III is the one which has made the marginal entries on ff. 56–63 (*Agricola*).[4] The hand is unique[5] and, although the facsimiles are inadequate in extent, a comparison of the writing in Annibaldi's Plate II with the two marginal readings in Plate V can leave little doubt that the latter are the work of this hand. In the marginalia we may observe a close similarity to hand III in the fineness of stroke and tendency to height rather than breadth, in the use of the tall *e*, in the relative height of *s*, in the length and fineness of the second transverse of *x*, in the tapering of the shafts of *m, n, r*, and in the line of suspension for *m*.

[1] 1907, 24.

[2] Facsimile of f. 28ʳ by Annibaldi 1907, Tav. II.

[3] The facsimile shows *st* once in ligature and once without.

[4] This is the hand which in my discussion of the text of the *Agricola*, following Annibaldi, I call m. 2.

[5] That is, it would be easy to find a score of MSS. whose writing bears a fairly close resemblance to hands I, IV, and V, but I have found nothing in published facsimiles which resembles hand III.

Hand IV: According to Annibaldi, this hand is found only on f. 29ᵛ.¹ It bears a general resemblance to hand I and a very close resemblance to hand V, but the letters are smaller and the writing is more compact than is the case with either of the other hands, while the *ductus* is more regular than that of hand I. There is only slight clubbing of the shafts, both bows of *g* are regularly closed,² and the only ligature employed is &.³ Abbreviations are rare, though $\bar{p}$ is found for *prae*,⁴ which Annibaldi says is not used by the other hands.⁵ The hand may give the general impression of being slightly more recent than the others, but there is no good reason for assigning it to a later date. It is chiefly the greater compactness of the script which is responsible for its slightly younger appearance.

I suspect that hand IV may in reality be identical with the one which I describe below as hand V. It is chiefly the greater compactness of the former which is responsible for its different appearance. A comparison of Annibaldi's Plates III and V shows that the formation of the letters in the two scripts is essentially the same. Only in the treatment of the final stroke of *m* and *n* do I note any marked dissimilarity, but this might be explained by the difference between the pens which the scribe employed.

Hand V: This is the hand which wrote the quaternion of the Hersfeld *Agricola*, preserved in ff. 56–63.⁶ It is a beautiful Carolingian minuscule and is the most elegant of all, being characterized by boldness of stroke, freedom from restraint, and a flowing quality. The clubbing of the shafts is frequent, though not always observed. Only the lower bow of *g* is open. The ligatures are limited to &, œ, ę, ℕ, and ꝣ, but with the

[1] 1907, 24 f. Facsimile, Tav. III.
[2] Note, however, col. 2, 18, *gens*, with both bows of *g* left open.
[3] *st* is not written in ligature: col. 1, 12, *post*, 17 *st* (?), 2, 24 *hostem*.
[4] Col. 2, 19 $\bar{p}$tio.
[5] 1907, 25. This abbreviation is, however, used by hand VI (f. 76ᵛ, 1, 8 $\bar{p}$ter), and in the marginalia of ff. 56–63 (63ᵛ, 1, 18 $\bar{p}$bere, 2, 15 $\bar{p}$sens, 60, 1, 21 $\bar{p}$bebantur), which I believe to have been written by hand III.
[6] Annibaldi 1907, 74 f. Facsimile of f. 58ʳ, Tav. V.

The Archetype of the Extant Manuscripts 23

exception of & all are infrequent. Annibaldi says that there is not a single example of *st* in ligature. There are fourteen examples of majuscule *N* aside from the *NT* ligature. Abbreviations are used very sparingly, and within a very limited scope.[1] I have already suggested that this hand may be the work of the same scribe as hand IV.

Hand VI: This is the hand whose writing is still decipherable on the partially erased f. 76ᵛ, and presumably the one which wrote the primary script on the palimpsest f. 69 and on the erased f. 76ʳ. Unfortunately Annibaldi gives neither a facsimile nor an adequate description of this writing. He says that the writing is more minute and compact than that of the other eight leaves of the *Agricola* (hand v), and, though giving the impression of being but slightly more recent, is certainly the work of a different scribe.[2] His statement that the hand is different should be accompanied by other evidence than the fact that the letters are smaller and the writing more compact, for this peculiarity of the script may be accounted for by the consideration that the scribe had only two sheets of parchment left upon which to complete the text of *Agricola*.[3] This circumstance would also account for the more frequent use of abbreviations by hand VI. We may note that hand VI has in common with hand IV the relative smallness of the letters and the compactness of the script, and the use of the abbreviation for *prae*. I have already suggested that the writing of hands IV and V may be the work of the same scribe. On the basis of such uncertain evidence it is doubtless rash to indulge in con-

[1] See table of abbreviations and ligatures in this portion of the MS. on p. 357.

[2] Annibaldi 1907, 140: "... vi si riconosce una minoscola piu serrata e minuta, direbbesi di poco posteriore, ma certo di mano diversa da quella delle altre otto." *Id.*, 1910, p. 24: "Avverto poi ... che cioè la grafia delle ultime carte dell' *Agricola* era diversa da quella delle otto carte conservate. ..." I do not understand Annibaldi to mean that he regards hand VI as actually belonging to a different period from hand v.

[3] It would have been impossible to complete the *Agricola* on the two leaves if the same scale of writing had been followed as on ff. 56–63. In ff. 56–63 most of the lines have from 22 to 28 letters each. On f. 76ᵛ there is an average of 34 or 35 letters to the line. Only toward the end of the second column, as the scribe found that he had plenty of room, did he make his writing less compact (see p. 78, note 2).

jectures, yet I wonder if one and the same scribe may not be responsible for all three hands, IV, V, and VI. Certainly a re-examination of the palaeographical details of the Aesinas is a *desideratum*.

The Date and Provenience of the Older Portions of the Aesinas

Perhaps in the actual light, or rather darkness, of palaeographical knowledge, nothing is more difficult than to determine whether a given piece of writing in Carolingian minuscule dates from the ninth or tenth century. I wish, however, to emphasize the fact that I can find no good reason why the hands which we have examined[1] should not be assigned to the ninth century, and even to a date as early as the middle of that century. In my opinion, they bear all the marks of the Carolingian minuscule of this period: writing in two columns to the page; general freedom from lateral compression and lack of uniformity in the joining of the letters; clubbing of the shafts extending above the line; the first shaft of *n* and the first two shafts of *m* tapering at the bottom and turning slightly toward the left, and the last shaft of both letters ending now in a curve to the left, now vertically, and again with a small hook to the right; occasional appearance of open *a* and *i-longa* (hand I), and of majuscule *N* both separately and in ligature with *T*; *g* with one or both bows left open; sparing use of abbreviations and their smallness of range; very imperfect word separation.

Doubtless many, perhaps all, of these features may be found in manuscripts of the tenth century, but there are numerous manuscripts generally accepted as dating from the ninth century which do not have the appearance of being older than the Aesinas. It is true that the manuscripts which I have in mind are not the products of German scriptoria, but of the scriptoria of central France. Some of them are known to have had a direct connection with Lupus of Ferrières.

[1] I have in mind hands I, IV, and V. Hands II and VI must remain out of the discussion, as we have no facsimiles of them. As I have stated, hand III appears to be unique, though I find no objection to assigning this also to the ninth century.

First of all we may take the Harleianus 2736 of Cicero, *de Oratore*, written by Lupus himself, perhaps between the years 829 and 836 when he was studying in Fulda, which has recently been made available for study in splendid facsimiles.[1] I find a striking resemblance between the writing of Lupus and that of hand v of our manuscript, though in certain details, such as the use of open *g*, of the *or* ligature at the end of the line, and of the hook added to the bow of *e*, giving it a cursive form,[2] the script of Lupus is closer to that of hand I. In fact our hand v seems to me to show just about the style of script one would expect of Lupus when writing at his best.[3]

Again, Bern 366, Valerius Maximus,[4] a manuscript corrected by Lupus, in general appearance is very similar to hand IV, though in certain details (*st* ligature, the relatively high *s* and *f*, the hooks added to the bow of *e*) it approaches more closely to hand I.

Another representative of the same general style of writing as that of our hands I, IV, and V is Paris, Lat. 8623, Symmachus, also bearing notes by the hand of Lupus.[5] I may also mention Bern 357, Petronius, perhaps from Auxerre, and the last two leaves of Leyden, Voss. Q. 30, said to be a part of the Bern manuscript.[6]

I realize that hands IV and V are freer from cursive elements than the manuscripts I have mentioned, but in this respect they find a counterpart in the manuscripts of Tours of the "regular" and "perfected" styles of the periods designated v

---

[1] Beeson, *op. cit.* on p. 20, note 4. Regarding the dating see Beeson, 3–5.

[2] *Ib.* 10.

[3] The Harleianus bears evidence of having been written in haste. See Beeson, 5. I am not, of course, suggesting that hand v is actually that of Lupus himself. Clearly it is not, at least if he was consistent in his manner of dividing words and in his use of reference symbols, etc.

[4] Facsimile of ff. 56ʳ and 64ʳ in Steffens, *Lateinische Paläographie*² (Berlin and Leipzig, 1909), Plate 60, "circa A.D. 860."

[5] Facsimile of f. 13ʳ (reduced) by Lowe, "Nugae Palaeographicae," *Persecution and Liberty*, Studies in honor of George Lincoln Burr (New York, 1931), 55–69.

[6] Facsimiles (f. 34ᵛ of the Bern MS., and f. 57ᶜ of the Leyden) by Chatelain, *Paléographie des classiques latins* (Paris, 1884–1892), Plate CXLIX, "fin du ixᵉ siècle."

and vi by Rand.[1] In fact the boldness of stroke and the freedom from restraint of hand v is to me reminiscent of Tours.[2] We may also wonder if the use of square capitals and of uncials,[3] without admixture of other elements, is not due to Turonian influence.[4]

Not only is the writing of the older portions of the Aesinas suggestive of central France, but in the *Agricola* at least [5] there are no errors to betray the German scribe,[6] as is the case with the Mediceus I of *Annals* i–vi. The latter, quite aside from its obviously German script, offers such errors as *turpidos* for *turbidos*, *epur* for *ebur*, *saturnio praecepta* for *saturni ob recepta*, *blebis* for *plebis*, *adbellerent* for *adpellerent*, *praedurae* corrected to *praeturae*, *conditionabundus* corrected to *contionabundus*, *dum* corrected to *tum*,[7] errors which one will seek in vain in the Aesinas of the *Agricola*.

The script of the major portion of the Aesinas is, as I have shown, French minuscule. But with the German Hersfeld as its mediaeval home,[8] what are we to say as to the place of its origin? One may naturally ask first if the place of writing was not the same as the mediaeval home. Surprisingly little is known of the library of the Hersfeld monastery. Lampert of Hersfeld states that the Abbot Gozbert, 970–985, greatly

[1] E. K. Rand, *A Survey of the Manuscripts of Tours* (Cambridge, 1929) 53-63. Periods v and vi extend roughly from 820 to 860 (pp. 53, 60).

[2] For comparison with our MS. I suggest Plates lxxxix, xciii, cxli, and cxliv, 2, of Rand's work.

[3] Rand, 41.

[4] Influence of the script of Tours on the writing of Lupus has been detected. See Beeson, 9, note.

[5] I have not examined the *Dictys* from this standpoint.

[6] I hardly think that the single instance of *uelud* can be taken as evidence for a German scribe. Certainly the writing of *haut*, *aput*, and *adque* cannot (see p. 251).

[7] See Rostagno, *Tacitus, Codex Laurentianus Mediceus 68 i, praefatus est Henricus Rostagno*, Codices Graeci et Latini phototypice depicti duce Scatone de Vries vii, 1 (Lugduni Bat., 1902), pp. ix f., xv.

[8] This is known only for the portion of the MS. containing the *Agricola*. However, the *Bellum Troianum* must be a product of the same scriptorium (cf. p. 19), though it was not necessarily in the same mediaeval repository.

enriched the library,[1] but this was more than a hundred years after the time in which I believe our manuscript to have been written. Of the Hersfeld library before Gozbert's time we know nothing, and even Lampert's notice says nothing about a scriptorium.

Aside from the fragment of the *Agricola* (and perhaps the *Bellum Troianum*), only one complete manuscript and one fragment of the former treasures of the Hersfeld library are known today.[2] The complete manuscript is Munich Lat. 3516, Paulus Diaconus, *Historia Miscella*, and Ephrem Syrus, *Sermo in Ioseph* ("*saec.* x"). The writing is, I should say, a good hundred years younger than that of the Aesinas,[3] and can hardly help us in our quest.

The other remnant of the Hersfeld library is the famous Marburg fragment of Ammianus Marcellinus, now preserved in the library at Kassel.[4] In point of time this fragment brings us nearer to the Aesinas. Traube dated it about the year 900,[5] but I wonder if it may not be some fifty years earlier. The script bears considerable resemblance to St. Gall 457, *Martyrologium* of Hrabanus Maurus, believed by Chroust to be the identical copy sent from Fulda by Hrabanus to Abbot Grimald of St. Gall between 840 and 852.[6] According to

[1] *De Institutione Hersveldensis Ecclesiae*, in *Lamperti Monachi Hersfeldenis Opera*, ed. O. Holder-Egger (Hanoverae et Lipsiae, 1894), 348: "Igitur Gozbertus abbas, etsi non morum, studii tamen sui erga locum Hersveldensem satis evidens ad nos transmisit documentum, magnam scilicet copiam librorum suo nomine ob monimentum sui attitulatorum."

[2] P. Lehmann, *Iohannes Sichardus und die von ihm benutzten Bibliotheken und Handschriften*, Quellen und Untersuchungen zur lateinischen Philologie des Mittelalters IV, 1 (Munich, 1911), 120–123.

[3] I have specimen photographs of this MS. in my possession.

[4] This is undoubtedly a fragment of the codex mentioned in the *Commentarium* of Niccolò Niccoli (see p. 7). The MS. was used by Sigismundus Gelenius for his edition of Ammianus, Basiliae, 1533 (Lehmann, *Johannes Sichardus*, 121; Clark, *op. cit.* [on p. 28], 11 f.), and must have been intact at that time. Of the Frontinus mentioned in the *Commentarium* all traces appear to have been lost. Partial facsimiles of the Marburg fragment will be found in the works of Nissen and of Clark mentioned below.

[5] L. Traube, *Die Ueberlieferung des Ammianus Marcellinus*, Mélanges Boissier (Paris, 1903), 443–448 (p. 448).

[6] Anton Chroust, *Monumenta Palaeographica, Denkmäler der Schreibkunst des Mittelalters* (Munich, 1902–), I Serie, XVII Lieferung, Tafel 8 (No. 168, Vol. III).

Traube[1] and Clark,[2] the Hersfeldensis of Ammianus was a twin brother of Vat. Lat. 1873,[3] which is known to have belonged to the library of Fulda,[4] though Nissen, the editor of the Marburg fragment, declares the Fuldensis to be a copy of the Hersfeldensis.[5] In either case, the two manuscripts of Ammianus offer a link connecting the library of Hersfeld with that of Fulda—a connection which one might reasonably assume even without direct evidence, in view of the proximity of the two foundations, and of the leading position occupied by Fulda as a center of learning.

Returning now to the Aesinas—we find no evidence that it originated in Hersfeld, even though this was its home (at least, the home of the Tacitus part of the manuscript) prior to its arrival in Rome. Of its connection with Fulda, quite apart from general probabilities or any fancied parallel between this and the Ammianus manuscript, we have an indication in the fact that around the middle of the ninth century Rudolph of Fulda had at his disposal a manuscript of the *Germania*.[6] How does the French character of the script of our manuscript fit in with the supposition that it once had its home in Fulda?

Evidence of relations between Fulda and central France is not difficult to find. Einhart, first a pupil in the school of Fulda, and later under Alcuin in the Palatine school,[7] Alcuin assuming the abbacy of St. Martin's in 796, Hrabanus Maurus,

[1] Traube, *op. cit.* 444 f.

[2] C. U. Clark, *The Text Tradition of Ammianus Marcellinus* (New Haven, 1904), 62 f.

[3] Facsimiles in Chatelain, *Pal. des class. lat.* II, Plate cxcv; Clark, *l.c.*, Plates 2 and 3.

[4] Clark, *op. cit.* 4.

[5] *Ammiani Marcellini Fragmenta Marburgensia*, edidit Henricus Nissen (Berlin, 1876), 18 ff. An examination of the evidence convinces me that Nissen's view is the better substantiated of the two. I hope to publish a detailed discussion of the matter within a short time.

[6] See p. 1, note 1. The suggestion of Fulda as the original home of our MS. is, of course, not new, but so far as I know the matter has never been examined before on palaeographical evidence.

[7] Max Manitius, *Geschichte der lateinischen Literatur des Mittelalters* (Munich, 1911–1931) I, 639.

the famous teacher of Fulda, twice sent to Alcuin in Tours,[1] and Lupus of Ferrières, a pupil of Hrabanus from 828 to 836,[2] probably offer but the merest suggestion of the intercourse which must have existed between Fulda and the valley of the Loire.[3] Are we to assume that the Aesinas was brought from central France to Fulda? Such an assumption, though possible enough, is quite unnecessary. Lupus is known to have written books while he was at Fulda.[4] He may well have instructed the native scribes in the technique of the French minuscule, and doubtless Lupus was not the only skilled French scribe who attended the school of Fulda, and copied books while there.

Are there manuscripts known to have been written in Fulda whose writing resembles that of the Aesinas? This question I cannot answer. The history of the various scripts of this monastery is still a closed book, and we must await with eagerness the work promised by Lehmann.[5] With a single exception, all manuscripts in non-Insular writing reputed to have had their origin in Fulda of which I have seen facsimiles may be said to differ markedly from the script of the Aesinas. The exception is the fragment of an old Fulda catalogue now preserved in ff. 35–43 of codex Pal. Lat. 1877. Lehmann, with excellent reason, has recently voiced the opinion that this fragment was written in Fulda before the year 850.[6] An examination of Lehmann's facsimile of f. 36^r will, I believe, show that the writing, like that of hands I, IV, and V of the Aesinas, is essentially of the French type, though cursive elements are more prevalent than in the Aesinas.

[1] *Ib.* I, 288 f.
[2] Beeson, *op. cit.* 3, note.
[3] P. Lehmann, *Modius als Handschriftenforscher*, Quellen und Untersuchungen zur lateinischen Philologie des Mittelalters III, 74: ". . . da wir schliesslich über den regen Handschriftenverkehr zwischen Lupus und Hrabanus, zwischen, um einen Namen für mehrere zu nennen, Tours und Fulda gut unterrichtet sind. . . ."
[4] Beeson, 3 and 9.
[5] P. Lehmann, *Quot et quorum libri fuerint in libraria Fuldensi*, Bok-Och Bibliotekshistoriska Studier tillagnäde Isak Collijn (Uppsala, 1925), 47–57 (p. 47).
[6] *Ib.* 50–52. Facsimiles of ff. 35^v and 36^r opposite p. 52.

Needless to say, I make no pretense to having proved that Fulda was the original home of the Aesinas, but in the light of present knowledge this does appear to offer a plausible answer to our problem.

3. Variant Readings and Sources of Corruption in the Hersfeld Agricola

I now turn to an examination of the text of the *Agricola* as found on ff. 56–63 and f. 76ᵛ of the Aesinas, with the view of determining, (1) the origin and relative antiquity of the marginal variants, and (2) the sources of corruption in the manuscript. Hereafter I shall refer to these portions of the Aesinas as "the Hersfeld *Agricola*" (or Hf.), though my references to the leaves will be according to their present numbering.

The bearing which the examination I am undertaking has upon the text of the *Germania* is, I believe, obvious, for we have seen that the lost ancestor of the *Germania* manuscripts was in the same codex as were the extant parts of the Hersfeld *Agricola*.[1] In the absence of evidence to the contrary, we are justified in adopting the hypothesis that in the Hersfeld codex both the *Agricola* and *Germania* were written by contemporary hands and were products of the same scriptorium, if not actually of the same scribe or scribes; that both texts had passed through the same line of tradition from antiquity; that both exhibited the same types of error and correction, the same peculiarities of script, the same orthography, etc. The validity of this hypothesis will, I believe, be established by the illustrative material which I draw from the *Germania* manuscripts in the ensuing discussion and from my detailed treatment of these manuscripts in part II. Herein, I am convinced, lies the real importance for the *Germania* of the discovery of the Aesinas.[2] The fact that the same codex contains a fifteenth-

---

[1] Note particularly in the *Commentarium* of Niccolò (see p. 7) the words, *Item in eodem codice*.

[2] I am pleased to note that this fundamental principle is recognized by the author of the latest article dealing with the text of the *Germania* that has come to my notice: Friedrich Frahm, "Neue Wege zur Textkritik von Tacitus' Ger-

century transcript of the *Germania* is a matter of secondary importance.[1]

Hands of Correctors in the Agricola

Preliminary to my discussion of the variant readings and sources of corruption a few words regarding the work of correctors in the Hersfeld *Agricola* are necessary.

In ff. 56–63 Annibaldi detects two hands besides that of the scribe who copied the text.[2] One of these (m. 2) is contemporary, the other (m. 3) is of the fifteenth century.

Fifteenth-century Corrector.—The fifteenth-century hand need not delay us long, and in reporting the readings of Hf. I have ignored the corrections made by this hand. Though it has corrected certain obvious errors of the manuscript, notably in the matter of word-separation and orthography, it has also introduced a few unintelligent interpolations. The most glaring of these is on f. 59^v, 2, 7 (*Agr.* 26), where *nonanis* has been changed to *romanis*.[3] This humanistic interpolation is the reading of A and B, and before the discovery of E and T[4] was the only reading with manuscript authority.

Contemporary Corrector.—The work of the contemporary hand (m. 2) is important for our investigation.[5] Performing

mania," *Hermes* LXIX (1934), 426–443. I fear, however, that the author's acceptance of the prevailing notions regarding the relationship of our extant manuscripts and his disregard for certain basic laws of palaeography and text criticism have led him far astray in his application of the principle.

[1] See pp. 15 f.

[2] We are left in the dark regarding f. 76^v. Although Annibaldi believes that the text of this page is by a hand different from that of ff. 56–63 (cf. p. 23), he does not state whether the corrections and marginal readings of this page are by the hand of the text. Perhaps the faded condition of the writing makes it impossible to determine this.

[3] The problem presents itself whether the Hersfeld *Germania* was likewise disfigured by the work of a fifteenth-century interpolator. I suspect such to have been the case, though definite proof seems to be lacking. (Cf. pp. 45–56.)

[4] The extant MSS. of the *Agricola* are, the Aesinas (E), the Toletanus (T), Vat. Lat. 3429 (A), and Vat. Lat. 4498 (B, which I have designated as Δ for the *Germania*). On the composition of E see pp. 15–18. T is a direct copy of E. A and B are probably copies of a lost fifteenth-century apograph of Hf.

[5] I have previously attempted to show that this hand is one of those found in the text of the *Bellum Troianum*. See p. 21.

the office of corrector, this hand has supplied in the margin or interlinear space words or letters omitted by the first scribe, has deleted letters[1] and made the necessary corrections above the line, has here and there added a comma to indicate the proper separation of words, and has made a large number of corrections in orthography by transforming the letters originally written. There can be little doubt that the corrector had before him the archetype from which the manuscript was copied, though in the numerous orthographical changes I believe that he corrected according to the rules of the scriptorium rather than according to the spelling of the archetype, since most of the orthographical peculiarities as written by the first scribe are characteristic of our oldest Latin manuscripts, and are, I think, due in part to phonetic changes of late Latin (confusion of b and consonant u, of e and i, ci and ti, etc.), and in part to an etymologizing trend in the orthography of late Roman times (*adque* for *atque*, unassimilated forms of prefixes).[2] Finally, all the marginal variants were written in by m. 2. The question at once arises whether these variants were creations of this contemporary corrector or were copied from the archetype, and we must therefore examine in detail the doublets of the Hersfeld *Agricola*.

Doublets in the Hersfeld Agricola

I first present a table of the doublets with the reference-symbols used. The dagger indicates the reading which is, in my opinion, corrupt.

(i)   f. 56, 1, 14 (*Agr.* 13, 9) †$\overline{praecipue}$ in text, $\overline{pcept\bar{u}}^{v}$ in mg.
(ii)   56, 2, 4 (14, 4), $\overline{co}gidumno$ in text, †- *Togidūno* in mg.

[1] In one place, f. 57, col. 1, 25 f., he has deleted several words (cf. p. 33, note 1). According to Annibaldi (1907, 87, note 14; 89, note 4), the mark of deletion, either by the first or second hand, is almost always a diagonal line drawn through the letter, though in the deletion just mentioned m. 2 used horizontal lines drawn above the letters.

In the facsimile of f. 58[r] I have noticed three deletions, all by the copyist himself. The diagonal line is used once (col. 2, 6), the dot placed underneath once (col. 1, 25), and both the dot and diagonal line once (col. 2, 26).

[2] Cf. p. 251, note 3.

The Archetype of the Extant Manuscripts 33

(iii)   56, 2, 10 (14, 8), *par/ta aprioribus* in text, †– *parta priore* in mg.

(iv)   56ᵛ, 1, 10, (15, 8), $\overline{mi}scere$ in text, †– $c\overset{y}{i}ere$ in mg.

(v)   56ᵛ, 2, 12 (16, 1), †$u\overline{o}$ *adicca* in text, †$\overline{bo}uid/icta$ in mg.

(vi)   56ᵛ, 2, 29 (16, 10), †$n\overline{e}quaqu\overline{a}$ in text, $\overline{N}equ\overline{a}$ in mg.

(vii)   57, 1, 2 (16, 11), $d\overline{u}rius$ in text, †– *dubius* in mg.

(viii)   57, 1, 25 f. (16, 22), †$f\overset{\cdot}{a}cta$ *ex/ercitus licentia ducis salute*¹ in text, $\overset{v}{—}pacti$ *exercitus licentiā dux salutem* in lower mg.

(ix)   58, 1, 8 (19, 6), *priuatis* in text, †*priuátus* in mg.

(x)   58, 1, 20 (19, 13), †$\overline{au}ction\overline{e}$ in text, $exction\overline{e}$ in mg.

(xi)   58ᵛ, 1, 2 (21, 3), †$\overline{in}otio$ in text, *et otio* in mg.

(xii)   58ᵛ, 1, 18 (21, 11), *balinea* in text, $b\overset{y}{a}lnea$ in mg.

(xiii)   58ᵛ, 1, 24 (22, 2), *adtanaum* in text, †*ad taum* in mg.

(xiv)   58ᵛ, 1, 29 (22, 5), $\overline{ca}stellis$ in text, †$t\overline{e}lis$ in mg.

(xv)   58ᵛ, 2, 6 (22, 8), *ac* in text, †$\overline{au}t$ in mg.

(xvi)   58ᵛ, 2, 21 (22, 15), †$\overline{con}uitiis$ in text, $\overline{con}uiciis$ in mg.

(xvii)   59, 1, 21 (24, 6), *válentissimam* in text, †$\overset{\cdot}{o}$ in mg.

(xviii)   59, 2, 2 (24, 12), $\overline{ge}ntis$ in text, †$\overline{ge}nte$ in mg.

(xix)   59, 2, 17 (25, 3), †$h\overline{os}tilis$ *exercitus* in text, $h\overline{os}tili$ *exercitu* in mg.

(xx)   59, 2, 21 (25, 5), $\overline{ui}rium$ in text, †$\overline{ui}num$ in mg.

(xxi)   59, 2, 25 (25, 7), $\overset{\cdot}{mi}xti$ in text, †$\overset{\cdot}{mi}xto$ in mg. (?)

(xxii)   59ᵛ, 1, 12 (25, 16), †$\overset{\cdot}{c}astellum$ in text, $\overset{\cdot}{c}astella$ in mg.

(xxiii)   59ᵛ, 1, 15 (25, 17), †$\overline{ex}cedendum$ in text, & in mg.

(xxiv)   59ᵛ, 2, 12 (26, 11), †*hostis* in text, $\overset{\cdot}{e}$ *in* mg.

(xxv)   60, 1, 15 (28, 4), $\overline{in}mixti$² in text, †$\overline{im}mixtis$ in mg.

(xxvi)   60, 1, 21 (28, 7), $\overline{prae}uehebantur$ in text, †$\overline{pb}ebantur\ y$ in mg.

(xxvii)   60, 2, 14 (29, 4), $\overline{in}luctu$ in text, †$\overset{\cdot}{in}lustrans$ in mg.

(xxviii)   60ᵛ, 1, 4 (29, 14), †$\overline{ui}ris$ in text, †– *uirens* in mg.

(xxix)   60ᵛ, 1, 27 (30, 8), $\overline{ac}$ (*subsidium*) in text, †– *ad* in mg.

(xxx)   60ᵛ, 2, 2 (30, 11) $\overline{co}Ntactu$ in text, †$\overline{con}pactu$ in mg.

(xxxi)   61ᵛ, 1, 12 f. (32, 19), $\overline{ta}mdeserentillos/ceteri\ germani$ *quam* in text, †$\overline{ty}$ *deserent illos/ceteri germani/tamquā* in mg.

(xxxii)   61ᵛ, 1, 18 (32, 22), $a\overline{eg}ramunicipia$ in text, †$t\overline{ae}tra$ *man-cipia* in mg.

(xxxiii)   61ᵛ, 2, 1 (33, 3) $\overline{in}struebatur$ in text, †*instituebatʳ* in mg.

---

[1] The reading of the text has been expunctuated by the second hand by means of horizontal lines drawn above the letters.

[2] The textual reading has been changed to *inmixtis*.

(xxxiv)   61ᵛ, 2, 3 (33, 4) †mōnitis in text, mūnimentis in mg.
(xxxv)   62, 1, 30 (34, 7), r̄uere in text, †r̄uebant in mg.
(xxxvi)   62, 2, 4 (34, 9), †d̄emtium in text, ēt metuentiū in mg.
(xxxvii)   62, 2, 16 (34, 16), r̄ebellandi in text, †b̄ellandi in mg.
(xxxviii)   62ᵛ, 1, 3, (35, 9), quōceteri in text, †y- quosteter in mg.
(xxxix)   62ᵛ, 1, 12 (35, 14) ārcessendas in text,—accersendas in mg.
(xl)   62ᵛ, 1, 24 (36, 5), †uataçuorum in text, batauorū in mg.
(xli)   62ᵛ, 2, 6 (36, 11), †f̄oedare & tratis in text, †- foede recti trates · uel traces in upper mg.
(xlii)   62ᵛ, 2, 20 (36, 17), †ēa in text, †ei in mg.
(xliii)   63, 1, 18 (37, 12), p̄raestare in text, †p̄bere in mg.
(xliv)   63, 1, 30 (37, 19),—dimissis equissimul in text, †- dimissis qui simulati in lower mg.
(xlv)   63ᵛ, 1, 9 (38, 13), d̄educit in text, †- reducit in mg.
(xlvi)   63ᵛ, 1, 18 (38, 18), t̄rucculensem in text, †- trutulensē in mg.
(xlvii)   63ᵛ, 1, 20 (38, 19), †l̄atere pre/lecta in text, †- latere lecto in mg.
(xlviii)   63ᵛ, 1, 24 (39, 2), †d̄omitianus in text, —domitiano/moris in mg.
(xlix)   63ᵛ, 2, 15 (39, 13), p̄raesentia in text, †- p̄sens in mg.
(l)   76ᵛ, 1, 13 (45, 20), figerem' in text, †pingéremus in mg.
(li)   76ᵛ, 1, 14 (45, 21), †túm in text, tám in mg.
(lii)   76ᵛ, 1, 19 (45, 24), compositus in text, †comploratus in mg.
(liii)   76ᵛ, 1, 26 (46, 6), potius in text, te p̄otius in mg.
(liv)   76ᵛ, 1, 27 (46, 6), †temporalībus in text, †temp̄orib in mg.

Origins of Doublets

I shall now examine these doublets for the purpose of determining their various origins and relative antiquity.

Doublets Derived from Marginal Index or from a Gloss.—A few of the doublets I believe to have arisen from the use of marginal indices to call attention to proper names found in the text.[1] We find evidence for the use of such marginal indices on f. 57, 2, 11 (ch. 17) *bregantum* m. 2 in mg. opposite the same word of the text, and again on f. 57ᵛ, 1, 3 (ch. 18), *Ordouicum* m. 2 in mg. opposite *ordouicum* in the text. When either the

[1] In *Germ.* 21, 14, a marginal caption, *uictus inter hospites*, conflated with a marginal variant, *comis*, found its way into the text.

word of the text or of the margin, or both, become corrupted doublets may arise. Such I believe to have been the origin of the variants shown in ii, v, xl, xlvi.

Again, the marginal index may stand in the nominative case opposite an oblique case of the same word in the text. The marginal index may then be misunderstood as a variant, and an exchange of the textual and marginal readings may be effected.[1] Such appears to be the origin of the textual reading (xlviii) *domitianus*.

A marginal (or interlinear) word, instead of serving as an index, may have been introduced as a gloss or explanation of some word in the text, and a later copyist may be misled into accepting this as a variant reading. An excellent example of a gloss mistaken for a variant is found in the marginal reading in xliii. The same doublets occur in *Germania* 26, 5.

Doublets Arising from Correction of Errors.—Most of the doublets in Hf. find their explanation in the correction of errors. That is, an error made in the transcription of a manuscript is later corrected, but both the error and correction are perpetuated in the apograph as though they were doublets. I have reserved for another section my account of the errors themselves and their causes, but will now show how the corrections may have been made in such a way as to give rise to doublets.

Correction from Another Manuscript.—It is noteworthy that in the *Agricola*[2] one of the doublets does as a rule offer the correct reading—at least insofar as we can determine what is correct. This may lead us to suspect that our text has been conflated from two manuscript sources. Such an hypothesis seems to me plausible enough, though hardly necessary. However, I am convinced that if such a conflation occurred it did not originate in the Hersfeld codex itself, but should rather be referred to some exemplar written in antiquity. The

---

[1] In *de Gram.* 22 the **X** family reads *tiberius uerbum* for *tiberi uerbum*. The **Y** family has *tiberium* (without *uerbum*). I suspect that the *tiberius* of the **X** family originated as a marginal index to a lost *tiberi* of the text.

[2] The same is true of the doublets in the *Germania* (see pp. 122 ff.).

very character of many of the doublets shows that if the corrector of Hf. had at his disposal some second manuscript it must have been a manuscript with a line of descent from antiquity distinct from that of the archetype of Hf. But that a ninth-century scribe had access to two manuscripts of the *Agricola* descending from antiquity by two different routes is *per se* improbable.

Correction by Conjectural Emendation.—The original scribe or the corrector (or some reader), finding a corruption in the text, may enter a variant reading which is a conjecture of his own, but naturally if he has the proper respect for the manuscript tradition he will not at the same time delete the reading which he found in his archetype. Again, the scribe may emend as he copies, while a corrector may enter in the margin the readings of the archetype.

However, conjectural emendations which betray themselves are rare in the Hersfeld *Agricola*. A clear case is found in xxviii, *uiris* in text, *uirens* in margin. The reading of the text is doubtless a corruption of *uiridis*, while that of the margin is a conjectural emendation. We have here an interesting example of the cycle through which a reading may pass, for the third (fifteenth-century) hand has actually restored *uiridis* by writing *di* above the line. One of the fifteenth-century decendants of Hf., **A**, has *uiridis* in the text and *uirens* in thes margin. Before the discovery of Hf. it would have been impossible to find a satisfactory explanation of the variant *uirens* in **A**.[1]

In another passage a double attempt at conjectural emendation is betrayed: (xli) *foedare & tratis* in text, *foede recti trates · uel traces* in mg. Any attempt to explain the origin of these doublets is doubtful, since we cannot be sure of the correct reading. Assuming, however, that *fodere et stratis* were the words of Tacitus, we see a progressive series of corruptions in

[1] The other fifteenth-century MSS. read only *uiridis*. This illustration shows how a variant which appears to be a needless gloss or an inexcusable interpolation may have had its origin at a time when there was a corruption in the text.

The Archetype of the Extant Manuscripts 37

the antecedents of Hf. Possibly the first stage was *FOE-DEREETSTRATIS*, in which an *E* was inserted by a scribe who had in mind the adverb *foede*. The next stage may have been the loss of the *S* of *STRATIS*. Then proceeding from *FOEDEREETTRATIS* there was perhaps a twofold attempt at emendation,[1] *foede recti* and *foedare et*,[2] but no attempt was made to heal *tratis*.[3]

A good example of a conjectural emendation in the *Germania* is in 45, 5, where *deorum* was meant as a correction of *eorum*, which is in reality a corruption of *equorum*. In the *de Gram.* we may note, 13 *hero suo Metrae* as a correction of *Eros nametra*, the latter probably being a corruption of *Eros < . . . > nam erat;* [4] 10 *hermam* as a variant of *haere*, the two together pointing to *haerem*, a corruption of *haeresin*.

The examples cited above all show unsuccessful attempts to heal a corrupted text. Sometimes the "correction" may assume the form of needless interpolation of a sound text.[5] Apparent interpolations of the genuine tradition [6] are found in the readings of the text in viii and xix, and in the readings of the margin in xxxv, xlix, lii.[7] There are also three orthograph-

[1] I am, of course, speaking of scribal "emendations," which often went no further than to make Latin words out of a meaningless jumble of letters.

[2] Naturally, there are other possibilities. The *i* of *recti* may have been the result of misreading the *s* of *stratis*, or it may point to an *istratis* (cf. p. 244) in the text at one point in its tradition.

[3] We are not here concerned with the graphical confusion between *trates* and *traces* (cf. p. 54), or with the phonetic confusion between *tratis* and *trates* (cf. p. 241).

[4] Here the interpolation may be of the fifteenth century, as it is found only in the Y family.

[5] It may not seem altogether consistent to group doublets arising from interpolation under those coming from correction of errors. Presumably, however, an interpolation is an *attempted* correction of a *fancied* error.

[6] I say *apparent* because I have just shown that a variant which appears to be a wanton interpolation may have originated at a time when there was a corruption in the text (see p. 36, note 1).

[7] On viii and xxxv see p. 41 and note 2. There is some doubt about the meaning in xix. I understand *infesta hostili exercitu* to mean, "marches by land fraught with danger to an invading (*i.e.* the Roman) army." If this is correct, *hostilis exercitus* was probably introduced by someone who thought that the reference should be to the Britons. Although some editors of the *Agricola*

ical variants which we may classify under interpolations (xii, xiv,[1] xxxix). While in xii and xxxix it may be impossible to tell which spelling is to be preferred, it is certain that the author did not use both in the same place, and accordingly one may be regarded as an interpolation.

Correction from the Archetype.—Still another source from which corrections may be made is the very archetype from which the manuscript was copied. The copyist may make an error *currente calamo* which he (or the reviser) corrects, but both the error and correction will be perpetuated in a later copy as though they were doublets. The objection may be raised that in a correction of this kind the error would be deleted, and consequently would not be copied into a later manuscript. Probably as a rule this was true, but it is possible to find various reasons why both the corruption and correction should be transmitted as doublets.

In the first place, the copyist may omit a word, which either he or the corrector will then add to the margin. But later in the transcription of an apograph the marginal correction may be mistaken for a variant of some word in the text. However, our manuscript offers no example of such a misunderstanding, unless it be that in *Agr.* 45, 24 (lii) we should read *paucioribus tamen lacrimis comploratus compositus es*.[2]

In the second place, because of some peculiarity of the archetype, such as an abbreviation, a ligature, an unfamiliar form of a letter, or through some blemish, such as a blot or a rubbing away of the ink, the scribe may be uncertain as to which is the true reading, and may therefore suggest two

prefer (lii) *comploratus*, I feel that this is unsound palaeographically. The preceding *lacrimis* might readily have suggested *comploratus* to a copyist or reader, but would hardly have suggested *compositus*. For another possible explanation of these doublets see p. 38.

[1] In xiv the marginal *telis* stands, of course, for *castelis*.

[2] Cf. p. 37 and note 7. In *de Gram.* 4, 3, *iam* and *tam* appear to have existed as doublets in Hf., though the correct reading is *iam tum*. The opposite error of accepting a variant as an addition to the text was, of course, common among ignorant scribes. On f. 62, 2, 4 (*Agr.* 34, 9), Hf. has *dementium* in the text and *et metuentium* in the margin. T, a direct copy, reads *dementium et metuentium*.

possibilities. That is, he deliberately creates doublets. Again, the corrector may not be satisfied that the original scribe has correctly deciphered the writing of the archetype, and so enters in the margin an alternative reading. The process may be illustrated by comparing Hf. with two of its fifteenth-century descendants. F. 56^v, 1, 8 (*Agr.* 15), Hf. reads *man'*. A has *manum*, B has only *manum*. Presumably the scribe of the archetype of **AB** was uncertain as to the significance of the abbreviation in Hf. and so offered both readings.[1]

Doublets which I believe to have arisen from the uncertainty of the scribe or corrector as to the true reading because of graphical peculiarities of the archetype, are to be seen in vii, ix, xvii, xx, xxi, xxii, xxiii, xxx, xxxi,[2] xli (*uel traces*), li.

Sometimes the scribe in making his corrections may have neglected to append the customary deletion symbols. Naturally in this case a future copyist would have understood the two readings as variants.

Finally, a copyist may have disregarded the deletion symbols which he found in the archetype, either because he did not understand them, or because he wished to omit nothing which was written in the parent manuscript. In either case, he would, of course, have copied both the corrupt reading and the correction.

In the fifteenth-century descendants of the Hersfeld *Agricola* I have found several instances in which the scribes have ignored the corrections of the archetype and have copied the corrupted readings, though I cannot cite any instance in which this has given rise to doublets. F. 58, 1, 21 (ch. 19), the scribe first wrote *auctione mae qualitate*. Perceiving his error, he drew a diagonal line through the *m* and made a line of sus-

[1] The superscript reading of **A** may, of course, be a conjectural restoration of its copyist, Pomponius Laetus.

[2] See my discussion of xxxi on p. 74. It is true that here the processes of error and correction are reversed, since it was really the corrector who made the error, but we may suppose that he intended the marginal reading as a possible correction of a possible error.

pension above the final *e* of *auctione*. Nevertheless, **A**, a copy of a lost apograph of Hf., reads *auctionem inaequalitate*; **B**, a copy of the same apograph, reads *exactionem in aequalitate*, having received into the text the marginal variant of *auctionem*. Had a corrector of the immediate archetype of **A** and **B** written the true reading *aequalitate* in the margin, we might find in **A**[1] the variants *aequalitate: inaequalitate*. Again, f. 59, 1, 9 (ch. 25), Hf. has *incolentĩs*. That one copyist disregarded the correction is shown by the reading *incolentis* in **A** and **B**. F. 60, 2, 17 (ch. 29), Hf. reads *praedatũm* with the deletion of *um* indicated. **A** reads *praedatam* with a dot above and below the *m*. This shows that the copyist of the archetype of **A** originally wrote *praedatam*, *i.e.* he failed to note the deletion of *m* in Hf. Finally, f. 57, 1, 25–26 (ch. 16), the second hand has deleted the reading of the text, *facta exercitus licentia ducis salute*, yet this reading is found as a variant in the margin of **A**.

Relative Antiquity of Doublets

It has, I trust, already become apparent that many of the marginal variants in Hf. did not originate with the corrector, but were copied in from the archetype. However, this matter of the relative antiquity of the doublets demands further investigation, and if possible some criterion must be found for determining which of the variants originated in the transcription of Hf. and which were copied in from the archetype. I now propose to examine those doublets which, in my opinion, declare their origin to antedate the transcription of the Hersfeld codex. In my discussion of these passages I adopt the hypothesis that neither the original copyist nor the corrector of Hf. had a second manuscript at his disposal. I grant that it is impossible to prove this hypothesis, but it appears to me inherently probable.[2]

v. †*uo adicca* in text, †*bouidicta* in mg. Both readings are older than Hf. The confusion of *b* and consonant *u* is ancient.

[1] B offers no marginal variants.
[2] Cf. p. 35.

As the name does not occur elsewhere in the text, the corrector of Hf. would have had no way of restoring the *b* in the marginal reading.

viii. †*facta exercitus licentia ducis salute* in text, *pacti exercitus licentiam dux salutem* in mg. The interpolated textual reading appears to show a secondary corruption, *pacta* > *facta*. In this case, it is older than Hf. The marginal reading, because of its very excellence, can hardly be a conjectural restoration.[1]

xxvii. *inluctu* in text, †*inlustrans* in mg. As Annibaldi has recognized, the marginal reading originally belonged with *inlustrauit* (l. 7). Since the marginal variant has been misplaced, it is obviously older than Hf.

xxxv. *ruere* in text, †*ruebant* in mg. The marginal reading is not an invention of the corrector of Hf., for the manuscript reads *quoque animal* for *quodque animal,* and it would be impossible to explain the plural form of the verb, unless the marginal reading had come into being before the corruption of *quodque* to *quoque*. It is unthinkable that the textual reading is a conjectural restoration.

xl. †*uatauorum* in text, *batauorum* in mg. The name occurs in but one other place in the text, f. 62ᵛ 2, 4, but here is corrupted to *uatabi*. Hence the marginal reading can hardly be a restoration of the corrector of Hf. Obviously the corruption of the textual reading is ancient.

xli. †*foedare & tratis* in text, †*foede recti trates uel traces* in mg. The *uel traces* of the marginal reading is a variant, not of the textual reading, but of the marginal *trates*. This shows that *trates* is older than Hf.[2] The *tratis* of the text likewise antedates Hf., since it points to the true reading *stratis*.

[1] I grant the other possibility that the copyist of Hf. deliberately changed the reading of his archetype as he wrote, and that the corrector added the reading of the archetype to the margin. An argument in support of this supposition may be found in the fact that the corrector has actually placed marks of deletion above the textual reading. However, I regard such wanton interpolation as contrary to the general practice of Carolingian scribes, and in particular contrary to the practice of the scribe of Hf.

[2] The *uel traces* of the margin originated with the corrector of Hf. See p. 43.

xlvii. *latere prelecta* in text, *latere lecto* in mg. If the corrector of Hf. had meant *lecto* to stand for *prelecto*, as a correction of *prelecta* in the text, he would hardly have prefixed *latere*. The marginal reading as it now stands is the outgrowth of a misunderstanding of an older correction of *prelecta* to (*pre*)*lecto*.[1] I suspect that in iv, vi, xiv, as well, the corrector of Hf. did not understand the true nature of the marginal variants.

xlviii. †*domitianus* in text, *domitiano moris* in mg. It is out of the question that the marginal reading is a conjectural emendation. Since the original marginal index and the reading of the text have exchanged places, both must be recognized as older than Hf.

iii. iv. xxvi. xxxii. xliv. In every case the reading of the text is correct, and that of the margin corrupt. Furthermore, the marginal readings all show secondary stages of corruption,[2] which is proof that the initial errors were older than Hf. Hence, both doublets must be older than Hf., unless we assume that the first scribe corrected the errors of the archetype as he wrote, and that the corrector preserved these errors by writing them in the margin. But I think it highly improbable, if not impossible, that the textual readings are conjectural restorations made from the actual marginal readings.

xiii. xviii. xxxiii. xxxvii. xlv. Here again the marginal readings are corrupt, but do not bear evidence of secondary stages of corruption. However, they can scarcely have been caused by the uncertainty of the corrector as to the true readings of the archetype, and must consequently be older than Hf. In other words, the marginal readings must at one time have stood in the text. Were they the readings of the text of the archetype of Hf., which were corrected by the copyist of the latter as he wrote, but added to the margin by the corrector? That the first scribe made the correction (xiii) from *taum* to *tanaum* I regarded as impossible. I grant that he may have made the restorations conjecturally in the other four cases,

---

[1] On the confusion of *o* and *a* see p. 53.
[2] See pp. 48, 50 f.

but this does not strike me as the more reasonable explanation

x. xxxiv. xxxvi. Here the marginal readings are correct and those of the text corrupt. Since the latter show secondary stages of corruption,[1] the initial errors must have originated before the transcription of Hf. Consequently the second hand could not have drawn its corrections from the archetype, unless they were already there in the form of variant readings—at least if we again exclude, on the ground of general probabilities, the explanation of conjectural restoration.

Reference-symbols Indicate Relative Antiquity.—We have found that twenty-one of the fifty-four doublets are probably older than Hf. Is there any way of determining the relative age of the remaining doublets? I believe that the answer is to be found in the reference-symbol. In all but two (xiii, xl) of these twenty-one readings the horizontal line is found as a *signe de renvoi*. What is more important, the dot is found with none of them.

Employment of the Dot as a Reference-symbol.—Turning to the use of the dot as a reference-symbol, we note first of all that it was used by the corrector, f. 58ᵛ, 2, 3 (*Agr.* 22, 6), both in the text and in the margin to call attention to the marginal entry *ab*. Presumably the corrector has merely added a word which was in the text of the archetype but had been omitted by the first scribe.

The dot is again employed before *uel traces* in the marginal reading of doublet xli. Here the marginal reading is in two parts. The first part, *foede recti trates*, bears evidence of being older than Hf.,[2] and has the horizontal line as a reference-symbol. The second part, ·*uel traces*, proposes a variant, not for the reading of the text, but for the marginal *trates*. In other words, I believe that in *uel traces* we have a variant which was created by the corrector of Hf., because he was not sure whether the marginal reading of his archetype was *trates* or *traces*.

[1] See pp. 50 f.
[2] Cf. pp. 36 f.

Dot Indicates Marginal Variants Originating with Corrector of Hf.—If we examine the other doublets which employ the dot as a reference-symbol (ix, xvii, xxi, xxii, xxiii, xxiv, xlii), we find that the corruptions, whether they stand in the margin or in the text, are but a single stage removed from the true readings[1]—*i.e.* they have nothing inherent to show that they could not have arisen in the transcription of Hf. itself. Moreover, all but two of the doublets (xxiv, xlii)[2] appear to be the result of graphical confusions,[3] as if the corrector were uncertain as to the reading of his exemplar.

Horizontal Line Indicates Variant Older than Hf.— I adopt the hypothesis, to which I shall return, that in ff. 56–63 the marginal variants accompanied by the dot originated with the corrector of Hf.[4] Other reference-symbols, almost without exception the horizontal line, indicate marginal variants which the corrector of Hf. copied in from the archetype.[5]

It is true that the marginal reading in xxxi is accompanied by the horizontal line, though I assign it *quâ* variant to the corrector of Hf. However, my explanation[6] assumes that there was already a marginal reading (words omitted from the text) in the archetype, and consequently the corrector may merely have copied the symbol which he found before him.

Reference-symbols on f. 76ᵛ.—On f. 76ᵛ two pairs of doublets (liii, liv) are found with the horizontal line. Here the text seems hopelessly corrupt, and we may readily believe that

[1] In xlii both readings seem corrupt.

[2] In xxiv the corrector has merely made in the margin an orthographical correction of his own, such as he has frequently made within the text itself. The marginal reading in xlii is puzzling. Is it an emendation proposed by the corrector, or is it due to some graphical peculiarity of the archetype?

[3] Naturally, not all doublets which appear to be the result of graphical confusions are accompanied by the dot, for this same source of error was doubtless potent during the transcriptions of the numerous antecedents of Hf.

[4] It will be found that this hypothesis conforms well with the theory of a minuscule archetype for Hf. See pp. 58 ff.

[5] The first scribe may, of course, sometimes have transferred the marginal reading of the archetype to the text, leaving it for the corrector to copy into the margin the reading which was formerly in the text.

[6] See my explanation on p. 74.

the doublets are older than Hf. For one pair (lii) no reference-symbol is reported.[1] The remaining pairs of doublets (l, li) are accompanied by a diagonal line. In li the confusion represented is purely graphical, and we may easily believe that the *tum* of the text was an error of the first scribe induced by the open *a* of his archetype. The doublets in l present more difficulty, for the marginal reading appears at first sight to be the result of a secondary stage of corruption: *figeremus* > *fingeremus* > *pingeremus*. However, this is not the only possible explanation. For instance, if the archetype of Hf. offered an *f* closely resembling *p*, the corrector may have decided that the reading was *pigeremus*, and then made the slight correction to *pingeremus*. The evidence afforded by this single page is insufficient, but I think it probable that for this part of the work the diagonal line indicates doublets created in the transcription of Hf.[2]

Sources of Corruption in the *Hersfeld* Agricola.

A study of the sources of corruption in the Hersfeld *Agricola* has an important bearing on the text of the *Germania*, for we may reasonably assume that such a study will give an index to the types of error existing in the Hersfeld manuscript of the *Germania*, and we shall thereby be enabled to determine within certain limits which of the mistakes in our fifteenth-century manuscripts were already in Hf., and which are of later origin.

Naturally any attempt to determine the sources of error in a manuscript which is the sole basis for the text, as is the case with the Hersfeld *Agricola*, is fraught with hazard. We may recognize a certain passage as indubitably corrupt, but any attempt to explain the corruption demands a knowledge of the true reading—information which is generally denied us.

In the Hersfeld *Agricola* the surest basis for studying the causes engendering errors is, I believe, to be found in the double

[1] See p. 37 and note 7; p. 38 and note 2.

[2] Annibaldi does not state whether the marginal readings on f. 76ᵛ are by a hand different from that of the text. The latter he believes to be different from the hand which wrote ff. 56–63 (see p. 23).

readings, where as a rule (at least to all appearances) the corruption is confronted by the genuine reading. Again, much may be gleaned regarding the errors made in the transcription of Hf. itself by examining the mistakes which the scribe made and corrected as he copied, or the mistakes of the scribe which were corrected by the reviser, though the results of such an examination have their weakness, since we cannot always be sure whether the scribe or reviser was correcting from the archetype or was emending *suo Marte*. Finally, there are some passages in which the corruptions are so slight and fall within such generally recognized categories as to leave no reasonable doubt regarding the correct restoration.

Scriptura Continua.—In the tradition of our Latin texts *scriptura continua* has played an important part in producing the varied mistakes of which copyists were capable. The scribe of the Hersfeld *Agricola* copied from an archetype in *scriptura continua*, or at least from one in which the word separation was very imperfect.[1] His work was of necessity largely mechanical. If he was to make any speed at all, he could not concern himself with the interpretation of the text as a whole, but only with the meanings of the individual words or of very small groups of words. Doubtless the thing uppermost in his mind was the formation of separate words from the continuous letters. All who have had experience in reading manuscripts in *scriptura continua* know how numerous are the opportunities for error. The careful and intelligent scribe would, of course, recognize and correct his mistakes as he proceeded. Our scribe did this in the majority of cases, though he left the final work of revision to the corrector.

Wrong Word-division.—The simplest type of mistake caused by *scriptura continua* is found in the erroneous separation of the letters. Thus, f. 59ᵛ, 2, 19, the copyist saw in his archetype *uirtutisuae*. He first read *uirtutis* and so wrote it. Then

---

[1] Among the numerous vestiges of *scriptura continua*, in addition to those given below, I will cite: 56, 2, 28 *&inter prae tando*; 56ᵛ, 1, 15 *nuncabignauis*; 57, 1, 21 *militesotiolasciuir&*; 57ᵛ, 1, 21 *quoceterispar*; 59ᵛ, 1, 5 *obstupe faciebant*; 61, 1, 23 *longin quitasac*.

perceiving his mistake he deleted the *s* and wrote *suae*. Other errors of this type are: 56ᵛ, 1, 13 *quis poliet*; 58, 1, 21 *auctionē maequalitate*; 61ᵛ, 1, 30 *procursus/ simul*; 62, 2, 18 *ardor,em inebat*; 62ᵛ, 2, 23 *exterritis/sine*; 63, 1, 13 *uulnera re,capere*; 2̄, 13 *in qui s,aulus*.

In many of the other types of error which I shall discuss *scriptura continua* must have exerted its influence, but was probably not the only factor at work.

Omission.—The most common type of error in the Hersfeld *Agricola* consists in the omission of letters, syllables, or even entire words:[1] 57, 1, 6 *nouusque* corr. to *nouus eoque; 57, 2, 20 *subiit omitted and added above the line; 29 *atate* corr. to *aestate*; 57ᵛ, 1, 22 *animosi/mili* corr. to *animus simili*;[2] 2, 20 *speritate* corr. to **prosperi-*; 58ᵛ, 2, 3 *ab omitted and added in margin; 24 *erat* corr. to *supererat; 58, 2, 13 *aesturia* corr. to *aestuaria*; 24 *&* added above; 60, 1, 30 *scitiam* corr. to *inscitiam; 61ᵛ, 1, 14 *nequicquam* corr. to *necquic-*; 62, 1, 4 *riculosissima* corr. to *pericu-*; 21 *recenset* corr. to *-sete*; 62ᵛ, 1, 6 *equetrepitu; 2, 29 *paucitate* corr. to **-tem*; 63, 1, 7 *pulsoinfugam* corr. to *pulsosin-*; 63ᵛ, 1, 6 **&* (*exacta*) added above; 2, 12 *quoque* corr. to *quodque; 76ᵛ, 1, 5 *oportunitate* corr. to *oppor-*; 15 *longe*[3] (*longe* corr. to *longae*).

I assume that the foregoing errors were made and corrected in the transcription of Hf., but naturally the same type of mistake was made in the transcriptions of its various antecedents as well. We may note, 62ᵛ, 1, 27 (ch. 36) *uetustatenniliae* for *uetustate militiae*; 2, 19 *equestres* for *aequa nostris* (?);[4]

---

[1] The asterisk indicates that the corrections were made by the second (contemporary) hand. The other corrections were made by the first copyist (in most cases *ex silentio* from Annibaldi's text). I am convinced that the corrector had the archetype before him, though it is possible that some minor corrections may have been his own emendations of the archetype's errors (cf. pp. 31 f.).

[2] A good example of the influence of *scriptura continua*. The copyist at first thought that he recognized the word *animosi*.

[3] Cf. p. 131.

[4] The stages of corruption were: *aequanostris > aequastris > equestris*, the second stage representing an "emendation." There was no compendium for *nostris* involved in the error.

63, 2, 11 *addecemilia*. However, the older errors of this type can best be detected in the places where Hf. offers doublets.[1] The omission of letters or syllables may be noted in the following doublets:[2] (vi) *nequamquam* > *nequaquam*; (xiii) *tanaum* > *taum*; (xxxvii) *rebellandi* > *bellandi*; (liv) *temporalibus*[3] > *temporibus*. Other variants as they now appear show a secondary stage of corruption, but it is probable that the intervening stage was due to this same type of error: (iii) *prioribus* > *prioris* > *priore*; (x) *exactionem* > *actionem* > *auctionem*; (xxxii) *municipia* > *muncipia* > *mancipià*; (xxxiv) *munimentis* > *munitis* > *monitis*; (xxxvi) *et metuentium* > *et mentium* > *dementium*; (xli) *foedare & tratis* etc. (see p. 37); (xliv) *dimissisequissimul* > *dimissisquisimul* > *dimissis qui simulati*.

Repetition.—Repetitions of words from other places in the text are to be seen in the following examples: 57, 1, 23 (ch. 16) *sed* (deleted) before *trebellius*, probably a repetition of *sed* in the third line above; 61ᵛ, 1, 1 (ch. 32) *circumtrepidos*, where *circum* appears to have been repeated from *circumspectantes* in the second line below;[4] 56ᵛ, 1, 18 (ch. 15) *&* (deleted) before *sese*, perhaps a repetition from the second line below. Possibly, 56ᵛ, 2, 20 (ch. 16) *ingeniis* is due to a fusion of *in* (*barbaris*) and *genus*.[5]

In the *Germania* we may compare 20, 12, the repetition of *in*, and 33, 9, of *gentibus*, from the preceding line.

The repetition of single letters or syllables (dittography) is rare, and most of the examples found are due to phonetic confusion[6] rather than to mere mechanical errors of transcription: 56, 1, 25 (ch. 13) *domitiae* for *domitae*; 2, 23 (ch. 14) *occansioni*; 25 (ch. 15) *brittania agitare* for *britanni agitare*; 57ᵛ, 1, 2 (ch. 18), 59, 2, 4 (ch. 24) *occansionem*; 59, 1, 8 (ch. 23) *proprior* for *propior*;[7] *brittania, brittannia, brittanni, brittani*.

[1] The Roman numerals refer to the table of doublets, pp. 32 ff.

[2] The symbol > denotes "corrupted to."

[3] *Temporalibus* is itself corrupt.

[4] The error is older than Hf. See p. 75, note 4.

[5] Cf. A. Schöne, *Woch. kl. Phil.*, 1912, 273. I think Schöne's hypothesis of an uncial forebear with sixteen letters to the line doubtful (cf. pp. 74 ff.).

[6] See p. 51.

[7] For the same error in the *Germania* see p. 103.

The Archetype of the Extant Manuscripts 49

Transposition.—Instances of transposition are not numerous. F. 57, 2, 23 (ch. 17) the copyist wrote *gentem* after *armis*, then expunctuated and wrote it before *armis* in the margin of the preceding line. F. 60ᵛ, 1, 15 (ch. 30) the copyist wrote *hodiernum diem* after *uestrum,* but the corrector expunctuated and wrote the words above (*i.e.* before) *consensumque*. In the archetype *hodiernum diem* was probably in the margin.[1] Uncertainty as to the true position of a marginal addition in the archetype gave rise to the variant reading in 61ᵛ, 1, 12 (xxxi).[1] F. 58ᵛ, 2, 7 (ch. 22) the words *craebrae eruptiones* appear to be misplaced. The disarrangement doubtless is older than Hf. The transposition of letters or syllables is rare: 60ᵛ, 2, 17 *sc utrantur* for *scrutantur*.

Assimilation.—The assimilation of a word-ending to that of the following word is seen, 59, 2, 3 (ch. 24) *spetiae amicitiae*; 60ᵛ, 2, 16 (ch. 30) *defuerae terrae* corr. to *defuere terram;[2] 58, 2, 10 (ch. 20) *contractu* (corr. to *-to*) *exercitu*.[3] A similar error antedating Hf. is to be seen in (xxv) *inmixtis* (*manipulis*) for *inmixti*. Assimilation of a word to the case of the following or preceding word is found, 58ᵛ, 1, 7 (ch. 21) *honor &aemulatio* corr. to **-ris aemu-*; 59ᵛ, 2, 18 (ch. 27) *cuius conscientiae*.

Confusion of Words Similar in Appearance.—Sometimes the scribe failed to grasp the word before him and quite unintentionally substituted another whose general appearance was the same, even though the error cannot definitely be attributed to any graphical peculiarity of the archetype: 56ᵛ, 1, 4 (ch. 15) *d̊*; 57ᵛ, 1, 28 (ch. 18) *cumius* corr. to *cuius*; 2, 23 *continuitsine* corr. to *continuisse ne*; 62ᵛ, 1, 29 (ch. 36) *inabitabile* corr. to *inabile*; 63ᵛ, 2, 12 *saeuire* corr. to *saeuae*; 62ᵛ, 2, 3 *aperto* for *arto*, where the error may be older than Hf., as it has not been corrected.[4]

---

[1] See my discussion, p. 74.

[2] Apparently *defuerae* (cf. p. 237) was the spelling of the archetype, so here the correction to *defuere* must have been made by the reviser.

[3] Cf. *Germ.* 38, 11 *formae sed innoxiae.*

[4] Cf. 76ᵛ, 1, 5 *perhiberent* for *perhibent*. The copyist quite unconsciously substituted the subjunctive for the indicative because of the preceding *ut*.

50   THE GERMANIA OF TACITUS

This same type of error in some of the antecedents of Hf. has produced doublets: (i) *praecipue* for *praeceptum*; (xi) *in otio* for *et otio*; (xv) *aut* for *ac*; (xxix) *ad* for *ac*; (xxxiii) *instituebatur* for *instruebatur*; (xlv) *reducit* for *deducit*.

Substitution of a Word of Similar or of Opposite Meaning.—Occasionally our copyist appears to have substituted quite unconsciously a word of similar or of opposite meaning to the one which he saw before him: 59ᵛ, 1, 23 (ch. 26) *incognitum* corr. to *cognitum*; 60ᵛ, 2, 7 (ch. 30) *tum* corr. to **Nunc*; 58, 2, 6 (ch. 20) *sine curia* corr. to *incuria*.[1] Probably a similar mistake in an earlier manuscript is to be seen in 63, 1, 25 (ch. 37) *ignari* for *gnari*.

Interpolation.—The text of the Hersfeld *Agricola* is comparatively free from interpolations,[2] and such as can be found appear to be an inheritance from earlier manuscripts rather than innovations of the copyist or corrector. We may detect two kinds of interpolation: (1) interpolation of a sound text, and (2) interpolation originating in an attempt to heal a corrupt text.[3] Examples of the former class, which are few in number, I have already adduced.[4] To these we may add the marginal *bouidicta* (57ᵛ, 2, 12, ch. 16) for *Boudicca*, perhaps due to the tendency of scribes to make Latin words out of names which meant nothing to them. Of the latter class, in addition to the two instances previously noted,[5] I may cite the following examples in which variants originating in some other form of corruption have become still further corrupted through attempts at emendation:[6] (iv) *miscire* > *misciere* > *ciere*; (x) *exactionem* > *actionem* > *auctionem*; (xxvi) *praeuehebantur*

---

[1] The copyist had in mind *sine cura*.

[2] The same was true of the text of the Hersfeld *Germania*. On a fifteenth-century interpolator in the Hersfeld codex see p. 31.

[3] Probably this distinction did not exist in the mind of the interpolator, for interpolation of a sound text implies that a corruption was suspected.

[4] See pp. 37 f.

[5] See pp. 36 f.

[6] For example, (x) *exactionem* became *actionem* through the unintentional omission of *ex* (first stage; cf. pp. 47 f.); *actionem* was then "emended" to *auctionem* (second stage).

The Archetype of the Extant Manuscripts 51

> *praebehebantur* [1] > *praebebantur*; (xxxii) *aegra* > *aecra* > *taetra*; [2] (xxxii) *municipia* > *muncipia* > *mancipia*; [2] (xxxiv) *munimentis* > *munitis* > *monitis*; [3] (xxxvi) *et metuentium* > *et mentium* > *dementium*; (xliv) *dimissisequissimul* > *dimissisquisimul* > *dimissis qui simulati*.

Phonetic Confusion.—At this point I will merely mention that errors induced by phonetic confusions in the pronunciation of Latin in late antiquity are found with some frequency in our manuscript. Such confusions involve a wide variety of orthographical details, which I have found it more convenient to discuss in another section in connection with the *Germania* manuscripts.[4]

Graphical Confusion.—I now turn to the graphical errors of the Hersfeld codex, which have special importance since it is upon them that we must depend in any attempt to determine the ancestry of our manuscript. By a "graphical error" I mean an error caused by the misunderstanding of an abbreviation or ligature, or of some peculiar form of letter or group of letters, in the archetype.

In discussing this type of error it will be well to proceed with great caution, for editors are, I suspect, sometimes prone to see mistakes of this kind where they do not exist. If a scribe wrote *instituebatur* for *instruebatur*,[5] it is not necessary to assume, nor does the assumption seem to me even probable, that he had before him an archetype in which the letter *r* resembled the group *it*. It is more reasonable to suppose that he failed to observe carefully and wrote a word whose general appearance and meaning were similar to the one which was actually before him.[6]

Even where we see evidence of graphical confusions, this was

---

[1] On the phonetic confusion producing the first stage of corruption see p. 246.

[2] The second stage may rather have resulted (at least in part) from a graphical peculiarity of the archetype (cf. p. 54).

[3] *Monitis* may rather be the result of a phonetic confusion (cf. p. 244).

[4] See pp. 235–260.

[5] See pp. 49 f.

[6] An error of this kind is in a sense "graphical," but not in the restricted meaning in which I am now using the word.

seldom the only influence at work. For instance, if a copyist had before him *aegrecliuoinstante* and wrote *aegre diu autstante*,[1] it seems fairly certain that in his archetype the letters *cl* resembled *d*, perhaps *o* resembled *a*, and possibly the group *in* bore a resemblance to *ut*.[2] Yet there were other factors at work. *Scriptura continua* was certainly one of the elements producing the errors, and perhaps conjectural emendation was the most important of all. That is, when the scribe thought he had extracted the word *diu*, he may have proceeded to "emend" the rest.

Errors Due to Abbreviations and Ligatures.—Errors in the Hersfeld *Agricola* pointing to abbreviations and ligatures in earlier manuscripts are very few,[3] and this is seldom the only explanation possible even for such examples as may be cited.[4] I submit the following instances, but feel that some are doubtful:

-en: 62ᵛ, 1, 3 *agminae quoceteri* for *agmen in aequo ceteri* (*ag-m̄inaequo* ?).

-er: 56, 1, 21 *auctoritate* for *auctor iterati* (*auctoritati* ?); 57ᵛ, 1, 3 *uterentur* for *uerterentur* (*ūterentur* ?).

est: 59ᵛ, 2, 27 *condicione* for *condicio est* (*condicioē*).[5]

---

[1] Cf. pp. 53, 55.

[2] Assuming, of course, that *instantes* is the correct restoration. *Adstantes* is simpler palaeographically, but hardly gives the desired meaning. I do not mean that all these errors were made in a single transcription. More probably they are successive corruptions.

[3] The Hersfeld *Agricola* is also very sparing in its use of abbreviations and ligatures. See my table on pp. 357 f. In the minor Tacitean works conjectural emendations based upon abbreviations supposed to have existed in Hf. or its antecedents can be tolerated only within the most restricted limits.

[4] For instance, we have seen that the omission of letters or syllables is the most common type of error in our MS. (see p. 47). Consequently such omissions as that of *er*, *en*, *ur*, can hardly be taken as definite proof that these letters were abbreviated in the archetype. Still another possible explanation is that the copyist of Hf. itself intended to use the abbreviation symbol, but forgot to append it.

[5] W. M. Lindsay, *Notae Latinae* (Cambridge, 1915), 352, states that prevocalic *n* is never symbolized in the period up to the year 850. Do we not here have an interesting bit of evidence to show that, even if scribes did not employ the symbol in this position in calligraphic MSS., they were at least familiar with such a usage?

The Archetype of the Extant Manuscripts 53

-it: 60, 2, 14 *inlustrans* in mg., a misplaced variant for *inlustrauit* (line 7). The error could best be explained on the assumption of an *s*-shaped abbreviation stroke for the final -*it* (*inlustrau̇*).

-m: 58ᵛ, 2, 30 *exercitus* corr. to *exercitum*. Does this point to the *s*-shaped symbol for *m* in the archetype? Cf. *Germ.* 36, 7, *aduersarios* as a variant of *aduersarum* (see p. 132).

-per: 59ᵛ, 1, 2 *comperarentur* for *compara-*.

uester: Perhaps, 60ᵛ, 1, 15 (ch. 30) $\overline{urm}$ in the immediate archetype as well as in Hf. See my discussion of this passage on p. 74.

-unt: 59, 1, 28 *differt* for *differunt* ($\overline{differt}$?).

-ur: 61, 1, 7 *conterunt* for *conteruntur*.

-us: 56, 1, 4 *primum* for *primus* (*prim'* ?) [1]; 76ᵛ, 1, 11 *excepissem* for *excepissemus*.

&: 59ᵛ, 1, 15 *excedendum* (& in mg. m. 2) for *et cedendum*.

ꝗ: 62, 2, 3 *reliquis* corr. to *reliquus*.[2] The opposite error (for which there seems to be less reason) occurs, 58, 1, 8, *priuatus* m. 2 in mg. opposite *priuatis* in text.

Confusion of Letters.—For the confusion of letters or of groups of letters at one period or another in the transmission of our text I submit the following evidence:[3]

A : O

(The confusion may be in part phonetic. See Schuchardt, *Der Vokalismus des Vulgärlateins* (Leipzig, 1866–1868) I, 177–185.)

(i) a for o

(1) 59ᵛ, 2, 11 (ch. 26) *partarum* (*o* add. m. 2)
(2) 62ᵛ, 2, 21 (ch. 36) *diu autstante* for *cliuo instantes* (?)
(3) 63ᵛ, 1, 20 (ch. 38) *prelecta* for *prelecto* (xlvii)
(4) 63ᵛ, 1, 29 (ch. 39) *quȧrum

(ii) o for a

(5) 58ᵛ, 1, 1 (ch. 21) *bello* for *bella* (?)[4]
(6) 59, 1, 21 (ch. 24) *ualentissimam*, in mg. m. 2 *o* (xvii)

[1] By way of illustration we may note that a fifteenth-century copyist wrote *manum* for the *man'* of Hf. See p. 39.

[2] *Agr.* 16, the three fifteenth-century MSS. all read *indecoris*, where Hf. has *indecorus* with the *us* ligature. Cf. *Germ.* 45, 25, where *radius* for *radiis* appears to have been the reading of Y (p. 103).

[3] The asterisk denotes corrections by the second hand. The Roman numerals to the right refer to the table of doublets shown on pp. 32 ff.

[4] *Bello* may be a phonetic corruption of *bellum*.

A : V
 (iii) **a for u**
  (7) 56ᵛ, 2, 13 (ch. 16) *uo adicca* for *boudicca* (v)
  (8) 58, 1, 3 (ch. 19) *primam* for *primum*
  (9) 61ᵛ, 1, 18 (ch. 32) *mancipia* [1] as variant of *municipia* (xxxii)
  (10) Germ. 45, 7 *saeuici* as variant of *sueuici*
  (11) de Gram. 4, 3 *tam* for *tum*
 (iv) **u for a**
  (12) 59ᵛ, 1, 12 (ch. 25) *castellum* as variant of *castella* (xxii)
  (13) 60, 2, 17 (ch. 29) *praedatum* (*magnum*) corr. to *praedata [2]
  (14) 76ᵛ, 1, 13 (ch. 45) *tum* as variant of *tam* (li)
  (15) Germ. 12, 7 *poenarum* for *poena nam* (?)

B : D
 (v) **d for b**
  (16) 58, 2, 29 (ch. 21) *adsumpta* for *absumpta*
  (17) Germ. 11, 10 *adsumitur* as variant of *absumitur* [3]

B : R
 (vi) **b for r**
  (18) 57, 1, 2 (ch. 16) *dubius* as variant of *durius* (vii)
 (vii) **r for b**
  (19) 58, 2, 19 (ch. 20) *inritamenta* for *inuitamenta* (i. e. *inuitamenta* > *inbitamenta*) [4]
  (20) Germ. 1, 9 *Arnobae* for *Abnobae*

C : E
 (viii) **e for c**
  (21) 57, 1, 1 (ch. 16) *eiusque* for *cuiusque*

C : G
 I regard the confusion as phonetic rather than graphical. See pp. 247 f.

C : T
 (ix) **c for t**
  (22) 62ᵛ, 2, 6 (ch. 36) *traces* as variant of *trates* [5] (xli)
  (23) 62, 2, 8 (ch. 34) *corpora* for *torpor* (?)
 (x) **t for c**
  (24) 56, 2, 4 (ch. 14) *Togidumno* as variant of *cogidumno* (ii)

---

[1] Perhaps an "emendation" rather than a graphical confusion (cf. pp. 50 f.).
[2] It may be questioned if the error is primarily graphical in origin.
[3] See p. 124.
[4] Cf. p. 247.
[5] See pp. 36 f.

The Archetype of the Extant Manuscripts 55

(25) 56ᵛ, 2, 13 (ch. 16) *bouidicta* for *boudicca* [1] (v)
(26) 62ᵛ, 1, 3, (ch. 35) *quosteter* as variant of *quoceter* (xxxviii)
(27) 61ᵛ, 1, 18 (ch. 32) *taetra* as variant of *aegra* (i.e *aegra* > *aecra*) (xxxii)
(28) 63ᵛ, 1, 18 (ch. 38) *trutulensem* as variant of *trucculensem* [2] (xlvi)

D : CL
  (xi) d for cl
(29) 62ᵛ, 2, 20 (ch. 36) *diu autstante* for *cliuo instantes* (?)

E : I
  I regard the confusion as phonetic rather than graphical. See pp. 240 f.

F : P
  (xii) f for p
(30) 57, 1, 25 (ch. 16) *facta* for *pacta* (? viii) [3]
  (xiii) p for f
(31) 76ᵛ, 1, 12 (ch. 45) *pingeremus* as variant of *figeremus* (l) [4]

H : L
  (xiv) l for h
(32) 63, 1, 21 (ch. 37) $\overset{h}{l}umus$

I : L
  (xv) i for l
(33) Germ. 22, 13 *ioci* as variant of *loci* [5]
  (xvi) l for i
(34) 60, 1, 22 (ch. 28) *utilla* for *utilia* (?)
(35) 61, 2, 4 (ch. 31) *laturi* for *ituri* (?)
(36) Germ. 28, 14 *neruli* for *neruii*

L : R
  (xvii) l for r
(37) Germ. 43, 18 *alii* for *Harii*
  (xviii) r for l
(38) 76ᵛ, 1, 28 (ch. 46) *militum decoramus* for *similitudine colamus* (?)

---

[1] Cf. however p. 50.
[2] The correct reading is doubtful, as the name does not occur elsewhere. I assume a corruption, *trucculensem* > *truculensem* > *trutu-*, but there may rather have been a confusion of *cc* and *t*.
[3] Cf. p. 41.
[4] Cf. p. 45.
[5] Cf. p. 298.

N : R
    (xix) r for n
        (39) *Gérm.* 40, 1 *largobardos* for *langobardos*
        (40) *Germ.* 46, 1 *peucurorum* as variant of *peucinorum*[1]

N : V
    (xx) n for u
        (41) 58, 1, 10 (ch. 19) *milites scire* for *militesue (ad)scire* (with *Ne* above) (?)
        (42) 61^v, 2, 9 (ch. 33) *nostra* for *uostra* (?)
        (43) 60, 2, 14 (ch. 29) *inlustrans* in mg., originally a variant of *inlustrauit*, line 7.[2]
        (44) *de Gram.* 24, 2 *minus* in **X** for *uiuus* (*nimis* Y)
    (xxi) u for n
        (45) 61^v, 1, 5 (ch. 32) *uobis* for *nobis*
        (46) 62^v, 1, 4 (ch. 35) *conuexi* for *connexi*

N : RI
    (xxii) n for ri
        (47) 59, 2, 21 (ch. 25) *uinum* as variant of *uirium* (xx)

NC : RA
    (xxiii) nc for ra
        (48) 56^v, 1, 1 (ch. 15) *tolencntibus* corr. to *tolerantibus*

P : T
    (xxiv) p for t
        (49) 60^v, 2, 2 (ch. 30) *conpactu* as variant of *contactu* (xxx)

R : S
    (xxv) s for r
        (50) 59^v, 1, 11 (ch. 25) *oppugnase* corr. to *oppugnare*[3]

R : T
    (xxvi) r for t
        (51) 60, 1, 4 (ch. 27) *locatura* corr. to **loca tuta*
        (52) 60^v, 2, 8 (ch. 30) *par&* corr. to **patet*

TI : TO
    (xxvii) to for ti
        (53) 59, 2, 25 (ch. 25) *mixto* (?)[4] as variant of *mixti* (xxi)
        (54) *Germ.* 46, 5 *mixtos* for *mixtis*

---

[1] See p. 137. Perhaps more accurately, a confusion of *in* and *ur*.

[2] See p. 41.

[3] Cf. Annibaldi, 94, note 3, who says that the corrected reading might be taken for *oppugnasse*, which is found in the three fifteenth-century MSS.

[4] Annibaldi (1907), 119: "La lezione marginale lascia dubbi nella lettura." Probably the corrector copied the word just as he saw it in the archetype.

4. The Ancestry of the Hersfeld Codex

We must now examine the graphical errors shown above for such clues as they may offer for determining the character of the script in which the immediate archetype of Hf. was written. Our first task is to distinguish, as best we may, between the mistakes caused by the script of the immediate archetype of Hf. and those engendered by the scripts of earlier antecedents.

I have previously adopted, on what appear to me adequate grounds, the hypothesis that the dot (or the diagonal line on f. 76^v) is the reference-symbol peculiar to the corrector of Hf., used to distinguish the readings which he added to the margin of the copy on his own initiative from those readings which he transcribed from the margin of the archetype.[1] If this hypothesis is correct, wherever we find doublets marked with the dot, the erroneous reading, be it in the text or in the margin,[2] originated in the transcription of Hf. Accordingly, we may assume that the errors shown in *6, 12, 14, 22, 31, 53*, were caused by graphical peculiarities of the immediate archetype, for in each case the dot or diagonal line is used. I now adopt a second hypothesis to the effect that the corrector in making his corrections within the column of writing, in so far as graphical errors are involved, drew from the archetype. This hypothesis carries with it the assumption that the corresponding errors of the first copyist were induced by peculiarities of the script from which he was copying, and we may now add to our list of mistakes made in the transcription of Hf. those shown in *4, 13, 51, 52*. Finally, I accept a third hypothesis to the effect that the corrections made by the original copyist are merely rectifications of his own errors. Accordingly, the errors themselves, if graphical in origin, were caused by

---

[1] See pp. 43 f.

[2] That is, if the error is in the text, it was made by the first copyist, while the marginal reading is a correction made from the archetype by the reviser. If the error is in the margin, it is due to the uncertainty of the reviser as to the accuracy with which the first copyist deciphered the script of the exemplar. In either case, the reviser has created doublets which did not exist in the archetype.

the script of the archetype, and we may yet increase our list of the mistakes made in the transcription of Hf. by the addition of those shown in *32, 48, 50*.

On the basis of the hypotheses stated above, we may assume tentatively that the following types of error were made in the transcription of Hf.: (i) *a* for *o*, (ii) *o* for *a*, (iv) *u* for *a*, (ix) *c* for *t*, (xiii) *p* for *f*, (xiv) *l* for *h*, (xxiii) *nc* for *ra*; (xxv) *s* for *r*; (xxvi) *r* for *t*; (xxvii) *to* for *ti*.

A glance at this list will probably suggest an archetype in minuscule script. I believe that this is the correct answer, yet the matter cannot be dismissed thus casually, for we must heed the timely warning sounded by Rand,[1] and examine the errors gathered by Ribbeck from the majuscule manuscripts of Vergil.[2] Strangely enough, all but three of these ten types of error find representation in Ribbeck's list. The three exceptions are (xiv) *l* for *h*, (xxiii) *nc* for *ra*, (xxvii) *to* for *ti*. Have we any other types of error which *per se* declare for a minuscule archetype and which bear the test of being absent from Ribbeck's list, even though they offer no direct evidence of having been made in the transcription of Hf.? I find but one: (xi) *d* for *cl*.[3] We have in all but four types of error which one would naturally refer to a minuscule archetype, and which do not occur in Ribbeck's list. Three of the four we have previously assumed occurred in the transcription of Hf.

The appearance of a given type of error in Ribbeck's list probably means that it occurred in transcribing from a majuscule archetype, but naturally cannot be taken as evidence

[1] E. K. Rand, "A Nest of Ancient Notae," *Spec.* II (1927), 160–176 (174 f.).

[2] O. Ribbeck, *Prolegomena Critica ad P. Vergili Maronis Opera Maiora* (Lipsiae, 1866), 235–264. Ribbeck was forced to the conclusion that the text of Vergil had passed through MSS. in majuscule cursive writing. Cf. p. 73.

[3] F. 60, 1, 28 (ch. 28, 11) Annibaldi reports *forte* for *sorte*, a peculiarly minuscule type of error (not found in Ribbeck's list). However, the descendants of Hf. (T *ex silentio*) know only *sorte*. I do not use this reading as evidence, for fear that it is a typographical error in Annibaldi's text.

From the *de Grammaticis* I can cite *y* for *r*, another minuscule type of error not occurring in Ribbeck's list: 14, 2 *santya* W for *Santra* (*satyra* or *satura* ω). However, we do not know that the Hersfeld codex drew the *de Grammaticis* from the same source that it did the Tacitean works.

The Archetype of the Extant Manuscripts 59

that the same error may not have been made in copying from a minuscule exemplar. Does any one of the ten types whose occurrence we have assumed for the transcription of Hf. really militate against the hypothesis of a minuscule archetype? I find that all are in harmony with such an hypothesis, with two possible exceptions, (i) *a* for *o*, and (xxvi) *r* for *t*. One of the instances of *a* for *o*, (3) *prelecta* for *prelecto*, is definitely older than Hf.,[1] and Ribbeck cites an unusually large number of examples (eleven in all) of this confusion. Yet we cannot get away from the single instance (4) in which we have assumed that the error was made in the copying of Hf. Perhaps we should modify our assumption regarding the source from which the corrector drew, and grant that here he made of his own initiative the obvious correction of *quarum* to *quorum*.[2] Or may the more probable solution be that some instances of this error remount to an ancient majuscule archetype, and others to the immediate minuscule archetype?[3]

Likewise, the error of *r* for *t* does not *per se* suggest a minuscule archetype.[4] As Constans has remarked,[5] the confusion of these two letters finds an easy explanation only in the majuscule cursive. But if the error is older than Hf., we must of course modify our opinion regarding the extent to which the corrector emended.

"*Minuscule*" *Errors*.—We are now in position to revise our original list of the types of error made in the transcription of Hf. I add to the list shown above (xi) *d* for *cl*, as a type peculiarly suited to a minuscule script, and I exclude (i) *a* for *o* and (xxvi) *r* for *t* as being doubtful for the reasons just set forth. With these corrections, my original list offers the types

---

[1] See p. 42.

[2] We should also note that in *1* the corrector did not delete the first *a* of *partarum*, which may be an indication either that he found the variants in the archetype, or that the emendation was one of his own.

[3] Again, this type of error may be phonetic in origin, at least in part. See p. 53.

[4] But cf. p. 65.

[5] L. A. Constans, *La "préhistoire" du texte de Tacite*, Extrait des Mémoires presentées par divers savants a L'Académie des Inscriptions et de Belles-Lettres XIII, 2 (1927), p. 12.

of error which I call "minuscule," and regard as originating in the copying of Hf. from its minuscule archetype.

"*Doubtful*" *Errors.*—This list of minuscule types of error does not, of course, include every type which may have occurred in the copying of Hf. from its minuscule archetype. There are several types, all of which are found in Ribbeck's list, but which from their very character I regard as "doubtful," *i.e.* the errors might have been made in copying either from a majuscule or from a minuscule manuscript: (iii) *a* for *u*. (viii) *e* for *c*; (x) *t* for *c*; (xii) *f* for *p*; (xv) *i* for *l*; (xvi) *l* for *i*; (xviii) *r* for *l*; (xix) *r* for *n*; (xx) *n* for *u*; (xxi) *u* for *n*; (xxii) *n* for *ri*. To this list of doubtful types I have already transferred from the minuscule group (i) *a* for *o* and (xxvi) *r* for *t*; On the other hand, we must at once exclude from the doubtful, and bring into the majuscule group mentioned below (xxii) *n* for *ri*, since the reference-symbol employed in the single instance of this mistake shows it to be older than Hf.[1] I am also inclined to believe that (x) *t* for *c*, (xv) *i* for *l*, (xvi) *l* for *i*, (xviii) *r* for *l*, should all be regarded as majuscule types of error.

"*Majuscule*" *Errors.*—There remain certain types of error which by their very character should be referred to some more remote archetype in majuscule script. Needless to say, these are well represented in Ribbeck's list: (v) *D* for *B*; (vi) *B* for *R*; (vii) *R* for *B*; (xvii) *L* for *R*;[2] (xxiv) *P* for *T*. To this list of majuscule errors I have already transferred from the doubtful group *N* for *RI*.

In What Kind of Minuscule Script was the Archetype of Hf. Written?

I have concluded that the immediate archetype of the Hersfeld codex was in a minuscule script, and I have established the types of error which I believe to have occurred in the transcription of Hf. itself. In what particular kind of

---

[1] Assuming that there was but *one* minuscule MS. among the ancestors of Hf.

[2] Perhaps more accurately, the group *AL* for *AR* (majuscule cursive?).

minuscule script was the archetype written? This I am unable to answer, for the evidence seems to me much too scanty. Only when the corruptions fairly screech forth from every page as in the Hersfeldensis and Fuldensis of Ammianus can we be sure as to the character of the archetype. But the scribe of our Hersfeldensis was of very different calibre from that of the Hersfeld Ammianus.[1] He did his work well, and carefully covered up the traces which might have given us a clue to his archetype.[2]

Doubtless our quest can be limited on the ground of general probabilities. In the tradition of the works of our classical authors there seems to be a gap of some two hundred years, roughly between 550 and 750, in which few, if any, manuscripts were transcribed.[3] If the archetype of Hf. antedated 550, it could have been in but one type of minuscule script, viz. the half-uncial,[4] a suggestion which has been made by Annibaldi.[5]

I hardly think that the half-uncial offers the solution to our problem,[6] though I must admit that most of the minuscule

[1] Assuming that the Hersfeldensis was the archetype of the Fuldensis (see p. 27; p. 28, note 5).

[2] Perhaps a re-examination of the MS. would throw new light on the script of the archetype. Annibaldi reports many erasures, but apparently these were so well made that there is no trace left of the original writing.

[3] I know only of the Milan Juvenal fragment, which Lowe, op. infra cit. (No. 58), on palaeographical grounds dates as saec. VI–VII.

[4] Many palaeographers are loath to call the half-uncial a minuscule script. I am unable to understand the reason for this, at least so far as the fully developed script is concerned.

[5] Annibaldi, 1907, 118.

[6] I purposely exclude any argument of the general improbability of a classical text having passed through a half-uncial stage, for I suspect that this belief, though perhaps still prevalent among palaeographers, will in time be abandoned. Lowe's list (E. A. Lowe, "A Hand-list of Half-uncial Manuscripts," Studi e testi XL [1924], 34–61) includes nine fragments of classical authors, ranging from the very early stage of the writing as found in the epitome of Livy (No. 34 of Lowe's list) to the fully developed minuscule script of the Milan Juvenal fragment (No. 58). The nine fragments of classical authors by no means exhaust the non-Christian writings, for the list includes law books, grammatical and mathematical treatises, and marginalia to pagan as well as to Christian authors. Only recently there has come to light a deed of sale in

types of corruption which I have found in Hf. would be explained by this script as well as by any other. Nevertheless, the mistake which seems to me most definitely graphical in origin, viz. (xxiii) *nc* for *ra*, could not well find its explanation in the half-uncial.[1]

A second reason for rejecting the half-uncial lies in the character of the abbreviations which I attribute to the archetype of Hf.,[2] though here we should proceed with the greatest caution. All the abbreviations which I suggest for our archetype find their counterparts in manuscripts of the sixth century or earlier,[3] and I should hesitate to assert that they could not have been employed in a half-uncial manuscript of a classical author. The investigations of Lindsay[4] and of Rand[5] and the discovery of three papyrus fragments of orations of Cicero[6] show that in non-calligraphic manuscripts the use of abbreviations in antiquity was far more extended than has commonly been supposed. My rejection of an ancient (half-uncial) exemplar is not due to any conviction that such a manuscript could not have had the abbreviations in question, but rather to the fact that the Hersfeld codex contains no traces of *obsolete* abbreviations.[7] Lindsay and Rand have found in

half-uncial writing (with cursive elements): E. Albertini, "Actes de vente du v⁰ siècle, trouvés dans la région de Tebessa (Algérie)," *Journal des savants* (1930), 23–30.

[1] At least it presupposes types of *r* and *a* which I have been unable to find in this script, but my search has been limited to published facsimiles.

[2] See pp. 52 f.

[3] See W. M. Lindsay, *Notae Latinae* (Cambridge, 1915) under the various abbreviations listed, and (on the *s*-form of *m*) p. xiii. I am, of course, referring to the letters, syllables, or words abbreviated, not to the particular forms the abbreviations may have taken (except for the *s*-shaped symbol).

[4] W. M. Lindsay, *Early Irish Minuscule Script*, St. Andrews University Publications VI (Oxford, 1910), 70–74; "The Abbreviation-Symbols of ergo, igitur," *Zentralblatt für Bibliothekswesen* XXIX (1912), 56–64, with supplement in *Notae Latinae*, xiii f.; "A New Clue to the Emendation of Latin Texts," *Class. Phil.* XI (1916), 270–277.

[5] E. K. Rand, *op. cit.* on p. 58, note 1.

[6] *Papiri Greci e Latini* (1912) I, No. 20, with facsimile, "saec. VI." *Oxyrhynchus Papyri* VIII (1911), No. 1097, with facsimile of recto; x (1914), No. 1251, "saec. v."

[7] The abbreviations in the Hersfeld *Agricola* are shown on pp. 357 f.

eighth- and ninth-century manuscripts corruptions due to abbreviations of the archetype which were no longer in use at that time, and also obsolete abbreviations which were taken over bodily. Now the abbreviations which I have suggested for the archetype of Hf. were all in common use in the late eighth and in the ninth centuries. If our manuscript had an ancient calligraphic exemplar, say of the fifth or sixth century, the latter presumably had no abbreviations beyond the few commonly admitted to such manuscripts.[1] If, on the other hand, the exemplar was non-calligraphic, and contained a wider range of abbreviations, it is improbable that these abbreviations were the very ones in use in the eighth and ninth centuries and only those, and it is even more improbable that the copyist of Hf. would have been led astray by compendia with which he should have been familiar but found no difficulty in resolving those which he could hardly have been expected to understand.

Since we have rejected the half-uncial, it follows that the minuscule archetype for which we are searching was probably not older than the second half of the eighth century, and in view of the imperfect word-division still noticeable in Hf. it is doubtful if it should be brought very far into the ninth century.[2]

For the late eighth and early ninth centuries we have a large variety of minuscule scripts from which to select—Visigothic, Beneventan, Insular, the various types somewhat loosely designated as "Merovingian," other precursors of the Carolingian minuscule in France, northern Italy, and Germany, and finally the Carolingian minuscule itself.

Unfortunately, the minuscule types [3] of error do not point in any one direction. Errors such as (xi) [4] *d* for *cl*, (xiii) *p* for *f*, (xiv) *l* for *h*, (xxv) *s* for *r*, and (xxvii) *to* for *ti* are, in my

---

[1] That is, the dot after -*b* and -*q* for -*bus* and -*que*, the suspension of *m* and *n* at the end of the line, *nomina sacra* (naturally not in our text), and certain abbreviations by suspension epigraphic in origin (*praenomina*, etc.).

[2] As I have tried to show (pp. 24 ff.), the Hersfeld codex itself may well have been as old as the middle of the ninth century, or even slightly older.

[3] See p. 59.

[4] The Roman numerals refer to the tabulations shown on pp. 53 ff.

opinion, to be referred to individual peculiarities of the exemplar which our copyist had before him rather than to definite features of some particular school of minuscule writing. We may, to be sure, gather that the archetype which we are seeking employed three forms of the letter *a:* (1) closed *a* with a full round bow (ii, *o* for *a*); (2) open *a* resembling *u* (iv, *u* for *a*); (3) open *a* (after *r*) resembling *ic* (xxiii, *nc* for *ra*). Yet the presence of these three types of *a* does not point to any one kind of script, though it suggests that we should eliminate those scripts which adhere consistently to a single form of this letter, such as Beneventan and Visigothic.[1] Again, the error of (ix) *c* for *t* might have been made in copying from any manuscript which employed the half-uncial form of *t*, but argues against those scripts in which *t* has a loop to the left of the shaft, *i.e.* Beneventan, Visigothic, and "Merovingian."

Our search seems to be narrowing down somewhat. We must find a script which admits the three types of *a* and the form of *t* previously mentioned. Let us now examine the Insular as a possibility.

Perhaps on external ground the Insular, or more particularly the Anglo-Saxon script, would have the best claim.[2] Along with others, I have suggested Fulda as the original home of the Hersfeld codex.[3] Now Fulda was the foundation of the Anglo-Saxon Bonifatius, and the native script of the founder is said to have been practiced there until toward the middle of the ninth century.[4] We might also seek a parallel in the

[1] General probabilities, as well as various details, would, I fancy, tend to exclude both these scripts from our search. The Beneventan was still in its infancy in the ninth century, and the great period of activity of Beneventan scribes in transmitting our classical texts was some two centuries later (E. A. Loew [Lowe], *The Beneventan Script* [Oxford, 1914], 16 ff., 334–370). Visigothic MSS. of classical authors are not only very few, but also very late (see list of Visigothic MSS. by Zacarías García Villada, *Paleografía Española* [Madrid, 1923], 94–128). Also certain abbreviations peculiar to this writing would almost certainly have left their imprint upon the apograph.

[2] E. Norden has recently declared in favor of an archetype in Insular script. A notice of his paper is given in *Sitzb. d. preuss. Akad. d. Wiss.*, phil.-hist. Klasse, 1927, 19, but no statement is given of the evidence upon which he bases his conclusions.

[3] See pp. 28 f.

[4] See L. Traube in *Mélanges Boissier* (1903), 446.

work of another historical writer, viz. Ammianus Marcellinus, whose tradition is through a lost exemplar in Insular script,[1] quite probably written in Fulda.[2]

Insular writing retains the half-uncial *t*, which is just the form of this letter for which we are searching. Likewise, the Insular might very well account for two of the three forms of *a* which we have posited. Perhaps the more usual type of *a* in this writing has the closed bow, and we may note in particular the full round bow reaching to the top of the shaft in the Anglo-Saxon script of Fulda.[3] But the Insular also admits the open *a*, which might be mistaken for *u*.[4] Possibly the mistake of *s* for *r* and of *p* for *f* would have occurred more easily in copying from Insular than from any other script,[5] and the writing of *to* for *ti* may indicate that in the exemplar there was some departure from the normal form of infrascript *i* which is so common in this writing.[6] Finally, the writing of *r* for *t*[7] may suggest the peculiar form of the latter letter sometimes used by Anglo-Saxon scribes.[8] All in all, however, I think the most we can say is that an Insular hand might account for the errors just mentioned, but hardly that it offers the only explanation possible. Furthermore, it is certain that one graphical error of Hf. militates against the hypothesis of an Insular archetype.

[1] Traube, *op. cit.* 444 ff.

[2] See p. 28.

[3] I have in mind the oldest Fulda chartulary (*c.* 828 A.D.) and the Ambrosian Columella. Facsimiles in Steffens, *Lateinische Paläographie*², Plate 54.

[4] For example, in the Leyden Priscian. Facsimiles in *New Palaeographical Society* (first series) I, 32 and 33.

[5] Cf. Lindsay, "The Letters in Early Latin Minuscule," *Palaeographia Latina* I (= St. Andrews University Publications xiv [1922], 7–61).

[6] The infrascript *i* in ligature with *t*, *s*, *m*, *n*, regularly assumes the form of a shallow curve opening to the left. I have noticed an instance in the St. Gall Priscian in which *i* in ligature with *s* is extended to the right in a curve opening toward the top, giving it a certain resemblance to *o*. See Steffens, Plate 50a, col. 2, 3 *pressi*. (The error has been corrected by a later hand.)

[7] See p. 59.

[8] I refer to the form of *t* lacking the right-hand half of the cross-stroke, as found in Vat. Pal. Lat. 195. See Lindsay, "The (Early) Lorsch Scriptorium," *Palaeographia Latina* III (= St. Andrews University Publications xix [1924]), 30 f. and Pl. ix. I am indebted to Dr. E. A. Lowe for the suggestion that this form of *t* might account for the error in question.

I refer to the writing of *nc* for *ra*. This error implies an *r* with a short shaft and a low shoulder extending downward to form the first shaft of an *a* of the *ic* type. Now the *ic* type of *a* is not a feature of Insular writing,[1] the shaft of *r* in this script regularly reaches below the line, and ligatures with *r* are avoided.

Turning now to the abbreviations which I have proposed for our archetype,[2] I find but one that is distinctively Insular, viz. -*rt* for -*runt*.[3] The others are definitely continental, in so far as these differ from the Insular.[4] Certainly the presence of one Insular abbreviation cannot be regarded as convincing, especially if our manuscript was written on German soil, where there was constant interchange of abbreviations between the Insular and continental schools.

The Mediceus I.—Some will seek to find a connection between Hf. and the unique manuscript of *Annals* I–VI, the ninth-century Mediceus I, which bears more definite Insular symptoms than does Hf. The Mediceus I was brought to Rome from the monastery of Corvey, a neighbor to Fulda, but was not necessarily written in Corvey. The idea of a common archetype containing *Annals* I–VI and the minor works, from which were derived the Mediceus I and the Hersfeldensis, is not new.

First let us examine the Mediceus I for Insular symptoms.[5]

[1] I have noticed this form of *a* in the Insular hand shown by Chroust, *Monumenta Palaeographica*, II Serie, XXII Lieferung, Tafel 8b (No. 458b, Vol. VI; Berlin, Lat. theol. qu. 139), but this hand shows strong continental influence in its use of cursive forms and ligatures. Note *Iudęam*, line 10; *extra*, line 13; *ea*, line 14; *demonstraret*, line 23.

[2] See the list on p. 52. Regarding the use of the various abbreviations, see Lindsay, *Notae Latinae*. Adequate data regarding the *s*-shaped stroke for *m* seems to be lacking. I have noted this stroke both for *m* and for a general abbreviation stroke in a Seneca from Lorsch, Vat. Pal. Lat. 1547 (facsimile in Chatelain, *Paléographie des classiques latins* II, 168a, "*saec.* IX"). An *m*-sign resembling a reversed *s* is found in several varieties of continental minuscule.

[3] See Lindsay, *Notae*, 369.

[4] Thus, the abbreviations for *est*, -*men*, and -*it* are all continental rather than Insular. See Lindsay, *Notae*, 69 ff., 331, 340. The use of the apostrophe for -*us* in Insular is declared by Lindsay to be an importation (*op. cit.* 383).

[5] The Mediceus I has been reproduced *in integro* in *Codices Graeci et Latini* VII, 1 (*op. cit.* on p. 26, note 7), with a preface by E. Rostagno.

We may note the use of *FINIT* for *EXPLICIT* at the end of each book,[1] ∼ for *est*, *q* with a hooked diagonal stroke cutting the shaft for *quod*, *-rt̄* for *-runt*, the infrascript *i* after *n*, ⁊ for *et*, *l* with the shaft cut by a transverse for *uel*.[2] Yet some of these features are found only in isolated cases,[3] and all suggest to me not so much that the Mediceus I was copied from an archetype in Insular script as that the scribe of the manuscript itself had not entirely broken away from Insular traditions.

Certain graphical errors in the Mediceus I may point to an Insular archetype. Most noteworthy is the writing of *p* for *r*,[4] a confusion which is easily made in reading the Insular script. Perhaps the writing of *confeltos*, Ann. IV, 73, 23 (f. 115) for *confectos* is reminiscent of the high narrow *c* sometimes found in Insular manuscripts.[5] The writing of *hiona* for *hiberna*, II, 26, 1 (f. 39) suggests the full round bow and short shaft of the Insular *b*.[6] Other minuscule errors of the Mediceus I not found in Hf., but which are not to me more suggestive of Insular than of other kinds of minuscule script are: Ann. II, 39, 13 (f. 44) *sermonilius* for *sermonibus*; II, 86, 4 (f. 61) *comicio* for *domitio*; IV, 19, 8 (f. 95ᵛ) *quo prium* for *proprium*; VI, 43, 5 (f. 134ᵛ) *haci* for *hau*; VI, 44, 19 (f. 135) *irastra* for *kastra*.[7] Without a more thorough investigation,[8] I should be unwilling to say that even the Mediceus I was copied from an archetype in Insular writing, though it does offer more symptoms of this script than the Hersfeldensis.

[1] See W. M. Lindsay, "Collectanea Varia," *Palaeographia Latina* II, 5–55 (pp. 5–10).

[2] See the list of abbreviations and ligatures given by Rostagno, *op. cit.* xv–xvii.

[3] Rostagno cites but one example of -r̄t̄ and ⁊, and but two of the infrascript *i*.

[4] See Rostagno, xii: Ann. III, 54, 32 (f. 81ᵛ) *prope* for *pro re*; IV, 3, 3 (f. 89ᵛ) *corpipere* for *corripere*.

[5] *E.g.* in the Leyden and St. Gall Priscians. Facsimile of the former in N. P. S. 32, 33; of the latter in Steffens², 50.

[6] It also suggests an abbreviation of *-ber-*, which according to Lindsay (*Notae*, 333–335), was avoided by Anglo-Saxon, but not by Irish, scribes.

[7] Ribbeck's list (see p. 58) gives one example of *L* written for *C*, but the other graphical errors I have cited from the Med. I are not found there.

[8] My investigation of the graphical errors of the Mediceus I makes no pretense to exhaustiveness.

Even if we grant that the Mediceus is a copy of an Insular archetype, do the graphical errors which it has in common with Hf. offer any basis for the establishment of the same exemplar for the two manuscripts? Of the nine types of error in Hf. which I believe to have been induced by a minuscule script,[1] I have found parallels for only five in the Mediceus: *o* for *a*, *u* for *a*, *c* for *t*, *d* for *cl*, *s* for *r*.[2] Of the twelve types of error in Hf. which I classify as doubtful,[3] nine are found in the Mediceus.[4] Of the six types of error in Hf. which I regard as originating in a majuscule script,[5] four are found in the Mediceus.[6]

[1] See pp. 58 f.

[2] *o* for *a*: *Ann.* I, 13, 21 (f. 8) *rogori* for *rogari*; I, 35, 5 (f. 15ᵛ) *uocationum* for *uaca*-; II, 8, 13 (f. 34) *angriuoriorum* for *-uari-*; II, 63, 1 (f. 53) *moroboduo* for *maro-*. The examples of this type of error are numerous.

u for *a*: See the examples given by Rostagno, p. ix. Note particularly, *Ann.* v, 8, 4 (f. 117ᵛ) *uelii* for *aelii*.

c for *t*: VI, 41, 13 (f. 134) *arca banum* for *artabanum*; III, 64, 7 (f. 84ᵛ) *sectum* for *set tum*.

d for *cl*: See examples given by Rostagno, p. x.

s for *r*: See examples given by Rostagno, p. xii. Also *r* for *s*.

[3] See p. 60.

[4] *a* for *u*: See examples given by Rostagno, p. ix.

a for *o*: *Ann.* I, 58, 2 (f. 23) *ramanum* for *ro-*; II, 70, 9 (f. 56) *maratus* for *mo-*; III, 12, 1 (f. 65) *temperamenta* for *-to*; IV, 28, 14 (f. 98ᵛ) *falsa* for *falso*; IV, 71, 14 (f. 114) *aperirentur* for *opperi-*.

e for *c*: *Ann.* I, 27, 6 (f. 12ᵛ) *eum* for *cum*.

t for *c*: See examples given by Rostagno, p. x.

f for *p*: III, 11, 4 (f. 65) *fulnicium* for *P. Vinicium*; III, 15, 17 (f. 67) *refertus* for *repertus*.

i for *l*; *l* for *i*: See examples cited by Rostagno, p. xi.

u for *n*: *Ann.* IV, 21, 7 (f. 96) *grauius* for *granius*. This error is certainly not common.

r for *n*: *Ann.* I, 34, 12 (f. 15) *uereratione* changed from *uene-* (!); III, 44, 3 (f. 77ᵛ) *hisparias* for *hispanias*; IV, 67, 9 (f. 112) *grano* for *gnaro*. Also *n* for *r*: VI, 8, 26 (f. 121ᵛ) *ianitonibus* for *-tori-*. The "correction" from *ueneratione* to *uere-* is significant. Surely the archetype must have had *-r-* and not merely an *n* resembling *r*. That is, the error of *r* for *n* antedates the immediate archetype, which I suspect to be the case for Hf. as well. I have not noted *n* for *u*, *r* for *l*, *r* for *t*.

[5] See p. 60.

[6] *D* for *B*: see examples given by Rostagno, p. ix. Also *B* for *D*.

B for *R*: *Ann.* IV, 65, 8 (f. 112) *aduenabum* for *aduenarum*. Also *R* for *B*: VI, 45, 11 (f. 135ᵛ) *rurellius* for *rubellius*.

The Archetype of the Extant Manuscripts 69

The value of the above evidence, if value it has, is not so much for the establishment of the identity of the immediate archetypes of the Mediceus and Hf. as for the indication that the two manuscripts had more remote archetypes in common.

My investigation has failed to establish an archetype in Insular script for the Hersfeld codex. I do not go so far as to deny that the archetype was in this style of writing, but I will say that if the copyist of Hf. had such an exemplar before him he managed to conceal it remarkably well.

Does the error of *nc* for *ra,* which seems to be the most significant of the graphical confusions in the Hersfeld codex, offer us a positive clue to the archetype that we are seeking? Although I do not pretend to have made a thorough investigation of all the possibilities, I suspect that the peculiar form of the combination *ra* which most resembles *nc* [1] is to be found in the north-Italian minuscule of the second half of the eighth and of the very early ninth centuries, and in the German minuscule of about the same period practiced in St. Gall, Reichenau, Chur, and Constance, to which Löffler [2] has given the name "rätisch." Of north-Italian manuscripts the one best illustrating the type of *ra* that I have in mind [3] is Vercelli CLXXXIII (Patristic writings).[4] In Raetian script it is best

P for T: *Ann.* IV, 45, 14 (f. 105) *per mestinorum* for *termestinorum.* Also T for P: II, 14, 2 (f. 35ᵛ) *res tersa* for *respersa.*

I have not noted L for R and N for RI.

I do not believe that errors in the Mediceus I resulting from the misunderstanding of abbreviations and ligatures are numerous, but my examination has been cursory. We may note, III, 20, 10 (f. 69) *romanis* for *-nus;* VI, 17, 11 (f. 124ᵛ) *fortunus* for *-nis;* I, 73, 14 (f. 29) *numinus* > *-num.* These types of error are also found in Hf. (see p. 53).

[1] I realize that the *ic*-form of *a* taken alone immediately suggests the Corbie *ab*-script, but in this script the shaft of *r* reaches well below the line so as to preclude confusion with *n.*

[2] K. Löffler, "Die Sankt Galler Schreibschule in der 2. Hälfte des 8. Jahrhunderts," *Palaeographia Latina* VI (1929), 5-66.

[3] Cf. p. 66.

[4] See E. A. Lowe (Loew), "Studia Palaeographica," *Sitzb. d. bayer. Akad., phil.-hist. Klasse,* 1910, 12 Abhandlung, 43 ("*saec.* VIII") and Pl. 1. Note: lines 4 and 8 *contra,* 11 *cooperantibus,* 14 *uestra.*

illustrated by a St. Gall document of the year 762[1] and St. Gall manuscript 126 (Hieronymus in *Evangelium Matthaei*).[2]

For continuing our investigation I have chosen the Raetian rather than the north-Italian minuscule,[3] partly because more facsimiles of the former are available, and partly because it may appear more natural to look for our archetype on German soil.

In Raetian minuscule the letter *a* appears in several forms—the *ic*-type (earlier period), the open *cc*-type, the closed *cc*-, and the *oc*-type being the more usual—none of which would as a rule be confused with *o* or *u*. However, the script also admits a form of uncial *a* with a round bow almost coextensive with the shaft, which might easily have suggested the letter *o* to a copyist.[4] Again, the open *a*, at least in isolated cases, is sufficiently like *u* to render possible the confusion of these two letters.[5]

Normally the *t* of the Raetian script would not be confused with *c*, since the shaft is perpendicular, with a hook at the end, and the horizontal bar extends well to the left of the shaft and is often brought around to form a loop. Nevertheless, the half-uncial *t* shaped like the Greek τ is sometimes

[1] St. Gall *Urkunde* I, 28. Facsimile by Chroust, *op. cit.*, I Serie, XIV Lieferung, Tafel 2b (No. 132b, Vol. II). Note: line 4 *maldra*, 5 *arata, brachare*, 9 *pondura*, 11 *traditionem*.

[2] Löffler, *op. cit.*, Pl. 1. Note: line 2 *temperat*.

[3] The north-Italian and Raetian minuscule have many peculiarities in common, and Löffler (p. 51) speaks for Italian rather than Frankish influence in the development of the latter. A north-Italian MS. in which most of the features for which we are looking are found is Carlsruhe Reichenau LVII. Facsimiles in Zimmermann, *Vorkarolingische Miniaturen* (Berlin, 1916) I, Pl. 31, and (reduced) Holder, "Der Isidorus-Codex Augiensis LVII," *Mélanges Chatelain* (Paris, 1910), 633–643. Also see Lindsay, *Palaeographia Latina* I, 9, and L. Schiaparelli, "Influenze straniere nella scrittura Italiana dei secoli VIII e IX," *Studi e testi* XLVII, 7–9.

[4] Cf. Zimmermann, *op. cit.*, Pl. 152c (St. Gall 731), line 9 *tam*; Chroust, *op. cit.*, I Serie, Lief. XVII, Tafel 7b (No. 167b, Vol. III; St. Gall 350), line 5 *carnalis*, line 18 *sacramentis*.

[5] Cf. Chroust, I Serie, Lief. XIV, Tafel 2b (St. Gall *Urkunde* I, 28), line 2 *talis*; Löffler, *op. cit.*, Pl. I (St. Gall 126), line 14 *natiuitatis*; Pl. III (St. Gall 11), line 11 *matri*. According to Löffler (p. 30), St. Gall 230 has an open *a* without the two knobs at the tops of the shafts. Presumably such an *a* would be similar to *u*.

admitted, and with this form there is always the possibility of confusion with c.[1]

For the error of -*se* for -*re* [2] no better explanation could be offered than that found in the *re* ligature of St. Gall 731.[3] Perhaps the type of *h* found in St. Gall 120 and 44, with its high shaft and relatively low and broad bow,[4] would account for the error of *l* for h.[5] Finally, the writing of *d* for *cl* and of *p* for *f* [6] may, I suspect, be explained by the Raetian [7] quite as well as by any other minuscule script.

It is possible to go further and find peculiarities in Raetian script which would account for some of the errors which I have called "doubtful" with reference to their origin in a minuscule or majuscule script.[8] Thus, the occasional imperfect joining of the bows of *o* might lead to confusion with a,[9] and the diagonal stroke sometimes used to cap the letter *c* might cause it to be mistaken for t.[10] We may go even further and try to establish a common ancestor in Raetian script for the Hersfeldensis and the Mediceus I, showing that the writing of *li* for *b* [11] may have had its origin in a carelessly made *b* such

[1] Cf. Zimmermann, Pl. 152a (St. Gall 731), line 3 *ita*; Chroust, I Serie, XVII Lief., Tafel 6b (No. 166b, Vol. III), line 12 *qualitatem*.

[2] See p. 56, xxv.

[3] Facsimiles in Zimmermann, Plates 150–152, and Chroust, I Serie, XVII Lief., Tafel 6 (No. 166, Vol. III). Note, p. 111 (Zimmermann, Pl. 151b, Chroust, 6a), line 2 *prodedire*, in which -*re* is scarcely distinguishable from *se* in the same line.

[4] Cf. Löffler, Pl. IV (St. Gall 120), line 14 *epiphanen*, 6 and 23 *habebat*; Chroust, I Serie, XIV Lief., Tafel 3 (No. 133, Vol. II; St. Gall 44), line 72 *habebant*.

[5] See p. 56, xiv.

[6] See pp. 56, xi, xiii.

[7] Note particularly the *f* with its bow even with the headline in the script of Winithar (facsimiles by Löffler, Plates VIII–X; Chroust, XIV Lief., 1 [No. 131, Vol. II]). Also note *f* with the bow closed in St. Gall 731 (*e.g.* Chroust XVII, 6a, line 8 *falsitate*, 9 *fuerit*).

[8] See p. 60.

[9] Cf. Zimmermann, Pl. 152c (St. Gall 731), line 10 *non*; Chroust XIV, 3 (St. Gall 44), line 104 (*ful*)*goris*; Chroust XIV, 1a (St. Gall 70, hand of Winithar), line 26 *dec*(*al*)*ogi*, b, 1 *spero*.

[10] Cf. Zimmermann, Pl. 151c (St. Gall 731), line 6 *conmentario*, 11–12 *substancia*.

[11] See p. 67.

as is to be seen in the crude hand of Winithar,[1] or again by showing instances in which this same scribe made *u* in such a way as to suggest *ci*.[2]

The abbreviations and ligatures which I have suggested for the archetype of the Hersfeld codex[3] are nearly all at home in the Raetian script.[4] The ones which I have not noted are -*r̄t* for -*runt*, the *s*-shaped symbol for *m* and as a general abbreviation stroke, and the -*us* ligature, but I suspect that a more thorough examination might establish all these.[5] If the *s*-shaped symbol is not found in Raetian, at least the symbol resembling a reversed *s* is common enough.[6]

The Raetian script offers an explanation for most, perhaps for all, of the errors originating in minuscule writing which I have observed in the Hersfeld codex, but I do not maintain that this is the only script which might afford an answer to our problem. Where uncertainty reigns, further indulgence in conjectures may seem unwise, yet in conclusion I will make a

[1] Cf. Löffler, Pl. VIII (St. Gall 907), line 14 *roborati*; Pl. X, 17–18 *inuestigabilibus, rebus*. Also in the calligraphic hand of St. Gall 120, Löffler, Pl. IV, line 4 *prioribus*.

[2] See p. 67. Cf. Chroust XIV, 1a, line 9 *causis*, 19 *epistulas*.

[3] See pp. 52 f.

[4] For the abbreviations of -*ter*, *est*, -*men*, *per*, -*tur*, -*mus*, *uestrum*, and the ligature &, it is sufficient to refer to the facsimiles cited above. The abbreviation *ū* for *uer* is found in St. Gall 350 (Chroust XVII, 7b, line 6 *conuersatione*); St. Gall 348 (Löffler, Pl. VI, 4 *aduersa*, 8–9 *aduersitate*); and very probably in other MSS. The suspension of -*it* (but not with the *s*-shaped symbol) I have noted in St. Gall 11 (Löffler, Pl. III, 20 *dixit*).

It may be noted that in the matter of abbreviations the Raetian script appears to offer a better solution for the problem of our archetype than does the north-Italian minuscule. At least, the very limited facsimile material which I have examined leads me to suspect that the earlier north-Italian minuscule did not employ so wide a range of abbreviations as I have posited for the archetype of Hf. However, these abbreviations (probably not the *s*-shaped symbol) are at home in the calligraphic Veronese minuscule of the ninth century (see A. Spagnolo, "Abbreviature nel minoscolo Veronese," *Zentralblatt für Bibliothekswesen* XXVII [1910], 531–548; Lindsay, *ibid*. 549–552).

[5] Regarding the -*us* ligature it may be noted that a similar ligature of *u* with a majuscule *T* is very common in St. Gall 193 (reproduced *in integro* in *Spicilegium Palimpsestorum* I [Beuron, 1913]).

[6] In the script of Winithar (see facsimiles cited on p. 71, note 7); in St. Gall 348 (Chroust XVII, 7a, Löffler, Pl. VI); St. Gall 193 (see above, note 5).

few suggestions, but insist that they are meant as nothing more. These suggestions are: that an ancient manuscript of the first part of the *Annals* and of the minor works, in capital or uncial script, was brought from Italy to St. Gall or some neighboring monastery, and was there transcribed in the late eighth or very early ninth century in the native Raetian writing; that this transcription was taken to Fulda, where, sometime before the year 850, copies were made of the minor works on the one hand and of the *Annals* on the other; that the copy of the minor works was our Hersfeldensis; that the copy of the *Annals*, perhaps in Anglo-Saxon script, was the exemplar from which the Mediceus I was transcribed at a slightly later date. With these suggestions I must reluctantly leave the problem of the immediate archetype of the Hersfeld codex with a *nescio*.

More Remote Ancestry of the Hersfeld Codex

Like all other classical texts, the minor works of Tacitus must have passed through several generations of manuscripts in majuscule script, and of these antecedents we have found traces in some of the graphical errors of the *Agricola* cited above.[1] L. A. Constans has recently attempted to show that the text of the Mediceus II (*Ann.* XI–XVI, *Hist.* I–V) passed through a stage in majuscule cursive of the second half of the second or first half of the third century.[2] While I think it questionable if this offers the only explanation possible for the errors he cites, it does in my opinion offer the best explanation for many of them. I do not attempt to carry the text of the Hersfeld codex back to so remote a date, but will merely say that I believe a majuscule cursive would afford a satisfactory explanation for some of the graphical faults which I have noticed.[3]

I believe that I can speak with rather more certainty re-

[1] See p. 60.

[2] *La "Préhistoire" du texte de Tacite*, Extrait des mémoires présentées par divers savants à L'Académie des Inscriptions et de Belles-Lettres, Tome XIII, IIe Partie, Paris, 1927.

[3] The copy in majuscule cursive would have been the "great-grandparent" of Hf., if not still more distantly removed.

garding the stichometry of one of the forebears of Hf., probably the archetype twice removed ("grandparent"), and I venture to assert that in this exemplar the text of the *Germania* and of the *Agricola* through ch. 40, 6 (f. 63ᵛ) was written in very short lines averaging thirteen letters each.[1] Let us examine the evidence.

F. 61ᵛ, 1, 12 (ch. 32) the text of the Hersfeld *Agricola* correctly reads, *tam deserent illos ceteri germani quam*, and in the margin (m. 2) is found, *deserent illos/ ceteri germani/ tamquam*. It will be noted that each of the first two lines of the marginal reading contains thirteen letters. I offer the following explanation of the marginal variant. In the archetype twice removed the words *deserent . . . germani* formed two lines. In the transcription of the immediate archetype these two lines were omitted and the words *tam* and *quam* were thereby brought together. The omitted lines were, however, added in the margin and a reference-symbol was placed over the *tamquam* of the text. The scribe of Hf. correctly restored the lines to their position between *tam* and *quam*, but the corrector thought that the marginal words might belong before *tamquam*, and so created the marginal variant as we now find it.[2]

F. 60ᵛ, 1, 14–15 (ch. 30) the copyist wrote *hodiernumdiem* (13 letters) after *consensumq.* $\overline{urm}$ (13 letters), while the corrector has deleted *hodiernumdiem* and restored the words to their proper place before *consensumq.* $\overline{urm}$. I believe that *hodiernumdiem* formed a single line of the archetype twice removed, which was omitted in the transcription of the immediate archetype but added to the margin. The copyist of Hf. restored the line to the text, but in the wrong position. If we may assume that the immediate archetype had the abbreviation $\overline{urm}$, just as it is found in Hf., the reason for the copyist's error is apparent. He mistook the abbreviation sign in $\overline{urm}$ for a symbol referring to the marginal reading.

[1] See p. 48, note 5. Naturally it was impossible to adhere rigidly to thirteen letters to the line, if any regard for syllable division was had. I think we may allow for a variation of from eleven to fourteen letters to the line.

[2] Cf. p. 44.

My next example is from *Germania* 39, 1. Here, as is shown by the evidence of the X family,[1] Hf. read *uetustissimos seu nobilissimosque sueuorum*. Now *seu* was clearly at one time a marginal variant of *sueuorum*.[2] In the archetype twice removed I imagine the situation to have been about as follows:

SEV   VETVSTISSIMOS (*13 letters*)
        NOBILISSIMOSQ. (*13 letters*)
        SVEVORUM

The scribe of the immediate archetype, totally ignorant of the origin of the marginal variant, incorporated it within the text between *uetustissimos* and *nobilissimosque*. I realize that in this case the same explanation might be offered if it was the *immediate* archetype of Hf. which had thirteen letters to the line, but the two preceding examples show that it was rather a more remote exemplar. Moreover, a minuscule manuscript with but thirteen letters to the line would be a rarity.

F. 61ᵛ, 1, 1 (ch. 32) Hf. reads *circum trepidos*, but *circum* is clearly out of place and appears to be a repetition from *circumspectantes* two lines below. This suggests that the scribe of the archetype glanced ahead four lines in copying from his exemplar. There are just 54 letters[3] (four lines) between *circum* and *circumspectantes*.[4]

Further evidence may perhaps be found in the position of the *NT* ligature, of which there are fifteen examples in Hf.

[1] See pp. 98 f.

[2] The variants *SVEVORUM:SEVORUM* are of the familiar type arising through correction of error (see p. 35). That is, *SVEVORUM* was corrupted to *SEVORUM* but later restored. However, in the transmission of the text the corruption as well as the restoration was perpetuated. For other instances in which only a part of one of the variants is written cf. p. 32, iv *ciere* for *misciere*, vi *Nequam* for *Ne quamquam*, xiv *telis* for *castelis*, p. 34, xlvii *lecto* for *praelecto*.

[3] Actually 52 letters in Hf., with the suspension of *m* in *caelum* and the use of the *et* ligature.

[4] The repetition of *circum* can hardly have occurred in the transcription of Hf. itself, for the copyist first wrote *cum* and then prefixed *cir* in the margin.

The supposition of an archetype of 11–14 letters lends support to Halm's conjecture in *Agr.* 24, 10: *in < teriora parum >, melius* . . .

The sporadic appearance of this ligature suggests that the scribe copied it from his exemplar. In our oldest manuscripts the *NT* ligature is, I believe, found only at the end of the line, while in Hf. itself it comes in this position in eleven of the fifteen cases. Particularly noteworthy is the double appearance of the ligature on f. 61, 2, 23–24, where *desierint* ends one line and the words *odisse incipient* (14 letters) form the next line, which is not filled out because it comes at the end of a paragraph. Again, in one of the four cases in which the ligature does not come at the end of the line it is found exactly in the middle of a line of twenty-five letters: f. 58, 2, 22 *exaequoegerant* (13 letters counting the ligature as a single letter). Since the ligature occurs once in a marginal reading (f. 62, 1, 30 *ruebant*) there are in all but two instances in which it does not come either at the end of the line or exactly in the middle.

This behavior of the *NT* ligature suggests an actual ratio between the length of lines in Hf. and in the archetype which had 11–14 letters to the line. More convincing evidence of this is found in the treatment of the large lacuna in *Dialogus* 35. I have attempted to show that at this point in Hf. itself three pages (one and a half leaves) were left vacant, but that there was a notice to the effect that in the exemplar six leaves were missing.[1] In other words, the copyist of Hf. left vacant one-fourth as many leaves as were missing from the archetype. This suggests that a single leaf of Hf. contained four times the amount of writing found in a leaf of the exemplar which we are attempting to restore. I find startling confirmation of this assumption in the evidence of codex **W** of the *Germania*.

Germ. 43, 12, after *helysios* **W** reads *haliosnas $\bar{q}$ uel alios*. *Haliosnas* and *alios* are, of course, variant readings which the copyist took into the text,[2] but what of $\bar{q}$ *uel?* At first sight one might suppose that *uel* merely introduced the variant reading, but this offers no explanation of $\bar{q}$. I am convinced that in $\bar{q}$ *uel* we have a corruption of an ancient quaternion-

[1] See pp. 12 f.
[2] On the origin of the variants see pp. 135 f.

signature, *i.e.* $\bar{q}$ $\bar{u}$, an abbreviation of *quaternio quintus*.[1] Let us now see how this fits in with the theory that a single leaf of Hf. contained the equivalent of four leaves of its archetype twice removed. Since the text of the *Germania* in Hf. occupied one and a half quaternions, it must have occupied six quaternions in the exemplar which had four times the bulk of Hf., and the text from the end of the fifth quaternion to the end of the *Germania* should have been slightly less than one-sixth of the whole—I say slightly less, since we must make some allowance for the subscription. Now I might well wish for the perfect working of my theory that there were just one-sixth (or only a little less) of the entire *Germania* from the place where $\bar{q}$ *uel* appears in **W** to the end of the book, but such is not the case. In reality there remains slightly less than one-eighth of the text according to the measurements which I have made in the Teubner text. But after all in a text so short as that of the *Germania* the difference between one-sixth and one-eighth is not so very great, and it need not tax our credence to suppose that in a fifteenth-century manuscript two degrees removed from Hf. this misunderstood quaternion-signature has become shifted somewhat from its original position.[2]

On ff. 56–63 of the Hersfeld *Agricola* the length of most of the lines falls within the limits of twenty-two to twenty-eight letters, and the norm of thirty lines to the column is rigidly maintained. I suggest that the archetype twice removed, like Hf., was written in two columns to the page, but with only

[1] In the oldest Latin MSS. the Roman numeral designating the quaternion is sometimes surmounted by one or more horizontal lines. For the data see the tables shown by Lowe, *opp. infra citt.* Consequently the quaternion-signature $\bar{u}$ might have been mistaken for the ancient *nota* for *uel* (cf. Lindsay, *Notae Latinae*, 310).

[2] The fact that in our oldest Latin MSS. the quire-signatures were written in the lower right hand corner of the last page of the gathering (see E. A. Lowe, "Some Facts about our Oldest Latin Manuscripts," *Class. Quart.* XIX [1925], 197–208 [p. 208], and, "More Facts about out Oldest Latin Manuscripts," *ib.* XXII, 43–62) lends probability to the assumption that in the copying of the immediate archetype of Hf. the signature of the fifth quaternion was in some way carried beyond its original position.

fifteen lines to the column.[1] For the *Germania* and part of the *Agricola* (through ch. 40, 6, f. 63ᵛ), as I have previously shown, the lines appear to have had from eleven to fourteen letters each.[2] Apparently the ratio of four to one was established by the immediate archetype of Hf., while Hf. must have maintained with considerable exactitude the stichometry of its exemplar.

[1] The famous palimpsest of Cicero, *de Republica*, Vat. Lat. 5757, affords the needed parallel from antiquity. Reproduced in *Codices e Vaticanis selecti* . . . XXIII (Bibliotheca Apostolica Vaticana, 1934).

[2] In ff. 56–63 of the Hersfeld *Agricola* there is considerable variation in the amount of text contained within the single columns, the limits being 119 cm. of Teubner text (reckoned line by line from the impression of 1922) on f. 57ʳ, 1, and 141 cm. on f. 63ʳ, 2. The average for this entire section is around 130 cm. The *Germania* in the Teubner text runs through about 5820 cm. In the Hersfeld codex it occupied 12 leaves or 48 columns. Allowing half a column each for the *incipit* and *explicit* (both, however, uncertain quantities), we have 47 columns of text. Dividing 5820 by 47, we arrive at an average of slightly under 124 cm. of Teubner text per column. The text formerly contained in the first four leaves (16 columns) of the Hersfeld *Agricola* runs through 1908 cm. of Teubner text. Allowing half a column for the *incipit* (in the fifteenth-century Aesinas there are thirteen lines of text in the first column), and dividing 1908 by 15.5 we arrive at an average of a little over 123 cm. of Teubner text per column. We see that in Hf. the average amount of text per column in the *Germania* and first four leaves of the *Agricola* was practically identical, while for the next eight leaves of the *Agricola* it was somewhat larger. However, through *Germania* ch. 16, paragraph-division, entailing incomplete lines, was probably much more frequent than in the *Agricola* (see p. 264 ff.). Consequently, so far as actual compactness of writing (*i.e.* the number of letters within a given linear space) is concerned, the *Germania* may have been nearer ff. 5–8 (56–63) of the *Agricola* than it was to ff. 1–4 of the same work. All in all, I think we may assume that the script of Hf. was of about the same compactness for the *Germania* and the first twelve leaves of the *Agricola*, but in the last two leaves of the *Agricola* the writing was more crowded. On the last two leaves of the Hersfeld *Agricola* were 1165 cm. of Teubner text in 7.6 columns (the text in the second column of f. 76ᵛ is in 18 lines). Dividing 1165 by 7.6 we find an average of a little more than 153 cm. of Teubner text per column. However, this average was not evenly distributed, for the first column of the last leaf (the partially erased f. 76ʳ) actually has about 190 cm. of Teubner text, leaving an average of about 146 cm. for the preceding six columns. By a similar calculation the *Dialogus* to the point of the lacuna (14 leaves) averaged 140 cm. of Teubner text per column, and after the lacuna (2.5 leaves) about 159 cm. per column.

II

THE EXTANT MANUSCRIPTS OF THE GERMANIA

1. DESCRIPTION[1]

A   Rome, Biblioteca Angelica, fondo antico 1172 (S. 4. 42), written in 1466. Massmann, 17-18; H. Narducci, *Catalogus Codicum Manuscriptorum . . . in Bibliotheca Angelica* I (Rome, 1892), 490. Ff. 1-23ᵛ *Germania;* 23ᵛ-57 Francesco Aretino's Latin translation of the *Letters* of the pseudo-Dio-

[1] I have included in this *conspectus codicum* two printed editions (**k, w**) which have the value of MSS., since they drew from manuscript sources now lost. On the Gensberg edition (1474?) and the Viennese edition of 1500(?), which likewise drew from lost manuscript sources, see p. 328 and pp. 209-211 respectively.

That many fifteenth-century MSS. of the *Germania* have been lost is of itself a reasonable supposition and one that is proved by the internal evidence of the existing MSS. I have little doubt that MSS. as yet unknown will from time to time be brought to light in European libraries, but, barring some rare good fortune which would restore to us the Hersfeld codex itself or one of its immediate apographs, I think it hardly probable that future discoveries will add greatly to our knowledge of the text of the *Germania*.

On a codex Bambergensis used by Lipsius, see p. 333. A reputed codex Mirandulanus is made the basis of a work, which I have not seen, entitled, *J. Lipsii in C. Cornelium Tacitum Notae cum Manuscripto Cod. Mirandulano collatae a Pompeio Lampugnano* (Bergomi, 1602), whose reputed author is identified with Marquard Freher by Ryckius (*ad Hist.* III, 13). Lipsius in his diatribe, *Dispunctio Notarum Mirandulani Codicis ad Corn. Tacitum* (Antwerp, 1602; reprinted in his edition of Tacitus, 1607), questions the very existence of this MS., and in any case it is not clear (at least from Lipsius' polemic) whether the MS. even purported to contain the *Germania*. Hieronymus Groslotius (Jérome Groslote) in notes sent to Ianus Dusa (Jan van der Does), published by Burmann, *Sylloge Epistolarum . . .* I (Leyden, 1720), 348-358, cites from a *uetus codex manuscribtus* of the *Germania*, which cannot be identified with any extant MS., though it seems to have been close kin of **E** and **T** (31, 2 *conventum*, 34, 8 *magnum*, 9 *consueuimus*). Another manuscript now lost is listed in the catalogue of the Sforza library in Pesaro compiled in 1500 (Annibaldi 1910, 15). This library was destroyed by fire in 1514. From the fact that the MS. contained, in addition to the *Germania*, Apicius and the pseudo-Diogenes we may suspect that it was closely related to **l**. Regarding a codex Grimmensis mentioned by Haase (p. lix, note 354) I have no information.

genes, prefaced by a dedicatory poem addressed to Pope Pius II (cf. **1Rz**). At the foot of f. 57: *finis 1466*. Collations: Massmann; G. Meynke for Holder (cf. *Mitth.* 45); R. Wünsch (1897, 46, 55). I collated this manuscript in the summer of 1924.

a   London, British Museum, Arundel MS. 277. *Catalogue of Manuscripts in the British Museum, New Series* I, part I (1834), *The Arundel Manuscripts*, 81 f. Ff. 1—Poggio, *Liber Facetiarum;* 68–82^v *Germania;* 83—miscellaneous (Latin translations from Lucian, etc.). Collations: *variae lectiones* excerpted by Isaac Voss (cf. A. Gronovius *ad lectorem*) published by A. Gronovius II, 576–578; collation (of Voss?) in Leyden, cod. Vossianus 7, edited by J. H. Nolte, 1853; Holder (cf. *Mitth.* 46). My collation is from photostats in my possession.

b   London, British Museum, Harley MS. 1895. *A Catalogue of the Harleian Collection of Manuscripts* (London, 1759). Ff. 1–22 Pomponius Mela; 23–34^v *Cento Probae;* 35–42 *Germania*. The lower margins of several pages of the *Germania* and the entire verso of f. 42 are filled with a Latin commentary on this work. Collations: A. Panizzi for Gerlach (*praef.* x), who in turn passed the collation on to Massmann (p. 4); Holder (*Mitth.* 46). My collation is from photostats in my possession.

c   Cesena, Biblioteca Malatestiana, plut. XVII, II, sec. fila. R. Wünsch, 1897, 54; M. Lehnerdt, 1898, 504; R. Zazzeri, *Sui codici e libri a stampa della Biblioteca Malatestiana di Cesena* (Cesena, 1887), 394. Ff. 1–27 Pomponius Mela; 27^v–35^v *Germania;* 36–207 Latin translation of Ptolemaeus, *Geographia*. I collated this manuscript in the summer of 1926.

d   Rome, Biblioteca Vaticana, Ottobonianus Lat. 1209. Description, facsimile of f. 135^v, list of double readings, and collation with the Aesinas (E), by F. Grat, 1925. Ff. 1–135 Sallust, *Catilina* and *Iugurtha;* 135^v–160 *Germania*. My collation is from photostats in my possession.

Δ   Rome, Biblioteca Vaticana, Vat. Lat. 4498. Massmann, 13–15. Ff. 1–20 Frontinus, *de Aquaeductibus;* 20^v–35^v Rufus,

de Prouinciis; 36–45 Suetonius, *de Grammaticis et Rhetoribus;* 45ᵛ–63 Plinius (!), *de Viris Illustribus;* 63ᵛ–77ᵛ Tacitus, *Agricola;* 78–97 *Dialogus;* 97ᵛ–109 *Germania;* 109ᵛ–110ᵛ M. Iunius Nypsus, *de Mensuris;* 111–112 anonymous, *de Ponderibus;* 112ᵛ–118ᵛ Seneca, *Apocolocyntosis;* 119–145 Censorinus, *de Die Natali.* Collations: Brotier (1771); Brunn for Massmann (pref. ix, note 1); Müllenhoff (pp. 72 ff.). My collation is from photostats in my possession.

E   Jesi, private library of Count A. Baldeschi Balleani, MS. Lat. No. 8. See description, and literature cited, on pp. 14 ff. My collation is from the diplomatic text (with facsimile of f. 69ʳ) published by C. Annibaldi, 1910.

e   Cambridge, Library of Harvard University, MS. Lat. 124 (L 25). Description and collation of *Germania* with text of Müllenhoff by Rand, 1905. The *Germania* is on ff. 36–55. This manuscript was formerly in the library of Sir Thomas Phillips of Middle Hill and Cheltenham, and was acquired by Harvard University in 1902. My collation is from photostats in my possession.

f   Vienna, Nationalbibliothek, 49. A. Wissowa, *Lectiones Tacitinae, Specimen* III (Ratibor, 1832),[1] whose description is repeated by Eckstein in his preface to Walther (IV, pp. xi f.); *Catalogus Codicum Manuscriptorum Bibliothecae Palatinae Vindobonensis* I (Vienna, 1836), 142. Ff. 1–204ᵛ Tacitus, *Annales* XI–XVI and *Historiae* (*Ann.* XVII–XXI); 205–217 *Germania;* 217–236ᵛ *Dialogus.* Collations: H. Schubart for Hess (1834); Tschopp for Fr. Passow (Massmann, p. 22; Tagmann, p. 22); Jahn for Massmann (22); K. Schenkl for Holder (*Mitth.* 45 f.). My collation is from photostats in my possession. This manuscript appears to be merely a copy of the *editio princeps* (see pp. 185 ff.).

h   Codex Hummelianus, now lost, named from its former owner, Bernhard Friedrich Hummel. A description of this manuscript with selected readings was published by Hummel in

---

[1] I have been unable to find this work. My citation is made from Massmann, p. 22.

his *Neue Bibliotheck von seltenen und sehr seltenen Büchern* (Nuremberg, 1776) I, 212 ff., and he again mentions it in passing in his *Bibliothek der deutschen Alterthümer* (Nuremberg, 1787), 41.[1] The manuscript passed by inheritance into the hands of Chr. Th. A. Dorfmüller, one time Pastor and Director of the Latin School in Weiden, in whose possession it was when Selling published his collation in 1830, but nothing seems to be known of its later history. Hummel's description of his manuscript is as follows: ". . . Es besteht aus 14. Quartblättern, deren jedes gegen 30. Zeilen aufzuweisen hat. Die Handschrift ist, der häufigen Abbreviaturen ohngeachtet, deutlich, durchaus gleichförmig, das Papier aber so weisz und steif, dasz es dem Holländischen nichts nachgibt. Die *Diphthongi ae, oe* werden allezeit nur durch einen einfachen *uocalem* ausgedruckt. Das *i* ist zuweilen mit einen Pünctgen versehen, zuweilen auch nicht. In Ansehung des *u* ist die sogenannte Cellarianische Orthographie beobachtet, nehmlich am Anfang des Worts *v*, in der Mitte *u*, am Ende der Wörter, aber, die sich mit *s* endigen, erblicket man bald ein langes, bald ein kurzes. *Commata* findet man gar nicht; sondern *punctum* und Fragzeichen müssen die Stelle der Unterscheidungszeichen allein vertretten. Der Context gehet ohne Capiteleintheilung und Absätze in einem beständigen Zusammenhange fort: der Abschreiber aber nennet sich nirgends. Soll ich von seinem Alter etwas muthmassen: so wollte ich es gleichwohl nicht viel über 300. oder 350. Jahre hinauf setzen. Vielleicht liesze sich aus dem Papierzeichen, welches in einem Zirkel 2. kreutzweis über einander gelegte Pfeile vorstellt, auf dessen Alter schlieszen, wenn man der Sache weiter nachspüren wollte. . ."

Aside from the selected readings published by Hummel (see above), two collations of **h** are extant: one entered by P. D. Longolius in a copy of the Leipzig edition of Melchior Lotter (1509), which is now in the Munich library;[2] another

---

[1] See Wünsch 1893, 4. I have not had access to the later work of Hummel.
[2] Bound with MS. Lat. 947 (see below under Mon.).

published by C. F. G. C. Selling at the end of his *Observationes Criticae* (Augsburg, 1830). The collation of Longolius (together with the collations of Hummel and Selling) has been published by R. Wünsch (1893, 7–23). My own restoration of h is based upon a re-examination of the three sources, the Munich library having kindly provided me with photostats of Longolius' collation. For the plan which I follow in restoring the readings of h see pp. 171 ff.

I   Rome, Biblioteca Vaticana, Vat. Lat. 1518. Massmann, 16 f.; B. Nogara, *Codices Vaticani Latini* III (Rome, 1912) 40 f. Ff. 1–108^v Porphyrio *in Horatium* (a manuscript distinct from the rest); 110–166^v a commentary on Persius; 166^v–173^v Suetonius, *de Grammaticis et Rhetoribus;* 173^v–189 dupl. Tacitus, *Dialogus;* 189 dupl.-198^v *Germania.* Collations: Brotier (1771); Massmann; A. Reifferscheid (1867, 623); A. Michaelis, whose collation was used by Müllenhoff (1873); Andresen in 1898 (II, 222); F. F. Abbott (1903, 5, note 7; corrections of Mf.'s critical apparatus, 42 f.); C. Annibaldi (1910, 49, note 1). My collation is from photostats in my possession.

k   The printed edition said to have issued from the press of Fr. Creusner, Nuremberg, c. 1473 (see description in Bibliography). A collation of three Munich copies (differing from one another in unimportant details) with Müllenhoff's edition is published by M. Rödiger at the end of *DA* IV^2, 695 f. I collated a copy in the national library of Vienna (6.F.22) in the summer of 1926, but have found the collation of Rödiger useful, since my own was rather hastily made.

Mon. The fragmentary manuscript, Munich, Staatsbibliothek, Lat. 947 (*Germania* 8, 8 *diu apud*—43, 11 *diffusum*) is a copy of k (see p. 209). Massmann, 4; *Catalogus Codicum Latinorum Bibliothecae Regiae Monacensis*, ed. alt. I, 1 (Munich, 1892), 213 f. It was once the property of P. D. Longolius, and later came into the possession of J. Kapp. Longolius used it in preparing his notes upon the *Germania*, which were gathered into an edition after his death by J. Kapp (1788; 2d ed. by Hess,

1824). The manuscript is bound with the copy of Lotter's edition which contains Longolius' collation of **h**. I have photostats of this manuscript at my disposal.

L   Leyden, University Library, XVIII Periz. Q. 21 ("Perizonianus"), written in 1460 (?). Massmann, 7–13; J. Geel, *Catalogus Librorum Manuscriptorum qui inde Anno 1741 Bibliothecae Lugduno-Batavae Accesserunt* (Leyden, 1852), 121 f.; complete photographic facsimiles with elaborate preface by G. Wissowa in *Codices Graeci et Latini Photographice Depicti*, Suppl. IV (Leyden, 1907); facsimile of f. 41^r by Chatelain, *Paléographie des classiques latins* (Paris, 1894–1900), II, Pl. CXLVII, 1. Ff. 2–30 *Dialogus;* 31–47 *Germania;* 47–59^v Suetonius, *de Grammaticis et Rhetoribus*. A note on f. 2^v states that the manuscript was written by Iovianus Pontanus in March, 1460,[1] but it is doubtful whether the actual manuscript is the autograph copy of Pontanus or a transcript of the same (see p. 203). Collations: L. Tross, who made this manuscript the sole basis for his edition (1841); F. Ritter (1848, xii); Geel for Massmann and later Massmann himself; K. Meiser (1871, 5); anonymous for O. Jahn, who loaned the collation to Mf. (1873); W. N. du Rieu for Holder (1873, iii); Holder (*Mitth*. 46). My collation is from the facsimiles in *Codd. Gr. et Lat.*

1   Florence, Biblioteca Medicea Laurenziana, plut. LXXIII, cod. 20. A. M. Bandini, *Catalogus Codicum Latinorum Bibliothecae Mediceae Laurentianae* III (Florence, 1776), 44 f.; Massmann, 2 f.; E. Rostagno, *Atene e Roma* XV (1912), 81; facsimile of ff. 45^v–46 by Chatelain, *op. cit.*, II, Pl. CXLVII, 2. Ff. 1–45 *Apicius;* 45–61 *Germania;* 61^v–83 Francesco Aretino's Latin translation of the *Letters* of the pseudo-Diogenes, prefaced by the dedicatory poem to Pius II (cf. **ARz**). Collations: Massmann; G. Meynke for Holder (*Mitth*. 45); R. Wünsch (1897, 46, 55). I collated this manuscript in the summer of 1924.

[1] See transcription on pp. 351 f.

M Venice, Biblioteca Marciana, class. xiv, 1, MSS. Lat. colloc. 4266, of the year 1464. J. P. Tomasini, *Bibliothecae Patavinae Manuscriptae Publicae et Privatae* (Utini, 1639), 16; Massmann, 19–21; G. M. Thomas, 1853; E. Philipp, 1904; G. Funaioli, "Due codice di Svetonio," *Studi Italiani* xvii (1909), 265–283 (267). Ff. 1–166^v various works of Aeneas Silvius; 166^v–172^v Suetonius, *de Grammaticis et Rhetoribus;* 172^v–184^v Tacitus, *Dialogus;* 186–193^v *Germania;* 196–222, Josephus, *de Bello Iudaico.* Notes on ff. 184^v, 193, and 222, state that the manuscript was written in 1464 at Bologna for Dr. Iohannes Marcanova. Collations: anonymous for Fr. Passow, who loaned the collation to Bach (Bach, x); Heubach for Massmann; Thomas (correction of errors in Massmann's critical apparatus). My collation is from photostats in my possession.

m Munich; Staatsbibliothek, Lat. 5307. Massmann, 4 f.; *Catalogus Codicum Latinorum Bibliothecae Regiae Monacensis* i, 3 (Munich, 1873), 3; R. Wünsch, 1893, 80. Ff. 1—Petrus Lombardus, *Compendium Librorum Sententiarum*, and three tractates on the Holy Land; ff. 153–168 *Germania*. Collations: Massmann; Holder (*Mitth.* 46); Wünsch. My own collation is from photostats in my possession.

N Naples, Biblioteca Nazionale, iv. C. 21 (Farnesianus). C. Jannelli, *Catalogus Bibliothecae Latinae Veteris et Classicae Manuscriptae quae in Regio Neapolitano Museo Borbonico adservatur* (Naples, 1827), whose description is repeated by Eckstein in his preface to Walther iv, ix f., and by Orelli i, xv; Massmann, 5–7. Tacitus, *Annales* xi–xvi, *Historiae* i–v (*Annales* xvii–xxi), *Dialogus, Germania;* Suetonius, *de Grammaticis et Rhetoribus.* Collations: Lipsius; Massmann; E. Martin and U. von Wilamowitz-Möllendorf for Mf. (1873); E. Böckel for Holder (*Mitth.* 45); Andresen in 1898 (ii, 222). My collation is from photostats in my possession.

o Rome, Biblioteca Vaticana, Ottobonianus Lat. 1795. Paper MS. in 8°, ff. 88+several blank leaves. Massmann, 17. Ff. 1–23^v *de primis Italiae regibus;* ff. 24–30^v *Germania*, chaps. 1–13, 19 *et ipsa plerumque*, followed by five blank leaves unnumbered; 31–76 Hyginus, *de Astris;* 77–83^v *Opusculum de Orthographia et figuris* (incomplete). Collations: Massmann; R. Wünsch (1897, 46). My collation is from photostats in my possession.

p   Paris, Bibliothèque Nationale, Nouvelles Acquisitions 1180. L. Delisle, "Inventaire des manuscrits latins de la Bibliothèque Nationale insérés au fonds des nouvelles acquisitions du 1er août 1871 au 1er mars 1874," *Bibliothèque de l'École des Chartes* xxxv (1874), 76–92 (84); R. Wünsch (1897, 48). Ff. 1–32 Pomponius Mela; 33–40 *Germania*, chaps. 1–44, 19 *regia utilitas;* f. 41 document of Jan. 19, 1454 (copy). Collated by Wünsch, *l. c.* 48–53. My collation is from photostats in my possession.

R   Florence, Biblioteca Riccardiana, MS. 158 (N. iii. 14). J. Lamius, *Catalogus Codicum Manuscriptorum qui in Bibliotheca Riccardiana Florentiae Adservantur* (Livorno, 1756), 359; R. Sabbadini, "Spogli Ambrosiani Latini," *Studi Italiani* xi (1903), 165–388 (228). Ff. 1–55 Francesco Aretino's Latin Translation of the *Letters* of the pseudo-Phalaris (cf. **z**); 56–71 Latin translation of the *Letters* of the pseudo-Brutus by Rinuccio da Castiglione, with prefaces; 71^v–96 Francesco Aretino's Latin translation of the *Letters* of the pseudo-Diogenes prefaced by his dedicatory poem to Pius II (cf. **Alz**); ff. 96^v–112 *Germania*. Collation of *Germ.*, chaps. 1–3 only, by Sabbadini, *l.c.* 228 f. I collated this manuscript in the summer of 1924.

r   Rimini, Biblioteca Comunale (Gambalunghiana), IV. D. 112, of the year 1476. G. Mazzatinti, *Inventari dei manoscritti delle biblioteche d'Italia* ii (Forlì, 1893), 165, with date wrongly given as 1426; R. Reitzenstein, 1898; M. Lehnerdt, 1898, 505. Ff. 1–59 *Mirabilia Vrbis;* 61–77 *Dicta quorundam philosophorum . . . per Iohannem Stephanum . . . in Latinum . . . versa;* 77^v–93^v *Germania*.[1] A note at the end of the *Germania* states that the manuscript was written in Rome by

[1] There seems to be some confusion in the numbering of the leaves. The numbers written on my photographs are 79^v–95^v.

Ranerius Maschius of Rimini, March, 1476.[1] Collations: H. Bresslau for Reitzenstein (1898, 307 ff.); M. Lehnerdt for A. Holder (cf. Lehnerdt, 1898, 505); C. Annibaldi (1910, 49, note 1). My collation is from photographs in my possession.

S   Stuttgart, Landesbibliothek, Hist. Q. 152. Massmann, 18 f.; W. von Heyd, *Die historischen Handschriften der Königlichen öffentlichen Bibliothek zu Stuttgart* II (1891), 69; Wünsch (1893), 82 f. Ff. 1–75 Florus, *Epitome;* 77–89 Petrus Candidus Decembrius, *Romanae Historiae Breuis Epitome;* 90ᵛ–99ᵛ Sextus Rufus, *Breviarium;* 100ᵛ–119 Benevenutus de Imola, *Libellus Augustalis;* 120–134 *Germania; Index Summorum Pontificum,* etc. Collations: Moser for Hess (1828, iii); Gerlach (1835, xiii); Osiander, whose collation was used by Tagmann (17); Fellner for Massmann; Holder (pref. to Holtzmann, iii–iv; *Mitth.* 46); Wünsch. My collation is from photostats in my possession.

T   Toledo, Chapter Library, 49, 2, of the year 1474. O. Leuze, "Die Agricola-Handschrift in Toledo," *Philologus,* Supplementband VIII (1899–1901), 513–556 (collation of *Agricola*); F. F. Abbott, 1903; J. M. Octavio de Toledo, *Catálogo de la Librería del Cabildo Toledano* (= Biblioteca de la Revista de Archivos, Bibliotecas y Museos III), Madrid, 1903, 191 f. Ff. 1–15ᵛ *Germania;* 16–36ᵛ *Agricola;* 37–63ᵛ Io. Ant. Campanus, *Oratio de Laudibus Scientiarum;* 64–65 anonymous Latin fragment; 66–222 Plinius, *Epistulae* (selections); 222–223ᵛ *Epistola sive Apologia pro Episcopo Caietano.* On f. 15ᵛ is found the subscription: *FVLGINIE SCRIPTVM GE/RENTE ME MAGISTRATVM/ PV. SCRIBE KAL. IVN. 1474.* Collation by Abbott with Müllenhoff's edition.

---

[1] I quote the note in full, since there are a few errors in the transcription published by Lehnerdt: "Scripsi rome expedito sindicatu senatus 1476 de mense martii dum expectarem solutionem salarii et vexillum quo etiam tempore dicebatur oratores Imperatoris et regis gallorum et aliorum ultramontanorum uenire ad citandum Sixtum iiii pontificem ad concilium quod fuit causa dilatationis expeditionis mee cum magna mei impensa quia habebam in hospitio decem equos et totidem famulos Ranerius Maschius Ariminensis manu propria." The note is in the same cursive hand that has written the *Germania* from f. 86 (*Germ.* 22, 13 *et nuda*) to the end.

My collation is from photostats in my possession. The manuscript is a copy of **E** (see pp. 206 ff.).

t   Zürich, Zentralbibliothek, Car. C. 56, of the year 1502. C. Mohlberg, *Katalog der Handschriften der Zentralbibliothek Zürich* I (Zürich, 1932), No. 251. Ff. 1–5ᵛ Giasone del Maino, *Ad . . . Maximilianum . . . Regem, in Eius et Auguste Blance Marie Nupciis Epithalamium;* 5ᵛ–6ᵛ Sebastian Brant, *Epithalamion;* 6ᵛ—Jacob Wimpheling, *Distichum in Blancam Mariam;* 9–14ᵛ *Germania*, with lacuna from ch. 8, 3 *quam longe* to 16, 10 *Solent;* 16–131 Conrad de Mure, *Fabularius;* 132 autograph note of Felix Hemerli. F. 131ᵛ, at the end of the *Fabularius*, is the following subscription: "Transcriptum manu Petri Numagen Treveren. Capellani sancti Leonardi prope Turegum Anno domini millesimo quingentesimo secundo. Die xii mensis junii." Collations: J. J. Breitinger for Ernesti (1752, *praef.*); J. C. Orelli (1819), Kellner for Passow, who loaned the collation to Tagmann (22); Holder (*Mitth.* 46). My collation is from photostats in my possession.

u   Rome, Biblioteca Vaticana, Urbinas Lat. 412 (655). Massmann, 15 f.; C. Stornajolo, *Codices Vrbinates Latini* I (Rome, 1902), 425. Ff. 2–201ᵛ Tacitus, *Annales* XI–XVI and *Historiae* (*Ann.* XVII–XXI); 204–214ᵛ *Germania*. Collations: Massmann; R. Wünsch (1897, 46, 55). My own collation is from photostats in my possession.

V   Rome, Biblioteca Vaticana, Vat. Lat. 1862. Massmann, 15; B. Nogara, *Codices Vaticani Latini* III (Rome, 1912), 305 f. Ff. 1–13 *Germania;* 13ᵛ–23 *de Grammaticis et Rhetoribus;* 23ᵛ–43 *Dialogus*. Collations: Brotier (1771); Massmann; A. Reifferscheid (1867, 623); A. Michaelis for Mf. (1873); L. Urlichs in 1872 (1876, 509); G. Meynke for Holder (*Mitth.* 45); Andresen in 1898 (II, 222); F. F. Abbott (1903, 5, note 7; corrections of Mf.'s critical apparatus on pp. 42–43); C. Annibaldi (1910, 49, note 1). My collation is from photostats in my possession.

v   Rome, Biblioteca Vaticana, Vat. Lat. 2964. Massmann, 17. Ff. 1–11 *Germania;* 12–18 *Dialogus* from ch. 26, 25 *expectabam* to the end. Collations: Brotier (1771); Massmann; Wilamowitz-Möllendorf for Mf. (*DA* IV², 78); R. Wünsch (1897, 46); W. Friedensburg for R. Reitzenstein (1898, 308). My collation is from photostats in my possession.

W Vienna, Staatsarchiv, 711, of the year 1466. J. Hümer, 1878, 801 ff.; E. Philipp, 1889, 288-290; Fr. Scheuer, 1901, 11 f. Paper manuscript of three large quarto volumes, all written by the same hand,[1] containing the works of Blondus Flavius Forliviensis. I, ff. 200–211ᵛ *Germania;* 212–230ᵛ *Dialogus;* 231–239 Suetonius, *de Grammaticis et Rhetoribus*. On the last leaf of Vol. II (f. 331) is found the following note: *Hugo haemste scripsit Rome Anno salutis 1466./ impensis Reverendissimi in Christo patris et domini: domini Jo. dei & apostolice/ sedis gratia Epyscopi. Tridentini: 2 c̄ (et cetera ?)*. As Lehnerdt (1898, 503) has seen, this manuscript was written for Johann Hinderbach, Bishop of Trent, 1465–1486. Throughout the manuscript are copious marginal notes in a hand different from that of the text, some of which bear the signatures, *Johannes Hinderbach* (I, f. 19ᵛ), *Joh. hin., Joh. Trid.*, etc. (cf. pp. 156 f.). Presumably these marginal notes were written by Hinderbach himself. Collations: Hümer, 1878; H. Schefczik, 1886 (corrections of Hümer's collation and additions, 4, note 8). My collation is from photostats in my possession. I also examined this manuscript in the summer of 1926.

w The *editio princeps*, said to have issued from the press of Vindelin of Spire, Venice, *ca.* 1469 (see Bibliography for description). My collation is from photostats of a copy in the British Museum (IB. 19592).

z Madrid, Biblioteca Nacional, 10037, formerly in the Chapter Library of Toledo. Octavio de Toledo, *op. cit.* (p. 87), 150. The manuscript is from the collection of Cardinal Zelada. Ff. 1–46ᵛ Francesco Aretino's Latin translation of the *Letters* of the pseudo-Phalaris (cf. **R**); 47–67ᵛ Aretino's translation of the *Letters* of the pseudo-Diogenes (cf. **A1R**); 68–83 *Germania;*

---

[1] Save for a few additions at the end of Vol. III.

83ʳ–84ᵛ Aretino's elegiac poem in honor of Pius II, usually prefaced to the Diogenes. I have seen no mention of this manuscript other than Octavio's description. My collation is from photostats in my possession.

2. Classification of the Manuscripts

> A *stemma codicum* will be found at the end of this volume.

Although the manuscripts and editions described above show considerable diversity of text, the presence of certain errors in all proves that they are offshoots of a single line of descent: 2, 11 *conditorisque;* 6, 10 *galeae;* 10, 5 *consuletur;* 12, 7 *poenarum;* 16, 13 *locis;* 21, 14 *uictus inter hospites comis;* 26, 3 *uices;* 26, 7 *et prata;* 28, 14 *Neruli;* 28, 18 *Nubii;* 30, 15 *peditum* (?) om.; 31, 10 lacuna after *habitus;* 35, 2 *redit;* 36, 4 *nomine superioris;* 37, 17 *Marcoque;* 38, 11 *innoxiae;* 39, 4 *eiusdem* om.; 39, 12 *habitantur;* 40, 9 *ea;* 40, 17 *uestes;* 41, 1 *pars uerborum;* 43, 1 and 3 *Gotini, Gotinos;* 43, 8 *iugumque;* 43, 19 *trucis;* 44, 17 *ociosa;* 45, 10 *omniumque;* 46, 1 *fines; Sueui,* etc. throughout. Furthermore, numerous variants scattered throughout our MSS. point clearly to double readings in a common archetype (see pp. 121–141). It is, I believe, no longer doubted that this line of descent culminated in the Hersfeld codex, from which all extant manuscripts derive by varying degrees.[1] These manuscripts, save for the few which were but recently discovered or have never before been collated, have been examined by various scholars with a view to establishing a *stemma codicum*. But the results seem far from satisfactory.

The more logical procedure, I suppose, would be to state the views of my predecessors in the field, and then to pass to my own classification of the manuscripts. But such a method would produce needless confusion in an investigation which is at best complicated. Accordingly, I find it preferable to proceed forthwith to the presentation of my own classification, and to reserve for an appendix a brief survey of former endeavors to group our manuscripts.

a. *The Division of the Manuscripts into the* **X** *and* **Y** *Families*

My investigation, based upon a careful examination of all the manuscript evidence, has convinced me that the extant manuscripts of the *Germania* descend from two lost apographs of the Hersfeld codex, which I call **X** and **Y**. From **X** have come by three independent lines of descent **Wmh**. From **Y** have descended the twenty-eight remaining manuscripts (and editions), which, however, readily group themselves into four divisions as follows: α, including **NΔIpMtwf**; β, including **VLdETvrok**; φ, including **balezuRAc**; and **s**, which cannot be classified with any of the three preceding groups. The sigla α, β, φ, indicate three lost apographs of **Y** from which the extant manuscripts within the respective groups derive. The manuscripts of the groups α, β, φ, may in turn be divided into various branches, as is indicated by the table of sigla on p. 270 and by the *stemma codicum* at the end of this volume.

My division of the manuscripts into two major families, **X** and **Y**, as stated above, must, however, be slightly modified, owing to evidence in certain manuscripts of the process known as "contamination." I find that **NΔI**, which form the σ

[1] As positive evidence of this, we may note that the character of the errors common to all the MSS. and the character of certain variant readings conform with the errors and double readings of the Hersfeld *Agricola* (see pp. 30–56).

branch of the α group, and the second hand in **s** (s²) show an infiltration of readings from the **X** family, and are accordingly to be classified with this family wherever they agree with **Wmh** in opposition to the remaining manuscripts. Contamination in the opposite direction is perhaps to be seen in **h**, which appears to show a certain affinity to the α group, but the existing collations of this lost manuscript are inadequate to warrant a definite conclusion.

I well realize that a grouping of our manuscripts which causes three of them (Wmh) to assume an importance equal to that of all other manuscripts combined must be shown to rest upon sound evidence. It will not be sufficient merely to list the readings peculiar to the **X** family. The past history of the text criticism of the *Germania* illustrates only too well the danger of such a procedure. I must show that the **X** family is an *ultimate* group, *i.e.*, that it does not form a subdivision of some larger group of manuscripts which has a common archetype later than Hf. Such proof will have to be twofold. First, I must prove that the **X** family contributes something toward the restoration of Hf. that is not found in the other manuscripts; second, that the **X** family does not concur with any of the other groups in corruptions which are demonstrably of later origin than Hf.[1]

Likewise, I well realize that an hypothesis which demands that four groups of manuscripts, presenting such a diversity of readings as do α, β, φ, **s**, be referred to a single fifteenth-century archetype, and which is so at variance with all accepted theories regarding the relationship of the *Germania* manuscripts, must also be shown to rest upon a firm foundation. The restoration of **Y** undoubtedly presents greater difficulties than does the restoration of **X**. Nevertheless, I hope to be able to establish the following points: (1) in certain places in our text

[1] That is, the agreement of the **X** family with one or more of the groups, α, β, φ, **s**, must, as a rule, be shown to offer the readings of Hf. I realize the inconsistency of referring to the single MS. **s** as a group, but have taken this liberty, since I find this MS. to represent a line of descent from **Y** parallel to the lines represented by α, β, φ.

the groups α, β, φ, s, offer essentially the same corruptions, whereas the **X** family appears to have maintained the better tradition; (2) certain corruptions, which by their very character betray a late (fifteenth-century) origin are unknown to the **X** family, but find representation (though not to the exclusion of the better readings) in all four groups, α, β, φ, s, or in three of these groups, or in two of them, offering as it were threads which lead the four groups back to one manuscript later than Hf.; (3) the readings peculiar to each of the groups, α, β, φ, s, offer little or nothing toward the restoration of Hf., whereas, if any of these groups represented an independent line of tradition from the parent manuscript, it might reasonably be expected to make some significant contribution toward its restoration.

I now submit the evidence of our extant manuscripts, which will, I believe, confirm my two hypotheses, (1) that **Wmh** (X) represent a line of tradition from Hf. distinct from the other manuscripts; (2) that the other manuscripts are to be referred to a common archetype (Y) later than Hf. Whether or not all will agree with my interpretation of the evidence, I cannot say, but I do feel confident that I shall not be open to the charge of suppressing any evidence which may seem to militate against my hypotheses.

X *opposed to* Y

In the following table I show the readings in which **Wmh**, with or without σ (NΔI) [1] and s², conspire against the other manuscripts. As I have stated, σ and s² are to be regarded as belonging to the **X** family wherever they agree with **Wmh** in opposition to the rest of the manuscripts. In a few instances I have admitted to the left hand column (X) readings which are found in one or two members of the **Y** family, duly indicating the concurrence, which I regard as accidental (ii, ix, xi, xiii, xxv, xxix, xxx).[2]

[1] The interlinear readings in **N** are by the hand of the text (see p. 189, note 1).
[2] Yet it is possible that in ix and xxix the MS. **Y**, as well as **X**, read *idem* and *temptes*.

		X	Y
(i)	2, 10	bistonem,² *in mg.* tuistonem (-sco- *h*) **Wh**, Bistonem **NΔ**, bisbonem **m**, histonem **s**²	tuistonem (*uarietas lectionum in p. 115 uidenda est. Scriptura bistonem in Y nusquam reperitur.*)
(ii)	11	conditorisque **W**, conditoremque **hs**² (= *a*), conditorisque **m** [with *em* superscr.]	conditorisque
(iii)	3, 12	incolatur **Wmh**	incolitur
(iv)	15	reperta¹ **WmhNΔ**	repertam
(v)	5, 17	serratos **W** [with *a* superscr.], sarratos **m**, serratos **h** *ex sil.*	serratos
(vi)	10, 4	temere, *in mg.* tenent **W**, tenent **hs²Δ**, temere, *superscr.* tenere **N**, temere **m**	temere
(vii)	13	contacti, *in mg.* contactis **W**, contractis **m**, contactis **s**², contacti **h** *ex sil.*	contacti
(viii)	14, 3	principi **W** [with *e* superscr.], principe **h**, principi **m**	principi
(ix)	15, 5	idem **Wmh** (= *b*)	iidem (iisdem *dk* ψ, hidem *r*, hisdem *l*)
(x)	11	singulis **Wmhs**²	a singulis
(xi)	16, 7	Nec **Wm**, **h** *ex sil.*,² **Ns**² (= *c*)	Ne
(xii)	9	inliniunt (-nunt *W*) **Wmh**	illinunt (*uel* -niunt)
(xiii)	25, 11	regnant **Wmhs**² (= *lu*²)	regnantur

¹ **W** reads *repertā*, but the line of suspension is probably by the second hand. The same correction is reported for the second hand in **h**.

² On the reading of **h** see p. 167.

The Extant Manuscripts of the Germania 95

			X	Y
(xiv)	26,	3	uices, *in mg.* vice **W**, uices **m**, uice **hs**², uite **Δ**, uice *e* uices **N**	uices (in uices β *pM*)
(xv)	28,	8	bohemi[1] *in tex.* **mNΔ**, *in mg.* **Wh**	boihemi
(xvi)	28,	8	signatque **WmhNΔs**²	significatque (sig, que *L*) t
(xvii)	29,	1	batauii, *in mg.* bathi **W**, batami **m**, bathi, *in mg.* bataui **h**, bathi **s**², batauii, *superscr.* batii **N**	batauii
(xviii)	30,	1	hercynio, *in mg.* herquinio **W**, herquinio **mh**	hercynio (*uel* -cin-)
(xix)		6	animis **Wh**, *om.* **m**	animi
(xx)		14	rari **W**, raro **hσ**, rari **m**	rari
(xxi)	36,	7	Tracti **WmhNΔs**²	Tacti
(xxii)	38,	8	saepius **Wmh**	saepe
(xxiii)		10	religant **mhs**², rei ligant **W**	ligant α **s**, religatur β, ne legant φ
(xxiv)	39,	1	uetustissimos (-mo *m*) seu **Wmhs**²	uetustissimos (-mo *I*) se (se *om. N r*) α β, uetustissimosque (-que *om. al*) φ, uetustissimos **N r al s**
(xxv)		3	sacrum, *in mg.* sacram **W**, sacrum **m**, sacram **h** *ex sil.*, **Δs**² (= χ), sacrum **N**	sacrum (sac.ᵐ *b*, sacrorum *s*, *in* sacrum *corr.* s²)
(xxvi)	40,	1	nobilitat **Wm**, **h** *ex sil.*,² **NΔs**²	nobilitas

[1] For a complete list of the readings see p. 128.
[2] See p. 170.

		X	Y
(xxvii)	43, 3	cultu **Wmh**	cultuque
(xxviii)	43, 10	legiorum, *in mg.* vegiorum **W**, legiorum **m**, regiorum **h**, uegiorum Δ**s**², legiorum **N**, leugiorum **I**	legiorum M𝛘 vk s, legiorum VdE, legiorum p L, ligiorum r bal, lignorum ψ
(xxix)	45, 28	temptes **Wmhs**² (= *t ae*)	tentes
(xxx)	46, 3	quidem **Wh** (= *v*), quidem *in* quidam *corr. ut uid.* **m**	quidam

From this table we are enabled to restore to **X** twelve pairs of doublets, each offering a variant reading that is not attested for **Y**. I shall now examine these variants for the purpose of determining which of them may with probability be referred to Hf., and which to all appearances had their origin in **X** itself.

i. *tuistonem: bistonem:* I explain *bistonem* as a corruption of *tuistonem*, i.e. *tuistonem > uistonem > bistonem*. Since the phonetic confusion between consonant-*u* and *b* is ancient (cf. pp. 246 f.), both readings should be assigned to Hf.

v. *serratos: sarratos:* Again, I believe, we are dealing with an ancient phonetic confusion of which traces are to be found in the Hersfeld *Agricola* (see p. 236).

vii. *contacti: contactis:* The variant *contactis* occurring in an excellent manuscript, such as the evidence proves **X** to have been, cannot be neglected. My own explanation is that *contactis* offers the better tradition, pointing to *contacti sunt* as the true reading. The abbreviation $\bar{s}$ for *sunt* is found once in the Hersfeld *Agricola*, and may of course have been used in its minuscule archetype (see pp. 57 ff.).

viii. *principi: principe:* Here too the nonsensical variant (*principe*) cannot be summarily dismissed. The confusion of *i* and *e* is common in the Hersfeld *Agricola*, though it is almost always the open *i*, and not the close *i* as found here, which has been displaced by *e* (see pp. 240 ff.). May not *principe* point rather to *principis* as the true reading? (On the confusion between final *-is* and *e* see p. 239.)

xvii. *batauii: bathi:* The variant *bathi* bears the mark of antiquity. The original form of the variant may have been *bath(auii)*, which was later changed to *bathi* in an effort to assimilate the two readings, or the process of corruption may have been, *batauii>bati>bathi*. In either case the variant *bathi* implies a progressive corruption of two or more stages, and this is a good reason for believing it to be as old as, or older than Hf.[1]

xviii. *hercynio: herquinio:* The orthographical variant *herquinio* is ancient. Manuscripts and inscriptions frequently show *qui* for the Greek κυ. In the glossaries we find *quigneum* (κύκνειον), *quinici* (*cynici*), *quines* (κύνες), *quilismata* (κυλίσματα), *quinoclosa* (*cynoglossa*), *quinoroda* (*cynorrhoda*), *Coquitus* (*Cocytus*).[2] From inscriptions may be cited *QVIRENARICE*[3] and *QVIRILLVS*[4] for *Cyrenaice* and *Cyrillus*. Conversely, Greek transliterations of Latin words sometimes have κυ for *qui:* ΚΥΡΕΙΝΑ[5] and ΚΥΝΤΗΛΙΟC[6] for *Quirina* and *Quintilius*. The manuscripts of Nonius, 27, 3 M, of which the oldest are saec. IX, give *helquisticon* or *helquesticon* for ἑλκυστικόν. See L. Duvau, *Mémoires de la société de linguistique de Paris* VIII (1894), 188 f. I have also noted *quirie* (κύριε) in St. Gall MS. 914, *saec.* VIII–IX (Plate 4, line 12, in Traube, *Textgesch. d. Regula S. Benedicti*, 2d ed., Munich, 1910). Finally, the oldest manuscript (*saec.* VIII–IX) of Jordanes, *Romana* (*M.G., A.A.* V, 148, ed. Mommsen), read *herquinius*. According to Duvau, *op. cit.*, the Latin name for the letter *y* was *ui*, which

---

[1] It is interesting to note how N has assimilated the two variants.
[2] See Löwe, *Prodromus Corporis Glossariorum Latinorum* (Leipzig, 1876), 376 f. The MSS. cited by Löwe are *saec.* VII–X.
[3] *C.I.L.* III, 2063.
[4] De Rossi, *Inscr. Christ. Vrbis Romae* (Rome, 1857–1861) I, 355.
[5] *I.G.* XII, 3, 522; 523; 528.
[6] Boeckh, *C.I.G.* II, 2588.

in old French was pronounced *gui*. The phonetic change producing the *g* shows that name *ui* goes back to ancient times.

xxviii. *legiorum: uegiorum:* The character of the variant *uegiorum* shows that it was not an innovation of **X**. Presumably we should ascribe to Hf. the reading *legiorum*, which points to *Lugiorum* as the correct form. The copyist of **X** misunderstood the superscript *u* as displacing the initial *l*. The copyist of **Y** may have written a superscript *v* so carelessly that it was indistinguishable from *y*, thereby giving rise to the reading *Lygiorum*, of which the spelling *Ligiorum* appears to be a corruption.[1]

ii. vi. xiv. xx. xxv: I think it doubtful if the variants peculiar to **X**, shown in these five pairs of doublets, are older than this lost manuscript. *Conditoremque* (ii) and *uice* (xiv) are obviously unsuccessful attempts to heal earlier corruptions,[2] and the variant *raro* (xx) has nothing to recommend it. It is true that *sacram* (xxv) is a necessary correction, but I suspect that Hf. knew only *sacrum*, a corruption which may have been induced by the preceding *patrium* (!) or by the similarity between open *a* and *u* in the minuscule archetype of Hf. (cf. p. 54). On the other hand, I am hesitant in the case of *tenent* (vi), for I feel that this reading may be quite as authoritative as the variant *temere*.[3]

Of the twelve doublets peculiar to the **X** family I find that at least seven make their contribution toward the restoration of Hf., and may accordingly be used as evidence that the **X** family represents a line of descent distinct from the remaining manuscripts.

I now turn to the other readings in which **X** presented a contrast to **Y**.

xxiv. In *uetustissimos seu* we have a striking instance of the

[1] However, it should be noted that *Lygiorum* as well as *Lugiorum* seems to have been an ancient spelling. See *A.P.V. s.v. Lugii*.

[2] See critical notes to the passages.

[3] See critical notes to the passage.

merit of the **X** family. *Seu* seems originally to have been a variant reading belonging with the following *Sueuorum* (*i.e. seu*[*orum*]: *sueuorum*),[1] though even in Hf. it must have been in the text.[2] The various attempts at emendation shown in the column to the right indicate a connection between α and β, but do not offer evidence for the restoration of an archetype (Y) common to all four groups. Still a different attempt at emendation is found in two members of the **X** family, **m** and **h**, which omit the *-que* of the following *nobilissimosque*. The fact that **W** alone gives the reading of Hf., *uetustissimos seu nobilissimosque sueuorum*, is but one of the numerous proofs of the excellence of this manuscript.[3]

xxi. xxvi: The readings of **X**, *Tracti* and *nobilitat* have long deservedly held their place in our editions of the *Germania*. To assume that these are merely fifteenth-century corrections would be gratuitous. The corresponding *Tacti* and *nobilitas* of Y are easily explained as a copyist's errors, but the readings of **X** are rather too good to be scribal emendations.[4]

xvi: Here again I believe that only the reading of **X**, *si-*

---

[1] In ch. 45, 7, our MSS. actually show the doublets *sueuici: saeuici*, though the origin of the corruption may not have been the same. *Saeuici* is probably due to the confusion of *u* and open *a* in the immediate archetype of Hf. (cf. p. 54), while *seuorum* was produced merely by the omission of *u*, and the corruption certainly antedates Hf.

[2] Cf. p. 75.

[3] Commentators have hitherto regarded only the interpolated reading of α β, and some have rightly found difficulties inherent in it. Heraeus (1880) sets forth the objections to *se*. The subject of *memorant* should not be the Suebi, but the antiquarians from whom Tacitus drew his material, as in *Germ.* 3, 1; 34, 2; 43, 15; *Hist.* v, 2, 3. Again, one would hardly expect the Suebi to *mention* their antiquity and fame; they would rather *boast* of it. I may add that the position of *se* appears to me awkward. Of course, these arguments might not of themselves be compelling, but a comparison of the readings of the two families can leave no doubt that *se* is an interpolation.

[4] We may note that of the twenty-two MSS. which read *nobilitas* only two (χ) show any attempt to correct the passage. These read *Longobardis* for *Longobardos*. Only **t** has tried to correct *Tacti*, and this by writing *Chatti*, which is about as intelligent as most scribal emendations! Hummel's *fracti*, which I regard as quite unnecessary, though adopted by Gudeman (1928), proceeds from *tracti* and not from *tacti*.

gnatque, offers a satisfactory meaning, and that the *significatque* of **Y** should definitely be discarded.[1]

xix: Here I feel that the *animis* of **X** is preferable to the *animi* of **Y**, at least on palaeographical grounds. (For a striking parallel cf. *Hist.* II, 99, 5 *non uigor corporibus, non ardor animis*.)

ix. xii. xxix: In *idem, inlinunt* (or *-niunt*), and *temptes* the orthography of the **X** family conforms with that of the Hersfeld *Agricola*, and I see no reason for doubting that **X** here preserved the spelling of the archetype. I realize the uncertainty of orthographical details, especially if one is dealing with late manuscripts, and did we have but these isolated instances of the superiority of **X** I should attach but little importance to them. However, as we proceed, we shall again and again have occasion to observe the fidelity with which **X** maintained the orthography of Hf.[2]

iii. x. xxii. xxvii: I find it quite impossible to determine on the respective merits of the readings themselves whether **X** or **Y** has preserved the better tradition. In my text I adopt (iii) *incolatur* and (xxii) *saepius* because I feel that on the whole **X** is more trustworthy than **Y**. On the other hand, I adopt (perhaps wrongly) the (x) *a singulis* and (xxvii) *cultuque* of **Y** on the general principle that in the tradition of a text words or letters were more easily lost than added.

iv. xi. xiii. xv. xxx: The readings of the **X** family, *reperta, Nec, regnant, bohemi, quidem*, are clearly erroneous, and there is no reason for attributing the errors to Hf. In *bohemi* I see a fifteenth-century "correction," and in the other readings mistakes made by the copyist of **X** as he transcribed from his exemplar.[3]

xxiii: Although the true reading *religant* is to be found only

---

[1] See critical note to the passage.

[2] Cf. pp. 142, 144. f., 146 f., 154.

[3] Yet *regnant* may be an intentional change made by one who did not understand the passage. We should note that this is the reading of l, and that it was also added to the margin of u by the scholar who revised this MS. Cf. p. 151.

in the **X** family, I believe that the lost **X** and **Y** themselves agreed in giving the reading of Hf., which was probably $\overset{i}{re}$ legant. The *rei ligant* of **W** appears to be the result of a double use of the superscript *i*.[1] In **Y** *re* probably resembled *ne*, which would account for *ne* of ϕ and the omission of the prefix in α s. The *religatur* of β is of course a secondary corruption due to the fact that the line of suspension for *n* was placed too far to the right (cf. p. 201).

To sum up our evidence, I find that in fourteen readings out of twenty-nine (eliminating xxiii from consideration) the **X** family makes contributions of its own toward the restoration of Hf. (i, v, vii, viii, ix, xii, xvi, xvii, xviii, xix, xxi, xxvi, xxviii, xxix), and that it quite possibly does so in four more readings (iii, x, xxii, xxvii).

The evidence for referring the four groups, α, β, ϕ, s, to a single apograph (**Y**) of Hf. is thus far as follows. There are seven readings in which I believe that these groups agree in offering corruptions (or deviations from Hf.) in contrast to the good readings of the **X** family (ix, xii, xvi, xix, xxi, xxvi, xxix), and four more in which the same situation may obtain (iii, x, xxii, xxvii).

XY *opposed to* **Y**

I now turn to an examination of those readings in which the manuscripts of the **X** family agree with part of the **Y** family in opposition to the remainder of **Y**. The presentation of the readings in this section is complicated, there being in all eleven different combinations determined by the division of the **Y** family into the four groups, α, β, ϕ, s. First I discuss those places of the text in which all four groups, though offering in part the readings of the **X** family, also show readings unknown to this family. Second I discuss those passages in which three of the groups α, β, ϕ, s, exhibit readings unknown to the other

---

[1] That is, after **X** was copied some reader may have changed *legant* to *ligant* without deleting the superscript (or marginal?) *i*. The scribe of **W** would then have found in his archetype $re\ \overset{i}{ligant}$, which he transcribed as *rei ligant*.

group and to the **X** family, and finally those passages in which two of the groups **α, β, φ, s**, present readings not found in the two remaining groups or in the **X** family.[1]

              X   **Y**
(i) 6, 16 Definitur   **α** Diffinitur χ, Definitur σpM
                                  β Difinitur d, Diffinitur v, Definitur λErok
                                  φ Diffinitur (differunt *a*)
                                  s Diffinitur (*corr. s²*)

Although **X** and the conspiring manuscripts of **Y** give the correct reading, we may suspect that Hf. had *defínitur*, in view of the frequent confusion of *e* and *i* in that manuscript. For the manuscript **Y** we may assume *defínitur*.

              X   **Y**
(ii) 20, 2 miramur (*h ex sil.*)   **α** mirantur[2] Ip, mirantur, *in mg.* ramur M, miramur NΔχ
                                  β mirantur v, miramur ω
                                  φ mirantur (nutriuntur *a*)
                                  s mirantur *e* minantur *corr.*

Here each group of the **Y** family shows the corrupt variant *mirantur*, which I believe to have had its origin in a fifteenth-century Gothic script.[3] It should be noted, however, that *mirantur* is but poorly attested for **β**.

              X   **Y**
(iii) 37, 14 et ipse   **α** et ipso et ipse ω, et ipse Δ, et ipso t
                                  β et ipso et ipse
                                  φ et ipso et ipse b, ipso *a*, et ipse π
                                  s in ipso et ipse

[1] In these tables I group σ (NΔI) with the rest of the **α** group, though wherever σ departs from **α** and agrees with **X** its readings have very probably been drawn from the latter source. I also list corrections of s² immediately after the readings of **s**, though these corrections have, almost without exception, been taken from **X**.

[2] In p a reference-symbol is placed above the *mirantur* of the text and in the margin, as though the scribe intended to write in the variant *miramur* but neglected to do so.

[3] Cf. 16, 12 *suffugiunt*, the reading of **φ** (except a1) for *suffugium*.

We may restore *et ipse* to **X** and *et ipso et ipse* to **Y**. Originally *et ipso* must have been meant as a "correction" of *et ipse*,[1] but was it already in Hf., or did it originate in **Y**? The fact that these words (*et ipso*) appear in the text of members of the **Y** family, and not as a variant, lends support to the former hypothesis. Though proof is lacking, I strongly suspect that in *et ipso* we have the work of a fifteenth-century interpolator in Hf.,[2] just as we have noted a similar mutilation of the text of the *Agricola*.[3]

		X	**Y**
(iv)	41, 2	proprior	α propior (propero *t*) ω, propius est Δ, proprior **N**
			β propior **Lvrk**, propior̃ⁱ **VdE**
			φ propior **lR**, proprior ω
			s Propior

My division of the manuscripts into two major families demands that we accept *proprior* as the reading of Hf. Since the same error is found in the Hersfeld *Agricola*,[4] this assumption seems probable enough.

		X	**Y**
(v)	45, 25	radiis (*h ex sil.*)	α radius I, radiis ω
			β radius λEvk, radiis dr
			φ radius (*om. Ac*) bπ, radiis a
			s radius (*corr. s²*)

Presumably *radiis* was the reading of **X** and *radius* the reading of **Y**. However, the difference may well be referred to doublets in Hf., since there is a parallel instance in the

---

[1] For other instances of this somewhat unusual use of the nominative in connection with an ablative absolute cf. *Agr.* 25, *diuiso et ipse in tres partes exercitu incessit; Ann.* XIII, 9 *forte prior ea de causa adito rege*.

[2] In this case the *et ipse* of **X** may represent the genuine tradition from Hf., but the same reading in π would of course be a correction of the reading of **Y**.

[3] See p. 31. It may be noted that the "correction" of *et ipse* to *et ipso* shows just about as good an understanding of the text as does the late interpolation of *Romanis* for *Nonanis* in *Agr.* 26, 8. For other possible instances of fifteenth-century interpolations in the Hersfeld *Germania* see pp. 150 f.

[4] F. 59, 1, 8 (ch. 23) *proprior* for *propior*.

104   The Germania of Tacitus

Agricola.[1] Again, *radius* may be an error of the copyist of **Y**, who mistook -*is* for the -*us* ligature.

	X	**Y**
(vi) 45, 31	differuntur	α differunt ξ, differuntur σ
		β differunt
		φ differunt ae, u² *in mg.*, differuntur ω
		s differunt

Here I am forced to assume that the corruption *differuntur* existed in Hf., just as in iv I accept *proprior* as the reading of this archetype. The obvious correction to *differunt* need occasion no surprise. With *differuntur* we may compare ch. 39, 12 *habitantur*, and possibly 44, 10 *ministrantur*, though I am not convinced that in the latter case the change to the active voice is necessary.[2]

	X s	α β φ
(vii) 1, 9	arnobae (abnobe *h*)	α Arbonae **ΔI**χ, arbonae *et in tex. et superscr., sed illic* -bon- *in ras.* **N**, Arnobae **M**, Arbonę, *in mg.* arnobę p
		β Arbonae **Lro**, Arnobae, *in mg.* Arbonae **VE**, Arnobę al' Arbonę, *in mg.* arbonę **d**, Arnobae **vk**
		φ Arbone **bzRAc**, Arnobe, *in mg.* Arbone **leu**, armbae **a**

---

[1] See p. 53.

[2] I suggest that the error was due to a misunderstanding of an upward flourish given to the horizontal bar of *t* coming at the end of the line. Among half-uncial MSS. I have noted such a flourish (easily mistakable for the -*ur* symbol) in the Basilican Hilary (complete facsimile, *Corpus Extravagantium Codicum D. Ambrosius M. Amelli . . . conlegit et edidit* i–ii [Rome, 1922]; cf. *rediderunt*, p. 155, last line, *et passim*). For an instance in Insular writing see W. M. Lindsay, *Early Irish Minuscule Script* [Oxford, 1910], Pl. 6, col. 1, line 4, *aut*. The same flourish was also employed by "Raetian" (cf. pp. 69 ff.) scribes, and is particularly frequent in the secondary writing of St. Gall 193 (complete facsimile, *Spicilegium Palimpsestorum arte photographica paratum per S. Benedicti Monachos Archiabbatiae Beuronensis* i [Beuron, 1913]).

Arnobae is the "good" form, since it approximates the true spelling *Abnobae*[1] more closely than does the *Arbonae* of α, β, φ. As Mf. has seen, *Arbonae* is the interpolation of someone who had in mind the town of Arbon on the Bodensee, a well known place of pilgrimage. I find no reason for supposing the interpolation to be older than Y.

     X s   α β φ
(viii) 6, 12 cuncto   α coniuncto pχ, coniuncto, *in mg.* cuncto M, cuncto, *superscr.* coniucto N, cuncto Δ, concto I
          β coniuncto, *in mg.* cuncto VEo, coniuncto (orbe) al' cuncto d, cuncto Lvr
          φ coniuncto

I regard this as one of the most doubtful passages of the entire *Germania* (see critical note). Apparently *coniuncto* is to be given preference, though I find it difficult to look at it as other than a fifteenth-century correction.

     X s   α β φ
(ix) 6, 22 concilium (*ex sil. h*)   α consilium I, concilium, *in mg.* consi pM, concilium NΔχ
          β consilium (s *super* c *in* o) vrok, concilium V, conscilium d, concilium LE
          φ consilium (-cil- a)

Consilium appears to be an error of the copyist of Y, but whether the correction to *concilium* was first made in this manuscript or in the various descendants is uncertain.

     X s   α β φ
(x) 8, 9 auriniam (*ex sil. h;*   α Albriniam Δ, fluriniam, *superscr.* albriniam N, Auriniam IpMχ
    auarimam *m*)
          β Albriniam r, Auriniam, *in mg.* uel *superscr.* Albriniam λdEo, *om.* v, auriniam k

[1] *Abnobae*, reported for h, can scarcely be more than a humanistic correction.

106   THE GERMANIA OF TACITUS

               X s   α β φ
                                   φ albriniam b, albrimam zA,
                                     auriniam (-mam e), in mg.
                                     albrimam (-nam u) eu,
                                     auriniam c, aurimam l,
                                     aurinam R, om. a

The choice between *Auriniam* and *Albriniam* is difficult, since neither form is found elsewhere. Did Hf. have the doublets *albriniam:auriniam*, or is *Albriniam* a fifteenth-century interpolation in Y? In favor of the former supposition it may be noted that *auriniam* can be explained as a corruption of *albriniam* (*albriniam* > *aluriniam* [1] > *auriniam*).[2] On the other hand *Albriniam* may come from the fifteenth-century "Germanist" who appears to have added to Y the forms (vii) *Arbonae* and (liii) *Tuisman*.[3]

             X s   α β φ
(xi) 11, 9   ut iussi   α iussi Δχ (*lac. in t*), iniussi p, in iussu M,
                                  ut iussi NI
                            β ut iussi λr, iniussi τ
                            φ ut iussi (-su a) al, iussi bψ

Vt iussi is unquestionably the correct tradition, but the restoration of Y is doubtful. I suggest that Y had an abbreviation for *ut* (*ū*?) which led to the omission of *ut* in abψ and to the corrupt *iniussi* of τ. (Probably the *ut iussi* of NΔ was borrowed from X [cf. pp. 91 f.], and the *iniussi* of pM from τ [cf. pp. 186 f.].)

             X s   α β φ
(xii) 15, 5   idem X, iidem s   α (cum) iisdem *in* iidem corr. M,
                                     iidem ω
                            β iisdem (*corr. E*) dEk, iidem λv,
                               hidem r
                            φ hisdem l, iisdem (*corr. u*) ψ,
                               idem b, quod a

[1] On the confusion of *b* and consonant-*u* in Hf. see pp. 246 f.

[2] Schweizer-Sidler suggests a phonetic corruption of *al-* to *au-* (cf. Fr. *aube* from Lat. *alba*).

[3] Note also the curious reworking of *Albriniam* into the *fluriniam* of N.

It is doubtful if the corruption *iisdem* is to be referred to Y. Because of the preceding *cum* the error might well have occurred independently in several manuscripts.

              X s   α β φ
(xiii) 24, 5 expectantium   α spectantium Mχ, expectantium,
                                   superscr. spec p, expectantium
                                           σ
                                   β spectantium Lτ, expectantium V
                                   φ spe expectantium ψ, expectantium ba, spec- l

I accept *expectantium* as the reading of Hf. and *spectantium* as a restoration of Y. The original corruption was probably phonetic, *spectantium* > *ispectantium*.[1] *Expectantium* represents an attempt to emend *ispectantium*.

              X s   α β φ
(xiv) 29, 15 decumathes (de   α decumates ΔIξ, decumathes N
                  eumathes W,   β decumates Lr, decumathes ω
                  deum athes *m*)   φ decumates

Since the etymology of the word is uncertain (see critical note), *decumathes* has quite as good a claim to being the correct form as does the commonly accepted *decumates*.

              X s   α β φ
(xv) 31, 6 nascendi (*h ex sil.*)   α noscendi IpM, nascendi NΔχ
                                                   a
                                   β noscendi Ldrk, noscendi V,
                                            o
                                      nascendi E, nascendi v
                                   φ noscendi b, nascendi ω

The illegibility of the script of Y appears to have given rise to the corrupt variant *noscendi*.

              X s   α β φ
(xvi) 33, 9 in gentibus   α in urgentibus (ingentibus *superscr.*
                                      N)
                                  β urgentibus iam
                                  φ in urgentibus (in verg- *a*)

[1] See p. 244.

I believe that an impartial examination of the evidence will show that *in gentibus* is the better tradition, *gentibus* being merely a repetition of the same word in the preceding line.[1] In **Y** (after the transcription of s?) *gentibus* was "corrected" to *urgentibus*. The *urgentibus iam* of β is probably the result of an attempt to emend *in urgentibus*. See critical note to the passage. (The superscript reading of **N** was borrowed from **X**.)

	X s		α β φ
(xvii)	34, 7	temptauimus	α tentauimus (temta- *t*)
			β tentauimus
			φ tentauimus (tempta- *c*)
(xviii)	46, 19	inlaborare	α illaborare ξ, inlaborare σ
			β illaborare d**Evrk**, inla- λ
			φ illaborare l**e**, inla- ω

Temptauimus and *inlaborare* show the orthography attested for Hf.,[2] the change to the more usual fifteenth-century spelling having been made either in **Y** or independently in three of its apographs.

	X φ		α β s
(xix)	28, 10	a bois (abors u*Az*, ab hoc	α a Boiis ω, ab Osis χ
		c, abora *e*, arbores *R*,	β a Boiis λv, a Bois d**Erk**
		ab osis *a*)	s a boiis

The reading *a bois* unquestionably represents the better tradition, since it approaches the true reading, *ab Osis*, more closely than does *a Boiis*. The "correction" to *Boiis* has been made from *Boii*, ch. 28, 7,[3] but it is not clear whether in **Y** or independently in its descendants.

	X φ		α β s
(xx)	34, 3	frisi (fusi ψ)	α frisii (fra- *M*) ξ, frisi (-sci *I*) σ
			β frisii
			s frisii

---

[1] For similar errors in the Hersfeld *Agricola* cf. p. 48.

[2] See pp. 254, 259.

[3] Observe that τ, which with the exception of v retains *bois*, has in 28, 7, changed *boii* to *boi*. Cf. p. 205.

The Extant Manuscripts of the Germania

Here it is just possible that *frisii* is the better tradition, since in the same line all manuscripts offer *frisis* (*frisiis* L), and the *frisi* of Xφ may be a restoration from this.

              X φ   α β s
(xxi) 38, 11 ornatorem **Wmhs²**,   α ornatiorem ω, ornatorem **N**
              hornatorem φ   β ornatiorem
                                    s ornatiorem

I not only believe that *ornatorem* was the reading of Hf., but also that it is better suited to the context than *ornatiorem* (see critical note to passage). **Y**, I believe, had *ornatorem* changed to *ornatiorem*. (Presumably the reading of **N** derives from **X**.)

             X α   β φ s
(xxii) 2, 17   primi (*h ex sil.*)   β primum **vr**, primi enim **k**,
                                 primi λdEo
                               φ primum ω, primi **bl**
                               s primum *in* primi *corr.*

Primi is undoubtedly the correct reading, and there is no reason why the variant *primum* should be carried beyond **Y**. Is the *primi enim* of **k** an attempt to conflate the doublets?

            X α   β φ s
                                          u   int
(xxiii) 4, 8   assueuerunt   β assueuerint **E**, assuerunt
          (*h ex sil.;* -rmtt *m*)   **V**, assueuerint **k**, assue-
                                    uerunt **dvro**, assuerunt **L**
                               φ assueuerint **bzuR**, -runt ω
                               s assueuerint *ex* -runt *corr.*[1]

Probably the illegibility of the script of **Y** was responsible for the corrupt *assueuerint*.

            X α   β φ s
(xxiv) 22, 12 adhuc (*h ex sil.*)   β ad hec λd, ad^he **r**, ad hoc **k**,
                                  adhuc **Ev**
                               φ ad haec **b**, ad hec **l**, ad hoc **a**ψ
                               s ad hoc (ad huc s²)

---

[1] Possibly the correction in s is by the second hand.

110   The Germania of Tacitus

The corrupt *ad hec* or *ad hoc* may have resulted from an abbreviation in Y.

	X α	**β φ s**
(xxv) 30, 1	hercynio, *in mg.* herquinio **W**, herquinio **mh**, hercinio **α**	β Hircynio **V**, hircinio **L**, hercinio (-cyn- *E*, -tin- *v*, Irano *r*) τ
		φ h'cynio (-cin- *u*) **zuAc**, hoc cuno **b**, hercynio (*uel* -ci-) **leR**, hermo **a**
		s hircinio
(xxvi) 30, 4	hercynius, *in mg.* herquinius **W**, herquinius **mh**, hercinius **α**	β Hircynius **V**, hirtinus **v**, hercinius (-cyn- *E*) ω
		φ h'cynius (*uel* -ci-) **zuAc**, hercinius (*uel* -cy-) **aleR**, quimus[1] **b**
		s hircinius

In both places the readings of βφs point to an abbreviation for *her-* in a common archetype.

	X α	**β φ s**
(xxvii) 45, 8	adluuntur (all- *N*ξ)	β abluuntur λ**E**, adluuntur **dvrk**
		φ abluuntur **a**, adluuntur (d *ex* b) **b**, alluuntur π
		s adbuuntur (b *leuiter inducto quasi* adbu- *in* adlu- *corr.*)

While the variant *abluuntur* is meaningless, it is just possible that Y preserved doublets of Hf. On the confusion of *B* and *D* in Hf. see p. 54.

	X β	**α φ s**
(xxviii) 2, 19	sint (*de lect. cod. h uide p. 167*)	α sunt **I**, sint ω
		φ sunt (st' *ec*)
		s sunt

[1] See p. 130.

The Extant Manuscripts of the Germania

                    X β   α φ s

(xxix)   18, 16   hoc (*h ex sil.*)   α hęc (data) I, hę̊c p, hęc M, hoc NΔχ
                                                   φ haec *uel* hec (hoc *a*)
                                                   s hec

(xxx)   31, 3   adoleuerint   α adoleuerit I, -rint ω
                        (*h ex sil.*)   φ adoleuerit aAc, -rint ω
                                                   s adoleuerit

(xxxi)   35, 11   assequuntur   α assequantur σ, assequuntur ξ
                        (*h ex sil.;*   φ assequentur (-quun- *e*)
                        ads- *W*)   s assequantur

In all these places the deviations from the correct readings in αφs may well be due to abbreviations or some other peculiarity of the script of an archetype common to these three groups.

                    X β   α φ s
(xxxii)   37, 15   deiectus (*ex sil. h*)   α derectus I, deiectus ω
                                                    φ derectus (di- *l*, deuetus *R*)
                                                        bπ, deiectus **a**
                                                     s derectus

The variant *derectus* appears to have arisen from a peculiarity of the script of Y, though the confusion of *i* and *r* is so common in late manuscripts [1] that the independent occurrence of the error in the three groups is not beyond the range of probability.

                    X β   α φ s
(xxxiii)   38, 11   innoxiae (*ex sil. h*)   α inopię I, inopię, *in mg.* innoxię pM, innoxiae NΔχ
                                                            φ inopie
                                                            s inopie (innoxie s[2])

The appearance of the corrupt *inopiae* in αφs can hardly be accidental. I suggest that in Y *innoxiae* was written with an *x* resembling *p*, and that some corrector changed a supposed *innopiae* to *inopiae*.

[1] Cf. 14, 17 *in eis* ψ for *iners*; 28, 10 *abors* ψ for *a bois*; 28, 18 *triborci* π (*triboici* ba); 30, 1 *carti* ψ (*caiti* bal); 40, 5 *nurchones* W, *nurtones* L, for *nuithones*; 40, 7 *Neithum* λ for *Nerthum*; 40, 16 *sacratam* bπ, (-*tum*) s, for *saciatam*.

			X β		α φ s
(xxxiv)	42, 6	Quadisque	α Quadisue Iξ, Quadisque NΔ
			φ Quadisue a, Quadisque bπ
			s Quadis ue

The reading of Y may have been *Quadisue* (cf. *Quadiue* in the preceding line) corrected to *Quadisque*.

			X φ s		α β
(xxxv)	2, 11	tres	α tris Mχ, Tres p, tres σ
			β tris ω, tres Vv

(xxxvi) 2, 14 plures α pluris Mχ, plures p, plures σ
β pluris

The groups αβ here depart from the orthography of Hf., as is shown by the *Agricola* (see p. 241).

(xxxvii) 2, 13 herminones X s, α hermiones ΔIM, herminones
hermimones   Npχ
(homines *b*) φ β hermiones

I restore to Y *hermiones*, which offers an explanation for the variations found in the several groups α, β, φ, s.

(xxxviii) 2, 20 mox et a α mox a Npχ, mox & a M, mox & a
ΔI
β mox a τ, mox etiam a λ

Apparently in the common forebear of αβ the word *et* was expunctuated, perhaps by some reader who hoped thereby to make this obscure passage more intelligible.

(xxxix) 6, 11 uariare (*ex sil. h*) α uarietate ξ, uariare σ
β uarietate Lτ, uariare V

The agreement of αβ in offering the corrupt *uarietate* can hardly be accidental. Probably in the archetype of these groups there was an abbreviation for *uariare* (*uari*ᵉ?).

The Extant Manuscripts of the Germania

                X ϕ s   α β
(xl)   30, 1   catti **X s**, caiti *uel* carti ϕ   α chatti **NMχ**, catti^h **p**, catti **ΔI**
                                                 β chatti **Vk**, chacti **dr**, Cathi **E**, Cacti **v**, catti **L**

I have little doubt that Hf. here read *catti* (the *caiti* or *carti* of ϕ is of course a corruption of *catti*). In αβ the *h* has been restored from the other passages in which the name occurs.

                X ϕ s   α β
(xli)   30, 10   romanae (-ne)   α ratione (rone *p*, r̄oē *I*)
                                                   β ratione (r̄oē *E*) **dEvk**, romanae **λr**

I find it surprising that some editors of the *Germania* give preference to *ratione*, which is so clearly a corruption of *ro.ᵉ*, a common abbreviation for *Romanae*.[1]

                X ϕ s   α β
(xlii)   37, 17   marcoque   α .M. (mi *I*) quoque **Iξ**, .M. **NΔ**
                                      β Marco quoque **Ldrk**, Marcoquoque, *superscr.* q **V**, Marcoque **Ev**

The *quoque* of αβ is probably due to a misunderstanding of the compendium for *-que* in a common fifteenth-century archetype, though there is a possibility that the doublets *-que:quoque* were in Hf. See my critical note to the passage.

                X ϕ s   α β
(xliii)   37, 24   nam   α inde **IpMχ**, nam **NΔ**
                                β inde **Lk**, inde, *in mg. uel superscr.* nam **VdE**, nam **vr**

Although *inde* has always remained the *vulgata*, I have no hesitation in declaring *nam* to be the correct reading (see critical note). Probably *inde* is nothing more than a repetition

---

[1] Thus ch. 33, 6 *Ro.*ⁱˢ is the abbreviation found in **ΔI** for *Romanis*, while a similar abbreviation gave rise to *roboris* in **s**. Again in ch. 29, 10 **Δ** alone has *ro.*ⁿⁱ as an abbreviation of *Romani*. Ch. 41, 3 **m** reads r̄onis (i.e. *rationis*) for *Romanis*. On the other hand, ch. 30, 7, the abbreviation r̄ois or r̄onis (*rationis*) has produced *romanis* in **I**.

of the same word two lines above. We may assume that in the archetype common to αβ (Y as I believe), the scribe first copied *inde* and then made the correction to *nam*.

		X ϕ s	α β
(xliv)	39, 1	uetustissimos (-mo *m*) seu X s², uetustissimosque ϕ, uetustissimos s	α uetustissimos (-mo *I*) se (se *om. N*) β uetustissimos se (se *om. r*)

See my discussion of this passage on pp. 98 f. The *se* of αβ indicates a relationship between these two groups.

		X ϕ s	α β
(xlv)	45, 3	in ortu se durat Wh s, in ortu sedurat (se- *om.* *l*) m ϕ	α in ortus edurat β in ortus (-tum λ) edurat

In the readings of Xϕs I find sure traces of *scriptura continua*, such as exist in the Hersfeld *Agricola* (see p. 46).

		X ϕ s	α β
(xlvi)	46, 1	sueuiae (*ex sil. h;* sūtuie *m*)	α Sueuę Δ, sueuiae, *superscr.* sueuae N, Sueuiae Iξ β Sueuię, *superscr.* sueuę V, Sueuiae L τ

Perhaps in the common forebear of αβ *Sueuae* was first written and then corrected to *Sueuiae*.

		X ϕ s	α β
(xlvii)	46, 24	uultusque (*de lect.* *cod. h uide p. 171*)	α uultusque et β uultusque et τ, uultusque λ

The *et* of αβ was perhaps added to the margin or interlinear space of their common archetype.

		X α ϕ	β s
(xlviii)	2, 5	orbe (*ex sil. h*)	β urbe vr, orbe ω s urbe (o *fortasse s²*)
(xlix)	5, 11	proinde (*ex sil. h*)	β proinde E, perinde V, perinde al' proinde d, perinde Lvro, proinde k

(superscript *per* above proinde E, *pro* above perinde V)

The Extant Manuscripts of the Germania

		X a φ	β s
			s perinde (proinde s^2)
(l)	22, 1	e (é, *in mg.* enim p, enim, *in mg.* é M)[2]	β enim (e r)[1] s ē (e s^2)
(li)	45, 19	perfertur (*ex sil.* h)	β profertur L τ, perfertur Vk s profertur
(lii)	45, 23	igitur (*ex sil.* h)	β ergo τ, igitur λ s ergo

I am by no means sure that the above readings show a connection between β and s. s is very corrupt and not infrequently shows errors which also occur in unrelated manuscripts.[3] In l it is possible that an accent mark over *e* in a common archetype has produced the *enim* of β and the *est* of s. I will state that I regard (xlix) *proinde* as unquestionably the reading of Hf., and that I see no reason for changing to *perinde* (cf. critical note).

		X a s	β φ
(liii)	2, 10	tuistonem *uel* bistonem (*uide p. 94*)	β Tristonem, *in mg.* Tuisman V, Tuisconem, *in mg.* Tuisin/d, tristonem L, Tuisconem (Thu- v) ω φ Tyistonem, *in mg.* tirstonem pro tuisman u, Tyisconem, *in mg.* al' tirfonem pro Tuisinan e, Tirstonem zR, tistonem b, Thyestenem a, Tyistonem lA, Thyistonem c
(liv)	2, 14	deo (de eo, *in mg.* deo h, deos s^2)	β deos Er, deo ω φ deos

[1] The true reading has been restored in r from some member of the φ group (cf. p. 208).

[2] The *enim* of pM is borrowed from τ (see pp. 186 f.).

[3] See p. 162.

			X α s	β φ
(lv)	28,	7	boii (*ex sil. h*)	β Boi τ, Boii λ
				φ boi **ba**, beii (boii *e*) π
(lvi)	37,	1	sinum (*ex sil. h;* finum *m*, situm *superscr. M*)[1]	β situm
				φ situm
(lvii)	37,	8	ac (*ex sil. h*)	β et
				φ et ψ, ac **bal**
(lviii)	38,	4	quamquam (*ex sil. h*)	β quam ω, quamquam r
				φ quam π, quamquam **ba**

The appearance of (liii) *Tuisman* and (lvi) *situm* in βφ points to a common archetype later than Hf. In the other cases the correspondence between these groups may be accidental.

			X β s	α φ
(lix)	5,	8	propitii ne (propitiine *β*)	α propitii σχ, propitii ne pM
				φ propitii
(lx)	6,	13	aestimanti (*ex sil. h*)	α existimanti σp, existimanti, *in mg.* ęsti M, estimanti χ
				φ exstimanti b, extimati ψ, aestimanti **al**
(lxi)	10,	11	equorum quoque (*ex sil. h;* equorumque *r*)[2]	α equorumque I, equorum quoque N Δ ξ
				φ equorum que
(lxii)	10,	14	hinnitusque (*de lect. cod. h uide p. 167*)	α hinnitus
				φ hinnitus ψ, hinnitusque (-tus que *b*) **bal**
(lxiii)	15,	11	sed et	α sed (publice) Iξ, & si Δ, sed et N
				φ sed π, sed et **ba**
(lxiv)	21,	11	quantum (*ex sil. h*)	α quam (*per compendium*) ΔI, quantum ω

[1] *Situm* in **M** was doubtless taken over from τ (cf. pp. 186 f.).

[2] The reading of r may have been taken from a MS. of the φ group (cf. p. 208).

THE EXTANT MANUSCRIPTS OF THE GERMANIA 117

			X β s	a φ
				φ quam (*per compendium*) ω, quantum a, *om.* l
(lxv)	27,	4	igni (*ex sil. h;* igitur *in mg. r*)[1]	a igitur I, igni ω
				φ igitur
(lxvi)	28,	5	diuisas	a diuersas Iξ, diuisas NΔ
				φ diuersas (-sis *a*)
(lxvii)	34,	1	Chamauos (*ex sil. h;* -nos *m L s,* -uos *s*²)	a chammatos I, Chamautos[2] Δ, chamauos Nξ
				φ camattos b, camactos l, chamateos z, chamatteos ue, chamatteo c, chamatheos R, chamattes A, Camouos a
(lxviii)	40, 20		illud	a id Iξ, illud N
				φ id

I doubt very much if the agreement between a and φ is accidental in (lx) *existimanti* and *extimanti*, (lxvi) *diuersas*, (lxvii) *chammatos*, etc. In the common archetype there were perhaps *extimanti*,[3] *diu.*ᵃˢ, *chamattos* corr. to *chamauos*. The other errors are of the kind constantly occurring in late manuscripts (misunderstanding of abbreviations, omission of *-ne, -que*), yet the number may be rather too large to admit of a chance agreement between a and φ in every case. It will be noted that in two cases only I of the a group agrees with φ. This may be because I is the most corrupt manuscript of the a group, and consequently is more likely to show chance agreement with unrelated manuscripts, or again because I alone in these two instances has preserved the reading of the lost a.[4]

[1] The marginal reading of r has been taken from a member of the φ group (cf. p. 208).

[2] Observe that the copyist of Δ must have had the doublets before him.

[3] Perhaps here Y recorded the reading of the archetype more accurately than X, for the same confusion between *s* and *x* is found in the *Agricola* (cf. p. 255).

[4] It is quite possible according to my classification of the MSS. for I alone to give the reading of a, since all MSS. of this group (though I but very rarely) show conflated texts (see p. 177).

118 The Germania of Tacitus

			X β φ	a s
(lxix)	12,	1	concilium (*ex sil. h;* -sil- *c*)	a consilium σpM, concilium χ s concilium *in* -sil- *mut.*
(lxx)	18,	15	(*bis*) hoc (*ex sil. h*)	a hec I, hęc p, hoc M, hoc NΔχ s hec
(lxxi)	24,	3	parauit	a parat Iχ, parat, *in mg.* parauit pM, parauit NΔ s parat
(lxxii)	24,	6	mirere (*ex sil h;* mirifice *a*, inicere ψ)	a miretur I, mirere ω s miretur (*corr. s²*)
(lxxiii)	38,	10	religant mh, rei ligant W, religatur β, ne legant φ	a ligant s ligant (reli- *s²*)

The readings peculiar to as are hardly numerous enough to afford evidence of relationship between these groups, particularly in view of the corruptions in which s abounds, yet (lxxi) *parat* and (lxxii) *miretur* suggest *parat* and *mirer* in a common archetype. On *ligant* see pp. 100 f.

			X a β	φ s
(lxxiv)	16,	4	nostrum (*ex sil. h*)	φ nostri (-tro *a*) s nri
(lxxv)	20,	11	hunc (*ex sil. h*)	φ habet ψ, hunc a, *om.* bl s habet (hunc *s²*)
(lxxvi)	40,	16	saciatam (*ex sil. h;* -ta *IpM*)	φ sacratam bπ, saciatam a s sacratum (saciatam *s²*)
(lxxvii)	46,	1	Peucinorum, *lect. uar.* Peucurorum (*u. p. 137*)	φ Prucinorum (PVr- *R*, prutiorum *a*) s Prutinorum (peucurorum, peucinorum *s²*)
(lxxviii)	46,	3	peucini (*ex sil. h;* pencini *m*)	φ prucini l, prutini a, prittini c, prugini ezuA, purgini R, pencini b s prutini (peucini *s²*)

The readings peculiar to φs are few in number and do not give convincing evidence of relationship between the two groups. *Prutini, Prucini*, etc., evidently represent conscious attempts to assimilate *Peucini* to *Pruteni* ("Prussians"), but naturally the interpolations may be independent. Likewise *nostri* and *habet* for *nostrum* and *hunc* point to the abbreviations n̄m and h̄c, but not necessarily to a common archetype. Finally, *sacratam* for *saciatam* represents a type of error which is very common in our manuscripts.[1]

The readings which we have passed in review fail to establish kinship between the X family and any of the groups, α, β, φ, s, other than their common ancestry in the Hersfeld codex. Sixty-nine of the seventy-eight readings common to X and to part of Y, either by their very excellence or on strong palaeographical grounds, declare themselves to have been the readings of the Hersfeld codex, whereas the dissenting manuscripts of the Y family offer errors which, with four possible exceptions (i, v, xxvii, lx), appear to be of fifteenth-century origin.[2]

In only six of the seventy-eight cases (iv, vi, viii, xiii, xl, xlii) does the X family with part of the Y family show erroneous readings in contrast to the seemingly correct readings of the dissenting manuscripts of Y. Obviously it is impossible to establish a relationship between the X family and any of the groups of the Y family on the basis of these six readings, for it is not always the same groups that side with X. Accordingly, we are here forced to adopt one of the following explanations for the agreement of X with part of Y: (1) these manuscripts have merely repeated errors of the Hersfeld codex, which were successfully corrected in the dissenting manuscripts; (2) the same errors were made independently in X and in the conspiring manuscripts of Y; (3) there were double

[1] Cf. p. 111, note 1.
[2] In these four instances the variants should perhaps be referred to doublets in Hf. If this assumption is correct, we have evidence of the merit of Y, but the hypothesis of the *independence* of X is in no way invalidated.

readings in Hf., X and part of Y accepting one variant, and the remainder of Y accepting the other variant. I find the first explanation satisfactory in all six cases, since the types of error involved are in accord either with the Hersfeld *Agricola* or with older Latin manuscripts in general, though I admit the third explanation as a possibility in viii and xlii. Finally, there remain three cases (x, xiv, xx) in which it seems impossible to determine whether XY or the dissenting manuscripts of Y have maintained the better tradition.

I believe that my hypothesis of the independence of the X family continues to hold good. That is to say, it is impossible to restore a common archetype later than Hf. for X and any *one* or any *two* of the groups, α, β, φ, s. Is it possible to establish such an archetype for X and any *three* of the four groups? The answer to this question must await the presentation of the readings which will establish the respective identities of the groups, α, β, φ, s.[1]

I now turn to my second hypothesis, viz. that the groups, α, β, φ, s, are to be referred to a common archetype Y. Though the closest relationship appears to be between α and β, and though s has the least in common with the other three groups, we have found threads binding all four groups together and leading to a common archetype later than Hf. If I have not fully proved my hypothesis of the archetype Y, at least I venture to believe that I have made it plausible. What is more important for establishing the text of the *Germania*, I have shown that when two or three of the four groups combine against X they almost always offer corruptions which could not have been in Hf., but clearly betray their late origin.

I believe the lost manuscript Y to have been a reasonably accurate copy of Hf., but one which presented considerable

[1] See pp. 177–235. If it could be demonstrated that one of the groups, α, β, φ, s, descends directly from Hf. (and not from Y), it might then be possible to show that X and the three remaining groups had an ancestor more recent than Hf.

difficulty to the reader because of its abbreviations and other peculiarities of script (cursive Gothic?). Apparently these difficulties were responsible for a gradual accumulation of marginal and interlinear words added by various readers of the manuscript who sought to make the text more legible.[1] We must also recognize a further accumulation of the conjectures of fifteenth-century scholars, some of which, to be sure, successfully healed corruptions inherited from Hf., but the greater number of which can be regarded only as unfortunate interpolations.[2]

XY *opposed to* XY

In the preceding section I presented those readings in which there is congruence among the manuscripts of the X family but a division among those of the Y family. Let us now turn to those readings in which the line of demarcation between the two families is completely eliminated, with the result that the same variants are known to both families.

It is obvious that readings of this kind cannot offer confirmation of my classification of our manuscripts, but I hope to show that they do not constitute a real obstacle in its path, as the interchange of readings between the two families can be reasonably explained away. First, the variants may derive from double readings in Hf. Again, the variants may be due to errors or corrections made independently in the two families.

[1] Naturally it is quite impossible to tell just how far this process of expanding abbreviations and of rewriting illegible words had gone in Y itself. The peculiarities of the script of Y may sometimes have misled the copyists of its apographs into making the same errors of transcription quite independently.

[2] Although it would be difficult to prove, the evidence suggests that Y was the closest to its original state of integrity at the time s (or rather the immediate archetype of s) was copied, that the interlinear and marginal additions had become more numerous when φ was transcribed, but were the most numerous of all when the apographs α and β were made. This does not, of course, mean that s and the MSS. of the φ group are better than those of the α and β groups. They are, as a matter of fact, far more corrupt than either α or β, but the corruptions are later in origin than Y itself.

122   The Germania of Tacitus

Finally, the presence of the same variants in both families may be due to "contamination." The first explanation will, I believe, account for the great majority of the readings now under consideration. The second explanation seems unquestionably correct in a few instances, while the third explanation is in my opinion scarcely tenable, save for the relationship previously mentioned between X, s², and σ.[1]

The following tabulations show the variant readings known to both families from which I am inclined to restore double readings to the Hersfeld codex. As a rule, if the same variants, in addition to appearing in both families, occur *as doublets* in one or more of the extant manuscripts, I regard them as pointing to doublets in Hf. This evidence will of course be strengthened, if it can be shown that the double readings which I restore to the Hersfeld *Germania* conform in their general character with the doublets which form so striking a feature of the Hersfeld *Agricola*.

1, 9   Hersfeld
                                     b
                                  danuuius
             X   Y
      b
W DAnuuius   α Dannuuius I, Danubius NΔξ
m Danubius   β Danubius
h Danuuius   φ Danuuius (*in* -b- *corr. c*, -uis *z*)
                                     ezuRAc, Danubius bal
                                  s danubius

This is a type of doublet found in the *Agricola* (see p. 246). Naturally, not every instance in which our manuscripts vary between the two spellings is to be attributed to doublets in Hf. (cf. p. 247), but here, on the evidence of W, I suspect that both spellings were indicated in the parent manuscript.

[1] See pp. 91 f. Throughout I treat s² and σ as belonging to the X family wherever they have readings peculiar to this family. Naturally, if both families have the same variants it is quite impossible to determine from which source (X or Y) σ drew.

3, 3   Hersfeld
       barditum : baritum

X	Y
W Barditum, *in mg.* baritum	a Barditum, *superscr.* baritum
m barditum	N, Baritum, *in mg.* bardi-
h Baritum *ex sil.*	tum p, barditum IM, bari-
s² baritum	tum Δχ
	β Barditum, *in mg.* Baritum
	dE, Barditum λ vk, bari-
	tum ro
	φ bardicum (blandicum *a*)
	s barditum

Baritum is probably a corruption of *barditum*. (See p. 47, and critical note to passage).

4, 4   Hersfeld
       tamquam : quamquam

X	Y
W tanquam, *in mg.* quamquam	a tanquam, *superscr.* quam-
m tamquam	quam N, quamquam, *in*
h quamquam	*mg.* tanquam p, tanquam
	(taq- *I*) IM, quanquam Δχ
	β quamquam, *in mg.* tanquam
	Vd, tamquam v, quamquam
	LEork
	φ quamquam
	s quamquam

Quamquam appears to be an interpolation for *tamquam*. (See p. 50, and critical note to passage.)

4, 5   Hersfeld
       caeruli : caerulei

X	Y
W caeruli, *in mg.* cerulei	a caerulei (crudeli, *in mg.* ceru-
m cerulei	lei *M*)
h ceruli	β caerulí V, cerulei E, caeruli
	uel lei d, caeruli Lvor,
	caerulei k
	φ cerulei
	s cerulei

124   THE GERMANIA OF TACITUS

These are orthographical variants of the type found in the Hersfeld *Agricola*. (See pp. 37 f.)

6, 16   Hersfeld
                        dilectos
                           e
      X   Y
W delectos   α delectos
  i   di
m delectos   β delectos V, delectos L⁒
h dilectos   φ dilectos b, delectos aπ
                                s delectos

On the confusion between *i* and close *e* in the Hersfeld *Agricola* see p. 240.

6, 18   Hersfeld
                    primum : primo
      X   Y
W primum   α primo, *in mg.* primum M,
m primo   primo (*om. I*) ω
h primum (*uide p. 167*)   β primo, *superscr.*[1] um (mum)
                                   λdE, primo **vork**
                                φ primo
                                s primum

Primo is probably a corruption of *primum*, induced by the vulgar pronunciation of final *-um*. (See critical note to passage.)

11, 11   Hersfeld
                 absumitur : adsumitur
      X   Y
  b
W adsumitur   α absumitur
m assumitur   β absumitur (ass- *T*)
h absumitur *ex sil.*   φ absumitur **ba**, assumitur (ads-
s² adsumitur   *R*) π
                                s absumitur

[1] The superscript reading in Vd is *u;*, which stands for *um*, not for *us* as reported for V by Andresen. The superscript reading in L has been erased so thoroughly that it cannot be deciphered in the facsimile. Andresen again reports *-us*.

On the confusion between *B* and *D* in a majuscule forebear of Hf. see p. 54. Here the variant *adsumitur* (*ass-*) is poorly attested for **Y**, as the *assumitur* of π may well be due to a secondary corruption. We should note that **T**, although unquestionably a copy of **E** (see p. 206), reads *assumitur* (*i.e.* its reading must be independent of **Y**). For a similar doublet found only in **Y** see p. 110.

12, 4   Hersfeld
                     crate : grate

X		**Y**	
W	grate, *in mg.* crate	α	crate (create *I*)
m	gratem [1]	β	crate, *superscr.* g V, crate L τ
h	crate	φ	(po)crate [2]
s²	crate	s	grate

The confusion between *c* and *g* is probably phonetic. (See p. 244.)

13, 3   Hersfeld
                     tum : cum

X		**Y**	
W	cum (?)	α	cum tum N, tum ΔI, cum pM, Tum eum χ
m	tum eutu	β	Cum (Tum *r*)
h	tum	φ	Tum b, tum cum aπ
		s	tum

On the error of *c* for *t* in the Hersfeld *Agricola* see pp. 54 f. On the reading of **m** see pp. 157 f.

13, 4   Hersfeld
                     propinquus : qui

X		**Y**	
W	propinqui, *in mg.* quus	α	propinquus, *in mg.* propinqui [3] pM, propinquus ω
m	propinquus	β	propinqui
h	propinquus	φ	propinquus
s²	propinquus	s	propinqui

[1] Cf. p. 157.
[2] See p. 145.
[3] **pM** have probably derived *propinqui* from τ (see pp. 186 f.) rather than from **Y** through α.

I am inclined to regard *propinqui* as an interpolation introduced because of the plural verb, but the choice between the variants is difficult (see critical note).

13, 9   Hersfeld
                     rubor : robur (robor?)

X	Y
W robur, *in mg.* rubor	α rubor N, rŏbur ω
m robur	β robur d, rubor ω
h rubor, *in mg.* robur	φ rubor (robur c)
	s robor

On the phonetic confusion between *o* and *u* in the Hersfeld *Agricola* see p. 246.

13, 12   Hersfeld
                     principium : pum

X	Y
W principium, *in mg.* pum	α principium NI, principum ω
m principium	β principum (-pium r)
h principum, *in mg.* principium	φ principium
	s principum

That *principium* is at least as old as Hf. is shown by the sentence division found in almost every manuscript: *quibus primus apud principem suum locus et principium (-pum). Cui plurimi. . . .* (In **Wm V A** *Cui* begins a new paragraph.) We may compare *patrium*, ch. 39, 3 (see p. 141, note 2), and *ciuitatium* (see p. 244) in the Hersfeld *Agricola*.

15, 5   Hersfeld
                     hebent : habent

X	Y
W hăbent	α hebent N, habent (h̄nt) ω
m habent	β hebent VEk, habent ω
h ebent	φ habent
	s hebent

On the phonetic confusion between *a* and *e* see p. 236.

The Extant Manuscripts of the Germania 127

20, 17   Hersfeld
                  gratiosior : gratior
      X   Y
W gratiosior   α gratiosior, *superscr.* gratior N,
m gracior   gratior, *in mg.* gratiosior
h gratior   pM, gratior Δχ, gratiosior I
                         β gratiosior, *in mg. uel superscr.*
                             gratior VdE, gratiosior Lk,
                             gratior vr
                         φ generosior
                         s graciosior

On this type of variant see p. 48.

22, 13   Hersfeld
                     loci : ioci
      X   Y
W loci, *superscr.* ioci   α ioci
m loci   β ioci, *superscr.* loci λ, ioci τ
h loci   φ ioci
s² ioci   s loci

The writing of *i* for *l* probably goes back to a majuscule archetype (see p. 55, and critical note to passage).

26, 5   Hersfeld
                  praestant : praebent
      X   Y
W praestant, *in mg.* prebent   α praestant, *in mg.* prebent pM,
m prestant   praebent NΔ, praestant Iχ
h praebent   β prestant, *in mg. uel superscr.*
s² praebent   prebent VdE, prebent Lvr,
                                prestant k
                         φ praestant
                         s prestant

The same gloss for *praestare* is found in the Hersfeld *Agricola*. (See p. 35.)

26, 6   Hersfeld
                   labore : laborare
      X   Y
W laborare, *in mg.* labore   α labore, *superscr.* rare N, la-
m laborare   bqre I, laborare Δξ

	X		Y
h	labore	β	labore, *in mg. uel superscr.* laborare **Vd**, laborare, *in mg. uel superscr.* labore **LE**, labore **k**, laborare **vr**
		φ	laborare
		s	labore

Laborare may be an "emendation" of someone who did not understand the meaning of *contendunt*, or it may represent a simple error of carelessness of a type noted in the Hersfeld *Agricola* (see pp. 49 f.).

27, 5   Hersfeld
                  operosum : opesum

	X		Y
W	operosum, *in mg.* opesum	α	peroperosum ξ, operosum σ
m	operosum	β	operosum
h	operosum	φ	operosum
		s	operosum

The corruption of *operosum > opesum* is so in keeping with the character of Hf. that I do not hesitate to assign these doublets to the parent manuscript. I suggest that **α** had a marginal *opesum* copied in from **Y**. This was corrected from the textual reading to *o̅pesum* (pero). A misunderstanding of this correction produced the *peroperosum* of ξ.

28, 8   Hersfeld
               boiihaemionem : boihemi nomen (u)

	X		Y
W	boiihaemionem, *in mg.* bouhemi al' bohemi [1]	α	Boihemi nomen, *in mg.* Boii a quibus bohiemi **p**, nomen bohemi **N**, Boihemi (Boiemi χ) nomen **IM**χ, Bohemi Boienorum nomen **Δ**
m	bohemi nomen (adhuc) boii hemionem		
h	boiihemi nomen, *rubr. in mg.* bohemi	β	Boihemi nomen, *in mg.* Boiiemionem **V**, Boihemi nomen **dEvk**, boieminomen **L**, boemi nomen **r**
s²	bohvemi, *del.* nomen		

[1] The addition of *nomen* in the right margin is probably by the second hand.

The Extant Manuscripts of the Germania

X	Y
	φ boiiemionem nomen, *in mg.* borhenum u, boemionem al' borhenum nomen A, boiiemionem nomen l, Bonennonem nomen c, borhenum nomen zeR, borrenum nomen b, bois .e. munere nomen a
	s bohiemi nomen

The process of corruption appears to have been *boiihaeminomen* > *-miomen* > *-mionem*. The restoration, of course, already stood in Hf., but apparently with a slightly different spelling (*boihemi* instead of *boiihaemi*). The *bohemi* of X is probably a fifteenth-century correction, while Y copied the corrupted variant without the aspirate and the diphthong (*boiiemionem*). The *bouhemi* of W and the *bohvemi* of s^2 show a misplaced *u* which may have stood in Hf. as a variant for the initial *b*.[1] The manuscripts of the φ group show a conflation of the two variants, and also a misplaced marginal index-word (*boihemum* corrupted to *borhenum*).

29, 6　　　　　　　　　　Hersfeld
　　　　　collationibus : collocationibus

X	Y
W collocationibus, *in mg.* collationibus	α collationibus, *superscr.* (*in mg.* M) collocationibus NM, collationibus Ipχ, collocationibus Δ
m collacionibus	
h collacionibus	β collationibus, *in mg.* collocationibus VdEr, collationibus Lvk
	φ collationibus b, collocationibus aπ
	s collacionibus

For this type of variants in the Hersfeld *Agricola* see p. 49.

[1] See p. 147.

30, 4   Hersfeld
                       hercynius : herquinius

X	Y
W hercynius, *in mg.* herquinius	α hercinius
m herquinius	β hercinius (-cy- *E*, Hircy- *V*)
h herquinius	φ quimus b, hercinius (*uel* -cy-)
	aπ
	s hircinius

The reading of **b** cannot be accidental. The variant *herquinius* is ancient, and is again found in the **X** family alone, ch. 30, 1 (see p. 97).

30, 12   Hersfeld
                       quem : quam

X	Y
W quam	α quam N Δ, quem Iξ
m qm̄ (quem ?)	β quem, *in mg. uel superscr.*
h quam, *in mg.* quem	quam Vd, quam, *in mg.*
s² qm̄ (quem ?)	quem r, quam v, quem LEk
	φ quam uR, quem ω
	s q̄ (quae)

Since it is not permissible to attribute an abbreviation for *quem* or *quam* to Hf. or its antecedents, the confusion appears to be phonetic (see p. 236).

31, 1   Hersfeld
                       raro : rara

X	Y
W raro *in* rara *corr.*	α Raro, *in mg.* rara pM, Raro
m raro	Iχ, rara NΔ
h rara *ex sil.*	β rara V, raro⁽ᵒ⁾ E, raro Lv, rara⁽ᵃ⁾ drk
	φ rara
	s rara

I have little doubt that the doublets stood in Hf. By the canon of the *lectio difficilior* we must adopt *raro*. Whether *rara* is an emendation of *raro* or a graphical error (cf. p. 53) is uncertain.

31, 16   Hersfeld
                            e
                          dura
              X   Y
      e
   dura Wh, dure m   α durae (-re)
                           β durae (-re)
                           φ durae (-re) bal, durare ψ
                           s dure

Strictly speaking, we are not dealing with doublets in Hf., but with a correction of *dura* to *durae*, just as *Agr.* 45, 21 (cf. p. 47) we find *longe*, i.e. *longe* corrected to *longae*. Apparently the copyists of both X and Y copied the reading just as it was in Hf. The *durare* of ψ is of course due to a misunderstanding of the superscript *e*.

34, 1   Hersfeld
                      dulgibini : dulcubuni
          X   Y
W dulgibini, *in mg.* dulcubuni   α dulgibini, *in mg. uel superscr.*
m dulcubuni   dulcubuni Np, dulgibini, *in*
h Dulcubimi (*cf. p. 169*)   *mg.* dulcubimi M, dulgibini
s² dulcubimi   IΔχ
                                     β Dulgibini, *in mg. uel superscr.*
                                         dulgicubini Vd, Dulgicu-
                                         buni, *in mg.* dulgibini E,
                                         dulgicubuni v, dulgicubini
                                         r, dulgitubini L, dulgibini k
                                     φ dulciboni (-borni a, dulci
                                         homini c)
                                     s dulgibini cubrini

Again, there appears to have been a phonetic confusion between *c* and *g*. Each of the variants has undergone a secondary corruption (-gu- > -gi-, and -bi- > -bu-), so that both are necessary for the restoration of the true form. On the conflation of the variants in β see p. 194.

35, 5   Hersfeld
                       sinuetur : sinatur
          X   Y
W sinuetur, *in mg.* sinatur   α sinatur, *in mg.* sinuetur pM,
m sinuetur   sinuetur χ, sinatur σ

10

	X		Y
h	sinuetur, *in mg.* sinatur	β	sinuetur, *in mg.* sinatur **dE**, sinuetur **λk**, sinant **v**, sinuatur **r**
		φ	sinuetur
		s	sinnetur

If *sinuetur* is the correct reading, the original corruption may have been *sinuetur* > *sinutur*. *Sinatur* would then be due either to the resemblance between *u* and *a* in the immediate archetype of Hf.,[1] or to the general tendency of scribes to tamper with meaningless forms, so as to make them at least resemble Latin words.

36, 7 Hersfeld
aduersarum : aduersarios

	X		Y
W	aduersarum (rios)	α	aduersarum **Nξ**, aduersarium **I**, aduersarios **Δ**
m	aduersarum		
h	aduersarum *ex sil.*	β	aduersarum, *in mg. uel superscr.* aduersariis **λdE**, aduersariis **v**, aduersarios **r**
s²	aduersarum (rerum)		
		φ	aduersarios
		s	aduersariorum (pares et equi)

Aduersarios must be a corruption of *aduersarum*, though the reason for the error is not clear. Possibly an *s*-shaped stroke for the final *m* of *aduersarum* was responsible (cf. p. 53).

38, 13 Hersfeld
ornantur : armantur

	X		Y
W	armantur, *in mg.* ornantur	α	ornantur, *superscr.* armantur **N**, armantur, (arina- **p**) *in mg.* ornantur **pM**, ornantur **Iχ**, armantur **Δ**
m	armantur		
h	ornantur *ex sil.*		
s²	ornantur		
		β	armantur, *in mg. uel superscr.* ornantur **VdEr**, ornantur, *superscr.* arm **L**, ornatum **v**, armantur **k**
		φ	armantur
		s	armantur

[1] Cf. p. 54.

The Extant Manuscripts of the Germania

Armantur appears to be an unintelligent "correction" of *ornantur*.

39, 1   Hersfeld
                    semnones : semones

X   **Y**

W semones, *in mg.* semnones   α semones, *superscr.* semnones
m semones   N, semnones Δξ, semones I
h semnones   β Semones, *in mg. uel superscr.*
s² semnones   semnones VdE, sėnones L,
                                         semones k, Senones v, sem-
                                         nones r
                                  φ semone ba, semnone (seno-
                                         R) π
                                  s semones

The nature of the corruption is obvious (cf. p. 47).

39, 2   Hersfeld
                    stato : statuto

X   **Y**

W stato   α stato σ, statuto ξ
m statuto   β Statuto, *in mg.* stato E,
h statuto *ex sil. coll. Long.*,   stato ω
      stato *ex sil. coll. Sell.* (*cf. p.* φ stato b, statuto ω
      170)   s Estiuo
s² stato

Statuto appears to be an unintelligent emendation of *stato*, though both are doubtless as old as Hf.

39, 4   Hersfeld
                    nominis : omnis

X   **Y**

W omnis, *in mg.* nominis   α omnis, *superscr.* nominis N,
m omnis   nominis Δ, omnis Iξ
h omnis, *in mg.* nominis   β omnes, *in mg. uel superscr.*
s² omnis   nominis l' numinis VdE,
                                     omnes Lk, numinis vr
                                  φ nominis
                                  s nominibusque

The process of corruption seems to have been, *nominis > ominis > omnis*. Observe that in β the corruption has gone still further through interpolation (*omnis* > *omnes*). The variant *numinis* found only in β is doubtless of secondary origin (cf. p. 194).

39, 13   Hersfeld
                          corpore : tempore

X   Y

W corpore, *in mg.* tempore   α tempore, *in mg.* corpore pM,
m corpore   corpore NIχ, tempore Δ
h tempore, *in mg.* corpore nu- β corpore, *in mg. uel superscr.*
     mero   tempore λdE, corpore rk,
s² tempore   tempore v
                                 φ corpore
                                 s corpore

Tempore is perhaps an interpolation on the part of someone who did not understand *corpore* in the sense of the *body politic*, though similarity between *c* and *t* in the archetype (cf. pp. 54 f.) may have been a contributing factor.

40, 5   Hersfeld
                          suardones : suarines

X   Y

W suarines, *in mg.* suardones   α Suarines σ, Suardones ξ
m smarines   β Suarines, *in mg.* Suardones
h suardones   dE, Suardones r, Suarines
s² suardones   λk, *om.* v
                                  φ suardones aπ, suarines b
                                  s suarines seu suardones

As neither of these forms can well be explained as a corruption of the other, I suspect that *suarines* is a misplaced variant,[1] and suggest that it was originally *uarines*, belonging to the preceding *Varini*. The *s* was, of course, prefixed by someone who understood the variant to belong to *Suardones*.

43, 1   Hersfeld
                           osiburi : siburi

X   Y

W osiburi, *in mg.* siburi   α Osi.Burii, *in mg.* siburii M,
m osiburi   osiburi, *superscr.* osi Buri

[1] Cf. p. 41.

	X		Y
h	osi buri, *in mg.* siburi	N,	Osi.Burii Ipχ, osiburi
s²	siburi		(*corr. in* osi b-) Δ
		β	Osi Buri
		φ	osiburi
		s	osiburi (*corr. in* osi b-)

The nature of the corruption is apparent. The fact that only **M** of the **Y** family has the variant *siburi(i)* affords a striking instance of the manner in which variants may crop out in unexpected places.

43, 6 Hersfeld
cotini : gotini (?)

	X		Y
W	Gotini	α	Cotini σ, Gothini ξ
m	Cotini	β	Gotini
h	Gotini, *rubr. in mg.* Cotini	φ	Cotini bπ, gotini a
		s	Gotini

There is no question that *Cotini* was in Hf., but we cannot be quite sure whether *Gotini* has come from the parent manuscript or is a fifteenth-century "correction" made from 43, 1 and 3, where the manuscripts know only *Gotini* and *Gotinos*. On the confusion between *C* and *G* see pp. 247 f.

43, 12 Hersfeld
helysios : haliosnas : alios (?)

	X		Y
W	helysios haliosnas $\bar{q}$ uel alios	α	Helysios (Ely- ξ)
m	helisios	β	Helysios, *superscr.* halisiosnas
h	Helisios, *superscr.* Heliosnas		V, Alisionas, *in mg.* helisios
	(*uide p. 171*)		r, Helisios, *in mg.* halisionas¹
s²	haliosnas (*quasi ad* helueca-		(-ion- *E*) d$\overset{s}{E}$, Alisiosnas v,
	nas *pertinens*)		helisios (el- *L*) Lk
		φ	heli$\overset{s}{c}$iosna a, helysios (-li- *blR*,
			el- *zR*, -sos *b*) bπ
		s	helisios

Neither *helysios* nor *haliosnas* can be explained as a corruption of the other. The clue to *haliosnas* is to be found in 43,

¹ In **E** *halisionas* serves as a variant of *heluetonas*.

18, where all manuscripts read *alii* for *Harii*. This suggested *alios* as a variant for *harios* in 43, 12. Later *alios* in some way became conflated with the *-nas* of *helueconas* in the same line, and finally the initial *h* was prefixed in order to assimilate the variant to *helysios* (i.e. *alios*>*aliosnas*>*haliosnas*). It will be observed that W actually has the variant *alios*. Has it preserved intact the original form of the variant, or is *alios* but a second (fifteenth-century?) attempt to correct *Harios* after the *alii* of 18?[1] In the reading of a we again have an interesting example of the outcropping of a variant in an unexpected place (cf. p. 135).

45, 4   Hersfeld
                    eorum : deorum

X	Y
W eorum, *in mg.* deorum	α deorum
m eorum	β deorum, *in mg.* eorum dE,
h deorum	deorum λk, eorum vr
s² deorum	φ eorum
	s eorum

Eorum is a corruption of *equorum*, and *deorum* a clumsy attempt at emendation. On this type of variant in the Hersfeld *Agricola* see pp. 36 f.

45, 7   Hersfeld
                    sueuici : saeuici

X	Y
W saeuici, *in mg.* sueuici	α saeuici, *superscr.* sueuici N,
m seuici	saeuici I, sueuici Δξ
h sueuici *ex sil.*	β Saeuici, *in mg. uel superscr.*
	sueuici λdE, Sueuici vr,
	Saeuici k
	φ sueuici
	s sueuici

The form *saeuici* appears to be due to the similarity between *a* and *u* in the immediate archetype of Hf. (see p. 54). Also see on *seu(orum)* for *sueuorum*, ch. 39, 1 (pp. 98 f.).

[1] On the q̄ *uel* of W, an ancient quaternion signature (*quaternio quintus*), see pp. 76 f.

46, 1   Hersfeld
                 peucinorum : peucurorum

        X   Y

W Peucinorum, *in mg.* peucuro-   α Peucinorum, *superscr.* peucu-
     rum   rorum **N**, peucinorum **Iξ**,
m pencinorum   Peucurorum **Δ**
       cini
h Peucurorum, *in mg.* Peucini   β Peucinorum, *superscr.* curo λ,
s² peucurorum / peucinorum   Peucinorum τ
                                        φ Prucinorum (prutiorum *a*)
                                        s Prutinorum

The origin of *peucurorum* is not altogether clear, though confusion between *N* and *R* in one of the ancestors of Hf. may well have been a contributing factor (see p. 56). The spellings of φ and s are doubtless fifteenth-century " corrections," trying to assimilate the word to *Pruteni* (cf. pp. 118 f.).

46, 23   Hersfeld
                 (et) oxionas : etionas

       X   Y

W oxionas, *in mg.* etionas   α oxionas **Nχ**, exionas **IM**,
m oxianas   Etionas **Δ**
h oxionas, *rubr. in mg. al.* etione   β Oxionas, *in mg. uel superscr.*
                                             etionas λd**E**, Oxionas **k**,
                                             etionas **v**, Ethionas **r**
                                        φ oxionas (esi- *R*, obsi- *z*)
                                        s exionas

Neither form is found elsewhere, though the Germanists have succeeded in finding etymologies for both. I follow Much (1901) in regarding *etionas* as a corruption of *et oxionas*. This is the most common type of error in the Hersfeld *Agricola*.

We have passed in review forty pairs of variant readings which I accept as pointing to doublets in the Hersfeld codex.[1]

[1] These forty double readings and the nine doubtful cases discussed immediately below do not, of course, offer a complete list of the doublets which may be attributed to the parent MS. Another fairly certain restoration on the evidence of both families is, 38, 10 *re legant* (cf. pp. 100 f.). From the **X** family alone I have previously restored (cf. pp. 96 ff.): 2, 10 *tuistonem: bistonem*, 5, 17 *serratos*, 10, 13 *contacti: contactis*, 14, 3 *principe*, 14, 11 *principes*, 29, 1 *batauii:*

There remain some twenty-two pairs of variants,[1] which to my mind do not declare so strongly for doublets in the parent manuscript, though certainly this explanation cannot be excluded in every case. It will be observed that the variants shown in the following table, with but three exceptions (ix, xvi, xx), do not occur *as doublets* in any of the extant manuscripts.

		X	Y
(i)	2, 8	nisi sibi **Wh**, nisi si m	nisi sibi t s, nisi si (si om. L φ) ω
(ii)	11	ei **Wms**², et h *ex sil*.	ei β, et α s, eius φ

bathi, 30, 1 *hercynio: herquinio*. More doubtful restorations from the evidence of the **X** family are: 10, 4 *temere: tenent* (cf. p. 98), 22, 9 *adsciscendis: aspiciendis* (cf. p. 154), 26, 10 *perinde: proinde* (cf. p. 143), 30, 16 *propriora: proprior* (cf. p. 143). On the basis of the **Y** family alone there are the following possibilities, though some of these seem to me very doubtful (see the readings numbered viii, lx, i, x, iii, xlii, xxvii, v, on pp. 102–116): 6, 12 *coniuncto: cuncto*, 6, 13 *extimanti*, 6, 16 *definitur*, 8, 9 *auriniam: albriniam*, 16, 4 *locant: longant* (see p. 194), 28, 18 *Treboci* (cf. p. 182), 29, 12 *batauis: uatauis* (cf. p. 222, note 4), 35, 10 *praecipuum: precuum* (cf. p. 176), 37, 14 *et ipse: et ipso*, 37, 17 *marcoque: marco quoque*, 45, 8 *abluuntur*, 45, 25 *radius: radiis*.

We now have a total of seventy-three doublets for the Hersfeld *Germania*, if we include some rather doubtful cases. Now on ff. 56–63ᵛ of the Aesinas (= Hersfeld *Agricola*) there are forty-nine double readings (see pp. 32 ff.), or an average of slightly over six to a leaf. The Hersfeld *Germania* was written on twelve leaves, with approximately the same amount of text to the leaf as is found in the extant quaternion of the *Agricola* just mentioned (see p. 78, note 2). Accordingly, it would be permissible to restore about seventy-two doublets to the Hersfeld *Germania*, on the assumption that its double readings were as frequent as those of the *Agricola*. However, it should be noted that for the *Agricola* I have counted only *bona fide* doublets, and not the numerous marginal and interlinear corrections (see pp. 31 f.), whereas for the *Germania* I have made no attempt to distinguish between the genuine doublets of the archetype and the corrections which may have given rise to doublets in the apographs. Consequently, it would be possible to restore to the Hersfeld *Germania* considerably more than the seventy-three double readings (and corrections) that I have suggested, without going beyond the range of probability.

[1] I have excluded from the following table a large number of orthographical variants, which may be seen on pp. 235–260. See also readings i and iii on p. 150, and the readings shown on pp. 156, 160 f., 174 f.

The Extant Manuscripts of the Germania

		X	Y
(iii)	3, 1	et apud eos **W**, apud eos et **m**, **h** *ex sil*.	et apud eos π, apud eos et ω, et a. e. et b
(iv)	6, 7	īmensum **W**, in mensum **m**, in immensum **h** *ex sil*.	in mensum λR, in immensum (mensum b, minime A, minime usum c) ω
(v)	14, 11	in bello que **Wm**, vi belloque **h** *ex sil*.	in belloque (-que *om. a*, in *in* vi *corr. s²*) r ba s, ui belloque (bello uique π) ω
(vi)	17, 12	vnde **Wm**, nude **h** *ex sil*.	unde b, nude (-ae) ω, nudant ψ, nudet (*corr. s²*) s
(vii)	19, 5	abscisis **Wm**, accisis **h** *ex sil*.	abscisis t Ev le R s, adcisis Vdrk b, accisis a L, adscissis zu, adsissis Ac, Incisis a
(viii)	22, 8	sed **W**, sed et **mh**	sed a φ s, sed et β
(ix)	24, 10	parua **W**, parua, *in mg.* al. praua[1] **h**, praua **m**	parua (*corr. M²*) M bazA, praua ω
(x)	25, 4	aut colono **Wm**, ut colono **h** *ex sil*.	aut colono Δ v z, ut colono ω
(xi)	28, 14	affectionem **mh**, adfectationem **W**	affectionem k ψ s, affectationem a β bal
(xii)	14	germanie **m**, germanicae **W**, **h** *ex sil*.[1]	germaniae (-nę L) Iξ Lr φ, germanicae (-ci N) NΔt β s
(xiii)	30, 12	impedite **Wm**, in pedite **h** *ex sil*.	impedite NΔ dv RA s, in pedite ω
(xiv)	31, 13	vultu **h** *ex sil*., cultu **Wm**	uultu ξ β, cultu σ φ s
(xv)	33, 8	ac **Wm**, at **h**	ac w b, ac *in* at *corr*. s (*an s²?*), at ω

[1] On the reading of **h** see p. 168.

140   THE GERMANIA OF TACITUS

		X	Y
(xvi)	34, 9	consuevimus h, consen-simus Wm	consueuimus E *in mg.*, aR, consensimus ω
(xvii)	39, 3	patrum W, h *ex sil.*, patrium m	patrum χ bazRc s, pa-trium IpM β 1, u² *in mg.*, patruum NΔ euA
(xviii)	40, 1	longobardos W, largo-bardos (-ga- *m*) mh	longobardos α L φ, lar-gobardos Vτ s (lango- s²)
(xix)	3	ac (periclitando) mh, et W	ac β, et ω
(xx)	43, 13	religionis h *ex sil.*, re-gionis Wm	religionis ξ λE al s, re-gionis σ dvrk, E *in mg.*, b ψ
(xxi)	44, 7	ipsae in oceano h *ex sil.*, ipso in oceanum Wm	ipsae in oceanum β ale, ipsae in oceano ξ, ipso in oceanum bzuRAc s, ipso in oceano σ
(xxii)	45, 26	in Wm, vi h *ex sil.*	in I RA s (*corr. s²*), ui ω

It would, I believe, be quite wrong to attribute the variants in v, vi, x, xiii, xv, xix, xxii, to double readings in Hf. Not only are the erroneous variants poorly attested for Y, but they also represent types of error constantly recurring in unrelated manuscripts.[1] Likewise in i, iv, ix, xvi, I am inclined to reject the explanation afforded by doublets, though here with less assurance.[2] Again, in iii and viii the variants seem to be due

[1] For this reason I do not even accept the agreement of W and m in v, vi, x, xv, xxii, or of m and h in xix, for the restoration of X, save in so far as the errors involved give a clue to the character of the writing in this lost MS.

[2] In i X appears to have had the doublets *si: sibi*, though the latter has little to recommend it (see critical note). The appearance of *sibi* in t and s (both badly interpolated MSS.) I regard as independent of X. In iv we should per-haps restore to X *in mensum*. In ix, *parua* for *praua* is probably due to a misunderstanding (independent in X and Y) of the abbreviation p̄ua (actually occurring in c). (xvi) *consueuimus* for *consensimus* is an interpolation which might easily have occurred to more than one fifteenth-century scholar.

The Extant Manuscripts of the Germania 141

not so much to doublets in Hf. as to a marginal or interlinear *et*,[1] which was retained in the same position in both **X** and **Y**. In the nine remaining cases (ii, vii, xi, xii, xiv, xvii, xviii, xx, xxi) the arguments for double readings in Hf. appear stronger, though this is certainly not the only possible explanation.[2] Our uncertainty is of course increased by the fact that in all but two (xi, xviii) of these nine readings the testimony of **h** is *ex silentio*, and consequently open to suspicion.[3]

X *opposed to* **XY**

So far in my restoration of **X** and **Y** I have considered the readings of our manuscripts according to the following classifications (the colon denotes "in opposition to"), **X:Y**, **XY:Y**, **XY:XY**. I now turn to the contrast indicated by **X:XY**, that is, the readings in which there is a division in the **X** family, part of its manuscripts agreeing with **Y** and part (two or more manuscripts)[4] departing from **Y**.[5]

In the following readings **Wm** (sometimes with **s**² or **σ**) conspire against **h** and **Y**:

---

[1] With viii we may compare the Hersfeld *Agricola*, f. 57, 2, 20 (*Agr.* 17), where *subiit* was added above the line by the second (contemporary) hand, but was nevertheless omitted in the archetype of **AB**.

[2] In vii, xvii, xviii, I attribute the readings, *adcisis* (see critical note), *patrium* (cf. pp. 126 and 244), and *largobardos* (see p. 60) to Hf., but it is less certain whether the corresponding corrections (or attempted corrections) come from this archetype or date from the fifteenth century (independently in **X** and **Y**?).

In xvii we may restore to **Y** *patri̊um*. In xi, xii, xx, if the theory of doublets is discarded, it seems impossible to determine which of the variants were the readings of Hf. The alternate readings might easily have arisen independently in the two families, either as errors or as corrections. In xxi, if the *ex silentio* reading of **h** is trustworthy, I am inclined to restore the doublets *ipso:ipsae* to Hf., but can regard *oceano* for *oceanum* only as a fifteenth-century correction.

[3] See my discussion on pp. 175 f.

[4] The readings in which but *one* MS. of the **X** family departs from all other MSS., *i.e.* the readings peculiar to **W**, **m**, **h**, respectively, do not of course belong here, but in my treatment of these individual MSS.

[5] Naturally **s**² and **σ** can be grouped with the **X** family only when they conspire with **W** or **m** or **h** in departing from the readings of **Y**, *i.e.* when they share in the readings shown in the left hand column (cf. pp. 91 f.).

		Wm̄	hY
(i)	2, 19	gentis & valuis se W, genti se valuisse m	gentis eualuisse (*ex sil. h*)
(ii)	8, 7	concilia Wm	consilia (*ex sil. h*)
(iii)	13, 9	adgregantur Wms²	aggregantur (*ex sil. h*)
(iv)	14, 12	equom Wm	equum (*ex sil. h*)
(v)	22, 15	Deliberandum Wm	Deliberant dum (*ex sil. h*)
(vi)	24, 1	nouum W, in (*om.* omni) m	in omni (*ex sil. h*)
(vii)	8	deliberate W, de liberate m	de libertate (*ex sil. h*)
(viii)	26, 10	proinde Wm	perinde (*ex sil. h*)
(ix)	29, 15	de eumathes agros W, deum athesagros m	decumathes (*uel* -mates) agros
(x)	30, 16	propriora constantiae Wm, propiora constantiae σ	proprior (propior ξ λdk le) constantiae
(xi)	39, 8	esta Wm	est (*om.* Iξ)
(xii)	44, 8	nauis Wm	nauium (*ex sil. h*)
(xiii)	9	adpulsui W, ad pulsui m	appulsui (*ex sil. h,* appulsum φ)
(xiv)	15	promisco WmNΔ	promiscuo (*ex sil. h*)
(xv)	45, 1	Transsuionos W, Transsuiones m, tnsuionas s²	Trans (Terras φ) suionas (*ex sil. h*)

Normally the agreement of **W** and **m** should give us the readings of **X**, for it will become clear in the course of my discussion that no lost manuscript intervening between **Wm** and **X** can be posited. However, in two cases (ii, vi) we may assume that the errors are independent in **W** and **m**.[1] Accept-

[1] **W** again writes *concilii* for *consilii*, ch. 6, 20. In both places the correction to *cons-* has been made, but probably by the second hand. In vi one may restore *inomi* to **X**.

ing the evidence of **Wm** for restoring **X** in all other cases, let us compare these readings of **X** with those of **Y**.

First we find that in a number of orthographical details **X** appears to have maintained the tradition better than **Y**. Thus, (iii) *adgregantur* and (xiii) *adpulsui* represent the type of spelling attested by the Hersfeld *Agricola*, and a comparison with the Medicean manuscripts of the *Annals* and *Histories* suggests that (xiv) *promisco* is the better tradition.[1] Even (iv) *equom*[2] deserves consideration, as conforming to the archaizing trend of the orthography in Hf.[3]

We may also suspect that **X** preserved some traces of *scriptura continua*,[4] which were smoothed out in **Y**: (i) *genti se ualuisse*, (ix) *de cumathesagros* (?), (xv) *Transsuionas*, and perhaps (v) *Deliberantdum* changed to *Deliberandum*.

More noteworthy, however, than the details mentioned above is the variant (x) *propriora*, which in my opinion points to *propior a constantia* as the true reading.[5]

Aside from (viii) *proinde*, which leaves us in doubt,[6] the remaining readings of **X** as restored from **Wm** appear to be errors which we should not be justified in referring to Hf., though (xi) *esta* is curious, and the omission of *est* in Iξ may not be without significance.[7]

[1] *Promiscus* is the only spelling known to the ninth-century Mediceus I (*Ann.* I–VI): *promiscum, promiso, -scis, -scas, -sca.* (*Ann.* I, 48, 5, the addition of *u* is, I believe, by a later hand.) The Mediceus II (*Ann.* XI–XVI, *Hist.* I–V), some hundred and fifty or more years younger than Mediceus I, offers both spellings: *promisco, -sca, -scas, -sce; promiscuum, -scui, -scuis, -scuas, -scua.* (*Ann.* XII, 7, 2; XIV, 14, 10 and 20, 23, the addition of *u* is unquestionably by a later hand.)

[2] The Hersfeld *Agricola* offers no parallel, as it does not have *equus* in the accusative singular. I have, however, noted *aecum* for *aequum* (see p. 248).

[3] Also note the following spellings, in which **Wm** do not stand entirely alone: 31, 15 *exsanguis* (cf. p. 258), 45, 19 *Sucum* and 27 *sucini* **Wσ**, *sucum* (a corruption of *sucini* not of *succini*) **m** (see pp. 245 f.).

[4] See p. 46.

[5] Cf. *Ann.* II, 47, 9 *Magnetes a Sipylo proximi*; *Hist.* I, 10, 5 *tam prope ab exsule*; *Dial.* 23, 17 *prope abest ab infirmitate*. Regarding *propriora* for *propiora* see p. 103.

[6] Either *perinde* or *proinde* in this passage is in accordance with Tacitean usage.

[7] It may be noted that in **W** *esta* comes at the end of a line (*esta/ad colli.*) Yet **m** cannot be a descendant of **W**.

How does it happen that in all the readings shown above h agrees with Y against Wm? First we may assume that h has kept the correct tradition (ii, vi), merely avoiding the errors made by the copyists of W and m. Second, the copyist of h (or of its immediate archetype) [1] may have adopted quite independently of Y the more usual spellings of the fifteenth century (iii, iv, xiii, xiv), and may have smoothed out certain irregularities due to *scriptura continua* (i, ix, xv). Yet in some six cases (v, vii, viii, x, xi, xii) the agreement of h with Y is puzzling. Various explanations may of course be suggested: (1) double readings in X (? *proinde:perinde*, ? *propriora:proprior*, ? *Deliberantdum*); (2) independent corrections made by the copyist of h (xi, xii); (3) contamination between h and some manuscript of the Y family. However, speculation seems idle, for in all but two (x, xi) of these six cases the readings of h are *ex silentio*. Did we but have access to the manuscript itself, I strongly suspect that some of these discrepancies would vanish.[2]

In the following readings Wh (sometimes with s^2 or σ) conspire against mY:

		Wh	mY
(i)	1, 2	ac	et
(ii)	2, 15	çambriuios W, ʒam- h, ʒam- s^2	gambriuios
(iii)	12, 4	insuper et grate, *in mg.* crate W, insuper et crate h	insuper crate (*lect. uar.* grate[gratem *m*]) m α β e s, insuper pro crate b, insuper pocrate (insuper proiecte R) π, insuper positos rate a
(iv)	14, 3	infamem Ws^2, infamem *in* infame in *corr.* h	infame in m α β b s, infamem in aπ
(v)	5	adsignare Wh	assignare

[1] See p. 173.
[2] See my discussion on pp. 175 ff.

The Extant Manuscripts of the Germania 145

		Wh	mY
(vi)	11	principes ¹ **Whs**², -pes *in* -pis *corr.* I	principis
(vii)	18, 10	adfert **Wh**	affert
(viii)	21, 12	abeunt ² **Whs**²	abeunti

The agreement of **Wh**, like that of **Wm**, in opposition to **Y** should normally give us the readings of **X**. I believe this to be the case with the single exception of i, where the same error was more probably made independently by the copyists of **W** and of **h**.[3]

Turning to an examination of the readings of **X** as restored from **Wh**, we again notice the superiority of this lost manuscript in orthography (v, vii).[4] Likewise in iii and iv only **W** and **h**, in my judgment, offer the readings of Hf., though the manuscript **Y** itself seems to have agreed with **X** in offering the genuine tradition, *et crate* (variant *grate*) and *infamem*. The *& crate* of **Y** gave rise to the absurd *pro crate* or *pocrate* of ϕ,[5] while the illegible *&* was merely omitted by the other apographs of **Y**. Again, the *infamem* of **Y** was corrected by the expunctuation of the final *m* and the addition of *in* above the line, whence the *infamem in* of ϕ.

In view of the numerous parallels offered by the Hersfeld *Agricola* it is reasonable to attribute to **X** and to Hf. the variant (vi) *principes*. In (ii) *gambriuios* **X** appears to have had an unusual form of *g*, which may have been an inheritance from a much older minuscule manuscript (*i.e.* Hf. or its archetype). Only in (viii) *abeunt* does **X** as restored from **Wh** appear to have been in error.

---

[1] **W** has *i* above the *e*, but the addition seems to be by the second hand.

[2] In the margin **W** has *cum*, hardly by the same hand as the text.

[3] *Ac* for *et* occurs several times in **h** alone (see p. 173).

[4] I will also call attention to the agreement of **W** and **h**, 24, 12 *exsoluant* (see p. 258), 31, 3 *submittere* (see p. 259), 46, 21 *adsecuti* (see p. 256), though in these instances they do not stand entirely alone.

[5] Apparently in **Y** the ligature *&* was so written as to suggest to the copyist of ϕ the compendium for *pro*.

In general the agreement of **m** with **Y** offers little difficulty. It has kept the true tradition in i, has adopted the more usual spelling in v, vii, has discarded an unusual form of *g* in ii, and has chosen the variant rejected by **Wh** in vi. In iii, iv, and viii, the reasons for the correspondence between **m** and **Y** are not quite so obvious. Perhaps we may assume that **m** accidentally omitted (iii) *et*, and independently corrected (iv) *infamem* and (viii) *abeunt*.[1]

I have found but a single instance in which **mh** stand together in opposition to **W** and **Y**: 39, 1 *nobilissimos* **mh**, *nobilissimosque* **WY**. Presumably we should posit for **X** *nobilissimosque* with the *-que* deleted.[2] The fact that **W** combines so often with **m** and with **h** in offering the readings of **X**, but sides with **Y** against **mh** in but a single instance (and even here maintains the genuine tradition), is one of the numerous proofs of the singular excellence of this much-neglected manuscript.

We have seen the readings in which two of the manuscripts **Wmh** conspire (sometimes with s^2 or σ) in contrast to the third manuscript and **Y**. Let us now consider the readings in which *one* of the manuscripts **Wmh** combines with s^2 in contrast to the other two manuscripts and **Y**.

W and s^2 offer the following readings in contrast to **mhY**:

		Ws^2	mh Y
(i)	4, 8	in aedia in **W**, in edia in s^2	inediam (*ex sil. h*; mediam *m*)
(ii)	6, 21	& iam **W**, et iam s^2	etiam (*ex sil. h*)
(iii)	9, 8	adsimulare **W**s^2	assimulare (*uel* -mil-; *ex sil. h*)

[1] The corrections could hardly have been made by the blundering copyist of m itself, but rather in its immediate archetype, m_1, which seems to have been the work of a scholar (cf. pp. 157 f.). I grant, however, that the presence of *abeunti* in m offers difficulty. In any classification of MSS. there is always, I believe, a residue of readings which do not find an altogether satisfactory explanation.

[2] See my discussion of this passage on pp. 98 f.

The Extant Manuscripts of the Germania

	Ws²	mh Y
(iv) 28, 8	bouhemi *in mg.* W, bohvemi s²	boiihemi h, boihemi Y, bohiemi s (*lectionis uarietas in pp. 128 f. est uidenda*)
(v) 39, 8	preesse (*in* pre se *corr.* W) Ws²	prae (pre) se (*ex sil. h*)

I think it fairly certain that in none of these readings is the agreement between **W** and **s²** accidental. For example, it would be absurd to suppose that anyone changed the (i) *inediam* of his manuscript to *inedia in*, unless he found this reading in the exemplar from which he was making his "corrections." In view of the instances of *ae* written for *e* and of the vestiges of *scriptura continua* found in the Hersfeld *Agricola*, I strongly suspect that *in aedia in* was not only the reading of **X** but also of Hf. The writing of (ii) *et iam* for *etiam* appears to have been a feature of **X**.[1] In (iii) *adsimulare* we have another example of the orthography of the parent manuscript which was preserved by **X**. In iv **W** and **s²** stand alone in offering the letter *u*, while the fact that they do not have the letter at the same place in the word is good evidence that it was marginal or superscript in the common source. Do we not have here an instance of the ancient confusion of *b* and consonant-*u* (i.e. *boihemi:uoihemi*), of which there are examples in the Hersfeld *Agricola?*[2] There is nothing inherent in the reading *preesse* to make us attribute it to **X**, but we are forced to this conclusion, since **s²** certainly did not draw from **W** itself.[3]

I have found only the following readings peculiar to **s²** and **m**:

---

[1] See the examples cited on p. 262.

[2] See pp. 246 f.

[3] As evidence of this, note the readings (vi–xiii) which s² shares with m and h, but not with W. Also note the following passages in which s² could not have corrected the errors of s from W: ch. 7, 15 *Aliique* s, *cibos* W, *cibosque* s² ω; 30, 12 *quae* s, *quam* W, *quem* s² (cf. p. 130); 38, 10 *ligant* s, *rei ligant* W, *religant* s²mh (cf. pp. 100 f.); 45, 7 *Aestorum* s, *aestiorum* W, *estiorum* s²mh φ.

148　　　The Germania of Tacitus

		m s²	Wh Y
(vi)	32, 5	hii (= It)	hi (ex sil. h; hic s)
(vii)	37, 24	et iam	etiam (ex sil. h)
(viii)	38, 2	uëgens teneterorum m, tenetterorum ue gens s²	tencterorum ue gens (fecterorum ue gens s; de lect. cod. h uide pp. 169)

In vi and vii we probably have readings of X,[1] though m and s² offer nothing of importance toward the restoration of this lost manuscript.

The following readings are peculiar to s² and h:

		h s²	Wm Y
(ix)	2, 15	vandalos, in mg. vandileos h, wandileos (fortasse wandaleos) s²	uandilios (uel-dal-; wandilios s)
(x)	28, 15	et (de lect. cod. h u. p. 168)	a
(xi)	34, 1	dulcubimi (= M in mg. De lect. cod. h u. p. 169)	dulcubuni uel dulgibini (dulgibini cubrini s)
(xii)	40, 5	Vuithones	nuithones (nurchones W, muthones m)
(xiii)	45, 4	ebetet et sonum	hebetet sonum (habet et sonum m, habet sonum s)

I think it out of the question that the agreement between s² and h is accidental in x and xiii, while for the other three readings this would at least be the more difficult assumption. It will be noticed at once that, whereas the readings peculiar to s² and W, and in part those peculiar to s² and m, can with probability be restored to X, not one of the readings peculiar to s² and h has any claim to a place in this lost archetype. That is, s² and h agree in corruptions which are later than X, though Holder's assumption that s² drew directly from h is

---

[1] On *hii* see p. 242; on *et iam* see p. 262.

clearly erroneous.[1] While the evidence may be regarded as meagre, I think it probable that s^2 drew from a lost manuscript (h_1) intervening between **X** and **h**. Naturally h_1 offered the text of **X** more accurately than does **h** itself.

It will be convenient to complete my discussion of s^2 at this point. In addition to transcribing readings peculiar to **X** and to h_1, s^2 doubtless drew from the latter manuscript in correcting according to ω numerous errors in **s**, though nothing could be further from the truth than to suppose that all the entries by s^2 were drawn from h_1. Occasionally its readings agree with members of the **Y** family, but in such a way as to show that the correspondence is accidental: 1, 6 *reticarum* changed to *rethicarum* s^2 (= v); 2, 14 *deos* in mg. s^2 (= Er φ in text); 28, 1 *auctor* s^2 in mg. (= *autor* λ in text); 36, 4 *superiores* s^2 (= t a). Other readings are peculiar to s^2 alone: 10, 1 $\overline{qm}$ (*quam?*) above *qui*; 12, 1 *quemque* as variant of *quoque*; 18, 7 *cultus* inserted after *muliebres* (*delicias* om. s); 19, 12 *tum* in mg. as variant of *quo modo*; 28, 2 *qd* (*quod?*) above *eoque*. Still other entries of s^2 are merely glosses upon words of the text: 21, 14 *accusant* above *imputant*; 24, 9 *ludendo* above *uictus*; 24, 10 *uendi* above *uenire*; 28, 18 *wormaticen(ses)* above *vangiones*, *argenturen(ses)* above *triboci*, *colonien(ses)* above *nubii*; 38, 6 *nobiles* above *ingenui*. The same hand entered elaborate marginal indices and numerous notes, showing the work of a learned German who was particularly interested in drawing parallels between ancient and modern Germany.[2]

The final step in our discussion of the opposition indicated by **X:XY** is an examination of the readings in which *one of*

---

[1] In addition to the readings peculiar to s^2 and **W** and to s^2 and **m** (i–viii), where to be sure the testimony of **h** is mostly *ex silentio*, note the following readings which s^2 could not have taken from **h**: ch. 3, 13 'Ασκιπύργιον omitted without a lacuna **s**, omitted with a lacuna **h**, in mg. *graecum* s^2 (only **W** of the **X** family has the Greek word); 22, 13 *loci* **s h**, *ioci* s^2 (cf. p. 127).

[2] Wünsch, 83, states that the marginal notes are by the hand of the text, but I cannot agree. The writing of the marginal notes bears a much closer resemblance to s^2 than it does to the first hand. Furthermore, the notes, some of which reveal considerable learning, could hardly have been the work of the blundering scribe of **s** (cf. pp. 234 f.).

the three manuscripts **Wmh** agrees with σ in contrast with the two remaining manuscripts and **Y**. The exact relationship of σ to **X** is more difficult to determine than is that of s². In the case of the latter we can, so to speak, follow the corrector in his work of borrowing readings from the **X** family, since we actually have the manuscript into which he entered these readings, while in the case of the σ branch the readings of the **X** family were not added directly to any of the existing manuscripts, but to the lost archetype σ, from which they were drawn, now by **N**, now by Δ, and very rarely by **I**.

I have noted only the following readings in which **W**σ agree against **mhY**:

		Wσ		mh Y
(i)	11, 3	praetractentur **W**σ		pertractentur
		(= *A*, pretactantur *b*)		
(ii)	44, 1	regnantur *in* regnant *mut.*		regnant
		W, regnantur **N**Δ		
(iii)	4	lemouii **W**σ (= *w Vv eu*)		lemonii

i. Presumably the agreement between **W** and σ goes back to **X**, but the situation is puzzling. *Praetractentur* is unquestionably the better reading—one which an editor would be justified in adopting even if it had no manuscript authority. But was it the reading of Hf.? The appearance of *praetractentur* in two corrupt manuscripts of the **Y** family is perhaps merely accidental, due to the misreading of *p̄tractentur* (*per-*).[1] On the other hand, the same reading in **W**σ may well represent the genuine tradition.[2] This is one of the passages which makes me suspect that the Hersfeld *Germania* was tampered with by a fifteenth-century interpolator, just as we know

[1] I have noted the superscript *r* closing a syllable in **z**, ch. 2, 1 *gēmanos* (*germanos*). Also 19, 5, **z** reads *premissa* for *permissa*, and 10, 9, **m v** have *p̄missum* (*premissum*) for *permissum*. These examples show the possibility of an unintentional change of *pertractentur* to *pre-*. On the other hand an abbreviation such as *ultā* (*ultra*), with the superscript *r* before the vowel, found in **z**, ch. 2, 4, suggests the possibility of the opposite error, *pretractentur > per-*.

[2] It should be noted, however, that in *de Gram.* 15 **W** with most of **Y** reads *praeceptisque*, where the sense clearly demands *perceptisque*.

this to have been the case with the *Agricola*.[1] I suggest that this interpolator changed the unfamiliar *praetractentur* of Hf. to the more common *pertractentur*, and that both readings found their way into **X** (and into **Y** ?).

ii. I do not believe that the agreement between **W** and **N**△ is accidental, and am inclined to think that these manuscripts alone have maintained the genuine tradition. Some may consider that *regnantur*, which is supported by so few manuscripts, should be regarded as a fifteenth-century correction in **X**. I doubt this very much. Such a restoration would show rather more critical acumen than is elsewhere manifest in our manuscripts. Even in **W** the change to *regnant* has been made, as though the copyist or a later corrector had failed to appreciate the irony of the passage. We should also compare ch. 25, 11, where the entire **X** family (Wmh) reads *regnant* for *regnantur*, and the same error occurs quite independently in two members of the **Y** family (lu²).[2] Therefore I strongly suspect that the fifteenth-century "correction" has been from *regnantur* to *regnant*. Even more convincingly than in the case of *pertractentur* just discussed does this passage point to the work of a fifteenth-century interpolator in the Hersfeld *Germania*. I suggest that *regnantur* was the reading of Hf., and that the -*ur* was expunctuated by the fifteenth-century interpolator. The scribe of **Y** copied only *regnant*, but the copyist of **X** wrote *regnantur* with the expunctuation of -*ur* just as he found it in his archetype.

iii. Here I think it doubtful if the agreement of **W** and **σ** should be accepted for the restoration of **X**, since the confusion of *u* and *n* is so common in late manuscripts. In the absence of other testimony regarding the name of this tribe, I accept the reading *lemonii*, which appears to have the stronger manuscript evidence in both families, but freely grant that the true reading is doubtful.

[1] See p. 31, p. 103, and immediately below on *regnantur*.
[2] See p. 100.

The following readings are peculiar to **m** and one or more members of the σ branch:

		m σ	Wh Y
(i)	5, 7	atque **m**, eatque **N∆**, eantque **I**	eaeque (*uel* eeque)
(ii)	9, 4	sacrificant **m I** (= *v*)	sacrificat (*ex sil. h*)
(iii)	10, 6	suscipiens **m ∆**	suspiciens (suppliciens *I*)
(iv)	19, 10	esse **m N**	eae (ee, he; *ex sil. h*)
(v)	20, 3	aut **m ∆** (= λ)	ac (nec *v*, non π)
(vi)	28, 10	onosi **m**, anosi **∆**	an osi
(vii)	38, 3	obtinet **m I**	obtinent
(viii)	39, 1	uetustissimo **m I**	uetustissimos
(ix)	40, 9	castrum **m σ** (*corr. N*)	castum

We must not be misled by the number of these readings, but should look rather to the character both of the readings and of the manuscripts which offer them. The errors are almost without exception of the types which are constantly found in unrelated manuscripts, and the four manuscripts involved are all corrupt, though **N∆** to a lesser degree than **m I**. In fact, I find but one reading which could not be explained as an independent error in **m** and σ, viz. (i) *eatque* (*atque*). The initial error must have been *eaeque* > *eatque* (an easy mistake for a scribe copying from a manuscript in Gothic writing), while the *atque* of **m** appears to be an emendation of *eatque*. It may also seem doubtful if (ix) *castrum* is of independent occurrence in **m** and σ.

As is the case with **s²** and **h**, we find evidence, though it is slight, of a relationship between σ and **m** which cannot be traced to **X**. In my discussion of **m** I shall show that this manuscript is a very corrupt copy of a much better manuscript (**m₁**) intervening between it and **X**. It is possible that σ drew from **m₁**, but the evidence is quite insufficient to warrant a definite conclusion.

I have found no readings peculiar to **h** and **σ**. Any attempt to find readings of **X** in **σ** alone would be more than doubtful, though I will merely mention, ch. 10, 19, *captiuo in* found in **Δ**, obviously a corruption of *captiuom* (= V), with which we may compare 14, 12 *equom* in **Wm**.

b.   Codex Vindobonensis 711 (**W**)

I have had frequent occasion to mention the excellence of this manuscript. As a rule, the agreement of **W** with one or more of the manuscripts **mhs²σ** establishes the readings of **X**, and more often than not of Hf. itself. On the other hand, combinations among **mhs²σ** in which **W** does not figure, in so far as they occur, offer little toward the restoration of **X**, and still less toward the restoration of Hf. This is definite proof that **W** is the best representative of the **X** family.

In fact, **W** is the only manuscript of the *Germania* which has independent value. Of the seven manuscripts which have the *Germania, Dialogus,* and *de Grammaticis,* **W** alone offers these three works in the order in which they were found in the Hersfeld codex.[1] **W** alone solves the problems of the extent of the large lacuna in the *Dialogus,*[2] and of the testimony of Hf. regarding the authorship of this work.[3]

In 39, 1, only **W** has preserved the reading of Hf., *uetustissimos seu nobilissimosque.*[4] In 39, 11, this manuscript alone reads *ad quod* (*quod* in an erasure) for *atque,* an error which was induced by *adq.* in the archetype—the usual manner of writing *atque* in Hf.[5] As we have previously seen, 43, 12, in the reading $\bar{q}$ *uel* **W** has preserved a quaternion-signature of one of the antecedents of Hf.[6]

With few exceptions **W** has faithfully recorded the doublets which **X** took over from Hf.,[7] and in 27, 5 it alone preserves

[1] See p. 19.
[2] See pp. 12 f.
[3] See p. 12.
[4] See p. 99.
[5] See p. 251.
[6] See pp. 76 f.
[7] See pp. 94–98, 122–141.

the doublets *operosum:opesum*.[1] Again, 43, 12, the word *alios*, which has crept into the text of W, may well be an old variant of *Harios*.[2] Still another noteworthy variant of W is, 22, 9, *aspiciendis* in the margin opposite *adsciscendis* of the text, though it is impossible to trace these doublets back to Hf.[3]

The superiority of X in maintaining the orthography of Hf. which we have already noticed [4] is now greatly enhanced by the following examples peculiar to W: 2, 15 *adfirmant*, 3, 7 *adfectatur*, 4, 8 *adsueuerunt*, 5, 11 *adficiuntur*, 11, 17 *ad sensus*, 20, 6 *adgnoscat* (*d* expunctuated), 20, 16 *ad finium*, 28, 14 *adfectationem*, 35, 11 *adsequuntur*, 39, 8 *ad colli*,[5] perhaps 46, 17 *subfugium*.[6] W also stands either alone or nearly alone in offering the better spelling in the following words: *proelium*, etc., *caeno*, *coetu*, *Raeticarum*, *Raetiae*, *Caecilio*, *Caepione*, *otium*, *conubiis*, *adulescentulis*, *adulescentium*, *saepta*, *boiihaemionem*,[7] *sollertiae*. Even in the writing of *ae* for *e* we may well suspect that W is merely maintaining the norm of Hf.: *interpraetatur*, *aepulis*, *saeparatae*, *paenates*, *paenes*, *in aedia in* (*inediam*).[8]

In view of the indisputable excellence of W, I have even ventured in one place to restore the text on the basis of this manuscript alone, ch. 31, 10 *et hic*, since this reading appears to offer a satisfactory solution to an otherwise unintelligible text.[9]

---

[1] See my discussion on p. 182.

[2] See my discussion on pp. 135 f.

[3] Possibly there is a connection between the *aspiciendis* of W and the *adpiscendis* of s².

[4] See pp. 100, 143, 145, 147.

[5] The very error of *ad colli* for *adtolli* is good evidence that the unassimilated form of the prefix was not an innovation of W.

[6] I will also mention that W frequently writes the prefix *in* without assimilation, just as it is found in the Hersfeld *Agricola*, but for the reason stated on pp. 258 f. I cannot feel sure that it here preserves the orthography of Hf.

[7] Only W preserves the diphthong *ae*.

[8] On orthographical details in general see pp. 235-260.

[9] See critical note to the passage. Perhaps in Hf. the word *et* was in the margin or interlinear space.

The Extant Manuscripts of the Germania

Finally, I will say that interpolations are almost wholly absent from **W**,[1] and that the errors of carelessness are not very numerous.[2]

Because of the singular merit of the manuscript, and in the absence of any evidence to the contrary, I regard **W** as a direct copy of **X**. Although the omissions in **W** are confined to single words, two errors suggest that its immediate archetype (X) was written in lines of 30 to 35 letters. At 24, 12, before *uictoriae* the scribe wrote *commerciae*, which he expunctuated. This was because his eye fell upon the preceding *commercia*. From the beginning of *commercia* to *uictoriae* there are 32 letters. Again, ch. 19, 9, **W** reads *nec* for *et*, while in the line below it has a superfluous *&* between *quidem* and *adhuc*. From *nec* to *adhuc* there are thirty-five letters. I suggest the following arrangement in **X**:

illic uitia ridet, nec corrumpere nec
...
               et
corrumpi saeculum uocatur. melius quidem
adhuc - - - -

That is, the copyist of **W** disregarded the expunctuation of *nec* and wrongly inserted the marginal *et* between *quidem* and *adhuc*.

m and **h** cannot be copies of **W**, as is shown by the following errors peculiar to **W**: 3, 17 *neque* om.; 7, 15 *-que* om.; 8, 9 *ut* for *et*; 14, 7 *torqueat* for *torpeat*; 19, 10 *& adhuc*; 20, 5 *separaret*; 29, 3 *olim* for *quondam*; 29, 16 *leuissimusque*; 32, 5 *usus* for *lusus*; 37, 8 *ad* om.; 38, 13 *bello*; 40, 7 *deum* for *terram*; 45, 22 *implicate*; 26 *litore*.

In the following readings **W** agrees with scattered manuscripts of the **Y** family, or with an entire group or branch of

---

[1] Excluding, naturally, the work of the second hand (see pp. 156 f.).

[2] My *apparatus criticus* gives all the peculiar readings of **W** (but not readings by the second hand [W²]), aside from orthographical details and mistakes which the copyist made and corrected as he wrote.

this family.[1] I regard the concurrence as fortuitous in every case:[2]

	W Y	hm Y
11, 3	quod W, quoḋ b s	quid
12, 11	concilium W a	consilium
13, 13	hec WI v Ac, hęc *in* hę *corr.* L	hae (hee *m*, h *ex sil.*, R *s*)
14, 8	cum W I E ψ	tum
19, 9	nec W v φ	et
21, 2	enim *om.* W A	enim
22, 6	ut *om.* W u	ut
30, 10	cetera, *del. et in mg.* certa W, cetera e	certa
38, 13	bello W, bello *in* bella *corr.* s	bella
46, 11	palustro W zuR, c² *in mg.*	plaustro

The second hand, which I believe to be that of Johann Hinderbach,[3] has made numerous changes in the text, but apparently did not draw either from another manuscript or from a printed edition. Although Hinderbach has frequently made successful corrections *ad sensum*,[4] other readings are either peculiar to him alone or found only in isolated manuscripts: 42, 1 and 4 *naristi* > *noristi* (= s in 42, 1); 43, 1 *siburi* in mg. > *osiburgi*; 45, 3 *sui* in mg. opposite *in ortu se durat* of text; 6 *natura* > *natiua*; 45, 10 *omniumque* > *omnique* (= t);

---

[1] Also see pp. 138 ff.
[2] In this table the readings of h are all *ex silentio*.
[3] See p. 89.
[4] Ch. 1, 5 *bellum* in mg. opposite *regnum* in text; 2, 20 *& valuis se* > *evaluisse*; 3, 14 *reperta* > *-tam*; 4, 8 *in aedia in* > *in ediam*; 6, 7 *immensum* > *in immensum*; 6, 19 *concilii* > *consilii*; 8, 7 *concilia* > *consilia*; 28, 8 *boii haemionem* > *boiihaemi nomen*; 28, 6 *hercuniam* > *hercyniam*; 41, 7 *hic* > *his*; 45, 26 *in* > *vi*; 31 *differuntur* > *-unt*. There are also numerous corrections in orthography and word-division: *inbelles* > *imb-*; *inprocera* > *imp-*; *et iam* > *etiam*; *promisco* > *-cuo*; *lictoris* > *litoris*; *batauii* > *bataui*; etc., etc.

20 *terrena>terrestria*; 45, 31 *ut* added after *tantum*; 45, 30 *Suionibus>Liuonibus*, *scitharum* above *sitonum*; 46, 4 *omnium>hominum* (= v). As a rule I have disregarded the second hand in my treatment of **W**.

Besides his changes in the text, Hinderbach has added copious marginal indices and notes. The notes generally deal with parallels between ancient and modern German customs. I quote the following as illustrative:

Germ. 2, 10 (*Tuistonem*): consonat vulgari italicorum qui omnes nos germanos dudeschos sive duischos vocant. a quo tractum existimo. Io. hin.

Germ. 6, 3 (*frameas*): framea germanicum verbum dicit cum et in psalmista habeatur. et sic iudeis commune fuerit potuit tamen interpres beatus iheronimus ex germanis ad sumpsisse apud quos versatus est ut ex epistulis eius colligitur.

Germ. 11, 6: hoc hodie servatur in partibus rheni et hassie patria mea nativa vbi noctes imprecantur bonas. non dies et tempora secundum noctes computant non secundum dies. Ioh'. hin.

c. Codex Monacensis 5307 (m)

To judge from the twofold character of its peculiar readings, this manuscript cannot be a direct copy of **X**. It exhibits two strata of corruptions, one of which betrays conscious interpolation, while the other shows errors of a purely mechanical type, such as could scarcely have been made by the copyist who was guilty of the interpolations.

Possible examples of interpolation are: 1, 8 *in miscetur* for *miscetur*; 3, 8 *repercussa*; 13, 16 *Non* for *Nec*; 19 *plurimique* for *plerumque*; 15, 4 *senibus*; 17, 11 *et manicas*; 20, 3 *aut* for *ac*; 12 *et animum*; 24, 1 *idem est*; 28, 19 *meruerunt*; 38, 10 *solo* om.; 42, 3 *boiis*;[1] 45, 22 *indurescente*; 5, 7 *atque* for *eatque* (a misreading of *eaeque*).[2] We may also note that some of the blunders made by the copyist of **m** itself seem to represent secondary stages of corruption: 12, 4 *gratem mergunt*, pointing to *grate in mergunt* in the immediate archetype (cf. above, *in miscetur, indurescente*); 13, 3 *tum eutu*, a meaningless reading

---
[1] A correction made from 28, 7, where most of the MSS. read *boii*.
[2] See my discussion on p. 152.

suggesting the interpolation [1] of *eum* in the immediate archetype and the incorporation within the text of the marginal variant *cum* [2] (misread as *tum*) by the ignorant copyist of **m** itself.

Certain orthographical peculiarities of **m** also point to an immediate archetype other than **X**: always *oceanus*, regularly *nichil, quamquam, tamquam, aput, haut*; also *conubiis, monumentaque, circumdari, circumdat, indigines, suiones*; [3] 23, 6 *hanc* for *haud*, pointing to *haut* in the archetype.

Stichometry leads in the same direction. There are four longer omissions in **m**: 28, 3–4 *quo . . . eualuerat* (30 letters); 36, 5–6 *nunc . . . uictoribus* (44 letters); 40, 12–13 *prosequitur . . . aduentu* (50 letters); 46, 16 *partemque . . . infantibus* (40 letters). The first of these omissions suggests an archetype with thirty letters to the line, which is approximately the length of line that I have proposed for **X**.[4] On the other hand, the two lacunae of 40–44 letters may represent the length of the line in the immediate archetype of **m**. To be sure, the omission of 50 letters does not fit in so well, but conclusions drawn from stichometry, if one is dealing with late manuscripts, are at best unsatisfactory.

Finally, I have previously suggested that σ drew from a lost manuscript (m_1) intervening between **m** and **X**, though this is at best doubtful.[5]

The errors in **m** which betray the purely mechanical work of a scribe who could have had but little idea of the meaning of his text are very numerous, and it would be idle to list them all. Some of these are due to a misunderstanding of abbreviations, though there is nothing to indicate that these were

[1] Yet the sentence is better grammatically if *eum* is inserted before or after *suffecturum*. Is it possible that **m** here preserves traces of a genuine reading?

[2] See p. 125.

[3] In general these are not the spellings indicated for **X**, and imply the work of a scholar rather than of the illiterate copyist of **m**.

[4] See p. 155.

[5] See p. 152. **m** impresses me as a very careless copy of a good MS. Although **m** itself did not record doublets, its archetype did, as is shown by the reading, 28, 8 *adhuc bohemi nomen adhuc boii hemionem*.

especially numerous or unusual: 1, 9 *clementi* for *clementer*;
3, 1, and 39, 2 *memorantur* for *memorant*; 5, 11 *uide* for *uidere*;
13, 7 *donacione* for *dignationem*; 18, 13 *Venie* for *uenire*; 29, 17
passionis for *possessionis*; 30, 8 *actiones* for *occasiones* (i.e.
occiones); 34, 5 *praetexunt* for *praetexuntur*; 37, 2 *perua* for
parua; 37, 8 *Comes* for *consulibus*; 37, 14 *nō* for *nobis*; 39, 13
efficiunt for *efficitur*; 40, 20 *parituri* for *perituri*; 41, 3 *rōnis* for
Romanis; 45, 22 *ūia* for *materia* (i.e. *m̄a*).

By far the greater part of the errors in **m** were caused by
the difficulty of the script of its archetype, which must have
been a carelessly written (cursive?) Gothic. We see the confusion of *u* and *n*, *m* and *ni*, *m* and *nt*, *r* and *c*, *e* and *t*, *o* and *a*,
t and *b*, etc., etc. The following errors are illustrative: 2, 4
roris for *raris*; 10 *bisbonem* for *bistonem*; 13 *isrenones* for *isteuones*; 15 *gambrunos* for *gambriuios*; 4, 8 *assueuermtt* for *assucuerunt*; 5, 11 *afficimur* for *afficiuntur*; 6, 11 *narrare* for *uariare*;
13, 16 *finitiuas* for *finitimas*; 16, 7 *renmtorium* for *cementorum*;
20, 7 *iumenta* for *iuuenta*; 21, 2 *linitur* for *luitur*; 22, 2 *accupat*
for *occupat*; 28, 4 *permnbaretque* for *permutaretque*; 37, 1 *finum*
for *sinum*; 40, 5 *smarines* for *suarines*; 46, 1 *sūtuie* for *sueuie*;
24, *gerese* for *gerere*.

Aside from the longer omissions mentioned above, we may
note: 13, 11 *-que*; 14, 9 *et* (*ingrata*); 16, 13 *frigorum*; 18, 10 *uiro*;
24, 1 *omni*; 30, 6 *animis*; 31, 4 *-que*; 7 *et*; 39, 12 *pagis* with
lacuna; 40, 16 *mortalium*; 45, 32 *a*.

It would be rash to seek the restoration of **X** or of **Hf.** in
any of the readings peculiar to **m** alone. Yet in the bizarre
word-division sometimes found in this manuscript there is at
least the possibility that we have traces of *scriptura continua*.[1]

The list of readings in which **m** agrees with isolated members
or with a single group of the **Y** family is much longer than the
corresponding lists for **W** and **h**.[2] This is because **m** is far

[1] See my discussion on pp. 260 f.

[2] For the readings in which **m** agrees with all the **Y** family against **Wh** see pp. 144 f. For the readings which **m** shares with more than one group of the **Y** family in opposition to **Wh** and the remainder of **Y** see pp. 138 f.

more corrupt than either of the other members of the **X** family, and we here find convincing evidence that the copyists of unrelated manuscripts were constantly making identical errors. It should be noted that the members of the **Y** family agreeing with **m** are generally those in which corruptions are the most numerous, *i.e.* the greater the number of errors on both sides, the greater the chances that some of these errors will be identical. The following is a partial list of the readings in which **m** agrees with a minority of **Y** against **Wh**[1] and the majority of **Y**:

		m Y	Wh Y
(i)	1, 5	et m s	ac
(ii)	2, 12	ingenoues m, ingaenones pM π s	ingaeuones (-ge-)
(iii)	3, 1	memorantur m s (*corr. s²*)	memorant
(iv)	8	eos m p A, eos > os V c	os
(v)	8	repercussa m s (*corr. s²*)	repercussu
(vi)	7, 2	aut libera m M β	ac libera
(vii)	5	uincere m M vro (*corr. v*), zRAc s	uincire
(viii)	10, 4	fortuitu m τ	fortuito
(ix)	11, 12	tamen m β Ac, tamen > tum s	tum
(x)	18, 17	seque m π	se quae
(xi)	25, 5	et m s	ac (liberi)
(xii)	10	hiis m vr b s	his Wh dEk π, iis a λ a
(xiii)	26, 9	degerunt (*corr. s²*) m s	digerunt
(xiv)	27, 8	omni (*om. b*) m φ	omnium
(xv)	30, 11	concensum m, consensum s	concessum

[1] The readings of h are *ex silentio* except in viii, xii, xxviii, xxix, xxxi.

The Extant Manuscripts of the Germania 161

		m Y	Wh Y
(xvi)	33, 2	chamanos m t Lr π s (*corr. s²*)	chamauos
(xvii)	2	augrinarios m, auginarios s (*corr. s²*)	angriuarios
(xviii)	34, 1	Augriuarios m Augrinarios s	angriuarios
(xix)	1	chamanos m L t s (*corr. s²*)	chamauos
(xx)	35, 11	agunt m s	agant
(xxi)	37, 15	abiecerit (ab- > ob- *s*) m s	obiecerit (*cf. p. 192*)
(xxii)	17	malio m, Mallio (Malio v) τ	manlio Wh α λ s, manilio φ
(xxiii)	38, 10	in ipso m Lr s (solo *add. s²*), in ipsa v	in ipso solo Wh α φ, in solo (*lect. uar.* ipso *VdE*) VdEk
(xxiv)	40, 4	uarmi m I s	uarini
(xxv)	15	armata m φ r	amata
(xxvi)	20	parituri m b ψ	perituri
(xxvii)	41, 7	hiis m It vr s	his
(xxviii)	42, 3	boiis m L s	bois
(xxix)	43, 1	gothini m ξ Rc	gotini
(xxx)	12	heluetonas m Ek, heluethonas r, heluectonas dv, heluectoras Δ, heluetonas V	helueconas
(xxxi)	19	feritate m s	feritati (-tis *h* ψ)
(xxxii)	45, 9	propriorm E bzuAc	propior

This list might be increased, but it is quite sufficient to show the character of the readings shared by **m** and scattered manuscripts of the **Y** family. Chance agreement, I believe, offers a satisfactory explanation in every case. I have attempted to include all the readings peculiar to **m** and **s**, partly because **s** stands alone in the **Y** family, and partly because of Holder's belief that **m** and **s** descended from a common archetype.[1]

Holder, apparently misled by insufficient manuscript authority, assumed that many readings were peculiar to **m** and **s** alone which are in reality found in other manuscripts as well. There are in all eleven readings found only in **m** and **s** (i, iii, v, xi, xiii, xv, xvii, xviii, xx, xxi, xxxi). To be sure, so large a number might give us pause, were it not for the character both of the readings and of the two manuscripts. It would be strange indeed if two manuscripts so corrupt as **m** and **s**, both presumably copied from archetypes in Gothic script, had not occasionally admitted the same errors quite independently. The appearance of similarity between the two is further enhanced by the fact that they follow the same style of orthography (*e* for *ae*, *ci* for assibilated *ti*, *w* for *u* and *uu*).[2] It is my belief that not one of the readings shown above indicates a connection between **m** and any member of the **Y** family.[3]

d. Codex Hummelianus (h)

Although this valuable manuscript is lost, it is possible to make a fairly satisfactory restoration of its readings from the extant collations. Of these three collations, that of Hummel is by far the most incomplete, offering only relatively few selected readings, and its importance lies in the valuable confirmatory evidence which it sometimes affords where there are discrepancies between the collations of Longolius and of Selling. In fact, Hummel reports but three readings contradictory to both the other collations: 5, 8 *propitii ne* (*propitiine* Selling, *propitii* Longolius *ex silentio*), 6, 9 *distinguuntur* (*distinguunt* Longolius and Selling *ex silentio*), 36, 7 *fracti* (*tracti* Longolius and Selling). In the first case we may accept the evidence of

---
[1] Holder's theory was refuted by Wünsch, 80 ff.
[2] Both MSS. appear to be the work of German scribes.
[3] On (xxii) *Malio* cf. p. 206.

Hummel,[1] but in the other two instances his evidence must be rejected. These errors may have been due to a confusion in his notes between conjectures of his own and the readings of the manuscript.

The collation of Selling, printed at the end of his *Observationes Criticae*, is based upon the edition of Teubert, Leipzig, 1826. The collation of Longolius is to be found in his own handwriting on the pages of a copy of the Leipzig edition of Melchior Lotter, 1509, which is now in the *Staatsbibliothek* in Munich.

A few words regarding Longolius' technical procedure will be apropos. Letters or words of the printed text differing from those of the manuscript have been underscored and the corresponding readings of the manuscript added in the margin or interlinear space. Words found in the manuscript but omitted from the printed text have been added to the margin preceded by a caret, while the same symbol has been placed in the text at the place of omission. Words or letters in the printed text which were missing in the manuscript have been deleted by the use of diagonal lines or parentheses with the deletion symbol placed above. Frequently words or letters of the text are underscored without any corresponding interlinear or marginal reading. I believe that such underscoring is meant to indicate that the reading of the printed edition agrees with that of the manuscript, though I treat such readings as *ex silentio*. In reporting corrections made in the manuscript Longolius indicates whether these are by the first or second hand, using *ead. m.* to designate the former, and *m. sec. rec.* or *rec. m.* to indicate the latter. In reporting doublets he has indicated which reading was in the text and which was in the margin of the manuscript. In general Longolius' collation of h offers not the slightest difficulty of interpretation, though occasionally one is left in doubt as to which readings were in the text and which were in the margin, but a comparison with the collation of Selling will make the matter clear.

[1] On the separation of the enclitic see pp. 261 f.

Beginning with ch. 28 Longolius has written in the margin in red ink[1] the names of the Germanic tribes opposite the places of their occurrence in the text. There can be no doubt that he has taken over these marginal indices bodily from h. Selling (p. 25) reports that h had such marginal indices in red, and mentions in particular the marginal entry *Tracti*, as indicating that the copyist thought this to be the name of a tribe. Longolius has made the same marginal entry. Furthermore, wherever the spelling of the name in the text of the manuscript departs from the printed edition the corresponding entry in the margin agrees with the manuscript and not with the edition.[2] Finally, in two instances the marginal entries offer variants which we know to have been transmitted from Hf.[3]

By means of Roman numerals in the margin Longolius has indicated the division into chapters according to the norm of later editions.[4] In chapters 1–13, 15–16, 40, 45, below the Roman numerals he has added at intervals Arabic numerals in serial. I suspect that these Arabic numerals correspond with the divisions into paragraphs indicated in h,[5] though in my discussion of the paragraph-division of our manuscripts I have left h out of consideration.[6]

To what extent are the collations of Longolius and of Selling in accord? As might be expected, certain allowances must be made for differences in the technique of the two collators, of which the most important is that Selling makes no attempt to record orthographical variations. Consequently, for our

[1] I assume that these entries are in red, since in my rotographs they appear much paler than do the other notations of Longolius.

[2] *E.g.* 43, 10, the edition reads *legiorum*, Longolius reports *regiorum* for the text of h, the marginal rubric is *Regii*.

[3] Ch. 43, 6 *Gotini* in text, *Cotini* rubr. in mg.; 46, 23 *Oxionas* in text, *al. etione* rubr. in mg. See pp. 135, 137.

[4] The edition of Lotter, like the other early editions, has no division into chapters.

[5] It is true that Hummel states that the text of h is continuous without division into chapters and paragraphs (see p. 82), but this statement hardly precludes the possibility that the paragraph-symbol was interspersed at frequent intervals in the text.

[6] See pp. 264 ff.

knowledge of orthographical details we are dependent on the collation of Longolius alone. Since we may well doubt if even he has noted every instance in which the orthography of h varied from that of the edition which he used, all *ex silentio* readings of h in orthographical matters must be viewed with suspicion. Other minor differences in the scope of the two collations will be noted after I have shown the table of their discrepancies. Even after we have eliminated purely orthographical details, we still find many differences in the two collations, but these are rarely positive, *i.e.* it seldom happens that either reports a reading which is contrary to the direct testimony of the other. In the great majority of cases where discrepancies occur the reading reported by Longolius or Selling is in opposition to the *ex silentio* testimony of the other. But occasionally both collators fail to report the readings of h at points where the texts of Lotter and of Teubert disagree, so that we here have conflicts in the *ex silentio* testimony of the two.[1]

Before listing the discrepancies in the collations of Longolius and of Selling, it is necessary to note that the following readings of h as given by Longolius are, in my judgment, incorrectly reported by Wünsch:[2] 2, 10 *bistonem*, in mg. *al. tuisconem* h; 11 *marnum* in text corr. to *mannum*, in mg. *al. mannum* h; *conditoremque* h; 3, 5 *trepidant ue*; 12 *asciburgium que*; 12 *hodie*

[1] The *ex silentio* readings are, of course, the readings of the texts of Lotter's and of Teubert's editions for which no variants in h are noted by Longolius and Selling respectively.

[2] Wünsch did not inspect Longolius' collation himself, but used a copy sent him by Heisenberg (p. 4, note 1). Although Wünsch clearly means to avoid *ex silentio* readings, keeping only to the positive testimony of Longolius and Selling, yet in many cases he ascribes to Longolius readings which are in reality *ex silentio*. I think this to be due to the manner in which Heisenberg copied the collation. In making my corrections of Wünsch's table I do not take into account these *ex silentio* readings which he has reported as if given on the positive testimony of Longolius, unless there is involved a conflict with the collation of Selling. It is perhaps needless to say that Wünsch's report, failing as it does to take into consideration *ex silentio* readings and the differences between the texts of Müllenhoff, Lotter, and Teubert, is quite inadequate for the complete restoration of h.

que; 16 *raecie germanie que*; 4, 2 *connubiis*; 6, 20 *instes consilii* [1] (*ex sil.*); 22 *a͏̈dire*; 11, 10 *tercius*; 11 *silencium*; 14, 3 *infamem* corr. to *infame in*; 15, 2 *ocium*; [2] 16, 8 *delectacionem*; 9 *inliniunt*; 18, 18 *rursus que*; 20, 15 *possessione* h, *successione* [3] h²; 16 *tanto* h, *quo* [4] h²; 26, 7 *seperent* h, *-par-* h², in mg. *al. secent* h; 28, 10 *a bois*; 18 *Nubii* in text and mg. in red h, *Nubii* in text corr. to *ubii* [5] h²; 34, 10 *simulatque* in text, *al. simulac que* in mg.; 37, 5 *fidem* in text, in mg. *al. fidem*; [6] 37, 9 *imperatoris* ex sil.; 23 *legionum* (*ni͏̈bus* h²); 39, 2 *statuto* ex sil.; 43, 1 *Buri* in text, in mg. *Siburi*; 6 *Gotini* in text, mg. in red *Cotini*; 10 *regiorum* in text, mg. in red *Regii*; *Heli͏̈sios*, mg. in red *Helisii al. Haliosii* (?); 12–13 *Nahanarualos* [7] ex sil. . . . *Naharualos*, mg. in red *Naharua͏̈li*; 45, 16 *que ue*; 20 *esse* om.; 46, 1 *Peucurorum*, mg. in red *Peucini*; 46, 23 *Oxionas* ex sil., mg. in red *al. etione*.

Having thus corrected the errors in Wünsch's report of Longolius' collation, we may examine the following table, which, except for orthographical matters, sets forth the discrepancies

---

[1] The edition of Lotter reads *instes magis consilii*. Longolius has merely deleted *magis*.

[2] Evidently the figure *2* placed in the margin by Longolius to indicate the beginning of a new paragraph was mistaken by Heisenberg for a *z*, which caused him to report the variant *ozium*. There is no evidence of *otium* corr. to *ocium*, as Wünsch reports.

[3] In the text of his edition Longolius has underscored *posse* in *possessione*; in the margin he writes, *succe a m. sec. rec. int. lin.*

[4] Longolius has underscored *quo* in the text, and written in the margin *tanto corr. a m. rec.* I take this to mean that the second hand has corrected *tanto* to *quo*, though in accordance with Longolius' usual procedure it might well mean *quo* changed to *tanto*, as Wünsch interprets it. See, however, pp. 173 f.

[5] Longolius has underscored *Ubii* in his text and written in the margin *Nubii*, but has drawn a diagonal line through the *N*. Above the marginal reading he has written *a sec. rec. m.* I take the superscript words to refer only to the deletion of *N*. Cf. p. 174.

[6] Doubtless Longolius meant to report *sedem* for the textual reading.

[7] In the first place *Nahanarualos* in the text of the edition is underscored, as if in confirmation of this spelling. In the second place diagonal lines have been drawn through *na* in the middle of the word and the deletion sign placed above.

between the two collations with my own restoration of the readings of **h**:

		Longolius	Selling	h restored
1,	2	ac	et *ex sil.*	ac
	10	effusus *ex sil.*	effusis	effusis
2,	10	bistonem (*in tex.*)	vistonem	bistonem
	11	Marnum *in* mannum *corr. in tex.*, *in mg.* al. Mannum	Marnum *in tex.*, *in mg.* Mannum	Marnum *in* Mannum *corr. in tex.* (*corr.* h²?), *in mg.* al. Mannum
	19	sunt *ex sil.*	sint *ex sil.*	sint
3,	13	nihil de lacuna	lacuna post nominatumque	lacuna post nominatumque
	15	repertam *ex sil.*	reperta *in* -tam *corr.* h²	reperta, *in* -tam *corr.* h²
5,	8	propitii *ex sil.*	propitiine (-tii ne *Hummel*)	propitii ne
6,	2	pastas	hastas *ex sil.*	pastas
	18	primo *ex sil.*	primum	primum
7,	2	ac libera *ex sil.*	aut libera *ex sil.*	ac libera
	5	neque uerberare *ex sil.*	ne verberare	ne verberare
	10	non casus *ex sil.*	non casus *bis*	non casus *bis*
	14	et (exigere)	aut *ex sil.*	et
9,	6	adiectam *ex sil.*	advectam *ex sil.*	advectam
10,	4	temere *ex sil.*	tenent	tenent
	14	Hinnitus *ex sil.*	hinnitusque *ex sil.*	hinnitusque
	16	sed (apud proceres) *ex sil.*	sed *om.*	sed *om.*
12,	5	illuc *ex sil.*	illud *in* illuc *corr.*	illud *in* illuc *corr.*
15,	5	miram diuersitatem *ex sil.*	mira diuersitate *ex sil.*	mira diuersitate
	11	sed et publice	sed publice *ex sil.*	sed et publice
16,	7	Nec *ex sil.*	Ne *ex sil.*	Nec
	9	et (splendente) *ex sil.*	ac *ex sil.*	ac
17,	2	ceteri	cetera *ex sil.*	ceteri
18,	4	ambiuntur *ex sil.*	ambiunt	ambiunt
19,	6	et (per)	ac *ex sil.*	et
20,	12	et in animum, *del. in* h²	et in animum	et in animum, *del. in* h²
	15	possessione h, succe(sione) h²	possessione *ex sil.*	possessione h, succe(sione) h²

		Longolius	Selling	h restored
	16	tanto (maior) h, quo h²	tanto	tanto h, quo h²
21,	12	abeunti *ex sil.*	abeunt, *in* abeunti *corr.* h²	abeunt, *in* abeunti *corr.* h²
24,	3	saltu *ex sil.*	se *del.*, saltu *in mg.* h	se *del.*, saltu *in mg.* h
	5	expectantium, s *add.* h²	expectantium	expectantium, s *add.* h²
	10	parua, *in* praua *corr.* h²	parua, *in mg.* al. praua	parua, *in mg.* al. praua h (?)
26,	5	prestant *ex sil.*	praebent	praebent
	5	et *ex sil.*	ut et	ut et
	6	laborare *ex sil.*	labore	labore
	7	seperent (*in tex.*), *in* -par- *corr.* h²	seperent	seperent, *in* -par- *corr.* h²
27,	7	est *ex sil.*	est *om.*	est *om.*
28,	10	a bois	ab ois	a bois
	14	Neruii h, Neruli h²	Neruli h	Neruli h, Neruii h² (?)
	14	affectionem h, affectationem h²	affectionem	affectionem h, affectationem h²
	14	Germanie *ex sil.*	Germanicae *ex sil.*	Germanicae (?)
	15	et (similitudine) h, a h²	a¹	et h, a h²
	18	Nubii h, ubii h²	Nubii	Nubii h, ubii h²
29,	1	Bathi h, Bataui h²	bathi, *in mg.* Bataui h	Bathi h, *in* Bataui *corr.* h², *fortasse* Bataui *rubr. in mg.*
	9	mactiacorum	r mactiacorum	r mactiacorum
	14	numeramus *ex sil.*	numerauerim	numerauerim
	15	decumathes	thecumates ²	decumathes
	17	acto h, aucto h²	acto *ex sil.*	acto h, aucto h²
30,	4	Herquinius	Hercynius *ex sil.*	Herquinius
	6	animi *ex sil.*	animis (*sic Hummel*)	animis
	12	ferramentis *ex sil.*	r fermamentis	r fermamentis
	14	raro	rari *ex sil.*	raro

¹ Selling's report is confused. He gives *et similitudine* as though it were the reading of Teubert's edition, which in reality reads *a simi-*.

² Selling's report is doubtless due to a misprint or a confusion.

The Extant Manuscripts of the Germania

	Longolius	Selling	h restored
16	proprior, *in* -pi- *corr.* h²	proprior	proprior, *in* -pi- *corr.* h²
31, 16	dure *ex sil.*	dŭra	dŭra
32, 4	laus *ex sil.*	laus est	laus est
33, 9	fortuna praestare	praestare fortuna *ex sil.*	fortuna praestare
9	in urgentibus *ex sil.*	in gentibus	in gentibus
34, 1	Dulcubini	Dulcubimi	Dulcubimi (?)
8	seu (adiit) *ex sil.*	sive *ex sil.*	sive
10	simul atque *in tex., in mg.* al. simulac que	simul atque *ex sil.*	simul atque *in tex., in mg.* al. simulac que
35, 5	Chattis	Chattos *ex sil.*	Chattis
10	virium precuum (?) [1]	virium *ex sil.*	virium precuum (?)
37, 4	ambitu *ex sil.*	ambitum	ambitum
5	fidem *in tex., in mg.* al. fidem	sedem, *in mg.* al. fidem	sedem, *in mg.* al. fidem
6	.xl.² *ex sil.*	quadragesimum *ex sil.*	.xl. (?) [2]
9	Traiani imperatoris	imperatoris Traiani *ex sil.*	Traiani imperatoris
17	M. quoque *ex sil.*	marcoque	marcoque
18	Po. Ro. *ex sil.*	populo Romano *ex sil.*	Po. Ro.
23	nibus legionum (nibus "a rec. ma.")	legionum, "sup. num scr. nibus ab ead. m. ut videtur"	nibus legionum (nibus h an h²?)
38, 2	Tenterorumue *ex sil.*	Tencterorumve *ex sil.*	Tencterorumve
5	obligare	obliquare *ex sil.*	obligare
8	sepius	saepe *ex sil.*	sepius
8	rarum *ex sil.*	eorum, *in mg.* rarum	eorum, *in mg.* rarum
11	ornatiorem *ex sil.*	ornatorem	ornatorem

[1] The edition of Lotter reads *virium precipuum*. Longolius has drawn cross lines through *ip* and placed a deletion-symbol above. This should mean *precuum* in h, but Selling's silence is noteworthy. Did Longolius mean to delete the entire word? See p. 176.

[2] Longolius has underscored the *.xl.* of the printed text, which may indicate that this was the reading of the MS. (cf. p. 163).

		Longolius	Selling	h restored
	11	habent *ex sil.*	habet	habet
39,	2	antiquitatis re-ligione *ex sil.*	te antiquitatis nis neligione	te antiquitatis nis religione
	2	statuto *ex sil.*	stato *ex sil.*	? ?
	4	eiusdemque	eiusdem *ex sil.*	eiusdemque
	8	prolapsus *ex sil.*	prolapsus est	prolapsus est
	12	Senonum *ex sil.*	Semnonum *ex sil.*	Semnonum (?)
	13	corpore *ex sil.*	tempore, *in mg.* al. corpore numero (numero *Hummel*)	tempore, *in mg.* al. corpore numero
40,	1	nobilitasque [1] *ex sil.*	nobilitat *ex sil.*	nobilitat [1]
	1	n Largobardos, *add.* n h[2]	Langobardos *ex sil.* (Langobardos *Hummel*)	n Largobardos, n *add.* h[2]
	3	ac (periclitando)	et *ex sil.*	ac
	7	Nerthum h, herthum h[2]	Nerthum *ex sil.*	Nerthum h, herthum h[2]
	9	ea *ex sil.*	eo *ex sil.*	ea
	11	uectamque *ex sil.*	e uictamque	e uictamque
	11	bobus *ex sil.*	duobus bobus, *sed* duobus *inducto*	duobus bobus, *sed* duobus *inducto*
	18	lacus *ex sil.*	lucus, *in* lacus *corr.* h[2]	lucus, *in* lacus *corr.* h[2]
41,	1	(pars) verborum h, sueuorum h[2]	verborum	verborum h, sueuorum h[2]
	2	proprior, *in* -pi- *corr.* h[2]	proprior	proprior, *in* -pi- *corr.* h[2]
	5	passim sine	passim et sine *ex sil.*	passim sine
	6	ut (cum) *ex sil.*	et *ex sil.*	et
42,	5	peragitur h, per-gitur h[2]	peragitur *ex sil.*	peragitur h, per-gitur h[2]
43,	2	Quadorumque *om.*	Quadorumque] retro *sed del.*	Quadorumque] retro *sed del.*
	3	cultu	cultuque *ex sil.*	cultu
	6	Gotini, *rubr. in mg.* Cotini	Gothini *ex sil.*	Gotini, *rubr. in mg.* Cotini
	10	regiorum, *rubr. in mg.* Regii	Lygiorum *ex sil.*	regiorum, *rubr. in mg.* Regii

[1] *Nobilitasque* is an emendation of Puteolanus. Y read *nobilitas*, X *nobilitat* (see p. 99).

		Longolius	Selling	h restored
	12	Nahanarualos *ex sil.* . . . Naharualos	Nahanarualos . . . Nahanarualos *ex sil.*	Nahanarualos . . . Naharualos
	12	Heliosnas Helisios, *rubr. in mg.* Helisii al. Haliosii	heliosuas helisios, *in mg.* haliosuae	Heliosnas Helisios, *rubr. in mg.* Helisii al. Haliosnae (?)
44,	4	Lemonii	Lemovii *ex sil.*	Lemonii
	14	exceptionibus h, exemptionibus h²	exceptionibus, "superscr. *exempt.*"	exceptionibus h, exempt- h²
	18	nec (libertinum) *ex sil.*	ne *ex sil.*	ne
45,	3	in ortu se durat, *in* in ortus edurat *corr.* h²	in ortu se durat	in ortu se durat, *corr.* h²
	9	deam *ex sil.*	deum *ex sil.*	deum
	21	uolucria *ex sil.*	uolucra	uolucra
	29	resinamque *ex sil.*	ve resinamque	ve resinamque
	31	differunt *ex sil.*	differuntur	differuntur
46,	1	cini Peucurorum, *rubr. in mg.* Peucini	Peucurorum, *in mg.* al. Peucini	cini Peucurorum, *rubr. in mg.* al. Peucini
	9	domus	domos *ex sil.*	domus
	9	ac (peditum)	et *ex sil.*	ac
	23	Oxionas *ex sil. in tex., rubr. in mg.* al. etione	Oxionas *ex sil.*	Oxionas *in tex., rubr. in mg.* al. etione
	24	uultusque et corpora *ex sil.*	uultusque corpora *ex sil.*	uultusque corpora

An examination of this table will show that Selling does not as a rule give the readings of the second hand (h²), a procedure which is justifiable if he was convinced that this hand did not draw from a manuscript source.[1] Longolius, on the other hand, does not as a rule report errors made and corrected by the copyist of h.

My method of restoring the readings of h where there are discrepancies between the two collations is, I believe, apparent. If there is a conflict between the positive statement of the one collation and the *ex silentio* evidence of the other, and this is

[1] See pp. 173 f.

the situation in the great majority of the discrepancies, the positive statement must in every case be accepted. In the few instances in which there is a conflict between the positive statements of both collations or between the *ex silentio* evidence of both, I adopt the reading which is attested for the other members of the X family. There are, to be sure, a few cases in which the restoration of **h** must remain uncertain.

With regard to my manner of reporting the readings of **h** throughout this edition, the following points should be observed. Orthographical details depend upon the collation of Longolius. All other readings which do not appear in the table given above, are based upon the agreement of the two collations. This agreement is determined by one of the following conditions: (1) the positive statements of the two collations coincide; (2) the positive statement of one collation coincides with the *ex silentio* evidence of the other; (3) the *ex silentio* evidence of both collations agrees. If the readings are *ex silentio*, I so note when citing under the symbols **h** and **X**, but not when **h** is included in ω.[1] Finally, wherever there is a discrepancy between the two collations, I adopt the reading which I have restored for **h** in the table shown above. If the discrepancy is between the positive statement of one collation and the *ex silentio* evidence of the other, I give no reference to this table, but if the discrepancy lies either in the positive statements of both collations or in the *ex silentio* evidence of both, I refer to the table when citing under the symbols **h** and **X**.

So far as we can judge from our two collations, **h** was a very good manuscript, though it was not entirely free from interpolation. Sometimes the interpolated reading has been substituted for the genuine tradition: ch. 11, 3 *principem* for *-pes*; 14, 3 *superstitem* corr. to *-te*;[2] 18, 4 *ambiunt* for *-tur*; 28, 10 *Osi* del., *boi* in mg.; 32, 4 *laus est* for *laus*; 38, 5 *obligare* for

---

[1] In orthographical matters, of course, the *ex silentio* readings are determined from the edition of Lotter alone.

[2] The interpolation is due to the preceding *principe* for *-pi* (cf. pp. 96 f.).

The Extant Manuscripts of the Germania 173

obliquare; 45, 20 *arboris* for *-rum*. The reading *abnobae*, 1, 9, found in **h** alone can hardly be more than a conjectural restoration.

Again, both the true reading and the interpolation are found as doublets: 2, 14 *de eo* in text, in mg. *deo*; 10, 21 *quemque* in text, in mg. *quoque*; 26, 5 *et*; 26, 7 *seperent* in text, in mg. *secent*; 29, 12 *mente* in text, in mg. *manente*;[1] 37, 5 *sedem* in text, in mg. *fidem*; 38, 8 *eorum* in text, in mg. *rarum*; 39, 2 *antiquitatis religione*; 39, 13 *tempore* in text, *corpore numero*[2] in mg.

Errors of carelessness are not very numerous. The most common are the transposition of words and the confusion of *ac* and *et*: 3, 16 *raecie germanie que*; 33, 9 *fortuna praestare*; 37, 9 *traiani imperatoris*; 45, 26 *labuntur mare*; 46, 16 *ferarumque imbrium*; *ac* for *et*,[3] 1, 9; 7, 8; 46, 9 (*ac peditum*); *et* for *ac*, 19, 6. Other errors of carelessness in **h** (not noted in the table of readings shown on pp. 167 ff.) are: 7, 3 *ac* for *si*; 33, 7 *oblectacione*; 43, 12 *lanimos* for *Manimos*; 45, 20 *esse* om.

I have previously suggested that **s**² drew from a manuscript (**h**₁) intervening between **h** and **X**. Perhaps evidence for the existence of **h**₁ is to be found in the character of some of the interpolations in **h**. Thus in 14, 3, the correction of *superstitem* to *-te* is due to the preceding *principe*. If the copyist of **h** had had before him the doublets of **X**, *principe*,[4] would he have made this change? Again, 29, 12, the marginal variant *manente* is clearly due to the fact that *animo* for *animoque* immediately follows. This implies an intervening manuscript, for **X** must have read *animoque* with ω.

The corrector in **h** (**h**²) drew from an early printed edition rather than from a manuscript. Thus, 20, 16 *quo* for *tanto*

---
[1] The marginal reading is due to *animo* for *animoque*.
[2] *Numero* is a gloss on *corpore*. The variants *corpore:tempore* are ancient (cf. p. 134).
[3] See also p. 145.
[4] See pp. 96 f.

of the manuscripts is the reading of χ (*ed. prin.*); 28, 18 *Vbii* for *nubii*, 42, 5 *pergitur* for *peragitur*, are both emendations of Puteolanus; 40, 1 *Langobardis* [1] (*largobardos, longo-* codd.) first appears in the edition of Beroaldus; 40, 7 *Herthum* is first printed in the margin of Rhenanus' edition of 1519; [2] 41, 1 *Sueuorum* (*uerborum* ω)appears in the Viennese edition of 1500, and again in Rhenanus' edition of 1533; [3] 29, 17 *aucto* for *acto* is an emendation proposed by Lipsius. Ch. 28, 14, Longolius reports *Neruii*, which first appears in the margin of Rhenanus' edition of 1519, as the reading of the first hand, and *Neruli*, which is found in all the manuscripts, as that of the second hand. Since Selling, who generally passes over the additions of the second hand, reports only *Neruli*, I think there can be little doubt that Longolius has here made an error and that we should restore, *Neruli* h, *Neruii* h².

Other readings of h² are to be found in many or in all manuscripts, but could also have been taken from one of the earlier printed editions, while a few are probably fictions of the corrector's own (20, 13 *in* del.; 20, 15 *successione*; 44, 14 *exemptionibus*). We may, I believe, totally disregard the corrections of h², since they are not drawn from a manuscript source.

In the following readings h agrees with scattered manuscripts of the Y family, or with an entire group or branch of this family, in opposition to Wm and the remainder of Y:

		h Y	Wm Y
(i)	1, 10	effusis h u	effusus
(ii)	11	septimum enim h *ex sil.*, ξ	septimum
(iii)	2, 10	tuisconem h t τ s	tuistonem [4]
(iv)	15	vandalos, *in mg.* vandileos h, Vandalos al, uandalios ξ L	uandilios (uandilos φ, uandulos r)

[1] *Langobardos* is the reading of s².

[2] *Herthum* is also found in p.

[3] Perhaps earlier, in Alciatus' edition of 1519 (cf. p. 330), which I have not seen. *Sueuorum* is also an emendation of the corrector in u.

[4] For the complete list of variants see p. 115.

		h Y	Wm Y
(v)	17	aditum **h v** l	additum (editum ψ)
(vi)	7, 5	ne (uerberare) **h** σ λ **a s**	neque (nec *b* ψ)
(vii)	17, 2	ceteri **h s**	cetera
(viii)	27, 7	est *om*. **h v**	est
(ix)	29, 1	bataui *rubr. in mg.* **h** (?),[2] bataui L, batani **e s**	batauii [1]
(x)	35, 10	praecipuum uirtutis ac uirium precuum argumentum **h** (?),[3] praecipuum (pręcium *I*) uirtutis ac uirium praecipuum argumentum *I* ξ	praecipuum uirtutis ac uirium argumentum
(xi)	42, 3	etiam ipsa **h L**, *olim in* **E**	ipsa etiam
(xii)	43, 19	feritatis **h** ψ	feritati
(xiii)	44, 7	ipsae in oceano **h** *ex sil.*, ξ	ipso in oceanum **Wm** bzuRAc **s**, ipsae (ipse) in oceanum β **ale**, ipso in oceano σ
(xiv)	45, 16	neque **h v**	nec quae (que)
(xv)	20	esse *om*. **h e**	esse
(xvi)	29	resinamque **h**, rasinam- que ξ (ve above)	resinamue

It is apparent that in most of these readings the agreement between h and the conspiring members of the **Y** family is accidental. To be sure, the correction in vi is necessary, but, in my opinion, *ne* is none the less merely a correction of the *neque* of Hf. However, the concurrence between h and α (or ξ) in

[1] For the complete list of variants see p. 95.
[2] On the reading of **h** see p. 168.
[3] On the reading of **h** see p. 169.

ii, x, xiii,[1] causes difficulty, for the theory of chance agreement is untenable. But we should observe that in ii and xiii the readings given for **h** are *ex silentio,* and that in x there may be a reasonable doubt as to the proper interpretation of Longolius' collation.[2] We have noted previously a similar difficulty with the *ex silentio* readings of **h**. In an unduly large number of cases they side with **Y** against **Wm**,[3] and again they side with **a** and one or two other groups of the **Y** family against **Wm** and the remainder of **Y**.[4] As I see the matter, there are but two alternatives: either the *ex silentio* readings of **h** are to be rejected in some cases (and the collation of Longolius in x does not mean what it ought to mean), or **h** has borrowed readings from **a**. Of the two alternatives the former seems to me the more probable. As we have seen, in many places the positive statement of Longolius or Selling is in opposition to the *ex silentio* reading of the other, and in a few instances the *ex silentio* readings of both collators are at a variance owing to the discrepancies between the respective printed editions which they used. It is then but natural to suppose that there are still other places in which the two editions agree but both collators failed to note the deviations in **h**.

In support of "contamination" between **h** and **a**, we may say that whatever Longolius had in mind his collation *ought* to mean that in x the reading of **h** was *uirium precuum,*[5] and

[1] The reading of Hf. was *ipso in oceanum,* the confusion between final *o* and *m* being phonetic. *Ipsae* is a clumsy attempt at emendation, which is at least as old as **Y**. On the other hand *oceano* is an emendation of **a**. It is of course possible that the same emendation was made independently in **h**.

[2] See p. 169 and note 1.

[3] See the readings shown on p. 142, and my discussion on p. 144.

[4] See the readings numbered ii, vii, xiv, xx, on pp. 138 f.

[5] If **h** really read *precuum,* this curious form would appear to be a corruption of *praecipuum (uirtutis),* and the doublets *praecipuum:precuum* would be quite in keeping with the character of Hf. The second *praecipuum* in Iξ would of course represent an attempt to emend *precuum,* and evidence for this may be found in the fact that **I** reads *pręcium* for the first *praecipuum.* Naturally, if Hf. had the doublets *praecipuum:precuum* the mere presence of the latter form in **h** would not declare for "contamination" between **h** and **a**, but the fact that the *precuum* of **h** and the second *praecipuum* of **a** appear in the same place in the text would indicate such a connection between the two MSS.

we may also cite the readings shown in iv and xvi, where the evidence for **h** is positive.

e. The α Group

The descendants of **α**, a symbol which I use to indicate one of the lost apographs of **Y**, divide themselves into two major branches: (1) σ, comprising **NΔI**, and (2) ξ, represented by **pMt** and the *editio princeps* (**w**) with its apograph the manuscript **f**. Among the members of the ξ branch there is again a line of cleavage between **pM** on the one hand and **tw** (χ) on the other.

Considerable difficulty attends the restoration of **α**, for all its descendants offer conflated texts. We have already seen that σ borrowed readings from the **X** family, which were taken over frequently by **NΔ** but only rarely by **I**. I shall show presently that **pM** adopted numerous readings of the τ branch, and that **tw** (χ) offer a "revised" text which probably drew from a manuscript source. The result is that most of the initial errors of **α** have been corrected in one or more of its descendants, so that the readings peculiar to all seven manuscripts are few in number and give no hint of the corruptions which must have existed in the archetype itself. In the following places the readings of **α** may be restored on the basis of all the manuscripts within the group:[1]

		α (NΔI pM wt)	ω
(i)	3, 12	hodie	hodieque
(ii)	10, 14	hinnitus (= ψ)	hinnitusque
(iii)	14, 2	aequare	adaequare
(iv)	39, 4	eiusdem (= *L s*)	eiusdemque
(v)	42, 7	manserunt	mansere
(vi)	44, 7	oceano (= *h ex sil.*, *u* [2])	oceanum

[1] In the following tabulations I have admitted as "peculiar" readings of **α** a few which are found in other MSS. as well, since I believe the concurrence to be accidental. (On the reading of **h** in ix see p. 175.) For readings found in **α** and other groups which may remount to **Y** see pp. 104 ff., 110 ff., 116 ff.

178   The Germania of Tacitus

		α (NΔI pM wt)	ω
(vii)	45, 4	formas	formasque
(viii)	16	gignit	gignat
(ix)	29	rasinamue σ, rasinamque (re- t) ξ	resinamue

In view of the fact that all manuscripts of the α group show conflated texts, the agreement of any manuscript of the σ branch with any manuscript of the ξ branch should, theoretically,[1] give us the readings of the lost α. On the basis of concurrence between members of the σ branch and members of the ξ branch I adduce the following readings for the restoration of α:[2]

		α	ω
(x)	2, 10	sit Iξ, est NΔ	est
(xi)	6, 13	existimanti σpM, estimanti χ, M *in mg.*	aestimanti (exstimanti *uel* -ati bπ)
(xii)	7, 12	ululatus foeminarum I pMχ, foeminarum (fe- Δ) ululatus NΔ	feminarum ululatus
(xiii)	9, 6	adiectam I pχ, aduectam NΔM	aduectam
(xiv)	10, 16	sed apud proceres Iξ (= α, E *superscr.*)	apud proceres
(xv)	11, 12	cum I p, cun *ex* cunque M, tum NΔχ	tum
(xvi)	14, 10	clarescant Iξ, clarescunt NΔ	clarescunt
(xvii)	16, 9	et ξ, ut I, ac NΔ	ac
(xviii)	19, 8	inuenit NIξ, inuenerit Δ	inuenerit (inuenitur s)
(xix)	22, 8	reconciliatis I pM w, reconciliandis NΔ t	reconciliandis

[1] As a matter of fact, there is only one reading (xl) in which ξ has but a single representative.

[2] Where the large lacuna occurs in t, 8, 3 *quam longe* through 16, 10 *imitetur*, I accept the readings of w alone for χ.

The Extant Manuscripts of the Germania

		α	ω
(xx)	8	inimicitiis Iξ, inimicis NΔ	inimicis
(xxi)	26, 7	et (hortos) Iξ (= d), ut NΔ	ut
(xxii)	28, 18	Treboci Iξ, (= treborci R), Treiboci [1] Δ, Triboci N	Triboci (triboici ba, triborci π)
(xxiii)	29, 14	numeramus Mχ, nuamus p, numerauimus I, numerauerim NΔ	numerauerim
(xxiv)	30, 5	arcus σpM, artus χ	artus (arctus dk c)
(xxv)	33, 1	Thencteros NpM, Theneteros (Tene-t) χ, tenc-I, tencteros Δ	tencteros
(xxvi)	35, 10	pręcium uirtutis ac uirium pręcipuum argumentum I, praecipuum u. ac u. praecipuum a. ξ, praecipuum u. ac u. a. NΔ	praecipuum uirtutis ac uirium (uirium precuum h ? uide p. 169) argumentum
(xxvii)	39, 8	est om. Iξ, est NΔ	est
(xxviii)	11	Adducit Δξ, Aducit I, Adducit, in mg. adiicit (aditiit p) pM, Adiicit N	adicit uel adiicit
(xxix)	40, 1	paucitas om. I pM, paucitas NΔχ	paucitas
(xxx)	10	uestae NΔ M w, ueste I p t	ueste
(xxxi)	15	Item (tantum amata) Iξ, om. N, tunc Δ	tunc

[1] We here have clear evidence that Δ was copied from a conflated text. Cf. also p. 117, lxvii.

13

			α	ω
(xxxii)		16	satiata I pM, satiatam NΔ χ	satiatam (sacratam φ, sacratum s)
(xxxiii)	41,	6	et sine NIξ, sine Δ	sine
(xxxiv)	43,	1	Burii[1] Iξ, Buri NΔ	Buri
(xxxv)		7	paucam I pM, pauca NΔχ	pauca
(xxxvi)		21	fertilis I pM, feralis NΔχ	feralis
(xxxvii)	44,	15	neque Iξ, in NΔ	in
(xxxviii)	45,	4	emergentis[2] *om.* ΔIξ, emergentis N	emergentis
(xxxix)	46,	5	mixtis Δ, mistis χ, *om.*[3] I, mistos M, mixtos N	mixtos
(xl)		23	Exionas I M, Oxionas Nχ, etionas Δ	Oxionas *uel* Etionas

The ξ Branch

So far I have regarded the evidence of one or more members of the σ branch as necessary for the restoration of α. It will be observed that the invariable representative[4] of σ has been I, which made little use of the corrections which had been entered into σ from X. There remain some twenty-five readings in which pMχ agree, but I as well as NΔ sides with the other manuscripts. Now it is possible to assume that in these readings all three manuscripts, NΔI, have restored the correct tradition from the marginal or interlinear corrections in σ, and that the consensus of pMχ offers the readings of α. On the other hand, it may be that pMχ are descendants of a lost apograph of α (ξ). I am quite unable to decide between the alternatives, but I adopt the symbol ξ, regardless of whether it

[1] Cf. pp. 181, lix.
[2] The text of p ends with 44, 18 *regia*.
[3] I omits, 46, 4–10 *ut . . . Sarmatis*.
[4] Except in xxx and xxxix.

really represents a lost manuscript, as convenient for indicating the consensus of **pMχ**:

		ξ (pMtw)	ω
(xli)	1, 11	septimum enim (= *h ex sil.*)	septimum
(xlii)	7, 14	nec p χ(= *a*), aut M	et (aut β)
(xliii)	14, 16	hostes	hostem
(xliv)	16, 9	&	ac (ut *I*)
(xlv)	18, 16	pereundum (= *L*)	pariendum
(xlvi)	27, 5	peroperosum	operosum (opesum *in mg. W; cf. p. 128*)
(xlvii)	30, 13	coonerant	onerant (honorant *I*)
(xlviii)	31, 5	frontes	frontem
(xlix)	34, 1	Chasuari (= *z*)	Chasuarii (Tha-β)
(l)	8	seu	siue
(li)	38, 2	Thencterorumue (Tencate- *t*)	Tencterorumue
(lii)	39, 5	coherent	coeunt (coheunt *I r bzRAc*)
(liii)	40, 12	cum *om.*	cum
(liv)	42, 1	Marconiani p M w (=*r*), -mani t	Marcomani
(lv)	2	Marconianorum	Marcomanorum
(lvi)	6	Marconianis	Marcomanis
(lvii)	43, 1	Gothini (= *m zR*)	Gotini
(lviii)	1	Marconianorum	Marcomanorum
(lix)	2	Burii	Buri
(lx)	3	Gothinos (= *zR*)	Gotinos
(lxi)	5	Sarmathae	Sarmatae
(lxii)	6	Gothini	Gotini, *lect. uar.* Cotini

		ξ (pMtw)	ω
(lxiii)	12	Arios (= R)	Harios
(lxiv)	12	Elysios (= z, eli- L, ęli- R)	Helysios uel Heli-
(lxv)	15	Eius (in mg. ea uis pM) numinis	ea uis numini
(lxvi)	45, 26	liquantia	liquentia
(lxvii)	46, 15	&	ac

The evidence for relating α to the groups β, φ, s, in the restoration of the common archetype Y has been adduced in my discussion of the X and Y families.[1] An examination of the readings peculiar to α (and ξ) fails to reveal any valid argument against such a relationship, since this group makes no independent contribution toward the restoration of Hf. I will grant that in a few instances α does assume a certain special importance, but only in connection with other manuscripts. Thus, the variants *siburi* and *dulcubuni* are attested by α alone[2] outside the X family; (xlvi) *peroperosum* in conjunction with the marginal *opesum* of W points to the doublets *operosum:opesum* in Hf.; (xxvi) *uirium praecipuum* in conjunction with the *uirium precuum* of h, if h really had this reading,[3] suggests the doublets *praecipuum:precuum*; and (xxii) *Treboci* in conjunction with the *triboici* of φ may point to *treboci* in Hf. Nevertheless, these readings need only mean that α copied variants which were either omitted or distorted by the other apographs of Y. I will also grant that two of the peculiar readings of α, (vi) *oceano* and (xxxix) *mixtis*, deserve to be received into our text of the *Germania*, but I can only regard them as fifteenth-century corrections. Save for the fact that the emender seems to have hit upon the truth, these two corrections belong to the same category as (i) *hodie*, (iv) *eiusdem*, (xiv) *sed apud proceres*, (xxi) *et hortos*, (xxxiii) *et sine*,

[1] See pp. 101–121.
[2] On the evidence of M alone (see pp. 134 and 131).
[3] See p. 169, note 1, pp. 176 f.

(xli) *septimum enim,* (xlv) *pereundum;* and perhaps (xviii) *inuenit,* (xxix) *paucitas* om. (*nobilitas* for *nobilitat* in Y), (xxxviii) *emergentis* om., (lxv) *numinis*.

The χ Branch

The manuscript t and the *editio princeps* (w) seem to be derived from a lost copy of ξ (or of α?),[1] which I call χ. The following readings may be used for the restoration of χ:[2]

			χ (tw)	ω
(i)	*Inscriptio*		Cornelii Taciti illustrissimi historici de situ moribus et populis Germaniae Libellus (libellus aureus w)	*Vide app. crit. ad loc.*
(ii)	1,	11	erumpit	erumpat
(iii)	2,	14	autem (= π)	ut in
(iv)	6,	7	plura	pluraque
(v)	13,	3	Tum eum	tum *uel* cum (tum eūtu m)
(vi)	14,	5	principum (= φ)	praecipuum
(vii)	20,	16	quo	tanto
(viii)	24,	9	iunior (= a, u in mg.)	iuuenior
(ix)	28,	6	Moeni w, Moemi t	Moenum
(x)		8	Boiemi	Boihemi
(xi)		10	ab Osis (= au[2])	a bois
(xii)	32,	2	Teneteri (= m s[2])	Tencteri
(xiii)		2	Teneteri (= m)	Tencteri
(xiv)		4	Teneteris (= m)	Tencteris
(xv)		8	extera	cetera

[1] See p. 180.
[2] The restoration of χ in v and vi rests on w alone, as there is a large lacuna n t (cf. p. 178, note 2).

			χ (tw)	ω
(xvi)	33,	1	Teneteros (= *m;* The- *w*)	Tencteros
(xvii)	37,	4	ambitu (= β *a*)	ambitum
(xviii)	39,	3	patrum (= *W, h ex sil. bazRc s*)	patrium *uel* patruum
(xix)	40,	1	longobardis (*cf.* Lombardis *u* ²)	longobardos *uel* largobardis
(xx)	45,	7	efluorum (*cf.* estuorum *M*)	Aestiorum
(xxi)	46,	3	Bastranas	Bastarnas

We see intentional changes in the text as transmitted by Hf. in i, vii, viii, xi, xvii, xviii, xix, and perhaps in ii, iii, vi. Furthermore, χ has sometimes restored the correct readings where α was in error:[1] 6, 13 *estimanti*, 11, 12 *tum*, 30, 5 *artus*, 40, 1 *paucitas*, 40, 16 *satiatam*, 43, 7 *pauca*, 43, 21 *feralis*, 46, 23 *Oxionas*. Some of these corrections must have been made from a manuscript source. The readings (iii) *autem* and (vi) *principum* suggest an affinity between χ and ϕ, while (viii) *iunior*, (xi) *ab Osis*, (xvii) *ambitu*, (xviii) *patrum*, would indicate that the manuscript of the ϕ group most closely related to χ is **a**. Also *estimanti* and *saciatam* are known only to **a** of the ϕ group. Yet (iii) **a** reads *ut in*, and the corrections (vii) *quo* and (xix) *longobardis* are peculiar to χ alone. I suspect that χ drew from some lost manuscript closely related to **a**.

Correction and interpolation have gone further in **t** than in χ. This manuscript has, 19, 5 *abscisis*, and 37, 14 *et ipso*, for the *accisis* and *et ipso et ipse* of **a**, 22, 8 *reconciliandis*, 28, 14 *germanice*, for the *reconciliatis* and *germaniae* of Iξ. It also has the following readings, unknown to **a**, but found here and there in other manuscripts: 2, 8 *sibi* (= Wh s) [2] for *si*, 36, 4 *nomine superiores* (= a s²) for *nomine superioris*, 43, 18 *Arii*

---

[1] See the readings numbered xi, xv, xxiv, xxix, xxxii, xxxv, xxxvi, xl, on pp. 178 ff.

[2] See p. 138.

in mg. (= s in text) for *alii* in ω, 45, 10 *omnique* (= W²) for *omniumque*, 46, 13 *sola* (= τ a s) for *solae*, 45, 28 *temptes* (= X ae) for *tentes*. Peculiar to **t** alone are, 36, 7 *Chatti* for the *Tacti* of **Y**, 41, 1 *neruorum* for the *uerborum* of ω. The agreement of **t** with **a** in some of these readings suggests that χ borrowed from **a** or a kindred manuscript more extensively than is indicated by the consensus of **tw**, but the source of the corrections in **t** is not a matter of importance.[1] The inadvertent errors in **t** are not numerous.

Unlike **t** the *editio princeps* (**w**) and its copy **f** depart from χ only in exhibiting a slightly larger number of careless mistakes:

		wf	ω
(i)	3, 8	stutis (= *A*)	scutis
(ii)	8, 3	peccatorum	pectorum
(iii)	27, 1	ut *om*.	ut
(iv)	33, 8	ac (= *Wm b*)	at
(v)	39, 11	auctorem	auctoritatem
(vi)	45, 18	ullo	nullo
(vii)	46, 2	femiorum (= *a*)	fennorum
(viii)	22	in illis	ut illis

I am reasonably sure that **f** is a copy of **w**. The former almost without exception offers a more corrupt text.[2] Ch. 31, 4, where **w** reads *exso* for *caeso*, **f** has *occiso*; 45, 27, where **w**

---

[1] The statement made by Schönemann (62) that **t** is a copy of the Venetian edition of 1476 seems even more unfounded than his statement that **w** is a copy of **f**. The edition of 1476 has none of the corrections and interpolations noted above for **t**. In fact, **t** bears no closer resemblance to this edition than it does to the *princeps* and its other reimpressions.

[2] The following partial list of the errors peculiar to **f** is sufficient to show that it cannot be the archetype of **w**: 5, 13 *utilitate* (= φ); 6, 14 *roboris* om.; 7, 10 *casu*; 9, 8 *imagine* for *magnitudine*; 13, 12 *principium* (= Wm, h in mg., NI φ); 21, 5 *amiciciae*; 24, 2 *lucrum* for *ludicrum*; 25, 4 *comunione* for *colono*; 31, 2 *consensu*; 31, 4 *exuere* om.; 34, 9 *in* om.; 35, 10 *ac* om.; 37, 17 *Manilio* (= φ); 38, 5 *crinem* om.; 43, 1–2 *terga* . . . *Buri* om.; 44, 10 *adiungunt* om.; 46, 8 *hi* om.

has *succin* for *succini*, **f** offers *succino*. These two readings show independent attempts on the part of the copyist of **f** to correct the errors of **w**. Ch. 46, 12, **f** reads *inita* for *mira*. Although a careful scribe would not have made this error in copying from **w**, yet in the exemplar of **w** from which my photographs were taken the first arc of the *m* of *mira* is broken and the *r* bears considerable resemblance to *t*. The few places in which **f** sides with the other manuscripts may be regarded as corrections of obvious typographical errors:[1] 2, 15 *suenos* **w**, *sueuos* **fω**; 13, 6 *uidenter* **w**, *uidentur* **fω**; 15, 4 *agiorum* **w**, *agrorum* **fω**; 31, 14 *Hulli* **w**, *Nulli* **fω**; 34, 2 *eludunt* **w**, *cludunt* **fω**; 34, 7 *tenrauimus* **w**, *tentauimus* **fω**.

The only valid evidence that I have been able to find against the supposition that **f** is a copy of **w** lies in the following readings of the former: 5, 13 *utilitate*, 13, 12 *principium*, 25, 4 *comunione*, 37, 17 *Manilio*. *Vtilitate* and *Manilio* are readings peculiar to φ, and we have previously noted a concurrence between χ and members of the φ group. *Principium* is found in φ and other manuscripts as well.[2] Yet I think it quite possible for all three errors to be of independent occurrence in **f**. As for *comunione*, there is certainly nothing in **w** to account for the error, but it would be vain to seek an explanation for all the peccadilloes of fifteenth-century copyists. In any event, **w** cannot be a copy of **f**, as has sometimes been suggested.

The MSS pM

A special affinity between **p** and **M** is indicated both by a short list of readings peculiar to them alone, and by a larger number of readings which show an infiltration from τ.

As for the readings found in **pM** alone, I have noted only the following: 1, 2 *Sarmathis*;[3] 10, 17 *consocios*, in mg. *con*-

---

[1] I believe that in early printed editions there are sometimes variations among different copies of the same impression. Possibly these errors are not to be found in all copies of **w**.

[2] See p. 126.

[3] Cf. 43, 5 *Sarmathae* ξ.

scios **M**, *consotios* with *ul' cŏnscios* inserted between *proceres* and *apud* **p**; 18, 6 *prebent*, in mg. *probant*; 27, 10 *quatŭs* **p**, *quantus* **M**; 28, 14 *Treneri*; 31, 6 *rettulisse* **M**, *rettu-*>*retu-* **p**.

Readings peculiar to β (the parent of τ) found in **pM** are as follows:[1] 1, 10 *plurĭs* **M**, *plures* **p**; 5, 19 *affectatione*; 22, 1 *enim* **M** in text, **p** in mg.; 26, 3 *in uices*; 37, 15 *obiecerunt*. In **M**, but not in **p**: 7, 14 *aut exigere*; 16, 4 *longant* in mg.; 37, 1 *situm* in mg. (= β φ in text).

Readings peculiar to τ found in **pM**:[2] 6, 16 *centini* **M**, *Centeịni* **p**; 11, 9 *iniussi* **p**, *in iussu* **M**; 13, 4 *ipsi* in mg.; 18, 16 *renuntiant*; 25, 5 *Verberant* in mg.; 8 *est* om.; 28, 21 *collati* in mg. In **M** but not in **p**: 10, 12 *candi*. In **p** but not in **M**: 16, 14 *ignoranter*; 18, 16 *sic uiuentes, sic parientes* in mg.

The readings shown above hardly offer proof of a lost manuscript intervening between **pM** and ξ. More probably both the readings peculiar to **pM** and those borrowed from τ were already in ξ (or α?).

The σ Branch

The apograph of α which I call σ has perished, but is represented by its three children **NΔI**. I have had occasion to mention this group frequently, since it has appropriated readings of the **X** family.[3] My assumption is that readings of **X** were inserted in the interlinear or marginal spaces of σ, from which they were drawn frequently by **N** and **Δ**, but only rarely by **I**. Obviously the agreement of two of these manuscripts may be taken for the restoration of σ, since the dissenting manuscript may have made the correction from the text of **X**.[4]

---

[1] See the table of readings shown on pp. 191 ff.

[2] See the table shown on pp. 203 ff.

[3] For the readings peculiar to **X** taken over by σ see pp. 94 f., 142, 144, 150 ff.

[4] Some of the corruptions found in any one of the three MSS. may have originated in the transcription of σ, but this is beyond our control.

188   The Germania of Tacitus

		σ (NΔI)	ω
(i)	2, 11	conditoris IΔ, conditorisque N	conditorisque
(ii)	4, 1	populis	populos
(iii)	5, 7	Eatque[1] NΔ, eantque I	eaeque (atque *m*)
(iv)	8, 2	praeco NΔ, pręc. I	precum
(v)	9, 9	consacrant	consecrant
(vi)	13, 12	primum	primus
(vii)	14, 7	populique Δ, plurique > populique (?) I, plerique N	plerique
(viii)	16, 15	ipsorum ΔI (*in* ipso *corr. I*), ipso N	ipso
(ix)	18, 10	id ΔI, a N	aliquid
(x)	10	haec	hoc
(xi)	19, 6	omne ΔI, omnem N	omnem
(xii)	21, 8	deficeret Δ, defecer& I, defecerit N	defecere
(xiii)	23, 6	uitiis *in* uinis *mut.* Δ, minis *in* uinis *corr.* I, uitiis N	uitiis
(xiv)	24, 3	excitatio NI, exercitatio Δ	exercitatio
(xv)	25, 2	Suam in Δ, Suam̄ N, Suam I	Suam
(xvi)	5	exequantur	exequuntur
(xvii)	13	est NΔ, *om.* I	sunt
(xviii)	28, 6	Hercinam (-cy- *N*) NI, hercyniam Δ	hercyniam (hircinam *a*)

[1] Apparently a reading borrowed from a member of the X family (see p. 152).

The Extant Manuscripts of the Germania 189

		σ (NΔI)	ω
(xix)	11	commigrauerunt	commigrauerint
(xx)	20	tsgressi Δ, Trasgressi I, Transgressi N	Transgressi
(xxi)	29, 3	populis NI, ppℓs Δ	populus
(xxii)	35, 4	obtendere NI, obtenditur Δ	obtenditur
(xxiii)	6	ppℓs Δ, ppℓis I, populus N	populus
(xxiv)	11	assequantur (= s)	assequuntur (-quen- φ)
(xxv)	39, 3	augurii NI, augurii ritu Δ	auguriis
(xxvi)	40, 8	propriis NI, populis Δ	populis
(xxvii)	43, 2	quodorumque	quadorumque
(xxviii)	13	nacharualos (antiquae) NI, Nahanarualos Δ	naharualos
(xxix)	20	praelium	proelia
(xxx)	44, 9	fronte	frontem
(xxxi)	12	nec NI, non Δ	non
(xxxii)	45, 7	dextera Δ, dextra I, dextro N	dextro
(xxxiii)	27	exudant I, exsudant (= E R) N, exundant Δ	exundant

The readings peculiar to the σ branch are without importance, and the prominence given NI in our editions [1] of the

[1] Since Mf. (71 f.) states that the interlinear variants in N are additions of a second hand, and since Andresen uses the symbol c^2 to distinguish these variants from the readings of the text (c), I wish to make clear my own conviction that these interlinear variants are by the hand which wrote the text. In fact, I fail to see how a comparison of the forms of the letters could lead to any other conclusion. N does show the work of a second hand in some marginal captions and in one marginal correction (37, 10 al' medio in mg. opposite Eedio in text), but the additions of this hand may be totally disregarded.

Germania is without justification, save in so far as these manuscripts offer readings of the **X** family.[1] Of the three manuscripts **I** is by far the most corrupt, yet it is the least interpolated, and in numerous places preserves corruptions of α which have been corrected in **N** or **Δ** or in both,[2] and in some cases **I** appears to be the only manuscript of the σ branch showing corruptions originating in **Y**.[3]

I take this opportunity to correct an error in my classification of the manuscripts of the *de Grammaticis* of Suetonius. The groups which I there called α and γ do not represent two lines of descent from **Y**, as I formerly supposed, but are to be referred to a single apograph of **Y**, which corresponds to α in my stemma of the *Germania* manuscripts. The group which I called α for the *de Gram.* is the same as σ, though it should be borne in mind that **Δ** for this work does not belong to the σ branch.[4] The group which I called γ for the *de Gram.* probably corresponds to ξ, though **M** is the only manuscript of the group containing both the *de Gram.* and the *Germania*.[5]

f. The β Group

To a second lost apograph of **Y** I have given the name of β. This manuscript appears to have had two apographs, both now missing, which I call λ and τ. From λ sprang **VL**, and from τ came **dETvro** and the printed edition **k**, but of these **T** may be disregarded, since it is a copy of **E**. The manuscript **r** presents a conflated text, having borrowed numerous readings from some member of the φ group, and having corrected, pre-

---

[1] **Δ** has not drawn the *Germania* from the same source as the *de Grammaticis*. The latter work was taken from an archetype far more corrupt than σ. Presumably the *Dialogus* was drawn from the same source as the *Germania* (*i.e.* σ) but this must await an investigation of the MSS. of the former work.

[2] See p. 180.

[3] See pp. 111, 116 f., 118.

[4] Robinson 1922, 176 f., 189.

[5] An investigation of the MSS. of the *Dialogus* will probably make the matter clear. One MS. (M) of the group contains *Germ.*, *Dial.*, *de Gram.*, four (KHUS for the *de Gram.*) contain the *Dialogus* and the *de Gram.*, while the *editio princeps* (w) has the *Germania* and *Dialogus*.

The Extant Manuscripts of the Germania

sumably from the same source, numerous errors originating in β and τ. The following readings may be used for the restoration of β:[1]

		β (VL dETvrok)	ω
(i)	1, 10	pluris (= *M*, plures *p*)ⁱ	plures
(ii)	5, 19	affectatione (= *pM*)	affectione
(iii)	7, 14	aut exigere (= *M*)	et (nec *p*χ *a*) exigere
(iv)	9, 2	et Martem [2]	ac Martem
(v)	14, 11	tuentur λ, tueantur k, tuere E, tueare dvr	tueare
(vi)	16, 4	longant k, longant, *in mg. uel superscr.* locant Vd, locant, *in mg.* longant (= *M*) E, locant Lvr	locant
(vii)	22, 1	enim (= *M*, *p in mg.*; e *r*, *M in mg.*)	e (ê *s*)
(viii)	25, 4	ut (et *r*) seruus	et seruus
(ix)	26, 3	in uices (= *pM*; inuicem L*r*)	uices (*lect. uar. in* X uice)
(x)	33, 9	urgentibus iam	in gentibus X s, *superscr.* N, in urgentibus ω
(xi)	34, 1	dulgicubini r, dulgicubuni v, dulgitubini L, Dulgicubuni, *in mg.* dulgibini E, Dulgibini, *in mg. uel superscr.* dulgicubini Vd, dulgibini k	Dulgibini, *lect. uar.* Dulcubuni (*uide p. 131*)
(xii)	1	Thasuarii (ta- *L*)	Chasuarii
(xiii)	8	magnum [3]	magnificum

[1] The frequent agreement of pM with β is due to the fact that the archetype of these MSS. borrowed readings from τ. See p. 186 f.

[2] Cf. p. 195.

[3] *Magnificum* now found in L is by the second hand in an erasure.

	β (VL dETvrok)	ω
(xiv)	36, 3 impotentis	impotentes
(xv)	7 aduersariis v, aduersarum, *in mg. uel superscr.* aduersariis VLdE, aduersarum k, aduersarios r	aduersarum, *lect. uar.* aduersarios (*uide, p. 132*)
(xvi)	37, 8 Sapirio (papirio *r*)	Papirio
(xvii)	15 obiecer͟ᵗ V, obiecerunt (obiecerentur *r*) Lτ (= *pM*)	obiecerit (obiecit Δ, obicitur *I*)
(xviii)	18 trisque	tresque
(xix)	38, 10 religat̄ V, religatur Lτ	religant X, ligant α s, ne legant φ
(xx)	39, 4 omnes,[1] *in mg. uel superscr.* nominis l' numinis VdE, omnes Lk, numinis vr	omnis, *lect: uar.* nominis
(xxi)	40, 4 Veudigni vdk, R͟ᵛeudigni E, Veusdigni λ, Reudigni r	Reudigni
(xxii)	43, 12 Naharualos (-uol- *v*) Lvrk (= *p*), Nahanarualos, *in mg. uel superscr.* naharualos VdE	Nahanarualos
(xxiii)	44, 4 Prot͟ᶦenus VdE, Protenus k, Protinus Lvr	protinus
(xxiv)	45, 11 hostis	hostes
(xxv)	27 igni	igne

Other readings which may, I believe, be regarded as independent corruptions or interpolations in β, though they are

[1] Observe that β has not only introduced a new variant, *numinis*, but has also changed *omnis*, a corruption of *nominis*, to *omnes*.

found in other manuscripts, are:

		β (VL dETvrok)	ω
(xxvi)	5, 11	perinde **Lr** (= s), perinde, *superscr.* pro **V**, proinde *superscr.* per **E**, peinde o, per perinde v, perinde al' proinde d, proinde k	proinde
(xxvii)	7, 2	aut libera (= m M)	ac libera
(xxviii)	11, 12	tamen (= m Ac, tamen > tum s)	tum
(xxix)	37, 4	ambitu **Lv** (= χ a), ambitum, *in mg. uel superscr.* ambitu **VdE**, ambitum rk	ambitum
(xxx)	8	et (= ψ)	ac
(xxxi)	38, 4	quam (= π)	quamquam
(xxxii)	10	in ipso **Lr** (= m s), in ipsa v, in solo, *in mg. uel superscr.* ipso **VdE**, in solo k	in ipso solo
(xxxiii)	39, 12	Semonum **k** (= a s), Semonum, *in mg. uel superscr.* Semnonum (Senno- V) **VdE**, senonumᵐ L, Senonum r, Sennonum v	Semnonum
(xxxiv)	45, 19	profertur **L**τ (= c s), perfertur **Vk**	perfertur

Though not free from interpolations and errors of carelessness, β was the best of the apographs of **Y**. Aside from the comparatively short list of its corruptions, the merit of this group is shown by the following readings in which it, with only a few other manuscripts, has maintained the correct tradition: 2, 11 *ei* (= Wm s²), 22, 8 *sed et* (= hm), 40, 1 *largobardos*

(= mh s), and perhaps 28, 14 *germanicae* (= Wh Δ).¹ Furthermore, as we shall see,² β probably maintained the paragraph-division transmitted from Hf. Finally, it transcribed most of the doublets which Y received from Hf.,³ though here and there it tampered with them (xi, xv, xx),⁴ and again created new doublets of its own (vi [?], xx [*numinis*], xxi, xxii, xxvi, xxix, xxxiii).⁵

In spite of the merit of β I can find no convincing evidence that its descent from Hf. was independent of Y. None of its peculiar readings seems to make any contribution toward the restoration of the parent manuscript, unless it be that (vi) *longant* is an ancient variant.⁶ The readings (xxix) *ambitu* and (xxxii) *in ipso* (neither the exclusive property of β), though presumably correct, are clearly late emendations.

A sharp cleavage is to be found between V and L on the one hand and the manuscripts of the τ branch on the other, but it is not quite clear whether L is a descendant of V or both V and L are derived from a common lost apograph (λ) of β.⁷

---

¹ See p. 141, note 2.
² See pp. 264 ff.
³ See pp. 122 ff.
⁴ A similar conflation of doublets is seen in the *halisiosnas* of β (43, 12) for *haliosnas*, a variant of *Helysios*, but this conflated form appears to be as old as Y, since a reads *heliciosna* (see pp. 135 f.). However, we know from the evidence of other MSS. that Y correctly reported the variants (xi) *dulcubuni*, (xv) *aduersarios*, and (xx) *omnis* (see pp. 131, 132, 133).
⁵ The variant (xxii) *Naharualos* was introduced from the second place of this name's occurrence in the next line, where the corruption of *Nahanarualos* to *Naharualos* is at least as old as Hf. Likewise (xxxiii) *Semonum* was taken from 39, 1, where Hf. had the doublets *semnones:semones* (see p. 133).
⁶ On the phonetic confusion between C and G see pp. 247 f.
⁷ The descent of L from V has been maintained by Sepp (1892, 1903), but his arguments are irrelevant, *i.e.* apply equally well to the hypothesis of a common archetype for the two MSS. As he had no facsimiles of the MSS., Sepp was unable to adduce the legitimate evidence for his thesis.

Wissowa (1905, 1–4) seeks to refute Sepp's theory. He maintains (with considerable probability) that the marginal notes in L on ff. 1ᵛ, and 47ᵛ (see p. 351) were copied in from the manuscript's archetype, and that L cannot be Pontanus' copy, but merely an apograph of it. Consequently, says Wissowa, L cannot be a copy of V, since V does not have these notes. But the essential

I first give the readings peculiar to **VL**, and then shall examine in detail the exact nature of the relationship of these two manuscripts.[1]

		VL	ω
(i)	2, 10	Tristonem (*in mg.* Tuisman [2] *V*)	Tuistonem (*uide p. 115*)
(ii)	20	etiam	*om.* τ N ξ, et ω
(iii)	4, 8	assuerunt (*superscr.* int *V*)	assueuerunt (*uel* -int, *cf. p. 109*)
(iv)	6, 17	quidem	quod
(v)	7, 2	etiam	et
(vi)	11	aut (pro-)	et
(vii)	9, 2	Martem concessis animalibus placant et Herculem	Herculem ac (et τ) Martem concessis animalibus placant
(viii)	10, 17	istos	illos
(ix)	19	exploratur (-antur > atur *L*)	explorant
(x)	12, 9	uindicauit	uindicatur

question is not whether **L** is a copy of **V**, but whether it is a *descendant* of **V**. Why could not the immediate archetype of **L**, *i.e.* Pontanus' MS., have been copied from **V**? This point is completely ignored by Wissowa. Neither side of the case has, in my judgment, been given an adequate presentation. But after all, the whole question has little importance for the textual criticism of the *Germania*, since VL can no longer maintain the high position which they have previously held.

[1] Wissowa (1907) and Schönemann have detected the hands of several correctors in **L**, though there is but one (styled *B*[2] by Wissowa) who undertook the task of correction to any noteworthy extent. Schönemann has shown that this corrector drew from the edition of Puteolanus, though not refraining from conjectures of his own. Since the changes made by the correctors are without importance for our classification of the MSS., I take account of them only where, in my judgment, Andresen has failed to distinguish between the original scribe and the corrector, or where the work of the corrector might not be apparent at first sight to one perusing the facsimile of the MS. I use the symbol L[2] indifferently to indicate any change in the text made by a hand other than that of the original scribe.

[2] On the variant *Tuisman* see p. 106.

	VL		ω
(xi)	13, 7	dignitatem (= a)	dignationem
(xii)	14, 11	tuentur	tueare (tuere E, tucantur k)
(xiii)	16, 11	supterraneos	subterraneos
(xiv)	17, 5	Ferunt	gerunt
(xv)	21, 6	aliqua	alia
(xvi)	12	poposcerunt [1]	poposcerit
(xvii)	25, 2	ministris	ministeriis
(xviii)	9–13	liberti... argumentum sunt [2] *ad finem c. 26*	liberti ... argumentum sunt
(xix)	28, 1	autor (= auctor s [2])	auctorum
(xx)	30, 1	Vlerahos (*corr. L* [2])	Vltra hos
(xxi)	1	incohatur (-choa L)	inchoant
(xxii)	5	ac	atque
(xxiii)	35, 5	Nam	tam
(xxiv)	7	maluit	malit
(xxv)	36, 7	fusi	fosi
(xxvi)	37, 6	Sescentesimum	Sexcentesimum
(xxvii)	38, 3	optinent (= Δ bc)	obtinent
(xxviii)	6	Sueuia	Sueui a
(xxix)	40, 4	Veusdigni	Reudigni (Veud- τ)
(xxx)	7	Neithum	Nerthum
(xxxi)	42, 3	parata (= R)	parta
(xxxii)	43, 15	memorat	memorant
(xxxiii)	45, 3	ortum	ortus
(xxxiv)	30	gens continuatur	gentes continuantur

[1] The correction to *poposcerit* in L is by a later hand.

[2] Andresen has failed to note that it is a later hand in L which has written these words in the margin opposite the place where they belong.

	VL		ω
(xxxv)	32	degeneratur[1]	degenerant
(xxxvi)	46, 10	pecudum	peditum
(xxxvii)	9	figunt	fingunt
(xxxviii)	21	difficilem	difficillimam

Other errors or corrections which are probably independent in **VL**, though found in other manuscripts, are: 6, 7 *in mensum* (= Wm); 7, 5 *ne uerberare* (= h σ a s; cf. p. 175); 20, 3 *aut* for *ac* (= m Δ k); 28, 6 *Hircyniam* **V** (= *hyr-* v), *hirciniam*[2] **L** (= s, *hircinam* a); 30, 1 *Hyrcinio* **V**, *hircinio*[3] **L** (= s); 38, 4 *quam* (= π).

These readings show a close relationship between **V** and **L** without indicating that either manuscript is descended from the other. I now turn to the evidence which may be used in favor of the hypothesis that **L** is a descendant of **V**.

i. Ch. 14, 2 *uero* **Vω**, *uiro* **L**. In **V** the back of the *e* is made with a heavy stroke, but the loop with a very fine stroke. The base-curve appears to be divided into two parts. The *uero* of **V** might easily be mistaken for *uiro*.

ii. Ch. 14, 5 **V** reads *ē* (*est* for *eius*) with a dot of deletion underneath. **L** has omitted the word.

iii. Ch. 27, 1 *obseruatur* **Vω**, *obseruant* **L**. In **V** the *-ur* symbol is pushed so far to the left as to cover the *a* as well as the *t*. This might be responsible for the *obseruant* of **L**, though the abbreviation of **V** suggests *-antur* rather than *-ant*.

iv. Ch. 28, 14 *circa* **Vω**, *citra* **L**. In **V** the shoulder of the *r* in conjunction with the following *c* bears a close resemblance to *r*.

v. Ch. 28, 12 *quia*. The reading of **V** is uncertain. After *qu* is a stroke somewhat like *i* or the shaft of *a*, yet sloping

---

[1] Andresen fails to note for **V**. The word is written with the usual *-ur* stroke above the *t* (cf. p. 201).

[2] The correction to *hercyniam* is probably by a later hand.

[3] The correction to *hercinio* is probably by a later hand. On *hir-* for *her-* cf. p. 110.

more to the left than is normal with these strokes in this manuscript. Between the base of this stroke and the *u* is a faint dot (or curve?) suggesting perhaps that the bow of an *a* has been crowded in. Again, at the top and to the right of the stroke there appears to be another very faint dot. In fact, one might read *qui, qua,* or *qux,* but at first sight the word would probably be taken for *qui,* which is the reading of L.

vi. Ch. 28, 14 *germanice* V, *germanę* L. In V the *c* is crowded against the *e* so as to suggest the *ae*-ligature.

vii. Ch. 31, 14 *cura* Vω, *rura* corr. to *cura* L. In general *c* and *r* in V bear considerable resemblance, and here the resemblance is perhaps more marked than usual.

viii. Ch. 40, 5 *Nuithones* Vω, *Nurtones*[1] L. In V the letter *i* bears a close resemblance to a type of *r* frequent in late manuscripts, though not the form of *r* used by the scribe of V.

ix. Ch. 45, 24 *sudantur* (?) V, *sudant* L. In V there seems to be a broken diagonal stroke above the final *t* of *sudant,* but it is quite different from the usual *-ur* stroke in this manuscript. Since Andresen reports *sudant* for both manuscripts, I suspect that what appears to be a pen stroke is really nothing more than a blemish in the paper.

If L is a descendant of V, the latter might be a direct copy of β. There are two or three details which would make such a supposition attractive. Ch. 37, 9, V reads *Con,* τ has *conuentum,* L has the reading of the other manuscripts, *consulatum.* Again, 37, 15 V has *obiecer* for *obiecerit;* τ and L have *obiecerunt.* Obviously in both places V has preserved the abbreviations of β which produced the errors in τ. While it is certainly not beyond the range of probability that these abbreviations were maintained through two generations of manuscripts ($\beta > \lambda > V$), yet it is simpler to suppose that they were taken over by V directly from β. Furthermore, the general excellence of V (cf. p. 202) makes it desirable to have as few manuscripts as possible intervening between it and Hf.

[1] The superscript *i* seems to be by the first hand.

Finally, I will mention one more bit of evidence, though I do not attach great importance to it. In V at the close of the *Dialogus* is found the following note: *Ego tantum repperi et meliusculum feci.* Now if **VL** are descended from a common archetype λ, **V** is a surprisingly accurate copy of this manuscript, and one is at a loss to understand the scribe's confession of interpolation. But the situation is very different if all the readings just noted as peculiar to **VL** originated with the copyist of **V**. Yet the very presence of the note could, I suppose, be taken as an indication of the conscientiousness of the scribe, while the diminutive *meliusculum* may have been used advisedly to refer to changes in orthography, etc.

I now pass to the evidence that **L** is not a descendant of **V**. First, it may be shown that some of the readings adduced above (i–ix) do not argue so strongly for the opposite hypothesis as might at first appear.

(i). With *uiro* in **L** we may compare 22, 6 *crebrae*. Here the copyist of **L** first wrote *cri*, then immediately (to judge from the spacing) changed *i* to *e* and wrote *i* above the line. At this point the *e* of **V** would not readily be taken for *i*. We may then suppose that an *e* resembling *i* was a feature of a common archetype of **VL**.

(viii). That the *Nurtones* of **L** was caused, not by the form of *i* in **V**, but by the form of that letter in a common archetype is suggested by the reading *Neithum* (for *Nerthum*) in both manuscripts, 40, 7.

Finally, in the other cases which may appear to show that **V** is the archetype of **L** this is not the only explanation possible. May we not rather suppose that the conscientious copyist of **V**, when in doubt as to the reading of his archetype, sought to give a diplomatic reproduction of its text?[1]

Let us now look at the readings in which **L** agrees with the other manuscripts in general or with the other manuscripts of the β group contrary to **V**:

[1] In 28, 12 (v) it seems almost certain that **V** has attempted to reproduce some abbreviation for *quia* found in the archetype. This would also seem to be the better explanation in iii (cf. below, p. 201).

200   The Germania of Tacitus

			V	L
(i)	5,	8	nauigauerint	negauerint (= ω)
(ii)		10	etiam	et (= ω)
(iii)	6,	11	uariare (= X σ φ s)	uarietate (= τ ξ)
(iv)	9,	3	suenorum	sueuorum (= ω)
(v)	10,	11	getis	gentis (= ω)
(vi)	15,	1	uotiens [1]	quotiens (= ω)
(vii)		5	hebent (= **Ek mh N s**)	habent (= *dvr m a φ*, haḃent **W**)
(viii)	30,	4	Hircynius (= hirtinus *v*, hircinius *s*)	hercinius (= ω)
(ix)	33,	2	bructeriis	bructeris (= ω)
(x)	35,	6	chāci	chauci (= ω)
(xi)	39,	5	celebant	celebrant (= ω)
(xii)	42,	6	arcomanis [1]	marcomanis (= ω)
(xiii)		7	Marabodui	marobodui (= ω)
(xiv)	44,	4	Lemouii (= *v W σ w eu*)	lemonii (= ω)
(xv)	45,	19	perfertur (= *k X a φ*)	profertur (= τ c s)

Now **L** is a scholarly edition, either the manuscript itself or its immediate archetype being the work of Pontanus. Certainly a scholar of far less critical acumen than Pontanus possessed could have corrected *suo Marte* most of the errors of **V** just shown.[2] Yet there are five readings which would hardly have made their way into **L** except from a manuscript

---

[1] The rubricator failed to place the initial letter in the margin.

[2] In iv, ix, x, xii, the correct forms could have been restored from other places in the text. On the supposition that **L** is a descendant, but not a *direct* copy of **V** the change (xiv) from *Lemouii* to *lemonii* might be accidental.

source: (iii) *uarietate*, (vii) *habent*, (viii) *hercinius*,[1] (xiii) *marobodui*,[2] (xv) *profertur*.

There are other bits of evidence which point to the existence of an archetype (λ) common to **VL**. Three of the errors peculiar to **VL**, (ix) [3] *exploratur*, (xxi) *incohatur*, (xxxiv) *continuatur*, were due to the misunderstanding of the line of suspension for *n* as the *-ur* symbol.[4] Now in ix **L** originally had *explorātur*, which implies that in its archetype the line of suspension was at first understood to do double duty for *n* and for *-ur*.[5] In this case the archetype of **L** was not **V**, for the latter has *exploratur* written out. Again, **VL** have twice written *p* for *b* before *t* (xiii, xxvii), but a third instance (35, 4 *optenditur*) is found in **L** alone, which suggests that this spelling was a feature of an archetype common to the two manuscripts rather than an innovation of **V** or **L**. Quite possibly a connection between **L** and **E** through β is to be found in the reading (42, 3) *etiam ipsa* (= h).[6]

All in all, I feel reasonably certain that **L** is not a descendant of **V**, but that both manuscripts are to be referred to a common archetype λ. Thus far I concur in the generally accepted view, but another belief which is commonly held must, in my opinion, be discarded. I refer to the hypothesis that the archetype of **VL** was a copy of **Hf**. As I have stated, to prove that a group of manuscripts has an independent line of descent from a given archetype, we must show that it is an "ultimate"

[1] Naturally a scholar might have been familiar with the spelling *Hercinius*, but why should he have made this change from *hir-* to *her-* but not in 28, 6, and 30, 1? In these two places the superscript *e* in **L** is, I am almost certain, by a later hand.

[2] The spelling *Maroboduus* is found in *Ann.* II and III, but this part of the *Annals* was unknown to Pontanus.

[3] The Roman numerals refer to the table of readings shown on pp. 195 ff.

[4] Also in xxxv the abbreviation in **V** cannot well mean anything other than *-ur*, though it is perhaps reminiscent of the line of suspension for *n* which existed in λ, just as seems to be the case with *religatur*, 38, 10 (see xix, p. 192).

[5] Conversely, 27, 1 *obseruatur*, the *-ur* symbol of the archetype, which seems to have been reproduced by **V**, has been mistaken for *n* by **L** (cf. p. 197).

[6] In **E** the correct order has been indicated by diagonal lines above the words. Was this so indicated in β?

group, *i.e.* that it does not form part of a larger division of manuscripts. Applying this test to λ, we find that it forms a part of the larger division β, which in turn is a part of the still larger division Y. Likewise, if we test λ on the merit of its peculiar readings we fail to find the slightest justification for the belief that it represents a distinct line of descent from Hf. Of the peculiar readings of λ only two can be said to possess *per se* any merit: (xxvi) *Sescentesimum*, (xxxvii) *figunt*.[1] This certainly does not mean that λ here preserved the readings of Hf., but merely that it successfully corrected errors which existed in the parent manuscript.

Among our manuscripts V can justly lay claim to an excellence second only to that of W. It is a surprisingly accurate copy of the lost λ, and whatever faults it has are almost all inherited ones rather than errors of its own copyist. Of the manuscripts of the β group V alone, in conjunction with the Viennese edition of 1500,[2] has preserved the title of the *Germania* as it existed in Hf.,[3] and, unless I am much mistaken, it alone of the entire Y family, again with the same edition, has maintained the paragraphing of Hf.[4] V also exhibits a certain excellence in orthographical matters,[5] though I think it doubtful whether it has therein kept an unbroken line of tradition from the parent manuscript.[6]

L has deservedly fallen from the high position of authority which it once held. As Wissowa has remarked, this manuscript's importance lies chiefly in the record that it offers of the labors of renaissance scholars in copying, interpreting, and

---

[1] See pp. 195 ff.
[2] See pp. 209 ff.
[3] See p. 11.
[4] See pp. 264 ff.
[5] See pp. 235 ff.
[6] It may be noted that 10, 22, V reads *pro iudicio*, which affords a paralle, with the *pro iudicio* of Rudolf of Fulda (see *testimonia ad loc.*). Likewise the MS. Δ offers *pro iudicio*. Naturally I regard these readings as mere coincidences, and do not feel the slightest doubt that Hf. read *pro praeiudicio* with the majority of our MSS.

emending their ancient authors.[1] It is generally believed that L is not the copy made by Pontanus, but only an apograph of this copy,[2] though Ullman is of the opinion that the writing is identical with a certain type of script employed by Pontanus.[3]

The τ Branch

The remaining manuscripts of the β group descend from a lost apograph of β which I call τ:[4]

		τ (dETvrok)	ω
(i)	5, 18	quoque *om.* (= *a*)	quoque
(ii)	6, 16	Centini **dvro** (= *M*, Centeini *p*) Centeni **Er**	centeni
(iii)	10, 12	candi **dvok** (= *M*), candi **E**, candidi [5] **r** (di above)	candidi
(iv)	11, 9	iniussi (= *p*, in iussu *M*; ut iussi *r*)	ut iussi (ut *om.* λχ *b*π)
(v)	10	coetium (-tuum *Eo*, coeuntium *r*)	coeuntium
(vi)	13, 4	ipsi (= *pM in mg.*; pater *r*)	pater
(vii)	14	et electorum	electorum

[1] Wissowa 1907, xxxii.
[2] See Wissowa 1907, xviii.
[3] Cf. W. Peterson, "The Dialogus of Tacitus," *American Journal of Philology* xxxiv (1913), 13, note 1. Professor Ullman has also expressed this conviction to me in person. Even if L is the work of Pontanus, it is not necessarily a direct copy of λ. I have found some evidence in the *de Grammaticis* to show that there was an intervening MS. (Robinson 1922, 181).
[4] At least this seems to be the most satisfactory explanation. Nevertheless, it is just possible that the readings which I ascribe to τ were already in β, and that λ corrected these errors from some source outside of β. But since this source does not reveal itself in the readings of λ, I reject the alternative. Yet cf. p. 211, note 2.
[5] On the restorations in r see pp. 190, 208. On the conflated text of **pM** see pp. 186 f.

204   The Germania of Tacitus

                    τ (dETvrok)   ω

(viii)	16	cuique *om*.	cuique
(ix)	14, 8	adolescentum	adolescentium
(x)	16, 4	et *om*.	et
(xi)	14	populatio (populatur *r*)	populatur
(xii)	14	ignoranter (= *p*; -tur *r*)	ignorantur
(xiii)	18, 16	renuntiant [1] (= *pM*)	denuntiant
(xiv)	16	sic uiuentes sic parientes (= *p in mg.*)	sic uiuendum sic pariendum
(xv)	19, 15	finere E, funere dv, finuere k, finire r	finire
(xvi)	20, 6	inexaucta E, inexauta dvk, inexhausta r	inexhausta
(xvii)	25, 5	Verberant (= *pM in mg.*)	uerberare
(xviii)	8	est *om*. (= *pM*)	est
(xix)	28, 21	collati (= *pM in mg.*; collocati *r*)	collocati
(xx)	29, 18	par	pars
(xxi)	35, 2	A (Ac *r*)	ac
(xxii)	6	sed	sed et
(xxiii)	11	iniuriam	iniurias
(xxiv)	37, 8	si *om*.	si
(xxv)	9	conuentum [2] (consulatum *r*)	consulatum
(xxvi)	39, 6	horrentia	horrenda
(xxvii)	42, 7	Trudi	Tudri

[1] The reading may have been a variant in β, as it is found in the edition of 1500 (see p. 210).

[2] Cf. *con*^(tu;) in V, which has evidently retained the abbreviation of β which produced the error in τ.

The Extant Manuscripts of the Germania

		τ (dETvrok)		ω
(xxviii)	45, 16	quae uero (queue, *in mg.* $\overline{uo}$ *E*)	*in*	quae ue [1]

The following readings, though found in other manuscripts, may be regarded as of independent origin in τ: [2]

(xxix)	2, 10	Tuisconem (= *h in mg.*, *t e s*)	Tuistonem (*uarietas lectionis in p. 115 est uidenda*)
(xxx)	28, 7	boi (= *ba*)	boii (beii π)
(xxxi)	37, 17	Mallio **dErk**, Malio **v** (= *m*)	manlio (manilio φ)
(xxxii)	45, 23	ergo (= *s*)	igitur
(xxxiii)	46, 13	Sola (= *t a s*)	solae
(xxxiv)	19	illaborare (= ξ *le*)	inlaborare

A few other variants, which are found in only part of the group, would seem to have had their origin in τ:[3] 2, 5 *urbe* **vr** (= *s*); 14 *deos* (= φ *s²*); 11, 4 *inciderit* **Ek**; 13, 10 *etiam et ipse* **Erk**; 15, 3 *penatum* **Er** (= *bRA*); 18, 15 *equs* **dk**, *equis* **v**; 16 *alr data parata arma* **v**, *parata*, in mg. *al' data* **d**, *parata* **k**.[4]

There is just one reading peculiar to the τ branch which *ceteris paribus* should be accepted as genuine, (vii) *et electorum*, for it can hardly be an interpolation. On the other hand, it is highly improbable that this group alone would preserve the true tradition. I suggest the following explanation for the presence of the *et*. In 16, 4 (x) τ omits *et*. Probably the omission was originally made in β, but the *et* was added in the extreme left margin of the page. In the transcription of τ this marginal *et* was erroneously incorporated in the text of the preceding page [5] (between *semper* and *electorum*).

---

[1] Cf. p. 261.

[2] Also see p. 114, xlvii.

[3] At least, save for **ro** (see p. 208), I can establish no relationship between the MSS. of the group other than their common descent from τ.

[4] Also see p. 328 on the Gensberg edition.

[5] We may note that in **E** there is almost exactly a page of writing intervening between the two passages.

Of the conjectural emendations of τ only (xxxi) *Mallio* should be accepted.[1] The correction of (xxxiii) *solac* to *sola* seems to me unnecessary.

E and T

Although not even the shadow of probability can, in my judgment, be attached to Annibaldi's contention that **E** is a direct copy of Hf.,[2] he is undoubtedly correct in declaring **T** to be a copy of **E**.[3] Those who have denied this [4] have been

[1] I suspect that even this, in its inception at least, was not an emendation but an error: *Mālio* (so in V) > *Malio* > *Mallio*.

[2] 1907, 165 ff.; 1910, 10 ff. To be sure, **E** and its more recently discovered cogener **d** are important for the restoration of β and τ, and possess considerable merit in the fidelity with which they have recorded the doublets transmitted from Hf. through **Y**, β, τ, but, if neither β nor τ can claim an independent line of descent from the parent MS., far less can such a claim be made for the single MS. **E**. Surely if **E** were a direct copy of Hf. it would make some contribution of its own toward the restoration of this lost archetype. But, as a matter of fact, the readings peculiar to **E** (and its copy **T**) are almost without exception the most inept blunders. Annibaldi's statement regarding the merit of the text of **E** is not substantiated by the evidence (1907, 165): "Nessuno degli altri codici, se si eccetui il Toledano . . . ci offre una lezione cosi corretta e completa come il nostro E. . . ." As it happens, the relative merit of the individual MSS. is not the primary concern of the editor of the *Germania*, but certainly **E** cannot compare in excellence with either **W** or **V**.

Even the external arguments adduced by Annibaldi are outweighed by another external argument, as Wissowa (1907, xii–xiii) has shown. The Hersfeld codex contained the *Germania*, *Agricola*, *Dialogus*, and *de Grammaticis et Rhetoribus*. Now six of our fifteenth-century MSS. (W, NIM, VL) have the *Germania*, *Dialogus*, and *de Grammaticis*, but do not have the *Agricola*. It is true that one MS. (Δ) does have all four works, but this is a MS. of miscellaneous content, and even inserts an extraneous work between the *de Grammaticis* and *Agricola* (see pp. 80 f.). The internal evidence of Δ shows that this MS. can neither be a copy of Hf. nor represent a line of tradition begun before the division of this lost archetype. In fact, Δ did not even draw the *de Grammaticis* from the same source from which it drew the *Germania* and *Dialogus*. For the *Germania*, and presumably for the *Dialogus*, the line of descent is: Hf. > Y > α > σ > Δ. The *de Grammaticis* in Δ is yet two degrees further removed from Hf.: > Y > α > ξ > θ > ε > Δ (see Robinson 1922, 171–177, 189 f., and p. 190 of the present work). If it is permissible to draw any conclusion from the *ex silentio* evidence of our extant MSS., this conclusion must be that the *Agricola* was separated from the rest of the Hersfeld codex before any copy was made.

[3] Annibaldi 1907, 168–170; 1910, 70–76.

[4] Gudeman 1928, 376, note 1; Jäkel, 29 ff.

led astray by Abbott's collation of **T**, which has failed to note some of the readings of this manuscript and at times to distinguish between the errors of the first hand and the corrections of the second.[1]

The following readings show how closely **T** has reproduced the errors of **E**: 1, 9 *norie* in mg. **E**, *none* in mg. **T**; 11 *Septimus* > *-mum*; 2, 12 *equorum* **E**, *é,quorum*[2] **T**; 3, 12 *asciburgumque*[2]; 12 *colitur* (corr. **T**[2]); 5, 1 $\overline{spe}$ **E**, *spem* > *spei* **T**; 7, 8 *-que* om. (= *W*); 10, 20 *depopularium*; 11, 12 *tantum* in mg.; 13, 8 *adolescentibus*; 14, 2 *virtute principem*; 10 *ancipiatia* > *ancipitia*; 12 *illamque*; 17, 10 *admictibus*; 19, 1 *pudicitię* **E**, *-tie*[2] **T**; 15 *finere* **E**, *sinere* > *finere* **T**; 20, 1 *atque* (= *R*); 6 *inexaucta*; 22, 2 *hyemis* (= ψ); 12 *aut* for *nec*; 27, 4 *equis*; 28, 19 *Aggripinenses*; 20 *Trangressi*[2]; 29, 1 *praecipui* om.[2]; 2 *Cathorum*, and so always except 30, 1 *Cathi* **E**, *cati* **T**, 35, 5 *chatos*, 36, 6 *Chattis*; 30, 8 *occīōes*, in mg. *occasiones*; 31, 2 *conuentum* for *consensum*; 32, 8 *natui*; 33, 5 *inuidere* om.; 5 *supra* **E**, *sūp*[2] **T**; 34, 7 *illis* in mg.; 9 *consueuimus* in mg. (= *h aR* in text); 35, 2 *Septemtrioni* **E**, *septentrioni* > *-nem* **T**; 10 *iurium*[2]; 36, 1 *et*, superscr. *ac*; 37, 10 *diu in Germania*; 22 *uersae* om.; 38, 4 *comuni* **E**, $\overline{comuni}$ **T**; 5 *Sicut*, in mg. *sic*; 8 $q\overline{d}$ (*quod*) **E**, *quid* **T**; 40, 2 *cuncti*; 7 *Nertum*; 18 *Seui*; 42, 3 *ët īpa*; 44, 15 *causa*; 45, 25 *terrisque . . . solis* om.; 27 *exsudant* (= *NR*); 46, 24 *ego* om.

Aside from a few purely orthographical variations, the readings in which **T** agrees with other manuscripts contrary to **E** are very few [3] and may easily be explained as independent corrections or errors of the scribe of the former manuscript: 2, 19 *sū* with an erasure following **E**, *sint* **T**ω; 6, 13 *ęstimanti* **E**, *extimanti* **T** (= ϕ); 11, 11 *absumitur* **E**, *assumitur* **T** (= *W ms*[2] π); [4]

---

[1] I have before me photostats of **T**. As for **E**, Annibaldi's diplomatic text, upon which I have had to rely, is not flawless, since two discrepancies are to be found between it and his photographic facsimile of f. 69[r]: 14, 8, the facsimile shows *cum* not *tum*; 15, 5 *cum iisdem* with *s* expunctuated, while the diplomatic text does not note the deletion.

[2] Not noted for **T** by Abbott.

[3] I suspect that a re-examination of **E** might reduce even this number.

[4] See pp. 124 f.

14, 8 *cum* **E**, *tum* **Tω**; 17, 6 *exquisitus* **E**, *exquisitius* **Tω**; 9 *iuris* **E**, *uiris* **Tω**; 39, 11 *auctoritate* **E**, *-tem* **Tω**.

Corruptions are, of course, more numerous in **T** than in **E**, as might be expected of the apograph. A few corrections have been made in **T** by a second hand, which may have drawn from **w**: 1, 11 *enim* added after *septimum*; 2, 11 *ei*>*et*; 13, 3 *Cum*> *Tum eum*; 16, 1 *Nullos* (*Nullis* **E**) . . . *populos*> *Nullas* . . . *populis*.

r and o

Yet another series of errors is found in **r** and **o**: 2, 13 *uocantur*; 3, 3 *carquorum* for *carmina quorum*; 5 *aurantur* for *augurantur*; 5, 12 *muneri* om.; 6, 13 *penes* om.; 12, 8 *coniuncti* (cf. *conuincti* v). **r** cannot be a copy of **o** since the latter is a mere fragment. The contrary cannot be the case, since **o** does not have the readings which **r** has borrowed from one of the φ group. Again, 12, 4, **r** has *insuper crate iniecta*, while **o** has the same order as the other manuscripts; 6, 14, **r** alone omits *congruente*; 6, 12, **r** has only *cuncto*, while **o** preserves the doublets *cuncto:coniuncto*. We must, therefore, assume that there was another manuscript, now lost, intervening between τ and **ro**.

An examination of the readings peculiar to β and τ shows that **r** has frequently corrected the errors originating in these manuscripts.[1] The source of these corrections appears to have been some manuscript of the φ group, as is shown by the following readings peculiar to **r** and φ: 10, 11 *equorumque* (= *I*); 14, 13 *compti*; 20, 7 *iuuentus* **r R**, *iuuentas* φ; 21, 8 *deficere*; 26, 4 *dignitatem*; 27, 4 *igitur* **r** in mg., φ (= *I*); 36, 6 *uagantur*; 38, 2 *partem germaniae* **r b** π; 8 *in mutatione* **r**, *mutatione* ψ; 43, 5 *aut emigenis* **r** in mg., φ; 45, 10 *omnium cuique* **r**, *omnium quique* φ. It is not clear from which particular manuscript of the φ group **r** borrowed. In 11, 9, **r** has restored *ut iussi*, which is known only to a1 of the extant manuscripts of φ, and in 2, 18, only **r** and **a** have *expulerunt*, yet **a** reads, 38, 2 *germanie partem*, 8 *imitatione*, 43, 5 *etiam emigenis*.

[1] See pp. 191 ff., 203 ff.

k and Mon. 947

The fragmentary manuscript, Monacensis 947, appears to be a copy of the Nuremberg edition of Creusner (**k**). The two are almost identical, offering the following readings in common: 15, 7 *iurium* (for *uiritim*); 16, 7 *scementorum*; 19, 9 *uocantur*; 15 *finuere*; 21, 4 *utilitate* (for *utiliter*); 22, 6 *probum*; 29, 4 *honus*; 30, 8 *necessitates* (for *occasiones*); 34, 7 *tentauerim*; 37, 8 *Sapino* (cf. *Sapiro* **v**); 40, 18 *Sueui* (for *serui*).

In addition to offering the complete text, the edition appears to be slightly less corrupt than the manuscript. Note the following variations: 10, 2 *descisam* Mon., *decisam* **k**; 11, 5 *auspicissimum* Mon., *auspicacissimum* **k**; 17 *ascensus* Mon., *assensus* **k**; 12, 4 *paludi* Mon., *palude* **k**; 13, 6 *reipuplicae* Mon., *reipublicae* **k**; 14, 11 *liberalite* Mon., *liberalitate* **k**; 18, 17 *inuoluta* Mon., *inuolata* **k**; 19, 5 *adcisam* Mon., *Adcisis* **k**; 20, 3 *aut* Mon., *ac* **k**; 25, 1 *seruis* om. Mon., *seruis* **k**; 37, 17 *Malleo* Mon., *Mallio* **k**; 21 *pertulerunt* Mon., *perculerunt* **k**.[1]

Vienna edition, 1500

There is another representative of the β group, which I have heretofore left out of consideration. I refer to the edition of the *Germania* said to have issued from the press of Johann Winterburg, Vienna, 1500 (*ed. Vind.*). This edition presents a conflated text drawn from **w** or one of its reimpressions and from some member of the β group. Its connection with **w** is shown by the readings, 7, 12 *ululatus feminarum*, 22, 8 *inimiciciis*, 40, 1 *longobardis*. The immediate source was probably the recension of Puteolanus,[2] as is indicated by 28, 18 *Vbii* (*nubii* ω). With β *ed. Vind.* has the following readings in common: 1, 10 *pluris*; 5, 11 *perinde*; 7, 2 *aut libera*; 14 *aut exigere*; 9, 2 *et Martem*; 11, 12 *tamen*; 16, 4 *longant*; 26, 3 *in uices*; 33, 9 *urgentibus iam*; 34, 1 *Thasuarii*; 8 *magnum*; 37, 8 *et*; 18 *trisque*; 39, 12 *Semonum*; 45, 11 *hostis*; 27 *igni*.

---

[1] Wherever *Mon.* presents a better reading than **k** (*e.g.* 40, 9, *nemus* repeated in *k*), it is merely because the scribe has corrected certain obvious typographical errors.

[2] See pp. 327 f.

210   THE GERMANIA OF TACITUS

In general the text of **w** and β will account for the readings of *ed. Vind.*, though there are numerous exceptions. In 2, 20, *ed. Vind.* reads *mox et*, where **w** (ξ) and τ omit *et* and λ has *mox etiam*; 38, 10, it reads *religant*, while **w** (α) has *ligant* and β *religatur*;[1] 31, 13 it offers *cultu*, though **w** (α) and β know only *uultu*, and 28, 8 *signatque*, which elsewhere occurs only in the **X** family. Furthermore, *ed. Vind.* has three readings peculiar to τ: 2, 10 *Tuisconem* (*tuistonem* **w**, *tristonem* λ), 14, 8 *adolescentum*, 18, 16 *renunciant;* also, 43, 13 it reads *regionis* with τ, where **w** (ξ) and λ have *religionis*.[2] With λ *ed. Vind.* has a larger number of readings in common: 7, 5 *ne uerberare*, 37, 6 *Sescentesimum*, 38, 3 *optinent*, 6, *Sueuia*, 45, 30 *gens continuatur*, 46, 10 *pecudum*, 46, 21 *difficilem*. It also reads with λ, 11, 9 *nec ut iussi* (*nec iniussi* τ, *nec iussi* **w**), 30, 10 *Romane* (*ratione* τ **w** [α]), 46, 24 *uultusque corpora* (*uultusque et corpora* τ **w** [α]). *Ed. Vind.* has none of the readings peculiar to **V** alone, but agrees with this manuscript in offering the title and paragraph-division as I believe them to have been in Hf.[3]

Finally, *ed. Vind.* has a number of conjectural emendations: 1, 1 *galiis* (= a, u², Lipsius); 2, 11 *Cui* for *ei* (β) or *et* (α); 13, 3 *Tum in* (*Cum in* β, *Tum eum* **w**); 15, 5 *habitant* (*habent* **w**, *habent* or *hebent* β); 20, 12 *et animum* (= m); 17 *tanto* (*gratior*) om.; 38, 10 *solo in uertice;* 41, 1 *pars Sueuorum* (= u², Rhenanus); 42, 5 *porrigitur;* 43, 15 *ei numini* (*eius numinis* **w** [ξ], *ea uis numini* β). *Ed. Vind.* is the work of a scholar, who as a rule employed sound critical judgment in selecting the readings of his two sources. It is perhaps significant that in 28, 10 *a Boiis*, 37, 1 *situm*, 39, 3 f. *patrium, sacrum, eiusdemque*, 44, 7 *ipse in oceanum*, 45, 7 *Seuici*, 25 *radius*, he preferred the readings of β to the *ab Osis, sinum, patrum, sacram, eiusdem, ipsae in oceano, Sueuici*, and *radiis* of **w**.[4] Apparently he

[1] Yet β itself may have had *religant* with the line of suspension for *n* easily mistakable for the *ur* symbol (cf. pp. 192, 201).

[2] See p. 140.

[3] See pp. 11 and 264 ff. In the matter of paragraph-division *ed. Vind.* assumes a certain importance for the restoration of Hf.

[4] But 13, 12 *principium. Cui* with **w**.

regarded β as the more authoritative of his two sources. *Ed. Vind.* is probably the best of the early printed editions of the *Germania*. Were it not marred by frequent typographical errors it would be incomparably superior to the other early editions.[1]

It is impossible to determine with exactitude from which member of the β group *ed. Vind.* drew. I believe that τ may be excluded, since it has so little in common with the edition.[2] I am also inclined to exclude **V**, since it and *ed. Vind.* conspire only where they give the genuine tradition, and since in a few instances the edition appears to have preserved the paragraph-division more faithfully than has **V**.[3] There remain as possible sources of *ed. Vind.* β itself and λ, and of the two λ seems to have rather the better claim.

g. The φ Group

The third apograph of **Y**, which I call φ,[4] and which, like the others, is missing, has left a numerous and very corrupt progeny, the manuscripts **baluezRAc**. Of these **b** and **a** may be regarded as independent copies of φ. The remaining manuscripts present a new series of corruptions which show that they are descended from a lost apograph of φ, which I style π. Again, there is a line of cleavage between **l** and the remaining manuscripts, which indicates that **l** was a copy of π, but that the rest are descended from a lost apograph of π, which I have named ψ. In the following table I attempt to give all the readings peculiar to the φ group as a whole, for this group in spite of its manifold corruptions does have importance in conjunction with other manuscripts for the restoration of Hf.

[1] See p. 329.

[2] Yet this forces us to assign 18, 16 *renuntiant* as a variant to β. Perhaps we here have evidence that τ was not an apograph of β, but that the MSS. of the τ branch really offer the text of β in contrast with a conflated text of λ (cf. p. 203, note 4).

[3] See p. 265, note 1.

[4] This is the symbol used by Rand (1905) for the MS. which I call **e**. Its extension to cover the entire groups seems appropriate, since Rand (309) has quite rightly regarded this MS. as typical of its *stirps*.

		φ	ω
(i)	1, 3	latus (= v)	latos
(ii)	11	haurit	hauritur
(iii)	2, 4	aduersis bπ, aduersus a	aduersus
(iv)	8	si *om.* (= L) ([quam] non a)	si (om. L)
(v)	11	eius	ei **Wms**² β, et h *ex sil.*, a s
(vi)	11	magno (manno a)	manno
(vii)	13	hermimones (homines b, -memo- u, -mino- A)	herminones *uel* hermiones [1]
(viii)	15	uandilos (-dal- *a l*)	uandilios (uandalios ξ L, vandalos h, uandulos r)
(ix)	20	omnis (*om. a*)	omnes
(x)	3, 3	Bardicum (blandicum a)	Barditum *uel* Baritum [2]
(xi)	4, 1	Item	Ipse
(xii)	7	potentia	patientia
(xiii)	5, 9	aurum argentumue (arg- au- b)	argentum aurumue
(xiv)	13	utilitate (= f)	uilitate
(xv)	6, 13	exstimanti b, extimati ψ, aestimanti al	aestimanti (existimanti σ pM)
(xvi)	7, 9	fortissimis	fortitudinis
(xvii)	8, 1	apud quasdam	quasdam
(xviii)	4	efficiati (offiti- a)	efficacius
(xix)	8	ueledum (uelle dum b, *om. R*)	Veledam

[1] See above, p. 112.
[2] See above, p. 123.

The Extant Manuscripts of the Germania

		φ	ω
(xx)	9	numerus b, minus a, nūīs ue, ūus R, nu̱me̱ri̱s̱ ruinis c, numeris z, numinis lA	numinis
(xxi)	9	habitatam (habitam lRe)	habitam
(xxii)	9	dum (olim a)	olim
(xxiii)	9, 2	hurnis (humanis a)	humanis
(xxiv)	8	& (= r) (ex al)	ex
(xxv)	10	id	illud
(xxvi)	10, 9	id (hic z)	illud
(xxvii)	11	equorumque (= I r)	equorum quoque
(xxviii)	11, 4	impletur luna aut inchoatur	inchoatur luna aut impletur
(xxix)	9	Id	Illud
(xxx)	9	iussi (= Δχ) (ut iussi l, ut iussu a)	ut iussi (iniussi τ)
(xxxi)	16	aspernatur (-ntur a)	aspernantur
(xxxii)	12, 1	discrimine	discrimen
(xxxiii)	4	pro crate b, proiecte R, pocrate ulAz, potrate c, rate a, crate e	et crate (gra-) Wh, crate (gr-) ω [1]
(xxxiv)	6	opinamur (opermium a)	puniuntur
(xxxv)	9	iudicantur (-catur a)	qui uindicatur
(xxxvi)	13, 1	nihil (nisi a)	nisi
(xxxvii)	6	par [2] (parum a, pro- c)	pars

[1] See above, pp. 144 f.
[2] My collation does not show this reading for R.

214 The Germania of Tacitus

			φ	ω
(xxxviii)		7	inclita (molita *b*, inclitaque *u*, indita *A*)	merita
(xxxix)		10	ipse etiam (etiam *om. R*, etiam ipse *e*)	etiam ipse
(xl)		13	super	semper
(xli)	14,	3	infamem in (infame in *b*)	infame in (infamem *Whs* [2])
(xlii)		3	probosum **b**ψ, probrosum **al**	probrosum
(xliii)		5	principum (= χ) **aule** *z*, principium **bRA**, princ.ᵐ **c**	praecipuum
(xliv)		6	Princeps ... pugnat	Principes ... pugnant
(xlv)		11	libertate [1]	liberalitate
(xlvi)		13	compti (= *r*)	incompti
(xlvii)	15,	3	delicata (deligata *b*, delicta *R*, *om. A*)	delegata
(xlviii)		4	seniliam **b**, senibus **a**, inseniliam (*om. l*) π	senibusque
(xlix)		10	sententiarum (suarum *a*, sententiam *Rz*) generum (-tum *A*, gentium *a*, gnūm *z*)	finitimarum gentium
(l)	16,	2	interest (inter eos *e*, inter se *a*)	inter se
(li)		12	suffugiunt (suffugium *ae*)	suffugium
(lii)	18,	2	laudis (laudant *a*, laudas *u*, laudes *e*)	laudaueris
(liii)		2	proprie	prope
(liv)		5	marito *om.*	marito

[1] The same error was made in **m**, but corrected by the first hand.

The Extant Manuscripts of the Germania

		φ		ω
(lv)		6	propinqui qui [1]	propinqui
(lvi)		10	armatorum (armorum *aec*)	armorum
(lvii)		17	inmolata ($\bar{y}$mo lata *b*, in violata *a*)	inuiolata
(lviii)	19,	6	urbem (uerberans *a*, u'bē *R*, urbis *e*)	uerbere
(lix)		8	enim *om.* [2]	enim
(lx)		9	nec (= *W v*)	et
(lxi)		12	nec (neque *R*)	ne
(lxii)		13	cognatio	cogitatio
(lxiii)	20,	3	non	nec
(lxiv)		4	dinoscas . . . uirtus *om.*	dinoscas . . . uirtus
(lxv)		6	agnoscas (cogn- *b*)	agnoscat
(lxvi)		6	cohique (cohitque *R*, coireque *l*, denique *a*)	eoque
(lxvii)		7	iuuentas (iuuentus *R*)	iuuenta
(lxviii)		8	partes	pares
(lxix)		12	accipiundis [2,1] (acapiundis *b*, accipiendis *a*, accipiens *A*)	accipiendis
(lxx)		16	quanto *om.*	quanto (plus)
(lxxi)		17	generosior [3]	gratiosior *uel* gratior
(lxxii)	21,	4	recipit	recipitque

[1] My collation does not show this reading for c.
[2] My collation does not show this reading for R.
[3] My collation does not show this reading for l.

			φ	ω
(lxxiii)		6	conuinctibus **Acz**, conuintibus **b**, comitibus **l**, coniunctionibus **R**, Coniunctis **u** Convictibus **a**	conuictibus
(lxxiv)		6	est	effusius
(lxxv)		6	indulget . . . excipit *om.*	indulget . . . excipit
(lxxvi)		8	deficere (= *r*) (deficit *e*, deficerem *b*, deficiem *A*, deffitiem *c*)	defecere (-rit *N*, -ret *I*, deficeret Δ)
(lxxvii)		10	in inuitati **aRu**, inuitati **le**, imitati **b**, in mutati **Ac**, inmuitati **z**	non inuitati
(lxxviii)	22,	2	calida aqua (aqua *om. b*)	calida (aqua calida *s*)
(lxxix)		6	conuiuiis (*om. a*)	conuiciis (-ti-)
(lxxx)		7	saepius *om.*	saepius
(lxxxi)		11	cognationes (cognatos *a*)	cogitationes
(lxxxii)	23,	3	simplicis	simplices
(lxxxiii)	24,	6	quidem	quod
(lxxxiv)		6	seua (sena *bA*, scena *c*, sua *z*, seria *a*)	seria
(lxxxv)	25,	9	aliquid [1] (*om. b*)	aliquod
(lxxxvi)	26,	2	ager **bl**, agrum **a**, agitur **uRAz**, igitur **c**, agri **e**, **l** *in mg.*	agri
(lxxxvii)		4	dignitatem (= *r*)	dignationem
(lxxxviii)	27,	1	nonnulla (non ulla *R*, uero nulla *e*)	nulla

[1] My collation does not show this reading for c.

The Extant Manuscripts of the Germania

		φ	ω
(lxxxix)	4	igitur (= *I*, *r in mg.*)	igni
(xc)	8	omni (= *m*) (*om. b*)	omnium
(xci)	28, 14	heruli (= *p*) (heculi *a*, hieruli *c*)	Neruli
(xcii)	18	triboici **ba**, triborci (tre- *R*, -rii *e*, -ti *c*) π	Triboci (Tre- *I*ξ, Trei- Δ)
(xciii)	19	inuenerint (uiue- *z*)	meruerint
(xciv)	29, 4	fieret (furam *b*, foret *a*, fuit *l*)	fierent
(xcv)	5	insigne *om.*	insigne
(xcvi)	6	honoribus	oneribus
(xcvii)	12	uatauis l, uacauis **Ac**, uaca ius **b**, uatanis u**Rez**, matiacis **a**	batauis
(xcviii)	13	nihil (nisi *e*)	nisi
(xcix)	13	ipse (ipsi *a*)	ipso
(c)	13	animatur (-ntur *ae*)	animantur
(ci)	30, 1	caiti **bal**, carti ψ	catti *uel* chatti
(cii)	4	et *om.*	et
(ciii)	8	dr̄e **b**, differentias **a**, differentia l, differentiae ψ	differre
(civ)	8	disponere *om.*	disponere
(cv)	10	non	nec
(cvi)	13	ne [1]	ire
(cvii)	31, 4	uirtutis (-tum *z*)	uirtuti
(cviii)	32, 2	Tenteri (teueri *pr. loco*, Teutones *alt. loc. a*, *om. alt. loc. c*)	Tencteri

[1] My collation does not show this reading for R.

			φ	ω
(cix)		4	Tenteris (teutones *a*)	Tencteris
(cx)		6	aemulatio perseuerat. Senes	aemulatio. perseuerant senes
(cxi)	33,	1	Tenteros (Teutones *a*)	Tencteros
(cxii)		2	agriuarios (agga- *a*, agerua- *l*, -nar- *e*)	angriuarios
(cxiii)	34,	1	agriuarios (-mar- *u*, Agerua- *l*)	angriuarios
(cxiv)		1	dulciboni (-borni *a*, dulci homini *c*)	dulgibini *uel* dulcubuni [1]
(cxv)		2	heque (de que *b*, aequae *a*, Neque *c*)	aliaeque
(cxvi)		5	et super (et *om. c*, ut super *l*, Insuper *a*)	insuper
(cxvii)		12	inuisum l, in vsum **b**, inuisis (-sus *u*) ψ, visum **a**	uisum
(cxviii)	35,	2	caueorum	Chaucorum
(cxix)		7	mauult	malit
(cxx)		9	appellantur	populantur
(cxxi)		11	assequentur (-quun- *e*)	assequuntur (-quan- σ *s*)
(cxxii)	36,	3	qui	quia
(cxxiii)		5	Itaque	Ita qui
(cxxiv)		6	uagantur (= *r*)	uocantur
(cxxv)		8	sunt hi (sunt ii *a*, sunt *expuncto*, scribi *c*, sunt *b*)	sunt
(cxxvi)	37,	9	computemus consulatum	consulatum computemus

[1] See above, p. 131.

The Extant Manuscripts of the Germania 219

		φ	ω
(cxxvii)	15	mafra **lueAz**, in afra **b**, in affra **R**, in asia **c**, *om.* **a**	infra
(cxxviii)	17	manilio	Manlio (mallio *Edrk*, Malio *m v*)
(cxxix)	17	confusis (confisis *b*, conss. fusis *e*, consulis *c*, fusis *a*)	fusis
(cxxx)	24	et	etiam
(cxxxi)	38, 2	partem germanie (= *r*) (ger- par- *a*)	germaniae partem
(cxxxii)	2	tenterorum ue (-que *a*) **bal**, tentecorum ve ψ	Tencterorumue [1]
(cxxxiii)	7	altis (aliis *l*)	aliis
(cxxxiv)	7	sueuorum *om.*	sueuorum
(cxxxv)	10	sequentur	sequuntur (sequentem *I*)
(cxxxvi)	10	ne legant (-tur *R*, negligant *a*)	religant [2]
(cxxxvii)	11	fortunae	formae
(cxxxviii)	12	Valitudinem **bl**, malitudinem **uARz**, multitudinem **c**, in altitudinem **ae**	in altitudinem
(cxxxix)	39, 1	uetustissimosque (-que *om. al*)	uetustissimos seu **X**, ue- se (se *om. Ns*) α β s
(cxl)	1	Semnone **lezuA**, semone **ba**, Senone **R**, Sennone **c**	Semnones *uel* Semones [3]
(cxli)	5	Caesosque (cas- *Ac*)	caesoque

[1] See below, p. 261.
[2] See above, pp. 100 f.
[3] See above, p. 133.

		φ	ω
(cxlii)	5	he b, hodie a, honore π	homine
(cxliii)	6	enim	nisi
(cxliv)	7	numīs a, numeris uRcz, muneris Ae, numerus b, numinis l	numinis
(cxlv)	40, 7	eaque (Eamque *a*)	eamque
(cxlvi)	15	armata (= *m r*)	amata
(cxlvii)	20	parituri (perituri *al*) (= *m*)	perituri
(cxlviii)	41, 3	Hermundororum (-dorum *bc*, Hermondiorum *a*, Nhere)	Hermundurorum (-dorum *E*)
(cxlix)	4	in *om.*	in
(cl)	42, 6	usque *om.* (= *N*)	usque
(cli)	7	Marobodetui (Marro-*b*) bl, Marcodetui a, Marchodemi uRA, Marcodemi ez, Marcodeni c	Marobodui
(clii)	10	ualenti	ualent
(cliii)	43, 5	aut (etiam *a*) emigenis (*om. c*) (= *r in mg.*)	ut alienigenis
(cliv)	6	et *om.*	et
(clv)	44, 4	et *om.*	et
(clvi)	7	Suiuonum zeR, Suluonum b, Suironum a, Suinonum Ac, Suiuorum u, Sueuonum l	Suionum
(clvii)	9	asper [1] (aspera *a*)	semper

[1] My collation does not show this reading for R.

		φ	ω
(clviii)	9	appulsum (pulsum *a*)	appulsui
(clix)	16	cursus	incursus
(clx)	18	neque (ne *a*)	ne
(clxi)	45, 1	Terras suiuonas (-non-*bz*, smuo- *c*)	Trans suionas
(clxii)	3	cadens **be**, calens π, radens **a**	cadentis
(clxiii)	4	fortunasque	formasque
(clxiv)	5	ut (ad *c*)	et (fama)
(clxv)	9	proprior (= *m E*) (propior *leR*, *e* -pri- corr. *a*)	propior
(clxvi)	10	omnium quique (om- nium quaeque *a*) (*cf.* omnium cuique *r*)	omniumque
(clxvii)	15	non [1]	ratio
(clxviii)	21	plerique [1] (plerumque *a*)	plerumque
(clxix)	24	credendum	crediderim
(clxx)	46, 7	quid **b**, qui π, quicquid **a**	quicquid
(clxxi)	16	imbrium	imbriumque
(clxxii)	22	ellusios (aluosios *a*)	Hellusios

In the presence of so many glaring errors it is inevitable that one or another of the manuscripts should occasionally have restored the correct reading,[2] but surprisingly enough not one

[1] My collation does not show this reading for **c**.

[2] This is most often true of **a** (vi, xv, xxii, xxiii, xxiv, xxxi, xxxvi, xlii, xlviii, l, li, lvi, lxix, lxxxiv, c, cxvi, cxxix, cxxxviii, cxlv, clxv), but the fact that the MS. has so often unsuccessfully attempted to restore the text is good evidence that it does not offer a conflated text. Next to **a**, the process of correction has been carried on to the greatest extent in **l** (xv, xxi, xxiv, xxx, xlii, lxxxvi, cxxxiii) and **e** (xxi, xxxiii, l, li, lvi, lxxxvi, xcviii, c, cxxi).

of the manuscripts gives the appearance of offering a conflated text.[1] Some of the readings listed above are not the results of actual errors in φ, but of abbreviations which were misunderstood by the copyists, giving rise to a considerable variety of absurd readings within the group (xx, xxxvi, lii, lviii, lxxxvi, ciii, cxlii, cxliv). Yet the greater part of the errors must have been made in the transcription of φ. We gather that its archetype abounded in abbreviations (cf. xvi, xxxii, xl, xlix, lxii, lxxi, xcviii, cxxxvii, cliii, clxii, clxiii, clxvii, etc.), that it was written in an illegible Gothic script (cf. xviii, xxxv, xxxviii, lxvi, cxviii, cxxvii, cxxxiii, clii, etc., etc.), and that the scribe was ignorant and careless.[2]

There are also instances of intentional changes, though generally unintelligent (v, xiv, xvii, xxxiv, xliv, lxvii, lxxviii, lxxxvii, cx, cxxxix, clxix).

As Rand has remarked, the corruptions of this group of manuscripts would amply illustrate an essay on the frailties of scribes, but as he also sagely observes, a multitude of errors in a manuscript need not discredit its good readings unless the text bears the marks of learned emendation.[3] Such emendations as are found in this group (taken as a group) are not "learned," but betray themselves by their very clumsiness, and the group has its due share of "good" readings. Naturally the good readings are not to be sought in the long list of corruptions exhibited above peculiar to φ alone,[4] but in the concurrence of φ with other groups of manuscripts. There is an imposing list of readings in which φ with X or with Xs maintains the better tradition,[5] and this group contributes its

[1] This conclusion regarding the group as a whole was also reached by Rand (1905, 316).

[2] If φ was a direct copy of Y (but I find this doubtful), we have an insight into the character of the latter MS.

[3] 1905, 308 f.

[4] Yet I suspect that (xcvii) *uatauis* φ preserves an ancient variant.

[5] 2, 11 *tres*; 14 *plures*; 20 *mox et*; 3, 1 *et apud eos*; 6, 11 *uariare*; 12, 4 *pro (po-)crate*; 14, 3 *infamem in*; 27, 4 *adicitur*; 28, 10 *a bois*; 30, 10 *Romanae*; 37, 24 *nam*; 38, 10 *ne legant*; 11 *hornatorem*; 39, 11 *adicit*; 43, 1 *osiburi*; 44, 7 *ipso in oceanum*; 45, 3 *in ortu sedurat*; 5 *adicit* (only bae); 46, 19 *inlaborare*; 24 *uultusque corpora*.

share toward the restoration of the doublets of the Hersfeld codex, sometimes in a rather startling manner.[1] In fact, we should have a very different impression of the lost **Y**, were it not for the φ group and **s**, which so often bring **Y** into closer relationship with Hf. than do α and β.

The first line of cleavage in the manuscripts of the φ group is between **ba** on the one hand and the remaining manuscripts on the other. The manuscripts **ba** either agree or show a certain resemblance in the following corruptions:

		ba	ω
(i)	2, 17	ut	et
(ii)	7, 10	fortuna (= *T*)	fortuita
(iii)	14, 11	in (= *Wm r s*)	ui
(iv)	18	sanguinem	sanguine
(v)	25, 3	more b, iure a (*cf.* mo$\overline{\text{um}}$ *uc*)	modum
(vi)	26, 2	si *om.*	si
(vii)	2	suetum b, sincerum a	uetitum
(viii)	28, 6	memini b, memimque a	Moenum
(ix)	18	triboici	triboci *uel* tre- (triborci π)
(x)	37, 11	dampna (= *m r*)	damna
(xi)	15	deiecerit	obiecerit (obiecit, obiecerunt)
(xii)	40, 9	in (insula) *om.*	in
(xiii)	43, 9	ultraque	ultra quod
(xiv)	15	$\overline{\text{mum}}$ b, ī vnum a	numini
(xv)	45, 4	insonum b, id est sonum a	sonum

[1] Consult the table of doublets on pp. 122–141, and note in particular 31, 16; 43, 6; 43, 12.

I cannot regard the readings shown in the column to the left as establishing an archetype later than φ for **ba**, in view of the manifold corruption in these two manuscripts. The concurrence may be in part accidental and in part the result of anomalies in the text of φ, though in one place (ix) **ba** give the reading of φ, which became further corrupted in π. The manuscripts **ba** sometimes assume an independent value within the φ group in those places where there were doublets in Hf.: 6, 16 *dilectos* **b**; 11, 11 *absumitur* **ba**; 29, 6 *collationibus* **b**; 30, 4 *quimus* **b** (alone of the **Y** family); 39, 2 *Stato* **b**; 40, 5 *Suarines* **b**; 43, 12 *heliciosna* **a**, and perhaps 43, 13 *religionis* **a**, though this is more probably an independent correction. These readings show that φ recorded doublets more faithfully than did its descendants. Likewise, where doublets may with plausibility be traced to **Y**, the manuscripts **ba**, or one of them, may give the variant unknown to the other members of their group: 28, 7 *boi* **ba**; 31, 6 *noscendi* **b**; 37, 15 *deiectus* **a**; 42, 6 *Quadisue* **a**; 45, 8 *abluuntur* **a**, *abluuntur*>*adl-* **b**. It is at least possible that the orthography in 15, 5 *idem* **b** (= X), and 45, 28 *temptes* **a** (= X t e) shows an unbroken line of tradition from Hf., but I do not insist.

The manuscripts **ba** may accordingly be regarded as separate copies of φ, but **a** at least cannot be a direct copy, as is shown both by the bewildering confusion in the disposition of its text, which must be due to a disarrangement of the leaves of the archetype, and by the character of its peculiar readings. The manuscript is clearly the work of an ignorant and careless scribe who copied from a much better, though badly interpolated, exemplar. Probably of all the manuscripts of the *Germania*, **a** enjoys the distinction of being the most corrupt, though it is not the least valuable.[1]

[1] In **b** there are several longer omissions which point to an immediate archetype of about 40 letters to the line: 3, 15 f. *et tumulos* . . . *inscriptos* (40 letters); 19, 11 f. *sic unum* . . . *corpus* (40 letters); 2, 5 f. *porro* . . . *Asia* (40 letters without *porro* which is omitted in π); 25, 9 f. *non multum* . . . *momentum* (43 letters); 27, 8 f. *in commune* . . . *moribus* (43 letters); 43, 22 f. *nouum* . . . *omnibus* (45 letters). At 43, 20 f. the copyist first wrote *ad prelia* . . . *formi-*

The π Branch

Although **ba** may be treated as independent copies of φ, the remaining manuscripts of the group, **lezuRAc**, descend from a single lost apograph of φ, which I call π, and whose identity is established by the following readings:[1]

		π (lezuRAc)	ba ω
(i)	1, 2	meatu	metu (uictu *a*)
(ii)	6	rateicarum	raeticarum (rhae-, rhe-, re-)
(iii)	2, 5	porro *om.*	porro (porro ... Asia *om. b*)
(iv)	13	instaenones (iust- RAc)	Istaeuones (Ineuones *b*, histeriones *a*)
(v)	14	autem (= χ)	ut in (in *om. ba s*)
(vi)	18	totungri (titu- *l*)	tungri (tingri *b*)
(vii)	3, 4	accendere	accendunt
(viii)	11	terrae	terras
(ix)	15	et *om.*	et (et ... inscriptos *om. b*)
(x)	5, 3	quam (= *N r*)	qua
(xi)	8	negarint	negauerint
(xii)	7, 7	imperitante	imperante (Inspirante *a*)
(xiii)	8, 5	puellaeque	puellae quoque
(xiv)	10, 2	frugiferi	frugiferae

dine between *populos* and *antecedunt* (43, 19), and then indicated the deletion of the words by *uacat*. From *populos* to *ad proelia* there are 85 letters. Apparently the scribe had glanced two lines ahead. At 40, 11 f. *is adesse ... feminis*, **b** has an omission of 52 letters. There is but one long omission in **a**: 22, 6 f. *crebrae ... transiguntur* (76 letters).

[1] This table and those which follow do not record a considerable number of unimportant variants found in individual MSS.

226   THE GERMANIA OF TACITUS

		π (lezuRAc)	ba ω
(xv)	10	hoc (h' *lc*, h³ *eA*, huius *z*)	hic
(xvi)	10	ciuium [1]	auium
(xvii)	11, 7	dum	diem
(xviii)	13	rerum	rex (etenim *b*)
(xix)	13	principes	princeps
(xx)	12, 11	singuli [2]	singulis
(xxi)	13, 5	hoc [3]	haec (hic *b*)
(xxii)	17	in numero	numero
(xxiii)	14, 10	auspicia	ancipitia
(xxiv)	11	bello uique (bello inque *Ac*)	ui (in *ba*) belloque
(xxv)	18, 5	offert	affert
(xxvi)	13	incipientis *om.*	incipientis
(xxvii)	15	epulis equus (ephippus equus *e*)	equus
(xxviii)	16	patrem (*om. cum lacuna l*)	pariendum (periende *b*, parentes *a*)
(xxix)	17	seque (sed *A*) (= *m*)	se quae (si, *om.* quae *a*)
(xxx)	19, 2	incitationibus (*om. A*)	irritationibus
(xxxi)	13	nec (longior)	ne
(xxxii)	20, 3	non (nutricibus)	ac (aut *m* Δ λ*k*)
(xxxiii)	4	educationum	educationis
(xxxiv)	11	habet (= *s*) (*om. l*)	hunc
(xxxv)	22, 7	et (uulneribus) *om.*	et

[1] My collation does not report for R. In z the word might be read as *acium*, save for the dot over the second shaft of the *a*.

[2] My collation does not report for R.

[3] My collation does not report for c.

The Extant Manuscripts of the Germania 227

			π (lezuRAc)	ba ω
(xxxvi)		12	nec (astuta)	non
(xxxvii)	24,	4	tamen *om*.	tamen
(xxxviii)		5	premium (pretium *z*)	pretium (patrum *a*)
(xxxix)	25,	2	in ministeriis	ministeriis
(xl)	28,	7	beii (boii *e*)	boii (boi *ba* τ)
(xli)		18	hemetes (herm- *c*)	Nemetes
(xlii)	29,	5	et *om*.	et
(xliii)	30,	16	cunctatior	cunctatio
(xliv)	31,	11	suis	suisque
(xlv)		12	intra (uitia *l*, uitia > initia *e*)	initia
(xlvi)		12	super	semper
(xlvii)		13	iam	nam
(xlviii)		15	alumni	alieni (alterni *b*)
(xlix)	34,	3	fusis	frisis
(l)		11	in *om*.[1] (= I)	in
(li)		11	sanctiusque reuerentius (sanctius reuerentiusque *le*)	sanctiusque ac retius
(lii)	35,	6	autem germanus	inter germanos
(liii)	36,	5	boi (boii *l*)	boni (*om. b*)
(liv)		7	certamina	contermina (continua *a*)
(lv)		8	seculis	secundis (serulis *b*, seculis > secudis *s*?)
(lvi)	37,	13	nisaris (uisaris *Ac*, cesaris *l*)	Arsacis (arsaris *b*)

[1] My collation does not report this reading for R.

16

228   The Germania of Tacitus

		π (lezuRAc)	ba ω
(lvii)	40, 8	populos [1] (-lus *l*)	populis
(lviii)	41, 8	Hermundoris	Hermunduris
(lix)	42, 1	Hermundoros	Hermunduros
(lx)	1	marcoemani (-cem-eRc, in arcoe- *A*)	Marcomani
(lxi)	43, 1	Marsigini (-gigni *c*)	Marsigni
(lxii)	2	ex	e
(lxiii)	9	sueuam	sueuiam
(lxiv)	11	sufficiat	sufficiet (-ceret *a*)
(lxv)	12	nabanarualos (-bolos *R*)	nahanarualos
(lxvi)	13	nabanarualos (-bolo *R*, om. *u*)	naharualos
(lxvii)	45, 9	Insignem	insigne
(lxviii)	10	formam	formas
(lxix)	25	quam	quae
(lxx)	46, 2	fesimorum	Fennorum

With scarcely an exception, the readings peculiar to π are the result of the copyist's blunders, and this branch is even less open to the charge of wilful interpolation than is the φ group as a whole.

Of π two transcriptions were made, l, and a lost manuscript which I call ψ, from which have issued **ezuRAc**. The readings peculiar to l need not delay us. The manuscript is the work of an intelligent copyist who had before him a very faulty exemplar. Although l has occasionally corrected the glaring errors of φ,[2] I do not believe that it offers a conflated text, and the interpolations are not numerous.

[1] My collation does not show this reading for c.
[2] See p. 221, note 2.

The ψ Branch

To establish the identity of ψ we have the following readings:

		ψ (ezuRAc)	ω
(i)	1, 10	se	sex
(ii)	2, 17	editum	additum (aditum *h l*)
(iii)	3, 3	huius	haec
(iv)	4	future (fortune *z*)	futuraeque
(v)	5, 2	gallicas	Gallias (gallie *l*)
(vi)	11	ualere **euR**, uidere ualere **Ac**	uidere
(vii)	17	veteram (-em *ecu* [2])	ueterem
(viii)	19	et	quia
(ix)	6, 16	et (ex *e*)	ex (e *a*)
(x)	19	dum nostro [1] (dum mɸ *z*, dum /// *e*)	dummodo
(xi)	24	finiuerunt [2]	finierunt
(xii)	7, 13	ludatores (adulatores *R*)	laudatores
(xiii)	10, 6	deumque	caelumque (ce-)
(xiv)	12, 4	et (= *v*)	ac
(xv)	8	rei	regi
(xvi)	14, 8	cum (= *W I*)	tum
(xvii)	17	in eis	iners (in omnes *a*)
(xviii)	16, 7	tegmentorum	cementorum
(xix)	17, 12	nudant	nudae (nudet *s*)
(xx)	19, 5	martis (maritis *e*)	maritis
(xxi)	20, 10	ad *om.*	ad
(xxii)	12	in *om.*	in

[1] My collation does not show this reading for **R**.
[2] My collation does not show this reading for **c**.

ψ (ezuRAc)   ω

(xxiii)	24, 3	fragmeas	frameas
(xxiv)	4	questu (equestu c)	quaestum (que-)
(xxv)	5	spe expectantium (spe asp- z)	expectantium *uel* spectantium [1]
(xxvi)	6	inicere (iniic- u)[2]	mirere (mirer l, mirifice a)
(xxvii)	27, 8	igitur mannorum **uz**, igitur inannorum **A**, igitur germanorum **Rc**, Germanorum **e**	germanorum
(xxviii)	10	e *om*.	e
(xxix)	28, 4	quoque (queque e)	quaeque
(xxx)	8	illuc	adhuc
(xxxi)	10	abors **zuA**, abora **e**, arbores **R**, ab hoc **c**	a bois
(xxxii)	14	affectionem (= h m k s)	affectationem
(xxxiii)	29, 2	annis (uis c, amnis e)	amnis (armis a)
(xxxiv)	3	mens (motus e)	in eas
(xxxv)	5	nec tam	nam nec
(xxxvi)	9	obsequi (obsequio e)	obsequio
(xxxvii)	30, 1	carti	Catti (caiti *bal*) *uel* Chatti
(xxxviii)	14	fortuna	fortuita
(xxxix)	31, 4	caseo (casio A, casuo c)	caeso (ce-)
(xl)	4	uotuum **uAc**, uotum **Rz**, uotiuum **e**	uotiuum

[1] See above, p. 107.
[2] My collation does not report this reading for **R**.

		ψ (ezuRAc)	ω
(xli)	10	namque	iamque
(xlii)	12	premia (= M)	prima
(xliii)	16	durare [1]	durae (-re)
(xliv)	34, 3	fusi	frisi *uel* frisii
(xlv)	5	praetereuntur (-run- R)	praetexuntur
(xlvi)	9	referri	referre
(xlvii)	35, 13	et quiescentibus ... Chaucorum *om.*	et quiescentibus ... Chaucorum
(xlviii)	38, 3	nobisque	nominibusque
(xlix)	7	cognationum (-tio A)	cognatione
(l)	8	mutatione	imitatione (Timtatrone b)
(li)	11	et *om.*	et
(lii)	39, 8	proferens	prae (pro I v) se ferens
(liii)	40, 7	Nehertum	Nerthum
(liv)	11	uehectamque (ucctamque e)	uectamque
(lv)	13	quacumque (quantumque A)	quaecumque (quem- a)
(lvi)	42, 9	ante	auctoritate
(lvii)	10	priuantur	iuuantur
(lviii)	43, 3	Pannonia (= v)	Pannonica
(lix)	8	insiderunt	insederunt (inciderunt b, Inscenderunt a)
(lx)	10	lignorum (lingorum e, Lig̊gum c)	legiorum (li-, ly-) *uel* uegiorum

[1] See above, p. 131.

		ψ (ezuRAc)	ω
(lxi)	19	feritatis [1] (= h)	feritati
(lxii)	19	ipse (tempore ze)	tempore
(lxiii)	44, 14	pauendi (cauendi R)	parendi
(lxiv)	46, 3	giros	quos

For the most part ψ merely increased the amazing list of errors previously noted for φ and π, though in xliii, *durare*, it preserved a reminiscence of Hf.,[2] and in xxv, *spe expectantium*,[3] and 2, 10 *tuisman* u, *Tuisinan* e,[4] it has retained doublets which seemingly originated in Y.

The manuscript e, like its kinsman l, is the work of a scholar who tried here and there to make a readable text, occasionally making the correct restoration *ad sensum*,[5] though the manuscript is not badly interpolated.

The chief interest of u lies in the marginal emendations of the second hand (u²), which form an interesting document showing to what lengths a fifteenth-century scholar might go in his efforts to make a readable text of a hopelessly corrupt manuscript. In a few instances, to be sure, he has arrived at felicitous emendations, as in 20, 16 *quanto maior*, and 41, 1 *pars sueuorum*.

The manuscript z, which up to the present time has remained entirely unknown, was perhaps transcribed with greater conscientiousness than any of the other apographs of ψ, since it sometimes seems to offer a diplomatic reproduction of the archetype.[6] R presents a number of interpolations, and, if the *ex silentio* readings of my collation are to be trusted, a few successful corrections.

[1] My collation does not report for c.
[2] See p. 131.
[3] See p. 107.
[4] See p. 115.
[5] Cf. p. 221, note 2, and in the preceding table, vii, ix, xx, xxvii, xxix, xxxvi, xl, liv.
[6] Cf. in the preceding table x; also p. 226, note 1.

One might wonder if it were possible for corruptions in manuscripts to go beyond the point reached by ψ. Yet **Ac** show in common some seventy or more additional corruptions,[1] which prove that they are not direct copies of ψ, but of some lost intervening manuscript.

h. Codex Stutgartiensis (s) [2]

The manuscript **s** is disfigured by a very large number of corruptions peculiar to itself alone. Though it bears no closer resemblance to any one of the groups, α, β, φ, than it does to the others, it may, I believe, be referred with all three groups to the common archetype **Y**. While **s** represents a distinct line of descent from **Y**, the extant manuscript can hardly be a direct copy, as is shown by the twofold character of its errors.

First we find a considerable number of readings which appear to be wilful interpolations: 2, 4 *atque (ut sic dixerim)*; 2, 5 *urbe nostra* (*urbe* in vr); 2, 8 *nisi sibi* (= Wh t); 2, 11 *conditoriosque fuisse*; 2, 15 *appellatores*; 2, 19 *coaluisse* for *eualuisse*; 3, 8 *uox repercussa* (= m); 4, 4 *toto* for *tanto*; 7, 5 *ne* (= h σ λ) for *neque* of the other manuscripts; 7, 15 *aliique* for *cibosque*; 16, 5 *Nam* for *suam*; 18, 7 *ornatur* for *comatur*; 19, 7 *Rupte* for *publicatae*; 19, 8 *maritus inuenitur*; 19, 9 *corrumpi sc*; 20, 11 *quod . . . habet nexum sanguinisque* (the misunderstanding of the abbreviation for *hunc* probably introduced

---

[1] The following are given *exempli causa:* 5, 13 *quam* for *quae*; 7, 11 *cuneum* om.; 10, 13 *morali* for *mortali*; 11, 6 *credant*; 12, 1 *ad* for *et*; 12, 6 *dum* om.; 13, 7 *aut* om.; 14, 15 *terram* om.; 14, 17 *pigrum* om.; 15, 8 *pro* om.; 16, 6 *casus* om.; 20, 7 *uestinantur* for *fes-*; 22, 13 *detracta* for *detecta*; 25, 11 *et super ingenuos* om. (= L); 26, 4 *facultatem* for *facilitatem*; 26, 6 *ubertatem*; 26, 9 *spes* for *species*; 30, 13 *Chattos* om.; 34, 4 *modo* om.; *uterque*; 36, 2 *in arcentem*; 39, 5 *barbara*; 44, 14 *nullus*; 45, 4 *emergens*; 45, 19 *mirantes accipiunt* om.; 45, 25 *solis radiis* om.; 46, 2 *Germanis* om.; etc., etc.

The archetype of **Ac** may have had 28–35 letters to the line. Thus **A** omits, 6, 13–14, *plus . . . mixti* (33 letters); 19, 2–3 *irritationibus . . . litterarum* (33 letters); 38, 7–8 *Sueborum . . . accidit* (33 letters, but only 25 without *Sueborum*, which was omitted in φ). **c** omits, 43, 5–6 *partem . . . imponunt* (56 letters); 21, 1–2 it has written *seu patris . . . amicitias* twice (34 letters).

[2] The following discussion is concerned only with the original text of **s**. The corrections and additions of the second hand, which drew from the **X** family, have been treated in connection with this family.

quod for *quidam* and the addition of *-que*); 22, 2 *aqua calida*; 25, 11 *illi* for *ibi*; 26, 8 *imponitur* for *imperatur*; 28, 10 *an boii* (reading *a boiis* with the other manuscripts); 31, 12 *hiis* for *haec*; 32, 5 *hic lusus*; 36, 7 *aduersariorum pares et equi*; 37, 14 *in ipso et ipse* (*et ipso et ipse* Y); 38, 4 *uniuersi* for *in commune*; 38, 10 *in ipso uertice*; 39, 2 *Estiuo tempore*; 39, 3 *auguriis patrum et prisca formidine sacrorum nominibusque eiusdem sanguinis*; 39, 12 *semonum* (= β a); 39, 12 *habitatur* for *habitantur* in ω; 43, 12–13 *nahauernales* and *nahauernalos*; 43, 18 *arii* for *alii* in ω; 46, 13 *Sola* (= a t τ); 46, 23 *exionas* (a conflated variant).

While some of these readings may be accidental, I do not believe that all can be the work of a scribe who had no idea of the meaning of the text. In other words they cannot be the work of the scribe who wrote *celitum* for *editum*, *ornatibus* for *uenatibus*, *dignos* for *dignationem*, and who in several places copied marginal variants into the text.

As illustrative of the long list of corruptions [1] which reveal the purely mechanical work of a scribe who had no idea of the meaning of his text, we may note the following: 3, 5 *enim* om.; 7, 12 (twice) *Vnum* for *unde*; 8, 6 *secundum* for *sanctum*; 12, 11 *plebibus* for *plebe*; 13, 1 *non* for *nisi*, 2 *nisi* for *non*; 13, 5 *viuente* for *iuuentae*; 15, 1 *ornatibus* for *uenatibus*; 15, 12

---

[1] The collation of Wünsch (84–107) is satisfactory, though the following corrections should be made: 2, 10 *celitū* s; 16, 14 *aut* (*autem*) s; 18, 16 *pieū*; 29, 13 *ipē* corr. to *ipō* s; 32, 1 *quiq3*, c add. s²; 36, 8 *pares et equi* (for *ex aequo*) s; 37, 5 *fidē* s; 37, 9 *ferime* del., in mg. *quam* (?) *ferme* s²; 37, 19 *nec* s. I am also inclined to disagree with Wünsch in the following readings, though I realize that it is sometimes impossible to distinguish between the corrections made by the first hand and those made by the second: 2, 10 *editum* superscr. s²; 2, 12 *inguenones* corr. to *ingaenones* s or s²?; 2, 14 *deos* in mg. s²; 3, 13 *g'cū* (*grecum*) in mg. s²; 6, 21 *eciam* corr. to *et iam* s²; 7, 12 *fagitus*, *v* add. s²; 8, 6 *scd'm* s, in mg. *al. sctm* s²; 9, 8 *assil'are*, *d* add. s²; 10, 21 *quēq3* in mg. s²; 12, 4 perhaps *mergāt* corr. to *mergūt* s²; 12, 8 *mlcte* in mg. s²; 13, 5 *iuuente* in mg. s²; 15, 3 *penalium* corr. to *penaerium* s; 19, 12 *tū* in mg. s²; 21, 1 *inimicicias* s, *amicicias* s²; 22, 9 perhaps *adsciscendis* changed to *adpiscendis* s² (cf. p. 154); 28, 1 *autor* in mg. s²; 38, 2 probably *tenetterorum* in mg. s²; 40, 5 *nuithones* changed to *vui-* s²; 40, 6 *inanime* s (but *Mamme* s² in marginal note); 43, 12 *haliosnas* superscr. s².

iam . . . docuimus om.; 18, 16 *perieum* for *pariendum*; 19, 1 *in* for *ergo*; 19, 9 *Meliusque* for *melius quidem*; 20, 13 *aman* for *animum*; 21, 1–2 *seu patris . . . amicitias* om. (corr. s²); 23, 6–7 *haud minus . . . uincentur* om. (add. s²); 26, 4 *dignos* for *dignationem*; 31, 2 *audiencia* for *audentia*; 31, 11 *suisque quisque* for *suisque*; 32, 3 *discipulus* for *disciplinae*; 33, 6 *roboris* for *Romanis*;[1] 40, 6 *inanime* for *in commune*; 40, 14–15 *clausum . . . amata* om. (add. s²); 40, 20 *pericia* for *perituri*; 43, 16 *suspicionis* for *superstitionis*; 45, 17 *eructamenta* for *eiectamenta*; 46, 20 f. *securi . . . deos* om. (add. s²).

In the following places the scribe of **s** has copied variants or glosses into the text: 10, 18 *aliud genus alia obseruacio*; 34, 1 *dulgibini cubrini*; 40, 5 *suarines seu suardones*; 40, 10 *conmissum seu concessum* (*conmissum* not found elsewhere).

This manuscript has occasionally found supporters, who have strangely misunderstood its true character.[2] Naturally, coming as it does by a distinct line of descent from **Y**, it is important for the restoration of Hf., but only in corroborating the evidence of other manuscripts,[3] and not in its peculiar readings.[4]

3. Orthography and Other Details

Orthography

In order to afford a convenient table of reference, I have grouped together orthographical details of the Hersfeld *Agri-*

---

[1] Cf. *ro.* in **ΔI**. (*is* written above)

[2] Holtzmann, Holder, Mosler, Holub, the last mentioned (to judge from the title of a work which I have been unable to find) even going so far as to defend the thesis that **s** is the best of the extant MSS. of the *Germania!* Perhaps the most startling example of misplaced confidence is to be found in Holtzmann's *Mammun Ertham* (40, 6)—a fiction based on the *inanime* (*Mamme* s² in mg.) *nerthum* of **s**, which is nothing more nor less than a corruption of *in commune nerthum*.

[3] E.g. 2, 13 *herminones*; 10, 12 *isdem*; 27, 4 *adicitur*; 30, 10 *romanae*; 31, 13 *cultu*; 33, 9 *in gentibus*; 34, 7 *temptauimus*; 37, 1 *sinum*; 37, 24 *nam*; 40, 1 *largobardos*; 43, 1 *osiburi*; 44, 6 *ipso in oceanum*; 45, 3 *in ortu se durat*; 46, 19 *inlaborare*. Also see the restoration of doublets on pp. 121–141.

[4] Only in the reading, 14, 17 *adquirere* (= L), **s** alone might conceivably lay claim to having maintained the better tradition. The spelling, 30, 7, *sollercie* (= *sollertie* W V), is also noteworthy.

cola (codex Aesinas) and of the *Germania* manuscripts, occasionally admitting illustrative material from the *de Grammaticis*. I realize, of course, that fifteenth-century copyists as a rule showed little conscience in changing the orthography of their exemplars, and that in many points (*e:ae, y:i, o:u, ci:ti, m:n* before a stop, doubling of consonants, etc.) the extant manuscripts offer no index to the orthography of the Hersfeld *Germania*. Only when a very good manuscript like **W**, free of learned correction, repeatedly follows the norm established by the extant portion of the Hersfeld codex can we have some assurance that it has kept the genuine tradition.

Vowels

A : E

   a for e [1]

      Hersfeld *Agricola:* f. 59, 2, 27 (ch. 25), *adtollerant;*
      62ᵛ, 2, 29 (ch. 37), *spernabant*. The corrections are by the second (contemporary) hand.

      Germania: 5, 17 *serratos* **W**, *sarratos* **m**, *serratos* ω; 15, 5 *habent* as variant for *hebent;* 30, 12 *quam* as variant for *quem*.

   e for a

      Germania: Perhaps ch. 36, 4 *nomine* for *nomina*.

A : O

      I regard the confusion as graphical rather than phonetic, but this may be questioned. See p. 53.

A : AV

   a for au

      Agricola: 56, 1, 13 (ch. 13) *agustus;* 63ᵛ, 1, 24 (ch. 39) *actum* for *auctum*.

---

[1] On the confusion of *a* and *e* see H. Schuchardt, *Der Vokalismus des Vulgärlateins* (Leipzig, 1866–1868) I, 185–205. The palimpsest of Cicero, *de Re Publica* (diplomatic transcription by A. W. Van Buren, *Supplementary Papers of the American School in Rome* II [1908], 111–262) shows *a* for *e* with astonishing frequency. For examples of the same confusion in the majuscule MSS. of Vergil see O. Ribbeck, *Prolegomena Critica ad P. Vergili Maronis Opera Maiora* (Leipzig, 1866), 384 f.

AE : E
  ae (oe) for e

  Agricola: 62, 2, 13 (ch. 34) *adprobatae;* 62ᵛ, 2, 13
  (ch. 36) *aequitum;* 62ᵛ, 2, 21 (ch. 36) *aequorum,*
  but elsewhere *eques, equus;* 56, 1, 30 (ch. 14),
  56ᵛ, 2, 30 (ch. 16) *aegregius,* but ch. 17, ch. 25,
  egregius; 63, 2, 12 (ch. 37) *caecidere;* 57, 2, 11
  (ch. 17) *caerealis;* 58ᵛ, 2, 7 (ch. 22) *craebrae,* but
  ch. 24 *crebris;* 60ᵛ, 2, 16 (ch. 30) *defuerae;* 56, 2,
  28 (ch. 15) *interpraetando;* 56ᵛ, 2, 1 (ch. 15)
  paenes; 57, 1, 24 (ch. 16) *praecario;* 58, 1, 9
  (ch. 19) *praecibus;* 58, 1, 27 (ch. 19) *praetio;* 59,
  2, 3 (ch. 24) *spetiae.*

  Always *ceterus* etc. (14 times); *femina* (ch. 16,
  ch. 31); *separare* (ch. 38).

  Germania: 21, 8 *aepulis* **W**, *epu-* ω; *aeques, aequus* (for
  equus), *aequaestris,* only in **N** (12, 7 *equorum* I);
  caeteri (*caeterum*) or *ceteri* (24 times) σ**Mw b**,
  sometimes **dE RA**, *ceteri* or *coe-* **p L uc** (*coe-*
  common only in L), *ceteri* ω; 45, 25 *expraessa* **W
  N**, *expressa* ω; *foemina* or *femina* (11 times) α
  except **t**, **LdE uR**, sometimes **R zA**, *femina* ω;
  4, 8 *in aedia in* (for *inediam*) **W**, *inediam* **I∆ dEo
  R**, *ined-* ω; 43, 14 *interpraetatione* **W** σ, *-pre-* ω;
  31, 12 *paenes* **W**, *poe-* **c**, *penes* ω; 25, 3 *paenates* **W**,
  poe- **zA**, *penates* ω; 44, 14 *praecario* (*pre-*) **N∆p**,
  precario (p̄c- **Lr a s**) ω; 5, 14· 20, 17· 24, 5· 31, 6·
  45, 19 *praetium* (*pre-*; 5, 14 *pretio* W) **W** σ**pM**,
  pretium ω; 22, 3 *saeparatae* **W ∆**, *sep-* ω; 22, 4
  saepae **W**, *saepe* or *sepe* ω.

  e (oe) for ae

  Agricola: The diphthong *ae* (or *e*) is always written,
  except 56, 1, 17 (ch. 13) *penitentiae;* 58, 1, 22
  (ch. 19) *questum;* 63ᵛ, 1, 20 (ch. 38) *prelecta;*
  76ᵛ, 1, 10 (ch. 45) *moestitiam.*

238   The Germania of Tacitus

Germania: In the following words *e* for *ae* is found in all, or nearly all the manuscripts: 14, 2 *adequare* ω, *adę-* LE, *aequare* N∆pMw; 28, 8 *boihemi nomen* or *boii(h)emionem* ω, *boii haemionem* W; 37, 7 *Cecilio* ω, *caecilio* W ∆p L; 16, 7 *cementorum* (*teg-* ψ) ω, *cac-* d; 12, 4 *ceno* ω, *caeno* W, *cęno* NM E, *coëno* Ldvo; 37, 16 *Cepione* ω, *caepione* W N∆p; 4, 5 *ceruli* (or *-lei*) ω, *caeruli* (or *-lei*) W ∆Iw do; 27, 4 *cespes* ω, *caespes* W ∆ 1; 16, 4 *coherentibus* ω, *cohae-* Mw Ld 1Rc; 13, 11 *emulatio* ω, *aemulatio* a dro; 45, 15 *glesum* ω; 1, 1 *retiisque* (*Rhe-*) ω, *ractiisque* (or *-ci-*) Wh NI, *rhaetiisque* pM dEro; 1, 6 *reticarum* (*rhe-*) ω, *raeticarum* Wh σ b, *Rhae-* M, *rateicarum* π; 41, 5 *retiae* (*rhe-*) ω; 19, 1 *septa* ω, *saepta* W σ d; 19, 9 *seculum* ω, *sae-* W Mw blu; 45, 28 *tedae* (*-de*) ω, *taedae* W ∆.

In hm t Vv e s *e* has virtually displaced *ae*. (V has, ch. 2, 13 *Istaeuones* and ch. 45, 7 *Aestiorum;* v has *Aestiorum;* e has, ch. 2, 12 *ingaerones*, ch. 37, 19 *Cęsari;* s has *ingaenones, istaenones*, and *Aestorum.*) In r ba *e* for *ae* is the more usual spelling, and it is common in W E uA. In the following instances W writes *e* (*oe*) for *ae* initially or medially:[1] 10, 6 *celumque;* 9, 8 *celestium;* 37, 19 *Cesari;* 21 *Cesaris;* 39, 5 *coesoque;* 6, 13 *estimanti;* 11, 13 *etas;* 3, 16 *grecis;* generally *hec*, but *haec* in 18, 10· 27, 8· 41, 1; generally *pre-* (*precipiti, precipuum, presagia, prestare*, etc.); 2, 3 *querebant;* 16, 15 *querenda;* 18, 7 *quesita;* 17, 10 *sepius*.

AV : V

claudere : cludere

Agricola: 59ᵛ, 1, 7 (ch. 25) *clauderetur;* 58, 1, 25 (ch. 19) *clausis;* 61ᵛ, 1, 3 (ch. 32) *clausos*.

[1] W does not, of course, stand alone in these readings, with the exception of *coesoque*.

The Extant Manuscripts of the Germania

Germania: 34, 2 *cludunt* ω, *claudunt* t ae s; 43, 2 *claudunt* ω, *cludunt* h, *clau-*>*clu-* s; 45, 2 *claudique* ω, *clu-* W, β except d; 45, 22 *cluduntur* ω, *clau-* h t ae; 40, 14 *clausum* ω; 44, 15 *clausa* ω.

E : IS
e for final is [1]

Agricola: 59, 2, 2 (ch. 24) *gente* as marginal variant of *gentis*. Perhaps 56, 2, 10 (ch. 14) *parta priore* in mg. opposite *parta aprioribus* in text (*i.e.* *prioribus* > *prioris* > *priore*).

Germania: Probably no example. Cf. however pp. 96 f. on ch. 14, 3 *principi*, and note on ch. 36, 4 *nomina*.

E : OE
e (ae) for oe

Agricola: 56ᵛ, 1, 12 (ch. 15) *praelio*, but elsewhere (chapters 15, 16, 17, 24, 27, 28, 29, 30, 33, 36) *proelium*. Also ch. 27 *coetibus;* 29 *foederibus;* 32 *poenae;* 36 *coepere;* 37 *coeperant*.

Germania: 24, 1 *cetu* ω, *coetu* WN L R, *cętu* ΔIpM E, *caetu* w; 5, 2 *feda* m, h ex sil., t λv φ s, *fęda* Δ E uc, *foeda* W NIξ dro; 46, 6 *fedantur* ω, *fę-* Δ, *foe-* W NMw (om. Ip) dEr R; 46, 12 *feda* m, h ex sil., t VvE aluzeA s, *fęda* Δ, *foeda* W NIMw Ldr Rc; *poena* (7, 6; 12, 2; 12, 7; 19, 4): *pena* (19, 4 *poena* > *pena* s) m, h ex sil., t Vv bale s, *pęna* Δ o, *pena* or *poena* zA, *pena*, *pęna*, *poena* u, *pęna*, *poena* I E c, *poena* W Nξ Ldr R; *proelium*, *proeliari* (3, 2; 6, 14; 6, 21; 7, 9; 18, 14; 29, 7; 30, 13; 33, 5; 40, 2; 43, 20; 43, 23): *prelium* mh t Vv le s, *prelium* or *p̄- r ba*, *p̄lium* L, *pręlium* (or *p̄-*) ΔIpM R, *praelium* (*proe-* 6, 21; 33, 5; 40, 2; *pre̜-* 6, 14) N, *pre-*, *prae-*, *pre̜-*, *proe-*, *p̄-*

---

[1] Cf. Lindsay, *Early Latin Prosody* (Oxford, 1922), 132; Max Bonnet, *Le Latin de Grégoire de Tours* (Paris, 1890), 341.

dE z Ac; *proelium* **W w u** (but *pre-* in **W**, 6, 14 and 21; *prae-* 18, 14; 29, 7; p̄- 43, 23).

oe for **e**. See *AE : E*

E : I

i for close e[1]

Agricola: 56, 1, 25 (ch. 13) **gentis* (nom.); 2, 4 (ch. 14) **ciuitatis* (nom.); 10 *regis* (acc.); 56ᵛ, 1, 9 (ch. 15) *centurionis* (acc.); 10 *miscere* in text, *ciere* in mg., i.e. *misc̦ire;* 15 *dilectus;* 22 **coniugis* (acc.); 57ᵛ, 1, 20 (ch. 18) *ordouic̦is* (nom.); 58, 1, 29 (ch. 19) **ciuitatis* (nom.); 58ᵛ, 2, 7 (ch. 22) *eruptionis* (nom.); 59ᵛ, 1, 9 (ch. 25) *incolentis* (nom.); 2, 12 (ch. 26) *hostis* (nom.), in mg. *e;* 27 (ch. 27) *omnis* (nom. plu.); 62ᵛ, 1, 13 (ch. 35) *legionis* (acc.); 2, 27 (ch. 37) *expertis* (nom.); 63ᵛ, 1, 26 (ch. 39) *excipit* (perf.). (ē > i > y: 59ᵛ, 1, 8 [ch. 25] *calydoniam;* 2, 20 [ch. 27] *calydoniam;* 61, 2, 5 [ch. 31] *calydonia.*) Note, 76ᵛ, 1, 11 (ch. 45) *ualetudini*.

Germania: 2, 11 *conditorisque* (acc.); 6, 16 *difinitur* **d**, *diffinitur* χ v ϕ s, *defi-* ω; 6, 16 *delectos* **W V**, *dilectos* **h b**, *de-* ω; 43, 19 *trucis* (nom. pl.).

e for open i[2]

Agricola: 57, 2, 11 and 16 (ch. 17) *bregantum* for *bri-;* 11 and 18 *cerealis* for *cerialis;* 62ᵛ, 2, 19 (ch. 36) *equestres;*[3] 63, 1, 28 (ch. 37) *indagines* (gen.).

---

[1] On this type of phonetic error see Schuchardt i, 244–328. I realize that the confusion of *E* and *I* may be partly graphical. The interlinear and marginal readings in the *Agr.* are all by the second (contemporary) hand. I have taken no account of the corrections by the third (fifteenth-century) hand. The asterisk denotes that the correction to *e* has been made in the text by the second hand.

[2] See Schuchardt ii, 1–69.

[3] The text is corrupt. *Equestris* appears to be a corruption of *aequa nostris*.

Germania: 10, 5 *consuletur* for *consulitur;* 14, 11 *principes* **Whs**², *-pes*>*-pis* I, *-pis* ω; 38, 10 *re_ilegant* in Hf. (?);¹ 40, 17 *uestes* (nom. sing.); 46, 1 *fines* (nom. sing.).

i for open e ²

Agricola: 57, 1, 22 (ch. 16) *tribellius*>**tre-*.

Germania: 8, 8 *negligunt* (*-gle-* V); 16, 10 *liniamenta* ω, *linea-* **m I VdErk**; 17, 5 *negligenter* (*-gle-* I); 30, 8 *intelligere;* 40, 11 *intelligit;* 45, 20 *intelligas;* 21, 15 *comis,* originally a marginal variant of *comes* (line 9).

e for close i ³

Agricola: 58, 1, 25 (ch. 19) *ads_iedere* (corr. m. 1); 62ᵛ, 2, 6 (ch. 36) *tratis* in text, *trates* in mg.;⁴ 63, 2, 5 (ch. 37) *seque*>**sequi;* 63ᵛ, 1, 4 (ch. 38) **d_iemissis.*

Germania: 26, 3 *uices* for *uicis* (abl.).

case forms

Agricola: The accusative plural of *i*-stems regularly ends in *-es:* ch. 21 *segnes;* 22 and 24 *gentes;* 25 *tres partes;* 26 *fugientes;* 28 *tres;* 29 *plures;* 35 *ruentesque;* 36 *enormes.* I have noted *-is* only in 57ᵛ, 2, 10 (ch. 18) *nauis,* 63ᵛ, 1, 8 (ch. 38) *finis.*

The ablative singular of nouns (but not adjectives) in *-is* ends in *-e:* ch. 24 *naue;* 25 and 29 *classe.*

Germania: 1, 10 *plures* ω, *pluris* ϐ; 2, 11 *tres* ω, *tr_ies* **M**χ **LdErok,** *Tres* **p**; 2, 14 *plures* ω, *pluris* **M**χ ϐ, *pl_iures* **p**; 2, 14 *pluresque* ω, *plurisque* v; 8, 10 *complures* ω, *-ris* **M**χ, ϐ (*-res* v), *-r_ies* **p**; 36, 3

---

¹ See pp. 100 f.
² Schuchardt I, 374–460.
³ Schuchardt II, 69–91.
⁴ See pp. 36 f.

impotentes ω, *-tis* β; 37, 17 *consularis* (*-res* t) ω; 37, 18 *tresque* ω, *trisque* β; 45, 11 *hostes* ω, *hostis* β; 43, 11 *plures* ω.

Ch. 45, 27 *igne* ω, *igni* β.

I : II

Agricola: 59ᵛ, 2, 5 (ch. 26) *adici;* 60, 2, 2 (ch. 28) *frisiis;* 62, 1, 25 (ch. 34) *hii* for *hi*, but above (22) *hi*, below (2, 8) *his;* 59, 2, 24 (ch. 25) *isdem* (abl.); 56, 2, 14 (ch. 14) *officii* > *offici*, but ch. 25 *officii*, ch. 15 *proelii*, ch. 24 and 33 *imperii;* 59ᵛ, 2, 8 (ch. 26) *redit* (perf. ?); 56ᵛ, 1, 18 (ch. 15) *transisse;* 62, 1, 2 (ch. 33) *transisse;* 57, 2, 20 (ch. 17) *subiit*.

Germania: 39, 11 *adicit* **Wm**, φ except **lu**, *adiicit* (*aducit* or *adducit* ΔIξ, *Aditur* s) ω; 27, 4 *adicitur* **Wm I**, φ except **lu, s**, *addicitur* **r**, *adiicitur* ω; 45, 5 *adicit* **Wm ba**, *addicit* **r**, *adiicit* ω; 3, 11 *adisse* ω, *adiisse* **lzuRc**; 34, 8 *adiit* ω; 29, 1 *batauii* ω, *bataui* **h L**, *batani* **e s**; 12 *batauis* ω; 28, 7 *boi* τ **ba**, *boii* (*beii* π) ω; 28, 8 *boihemi*, *boiihaemionem;* 42, 3 *bois* ω, *boiis* [1] **m L s**; 34, 3 *frisi* **X N Δ bal**, *frisci* **I**, *fusi* ψ, *frisii* ξ β **s**; 34, 3 *frisis* (*fusis* π) ω, *frisiis* **L**; 7, 13 *hi* ω, *hii* **h t v s**; 13 *hi* ω, *hii* **mh t v s**; 32, 5 *hi* ω, *hii* **m I t s**²; 43, 7 *hi* ω, *hii* **Wm I t r c s**, *ii* **a**; 46, 8 *hi* ω, *hii* **Wm v t s**; 25, 10 *his* **Wh dE** π, *hiis* **m vr b s**, *iis* **a λ a**; 10, 12 *isdem* **s**, *hisdem* **Wm l**, *iisdem* ω; 12, 10 *hisdem* **X I o bl**, *iisdem* ω; 15, 5 *idem* (plu.) **X b**, *hidem* **r**, *hisdem* **l**, *iidem* (or *iisdem*) ω. Genitive of nouns in *-ius* and *-ium* always in *-ii*—even *Cornelii* in the title.

I : V

i for u

Germania: 9, 8 *assimilare* **m ΔMw** τ **al**, *assimulare* (*ads-*) ω; 41, 9 *inclitum* ω, *inclytum* **ΔpMw λE a**,

---

[1] m regularly writes *ii* as *y*.

The Extant Manuscripts of the Germania 243

inclūtum d, melutum v; 3, 15 monimentaque **Wh a β**, monu- **m N L ɸ s** (monitos **b**); but, 27, 4 monumentorum **ω** (moni- **t**).

I : Y

i for y

Germania: 6, 11 *giros* **h It π s**, *gyros* **ω**; 28, 6 *herciniam* [1] **It Lr baA s**, -*cin*- > -*cyn*- **p**, -*cun*- **W**, -*cyn*- **ω**; 30, 1 *hercinio* [1] **a Ldv e s**, *hercynio* **W VE π**, *herquinio* **mh**, **W** in mg.; 30, 4 *hercinius* **a Ldvr aleuz s**, *hercynius* **W VE RA**, *herquinius* **mh**, in mg. **W**, *quimus* **b**; 43, 10 *ligiorum* **r ɸ** (*lignorum* **ψ**), *leg*- **p**; 44, 1 *ligios* **m p Lvr ɸ s**, *lygios* **Wh a V dE**; 43, 12 *helisios* [2] (*el-*) **mh t LdEr blR s**, *helysios* **W a V ezuAc**.

y for i

Agricola: *calydonia* ($\bar{e} > i > y$. See p. 240). Otherwise *i* correctly written (*hibernis, hiemps, hieme, hispaniam*).

Germania: 2, 6 *Asya* **W**; 37, 1 *cymbri* **W ξ L e**; 37, 7 *cymbrorum* **W ξ L e**; 37, 23 *hybernis* **W ΔIξ VdE c**; 16, 12 *hyemi* **ω**, *hiemi* **hm Nt Lr blu**; 22, 2 *hyems* (or *hyemps, hyemis* **E zAc**) **ω**, *hiems* (*hiemis* **N lu**) **h Nt L luR**; 26, 9 *hyems* (*hyemps*) **ω**, *hiems* **h t L lzuA**; 41, 9 *inclytum* (see on *i : u*); 46, 17 *hymbriumque* (*ym*-) **ΔIχ Vr buA s**; 14, 17 *ymmo* **Wm v b**, *ymo* **s**; 37, 12 *hyspaniae* **W I b**; 27, 6 *lachrymas* **Δ VdE**; 3, 10 *Vlyxem* (-*en*) **Mw Vro**, *Vlyssem* **L**, *Vli*- **ω**; 3, 14 *Vlyxi* **Mw Vdro**, *Vlyssi* **L**, *Vli*- **ω**.

---

[1] For variations other than in the syllable -*cy*- and for MSS. not here reported see p. 110.

[2] The true spelling is uncertain. **W** is here hardly a safe guide, because of the frequency with which it writes *y* for *i*.

prosthetic *i:* [1]

    Agricola: No clear case, but cf. p. 37, note 2 on ch. 36, 11 *foede recti trates.*

    Germania: 24, 5 *expectantium*, probably an attempted emendation of *ispectantium* (cf. p. 107).

    de Grammaticis: 11, 2 *is scripsit* or *inscripsit* for *scripsit;* 3, 1 *istilo* for *Stilo.*

IVM : VM

    Agricola: 60, 2, 29 (ch. 29) *ciuitatium.*

    Germania: 13, 12 *principium* (in mg. *pum* W) **Wm NI r φ, h** in mg., *principum* ω; 39, 3 *patrium* **m IpM β 1, u**^{2} in mg., *patrum* **W, h** ex sil., χ **bazRc s**, *patruum* **NΔ euA**.

O : V

u for close o [2]

    Agricola: 58, 2, 10 (ch. 20) *contractu (exercitu)* corr. to *contracto.* (The error is hardly phonetic.)

    Germania: 10, 4 *fortuitu* **m** τ, *fortuito* ω.

o for open u [3]

    Agricola: 57^v, 1, 22 (ch. 18) *animosi/mili* corr. to *animussi/mili.* (Again the error is hardly phonetic.)

    Germania: 13, 8 *adolescentulis* ω, *adulescentulis* **W dvo baz**; 14, 8 *adolescentium* (*adel-* **m**) ω, *adulescentium* **W bz**; 10, 19 *captiuom* **V**, *captiuo in* Δ; 11, 10 *conctatione* **h v s**, *conta-* Δ**I V b**, *conta-* > *cunta-* **p**, *cunctatione* (*cuncta-* > *cunta-* M, *cunta-* w z) ω; 30, 17 *conctatio* **V**, *contatio* **I b**, *cuntatio* (from *cuncta-* M) **pMw**, *cunctatio* ω; 22, 6 *uinolentos* **m, h** ex sil., λ π **s**, *uinu-* **W a** τ **s**^{2} (*multos* **b**, om. **a**); 13, 9 *robur*, in mg. *rubor* **W**, *rubor*, in mg. *robur* **h**, *ru̇bor* **N**, *robur* **m d c**, *robor* **s**, *rubor* ω. Also see *C : QV*.

---

[1] Cf. Schuchardt II, 337–353.
[2] Schuchardt II, 91–130.
[3] Schuchardt II, 149–180.

u for open o [1]
: *Agricola:* 56ᵛ, 1, 5 (ch. 15) *procuratur* > *procurator.*
o for close u [2]
: *Agricola:* 61, 2, 16 (ch. 32) *dicto* > *dictu;* 63, 2, 19 (ch. 38) *plorato* for *ploratu.*
  Germania: 36, 2 *iocundius* m Iξ VdE blzeRc, *iucundius* Wh N∆ Lvr auA.

(G)V : VV
: *Agricola:* 76ᵛ, 1, 22 (ch. 46) *extinguntur.*
  Germania: 6, 9 *distingunt* ω, *distinguunt* W, h ex sil.,[3] χ a; 17, 3 *distinguntur* ω, *distinguuntur* t v a. (Also see *C : QV*).

Consonants

consonants doubled
: *Agricola: Brittania, brittannia, brittanni, brittani,* are the usual spellings (only rarely *britannia, britanni*), but the correction to *britannia, britanni,* has been made in most places by the first or second hand. 63ᵛ, 2, 27 (ch. 40) *atilli* corr. to *atili,* but the former may be a corruption of *atilii.* Otherwise there is no doubling of consonants (ch. 15 *oceano*, 25 *oceanus;* 13 *litore,* 30 *litora;* 32 *germanos, germani*).
  Germania: 13, 13 *accerrimi* W p; 2, 6 *Affrica* W It aRc s; 17, 8 *belluarum* ∆M Er bz; 36, 7 *fossi* W R; 41, 4 *germannorum* W; 35, 3 *littoris* ∆pχ, ϛ except r, bauA s, *lictoris* W cz, *litoris* (*literis* m) ω; 45, 7 *littore* h ex sil., NIχ dEv azRA s, *litore* ω; 45, 15 *littore* h ex sil., NIχ VdEv aR s, *lictore* c, *litore* ω; 45, 27 *littora* as in 45, 15 (*littora* A, *lito-* c); 42, 1 *marchomanni* s; 42, 2 *marcomannorum* W L s; 42, 6 *marcomannis* W s; 43, 1

---

[1] Schuchardt II, 130–149.
[2] Schuchardt II, 180–191.
[3] See p. 162.

marcomannorum (corr. to *-ano-* in L) **W L** lzeu
s; *occeanus* so written regularly in **Wh NI Ev**,
ϕ except **b**, **s**; *oceanus* regularly in **m Δ ξ**, β
except **Ev**, **b**;[1] 45, 14 *succinum* ξ L τ, **h** ex sil., a,
sucinum **Wm** σ **V** bπ **s**; 45, 27 *succini* ω, *sucini*
(*sucum* m) **Wm** σ **Vr**; 45, 20 *succum* ω, *sucum* **Wm**
Vr le.

single consonant for double

Agricola: brittania (cf. above); 76ᵛ, 1, 5 (ch. 45)
o̓portunitate.

Germania: 22, 12 *calida* **W p r bc**, *cali->calli-* **I**,
callida ω; 31, 6 *retulisse* ω, *rettulisse* **pM** (*rettu-
>retu-* p); 30, 7 *solertiae* ω, *sollertiae* **W t V s**.

B : V (consonant)

u for b

Agricola:[2] 56, 1, 17 (ch. 13) *mouili; 56ᵛ, 2, 12 (ch. 16)
uo adicca in text, *bouidicta* in mg.; 57, 1, 28
(ch. 16) and 2, 3 *uolanus* for *Bolanus*; 59, 2, 14
(ch. 25) *uo dotriam*; 60ᵛ, 2, 18 (ch. 30) *amuitiosi;
62ᵛ, 1, 24 *uatauorum* in text, *batauorum* in mg.;
2, 4 *uatabi*.

Note that 60, 2, 2 (ch. 28) *suebis* is correctly
written.

Germania: Sueui, Sueuia, everywhere except 41, 1,
where the corruption *pars uerborum* for *pars Sueborum* is an index to the correct orthography.
Possibly, ch. 8, 9, *Auriniam* is a corruption of
Albriniam.[3] Ch. 28, 8, probably *boi̓hemi* in Hf.[4]

---

[1] *Occe-* **V** in 17, 8; **dr** in 1, 3; **r** in 2, 12· 3, 11· 44, 4 and 17; *occe->oce-* **p** in 1, 3 and 7; sometimes *occe-* in **t**; *occe-* **b** in 1, 7· 2, 4.

[2] The asterisk indicates that the correction to *b* has been made by the second (contemporary) hand. The marginal and interlinear readings are all by the second hand.

[3] See pp. 105 f.

[4] See p. 129.

The Extant Manuscripts of the Germania

de Gram.: 11, 1, *uburseni*, the reading of **W** for *Burseni*.

b for u:

Agricola: 59, 2, 19 (ch. 20) *explorab̊it;* 58, 2, 19 *inritamenta* for *inuitamenta;*[1] 60, 1, 21 (ch. 28) *praebebantur* in mg. as variant of *praeueheban-tur;*[2] 63ᵛ, 2, 17 (ch. 39) *fabor* (?).[3] Also cf. 57, 1, 25 (ch. 16) *praeḃuit*.

Germania: 1, 9 *DAnuuius*[4] **W**, *danubius* ω, *danuuius* **h I** zeu**RAc**; 1, 2 *danubio* ω, *danuuio* **h I v** ezu**RAc**; 29, 15 *danubium* ω, *danuuium* **Wh ΔI** ezu**Ac**; 41, 3 *danubium* ω, *danuuium* **Wh ΔI V** ezu**RAc**; 42, 5 *danubio* ω, *danuuio* **Wh I V** ezu**RAc**; 2, 10 *bistonem* as variant of *tuistonem*.[5]

C : D (before *q*)

Agricola: 63ᵛ, 2, 22 (ch. 40) *quidquid;* 76ᵛ, 2, 11 (ch. 46) *quidquid*.

Germania: 34, 8 *quidquid* **v**, *quicquid* (abbr. in m) ω; 40, 6 *quidquam* **h**, *quitquam* **m v**, *quicquam* ω; 46, 7 *quidquid* **m v**, *quitquid* **W t**, *quid* **b**, *qui* π, *quicquid* ω.

C : G

Agricola: 59ᵛ, 1, 19 (ch. 25) *acminibus*.[6] Possibly 61ᵛ, 1, 18 (ch. 32) *taetra* in mg. (i.e. *aegra* > *aecra* > *taetra;* cf. p. 51).

---

[1] The process of corruption was *INVITAMENTA* > *INBITAMENTA* > *INRITAMENTA*.

[2] Probably a series of corruptions: *PRAEVEHEBANTUR* > *PRAEBEHE-BANTUR* > *praebebantur*.

[3] Annibaldi reports *fauor*, with *u* in an erasure by the third (fifteenth century) hand.

[4] Only in 1, 9, are doublets indicated for Hf. In the other cases we can hardly say which was the spelling of the parent MS.

[5] See p. 96.

[6] The correction to *ag-* is by the fifteenth-century hand.

Germania: 12, 4 *crate,* variant *grate;* 34, 1 *dulgibini,* variant *dulcubuni;* 43, 1 *gotini* ω; 6 *gotini* **W, h** in text, ξ β **as,** *cotini* **m, h** mg. in red, σ φ; 43, 3 *gotinos* ω. Possibly 16, 4 *longant* in β as variant of *locant* (i.e. *locant* > *logant* > *longant*).

C : Q V

Agricola: 57ᵛ, 1, 20 (ch. 18) *aecum* for *aequum;* 61, 11, 12–13 (ch. 31) *cotidie* twice.

Germania: 14, 12 *equom* **Wm,** *equum* ω; 5, 18 *secuntur* σp**M** ro b π, *sequntur* **d,** *sequuntur* ω; 38, 10 *secuntur* **N**ξ, **r** in mg., **v,** *sequntur* **d,** *sequuntur* (*-quen-* φ) ω. See note to ch. 37, 16, *quoque.*

CI : TI (assibilated)
ci for ti

Agricola:[1] 62ᵛ, 1, 1 (ch. 35) *edicioribus;* 56ᵛ, 1, 8 (ch. 15) *exiciosam;* 56, 1, 23 (ch. 13) *inicium,* but elsewhere, chapters 18, 29, 30, *initium;* 56ᵛ, 1, 12 (ch. 15) *forciorem;* 59, 2, 26 (ch. 25) *laeticia;* 59, 1, 30 (ch. 24) *negociatores;* 56ᵛ, 2, 26 (ch. 16) *pacientiae,* but chapters 15 and 33, *patientia;* 58, 1, 27 (ch. 19) *praecio;* 60ᵛ, 2, 20 (ch. 30) *saciauerit,* but chapters 39 and 45, *satiatus* and *satiari.*

Germania: In **m** and **s** *ci* has virtually displaced assibilated *ti.* It occurs with great frequency[2] in **htbWvwuMVlR.** I list only the instances occurring in **W** or in six or more manuscripts of **Y**: 28, 15 *ambiciosi* **Wm t s;** 21, 2 *amicicias* **mh pt V au;** 14, 10 *ancipicia* **m s,** *auspicia* π; 38, 9 *caniciem* **Wm NMt** λ**v bu s;** 18, 16 *denunciant* (*re-* **r**) **Wm t Vr bu s;** 6, 22 *flagicium* **Wm t s;**

---

[1] The correction to *t* has everywhere been made by the second (contemporary) hand.

[2] The MSS. are listed according to the relative frequency with which *ci* occurs. It may well be doubted if Longolius reported every instance of *ci* in **h**.

The Extant Manuscripts of the Germania 249

2, 2 *hospiciis* X Mt v buA s; 21, 6 *hospiciis* X tM v b s; 21, 9 *hospicii* X t v A s; 5, 4 *impaciens* Wm t u s; 8, 3 *impacientius* W o, *impaciencius* m s; 39, 10 *inicia* X t v s; 21, 5 *inimiciciae* mh pt Vv u s; 28, 16 *inercia* Wm s; 35, 7 *iusticia* W Mt v bu s (*iusti*^{a} m p); 22, 4 *negocia* m ∆χ λE b s; 18, 4 *nupciis* Wm s; 14, 7 *ocio* X ∆χM λdEr be s; 15, 2 *ocium* X ∆χM LdEr bR s; 37, 22 *ocium* ω, *otium* W, h ex sil., Np vr au (om. I, *odio* b); 44, 17 *ociosa* ω, *otiosa* N azuc, h ex sil.; 4, 7 *pacientia* W M, *paciencia* m t s, *potencia* b; 7, 2 *pocius* Wm s; 26, 4 *parciuntur* Wm a; *parciendi* X t r ba; 31, 6 *precia* m χM λ uR; 24, 5 *precium* I ξ λ s (*premium* π); 43, 4 *paciuntur* Wm t a s; 19, 1 *pudicicia* mh χ V auR s, 19, 7 *pudiciciae* mh t V uR s; 40, 16 *saciatam* Wms² ∆tM Ev (*sacratam* bπ, *sacratum* s); 16, 5 *spacio* Wm M ue s; 37, 3 *spacia* Wm It bu s; 11, 10 *tercius* X M b Rs; 27, 6 *tristiciam* Wm It v bu; 19, 8 *uicia* X Mt v buR s; 23, 6 *uiciis* X t R; 11, 9 *uicium* Wm ∆M s.

ti for ci

Agricola: 59, 1, 29 (ch. 24), 60, 2, 4 (ch. 28), 63^v, 1, 28 (ch. 39) *commertia;* 59^v, 2, 27 (ch. 27), 76^v, 1, 15 (ch. 45) *conditione;* 58^v, 2, 21 (ch. 22) *conuitiis* in text, *conuiciis* m. 2 in mg.; 63, 2, 15 (ch. 37) *ferotia,* but ch. 31 *ferocia;* 60, 2, 6 (ch. 28), 63^v, 2, 13 (ch. 39) *inditium;* 57, 1, 9 and 14 (ch. 16), 57, 2, 13 (ch. 17), 57^v, 1, 12 and 2, 16 (ch. 18) and 28 (ch. 19), 58, 1, 6 (ch. 19) *prouintia,* but *prouincia* chapters 14 and 16; 59, 2, 3 (ch. 24) *spetie,* but ch. 25 (twice) *specie,* ch. 35 *speciem.*

Germania: Examples occurring in W or in six or more manuscripts of the Y family are listed. Elsewhere -*ti*- for -*ci*- is common only in Ip ba, but appears occasionally in NM A. 5, 14 *commer-*

tiorum **W σM τ φ**, *commerciorum* **hm pχ λ s**; 17, 6 *commertia* **ω**, *commercia* **hm χ V s**; 24, 12 *commertia* **ω**, *commercia* **hm χ λ baR s**; 41, 4 *commertium* **ω**, *commercium* **m χ L s**; 24, 11 *conditionis* **ω**, *condicionis* **m pt a s**, *condictionis* **v**; 22, 6 *conuitiis* **σpM VdE**, *conuiciis* **X χ Lvr s** (*conuiuiis* **φ**); 20, 4 *delitiis* **a** (-ci- t), **τ lzuc**, *deliciis* **X λ baeRA s**; 18, 7 *delitias* (om. s) **σpw dvr balzec**, *delicias* **X Mt λE uRA**; 8, 4 *efficatius* **W IM Vor**, -ti- to -ci- p, (*efficiati* **φ**); 13, 10 *iuditio* **W IM ba** (-ti- >-ci- p); 5, 16 *mertium* **W IMw v bauAc**; 25, 5 *offitia* **W NIM r a** (*offa* p); 29, 18 *prouintiae* **p vr aAc s**; 41, 5 *prouintiae* **pM vr aAuR s**; 24, 11 *peruicatia* **W IM baAc**; 5, 1 *spetie* **NΔp dor aRzeAc** (*spē* I LE s); 9, 8 *spetiem* **N dEr aec** (*spēm* ΔIp L); 16, 8 *spetiem* **NΔ VE a** (*spēm* Ip L); 26, 9 *speties* **N dvE baz** (*spēs* Δ L eAc s).

CT : T
t for ct
Agricola: 56, 2, 16 (ch. 14) *extintus*.
Germania: Tenteri (32, 2; 33, 1; 38, 2) **φ**.

ct for t
Agricola: No examples. Note, 63, 1, 29 (ch. 37) *artiora*.
Germania: 20, 11 *arctioremque* **ω**, *arti-* **ΔIt Vr a**, *arci-* **mh**; 11, 10 *contatione* **ΔIp V bz**, *cunta-* (-nct->-nt- M) **Mw**; 30, 16 *contatio* **I b**, *cuntatio* (*cuncta->cunta-* M) **pMw**; 12, 8 *mulctantur* **ω**, *multantur* **NIpw V b**; *mulctae* **ω**, *multae* **pw b**.

CT : TT
Germania: 3, 16 *licteris* **W**; 19, 2 *licterarum*, 35, 3 *lictoris* **W**; 29, 9 *Mactiacorum* **h φ**.

D : T
   d for t

      Agricola: *adque*[1] (*adq.*) for *atque* was originally written everywhere[2] except 61, 1, 3 (ch. 31), where it is written as part of the preceding word, *ageratque*.[3] In all but three cases[4] the correction to *atque* has been made by the second (contemporary) hand. 76ᵛ, 2, 16 (ch. 46) *uelud*.

      Germania: 39, 11 *ad quod* **W**, *atque* ω. Elsewhere only *atque*, and always *uelut* (*uelud* b).

   t for d

      Agricola: *haut* is always written for *haud:* 57ᵛ, 1, 4 (ch. 18) *haut multo;* 58, 1, 5 (ch. 19), 2, 8 (ch. 20) *hautminus;* 59, 1, 27 (ch. 24) *haut multum;* Likewise *aput* for *apud* was the original writing, but the correction to *apud* was made by the second hand:[5] 57ᵛ, 1, 13 (ch. 18); 58, 2, 15 (ch. 20); 58ᵛ, 1, 20 (ch. 21); 2, 20 (ch. 22); 60ᵛ, 1, 8 (ch. 29).

      Germania: *haut* (*aut* b) is found only in **m baR**. *Aput* is found only in **m a s**, but is not used exclusively even in these manuscripts.

F : PH

      Agricola: 63ᵛ, 2, 20 (ch. 40) *triumfalia;* 63ᵛ, 1, 28 (ch. 39) *triumfum,* but *triumpho* 63ᵛ, 2, 22 (ch. 40).

---

[1] This spelling is found in our oldest Latin MSS., and is said to occur in inscriptions from the first century of our era. Cf. Kühner-Holzweissig, *Ausführliche Grammatik der lateinischen Sprache* i (Hanover, 1912), 35.

[2] 56ᵛ, 2, 11 (ch. 16); 59, 1, 7 (ch. 23); 60, 1, 6 (ch. 27); 22 (ch. 28); 29; 60ᵛ, 2, 8 (ch. 30); 24; 61, 1, 1 (ch. 31); 9; 61ᵛ, 2, 8 (ch. 33); 62, 1, 18 (ch. 34); 63, 1, 14 (ch. 37).

[3] The fact that the sole appearance of *atque* is in a place where it might have been understood as forming part of the preceding word leads me to suspect that elsewhere there was an intentional change from *atque* to *adque*—i.e. an "orthographical revision" in late antiquity (cf. p. 256).

[4] 56ᵛ, 2, 11; 60, 1, 22; 60ᵛ, 2, 24.

[5] 58, 2, 15 the correction is by the third (fifteenth-century) hand.

Germania: 21, 7 *nephas* **Wm pI v** (corr. to *nefas* I), om. ɸ, *nefas* ω; 6, 23 *phas* **m**, *fas* ω; 15, 12 *falerae* **X** ψ, *pha-* ω. Note, 37, 25 *triumphati* (-*mfa-* I) ω.

H

    h omitted:

        Agricola: 59, 1, 28 (ch. 24) *h aut* (*h* in mg.); 58, 1, 25 (ch. 19) *orreis;* 62ᵛ, 1, 29 (ch. 36) *inabile*. (with *h* superscript marks above *orreis* and *inabile*)

        Germania: 30, 1 *catti* **X ΔI Lv s**, *catti*>*cha-* **p**, *caiti* or *carti* ɸ, *Cathi* **E**, *Chatti* **NM**χ **Vdr**; elsewhere *Catti* (*cacti* l) is regular only in **L bl**.[1] (On the spelling *Cathi* see below.) 35, 2 *caucorum* **Ldr**, caueorum **b**π, *chau-* ω; 36, 1 *caucorum* **r ba**, om. ψ, *chau-* ω; 35, 6 *cauci* **r balR**, *cauci* **IM**, *chau-* ω; 29, 15 *decumates*[2] **ΔI**ξ **Lr** ɸ, *decumathes* **XN**, β except **Lr**, **s**; 6, 4 *abili* **h v b s**, *abili*>*ha-* **M u**, *alibi* **m**, *ha-* ω; 43, 18 *alii* for *harii* ω, *arii* in mg. **t**; 43, 12 *Elysios* (*Eli-*) ξ **L Rz**; 23, 1 *ordeo* ω, *hordeo* **m NΔ λdE**; 26, 7 *ortos* **X p**χ **vr alezuA s**, *hortos* σ**M**, β except **vr**, **bRc**; 2, 17 *renum* **mh t v l** (always *re-* in **m**, usually in **r z**, sometimes in **v**); 46, 1 *uenetorumque*[2] **m**, α except **N**, β except **V**, **balR s**, *uenethorumque* **Wh N V ezuAc s**²; 46, 6 *ueneti* **m α** β ɸ, *uenethi* **Wh N V s**.

    h transposed

        Agricola: 59, 2, 13 (ch. 25) *incohabat;* 57ᵛ, 1, 15 (ch. 18) *incoaturo*. (with *h* superscript above *incoaturo*)

        Germania: Generally *cathi*, etc. in **E aR**; 11, 4 *inchoatur* ω, *incohatur* **N VEr bAz**, *incoa-* **do**; 30, 1 *inchoant* **X ΔIM**χ **L luRc**, *incohant* **Np VEvr baezA s**, *incoant* **d**.

---

[1] 29, 2 *cattorum* (*cot-* v) **Ldvr lz**, *Ca-*>*Cha-* **V**, *hactorum* **b**; 30, 4 *cha-* **b**; 30, 4· 31, 2· 31, 10 *ca-* **s**; 31, 2 *ca-* **h**.

[2] The correct spelling is uncertain.

h added:

Agricola: 58, 2, 12 (ch. 20) *cohercere;* 58, 1, 4 (ch. 19) *cohercuit;* 61ᵛ, 2, 3 (ch. 33) *cohercitum.* Note, 76ᵛ, 1, 18 (ch. 45) *lacrimis;* 2, 7 (ch. 46) *simulacra.*

Germania: 40, 19 *archanus* **mh It r ɸ s,** *arcanus* **W α β b**; 18, 10 *archana* **X ΔMt v aleuA s,** *arcana* **NIpw β bRzc**; 11, 12 *cohercendi* **W NI r ɸ s,** *coercendi* ω; 25, 6 *cohercere* **m NIt r, ɸ** except u, s, *coer-* ω; 39, 5 *coheunt* **I r bzRAc,** *coherent* ξ, *coeunt* ω; 44, 1 *gothones* ω, *gotones* **bluAz**; 46, 17 *himbriumque (hy-)* **ΔI w Vr bzuRA s**; 5, 2 *humidior* ω; 27, 6 *lachrimas (-ry-)* **NΔw VdE R**; 1, 1 *rhaetiisque (rhe-)* **ξ L⸚ ae,** *raetiisque (re-)* **Xσ Vv ɸ s**; 1, 6 *rhaeticarum (rhe-)* **ξ L⸚ a** *(rethi- v)*; 3, 16 *rhaetiaeque (rhe-)* **ξ L⸚ ɸ** *(rethi- b, reti- z)*; 41, 5 *rhaetiae (rhe-)* **ξ LE,** *(rhenae b)* **bae**; 27, 4 *sepulchrum* **Wm ΔMw E auRA s**; 43, 16 *simulachra* **W M r lu s**; 17, 4 *sarmathae* **ξ s**;[1] 43, 5 *sarmathae* ξ; 46, 5 *sarmatharum* **ξ dvr ezuA**; 46, 10 *sarmathis* **ξ dvr**; 45, 24 *thura* **m, h** ex sil., **NΔt π s.**

M : N (before a stop)

Agricola: 76ᵛ, 1, 7 (ch. 46) *tanquam;* 63, 2, 28 (ch. 38) *tāquā;* 56, 1, 6 (ch. 13) *quāquam;* 62ᵛ, 2, 15 (ch. 36) *quāquā.* Otherwise always *m: circumcisis; circumdedit; circumdatae; quamquam* (six times); *quemque; numquam; plerumque, tamquam.*

Germania: I do not give a detailed report, since none of our manuscripts is a direct copy of Hf. and the line of suspension, standing either for *m* or *n,* may have been used in the intervening manuscripts. In *quamquam, numquam, quemquam, plerumque, tamquam;* only **t ba** write *-mq-* consistently, **m I s** abbreviate or write *-mq-;*

---

[1] Ch. 1, 2 *sarmathis* only in **pM**.

NΔMw u prefer -*nq*-, though N usually abbreviates *quamquam*. VdEr write -*nq*- or abbreviate; the other manuscripts show -*mq*-, -*nq*-, and the line of suspension. W writes: *tanquam* (8, 10; 12, 5; 19, 13 and 14; 20, 12; 22, 10; 28, 15; 39, 10); *plerumque* (5, 5; 13, 19); *quemquam* (19, 15); *quemque* (20, 2); *utrimque* (44, 8); *quēcunque* (21, 7); *nunquam* (25, 10); elsewhere uses the line of suspension or abbreviates. Ch. 25, 10 *dumtaxat* is the reading of ω (*dūtaxat* Npw Lr b s, *duntaxat* M e).

MN : MPN

Germania: 29, 5 *contempnuntur* Wm v R, *contemnuntur* ω.

MPT : NT

Agricola: 58, 2, 14 (ch. 20), *praetemptare*.
Germania: 34, 7 *temptauimus* X c s, *tentauimus* (-*mtat*) ω; 34, 11 *temptauit* X Iξ r, φ except bl, s, *tenta-* NΔ β bl; 45, 28 *temptes* X s² t ae, *tentes* ω; 31, 15 *contentores* IΔ bzuRAc, *contempt-* (-*npte*, -*mt-* t) ω.

MS : MPS

Agricola: 58, 2, 28 (ch. 21), 58ᵛ, 2, 10 (ch. 22) *hiemps*.
Germania: 22, 2 *hiems* h t L lR, *hiemis* N lu, *hyemps* m v e s, *hyems* (*hyemis* E Ac) ω; 26, 9 *hiems* h t L lzuA, *hyemps* m v ae, *hyems* ω.

S : NS [1]

Agricola: 56, 2, 23 (ch. 14) *occansioni*; 57ᵛ, 1, 2 (ch. 18) *occansionem*; 59, 2, 4 (ch. 24) *occansionem*; 59ᵛ, 2, 30 (ch. 27) *occansione*.
Germania: 30, 8 *occasiones* ω; 37, 22 *occasione* ω.

---

[1] See W. Brambach, *Die Neugestaltung der lateinischen Orthographie* (Leipzig, 1868), 266 ff.

S : X

Agricola: f. 58ᵛ, 1, 28 (ch. 22) aŭxi (for ausi).

Germania: 37, 6 *sescentesimum* λ, *secen-* I, *sexcen-* ω; 6, 13 *exstimanti* b, *extimati* ψ, *existimanti* σ pM, for *aestimanti* (i.e. eẋtimanti; cf. p. 116).

Prefixes

adc-

Agricola: 62ᵛ, 1, 3 (ch. 35) *adcliue*. Otherwise only *acc-*: *accendere, accendunt, accendendum, accucurrerant* (63, 1, 6, ch. 37).

Germania: 19, 5 *Adcisis* Vdr buc, *Adcisam* k, *accisis* h *ex sil.*, a L (*abscisis* Wm t Ev lR), *adscissis* zu, *Adsissis* Ac. Otherwise *acc-*: *accedo, accendunt, accidit, accipere*.

adf-

Agricola: 60ᵛ, 2, 21 (ch. 30) *adfectu;* 61, 2, 20 (ch. 32) *adfectu* corr. from *aff-;* 60ᵛ, 1, 2 (ch. 29) *adfluebant;* 62, 2, 25 (ch. 35) *adfunderentur*.

Germania: 3, 7 *adfectatur* W, *aff-* ω; 28, 14 *adfectationem* W, *aff-* ω; 18, 10 *adfert* Wh, *aff-* ω; 5, 11 *adficiuntur* W, *aff-* ω; 20, 16 *adfinium* W, *aff-* ω; 2, 15 *adfirmant* W, aff- ω; 5, 8 *adfirmauerim* W, *aff-* ω.

37, 24 *affectauere*, 5, 19 *affectione*, 22, 8 *affinitatibus* ω.

adg-

Agricola: 56, 2, 23 (ch. 14), 57, 2, 14 (ch. 17) *adgressus;* 59ᵛ, 1, 26 (ch. 26) *adgressi;* 62, 1, 24 (ch. 34) *adgressos*.

61ᵛ, 1, 10 (ch. 32) *agnoscent*.

Germania: 19, 15 *adgnatis* Ws² b, *agna-* ω; 20, 6 *adgnoscat* W, *agno-* ω; 13, 9 *adgregantur* Wms², *aggr-* ω. 5, 15 *agnoscunt* ω.

adl-
    Agricola: 62, 2, 17 (ch. 35) *adloquente.*
    Germania: 45, 8 *adluuntur* **X ΔI dvrk b s,** *allu-* **N ξ π,**
    (*abluuntur* λE a); 24, 10 *alligari* ω.

adn-
    Agricola: Note, 58^v, 2, 9 (ch. 22) *adnuis* for *annuis*, evidence, I believe, that our text went through an "orthographical" revision at some point in its history (cf. p. 251, note 3).
    Germania: Always *adn-*.

adp-
    Agricola: 62, 2, 13 (ch. 34) *adprobatae;* 63, 1, 23 (ch. 37) *adpropinquauerunt.* (Ch. 30 *appellant.*)
    Germania: 44, 9 *adpulsui* **Wm,** *app-* ω. (*Apparatu, apparatus, apparatis, appellationes, appellant* ω.)

adq- (For *adque* see *D : T.*)
    Germania: 14, 17 *adquirere* **Δ L s,** *aquirere* >*acq-* **W,** *acq-* ω.

adr-
    Agricola: 60, 1, 1 (ch. 27) *adrogantia;* 56^v, 2, 30 (ch. 16) *adroganter.*

ads-
    Agricola: 58, 1, 25 (ch. 19), 76^v, 1, 10 (ch. 45) *adsidere;* 76^v, 1, 17 (ch. 45) *adsidente;* 58^v, 1, 2 (ch. 21) *adsuescerent;* 57, 1, 20 (ch. 16) *adsuetus;* 59, 2, 20 (ch. 25) *adsumpta;* 56, 1, 22 (ch. 13) *adsumpto;* 59^v, 2, 3 (ch. 26) *adsultare;* 62^v, 2, 7 (ch. 36) *adstiterant.* Ch. 28 *ascendere;* 30 *aspicientes;* 32 *aspectus;* 38 *aspectu;* 24 *aspicit;* 29 *aspiciebantur.*
    Germania: 22, 9 *adsciscendis* ω, *ascis-* **Nt r l**; 46, 2 *adscribam* **WN I V b π s,** *ascr-* **h** ex sil., **Δ ξ L τ aR**; 46, 22 *adsecuti* **Wh R,** *ass-* ω; 35, 11 *adsequuntur* **W,** *asse-* ω; 11, 17 *adsensus* **W,** *ass-* ω; 2, 12 *adsignant* **W,** *assig-* ω; 13, 8 *adsignant* **W,** *assig-* ω; 9, 8 *adsimulare* **W s^2,** *assi-* ω; 4, 8 *adsueuerunt* **W,** *assu-* ω; 11, 10 *adsumitur* **W s^2 R,** *assumitur* φ

(*absumitur* ω); 12, 12 *adsunt* ω, *assunt* **m N L**;
14, 5 *adsignare* **Wh**, ass- ω. 25, 12 *ascendunt*,
43, 23 *aspectum*, 2, 8 *aspectuque*, 13, 10 *aspici*,
45, 5 *aspici*, 5, 3 *aspicit*, ω.

adt-
Agricola: 63ᵛ, 2, 5 (ch. 39) *adtolli;* 59, 2, 27 (ch. 25)
adtollerent. 62, 1, 10 (ch. 33) *attinet.*
Germania: 39, 8 *adtolli* **I V**, *ad colli* **W**, *attolli* ω.
29, 6 *atterit*, 40, 10 *attingere* ω.

conf-
Agricola: 56, 2, 27 (ch. 15) *comferre*, but ch. 22
conflictatum.
Germania: conſ- or cōf- (*conferre, confinio, confirmare*).

conl-
Agricola: 63, 1, 25 (ch. 37) *collecti.*
Germania: 28, 21 *conlocati* **W**, coll- ω. 6, 2 *colligitur,*
37, 10 *colliguntur*, 29, 6 *collationibus* ω.

conm-
Agricola: Always comm- (*commendatione, commertia,
commodare, commendent, commilitones, commea-
tuum*), except 60, 2, 27 (ch. 29) cō *mune.*
Germania: 5, 14 *commertiorum* (cōme-, -ci-) **W**, **h** ex
sil., a λ **R s**, *conme-* **m**, *come-* ω; 17, 6 *commertia*
(cōme-, -ci-) **X** (h ex sil.), σt λ au**R**, *conme-* **s**, *come-*
ω; 24, 12 *commertia* (cōme-, -ci-) **X** (h ex sil.),
σt λ a**R s**, *come-* ω; 41, 4 *commertium* (cōme-, -ci-)
X (h ex sil.), **N∆Mt** λ a**RAc s**, *come-* ω; 6, 5 *comminus* (cōmi-) **NI Vdvo**, *cominus* ω; 8, 3 *comminus*
(cōmi-) **W N Vdvro**, *cominus* ω. Elsewhere
comm- or cōm- (*commigrauerint, committunt,
commune* abbreviated in many manuscripts)
without noteworthy exceptions.

conn-
Agricola: 62ᵛ, 2, 9 (ch. 36) *conisae;* 62ᵛ, 1, 4 (ch. 35)
conuexi for *connexi.*

Germania: 16, 4 *connexis* ω; 4, 2 *conubiis* **m M**, *connu-* ω; 46, 5 *conubiis* **W v**, *connu-* ω.

conp-

Agricola: 62ᵛ, 1, 6 (ch. 35) *conplebat*. Otherwise only *comp-* (*compararentur, comparetur, compertum, complexus, complexum, comploratus, compositus, compositum, compositos, compositis, comprimendo*).

Germania: (*complectens, complures, componitur, computant, comperi, compertum*.) **W z** regularly write *conp-*, while the other manuscripts have *comp-* or *côp-*, but ch. 37, 9 *conputemus* **m z**, *computemus* **W** ω.

exs-

Agricola: 58, 1, 12 (ch. 19) *exequi;* 57ᵛ, 2, 11 (ch. 18) *expectabant;* 76ᵛ, 1, 22 (ch. 45) *extinguntur;* 56, 2, 16 (ch. 14) *extintus;* 58ᵛ, 1, 5 (ch. 21) *extruerent.*

Germania: 12, 9 *exsoluitur* **W N k bzc**, *exól-* ω; 24, 12 *exsoluant* **Wh lu s**, *exol-* ω; 31, 15 *exsanguis* **Wm l**, *exa-* ω. 25, 5 *exequuntur*, 14, 15 *expectare*, 24, 5 *expectantium* (or *spec-*), 3, 17 *extare*, 4, 3 *extitisse* ω.

inb-, inm-, inp-

Agricola: There is no consistency in the use of the assimilated and unassimilated forms of the prefix, and apparently no distinction between *in-* negative and the prepositional prefix. We find *inminente, inmixtis, inperiis, inperantibus, inponi, inputari, inputantur, inbellibus*, but *impellitur, impellerentur, inmixtis* (m. 2 in mg.); *impigre, immensum, imperentur, impetu, imperitos, imperii, imperantes.*

Germania: The evidence of our manuscripts on this point is useless, since none is a direct copy of Hf. If a scribe found *ib-* etc. in his archetype, he could not tell whether it stood for *inb-* or *imb-*, etc., and would naturally employ the spelling which he preferred.[1] W writes *inb-*[2], *inp-* frequently, *inm-*[3] but once.

inl-

Agricola: 58, 2, 26 (ch. 20) *inlacessita;* 63ʳ, 2, 21 (ch. 40) *inlustris;* 60, 2, 7 (ch. 28) *inlustrauit;* 15 *inlustrans* in mg.; 63, 2, 15 (ch. 37) *inlatus.*

Germania: 46, 19 *inlaborare* X σ λ φ s, *illa-* ξ τ le; 36, 2 *inlacessiti* X σ λ φ s, *illa-* ξ τ; 16, 9 *inlinunt* X, *illi-* Y. 19, 1 *illecebris* ω.

inr-

Agricola: 58, 2, 19 (ch. 20) *inritamenta* (corr. to *irr-*); 60, 1, 7 (ch. 27) *inritatis;* 58ᵛ, 2, 11 (ch. 22) *inritis;* 59ʳ, 1, 28 (ch. 26) *inrupere;* 1, 19 (ch. 25) *inrupturos.*

Germania: 19, 2 *irritationibus* ω, *incitationibus* π.

subf-

Agricola: 76ᵛ, 1, 1 (ch. 45) *sufficeret.*

Germania: 43, 11 *sufficiet;* 32, 2 *sufficiat;* 13, 3 *suffecturum;* 16, 12 *suffugium* ω; 46, 17 *subfugium* W, *suff-* ω.

subm-

Agricola: 59, 1, 9 (ch. 23) *summotis.*

Germania: 31, 3 *submittere* Wh Nt Er alz, *summ-* ω.

trans-

Agricola: 57ᵛ, 2, 4 (ch. 18) *transuexit*, but 62ᵛ, 2, 25 (ch. 36) *transuersos;* 59, 1, 12 (ch. 24) *trangressus,* but 57, 2, 29 (ch. 18) *transgressus.*

Germania: 2, 18 *transgressi* (*-ngr-* b) ω; 28, 3 *transgressos* ω; 28, 20 *Transgressi* (*Trang-* E z, *Trasg-* I, *Trag-* v) ω; 29, 3 *transgressus* (*trang-* m) ω.

---

[1] The same is true of *cŏ-* before a labial. On the other hand, *cŏl-* and *ĭl-* could stand only for *conl-* and *inl-*, not for *coll-* and *ill-*.

[2] 12, 3 *inbelles* (= m p o bazA s); 31, 7 *inbellibus* (= m It bazc s); even *inbriumque*, 46, 17.

[3] 45, 1 *inmotum* (= m It v ze).

Other prefixes are written according to the usual norm in both the *Agricola* and *Germania: adm-, corr-, occ-, off-, obl-, obs-, obr-, succ-, sugg-, subl-, supp-, susp-, subst-* (Germ. 38, 5 *substringere*), *sust-* (43, 22 *substinente* N r a).

Traces of *Scriptura Continua*

As we have already observed, traces of *scriptura continua* form one of the most striking features of the Hersfeld *Agricola*.[1] Turning to the manuscripts of the *Germania*, we find the following readings sufficiently represented in both the X and Y families to leave no doubt that they are to be referred to the parent manuscript: 28, 8 *boiihaemionem* (*boiiemi-*)[2] as a variant for *boihemi nomen;* 43, 1 *osiburi* Wm NΔ φ s (*siburi* as variant in Whs[2] M); 45, 3 *in ortu se durat* Wh s a, *in ortu sedurat* m bπ; 14, 3 *infamem* Wh, *infamem in* aπ.

In two or more members of the X family we find the following instances of faulty word division: 2, 19 *genti se valuisse* m, *gentis & valuis se* W; 4, 8 *in aedia* (*in ed-* s[2]) *in* Ws[2]; 22, 15 *Deliberandum* Wm; 29, 15 *de eumathes agros* W, *deum athesagros* m; 10, 13 *contactis*[3] W, *contractis* m; 30, 16 *propriora*[4] Wm, *propiora* σ; 45, 1 *transsuionas* (*-nos* W, *-nes* m, *tn̄su-* s[2]) Wms[2]. In view of the numerous archaic features found in the X family, I have little hesitation in referring these readings to traces of *scriptura continua* in Hf., but do not, of course, assign the secondary corruptions, such as *deeum-* for *decum-*, to the parent manuscript.

Finally, m alone offers numerous examples of bizarre word division: 2, 20 *metu minorum* (?) for *metum mox;* 9, 5 *liburna efiguratum*[5] for *-nae fi-;* 16, 10 *adlineamenta* for *ac li-;* 24, 3 *aut temporauit* for *artem parauit;* 30, 1 *Vltrochos* (cf. *Vlerahos* λ) for *Vltra hos;* 31, 5 *sequentum* for *seque tum;* 36, 7 *cheriis eorum* for

---

[1] See p. 46.
[2] For a detailed list of readings see pp. 128 f.
[3] See my discussion on p. 96.
[4] See my discussion on p. 143.
[5] It should be observed that m regularly writes *e* for *ae* (see p. 238).

cheruscorum; 45, 23 *secundi ora* for *fecundiora;* 46, 4 *actor pro* for *ac torpor;* 44, 7 *Sui onn* for *Suionum*. Although carelessly written fifteenth-century manuscripts sometimes fail to give proper attention to the separation of words, I think it quite possible that in some of these instances **m** alone has preserved traces of *scriptura continua* inherited from Hf. Naturally such corruptions as *cheriis eorum* for *cherus corum* and *actor pro* for *actor por* are quite secondary in origin.

Separation of Prefixes and Enclitics

The writing of prefixes and enclitics as separate words is not, to judge from Annibaldi's diplomatic text, a very definite feature of the Hersfeld *Agricola*. I have noted the following instances: 56, 1, 29 (ch. 14) *uter que;* 57, 1, 17 (ch. 16) *inter uentus;* 60, 2, 27 (ch. 29) *pro pulsandum;* 61, 1, 14 (ch. 31) *& iam;* 61, 2, 6 (ch. 31) *se posuerit;* 61^v, 2, 28 *omnia quae* for *omniaque;* 63^v, 2, 21 *in lacessita*. There are also numerous instances in which the prefix ends the line, as in 61, 1, 19 (ch. 31) *re/seruemur*. Since the Hersfeld codex, like other manuscripts of the period, does not employ the hyphen, such a division at the end of the line might lead to the separation of the prefix (or enclitic) from its word in the apographs.

In the *Germania* manuscripts the writing of the enclitics -*ue* and -*ne* as separate words is almost universal.[1] Some of our manuscripts show corruptions which must have been caused by the separation of -*ne* or -*ue* in their respective archetypes: 5, 8 *propitii* (-*ne* om.) σχ φ; 4, 8 *solo ire* for *soloue* **m**; 38, 2 *tenterorum uegens* **b**, *uegens teneterorum* **m**; 24, 7 *lucrandi ne* for *lucrandi perdendiue* **m**; 45, 16 *quae uero* (*ratio*) for *quaeue* (i.e. *quae ue ro*) τ.

The only instance of the separation of -*que* in a considerable number of manuscripts is in ch. 18, 18 *rursus que* (or *quae*) **mh a VdE k s,** *rursusque* **W Lvr** φ. Instances of *que* for -*que* in the **X** family are: 3, 16 *germaniae raeciae que* **W**, *raecie germanie que* **h;** 5, 15 *formas que* **Wm;** 6, 7 *at que* **W;** 12, 8 *pecorum que* **m;**

---

[1] The enclitic -*ne* is, however, used but once in the *Germania*, ch. 5, 8.

14, 11 *bello que* **Wm**; 17, 10 *eos que* **W**; 39, 11 *ad quod* for *atque* (cf. p. 153) **W**.

The more noteworthy instances of the separation of the prefix *in-* are: 1, 6 *in accesso* (*-su* I) **Wm △IMw dEvo RA** (cf. *inaccessu* u); 14, 17 *in ers* **m**, *in omnes* **a**, *in eis* ψ; 36, 2 *in lacessiti* (corr. to *inl-* s) **Wm △I c s**, *ui la-* **a**. Elsewhere this prefix is sometimes written separately in **Wm △I Vvr a**.

Ch. 38, 10 *re legant* appears to have been the reading of Hf.,[1] with which we may compare 22, 8 *re conciliandis* **W**. I have noted the separation of other prefixes as follows: 7, 4 *ad miracione* **m**; 11, 17 *ad sensus* **W**; 13, 9 *ad gregantur* **m**; 20, 16 *ad finium* **W**; 36, 7 *ad uersarum* **m**; 39, 8 *ad colli* **W**; 44, 9 *ad pulsui* **m** (cf. *appulsum* φ); 43, 19 *ante cedunt* **W**; 6, 1 *super est* **m △I**; 26, 5 *super est* **m △I vr**; 34, 7 *super esse* **m △ r**, *sub esse* corr. to *supesse* (?) **v**.

The writing of *et iam* for *etiam* is confined to the **X** family: 3, 14 *& iam* **W**; 6, 21 *& iam* **W**, *et iam* **s²**; 28, 2 *& iam* **W**; 37, 19 *et iam* **m**; 37, 24 *et iam* **m s²**; 42, 3 *& iam* **W**; 45, 11 *et iam* **m**. Also note, 21, 4 *satis factionem* **W**.

Apparently the separation of prefixes and enclitics from their words and the writing of *et iam* were more prevalent in **X** than in **Y**. In the light of our present knowledge, it is doubtful if the evidence of the **X** family in this matter should be accepted for the restoration of Hf., unless it is confirmed by the testimony of authoritative manuscripts of the **Y** family.

Punctuation

Punctuation is employed sparingly in the Hersfeld *Agricola*, though there is some attempt to group the words according to phrases, clauses, and sentences—an attempt which is not carried out consistently.[2] The following passage may

---

[1] See pp. 100 f.

[2] The most common mark of punctuation is the dot, sometimes on the baseline, sometimes midway between the two lines, and sometimes on the headline. The colon, semicolon, and interrogation point (√) are also found. It would be difficult to find any principle determining the choice of the dot, colon, and semicolon. Cf. Annibaldi, 25.

be taken as illustrative (f. 58, col. 1, *Agr.* ch. 19): . . . sequerentur:[1] causas bellorum statuit excidere[2] a se suisque orsus:[3] primam domum suam cohercuit quod plerisque haut minus arduum est quam prouintiam regere nihil per libertos seruosque publicae rei non studiis priuatis nec ex commendatione aut praecibus. centurionem milites(Ne) scire sed optimum quemque fidissimum putare. omnia scire non omnia exequi. paruis peccatis ueniam. magnis seueritatem commodare. nec poena semper sed saepius paenitentia contentus esse officiis & administrationibus potius non peccaturos praeponere quam damnare cum peccassent.

As is to be expected, the manuscripts of the *Germania*, being centuries later, employ punctuation much more frequently than does the Hersfeld *Agricola*, yet in the larger groupings of words into clauses and sentences they exhibit such uniformity as to show that the initial impulse has come from the parent manuscript itself. As a rule the punctuation is quite in accord with the meaning of the text. The following are the more noteworthy variations in the punctuation of the manuscripts from that which I have for obvious reasons adopted in my text:[4] 2, 10 f. *editum ei* (*et* h ex sil., a s, *eius* φ) ω, *editum. Ei* β; 2, 11 *conditorisque. Manno* ω; 4, 5 *idem omnibus truces*[5] ω, *idem. Omnibus* **Vd** v o **pM** χ, *idem omnibus. truces* **L u s**; 5, 13–16 *finguntur, quamquam . . . eligunt. Interiores* ω; 6, 13 *sit in uniuersum aestimanti* **Wm v a s**; 10, 4 *spargunt mox* **Wm I a**; 13, 12 *principium* (or *-pum*). *Cui* ω, *principum cui* **Ev a**, *principum, cui* **M L**; 18, 11 *arbitrantur, ne se . . . putet. Ipsis* ω; 22, 14 *mens postera die* ω, *mens, postera die* **Vd s**, *mens: postera*

---

[1] Annibaldi states that the lower dot was added by the second (contemporary) hand.

[2] After *excidere* Annibaldi prints a dot on the headline, but I find nothing in the facsimile which I should interpret as a mark of punctuation.

[3] The colon is very faint in the facsimile, as though it had been erased. Annibaldi does not print it in his text.

[4] The list is not exhaustive. No details are given for h, and my collations of IRAc do not as a rule report punctuation.

[5] W has a diagonal line after *omnibus*, perhaps the work of the second hand.

die u; 30, 3 *patescit durant. Siquidem* (*si-* W) ω, *patescit durant siquidem* m b; 30, 5 *deponit duriora* ω, *deponit. Duriora* V⸝ pt s; 30, 16 f. *constantiae est et aliis* ω, *constantiae est. et aliis* W N ξ VLr zu; 37, 24 *pulsi nam* (or *inde*) ω, *pulsi. Nam* (*nam* W N M ezu) WNM r baeuzc s.

Paragraphing

In the Hersfeld *Agricola* each paragraph begins on a new line with a large initial letter—usually a square capital, but sometimes a minuscule letter larger than those of the text. Sometimes these breaks in the text occur with considerable frequency, as in *Agricola* 33: *Excepere* ... *Octauus* ... *ergo* ... *equidem*, while again the text extends for many lines without a break, as *Agricola* 35, 11 *Tumagricola* ... 37, 9 *Tumuero*.

Any attempt to restore the paragraph division of the Hersfeld *Germania* must be based on the evidence of Wms[2] V and the Viennese edition of 1500 (*ed. Vind.*).[1] I prefer to eliminate h from this discussion, though its paragraphs may perhaps be partially restored from the Arabic numerals which Longolius placed in the margin of his edition through ch. 16 and in ch. 40 and ch. 45.[2] The other manuscripts with the exception of certain members of the φ group (notably 1A), either employ no paragraph division whatever, or use it with the greatest rarity.[3] The division in members of the φ group is, I believe, quite independent of Wms[2] V *ed. Vind.*, though A, which employs the paragraph symbol with almost every sentence, must inevitably agree with these manuscripts in many instances.

The manuscripts Wms[2], or two of the three, agree with V and *ed. Vind.* in showing paragraph division at the following

---

[1] On this edition see pp. 209 ff. I believe it to have drawn from λ, the archetype of VL.

[2] See p. 164. The division into paragraphs in h through ch. 16 seems to have been more frequent than in Wms[2].

[3] A number of MSS. (I dE aeu) follow the practice of extending into the margin any capital letter which falls at the beginning of the line, but since the preceding line is always filled out this cannot be regarded as paragraph division.

points.[1] The asterisk indicates correspondence with the paragraph divisions in my edition of the text.

Ch. 1, 6 *¶*Rhenus* **Ws²V** (= b); 2, 9 *¶*Celebrant* **Ws²V** (= b); ch. 3 *¶*Fuisse* **Wms²V**; 3, 2 *¶*Sunt* **Ws²V**; 3, 10 *¶*Ceterum* **Wms²V** (= b); ch. 5 *¶*Terra* **Ws² V**; 5, 6 *¶*Ne armentis* **Wms² V**; 5, 8 *¶*Argentum* **Wms² V**; 5, 9 ¶*Nec tamen* **Wm V**; 5, 11 ¶*Est uidere* **Ws² V**; 5, 16 ¶*Interiores* **Wm V**; 5, 17 ¶*Pecuniam* **Wm V**; 5, 18 ¶*Argentum* **Wms² V**; 6, 2 ¶*Rari* **Wms² V**; 6, 5 ¶*Et eques* **Wms² V**; 6, 11 ¶*Sed nec* **Ws² V**; 6, 16 ¶*Definitur* **Wms² V**; 6,19 *¶*Acies* **Wms² V**; ch. 7 *¶*Reges* **Ws² V**; 7, 5 *¶*Ceterum* **Wms² V**; ch. 8 *¶*Memoriae* **Ws² V**; 8, 6 ¶*Inesse* **Wms² V**; ch. 9 *¶*Deorum* **Wms² V**; 9, 2 ¶*Herculem* **Wms² V**; 9, 3 ¶*Pars* **Wms² V**; 9, 4 ¶*Vnde* **Wms² V**; 9, 7 *¶*Ceterum* **Wms² V**; 9, 9 ¶*Lucos* **Wms² V**; ch. 10 *¶*Auspicia* **Ws² V**; 10, 18 *¶*Est* **Wms² V**; 10, 19 ¶*Eius gentis* **Wm V**; ch. 11 *¶*De minoribus* **Wms² V**; 11, 3 ¶*Coeunt* **Wms² V**; 11, 5 ¶*Nam agendis* **Wm V**; 11, 6 ¶*Nec dierum* **Wms² V**; 11, 7 ¶*Nox* **Wm V**; 11, 9 *¶*Illud* **Wms² V**; 11, 11 ¶*Silentium* **Wms² V**; 12, 2 ¶*Proditores* **Wm V**; 12, 7 *¶*Sed et* **Wms² V**; 12, 10 *¶*Eliguntur* **Wm V**; 13, 7 *¶*Insignis* **Wm V**; 13, 10 ¶*Gradus* **Wms² V**; 13, 11 *¶*Magnaque* **Wm V**; 13, 12 ¶*Cui* **Wm V**; 13, 16 *¶*Nec solum* **Ws² V**; 13, 18 ¶*Expetuntur* **ms² V**; 14, 2 ¶*Iam uero* **Wm V**; 14, 6 ¶*Principes* **Wms² V**; 14, 7 *¶*Si ciuitas* **Ws² V**; 14, 11 ¶*Exigunt* **Wm**

---

[1] In this list the symbol V does double duty for the MS. V and for *ed. Vind.*, since the two agree except in 11, 7, where no paragraph is indicated in *ed. Vind.*, and in 22, 12, and 24, 6, where none is indicated in V.

In W and V the new paragraph begins with a majuscule letter in the margin, while the end of the preceding paragraph does not as a rule fill out the line of writing. In *ed. Vind.* the first word of the paragraph, preceded by the paragraph symbol, begins a new line. In m the only sure evidence of a new paragraph is the incomplete line of writing at the end of the old paragraph, as the initial (majuscule) letter does not extend into the margin. Wherever m has a majuscule letter beginning a line, with the preceding line filled with writing, I count this as the beginning of a paragraph if there is a break at the same point in W or s². The text of s originally was written without a break, except 27, 8 *Haec;* 35, 1 *Hactenus;* 41, 2 *Propior;* 46, 1 *PRutinorum,* but the marks indicating paragraphs have been intercalated, presumably by the second hand (s²). The mark used is a bracket, which has sometimes been covered by a paragraph symbol in red and sometimes allowed to stand unaltered. I count the presence of the bracket, with or without the addition in red, as an indication of a new paragraph.

V; ch. 15 *¶*Quotiens* **Wm** V; 15, 3 ¶*Delegata* **Wms**^{2} V; 15, 5 ¶*Ipsi* **Wms**^{2} V; 15, 7 *¶*Mos est* **Wms**^{2} V; 15, 10 *¶*Gaudent* **Wms**^{2} V; ch. 16 *¶*Nullas* **Wms**^{2} V; 16, 2 ¶*Colunt* **Wms**^{2} V; 16, 3 ¶*Vicos* **Wms**^{2} V; 16, 7 *¶*Ne caementorum* **Wm** V; 16, 9 ¶*Quaedam* **Wms**^{2} V; ch. 17 *¶*Tegumen* **Wms**^{2} V; 17, 3 ¶*Locupletissimi* **Wms**^{2} V; 17, 5 *¶*Gerunt* **Wms**^{2} V; ch. 18, 5 *¶*Dotem* **Wms**^{2} V; 19, 3 ¶*Paucissima* **Ws**^{2} V; 19, 15 *¶*Numerum* **Ws**^{2} V; 20, 10 *¶*Sororum* **Ws**^{2} V; ch. 21 *¶*Suscipere* **Wms**^{2} V; 21, 6 *¶*Conuictibus* **Wms**^{2} V; 21, 14 ¶*Victus* **Wms**^{2} V; 22, 8 *¶*Sed et* **Wm** V; 22, 12 ¶*Gens* **ms**^{2} ed. Vind.; ch. 23 *¶*Potui* **Wms**^{2} V; ch. 24 *¶*Genus* **Wms**^{2} V; 24, 6 *¶*Aleam* **Wms**^{2} ed. Vind.; 25, 9 *¶*Liberti* **Wms**^{2} V; ch. 26 *¶*Faenus* **Wms**^{2} V; ch. 27 *¶*Funerum* **Wms**^{2} V; 27, 8 *¶*Haec in* **Wm** V (=p E b s); ch. 28 *¶*Validiores* **Wms**^{2} V (=LEr lzRAc); 28, 6 ¶*Igitur* **Wms**^{2} V; 28, 14 *¶*Treueri* **Wm** V; 28, 16 *¶*Ipsam* **Wm** V; ch. 29 *¶*Omnium* **Wm** V; 29, 9 *¶*Est* **Wm** V; 29, 14 *¶*Non numerauerim* **Wms**^{2} V; ch. 30 *¶*Vltra* **Wms**^{2} V; 31, 10 *¶*Plurimis* **Wm** V; ch. 32 *¶*Proximi* **Wms**^{2} V; ch. 33 *¶*Iuxta* **Wms**^{2} V; ch. 34 *¶*Angriuarios* **Ws**^{2} V; ch. 35 *¶*Hactenus* **Wm** V (=bA s); 35, 5 ¶*Tam immensum* **Wms**^{2} V; 36, 7 *¶*Tracti* **Wm** V; ch. 37 *¶*Eundem* **Wms**^{2} V (=E); 37, 6 *¶*Sescentesimum* **Wm** V; 37, 10 ¶*Medio* **Wms**^{2} V; ch. 38 *¶*Nunc* **Wms**^{2} V (=E); 38, 5 *¶*Insigne* **Wms**^{2} V; ch. 39 *¶*Vetustissimos* **Ws**^{2} V (=E); ch. 40 *¶*Contra* **Wms**^{2} V; 40, 4 *¶*Reudigni* **Wms**^{2} V; 40, 9 *¶*Est in* **Wms**^{2} V; ch. 41 *¶*Et haec* **Wms**^{2} V; 41, 3 ¶*Hermundurorum* **Wm** V (=p LE blzRAc); 41, 8 ¶*In Hermunduris* **Wm** V; 42, 6 *¶*Marcomanis* **Wms**^{2} V; ch. 43 *¶*Retro* **Wms**^{2} V; 43, 18 *¶*Ceterum* **Wms**^{2} V; ch. 44 *¶*Trans* **Wms**^{2} V; 44, 4 *¶*Protinus* **Wms**^{2} V; 44, 7 *¶*Suionum* **Wms**^{2} V; 44, 13 *¶*Est apud* **Wms**^{2} V; ch. 45 *¶*Trans* **Wm** V; 45, 7 *¶*Ergo* **Wms**^{2} V; 45, 30 *¶*Suionibus* **Wm** V; 46, 1 ¶*Peucinorum* **Wm** V (=bRA s); 46, 11 *¶*Fennis* **Wms**^{2} V; 46, 23 *¶*Cetera* **Ws**^{2} V.

The instances in which **V** and *ed. Vind.* agree with but one of the group **Wms**^{2} are negligible: 1, 9 *¶*Danuuius* **W** V; 3, 13 ¶*Aram* **s**^{2} ed. Vind.; 10, 1 ¶*Sortium* **W** V; ch. 12 *¶*Licet* **W** V;

16, 13 ¶*Et si quando* **W V**; 19, 2 ¶*Litterarum* s² **V**; ch. 36 *¶*In latere* **W V**.

Are we to conclude that the paragraph divisions shown above give us the paragraphing of Hf.? I believe such a conclusion to be almost inevitable. The striking feature about the paragraphing which I have shown is its frequency through ch. 29 and its relative infrequency from ch. 30 to the end. I think it highly improbable that two or more copyists would independently have adopted the same elaborate system of paragraphs through the same chapters and then have abandoned it at just the same point. Furthermore, if the paragraphing is independent in the five sources, or (more probably) independent in **X** and λ, surely there would be many instances in which one or the other of the manuscripts would stand alone.[1] As a matter of fact the instances are relatively very few.[2]

While the agreement of **Wms**² may reasonably be taken for the restoration of the paragraphing of **X**, some may find it rash to accept the evidence of **V** and *ed. Vind.* for restoring that of **Y**. Yet I believe that stranger phenomena than this may be found in the behavior of manuscripts. I assume that **Y**, like **X**, observed the paragraphing of Hf., that of the four apographs of **Y** only β maintained the tradition, that of the two apographs of β the tradition was kept by λ but abandoned by τ, and finally that of the copies of λ it was continued by **V** and *ed. Vind.*, but not by **L**.[3]

[1] The MS. **A** will illustrate my point. Although it often indicates paragraphs where they are found in **Wms**² **V**, it also indicates them in an even larger number of places where they are not found in these MSS. It will be sufficient to show the paragraphing of **A** within a single chapter: 37, 2 ¶*Parua;* 3 ¶*Vtraque;* 6 ¶*Sexcentesimum;* 7 ¶*Cum;* 7 ¶*Cecilio;* 10 ¶*Medio;* 11 ¶*Non;* 15 ¶*At.*

[2] Ch. 2 *¶*Ipsos* **V** ed. Vind. (=b); 2, 11 ¶*Manno* **V** ed. Vind.; 5, 15 ¶*Formasque* s²; 6, 10 ¶*Equi* ed. Vind.; 6, 16 ¶*Centeni* **m**; 7, 1 ¶*Duces* s²; 10, 10 ¶*auium* s²; 10, 21 ¶*Victoria* **V**; 11, 17 ¶*Honoratissimum* **V** ed. Vind.; 12, 3 ¶*Ignauos* ed. Vind.; 13, 1 *¶*Nichil* **m**; 13, 8 ¶*Ceteris* **m**; 15, 13 ¶*Nam* **m**; 21, 2 ¶*Luitur* **Ws**²; 22, 2 ¶*lauantur* s²; 22, 6 ¶*Crebrae* **ms**²; 22, 15 ¶*Deliberant* **ms**²; 23, 2 ¶*Proximi* **m**; 23, 3 ¶*Cibi* **Wm**; 27, 9 ¶*Nunc* **m**; 31, 15 ¶*Prodigi* **m**; 35, 10 ¶*Id* **V**; 37, 18 ¶*Varum* **Ws**² (cf. *suarum* **m**); 40, 18 ¶*Serui* **m**.

[3] It may be noted in this connection that **V** and *ed. Vind.* alone of the β group (but not alone of the **Y** family) have the title of the *Germania* as it stood in Hf. (cf. p. 11).

In my text of the *Germania* I adhere to the customary division into chapters, said to have originated with Gruterus, save that I follow Halm in beginning ch. 44 with *Trans Lugios* instead of with *Suionum* (44, 6), and in beginning ch. 46 with *Hic* instead of with *Peucinorum*. In my division of the text into paragraphs within the various chapters I have in general followed my restoration of Hf., insofar as this is consistent with the sense and with the good appearance of the printed page.

Capitalization

In the Hersfeld *Agricola* capitalization is confined to the use of the majuscule letter placed in the margin at the beginning of a new paragraph.[1] Proper names are never capitalized.

The manuscripts of the *Germania* employ capitalization freely:[2] regularly at the beginning of the sentence, and sometimes even at the beginning of subordinate clauses. It may be noted that where **Wms²V** indicate paragraphs the other manuscripts as a rule have capitalization (and punctuation). The process of capitalization has gone considerably further in α and β than in **Xφs**. There is little consistency, even within individual manuscripts in the use of capitals with proper names.

[1] Annibaldi's text shows a few instances of majuscule *I* within the line, but these are probably a survival of *I-longa*. The few examples of the survival of majuscule *N* are also beside the point.

[2] Only L uses capitals very sparingly.

THE GERMANIA OF TACITUS
Text, Critical Apparatus, and Critical Notes

Sigla

Conspectus codicum in pp. 79–90 et stemma codicum in calce huius uoluminis uidenda sunt.

A	Angelicanus	W	Vindobonensis 711
a	Arundelianus	w	Editio princeps
b	Harleianus	z	Matritensis
c	Cesenas		
d	Ottobonianus 1209	X	Consensus codicum **Wmh**
Δ	Vaticanus 4498	Y	Consensus ceterorum omnium
E	Aesinas		
e	Haruardianus	α	Consensus codicum **NΔIpMtw**
h	Hummelianus		
I	Vaticanus 1518	ξ	Consensus codicum **pMtw**
k	Editio Norimbergensis	χ	Consensus codicum **tw**
L	Leidensis	σ	Consensus codicum **NΔI**
l	Laurentianus	β	Consensus codicum **VLdEvrok**
M	Marcianus		
m	Monacensis 5307	λ	Consensus codicum **VL**
N	Neapolitanus	τ	Consensus codicum **dEvrok**
o	Ottobonianus 1795	φ	Consensus codicum **balezuRAc**
p	Parisiensis		
R	Riccardianus	π	Consensus codicum **lezuRAc**
r	Ariminensis		
s	Stutgartiensis	ψ	Consensus codicum **ezuRAc**
t	Turicensis	ω	Consensus codicum omnium praeter nominatim prolatos
u	Vrbinas 412		
V	Vaticanus 1862		
v	Vaticanus 2964		

CORNELII TACITI
DE ORIGINE ET SITV GERMANORVM
LIBER

CORNELII (C. CORNELII *ΔI*) TACITI DE ORIGINE ET SITV GERMANORVM (LIBER INCIPIT *add. V*, LIBER INCIPIT FOELICISSIME *W*), *Cod. Hf. teste Nicolao*, Wm IΔV, CORNELII TACITI LIBER DE SITV ET ORIGINE GERMANORVM M, C. Cornelii taciti oratoris de origine et situ germanorum liber Incipit b, Cornelii TACITI DE ORIGINE RITV ET MORibus GeRMAnorum feliciter incipit s, CORNELII TACITI DE ORIGINE SITV MORIBVS AC POPVLIS GERMANORVM LIBER INCIPIT L, . . . INCIPIT EIVSDEM DE ORIGINE ET MORIBVS GERMANORVM E, C. CORNELII TACITI DE ORIGINE ET SITV GERMANIĘ LIBER INCIPIT N, *et sic fere (praenomine omisso) cod. Hf. teste Decembrio*, Cornelius Tacitus de situ germaniae et moribus germanorum p, Cornelii Taciti illustrissimi historici de situ moribus et populis Germanię libellus aureus χ, Cornelii Taciti viri consularis de situ ac moribus germanie libellus incipitur o, CORNELII TACITI VIRI CLARISSIMI LIBER DE SITV GERMANICO INCIPIT r, C. (C. *om. e*) cornelii taciti equitis .r. de origine et situ germanie liber incipit (INCIPIT FELICITER *e*) le, CORNELII TACITI DE SITV GERMANIE LIBER INCIPIT u, De Germanie Situ opusculum Foeliciter incipit A, COR: TACITI GERMANIAE DESCRIPTIO c, Cai Cornelii Taciti Equitis Ro. Germania incipit k, *inscriptio uel nulla uel manu recentiore addita* h dv a Rz.

1. Germania omnis a Gallis Raetisque et Pannoniis Rheno et Danuuio fluminibus, a Sarmatis Dacisque mutuo metu aut montibus separatur. Cetera Oceanus ambit, latos sinus et insularum immensa spatia complectens, nuper cognitis quibusdam gentibus ac regibus quos bellum aperuit.

Rhenus Raeticarum Alpium inaccesso ac praecipiti uertice ortus modico flexu in occidentem uersus septentrionali Oceano miscetur.

Danuuius molli et clementer edito montis Abnobae iugo effusus plures populos adit, donec in Ponticum mare sex meatibus erumpat; septimum os paludibus hauritur.

2. Ipsos Germanos indigenas crediderim minimeque aliarum gentium aduentibus et hospitiis mixtos, quia nec terra olim sed classibus aduehebantur qui mutare sedes quaerebant, et immensus ultra utque sic dixerim aduersus Oceanus raris ab orbe nostro nauibus aditur. Quis porro, praeter periculum

---

1, 1 A/ a **W**   Raetisque (Rhae-) *Cellarius*, Raetiisque (rhae-, re-, rhe-, raeci-, reci-, *uide p. 253*) ω   Rheno ac **Wh**
5 bellum] regnum (*in mg.* bellum *W*²) **W**   9 Danuuius (-uu- *in* -bu- *corr. c*, Danuuis z) **h euAcz**, Dannuuius **I R**, DAnuuius^b **W**, Danubius ω (*uide p. 122*)   Abnobae **h**, *Hermolaus Barbarus in ora ed. Pinc. a. 1497 teste Walther; Rhenanus ex Artolphi codice (cf. p. 331¹)*, Arnobae **Wm M vk s**, Arnobae, *in mg. uel superscr.* Arbonae **VE leu**, Arnobę al' Arbonę, *in mg.* arbonę **d**, arbonae *et in textu et superscr. sed lect. superscr. eras., et in textu* -bon- *in ras. super* -nob- *ut uid.* **N**, Arbonę, *in mg.* arnobę **p**, Arbonae **ΔIχ** Lro bzRAc, armbae a   10 plurimos *E. Wolff*

2, 4 aduersis **bπ**, auersus *Acidalius et sic ex* adu- *in p*

1, 9 Abnobae: This spelling is well established by the testimony of ancient authors and inscriptions (see Ihm in P.-W. and Holder *AC.S.*, *s.v.*). On the readings of our MSS. see pp. 104 f.

10 plures: Knoke (8) and Andresen (1916, 1135) understand in the sense of *plures quam Rhenus*, but I am unconvinced that the word may not be merely the equivalent of *complures* or *nonnullos*. Certainly I see no reason for changing the reading of the MSS.

2, 4 aduersus: The reading of the MSS. is beyond suspicion. I understand it in the sense of "unfriendly" or "forbidding."

8 nisi si: The variant *sibi* had best be regarded as a fifteenth-century interpolation (cf. p. 140, note 2). If, as the tense of *sit* suggests, the clause

horridi et ignoti maris, Asia aut Africa aut Italia relicta Germaniam peteret, informem terris, asperam caelo, tristem cultu aspectuque nisi si patria sit?

10 Celebrant carminibus antiquis, quod unum apud illos memoriae et annalium genus est, Tuistonem deum terra editum. Ei filium Mannum originem gentis, conditoresque Manno tres filios adsignant, e quorum nominibus proximi Oceano Ingaeuones, medii Herminones, ceteri Istaeuones uocentur. Quidam, ut in licentia uetustatis, plures deo ortos pluresque gentis

---

8 si] sibi **Wh** t s, *om.* **L** ɸ, cui *Sturm*   10 Tuistonem] bistonem, *in mg.* tuistonem (-sco- *h*) **Wh**, Bistonem **NΔ**, bisbonem **m**, histonem **s**², Tuisconem τ s, *reliqua uarietas lect. in p. 115 est uidenda*   11 ei **Wm**s² β, et **h** *ex sil.*, **a** s, eius ɸ   conditoresque *Rhenanus et forsitan sic in v*, conditorisque ω, conditorisque **W**, conditoremque hs² a em 13 Herminones **X** **Npx** s, hermimones ɸ, hermiones **ΔIM** β 14 de eo, *in mg.* deo **h**, deos **Er** ɸ s²

---

nisi . . . sit merely limits *tristem cultu aspectuque*, instead of forming a protasis to *peteret*, the reading *sibi* becomes impossible.

10 Tuistonem: The name is otherwise unknown. On the variant *bistonem* see p. 96.

11 conditoresque: This simple correction of the *conditorisque* (see p. 240) of the MSS. was long the *vulgata*, but with a preceding *et* instead of *Ei*. The presence of the corrupt *et* led to a curious misunderstanding of the passage, which is still prevalent. Tuisto and Mannus together were supposed to be the *origo* and *conditores*. When Andresen (1903, 276 ff.) restored *Ei* to its rightful place he strangely assumed that this necessitated the adoption of the interpolated *conditoremque*. (Thereby Mannus became both the *origo* and *conditor* of the race.)

As I interpret the passage, Mannus was the *origo gentis* and his three sons were the *conditores*. Similarly, Aeneas, Verg. *Aen.* xii, 166, is called *Romanae stirpis origo*, while Romulus is frequently designated as the *conditor* of Rome (e.g. *Hist.* i, 84, 27 *a parente et conditore urbis nostrae*; *Ann.* xi, 24, 19 *conditor nostri Romulus*). The parallel between Mannus and Aeneas on the one hand, and between the sons of Mannus and Romulus on the other, is obvious: Mannus and Aeneas were both of divine origin, the sons of Mannus and Romulus gave their names to their respective races. (Other passages of Tacitus in which *conditor* is used of the one who has given his name to a city or race are: *Germ.* 28, 20; *Hist.* v, 4, 15; *Ann.* vi, 42, 2. *Origo* and *conditor* are used together in *Ann.* iv, 9, 8 ff., though the parallel to our passage is not exact: *origo Iuliae gentis Aeneas . . . et conditor urbis Romulus*.) Reitzenstein (1913, 270), though reading *et* for *Ei*, correctly interprets *conditoresque* as referring to the three sons of Mannus.

12 Ingaeuones: In accordance with my usual treatment of tribal names, I adhere to the manuscript reading in the absence of inscriptional or other compelling evidence to the contrary. The Germanists, however, declare for *Inguaeones*, which is the spelling indicated by the MSS. of Pliny *N.H.* iv, 96, and of Solinus, p. 95, 19, ed. Mommsen. See *A.P.V. s.v.* Inguaeones.

13 Herminones: Cf. p. 112, and *A.P.V. s.v.*

Istaeuones: The Germanists declare for *Istuaeones*. (Cf. note on *Ingaeuones*, and *A.P.V. s.v.* Istuaeones.)

274   THE GERMANIA OF TACITUS

15   appellationes, Marsos Gambriuios Sue*bos* Vandilios adfirmant,
eaque uera et antiqua nomina. Ceterum Germaniae uocabulum recens et nuper additum, quoniam qui primi Rhenum

---

15 Suebos *Halm*[1], Sueuos ω   vandalos, *in mg.* vandileos h,
Vandalios ξ L, uandulos r, Vandilos (Vandalos *al*) φ   17 adi-
tum h v l, editum ψ, auditum *Lipsius*   primum vr aψ, *primi-*

15 **Vandilios:** Apparently this spelling is not found elsewhere, though the form *Vandili* is frequent. See *A.P.V. s.v.* Vandali and *Einl.* xxvi f., and Boissevain's note to Cassius Dio LXXII, 2, 4.

17 **additum:** I find no reason for mistrusting the manuscript reading. The various tribes of the Germans must already have had their individual names, so that the name *Germani* given to the entire race was in a sense an *addition*. However, *additum* may be the mere equivalent of *datum*, just as in 3, 18, *addat fidem* appears to be the equivalent of *det fidem*. For *addere = dare* Andresen (1916, 1136) cites *Hist.* I, 62, 10; III, 6, 4.

17 **quoniam . . . uocati sint:** "Since those who first crossed the Rhine drove out the Gauls and (though now called Tungri) were at that time given the name of Germans." I have little doubt that the manuscript tradition is corrupt. Grammatically it is possible only if we understand *transgressi* (*sunt* or *sint*) as the verb of the *qui*-clause, and construe with *quoniam*, (1) *expulerint*, (2) an implied *uocentur* after *Tungri*, and (3) *uocati sint*. (The ellipsis of the copula in relative sentences is common enough in Tacitus: *Ann.* XVI, 1, 8 f. *quae per tantum aeui occulta augendis praesentibus bonis;* III, 1, 9 f. *ubi primum ex alto uisa classis; Germ.* 14, 1 *cum uentum in aciem; Germ.* 13, 11 ff.; 17, 6.)

The logical difficulty in this construction of the clauses is obvious, for the "modern" name (*nunc Tungri* [*uocentur*]) cannot properly be adduced as a reason for the statement that the word *Germania* is new. Possibly this difficulty is obviated if *nunc Tungri* is regarded as a parenthetical bit of information, such as a modern writer would place in a footnote. (Other instances of parenthetical insertions are: *Germ.* 31, 8 *ignominiosum id genti;* 42, 8 *iam et externos patiuntur;* 46, 4 f. *sordes omnium ac torpor procerum.*) Some may find a similar logical difficulty in *quoniam . . . expulerint*, but in view of the scanty information provided by our author I doubt if such a judgment is warranted. In fact, the concluding part of the entire chapter seems to imply that the victory (*a uictore*) of the invading tribe was a definite step in the establishment of the name *Germani*.

Most commentators construe, *quoniam . . . uocati sint*, and, *qui . . . expulerint ac nunc Tungri* (*uocentur*). I do not believe that this is Latin, for it demands that *uocentur*, as verb of the adjectival *qui*-clause, be supplied from the verb of the temporal *quoniam*-clause. So far as I know, no parallels to so astounding an ellipsis have been adduced. Norden (313, note 1) cites as the most closely related passages in Tacitus, *Hist.* IV, 26, 8 f. *quod in pace fors seu natura, tunc fatum et ira deum uocabatur;* and *Germ.* 36, 5 f. *ita qui olim boni aequique Cherusci nunc inertes ac stulti uocantur.* In both cases the verb of the relative clause is to be supplied from the *principal* verb of the sentence—a common enough construction in Latin. An examination of the examples given by Leo, *Analecta Plautina* I (Göttingen, 1906), 33 ff. (cited by Norden) fails to show any instance parallel to our passage as it is commonly construed.

The ungrammatical character of the passage (as it is commonly construed) was seen by the humanist (Pontanus?) who substituted *ut* for *ac* in L. It is well stated by Jessen: "Dass in Correlatsätzen das Verbum im ersten weggelassen und aus dem zweiten ergänzt wird, hat für das

transgressi Gallos expulerint, ac (nunc Tungri) tunc Germani
uocati sint. Ita nationis nomen non gentis eualuisse paulatim,

| *tus in* s | 18 *post* expulerint *nonnulla excidisse suspicor* | ac] |
| ut *in ras.* L | ac nunc Tungri *secl. Gudeman* | 19 sunt |

Sprachgefühl gar keine Schwierigkeit. Hier aber hat der Relativsatz ein cignes Prädicat *expulerint,* aus dem die einzelnen Satztheile, die sich in derselben Gedankensphäre befinden, ihre Ergänzung nehmen müssen . . . ."

The passage becomes at once logical and grammatical if we follow Gudeman in deleting *ac nunc Tungri* (understanding *expulerint* as the verb of the *qui*-clause), but the remedy seems drastic. I am unable to subscribe to the arguments which Gudeman adduces for the deletion, except that of the ungrammatical (or rather, illogical) character of the clauses.

Sievers believes that the verbs *expulerint,* (*uocentur*), and *uocati sint* all belong with *qui,* and that the verb of the *quoniam*-clause has been lost. This is attractive, yet I find a serious objection in the tense of *uocati sint.* If this verb belongs with *qui,* the meaning ought to be that the tribe which first crossed the Rhine was already in possession of the name *Germani,* not that it received the name after coming into Gaul. To be sure, many scholars (among them Norden, 390) take this to be the meaning, but I am quite unable to see how the tense of the verb admits of such an interpretation. If Tacitus meant that the tribe brought the name *Germani* with them, he should have written *uocati fuerint* (cf. Cic. *Off.* 1, 57 *qui lacerarunt omni scelere patriam et in ea funditus delenda occupati et sunt et fuerunt*). Nevertheless, I strongly suspect that there is something missing in the passage (perhaps several lines), and suggest that the place of the lacuna is between *expulerint* and *ac.* In this case, of course, the regimen of *uocati sint* is uncertain.

19 Ita . . . uocarentur: "Thus it was that the name of a tribe, not of the race, gradually gained ground, so that all were called Germans, first by the victor for the purpose of inspiring fear, in time by themselves as well,

when once they had happened on the name." As the text stands, I deduce four stages in the adoption of the name *Germani.* (1) Those who first crossed the Rhine were successful in driving out the Gauls and were at that time given the name *Germani* (by the Gauls). (2) They adopted the name for themselves. (This stage is not expressly mentioned by Tacitus.) (3) They extended the name to the entire race (the *Transrhenani*) for the purpose of inspiring fear (within the Gauls). (4) The rest of the race (the *Transrhenani*) adopted the name for themselves when they heard of it.

The obscurity of the whole sentence affords a strong argument for the supposition of a lacuna in the sentence immediately preceding. Quite aside from the difficulty as to *why* the extension of the name *Germani* to the *Transrhenani* would be calculated to inspire fear, I find it highly doubtful if Tacitus would have employed *ob metum* in this context (as it now stands) for *ob metum incutiendum.* The words *a se ipsis* imply *ceteri* rather than *omnes* as the subject of *uocarentur,* but of course this is not the only place in which our author's logic is at fault. (In substantiation of the meanings which my translation assigns to *nationis, gentis, ob metum, inuento nomine,* see Norden 314 ff., 331 ff., 336 ff. I understand *a se ipsis* ἀπὸ κοινοῦ with *inuento* and *uocarentur,* not with the latter alone, as does Norden.)

Invaluable as I have found Norden's monumental work which he has written around this one sentence, I am quite unable to accept his major thesis (also advanced by numerous earlier commentators) that *a uictore* means ἀπὸ τοῦ νικήσαντος. As Gudeman (1927, 690) has pointed out, the mere presence of *et* (*etiam*) makes it necessary to give the same meaning to *a* in both places.

20　ut omnes primum a uictore ob metum, mox et a se ipsis inuento nomine Germani uocarentur.

3. Fuisse et apud eos Herculem memorant, primumque omnium uirorum fortium ituri in proelia canunt.

Sunt illis haec quoque carmina quorum relatu, quem barditum uocant, accendunt animos futuraeque pugnae fortunam
5　ipso cantu augurantur; terrent enim trepidantue prout sonuit acies, nec tam uoces illae quam uirtutis concentus

---

I ϕ s, sū *sequente litura* E　　*lacunam post* sint *statuit Sievers*　　gentis & valuis se W, genti se valuisse m　　20 a uicto *Leibnitz*, a uicto, reor *O. Hirschfeld*　　et X ΔI ϕ s, et *expunx.* M, *om.* Npχ τ z, etiam λ

3, 1 et apud eos W π, et apud eos et b, apud eos et ω　　3 illius *Hertlein*　　barditum m IM λvk s, barditum, *in mg. uel superscr.* baritum W N dE, baritum, *in mg.* barditum p, baritum h *ex sil.*, s² Δχ ro, bardicum ϕ, barritum *Cluuerius 1 (ch. 51) p. 386*　　6 uocis ille ... uidetur *Rhenanus*

3, 1 et apud eos Herculem: This reading, which admits of a more satisfactory interpretation than the *uulgata*, though adopted by Gudeman (1916) as an emendation, has in reality very respectable manuscript authority (see pp. 140 f.). I should, however, have little hesitation in retaining *apud eos et Herculem* if the manuscripts were unanimous in its support. (*Et Herculem* might be explained as "even Hercules." Thus Andresen, 1917, 89 f.; Norden, 182, note 1.)

3 Sunt illis: Hertlein's *illius*, which would make the *barditus* a song in honor of Hercules, is attractive, but unnecessary. Norden (180 ff.) explains the sentence as a παρενθήκη, "ein richtiger kleiner Excurs," in the fashion of Herodotus.

haec: This word has been suspected (*e.g.* Halm, 1864, 27 f.; Hachtmann), but quite needlessly. It is due to the vividness of the description: "these which I have in mind." Norden (181, note 1) cites *Germ.* 20, 1 f. *in hos artus, in haec corpora quae miramur;* 10, 9 *et illud quidem etiam hic notum;* Hor. *C.* II, 14, 22 *harum quas colis arborum.* Also see the parallels from Seneca given by J. Müller.

barditum: I adopt this reading on palaeographical grounds, since the variant *baritum* may be explained easily as a corruption of *barditum* (cf. p. 47). Nevertheless, *baritum* bears a close resemblance to *barritus*, the cry of the elephant, and a form of battle cry mentioned by later writers (Ammianus XVI, 12, 43; XXI, 13, 15; XXVI, 7, 17; XXXI, 7, 11; Vegetius, *Mil.* III, 18). Ihm in P.-W. *s.v. barditus* assumes that *barditus* is the earlier form, which because of its similarity in sound and meaning was assimilated to *barritus*, the cry of the elephant. H. Fischer favors *barritum*.

6 uoces illae ... uidetur: Rhenanus' *uocis ille ... uidetur* has found general favor, but the burden of proof rests with those who would change the manuscript reading. Valmaggi (1920, 14) is perhaps correct in supposing that it was Tacitus' fondness for asymmetry which led him to express himself as the MSS. indicate. (I naturally take *concentus* as plural. Cf. Vitr. v, 4, 7 *concentus, quos natura hominis modulari potest, graece quae* συμφωνίαι *dicuntur, sunt sex;* Apul. *Met.* XI, 7 *ut canorae etiam auiculae prolectatae uerno uapore concentus suaues adsonarent;* Stat. *Theb.* VII, 285

TEXT, CRITICAL APPARATUS, CRITICAL NOTES 277

uidentur. Adfectatur praecipue asperitas soni et fractum murmur obiectis ad os scutis quo plenior et grauior uox repercussu intumescat.

10 Ceterum et Vlixen quidam opinantur longo illo et fabuloso errore in hunc Oceanum delatum adisse Germaniae terras, Asciburgiumque, quod in ripa Rheni situm hodieque incolatur, ab illo constitutum nominatumque ['Ασκιπύργιον]; aram quin etiam Vlixi consecratam adiecto Laërtae patris nomine eodem
15 loco olim repertam, monumentaque et tumulos quosdam Graecis litteris inscriptos in confinio Germaniae Raetiaeque adhuc extare. Quae neque confirmare argumentis neque refellere in animo est: ex ingenio suo quisque demat uel addat fidem.

4. Ipse eorum opinionibus accedo qui Germaniae populos

---

8 ad eos **m p A**, ad eos *in* ad os *corr.* **V c**, *om.* **N**   10 Vlixen **Wmσ s**, Vlyxen **V**, Vlixem (*uel* -yx-) **ω**   12 incolatur **X**, incolitur **Y**   13 ΑCΚΙΠΤΡΓΙΟΝ (*corrupte in vk ba*) **W NIM Vτ ba**, *om. lac. rel.* **hm Δpw π**, *lac. ind. et in mg. scr. grecum* **s²**, *om. sine lac.* **t L s**, *secl. Wölfflin 1867, 160*   15 reperta **mh NΔ**, reperta *in* -tam *corr. alt. man. ut uid.* **W**   17 (Quae) neque *om.* **W**
4, 1 opinioni *Meiser*

---

patriis concentibus audis/ exultare gregem. . . .)

12 incolatur: I find it hard to choose between the *incolatur* of **X** and the *incolitur* of **Y**. Certainly the indicative is more usual in a relative clause of this kind, but perhaps for this very reason the subjunctive should here be adopted as the *lectio difficilior*. That Tacitus does occasionally treat relative clauses of "fact" as though they were an integral part of the *oratio obliqua* is shown by such passages as *Ann.* II, 60, 6 ff. *quem* (Herculem) *indigenae ortum aput se et antiquissimum perhibent eosque, qui postea pari uirtute FVERINT, in cognomentum eius adscitos;* xv, 64, 11 ff. *Statium Annaeum . . . orat prouisum pridem uenenum, quo damnati publico Atheniensium iudicio EXTINGVERENTVR, promeret.*

13 ['Ασκιπύργιον]: There is every reason to suppose that this word was in Hf., but I do not maintain that it derives from Tacitus himself, who regularly excludes Greek words (cf.

Wölfflin 1867, 160).

4, 1 opinionibus: Criticism of this, the reading of all MSS., has been voiced, on the ground that only a single opinion is adduced. I accept Mf.'s explanation that Tacitus was thinking of his individual authorities, though, as Gudeman (40) points out, these authorities may have differed in the reasons adduced for substantiating the claim that the Germans were an unmixed race. Schweizer-Sidler mentions that the use of the plural avoids an hiatus. In fact, it avoids three hiatuses in succession. J. Müller aptly cites the following: Sen. *Ben.* VI, 43, 1 *in magnis erroribus sunt, qui ingentis animi credunt proferre, donare, plurium sinum ac domum inplere;* Pliny, *N. H.* VII, 39 *et in Italia tales partus esse uitales, contra priscorum opiniones;* Val. Max. I, 6, 9 (M. Marcellus cum) . . . *solemnique sacrificio uoluntates deorum exploraret. . . .* He remarks: "Idem omnium error est, eadem priscorum opinio, una deorum uoluntas."

nullis aliis aliarum nationum conubiis infectos propriam et sinceram et tantum sui similem gentem extitisse arbitrantur. Vnde habitus quoque corporum, tamquam in tanto hominum
5 numero, idem omnibus: truces et caeruli oculi, rutilae comae, magna corpora et tantum ad impetum ualida, laboris atque operum non eadem patientia, minimeque sitim aestumque tolerare, frigora atque inediam caelo soloue adsueuerunt.

Rudolphus Fuldensis, *Translatio Sancti Alexandri*, M.G., SS. II, 675: "Generis quoque ac nobilitatis suae prouidissimam curam habentes, nec facile ullis aliarum gentium uel sibi inferiorum conubiis infecti, propriam et sinceram et tantum sui similem gentem facere conati sunt. Vnde habitus quoque ac magnitudo corporum comarumque color, tanquam in tanto hominum numero, idem pene omnibus."

---

2 aliis *del. Lipsius*　　　connubiis ω *praeter m M*　　　4 tamquam m IM v, tamquam, *in mg. uel superscr.* quamquam W N, quamquam, *in mg. uel superscr.* tanquam p Vd, quamquam ω
5 caeruli h Lvro, caeruli, *in mg. uel superscr.* caerulei W V, caeruli uel^{li} lei d, cerulei E, crudeli, *in mg. alt. m.* cerulei M, cerulei ω　　8 in aedia in W, in edia in s², mediam m　　　assueuerint (-rit z) k bzuR, *ex* -runt *inc. man.* s, assueuerint E, assue^{u}runt V, assue^{int}runt L, assueuermtt (t *priore loc. exp.*) m

---

2 aliis aliarum: I keep the *aliis* of the MSS., even though it is redundant. By way of comparison Döderlein cites *Dial.* 30, 19 *ut omnem omnium artium uarietatem complecteretur.* To this add Cic. *Mil.* 1 *haec noui iudicii noua forma.* Yet neither of these passages affords an exact parallel. Possibly Tacitus found in his Greek source ἄλλοις ἄλλων ἐθνῶν γάμοις. (Döderlein compares Plato *Phaedr.* 278a ἄλλαισιν ἄλλων ψυχαῖς. Norden, ch. II, *et passim*, has shown how closely the phraseology of the *Germania* follows Greek ethnographic literature. Cf. note on ch. 23, 5 ff.)

4 tamquam: By the canon of the *lectio difficilior* this is preferable to the variant *quamquam*. I follow Andresen (1916, 1137) and Persson (1927, 90 f.) in regarding *tamquam* as restrictive in sense: "in so far as the large number of inhabitants admits of so sweeping a statement." A similar use of the word is found in *Hist.* 1, 8, 1 f. *Et hic quidem Romae, tamquam in tanta multitudine, habitus animorum fuit.* Since Tacitus has just described a universal attitude of hostility toward Galba, the meaning must be, "making due allowance for so large a populace," or, "in so far as this can be determined in so large a populace," not, "as is to be expected in so large a populace." A similar restrictive use of *ut* is of course familiar to all (*e.g. Germ.* 30, 6 *ut inter Germanos*).

5 caeruli: On the doublets *caerulei:caeruli* see pp. 123 f. A choice between the two seems arbitrary, though Bährens (268) defends *caeruli* as the "poetic" and less usual form, and hence the one more likely to have appealed to Tacitus.

8 soloue: Wolff and Gudeman (1928) read *soloque*, but Tacitus ap-

5. Terra etsi aliquanto specie differt, in uniuersum tamen aut siluis horrida aut paludibus foeda, humidior qua Gallias, uentosior qua Noricum ac Pannoniam aspicit; satis ferax, frugiferarum arborum impatiens, pecorum fecunda, sed plerumque improcera.

Ne armentis quidem suus honor aut gloria frontis: numero gaudent, eaeque solae et gratissimae opes sunt.

Argentum et aurum propitiine an irati dii negauerint dubito. Nec tamen adfirmauerim nullam Germaniae uenam argentum aurumue gignere: quis enim scrutatus est? Possessione et usu haud proinde adficiuntur: est uidere apud illos argentea

---

5, 4 patiens *Tross 1828*   5 pleraque *Lipsius*   in improcera *Mitscherlich*   6 aut] et *Gudeman 1916*   7 eaeque Eatque N∆, eantque I, atque m   8 propitii σχφ (cf. p. 261)
11 perinde V, proinde E, perinde al' proinde d, perinde (proinde s²) Lr s, per perinde v, peinde o, proinde *ante* est *transp. Bährens*

---

pears purposely to have chosen the connective *-ue* because *caelo* looks to *frigora* and *solo* to *inediam.* John in *G.G.* 1740 cites an exact parallel in the use of *uel: Ann.* III, 36, 4 f. *libertique etiam ac serui, patrono uel domino cum uoces, cum manus intentarent, ultro metuebantur.*

5, 4 impatiens: Tross' *patiens* has found some adherents, but the fact that we here have two antithetical pairs, *ferax:impatiens::fecunda:improcera,* should serve as a warning against tampering with the manuscript tradition. It is true that *frugiferarum arborum impatiens* is in contradiction with 26, 7 *ut pomaria conserant,* where the implication is that the Germans might have orchards, if they would take the trouble to plant them. However, this is not the only place in which the text will have to be changed if we seek to establish the infallibility of our author.

pecorum . . . improcera: With *improcera* we have an astonishing change of subject. Mitscherlich's *in improcera,* which is simple palaeographically, is based on Sil. II, 498 *fecundum in fraudes hominum genus,* and Just. XLIV, 1, 4 *felicibus et tempestiuis imbribus in omnia frugum genera fecunda est* (Hispania).

6 aut: Regarding the use of *aut* in place of the more logical *et* or *ac* see Valmaggi (1923) and W. H. Kirk, "And and Or," *A.J.P.* XLII (1921), 1–11. Cf. *Germ.* 19, 15; 35, 9; 38, 12 (*amenturue*).

11 proinde: The variant *perinde*, found only in the β group and in s, is without adequate authority. An exact parallel to this passage seems to occur in *Agr.* 10, 18 ff. *sed mare pigrum et graue remigantibus perhibent ne uentis quidem proinde* (sic codd.) *attolli.* Probably in both cases *proinde* is the mere equivalent of *perinde*, as is so often true in the writings of Tacitus. (Unfortunately, all examples of *proinde* = *perinde* [some fifteen in number] must be sought in *G.G.* under the latter word, for the compilers of this lexicon have followed the third and fourth editions of Halm, who substituted *perinde* for *proinde* ad libitum.) We may understand an ellipsis of *atque expectemus* or some similar expression, and take *haud proinde* in the sense of "not especially," οὐχ οὕτως. (This is the meaning attributed to *haud perinde* by Mf., Gudeman [1928],

uasa legatis et principibus eorum muneri data non in alia
uilitate quam quae humo finguntur. Quamquam proximi ob
usum commerciorum aurum et argentum in pretio habent
formasque quasdam nostrae pecuniae agnoscunt atque eligunt,
interiores simplicius et antiquius permutatione mercium utuntur. Pecuniam probant ueterem et diu notam, serratos
bigatosque. Argentum quoque magis quam aurum sequuntur,
nulla affectione animi, sed quia numerus argenteorum facilior
usui est promiscua ac uilia mercantibus.

6. Ne ferrum quidem superest, sicut ex genere telorum
colligitur. Rari gladiis aut maioribus lanceis utuntur, hastas
uel ipsorum uocabulo frameas gerunt, angusto et breui
ferro, sed ita acri et ad usum habili ut eodem telo, prout
ratio poscit, uel comminus uel eminus pugnent. Et eques
quidem scuto frameaque contentus est, pedites et missilia

---

13 uilitate] utilitate φ   17 sarratos m, serrator^a W, cf. p. 96
18 quoque om. τ, -que Schütz

---

and others.) It should be noted, however, that aside from the two passages under discussion no such usage of either *proinde* or *perinde* can be cited from the works of Tacitus, since elsewhere the second part of the comparison, if not expressed in full, may always be supplied from the context.

Zöchbauer (reading *proinde*) understands our passage to mean: "the influence exerted over the Germans by the possession and utilization of gold and silver is not in accord with the total absence of mines among them." That is to say, because of the scarcity of these precious metals among them one would expect the Germans to attach more value to them than they actually do. *Non proinde* is similarly used in a letter of Plancus, Cic. *Fam.* x, 24, 5 . . . *uel quod ex tam insigni amicitia mea atque Caesaris hunc* (Caesarem Octauianum) *filii loco et illius et uestro iudicio supstitutum non proinde habere* (i.e. non ut filium habere) *turpe mihi uidetur.* Never-

theless, such an interpretation of our passage seems very strained.

Finally, it should be noted that the Forcellini lexicon cites this passage and *Agr.* 10, 18 ff., for *proinde* in the sense of *igitur, quapropter*. The meaning in the one passage would be: in consequence of the absence of gold and silver mines, the Germans are not influenced by the possession and use of these metals (i.e. they do not, as a general rule, possess and use them, and accordingly have no knowledge of their value). In the other passage: in consequence of its sluggishness and heaviness the sea is not even ruffled by the winds. Such a meaning of *proinde* in these two passages, though otherwise quite satisfactory, is condemned by the adverb's position. We should expect *proinde possessione et usu haud adficiuntur*, and, *et proinde ne uentis quidem attolli*.

18 quoque: This word is correctly interpreted by J. Müller: "ut pecuniam ueterem magis sequuntur quam nouam, ita argenteam magis quam auream."

Text, Critical Apparatus, Critical Notes 281

spargunt, pluraque singuli, atque in immensum uibrant nudi aut sagulo leues. Nulla cultus iactatio: scuta tantum lectissimis coloribus distinguunt. Paucis loricae, uix uni alteriue cassis aut galea e*st*. Equi non forma non uelocitate conspicui. Sed nec uariare gyros in morem nostrum docentur: in rectum aut uno flexu dextros agunt ita coniuncto orbe ut nemo posterior sit. In uniuersum aestimanti plus penes peditem roboris, eoque mixti proeliantur, apta et congruente ad equestrem pugnam uelocitate peditum quos ex omni iuuentute delectos ante aciem locant. Definitur et numerus: centeni ex

---

6, 7 in immensum] imensum **W L R**, in mensum **m V**, mensum **b**, minime **A**, minime usum (usum *ex* usara) **c**   10 galea est *Mützell* (*cf. p. 52*), galeae ω, galea t **a**, *Rhenanus*   11 uariare] narrare **m**, uarietate ξ **L**τ   12 coniuncto pχ k ϕ, coniuncto, *in mg. uel superscr.* cuncto **M VE**o, cuncto, *superscr.* coniucto **N**, coniuncto orbe al' cuncto **d**, cuncto **X Δ L**vr **s**, concto **I**, iuncto *Halm*² *ii, xxx*   13 aestimanti **X** (*h ex sil.*), χ β al **s**, exstimanti **b**, extimati ψ, existimanti σp, existimanti, *in mg.* ẹsti **M**, *cf. p. 117*
     i   di
16 delectos **W**, delectos **V**, dilectos h **b**   Diffinitur χv ϕ **s**, Difinitur **d**, *cf. p. 102*

6, 12 coniuncto: The variant *cuncto* has better manuscript authority (cf. p. 105) and is grammatically possible, but would force *orbe* into a meaning apparently not found elsewhere (see below). So with much hesitation I adopt *coniuncto*, though quite aside from its inferior manuscript authority it does not afford an altogether satisfactory meaning. With *coniuncto* the best interpretation, and the one now generally accepted, is as follows: a rank of horsemen acting as a radius with the man on the extreme right as pivot described a circle, with such skill that the line of the radius remained unbroken with no man lagging behind. The hypallage involved in the use of *coniuncto* is probably not a serious objection. Mf. (173) explains: "uno flexu dextros in orbem ita coniuncti agunt ut nemo posterior sit." More grave is the objection that the manœuvre described could hardly have been executed on the field of battle, but belongs rather to the riding school, though the entire chapter deals with the equipment used and the practices followed in actual conflict. Furthermore, it is difficult to see why they should have executed the manœuvre always to the right and never to the left.

Earlier commentators understood the manœuvre to be that of horsemen riding around clockwise in a circle. This interpretation is open to the last two objections mentioned above, and in addition makes the clause *ut nemo posterior sit* appear absurd. While it is doubtless true that in such a formation no man is *behind* the other, to make the statement is merely puerile.

A third interpretation, which perhaps deserves more consideration than it has received, is clearly and logically set forth by H. Schneider. He understands *orbe* to mean, not a circle, but a *mass formation* of cavalry

singulis pagis sunt, idque ipsum inter suos uocantur, et quod primum numerus fuit iam nomen et honor est.

Acies per cuneos componitur. Cedere loco dummodo rursus instes consilii quam formidinis arbitrantur. Corpora suorum etiam in dubiis proeliis referunt. Scutum reliquisse praecipuum flagitium; nec aut sacris adesse aut concilium inire ignominioso fas, multique superstites bellorum infamiam laqueo finierunt.

---

18 primum **Wh** s, primo, *in mg.* primum **M**, primo ʌd, primo **E**, primo ω   20 concilii **W**   22 consilium **I vrok**, φ *praeter a*, pM *in mg.*, **V** *superscr.*, conscilium d

---

(*Haufen*). The words *ita . . . sit* he takes with *in rectum* as well as with *dextros*. According to Schneider, Tacitus is merely describing the two methods of attack employed by the German cavalry—the frontal attack and the oblique attack (to the right naturally) against the enemy's right flank (the *latus apertum*). He translates (256): "Geradeaus oder mit der einzigen Schwenkung rechtshin reiten sie in so enggeschlossenen Haufen (Quarré), dass keiner zurückbleibt." Unfortunately, Schneider's explanation (in other respects admirable) demands a meaning for *orbis* which he does not substantiate, and for which I have been able to find no parallel. So far as I know, the word is used only of a defensive formation in the case of sudden attack by the enemy (cf. W. Rüstow, *Heerwesen und Kriegführung C. Julius Cäsars* ² [Nordhausen, 1862], 55–57).

Strangely enough, if Schneider's interpretation of *orbis* could be accepted, we might then adopt in place of *coniuncto* the better attested reading *cuncto*. I should. translate: "They ride straight ahead or in a single swerve to the right, with such skill (*ita*) that no man lags behind the entire mass formation." (The anastrophe of *ut* in Tacitus is much rarer than that of *ne*, though I can cite *Ann.* II, 6, 6 f. *conuerso ut repente remigio hinc uel illinc adpellerent; Hist.* II, 14, 13 f. *in ipso mari ut adnexa classis . . . praetenderetur;* perhaps *Ann.* VI, 31, 19 f. *nomine tantum et auctore opus,* [*ut*] *sponte Caesaris ut genus Arsacis ripam apud Euphratis cerneretur,* where J. Müller deletes the first *ut*.)

18 primum: Since the doublets *primum:primo* appear to have been in Hf., it is perhaps immaterial which is chosen, though I feel that the phonetic confusion (cf. p. 124) producing the variants implies the corruption *primum > primo* rather than the opposite. Yet in ch. 44, 7, the MSS. have *oceanum* for *oceano*. I think it doubtful if any hard and fast distinction between the Tacitean usage of *primum* and *primo* can be made. (The distinction attempted by Knoke, 10–12, is not borne out by all the passages which may be cited. For instance, in the following, *primum* is used, though according to Knoke's definition we should find *primo: Ann.* XIII, 46, 7; XIV, 37, 1; XV, 71, 16. In *Ann.* XVI, 4, 6 *primo* corresponds rather with his definition of *primum*.)

7. Reges ex nobilitate, duces ex uirtute sumunt. Nec regibus infinita ac libera potestas, et duces exemplo potius quam imperio, si prompti, si conspicui, si ante aciem agant, admiratione praesunt.

Ceterum neque animaduertere neque uincire, ne uerberare quidem nisi sacerdotibus permissum, non quasi in poenam nec ducis iussu, sed uelut deo imperante, quem adesse bellantibus credunt. Effigiesque et signa quaedam detracta lucis in proelium ferunt; quodque praecipuum fortitudinis incitamentum est, non casus nec fortuita conglobatio turmam aut cuneum facit, sed familiae et propinquitates; et in proximo pignora, unde feminarum ululatus audiri, unde uagitus infantium.

7, 2 ac] aut m M β   5 uincere m M, vro (*sed corr. in v*), zRAc s   ne (uerberare) h σ λ a s (*de lect. cod. h. uide p. 167*), neque Wm ξ ▼ lR, nec b ezuAc, *cf. p. 175*   12 est audire *Mähly*   possit *post* infantium *suppl. Heraeus*

7, 2 infinita ac libera: The reading *aut* for *ac* should be definitely discarded, as it is but poorly attested.

12 audiri: This form has frequently been questioned, but I think it may be regarded as an extension of the historical or descriptive infinitive. The difficulty lies not in the use of the historical infinitive in a subordinate clause, of which there are over twenty examples in Tacitus according to J. J. Schlicher ("The Historical Infinitive," *Class. Phil.* IX [1914], 279–294, 374–394, X [1915], 54–74 [see IX, 388]), but in its substitution for a present indicative, to which no exact parallel has been adduced. P. Kretschmer ("Zur Erklärung des sogenannten Infinitivus Historicus," *Glotta* II [1910], 270–287) regards the use of the infinitive in place of a finite verb as an extension of its substantival use. If this is the case, there is no inherent reason why the historical or descriptive infinitive should not refer to present time, since the substantival infinitive is of itself quite without temporal restrictions (cf. Persson, 109). In *Germ.* 30, 7 ff. the infinitive, though definitively substantival, might be replaced by the present indicative without any essential change in meaning. In Pliny, *N. H.* x, 108, cited by J. Müller in support of *audiri*, the infinitives differ scarcely at all from the present indicative, though their substantival origin is still discernible: *etiam ex uolatu* (gloria) *quaeritur* (a columbis)*: plaudere in caelo uarieque sulcare.* In Verg. *Geor.* I, 199 f. (also cited by Müller) the infinitive replaces a gnomic perfect, *i.e.* logically belongs to the present timesphere: *sic omnia fatis/ in peius ruere ac retro sublapsa referri.* The infinitive in Sallust, *Cat.* 20, 7, replaces a *perfectum praesens,* not a *perfectum historicum: nam postquam res publica in paucorum potentium ius atque dicionem concessit, semper illis reges tetrarchae uectigales esse, populi nationes stipendia pendere; ceteri omnes . . . uolgus fuimus sine gratia. . . .* (J. Müller further cites in support of *audiri* Pliny, *N. H.* XIV, 6, but here the infinitives seem to refer to past time. In defense of *audiri* as an historical or descriptive infinitive see Müller-Graupa and Persson [109 f.].)

Some understand *audiri* for *est audiri*, though Wölfflin ("Est uidere," *Archiv f. Lat. Lex.* II [1885], 135 f.)

Hi cuique sanctissimi testes, hi maximi laudatores: ad matres, ad coniuges uulnera ferunt, nec illae numerare et exigere plagas pauent, cibosque et hortamina pugnantibus gestant.

8. Memoriae proditur quasdam acies inclinatas iam et labantes a feminis restitutas constantia precum et obiectu pectorum et monstrata comminus captiuitate, quam longe impatientius feminarum suarum nomine timent, adeo ut efficacius obligentur animi ciuitatum quibus inter obsides puellae quoque nobiles imperantur. Inesse quin etiam sanctum aliquid et prouidum putant, nec aut consilia earum aspernantur aut responsa neglegunt. Vidimus sub diuo Vespasiano Veledam diu apud plerosque numinis loco habitam; sed et olim Auriniam et complures alias uenerati sunt, non adulatione nec tamquam facerent deas.

9. Deorum maxime Mercurium colunt, cui certis diebus humanis quoque hostiis litare fas habent. Herculem ac Martem concessis animalibus placant. Pars Sueborum et Isidi sacrificat. Vnde causa et origo peregrino sacro parum com-

---

14 et] aut **M** β, nec pχ a   15 cibos **W**
  8, 7 concilia **Wm**   8 Velaedam *Ritter*²   9 muminis **W**
9 et] ut **W**   Auriniam (auarimam *m*) **X I**ξ **k c s**, aurimam l, aurinam **R**, Auriniam, *in mg. (superscr. in L)* Albriniam λd**Eo**, fluriniam, *superscr.* albriniam **N**, auriniam, *in mg.* albrinam **u**, aurimam, *in mg.* albrimam **e**, Albriniam **Δ r b**, albrimam z**A**, *om.* **v a**, Albrunam *Wackernagel*
  9, 2 ac] et β   3 Sueborum *Halm*¹, Sueuorum ω

---

knows this use of the passive or deponent infinitive (type, *est uideri*) in no author earlier than Tertullian. Hauler ("Die Orléaner Palimpsestfragmente zu Sallusts Historien," *Wiener Studien* ix [1887], 25–50 [see 44]) finds a parallel in Sallust, *Hist.* ii, frag. 87D, ed. Maurenbrecher: *et in eo credebatur epulari diebus certis dea, cuius erat de nomine, exaudiri sonores*. . . . He is followed by A. Kunze, *Berl. Phil. Woch.* xxxix (1919), 622. I think it impossible to determine the construction of *exaudiri* in this mutilated fragment, but should expect it to depend upon an impersonal *credebatur* rather than upon an implied *est*.

8, 9 Auriniam: The choice between the two variants is uncertain. See my discussion on pp. 105 f.

9, 2 Herculem: Those who would delete the reference to Hercules can no longer find support on palaeographical grounds. The transposition of *Herculem* occurs only in λ (see pp. 194 ff.).

peri, nisi quod signum ipsum in modum liburnae figuratum docet aduectam religionem.

Ceterum nec cohibere parietibus deos neque in ullam humani oris speciem adsimulare ex magnitudine caelestium arbitrantur. Lucos ac nemora consecrant deorumque nominibus appellant secretum illud quod sola reuerentia uident.

10. Auspicia sortesque ut qui maxime obseruant. Sortium consuetudo simplex: uirgam frugiferae arbori decisam in surculos amputant eosque notis quibusdam discretos super candidam uestem temere ac fortuito spargunt. Mox, si publice consulitur, sacerdos ciuitatis, sin priuatim, ipse pater familiae

---

Rudolphus Fuldensis, *Translatio Sancti Alexandri*, ch. 2, *M.G.*, SS. II, 675: "Coluerunt enim eos, qui natura non erant dii: inter quos maxime Mercurium uenerabantur, cui certis diebus humanis quoque hostiis litare consueuerant. Deos suos neque templis includere, neque ullae humani oris speciei adsimilare ex magnitudine et dignitate coelestium arbitrati sunt. Lucos ac nemora consecrantes, deorumque nominibus appellantes, secretum illud sola reuerentia contemplabantur."

---

5 liburnicae *Gudeman* liburna efiguratum **m**
10, 4 temere, *in mg.* tenent **W**, tenent **hΔs²**, temere, *superscr.* tenere **N** fortuitu **m** τ 5 consulitur *Walch 1829*, consuletur ω (*uide p. 240*), consulatur *Rhenanus*, consultetur *Halm¹ II, xii*

---

5 liburnae: Gudeman (30 f.) insists that *liburnicae* should be written, since Tacitus elsewhere employs this form exclusively, but I hesitate to depart from the authority of the MSS.

10, 4 temere: Arguments may be found in favor of both variants, *tenent* and *temere*. In favor of *tenent* it may be said: (1) that *temere* has arisen through dittography because of the preceding *uestem;* (2) that the writing of *R* for *N* is an error which we know to have occurred in the transmission of our text (cf. ch. 40, 1 *largobardos*); (3) that the combination *temere ac fortuito* is not found elsewhere in Tacitus; (4) that the combination is so common in Latin that an ancient copyist might quite unconsciously have substituted *temere* for *tenent*. In support of *temere* we may say: (1) that this is the reading of Rudolph of Fulda, though certainly not a convincing argument, since he may have found both readings in his MS.; (2) that *tenent* is known only to the X family; (3) that the misreading of *temere* as *tenent* in a fifteenth-century Gothic script would be very easy. On the whole, I am inclined to give preference to *temere*.

5 consulitur: In view of the universal confusion between open *i* and close *e* in the tradition of our text, I adopt *consulitur* as the simplest emendation of the manuscript *consuletur*. Some object to the impersonal use of the verb on the ground that *consulere* in the sense of "ask advice" regularly takes the accusative of the person asked, but the following

precatus deos caelumque suspiciens ter singulos tollit, sublatos secundum impressam ante notam interpretatur. Si prohibuerunt, nulla de eadem re in eundem diem consultatio; sin permissum, auspiciorum adhuc fides exigitur. Et illud quidem etiam hic notum, auium uoces uolatusque interrogare; proprium gentis equorum quoque praesagia ac monitus experiri. Publice aluntur isdem nemoribus ac lucis; candidi et nullo mortali opere contacti *sunt*; quos pressos sacro curru sacerdos ac rex uel princeps ciuitatis comitantur hinnitusque ac fremitus obseruant. Nec ulli auspicio maior fides, non solum

Rudolphus Fuldensis, *l.c.*: "Auspicia et sortes quam maxime obseruabant. Sortium consuetudo simplex erat. Virgam frugiferae arbori decisam in surculos amputabant, eosque notis quibusdam discretos super candidam uestem temere ac fortuito spargebant; mox si publica consultatio fuit, sacerdos populi, si priuata, ipse paterfamilias precatus deos coelumque suspiciens ter singulos tulit, sublatisque secundum impressam ante notam interpretatus est. Si prohibuerunt, nulla de eadem re ipsa die consultatio, si permissum est, euentuum adhuc fides exigebatur. Auium uoces uolatusque interrogare, proprium gentis illius erat. Equorum quoque praesagia ac monitus experiri, hinnitusque ac fremitus obseruare; nec ulli auspicio maior fides non solum apud plebem, sed etiam apud proceres habebatur. Erat et alia obseruatio auspiciorum, qua grauium bellorum euentus explorare solebant; cius quippe gentis, cum qua bellandum fuit, captiuum quoquo modo interceptum, cum electo popularium suorum patriis quemque armis committere, et uictoriam huius uel illius pro iudicio habere."

12 isdem **s**, hisdem **Wm 1**, iisdem **ω**   13 contacti sunt *scripsi*, contacti, *in mg.* contactis **W**, contactis **s²**, contractis **m**, contacti **ω**
14 hinnitus **a ψ**

passages show that such is not always the case: *Ann.* xv, 25, 5 ff. . . . *consuluit inter primores ciuitatis Nero, bellum anceps an pax inhonesta placeret;* and Caesar *B.G.* i, 53, 7 (cited by E. Wolff) *Is* (C. Valerius Proculus) *se praesente de se ter sortibus consultum dicebat, utrum igni statim necaretur an in aliud tempus reseruaretur, sortium beneficio se esse incolumem.* For the use of the indicative with *si* as the equivalent of ἐάν or ὅταν cf. ch. 20, 14 *si liberi non sunt.*

13 contacti sunt: See p. 96.
15 non solum . . . sacerdotes: The asyndeton is very harsh and in the absence of punctuation would render the passage almost unintelligible. Probably the text is corrupt, but I suspect that the corruption is too deep to be healed by the simple expedient of inserting *sed* before *apud proceres*, as has been done in some of our MSS., or before *apud sacerdotes*, as some commentators have done. With or without the addition of *sed*, I believe the

apud plebem: apud proceres, apud sacerdotes: se enim ministros deorum, illos conscios putant.

Est et alia obseruatio auspiciorum, qua grauium bellorum euentus explorant. Eius gentis cum qua bellum est captiuum quoquo modo interceptum cum electo popularium suorum patriis quemque armis committunt: uictoria huius uel illius pro praeiudicio accipitur.

11. De minoribus rebus principes consultant, de maioribus omnes, ita tamen ut ea quoque quorum penes plebem arbitrium est apud principes praetractentur. Coëunt, nisi quid fortuitum et subitum incidit, certis diebus, cum aut inchoatur

---

Rudolphus Fuldensis, *l.c.*: "Quomodo autem certis diebus, cum aut inchoatur luna aut (ut *cod.*) impletur, agendis rebus auspicatissimum initium crediderint, et alia innumera uanarum superstitionum genera, quibus implicati sunt, obseruauerint, pretereo."

---

16 sed apud proceres (sed *superscr. in E*) I ξ **E a** sed apud proceres; sacerdotes enim *Perizonius* sed apud sacerdotes *Thomas teste Halm*, etiam apud sacerdotes *Hirschfelder*

19 captiuom **V**, captiuo in **Δ**, captum **m**   22 pro^pre iudicio **V**, pro iudicio **Δ** *et sic Rudolphus* (*cf. p. 202, adn. 6*)

11, 3 praetractentur (*ex per- in I*, -tactantur *b*) **Wσ bA**, pertractentur **ω**   quod **W**, quod^i **b s**

---

contrast to be between *plebem* on the one hand and *proceres* and *sacerdotes* on the other. Not only would the more enlightened *proceres* be expected to have the same opinion about the *auspicia* as did the *sacerdotes*, but their part in the ceremony has also been indicated in line 14 (*uel princeps ciuitatis*).

Hirschfelder's *etiam* (in my judgment it belongs before *apud proceres*, not before *apud sacerdotes*) is based upon a Tacitean usage found in *Ann.* III, 19, 4 ff.; IV, 35, 1 ff.; *Hist.* II, 27, 2 ff.

In support of the asyndeton Persson (95) cites Cic. *ad Q. Fr.* I, 3, 6 *sed hoc non solum, multa alia praetermisi;* Calp. *Ecl.* 7, 64 f. *Nec solum*

nobis siluestria cernere monstra/ Contigit: aequoreos ego cum certantibus ursis/ Spectaui uitulos . . .: Plaut. *Bacch.* 973 f. *sed Priamus hic multo illi praestat: non quinquaginta modo,/ quadringentos filios habet.* Also *Ann.* XVI, 26, 3 ff. (previously cited by Wölfflin 1867, 125) *non solum Cossutianum aut Eprium ad scelus promptos: superesse qui forsitan manus ictusque per immanitatem ingesturi <sint>*, where, however, Persson feels that the *super* of *superesse* may replace an *etiam*.

11, 3 **praetractentur**: This reading is not so well attested as the variant *pertractentur* (cf. p. 150), but is clearly required by the context.

luna aut impletur; nam agendis rebus hoc auspicatissimum initium credunt. Nec dierum numerum, ut nos, sed noctium computant; sic constituunt, sic condicunt: nox ducere diem uidetur.

Illud ex libertate uitium, quod non simul nec ut iussi conueniunt, sed et alter et tertius dies cunctatione coëuntium absumitur. Vt turbae placuit, considunt armati. Silentium per sacerdotes, quibus tum et coërcendi ius est, imperatur. Mox rex, uel princeps prout aetas cuique, prout nobilitas, prout decus bellorum, prout facundia est, audiuntur auctoritate suadendi magis quam iubendi potestate. Si displicuit sententia, fremitu aspernantur, sin placuit, frameas concutiunt: honoratissimum adsensus genus est armis laudare.

12. Licet apud concilium accusare quoque et discrimen capitis intendere. Distinctio poenarum ex delicto: proditores et transfugas arboribus suspendunt, ignauos et imbelles et corpore infames caeno ac palude iniecta insuper et crate mergunt. Diuersitas supplicii illuc respicit, tamquam scelera ostendi oporteat dum puniuntur, flagitia abscondi.

Sed et leuioribus delictis pro modo poena: *nam* equorum pecorumque numero conuicti multantur. Pars multae regi uel ciuitati, pars ipsi qui uindicatur uel propinquis eius exsoluitur.

---

5 auspicatis simum **W**   9 ut iussi **X NI** λr **al** (ut iussu *a*), iniussi **p** τ, in iussu **M**, iussi (ut *om.*) Δχ **b**ḇ   11 adsumitur **W**, adsumitur **s²R**, assumitur **m** π   turba *I.F. Gronouius*
12 tum] tamen **m ß Ac**, *primitus in* **s**, cum **Ip**, cun *ex* cunque **M**
13 principes π, *Perizonius*

12, 4 et crate **h**, & grate, *in mg.* crate **W**, pro crate **b**, pocrate (crate *c*, proiecte *R*) π, gratem **m**, c̍rate **V**, create **I**, positos rate **a**, grate (crate *s²*) **s**, crate ω   7 poena: nam *scripsi*, poenarum ω, poena *Acidalius*, poena rata *Mützell, uide p. 54*   9 absoluitur, *sed ab expunx. et ex add. in mg. ead. m.* **W**

---

13 princeps: Perhaps the passage would be smoother if we read *principes* (cf. *Ann.* xiv, 23, 7 *barbari, pro ingenio quisque*), but I doubt if the change is justifiable. The choice of the plural verb was probably influenced by *cuique*, but cf. ch. 13, 4 f. and note.

12, 4 iniecta insuper et crate: "with a hurdle too thrown above." *Et* (= *etiam*) marks the additional precaution taken to prevent escape. On the manuscript readings see pp. 140 f.

10   Eliguntur in isdem conciliis et principes qui iura per pagos vicosque reddunt.   Centeni singulis ex plebe comites consilium simul et auctoritas adsunt.

   13. Nihil autem neque publicae neque priuatae rei nisi armati agunt.   Sed arma sumere non ante cuiquam moris quam ciuitas suffecturum probauerit.   Tum in ipso concilio uel principum aliquis uel pater uel propinquus scuto frameaque
5   iuuenem ornant: haec apud illos toga, hic primus iuuentae honos; ante hoc domus pars uidentur, mox rei publicae.

   Insignis nobilitas aut magna patrum merita principis di-

---

10 isdem *Holder*, hisdem **X I o bl**, iisdem ω   11 concilium **W a**
   13, 3 tum h **Δ I r b s**, cum **W p M β**, tum eutum **m**, tum, *superscr.* cum **N**, Tum eum χ, tum cum a π, *fortasse* eum *ante* probauerit *inscrendum est*   4 propinquus (*ex* -quis *ut uid.* I) **hm**σs² χ φ, propinqui, *in mg.* quus **W**, propinquus, *in mg.* propinqui **pM**, propinqui β s   7 donacione **m**, dignitatem λ a

---

13, 4 propinquus: On the doublets *propinquus:propinqui* see p. 125. From a stylistic point of view *propinquus* seems to me slightly preferable to *propinqui*. A plural verb with singular subjects connected by *uel* is found in Quint. IX, 4, 107 *Apparet uero, quam bene eum* (creticum) *praecedant uel anapestos uel ille, qui uidetur fini aptior, paeon.* The same usage with *aut* is found in Tacitus *Ann.* I, 42, 1; II, 63, 10; VI, 1, 15; XI, 7, 12; with a connecting *neque . . . neque, Hist.* III, 28, 3. (These examples from Tacitus are cited by Gudeman *ad Dial.* 35, 6 f. For examples from other authors see *ibid.* and Menge, *Repertorium d. Lat. Syntax u. Stilistik* [10] [Wolfenbüttel, 1914] *zweiter Teil*, 9. Also cf. ch. 11, 13 ff., and note.)

7 principis dignationem: "Marked nobility of family or illustrious services of their sires accord even to striplings recognition from a prince. They are attached to the rest of his retinue, who are more mature and have sometime since been adjudged competent, and they feel no shame in being seen among the *comites*." The sense of the passage depends upon the meaning attached to *principis dignationem*. The interpretation which I have indicated is said first to have been advanced by Longolius (cf. Hess *ad loc.*) and Orelli (1819, 15), and has been ably defended by Baumstark, Müllenhoff, and Strache (1919, 68 f.), but best of all by A. Wiessner. Others, and so far as I can determine the greater number, understand *principis dignationem* to mean "the rank of a prince," believing that this is the only interpretation allowed by the Tacitean usage of *dignatio*. Since numerous proposals for changing the tradition of our MSS. have come from this group of commentators, it will not be beyond the bounds of a critical edition to state briefly the case for *dignationem* = "recognition."

With this interpretation, the entire chapter is a unified, coherent, and harmonious whole, and is at least as intelligible as the scanty information provided by the author permits. After a brief introductory sentence, Tacitus says that it is not usual for anyone to bear arms until the state shall have declared him competent. Then one of the *princes* or his father or a relative invests the *young man* with his shield and spear. This corresponds with the assumption of the toga among the Romans, and is the first public recognition of *young manhood*.

gnationem etiam adulescentulis adsignant: ceteris robustioribus
ac iam pridem probatis adgregantur, nec rubor inter comites
aspici. Gradus quin etiam ipse comitatus habet iudicio eius
quem sectantur, magnaque et comitum aemulatio, quibus
primus apud principem suum locus, et principum, cui plurimi
et acerrimi comites. Haec dignitas, hae uires, magno semper
electorum iuuenum globo circumdari, in pace decus, in bello
praesidium.

Nec solum in sua gente cuique, sed apud finitimas quoque
ciuitates id nomen, ea gloria est, si numero ac uirtute comitatus
emineat; expetuntur enim legationibus et muneribus ornantur
et ipsa plerumque fama bella profligant.

---

8 ceteri *Lipsius*, certis *Gudeman*   9 robur, *in mg.* rubor **W**,
rubor, *in mg.* robur **h**, robur **m d c**, rŭbor **N**, robor **s**   12 principium, *in mg.* pum **W**, principum, *in mg.* principium **h**, principium **m NI r ɸ** (p: e), *uide p. 126*   13 hae] hec (*sed corr. in L*) **W I Lv Ac**   semper et electorum **τ** (*cf. p. 205*)

However, even *striplings* (*adulescentulus* is of course purposely used in place of *adulescens*) may receive this recognition of competence at the hands of a *prince*, if they are recommended by outstanding nobility of family or illustrious services of their fathers. The boys who have been thus favored are attached to the rest of the prince's retinue, who are stronger because of their more advanced years and greater experience, and who some time before have received the sanction of the state to bear arms. In spite of their noble birth or the prominence of their families, these *adulescentuli* are not ashamed to be seen in the *comitatus*. It will be seen that the author's transition from the *probatio ciuitatis* to the *comitatus* is easy and natural.

The only legitimate objection to this interpretation is that elsewhere in Tacitus *dignatio*, though of frequent occurrence, has a meaning akin to that of *dignitas*. (I say *akin*, for some who defend *principis dignationem* in the sense of "the rank of a prince" carefully distinguish between *dignitas* and *dignatio*. Thus Karle: "dignatio = ἀξίωσις, das für werth halten, das würdigen; dignitas = würde." Gudeman [1928]: "he was a *princeps de iure*, not *de facto*.") Yet the active meaning of *dignatio* is one that is well attested in Latin literature, and in fact this must have been the original meaning of the word, as its formation shows (see Mf.'s discussion, 259 f.).

If, on the other hand, we attempt to force the meaning of "rank" upon *dignationem*, the unity and coherence of the chapter are destroyed. *Adulescentulis* no longer offers a contrast to *iuuenem* and *iuuentae*, the connection between *principum aliquis* (l. 4) and *principis* (l. 7) is lost, the parallel between *probauerit* (l. 3) and *iam pridem probatis* (l. 9) is vitiated. Quite without warning the author introduces the new and irrelevant matter of elevation to the rank of *princeps*, which he immediately abandons as he passes on to the discussion of the *comitatus*. Finally, *ceteris* becomes unintelligible. It is significant that those who accept *dignationem* in the sense of "recognition" are in essential agreement as to the meaning of the passage, whereas those who insist that it must have the meaning of

14. Cum uentum in aciem, turpe principi uirtute uinci, turpe comitatui uirtutem principis non adaequare. Iam uero infame in omnem uitam ac probrosum superstitem principi suo ex acie recessisse: illum defendere, tueri, sua quoque fortia facta gloriae eius adsignare praecipuum sacramentum est: principes pro uictoria pugnant, comites pro principe.

Si ciuitas in qua orti sunt longa pace et otio torpeat, plerique nobilium adulescentium petunt ultro eas nationes quae tum bellum aliquod gerunt, quia et ingrata genti quies et facilius inter ancipitia clarescunt magnumque comitatum non nisi ui belloque tueare. Exigunt enim <a> principis sui liberalitate illum bellatorem equom, illam cruentam uictricemque frameam; nam epulae et quamquam incompti largi tamen apparatus pro stipendio cedunt: materia munificentiae per bella et raptus. Nec arare terram aut expectare annum tam facile persuaseris quam uocare hostem et uulnera mereri; pigrum quin immo et iners uidetur sudore a*d*quirere quod possis sanguine parare.

15. Quotiens bella non ineunt, non multum uenatibus, plus

14, 3 infame in] infamem **Ws**², *primitus in* h, infamem in a π, *uide p. 145* (*cf. pp. 96 f.*) principi **W**, principe h, principis (sui) *suspicor* 7 torqueat **W** 8 tum] cum **W I E** ψ 11 in bello que **Wm**, in belloque r b s (*corr. s*²), bello uique π, in bello **a** a *add. Acidalius, om.* ω principes **Whs**², principes *in* -pis *corr.* **I** 12 equom **Wm**, equum ω

15, 1 non *ante* multum *del.* **Lipsius**

"rank" show the widest diversity of opinion on other details, and, as I have stated, can seldom refrain from tampering with the text. (Among those who attempt to defend *dignationem* in the meaning of "rank" without changing the text may be mentioned C. John, 1917, 842 f., Kettner, W. Schultze, and Haverfield, 1901. The last three begin a new sentence with *Nec rubor*, understanding that Tacitus is describing two ways of entering the service of the state: as a *princeps*, and as a *comes*.)

14, 11 <a> . . . liberalitate: To say, "they demand something *by virtue of* (*because of*) their chieftain's generosity," when the simple and natural expression is, "they demand something *of* their chieftain's generosity," seems to me very forced even for Tacitus. For *exigere ab aliqua re* cf. Quint. XII, 11, 29: *nisi indignum litteris esset ab opere pulcherrimo, . . . hanc minorem exigere mercedem*.

15, 1 non multum uenatibus: There is no reason for deleting *non* on the ground that Tacitus is here in contradiction with Caesar (*B.G.* IV, 1, 8: VI, 21, 3). As Strache (1919, 70) has pointed out, the train of thought throughout the paragraph is in contra-

per otium transigunt, dediti somno ciboque, fortissimus quisque ac bellicosissimus nihil agens, delegata domus et penatium et agrorum cura feminis senibusque et infirmissimo cuique ex familia. Ipsi hebent mira diuersitate naturae, cum idem homines sic ament inertiam et oderint quietem.

Mos est ciuitatibus ultro ac uiritim conferre principibus uel armentorum uel frugum quod pro honore acceptum etiam necessitatibus subuenit.

Gaudent praecipue finitimarum gentium donis, quae non modo a singulis, sed et publice mittuntur, electi equi, magna arma, phalerae torquesque; iam et pecuniam accipere docuimus.

16. Nullas Germanorum populus urbes habitari satis notum est, ne pati quidem inter se iunctas sedes. Colunt discreti ac diuersi, ut fons, ut campus, ut nemus placuit. Vicos locant non in nostrum morem conexis et cohaerentibus aedificiis: suam quisque domum spatio circumdat, siue aduersus casus ignis remedium siue inscitia aedificandi.

Ne caementorum quidem apud illos aut tegularum usus: materia ad omnia utuntur informi et citra speciem aut delectationem. Quaedam loca diligentius inlinunt terra ita pura ac

---

5 hebent **N VEk** s, ebent **h**, habent **W**, hab̄ent (hn̄t *Ipm eRc*) ω idem **X b**, hidem **r**, iidem **a λv** s, hisdem **l**, iisdem **dk** ψ, iidem *ex* iisdem **M E u**, quod **a**   7 principibus aliquid *ed Vind. a. 1515 teste Passow*   11 a *om.* **Xs**², *fortasse recte (cf. p. 100)*   et *om.* **Iξ π**   magna] magnifica *Meiser*

16, 4 locant, *in mg.* longant **M E**, longant, *in mg. uel superscr.* locant **Vd**, longant **k**, *cf. p. 194*   connexis ω   6 inscientia *cod. Hf. teste Decembrio, cf. p. 12*   7 Nec **X** (*de lect. cod. h. uide p. 167*), s² **N** c

---

diction with Caesar, who says of the Germans (*B.G.* VI, 21, 3): *uita omnis in uenationibus atque in studiis rei militaris consistit*. More reasonable is the criticism made by John (1917, 839) that only with a positive *multum* does *plus* assume its proper emphasis, for *more* than *not very much* need not necessarily be a great deal.

16, 9 inlinunt . . . imitetur: The passage is very difficult, but probably is in need of interpretation rather than emendation. The meaning may be, that the clay was so uniform in color (*pura*) and so bright (*splendente*) that it resembled the pigments used by painters (*ut picturam . . . imitetur*). When applied to the houses as trimmings (*quaedam loca*), it gave the impression of colored outlines made with paint (*ut picturam ac lineamenta colorum imitetur*). The closest parallel

splendente ut picturam ac lineamenta colorum imitetur. Solent et subterraneos specus aperire eosque multo insuper fimo onerant, suffugium hiemi et receptaculum frugibus, quia rigorem frigorum eius modi lacus molliunt, et si quando hostis aduenit, aperta populatur, abdita autem et defossa aut ignorantur aut eo ipso fallunt quod quaerenda sunt.

17. Tegumen omnibus sagum fibula aut, si desit, spina consertum: cetera intecti totos dies iuxta focum atque ignem agunt. Locupletissimi ueste distinguuntur non fluitante, sicut Sarmatae ac Parthi, sed stricta et singulos artus exprimente.

Gerunt et ferarum pelles, proximi ripae neglegenter, ulteriores exquisitius, ut quibus nullus per commercia cultus. Eligunt feras et detracta uelamina spargunt maculis pellibusque beluarum quas exterior Oceanus atque ignotum mare gignit. Nec alius feminis quam uiris habitus, nisi quod feminae saepius lineis amictibus uelantur eosque purpura uariant, partemque uestitus superioris in manicas non extendunt, nudae brachia ac lacertos, sed et proxima pars pectoris patet.

10 ac lineamenta] adline- m   imitentur N∆ E R   12 hiemis *Reifferscheid*   13 lacus *Bährens*, locis ω, lacis *Holder*, loci *Acidalius*, focis *Bywater*

17, 11 superiorem *P. Voss*   12 nudae] Vnde **Wm** b

to *lineamenta colorum* for *lineamenta colorata* that I have found is Pliny, *N. H.* xxxv, 81: *adreptoque penicillo lineam ex colore duxit summae tenuitatis per tabulam.* For *color purus* cf. x, 151: *quarto die post quam* (oua) *coepere incubari, si contra lumen cacumine ouorum adprehenso ima manu purus et unius modi perluceat color, sterilia existimantur esse.* . . .

12 **suffugium hiemi**: Reifferscheid's *hiemis* has found numerous adherents, but I see no reason why Tacitus could not have written *suffugium hiemi et receptaculum frugibus,* just as in English we may say "a retreat *for* winter and a storehouse *for* grain," though the force of the preposition is different in each case. Cf. Pliny, *N. H.* viii, 133 *praeparant hiemi et irenacei cibos,* and the other passages cited by J. Müller.

13 **lacus**: *Locis,* the reading of all MSS., should be rejected on stylistic grounds, but there is no apparent reason why this corruption should have arisen from *loci,* the *uulgata.* Bährens' *lacus* is sound palaeographically, and gives a satisfactory meaning. The misreading of the *-us* ligature as *is* and the writing of *o* for *a* are both errors which we know to have occurred in the copying of Hf. (see p. 53). *Lacus* is used to designate the bins of a granary by Columella, I, 6 *Sed et lacubus distinguuntur granaria, ut separatim quaeque legumina ponantur.* In Scriptural Latin it is used for a den (*lacus leonum*), a prison, and a tomb (see Forcellini, *s.v.* 18, 20, 22). Tacitus may well have read λάκκος in the Greek work which he was excerpting.

18. Quamquam seuera illic matrimonia, nec ullam morum partem magis laudaueris. Nam prope soli barbarorum singulis uxoribus contenti sunt, exceptis admodum paucis qui non libidine sed ob nobilitatem plurimis nuptiis ambiuntur.
 Dotem non uxor marito, sed uxori maritus offert. Intersunt parentes et propinqui ac munera probant: munera non ad delicias muliebres quaesita nec quibus noua nupta comatur, sed boues et frenatum equum et scutum cum framea gladioque. In haec munera uxor accipitur atque inuicem ipsa armorum aliquid uiro adfert: hoc maximum uinculum, haec arcana sacra, hos coniugales deos arbitrantur. Ne se mulier extra uirtutum cogitationes extraque bellorum casus putet, ipsis incipientis matrimonii auspiciis admonetur uenire se laborum periculorumque sociam, idem in pace, idem in proelio passuram ausuramque: hoc iuncti boues, hoc paratus equus, hoc data arma denuntiant. Sic uiuendum, sic pariendum: ac-

18, 4 pluribus *Halm²*, pluris (nuptiis ambiunt) *Weidner* 4 ambiunt h 6 ac] at **W** munera *priore loco del. Lachmann, altero loco Bernhardy apud Döderlein* 16 uiuendum] nubendum *Bährens* pariendum **XσV**, periendum al' pariendum **s²**, (sic uiuentes sic) parientes τ, p *in mg.*, pereundum ξ L, pieū **s**, piende **b**, parentes **a**, patrem (*om. l*) π, moriendum *Novák*

Ch. 18: Halm in his first and succeeding editions (so also Andresen) begins the chapter with *Dotem*. I agree with Gudeman (1928) that the skillful transition from the suggestion of moral laxity implied in the words, *sed et proxima pars pectoris patet*, to the discussion of German marriage customs is set forth better if we follow the older editions in making the chapter begin with *Quamquam*.

3 non libidine: The *ambiunt* of h shows that the difficulty of the passage was recognized by some humanistic scholar. Gudeman (1928) translates: "not for the purpose of gratifying their lust." Schweizer-Sidler: ". . . nicht mit Rücksicht auf ihre *libido*. . . ." Probably this is what Tacitus meant, but it is not what he says. Is it just possible that *non libidine* means "not because of laxity of morals (among the Germans)?"

4 plurimis: I see no excuse for adopting *pluribus*. Tacitus does not say that some of the nobles have very many wives, but that they receive very many offers of marriage.

16 uiuendum: Bährens' *nubendum* is not so difficult a change as might at first appear, in view of the frequent confusion between *b* and consonant-*u* in one of the antecedents of Hf. (cf. p. 246).

pariendum: This seems to me at least as satisfactory (note *liberis* in the next line) as the *uulgata, pereundum*, which is lacking in respectable manuscript authority.

cipere se quae liberis inuiolata ac digna reddat, quae nurus accipiant rursusque ad nepotes referantur.

19. Ergo saepta pudicitia agunt, nullis spectaculorum illecebris, nullis conuiuiorum irritationibus corruptae. Litterarum secreta uiri pariter ac feminae ignorant. Paucissima in tam numerosa gente adulteria, quorum poena praesens et maritis permissa. Adcisis crinibus nudatam coram propinquis expellit domo maritus ac per omnem uicum uerbere agit; publicatae enim pudicitiae nulla uenia: non forma, non aetate,

---

17 inuiolata reddat, ac digna quae *Acidalius* 18 rursus que **hm** t **VE**, rursus quae **σpMw d s**

19, 1 septe a, *unde* saeptae *Crollius* 3 ac] & **W** 5 adcisis **Vdrk** b, accisis **h** *cx sil* , a **L**, adscissis **zu**, adsissis **Ac**, abscisis **Wm** t **Ev leR** s, incisis **a** 7 enim] etiam *Lipsius*, enimuero *Madvig* ii, 565

19, 5 Adcisis crinibus: The choice between the variants *adcisis* and *abscisis* is difficult, as both may well have been in Hf. (on the confusion of B and D see p. 54). Yet the fact that β and φ appear to have had *adcisis* with the unassimilated prefix does in my opinion point to the antiquity of this reading, whereas *abscisis* may be a humanistic interpolation. The decision is rendered more difficult by the fact that we must depend upon the *ex silentio* reading of **h**, which is *accisis*.

All examples of *accidere* with *crinis* or *coma* cited by the *Thesaurus* are from late Latin (Paul. Nol. *Carm.* 24, 590 [Samuel] *neque accisus comam;* Sulp. *Chron.* I, 28, 4 [Samsoni] *accisus crinis crescere* . . . *occeperat;* Sid. *Ep.* IV, 13, 1 *crinis in rotae specimen accisus*), but I do not regard this as evidence that the verb could not have been so used in Tacitus' time. *Corp. Glos.* IV, p. 6, 1, gives *accisis = circumcisis* (glosses of cod. Vat. 3321). Wissowa (1916) believes that Tacitus had in mind the περικειρομένη, the faithless mistress whose hair had been shorn by her jealous lover. As Wissowa remarks, it is not a question of what was the actual custom among the Germans, but of what Tacitus, or his authorities, imagined it to be.

7: publicatae enim . . . inuenerit: Lipsius' *etiam* or Madvig's *enimuero* would mark a transition from the discussion of the *adultera* to a discussion of the *meretrix*. The objections found to the manuscript tradition are, (1) that *publicare pudicitiam* should be said of the *meretrix*, and not of the *adultera*, (2) that *maritum* must stand for *alterum maritum*, if *adultera* is the subject of *inuenerit*. whereas the mention of a second marriage in this connection seems incongruous. Nipperdey (1863, 343), proposing the deletion of *enim*, pointedly asks: "Wer hätte selbst in Rom eine nackt, mit abgeschnittenen Haaren durch die Strassen gepeitschte Person geheirathet?"

The first of these objections does not appear to me cogent. I suspect that in Tacitus' eyes the cases of the *adultera* and of the *meretrix* were nearly enough identical to warrant the use of *publicatae pudicitiae* with reference to the former, though quite probably with these words his point of view has shifted to the extent that he has in mind not merely the *adultera* but any woman of easy virtue. As for the second objection, I see no reason why the retention of *enim* involves the mention of a *second* marriage. To be sure, the author's

non opibus maritum inuenerit. Nemo enim illic uitia ridet, nec corrumpere et corrumpi saeculum uocatur. Melius quidem adhuc eae ciuitates in quibus tantum uirgines nubunt et cum spe uotoque uxoris semel transigitur. Sic unum accipiunt maritum quo modo unum corpus unamque uitam, ne ulla cogitatio ultra, ne longior cupiditas, ne tamquam maritum sed tamquam matrimonium ament.

Numerum liberorum finire aut quemquam ex adgnatis necare flagitium habetur, plusque ibi boni mores ualent quam alibi bonae leges.

---

8 inuenit **a** *praeter* Δ, (maritus) inuenitur **s**, leniuerit *Krafft*
9 et] nec **W v ϕ**   10 & adhuc **W**, *cf. p. 155*   13 ne tam maritum quam matrimonium] *Meiser*, ne tamquam matrimonium sed tamquam maritum *Grotius*

---

point of view has again changed somewhat, for the words *non forma . . . maritum inuenerit*, though used with special reference to the adultress, are equally applicable to the German woman in general. I believe Tacitus' line of thought to be: "Do not be surprised at the severity of the penalty, for violation of chastity finds no pardon: it is not by beauty, youth, or wealth that she can find her husband, and consequently she cannot make use of these advantages to win his forgiveness, if she prove unfaithful." The clause *non forma . . . inuenerit* serves to explain, not to expand, *nulla uenia*. With this interpretation the contrast between German and Roman morals, dominant in the author's mind throughout the chapter, is, I believe, brought more clearly into relief. A striking parallel in thought is offered by Horace's familiar lines (*C.* III, 24, 19–23): "nec dotata regit uirum/ coniunx, nec nitido fidit adultero./ dos est magna parentium/ uirtus et metuens alterius uiri/ certo foedere castitus." For the mood and tense of *inuenerit* cf. *Hist.* I, 79, 11 *ubi per turmas aduenere* (Sarmatae). *uix ulla acies obstiterit*; *Germ.* 37, 15 *obiecerit*.

13 ne tamquam . . . ament: The idea is strangely expressed, and the double *tamquam* may not be beyond suspicion. Yet, as usual, it is well to remember that we are dealing with Tacitus. If a woman marries more than once, it is probably because she wants a husband (*ne tamquam maritum . . . ament*); if on the other hand a woman loses her husband and refuses to marry again, she may well be influenced by the feeling that her marriage is a sacred bond holding her throughout life (*sed tamquam matrimonium ament*). Such I believe to be Tacitus' meaning. Cf. Andresen (1916, 1112 f.): "Ich bin meiner Sache nicht sicher, möchte aber glauben, dass *tamquam* hier, wie so oft, das subjective Empfinden der Person bezeichnet, von der die Rede ist, hier also der Frau. Der Sinn wäre dann, 'damit der Gedanke an den Ehebund, den sie geschlossen hat, ihr Dasein ausfülle, ihr Gefühl beherrsche, nicht die Person des Ehemanns, der ihr verloren gehen und durch einen andern ersetzt werden könne."

In defense of the double *tamquam* F. Walter (1885) cites Val. Max. VIII, 11, 3 . . . *quod stat* (Vulcanus) *dissimulatae claudicationis sub ueste leuiter uestigium repraesentans, ut non exprobratum tamquam uitium, ita tamquam certam propriamque dei notam decore significatam*; Seneca, *Ben.* IV, 28, 2 . . . *quidquid aliud est, quod tamquam ciui, non tamquam bono datur, ex aequo boni ac mali ferunt.* But these passages do not afford exact parallels to the one under discussion.

20. In omni domo nudi ac sordidi in hos artus, in haec corpora quae miramur excrescunt. Sua quemque mater uberibus alit, nec ancillis ac nutricibus delegantur. Dominum ac seruum nullis educationis deliciis di*g*noscas: inter eadem pecora, in eadem humo degunt, donec aetas separet ingenuos, uirtus adgnoscat. Sera iuuenum uenus, eoque inexhausta pubertas. Nec uirgines festinantur: eadem iuuenta, similis proceritas: pares ualidaeque miscentur, ac robora parentum liberi referunt.

Sororum filiis idem apud auunculum qui ad patrem honor. Quidam sanctiorem artioremque hunc nexum sanguinis arbitrantur et in accipiendis obsidibus magis exigunt, tamquam et [in] animum firmius et domum latius teneant. Heredes tamen successoresque sui cuique liberi, et nullum testamentum. Si liberi non sunt, proximus gradus in possessione fratres patrui auunculi. Quanto plus propinquorum, *qu*anto maior adfinium numerus, tanto gratiosior senectus, nec ulla orbitatis pretia.

21. Suscipere tam inimicitias seu patris seu propinqui quam amicitias necesse est. Nec implacabiles durant; luitur enim etiam homicidium certo armentorum ac pecorum numero recipitque satisfactionem uniuersa domus, utiliter in publicum, quia periculosiores sunt inimicitiae iuxta libertatem.

Conuictibus et hospitiis non alia gens effusius indulget. Quemcumque mortalium arcere tecto nefas habetur; pro fortuna quisque apparatis epulis excipit. Cum defecere, qui

---

20, 2 mirantur IpM v φ (*sed alr. ramur in mg. M*), mirantur *ex* minantur s   3 ac] aut m Δ λ, nec v, non π   5 separaret W   10 ad *om.* ψ, apud L, *Rhenanus*   13 in *om.* m, *del.* h[2] *et Gerlach*, inligent *P. Voss*, uinciant *Fritz Walter*   16 quanto u[2] *in mg.* (*Halm*[2] *II, xxxii*), tanto ω, tam m, quo ϰ   17 gratiosior W I Lk s, gratiosior, *in mg. uel superscr.* gratior N VdE, gratior, *in mg.* gratiosior pM, gratior hm Δχ vr, generosior φ
21, 2 enim *om.* W A

20, 10 ad patrem: I retain the *ad* of the MSS., feeling that Tacitus' fondness for asymmetry may have led him to express himself in this manner. However, I know of no exact parallel for such a use of *ad*.

12 et [in] animum: Andresen (1915, 308) is probably correct in regarding *in* as an intrusion from the preceding *et in*. (Cf. *ibid.* for instances of similar repetitions in the MSS. of Tacitus, and see p. 48.)

modo hospes fuerat monstrator hospitii et comes; proximam domum non inuitati adeunt. Nec interest: pari humanitate accipiuntur. Notum ignotumque quantum ad ius hospitis nemo discernit. Abeunti, si quid poposcerit, concedere moris; et poscendi inuicem eadem facilitas. Gaudent muneribus, sed nec data imputant nec acceptis obligantur. [uictus inter hospites comis.]

22. Statim e somno, quem plerumque in diem extrahunt, lauantur, saepius calida, ut apud quos plurimum hiems occupat. Lauti cibum capiunt: separatae singulis sedes et sua cuique mensa. Tum ad negotia nec minus saepe ad conuiuia procedunt armati. Diem noctemque continuare potando nulli probrum. Crebrae, ut inter uinulentos, rixae raro conuiciis, saepius caede et uulneribus transiguntur.

Sed et de reconciliandis inuicem inimicis et iungendis affinitatibus et adsciscendis principibus, de pace denique ac bello plerumque in conuiuiis consultant, tamquam nullo magis tempore aut ad simplices cogitationes pateat animus aut ad magnas incalescat. Gens non astuta nec callida aperit adhuc secreta pectoris licentia loci; ergo detecta et nuda omnium mens. Postera die retractatur, et salua utriusque temporis

---

12 abeunt, *in mg. inc. m.* cum W, abeunt hs²   14 uictus ... comis *secl. de la Bleterie*

22, 1 e] enim β *praeter* r, p *in mg.*, enim, *in mg.* e M, ē s, e s²   6 ut *om.* W u   8 sed et mh β, et *om.* ω   9 adsciscendis, *in mg.* aspiciendis W, adpiscendis *ut uid.* (*ex* adsciscendis) s²   12 adhuc] ad hec λdr bl, ad hoc k aψ s (*corr.* s²)   13 loci mh s, loci, *superscr.* ioci W, ioci V, ioci, *superscr.* loci L, ioci ω (s²)   14 res retractatur *Meiser*

21, 14 [uictus ... comis]: These words are so palpably spurious that it is unnecessary to mention the various attempts which have been made to save them. They are probably a fusion of a marginal index, *uictus inter hospites*, and a variant reading *comis* for *comes*, line 9 (cf. pp. 34 f.). This is essentially the explanation given by Andresen, 1915.

22, 13 licentia loci: As the variants *loci:ioci* are at least as old as Hf., and probably older, it may be a matter of individual preference which is adopted, though I personally have no hesitation in accepting *loci*.

14 mens. Postera: This punctuation was restored by Passow from the Viennese edition of 1515. Previously the text was commonly printed with a full stop before *ergo* and no punctuation after *mens*, which thereby

15   ratio est: deliberant dum fingere nesciunt, constituunt dum errare non possunt.

23. Potui humor ex hordeo aut frumento in quandam similitudinem uini corruptus; proximi ripae et uinum mercantur. Cibi simplices, agrestia poma, recens fera aut lac concretum: sine apparatu, sine blandimentis expellunt famem.
5   Aduersus sitim non eadem temperantia: si indulseris ebrietati suggerendo quantum concupiscunt, haud minus facile uitiis quam armis uincentur.

15 deliberant dum] Deliberandum **Wm**

became the subject of *retractatur* (so too in the MSS. [cf. p. 263]). Mf. defends the older punctuation, which is also retained by Reeb. I find it more logical to take *retractatur* as impersonal.

23, 5 si indulseris ... uincentur: Wiedemann compares Pompeius Trogus, as excerpted by Justinus I, 8, 7: *priusque Scythae ebrietate quam bello uincuntur*. It is interesting to note how Tacitus has embellished with his rhetorical flourishes this simple "catch-phrase" of ethnographic literature. He has made a highly rhetorical and sententious conclusion to his chapter without due regard to the *reductio ad absurdum* which results from a strictly logical interpretation of his words. He has done the same thing in the conclusions of chs. 16 and 24. (Also cf. 18, 3 f. *non libidine ... ambiuntur*.) Certainly the logical implication of *haud minus facile* is that the vanquishing of the Germans is an easy matter, which is in direct contradiction to 37, 8 ff., and which is not at all what our author meant to say. His fondness for litotes has caused him to say *haud minus facile* when he really means *facilius*, just as in 5, 12, he says *non in alia uilitate*, where the sense demands either *in eodem uilitate* or *non in alio pretio*. Gudeman thinks that Tacitus could not possibly have written this concluding sentence, and consequently brackets it. I doubt very much if anybody but Tacitus *could* have written it.

There is scarcely a word in the sentence with which Gudeman does not find fault. He says that nowhere in Latin does *indulgere* have the meaning of "come to the aid of" or "to encourage," but he does not state what he regards as the legitimate use of the word. He believes that in *ebrietati* we have an unparalleled use of this word for *ebriositas*. Yet with all the unpublished *Thesaurus* material at his disposal he finds only three examples of *ebriositas*, and each time it is used with *ebrietas* for the purpose of making a distinction between the two. I suspect this of being a grammarian's distinction, such as Remmius Palaemon's *gutta stat, stilla cadit*. Finally, Gudeman sees in the words *suggerendo quantum concupiscunt* two incredible suggestions: (1) that there was a beer famine in Germany; (2) that Tacitus, or rather the interpolator, has no better advice to offer than that the Romans should engage in the brewing and exportation of beer, in order to conquer their old enemy in this unique manner! I cannot take these objections seriously, but if the grammarian's plumb-line must be applied to this "purple patch" of Tacitean rhetoric, why may not Tacitus have had in mind the exportation to Germany, not of beer to be sure, but of Italian and Gallic wines, whose alcoholic content was doubtless stronger than that of German beer (cf. line 2, *proximi ripae et uinum mercantur*)?

24. Genus spectaculorum unum atque in omni coetu idem: nudi iuuenes, quibus id ludicrum est, inter gladios se atque infestas frameas saltu iaciunt. Exercitatio artem parauit, ars decorem, non in quaestum tamen aut mercedem: quamuis audacis lasciuiae pretium est uoluptas spectantium.

Aleam, quod mirere, sobrii inter seria exercent, tanta lucrandi perdendiue temeritate ut cum omnia defecerunt extremo ac nouissimo iactu de libertate ac de corpore contendant. Victus uoluntariam seruitutem adit: quamuis iuuenior, quamuis robustior, alligari se ac uenire patitur. Ea est in re praua peruicacia; ipsi fidem uocant. Seruos condicionis huius per commercia tradunt, ut se quoque pudore uictoriae exsoluant.

25. Ceteris seruis non in nostrum morem descriptis per familiam ministeriis utuntur: suam quisque sedem, suos penates regit. Frumenti modum dominus aut pecoris aut uestis ut colono iniungit, et seruus hactenus paret; cetera domus officia uxor ac liberi exequuntur. Verberare seruum ac uinculis et opere coërcere rarum: occidere solent non disciplina et seueritate sed impetu et ira, ut inimicum, nisi quod impune est.

Liberti non multum supra seruos sunt, raro aliquod momentum in domo, numquam in ciuitate, exceptis dumtaxat is

---

24, 1 in omni] nouum **W**, omni *om.* **m**   3 artem parauit] aut temporauit **m** .   parat I ξ s (parauit *in mg. pM*)   5 spectantium **M**χ **L**τ l, **p** *superscr.*, expectantium **X** σp **V** ba s, spe expectantium ψ, *cf. p. 107*   8 deliberate **W**, de liberate **m**   10 praua] parua **Wh** (*de lect. cod. h uide p. 168*), **M** baAz (*corr. M²*)

25, 1 Ceterum *E. Wolff*   discriptis *Reifferscheid*   4 ut] aut **Wm Δ v z**   10 is *ed. Vind. 1515 teste Holder*, his **Wh dEk** π, iis (hiis *m vr b s*)ω

25, 1 Ceteris: E. Wolff, followed by Andresen and Gudeman in their editions, changes to *Ceterum*, since he sees no reason why those who have sold themselves to pay their gambling debts should receive different treatment from the rest of the slaves. But is not the implication of the concluding sentence of ch. 24 that these debtors are sold out of the country? In this case, they could not well figure in Tacitus' account of the treatment of slaves among the Germans.

descriptis: I follow Vetter in the *Thesaurus* v. 662, who cites this passage under the heading, *definire, determinare, constituere*, but the change to *discriptis* is very simple (on confusion of *e* and *i* see pp. 240 f.), and perhaps justifiable (cf. F. Bücheler, "Coniectanea Critica," *Rh. Mus.* XIII [1858], 573–604 [598 ff.]).

gentibus quae regnantur. Ibi enim et super ingenuos et super nobiles ascendunt; apud ceteros impares libertini libertatis argumentum sunt.

26. Faenus agitare et in usuras extendere ignotum; ideoque magis seruatur quam si uetitum esset. Agri pro numero cultorum ab uniuersis uicis occupantur, quos mox inter se secundum dignationem partiuntur; facilitatem partiendi camporum spatia praestant. Arua per annos mutant, et superest ager. Nec enim cum ubertate et amplitudine soli labore contendunt, ut pomaria conserant, ut prata separent, ut hortos rigent: sola terrae seges imperatur. Vnde annum quoque ipsum non in totidem digerunt species: hiems et uer et aestas intellectum ac uocabula habent, autumni perinde nomen ac bona ignorantur.

27. Funerum nulla ambitio: id solum obseruatur ut corpora clarorum uirorum certis lignis crementur. Struem rogi nec uestibus nec odoribus cumulant: sua cuique arma, quorundam

---

11 regnant Xs² l

26, 3 uicis cod. *Bambergensis teste Lipsio, et probante Waitz, pp. 109 f.*, uices m Iχ ϕ s, uices, *in mg.* vice W, uice *ex* uices N, uice hs², uite Δ, in uices (in uicem *Lr*) ß pM, *del. Halm*⁴, per uicos *Pichena* 5 praestant m Iχ k ϕ s, praestant, *in mg. uel superscr.* praebent W pM VdE, praebent hs² NΔ Lvr   6 labore h I k s, labore, *in mg. uel superscr.* laborare N Vd, laborare, *in mg. uel superscr.* labore W LE, laborare ω   7 ut prata *Mützell*, et prata ω   et hortos Iξ d, aut hortos *Nipperdey 1876*   10 Antumni W, autipm m   proinde Wm

26, 2 seruatur: "Seruatur ne faenus agitetur aut in usuras extendatur." *Seruatur* is impersonal and is virtually the equivalent of *cauetur*. This explanation offered by J. Golling shows that the passage is not in need of emendation.

3 uicis: On the manuscript readings see p. 98. It is difficult to see why this simple emendation of the manuscript *uices*, ably defended by Waitz (145), has not found general acceptance. Mf.'s objection that *ab uniuersis uicis* would mean "by all the communities" rather than "by the (respective) communities as a whole" is without foundation. For *uniuersi* in the sense of *toti* cf. *Hist.* I. 63, 8 f. *isque terror Gallias inuasit, ut uenienti mox agmini uniuersae ciuitates cum magistratibus et precibus occurrerent;* Ann. xiv, 27, 8 ff. *non enim, ut olim, uniuersae legiones deducebantur cum tribunis et centurionibus et sui cuiusque ordinis militibus, . . . sed ignoti inter se, diuersis manipulis, . . . quasi ex alio genere mortalium repente in unum collecti . . . ;* Dial. 21, 15 ff. *ex Caelianis orationibus nempe eae placent, siue uniuersae siue partes earum (uniuersa parte serum codd.), in quibus nitorem et altitudinem horum temporum agnoscimus.*

igni et equus adicitur. Sepulcrum caespes erigit: monumentorum arduum et operosum honorem ut grauem defunctis
aspernantur. Lamenta ac lacrimas cito, dolorem et tristitiam
tarde ponunt. Feminis lugere honestum est, uiris meminisse.

Haec in commune de omnium Germanorum origine ac
moribus accepimus: nunc singularum gentium instituta ritusque quatenus differant, quae nationes e Germania in Gallias
commigrauerint, expediam.

28. Validiores olim Gallorum res fuisse summus auctorum
Diuus Iulius tradit; eoque credibile est etiam Gallos in Germaniam transgressos. Quantulum enim amnis obstabat quo
minus, ut quaeque gens eualuerat, occuparet permutaretque
sedes promiscuas adhuc et nulla regnorum potentia diuisas?
Igitur inter Hercyniam siluam Rhenumque et Moenum
amnes Heluetii, ulteriora Boii, Gallica utraque gens, tenuere.
Manet adhuc Boihaemi nomen signatque loci ueterem memo-

27, 5 operosum, *in mg.* opesum W, peroperosum ξ, *cf. p. 182*
10 quae . . . commigrauerint *secl. Reifferscheid, p. 624*   quae]
quaeque *Halm²*

28, 3 animis W, annus m, annis ΔM v zuRAc   5 diuisas]
diuersas Iξ φ   6 *post* igitur *inserendum* quantum *prop. Wölfflin
1867, 101*, cuncta *Prammer*   hercuniam W, hercinam I,
hercynam N, Hircyniam (-ci- L) λ, hyrcyniam v   7 *post*
amnes *inser.* citeriora *Möller*   8 Boihaemi nomen *Mf. 1853*,
boii haemionem, *in mg. sinist.* bouhemi al' bohemi, *et in mg. dextra
inc. man.* nomen W, boiihemi nomen, *in mg.* bohemi h, bohemi
nomen adhuc boii hemionem m, bohvemi (*del.* nomen) s², boihemi
nomen, *lect. uar.* boiiemionem Y (*uarietas lectionum in pp. 128 f. est
uidenda*)   8 signatque XNΔs² *ed. Vind. 1500*, significatque
(sig, que, *distinxit alt. man. in litura ut uid. L*) Y

**27, 10 quae nationes . . . com-
migrauerint**: Reifferscheid deletes this
clause on the ground that it is a
marginal note which has crept into
the text. Its authenticity is, I believe, proved by the adverb *etiam* in
28. 2. The asyndeton is not unduly
harsh if we understand *instituta
ritusque* as the subject of *differant* and
not as the object of *expediam*.

28, 6 inter . . . amnes Heluetii: It
is but natural to suspect that some
word parallel to *ulteriora* has been
lost, though the interpretation, τὰ
inter . . . amnes, offered by Reeb
seems satisfactory. See the parallels
from Tacitus and other authors which
he cites.

8 signatque . . . memoriam:
"and gives the seal of authenticity to
the ancient tradition regarding the
region." I do not understand Tacitus

riam quamuis mutatis cultoribus. Sed utrum Arauisci in
Pannoniam ab Osis Germanorum natione an Osi ab Arauiscis
in Germaniam commigrauerint, cum eodem adhuc sermone
institutis moribus utantur, incertum est, quia pari olim inopia
ac libertate eadem utriusque ripae bona malaque erant.

Treueri et Neruii circa adfectationem Germanicae originis
ultro ambitiosi sunt, tamquam per hanc gloriam sanguinis a
similitudine et inertia Gallorum separentur.

Ipsam Rheni ripam haud dubie Germanorum populi
colunt, Vangiones Triboci Nemetes. Ne Vbii quidem, quamquam Romana colonia esse meruerint ac libentius Agrippinen-

---

10 ab Osis χ a, u² *in mg.*, a bois **X τ bl**, abors (abora *e*, arbores
R, ab hoc *c*) ψ, a boiis σpM λv s   Germanorum natione *secl.
Passow*   14 Neruii *Rhenanus 1519 (et sic cod. h teste Longolio,
sed cf. p. 174)*, neruli (ueruli *m*, heruli *p* φ) ω   affectionem **mh**
ψ s   germaniae (-nice *t*, -nę *L*) **m Iξ Lr** φ   18 Triboci **X N**
β s, Treiboci **Δ**, treboci **Iξ**, triboici **ba**, triborci (tre- *R*) ψ   Ne
Vbii *Gruterus*, Nubii ω

---

to mean that the only evidence for the location of the ancient home of the Boii is to be found in the geographical name Boihaemum, but rather that there is a distinct tradition regarding the former location of this tribe, which in turn is *authenticated* by the survival of the name Boihaemum. The meaning which I attach to *signat* is a simple extension of the verb's original meaning of *signis notare* (cf. Paul. Fest. 341 Mül. "*Signare*" *significat . . . modo anulo signa inprimere, modo pecora signis notare*). For a similar use of the verb cf. Vell. II, 115 *In qua regione quali adiutore legatoque fratre meo Magio Celere Velleiano usus sit, ipsius patrisque eius praedicatione testatum est et amplissimorum honorum, quibus triumphans eum Caesar donauit, signat memoria.*

Significatque, the reading of the Y family, does not in my judgment give a satisfactory meaning. The name Boihaemum might be said to *make known* or *reveal*, i.e. *identify*, the ancient *inhabitants* of the region, but can hardly be said to reveal the ancient *tradition* concerning the place.

10 Germanorum natione: Passow's proposal to delete these words because of the contradiction with 43, 3, though generally adopted, is unsound. The problem confronting Tacitus is whether or not the two kindred tribes of the Osi and Aravisci are German. If the Aravisci have separated from the Osi and moved into Pannonia, the implication is that both tribes are German. The words *Germanorum natione* have no effect upon this implication, and with or without these words the passage still remains in contradiction with 43, 3 f. *Cotinos Gallica, Osos Pannonica lingua coarguit non esse Germanos, et quod tributa patiuntur.* I suspect that the contradiction is due to two different sources which Tacitus followed, and that it was precisely because he noticed the discrepancy that he added the words *Germanorum natione:* "in case they (the Osi) really are a German tribe." Whatmough (140 f.) defends the manuscript tradition on different grounds, finding in *natione* a geographical and political connotation —i.e. the Osi are reckoned as Germans because they reside on German soil and pay tribute to a German state.

ses conditoris sui nomine uocentur, origine erubescunt, transgressi olim et experimento fidei super ipsam Rheni ripam conlocati, ut arcerent, non ut custodirentur.

29. Omnium harum gentium uirtute praecipui Batauii non multum ex ripa, sed insulam Rheni amnis colunt, Chattorum quondam populus et seditione domestica in eas sedes transgressus in quibus pars Romani imperii fierent. Manet honos et antiquae societatis insigne; nam nec tributis contemnuntur nec publicanus atterit: exempti oneribus et collationibus et tantum in usum proeliorum sepositi, uelut tela atque arma, bellis reseruantur.

Est in eodem obsequio et Mattiacorum gens; protulit enim magnitudo populi Romani ultra Rhenum ultraque ueteres terminos imperii reuerentiam. Ita sede finibusque in sua ripa, mente animoque nobiscum agunt, cetera similes Batauis, nisi quod ipso adhuc terrae suae solo et caelo acrius animantur.

29, 1 batauii (*in* bataui *corr.*), *in mg.* bathi W, bathi, *in mg.* bataui h (*sed cf. p. 168*), bathi s², batauii, *superscr.* batii N, batami m, batanii (Bact- b) buRAc, batani (*in* -vi *corr. inc. man. s*) e s, bataui L   3 quondam] olim W   6 collationibus hm Ipχ Lvk b s, collationibus, *in mg. uel superscr.* collocationibus N M VdEr, collocationibus, *in mg.* collationibus W, collocationibus Δ aπ

9 mactiacorum h, mactiacorum φ   12 uatauis (uacauis, uatanis) φ   13 quod hi ipso *Riese*

29, 1 **Batauii**: On the interchange of -*i* and -*ii* in tribal names see *A.P.V.* Einl. xxvi. On the variant *bathi* see p. 97.

13 **quod ... animantur**: Mf. believes that the spirited temperament of the Mattiaci is ascribed to the fact that they are indigenous (*terrae suae*), whereas the Batavii have settled on foreign soil. This explanation not only appears fanciful, but is also rendered improbable by the choice of the words *solo et caelo* (cf. 4, 8). Better is the explanation offered by Gudeman (1928): "The plateau of the Mattiaci is contrasted with the level of the Batavian island, the resultant characteristics here mentioned being still observable in the mercurial temperament of the Rhinelanders as compared with the greater stolidity of the Dutch." Nevertheless Riese's proposal to insert *hi* after *quod* is attractive. This would make the *quod*-clause refer to the Batavii, whose vigor and bravery are frequently mentioned by Tacitus (*e.g. Hist.* I, 59, 2; IV, 15, 3 f.; IV, 28, 14) and other authors, rather than to the comparatively obscure Mattiaci. Moreover, as Riese points out, the geographical location of the Batavii, who dwelt further to the north and closer to the sea, would, according to ancient ethnographical notions, be more conducive to a vigorous temperament than would the situation of the Mattiaci. Cf. Strabo IV, 4, 2 *ad fin*

Non numerauerim inter Germaniae populos, quamquam
trans Rhenum Danuuiumque consederint, eos qui decumathes
agros exercent: leuissimus quisque Gallorum et inopia audax
dubiae possessionis solum occupauere; mox limite acto promotisque praesidiis sinus imperii et pars prouinciae habentur.

30. Vltra hos Chatti initium sedis ab Hercynio saltu inchoant, non ita effusis ac palustribus locis ut ceterae ciuitates in quas Germania patescit, durant siquidem colles, paulatim rarescunt, et Chattos suos saltus Hercynius prosequitur simul atque deponit. Duriora genti corpora, stricti artus, minax uultus et maior animis uigor. Multum, ut inter Germanos, rationis ac sollertiae: praeponere electos, audire praepositos, nosse ordines, intellegere occasiones, differre impetus, disponere diem, uallare noctem, fortunam inter dubia, uirtutem inter

---

15 decumathes h N β s, de eumathes W, deum athes(agros) m, decumates a Lr φ   16 leuissimusque quisque W

30, 1 Chatti] *de orthogr. uide p. 113*   hercynio, *in mg.* herquinio W, herquinio mh, *uide et p. 97*   3 patescit, durant siquidem *Rhenanus*, patescit durant (durat *m*). Siquidem ω   4 hercynius, *in mg.* herquinius W, herquinius mh, quimus b, *uide et p. 130*   6 animis Wh, *om.* m, animi Y, *uide p. 100*

ἀεὶ δὲ οἱ προσβορρότεροι καὶ παρωκεανῖται μαχιμώτεροι. In further support of his view Riese cites Plato *Rep.* IV, 435e; Lucan I, 458 ff.; VIII, 363 f.; Caesar, *B.G.* I, 1, 3. A similar use of *hi* to mark a contrast between two tribes is found in ch. 46, 8 (cf. note *ad loc.*).

15 **decumathes**: Until the etymology of this word has been established, it will be sounder to accept the reading which has the better manuscript authority. (See *A.C.S. s.v. decumates*, L. Schmidt, Hesselmeyer.)

30, 1 **Vltra hos . . . rarescunt**: I see no serious difficulty in the more commonly accepted punctuation and interpretation. The ablative absolute, *non ita effusis ac palustribus locis*, has only the loosest grammatical connection with the sentence ("their country being not so level and swampy"), and is really equivalent to an independent clause, as is frequently the case in Tacitus (*e.g. Germ.* 1, 4 f. *nuper cognitis quibusdam gentibus ac regibus*). Fault has been found with the postpositive *siquidem*, but certainly no criterion can be found in Tacitus' own writings, for he employs *siquidem* in but one other place (cf. G.G. 1323). In support of the usage cf. Pliny, *N.H.* XI, 2 (cited by Mf. and Persson) *in magnis siquidem corporibus*; Orosius, *Hist.* III, 5, 1 (cited by Persson) *sequitur hanc miseram luem . . . repente siquidem . . .* Even if a parallel were lacking, I should not regard a postpositive *siquidem* as the most unusual of Tacitus' stylistic peculiarities.

The MSS. place a full stop after *durant*, and begin *siquidem* with a majuscule *S* (cf. p. 264), making *Chatti* the subject of *durant* as well as of *inchoant*. This was the interpretation of editors before Rhenanus, and it has found favor with many after him (Passow, Dilthey, Bach, Kapp, Altenburg, Teubert, Gruber, Kiessling, Weishaupt, Kritz, Holder, to mention

certa numerare, quodque rarissimum nec nisi Romanae disciplinae concessum, plus reponere in duce quam in exercitu. Omne robur in pedite, quem super arma ferramentis quoque et copiis onerant: alios ad proelium ire uideas, Chattos ad bellum. Rari excursus et fortuita pugna: equestrium sane uirium id proprium, cito parare uictoriam, cito cedere; <*peditum*> uelocitas iuxta formidinem, cunctatio propior a constantia est.

31. Et aliis Germanorum populis usurpatum raro et priuata cuiusque audentia apud Chattos in consensum uertit, ut primum adoleuerint, crinem barbamque submittere nec nisi hoste caeso exuere uotiuum obligatumque uirtuti oris habitum. Super sanguinem et spolia reuelant frontem seque tum demum pretia nascendi ret*t*ulisse dignosque patria ac parentibus ferunt; ignauis et imbellibus manet squalor. Fortissimus quisque

---

10 certa] cetera, *del. et* certa *scr. in mg. inc. man.* W   Romanae] ratione a, τ *praeter* r, *cf. p. 113*   12 impedite Wm NΔ dv, 1RA (*corr. in* in pe- *l*) s   quem Iξ LEk, φ *praeter* uR, s², quem, *in mg. uel superscr.* quam Vd, quam, *in mg.* quem hr, quam W NΔ v uR, quae s   14 rari̊ W, raro hσ   15 peditum *suppl. Bährens, om.* ω, *ceteris Eussner 1877*   16 propior a constantia *scripsi*, propiora constantiae σ, propriora constantiae Wm, propior constantiae ξ λdk le, proprior constantiae h Evr φ, proprior est constancie s

31, 1 raro m Iχ Lv, rara *ex* raro W, raro, *in mg. uel superscr.* rara pM E, rara V̊, rara ω   4 ciso W   5 seque tum] sequentum m   6. nascendi E, nŏscendi V, noscendi IpM Ldrk b

only those of the nineteenth century). Strangely enough, within recent years this interpretation was advanced by W. Sternkopf (1922) as though it were something quite new. I disagree with Sternkopf's statement that *Chatti . . . durant* presents no greater difficulty than does *durant . . . colles*, and even find the former intolerable. It is the fact that the hills *last* or *continue* which distinguishes the land of the Chatti from the other territories which Tacitus has in mind. In *Chatti . . . durant* the verb would have to assume a colorless force such as would be expressed by *sedent, habitant,* or *colunt*. To find in (*Chatti*) *durant* an antithesis to *dubiae possessionis* (29, 17), as does Hirschfelder, or to see with Urlichs a contrast between the permanency of abode of the Chatti and the migrations of the various tribes mentioned in chs. 28 and 29, seems to me forced.

15 parare: J. Müller, E. Wolff, and Gudeman (1928, 389) have so ably defended the reading of the MSS. that nothing need be added.

<peditum> uelocitas: I have found no satisfactory explanation of the manuscript reading. Unless some such word as *peditum* is supplied, the point of contrast between the cavalry and infantry tactics is lost.

16 propior a constantia: See p. 143.

ferreum insuper anulum (ignominiosum id genti) uelut uinculum gestat, donec se caede hostis absoluat.

10 Plurimis Chattorum et hic placet habitus <***> iamque canent insignes et hostibus simul suisque monstrati. Omnium penes hos initia pugnarum; haec prima semper acies, uisu noua. Nam ne in pace quidem cultu mitiore mansuescunt. Nulli domus aut ager aut aliqua cura: prout ad quemque uenere
15 aluntur, prodigi alieni, contemptores sui, donec exsanguis senectus tam durae uirtuti impares faciat.

---

10 & hic **W**, et *om.* ω   *lacunam statui*   13 Nam] iam π

cultu **Wm**σ r φ s, uultu h *ex sil.*, ξ β   16 dur$\overset{e}{\text{a}}$ **Wh**, durare ψ
(*uide p. 131*)

31, 10 et hic placet habitus <*>:** The reading of **W**, whose independent value (see pp. 153 ff.) has been established, affords a clue to an otherwise unintelligible passage. Tacitus has just related that the young men of the Chatti allow their hair and beard to grow, until they have proved their valor by slaying their man. The cowards and shirkers are forced to keep the long hair and beard as a mark of disgrace. Furthermore, all the bravest wear an iron ring until they have freed themselves from this badge of ignominy by killing their enemy. Then (according to the universally accepted reading) our author tells us that *very many* of the Chatti allow the hair and beard to grow (and wear the ring?) until old age, and that these are the bravest of the brave, and that they enjoy special privileges! That which was but a moment before a brand of cowardice and ignominy has now become a sign of great valor and a mark of special distinction. I fail to see how absurdity in textual exegesis can go to greater lengths.

I am aware that upon the basis of passages in ancient and mediaeval literature attempts have been made to explain away this absurdity on the assumption that the bravest of the Chatti kept themselves under a perpetual vow by wearing the badges of disgrace, or that the vow was renewed each time an enemy was slain. Thus Civilis, after declaring war on Rome, allowed his hair to grow and did not cut it until he had won a victory (*Hist.* IV 61, 1 ff.). In later times six thousand Saxons made a vow that they would not shave their beards or cut their hair until they had avenged themselves against their Suebic enemies (Paul. Diac., *Hist. Lang.* III, 7). Even Julius Caesar after the destruction of the cohorts quartered in the land of the Eburones is said to have allowed his hair and beard to grow until he had wreaked vengeance (Suet. *Iul.* 67, 2). But these are all special cases, not a general practice or a perpetual vow. The persons concerned voluntarily assumed the ignominious garb as a greater incentive to conquer the enemy, and as long as they retained this garb it was a mark of defeat. If Tacitus had had in mind some such vow perpetually renewed, he would have made that fact plain.

With the reading *et* (= *etiam*) *hic* and the marking of a lacuna after *habitus* the difficulty is cleared away. In the lacuna Tacitus described some *other* manner of dress affected only by the bravest, or perhaps told of the retention of the long hair and beard as a perpetual vow, mentioning some mark whereby these, the bravest, might be distinguished from the *ignaui et imbelles*.

13 Nam: This particle presents a certain difficulty, for it seems to mark the transition to a new idea, instead of retaining its usual (in Tacitus) explanatory or corroborative force.

21

32. Proximi Chattis certum iam alueo Rhenum quique terminus esse sufficiat Vsipi ac Tencteri colunt. Tencteri super solitum bellorum decus equestris disciplinae arte praecellunt; nec maior apud Chattos peditum laus quam Tencteris equitum. Sic instituere maiores, posteri imitantur. Hi lusus infantium, haec iuuenum aemulatio, perseuerant senes. Inter familiam et penates et iura successionum equi traduntur: excipit filius, non ut cetera maximus natu, sed prout ferox bello et melior.

33. Iuxta Tencteros Bructeri olim occurrebant: nunc Chamauos et Angriuarios immigrasse narratur, pulsis Bructeris ac penitus excisis uicinarum consensu nationum, seu superbiae odio seu praedae dulcedine seu fauore quodam erga nos deorum; nam ne spectaculo quidem proelii inuidere. Super sexaginta milia non armis telisque Romanis, sed quod magnificentius est, oblectationi oculisque ceciderunt. Maneat, quaeso, duretque gentibus, si non amor nostri, at certe odium sui, quando in [gentibus] imperii fatis nihil iam praestare fortuna maius potest quam hostium discordiam.

32, 5 lusus] usus **W**
33, 2 augrinariosum migrasse **m**   8 at] ac **Wm b**   9 in gentibus **X s**, gentibus *seclusi*, inurgentibus, *superscr.* ingentibus **N**, in urgentibus α φ, urgentibus iam β, ingruentibus *Wölfflin 1867*, urgentibus *Rhenanus, uulgo, secl. Brunot*   iam] tam **W**

33, 9 in [gentibus] imperii fatis: On the manuscript readings see p. 108. For *praestare aliquid in aliqua re* (though with a slightly different meaning of the verb) cf. Cic. *Fam.* I, 9, 5 *neque hercule in iis ipsis rebus . . . in meis damnis . . . sarciendis eam uoluntatem, quam exspectaram, praestiterunt.* (I am indebted to Professor F. G. Moore for calling this parallel passage to my attention.) We may also compare Suet. *Aug.* 89, 1, though here the parallel is not so close, since *praestare* is used intransitively: *Ne Graecarum quidem disciplinarum leuiore studio tenebatur. In quibus et ipsis praestabat largiter. . . .*

Quite aside from the inherent palaeographical difficulties, a strong argument against the commonly accepted *urgentibus* (or *urgentibus iam*) is to be found in the mere fact that it admits of two diametrically opposed interpretations of the words *imperii fatis*. Some, as if they made a prophet of Tacitus, interpret *urgentibus imperii fatis* to mean "with the doom of the empire swooping down," while others believe that the meaning is, "with the destiny of the empire (to rule the world) sweeping on to fulfillment." To mention only two fairly recent discussions, Landi (1925) is an exponent of the former view, and Reitzenstein (1914) is a defender of the latter. It is gratifying to note that neither author can be accused of national bias in setting forth his view!

With my restoration of the text, there can be but one interpretation:

Text, Critical Apparatus, Critical Notes 309

34. Angriuarios et Chamauos a tergo Dulgubini et Chasuarii cludunt aliaeque gentes haud perinde memoratae, a fronte Frisi excipiunt. Maioribus minoribusque Frisis uocabulum est ex modo uirium. Vtraeque nationes usque ad Oceanum
5 Rheno praetexuntur ambiuntque immensos insuper lacus et Romanis classibus nauigatos. Ipsum quin etiam Oceanum illa temptauimus, et superesse adhuc Herculis columnas fama uulgauit, siue adiit Hercules, seu quicquid ubique magnificum est in claritatem eius referre consensimus. Nec defuit
10 audentia Druso Germanico, sed obstitit Oceanus in se simul

34, 1 chamanos m t L s (*corr.* s²), Chammatos I, Chamautos Δ, chamattos (*cf. p. 117*) φ   Dulgubini *Tross*, dulgibini ΔI χ k, dulgibini, *in mg. uel superscr.* dulcubuni (-bimi *M*) W NpM, Dulgibini, *in mg. uel superscr.* dulgicubini Vd, Dulgicubuni, *in mg.* dulgibini E, dulcubuni m, dulcubimi hs² (*de lect. cod. h uide p. 169*), M *in mg.*, dulgicubini (-tubi- *L*) Lr, dulgicubuni v, dulciboni φ, dulgibini cubrini s, Dulgubnii *J. Grimm*   3 Frisi (-sci *I*) Xσ bal, fusi ψ, Frisii ξ β s   9 consensimus] consueuimus h aR, E *in mg.*   10 Drusi *R. Borchardt*

imperii fatis means "the destiny of the empire," which is exactly what the context demands. What possible connotation can the words *ne spectaculo quidem proelii inuidere* have except that the gods (or Fortune) had already done their utmost to further the cause of Roman arms, and that as a final favor had *not even* begrudged the Romans the pleasure of witnessing (*oblectationi oculisque*) a great battle among their enemies, as though it were some giant *spectaculum?* If our author had really felt that Roman arms were powerless, and that the empire's only hope lay in the strife of its enemies, would he have styled such a situation as *magnificentius* than one in which Rome triumphed in battle over her foes?

This chapter is, to be sure, in contradiction with ch. 37. There Tacitus' love for rhetorical display seems to have led him to depict the German peril in more glowing colors than he could really have felt warranted by the situation, while here the same predilection has made him disregard the danger.

34, 1 Dulgubini: See *A.P.V. s.v.* On the doublets see p. 131.

10 Druso Germanico: The elder Drusus, brother of Tiberius, upon whom the cognomen Germanicus was bestowed by the senate after his death in 9 B.C. (Suet. *Claud.* 1, 3; Stein in P.-W. *s.v.* Claudius 139, col. 2705), is again called Drusus Germanicus by Tacitus in *Hist.* v, 19, 7.

Some commentators question the manuscript tradition, because they find it strange that Tacitus should mention only the voyage of Drusus in 12 B.C., to the exclusion both of the expedition under Tiberius in 5 A.D. and of the campaign of Germanicus, son of Drusus, in 16 A.D. If the reading of the MSS. offers a satisfactory meaning, it is hardly within the province of a critical edition to ask why the author did not write something else. We may, however, assume with Mf. that Tacitus mentions only Drusus because his was the pioneer expedition of discovery, and acquired such fame as to give it a semi-legendary character, witness the story told by Suetonius, *Claud.* 1, 2 (also cf. *Ann.* II, 8). Our

atque in Herculem inquiri. Mox nemo temptauit, sanctiusque ac reuerentius uisum de actis deorum credere quam scire.

35. Hactenus in occidentem Germaniam nouimus; in septentrionem ingenti flexu recedit. Ac primo statim Chauco-

---

35, 2 recedit *Heraeus*, redit ω

---

author's hatred for Tiberius may have been sufficient reason for the omission of the tyrant's name in this connection, even though his naval expedition went to the mouth of the Elbe (cf. Vell. II, 106, and, without mention of Tiberius' name, *Mon. Ancyr.* 26; Pliny, *N.H.* II, 167), while that of Drusus reached only the mouth of the Weser (Cass. Dio LIV, 32, 2; Stein *l.c.* 2710). As for the expedition of Germanicus, there is perhaps no reason why Tacitus should mention it. Germanicus was conducting a military campaign, not a voyage of discovery, and went by sea only to the mouth of the Ems (see Kroll in P.-W. *s.v.* Iulius 138, col. 448). Furthermore, the expedition ended in the deep humiliation of its commander owing to the dispersal and partial destruction of his fleet (*Ann.* II, 23 and 24). As Mf. pointedly remarks, if any of Germanicus' followers made discoveries (cf. *Ann.* II, 24, 16 ff.), it was quite by accident.

A possible objection to the sentence as it stands lies in the words *mox nemo temptauit*. Even Mf., strong advocate that he is of the reading *Druso Germanico*, finds an inaccuracy therein, as though there were no voyage into the North Sea after that of Drusus. But must these words be the mere equivalent of *nemo postea temptauit?* May they not rather mean, "in course of time men ceased making the attempt?" With this interpretation, other expeditions after that of Drusus are distinctly implied.

Though the manuscript tradition is tenable, as I have attempted to show, I must admit that I find Borchardt's *Nec defuit audentia Drusi Germanico* (such is the text implied by his translation) very tempting. The strongest argument in its favor is the striking parallel cited by Gudeman (1928) from *Ann.* II, 8, 3 ff. *precatusque Drusum patrem, ut se eadem AVSVM libens placatusque exemplo ac memoria consiliorum atque operum iuuaret.* . . . Again, I think that the latter half of the chapter may gain in force and coherence if this simple change is made. Mention in general terms of the expeditions of Drusus and Tiberius in *temptauimus* (line 7) would then be followed by a specific mention of Tacitus' hero Germanicus.

35, 2 recedit: I can make nothing of the manuscript reading *redit*. None of the passages which I have seen adduced in its support offers a parallel. Most frequently cited is Vergil, *Geor.* III, 351 *quaque redit medium Rhodope porrecta sub axem*, a passage which has been strangely misunderstood (by Servius among others). Goelzer correctly translates (*Vergile, Les Georgiques, texte établi et traduit par Henri Goelzer*, Collection des Universités de France, Paris [undated]): "et où le Rhodope revient sur lui-même après s'être étendu jusqu'au milieu du pôle." It will be observed that Tacitus has nothing corresponding to *porrecta*. The following passages cited in support of *redit* by Gudeman (1928) likewise fail to offer parallels. (1) Manilius IV, 626 f. *donec in Aegyptum redeunt curuata per undas/ litora Niliacis iterum morientia ripis.* These words can be understood only in their context. With line 595 the poet starts to trace the shoreline of the Mediterranean. From the Strait of Gibraltar he follows the northern coast of Africa as far as the mouth of the Nile (*usque ad Nilum*, line 601). Then he jumps back to the Strait, crosses to Spain, follows the coastline of Europe, passes through the Hellespont, around the Black Sea, then along Asia Minor and Syria, and finally *returns* to the mouth of the Nile. *Redeunt* is entirely suitable, for the circuit has been completed. (2) Mela I, 56 *tantum redeunte flexu quantum processerat.* The author

rum gens, quamquam incipiat a Frisis ac partem litoris occupet,
omnium quas exposui gentium lateribus obtenditur, donec in
Chattos usque sinuetur. Tam immensum terrarum spatium
non tenent tantum Chauci, sed et implent, populus inter
Germanos nobilissimus quique magnitudinem suam malit iusti-
tia tueri. Sine cupiditate, sine impotentia, quieti secretique
nulla prouocant bella, nullis raptibus aut latrociniis populantur.
Id praecipuum uirtutis ac uirium argumentum est, quod ut
superiores agant non per iniurias adsequuntur; prompta tamen
omnibus arma ac si res poscat exercitus plurimum uirorum
equorumque; et quiescentibus eadem fama.

36. In latere Chaucorum Chattorumque Cherusci nimiam ac
marcentem diu pacem inlacessiti nutrierunt; idque iucundius
quam tutius fuit, quia inter impotentes et ualidos falso quie-
scas: ubi manu agitur, modestia ac probitas nomina superioris

5 sinuetur mχ λk φ, sinnetur s, sinuetur, *in mg.* sinatur **Wh dE**,
sinatur, *in mg.* sinuetur (*corr. ex* sinuatur *M*) **pM**, sinatur σ, sinant
v, sinuatur r   10 Idque *Rhenanus 1544*   praecipuum]
pręcium **I**   uirium] uirium precuum *ut uid. teste Long.* (*uide
p. 169*) **h**, uirium praecipuum **Iξ**, *uide p. 176*   12 exercitus
del. Walch 1815   plurimorum *Gudeman 1916*, plurimum enim
Reifferscheid

36, 4 nomina *Pincius*, nomine ω, nomina et *F. Walter 1887*
4 nomina superiori *Heinsius*, nomine superiores t a s² (*Holder²*)

is describing the winding porticoes of the labyrinth of Psammeticus, which extend in one direction, and then *return* in the opposite direction. (3) Mela III, 1 . . . *ubi in omnia litora . . . terrarum insularumque ex medio pariter effusum est* (pelagus magnis aestibus concitum), *rursus ab illis colligitur in medium et in semet ipsum redit.* . . . The author is speaking of the rising (*effusum est*) and falling (*colligitur . . . redit*) of the tide. Naturally the sea may be said to *return to itself.*

Heraeus' *recedit* is recommended by its simplicity, but naturally is not the only possibility. Bearing in mind other supposed Vergilian reminiscences in Tacitus, we might write *in septentrionem <porrecta> ingenti flexu redit,* or *<porrigitur et>.*

5 sinuetur: On the doublets see pp. 131 f.

12 plurimum: The manuscript reading may be kept if this form is taken as a genitive, which is the explanation offered by Gruber. Cf. *Ann.* III, 72, 5 *posterum gloriam.* The cacophony in *exercitus plurimorum equorum uirorumque* is thereby avoided.

36, 4 nomina superioris: The true reading is uncertain, though the simple correction of *nomine* to *nomina* is perhaps the most satisfactory (on the confusion of *e* and *a* see p. 236). Palaeographically the simplest emendation is *nomine superiores* (on the confusion of *e* and *i* see p. 240), but I hardly think that it gives a suitable meaning. Presumably *nomine* would stand for *nomine tantum* (in contrast

sunt. Ita qui olim boni aequique Cherusci nunc inertes ac stulti uocantur; Chattis uictoribus fortuna in sapientiam cessit.

Tracti ruina Cheruscorum et Fosi, contermina gens, aduersarum rerum ex aequo socii sunt, cum in secundis minores fuissent.

37. Eundem Germaniae sinum proximi Oceano Cimbri tenent, parua nunc ciuitas, sed gloria ingens. Veterisque famae lata uestigia manent, utraque ripa castra ac spatia, quorum ambitu nunc quoque metiaris molem manusque gentis et tam magni exitus fidem.

Sescentesimum et quadragesimum annum urbs nostra agebat, cum primum Cimbrorum audita sunt arma Caecilio Metello ac Papirio Carbone consulibus. Ex quo si ad alterum imperatoris Traiani consulatum computemus, ducenti ferme et decem anni colliguntur: tam diu Germania uincitur. Medio tam longi aeui spatio multa inuicem damna. Non Samnis, non Poeni, non Hispaniae Galliaeue, ne Parthi quidem saepius admonuere: quippe regno Arsacis acrior est Germanorum libertas. Quid enim aliud nobis quam caedem Crassi amisso et ipse

---

7 Tracti XNΔs[2], Tacti ω   aduersarum mhs[2] Nξ, aduersarum rios W, aduersarios Δ r φ, aduersarum, *in mg. uel superscr.* aduersariis λdE, aduersariis v, aduersarium I, aduersariorum (pares et equi) s, *uide p. 132*

37, 1 sinum] situm β φ, M *superscr.*, finum m   4 ambitu χ Lv a, ambitum, *in mg. uel superscr.* ambitu VdE, ambitum ω   5 et tam] etiam W   6 quadragesimum N β, sexagesimum I, .xl. Wm Δpmχ φs, *de cod. h non liquet*   8 ac] et β ψ   ad *om.* W   14 et ipse X Δ π, et ipso (et *om.* a) t a, et (in s) ipso et ipse ω, *cf. p. 103*

---

with *manu*), and this would be the Tacitean version of *probitas laudatur et alget*. Such an interpretation is, I believe, in contradiction with *nunc inertes ac stulti uocantur*. Heinsius' *nomina superiori* ("mere names to the more powerful") is ingenious, but departs further from the manuscript authority, and like the other conjecture hardly seems suited to the sentence immediately following. May not the correct reading be *nominis superioris* (on the writing of *e* for final *is* see p. 239)? In this case *nomen* would be equivalent to *populus* or *potestas*, as in *Hist.* IV, 18, 6 *pulsum Batauorum insula Romanum nomen.* . . . Also cf. Sall., *Cat.* 52, 24 . . . *Gallorum gentem infestissumam nomini Romano ad bellum arcessunt*.

37, 4 ambitu: This correction of *ambitum*, which has been made in some of our MSS., is strengthened by *Ann.* I, 61, 7 f. *prima Vari castra lato*

TEXT, CRITICAL APPARATUS, CRITICAL NOTES 313

15 Pacoro infra Ventidium deiectus Oriens obiecerit? At Germani Carbone et Cassio et Scauro Aurelio et Seruilio Caepione Cn. quoque Ma*l*lio fusis uel captis quinque simul consular*es* exercitus po(pulo) Ro(mano), Varum tresque cum eo legiones etiam Caesari abstulerunt; nec impune C. Marius in Italia,
20 Diuus Iulius in Gallia, Drusus ac Nero et Germanicus in suis eos sedibus perculerunt; mox ingentes C. Caesaris minae in ludibrium uersae. Inde otium, donec occasione discordiae nostrae et ciuilium armorum expugnatis legionum hibernis etiam Gallias affectauere, ac rursus pulsi; nam proximis tem-
25 poribus triumphati magis quam uicti sunt.

---

15 obiecit Δ, obicitur I, obiecer V, obiecerunt (-cerentur *t* *r*) Lτ pM   17 Cn. quoque *Ernesti*, Marcoque X Ev φ s, Marco (mi *I*) quoque Iξ Ldrk, .M. NΔ, Marcoquoque, *superscr.* q *ut uid.* V, Gnaeoque *Halm 1864*   Mallio dErk (*Halm 1864*), malio m v, Manlio Wh α λ s, manilio φ *et primitus in* N   18 populo romano t L², po.ro. W w zuA, P.O.P.R m, p. Ro. bR, p.R. r ac, populi romani *uel exscriptum uel per compendia* ω, *de cod.* h *non liquet*   21 pertulerunt W t c s   22 ludibrum W   24 nam] inde Iξ Lk, inde, *in mg. uel superscr.* nam dVE

ambitu et dimensis principiis trium legionum manus ostentabant.

17 Cn. quoque Mallio: The praenomen *Cn.* and the nomen *Mallius* are attested by inscriptions (see Münzer in P.-W. *s.v.* Mallius 13). The correction to *Mallio* is so simple as to require no comment (cf. p. 206). The change in the *praenomen*, though more drastic, is equally necessary, unless we assume that the error emanates from Tacitus himself. Ernesti's *Cn. quoque* is not so difficult palaeographically as might at first appear. The initial corruption may have been *CNQVOQVE > CNCOQVE* (cf. *quoquos:cocus; quotidie:cotidie*). The second stage represents an emendation of *cncoque* to *marcoque*. The change of *cn* to *mar* may have been arbitrary, or may have been suggested by the resemblance of *cn* to an uncial *M* in the archetype (cf. pp. 57 ff.) of Hf. Whether the variant *quoque* found in some of our MSS. indicates that the true reading was already partially restored in Hf. or is due merely to a confusion between the fifteenth-century compendia for -*que* and *quoque* is uncertain, though I incline to the latter hypothesis.

24 nam: The variant *inde*, though it has always remained the *uulgata*, can scarcely antedate the fifteenth century (cf. pp. 113 f.). It is either a willful interpolation or an accidental repetition from the third line above. Our author's thought is: "I make no mention of any later reputed Roman victory over the Germans, *for* in recent times they were triumphed over rather than conquered." Tacitus is of course alluding to the triumph of Domitian over the Chatti, which he mentions slightingly in *Agr.* 39, 3 ff. *inerat conscientia derisui fuisse nuper falsum e Germania triumphum, emptis per commercia quorum habitus et crinis in captiuorum speciem formarentur.*

38. Nunc de Suebis dicendum est, quorum non una ut Chattorum Tencterorumue gens; maiorem enim Germaniae partem obtinent, propriis adhuc nationibus nominibusque discreti, quamquam in commune Suebi uocentur.

Insigne gentis obliquare crinem nodoque substringere: sic Suebi a ceteris Germanis, sic Sueborum ingenui a seruis separantur. In aliis gentibus seu cognatione aliqua Sueborum seu, quod saepius accidit, imitatione, rarum et intra iuuentae spatium, apud Suebos usque ad canitiem horrentem capillum retro sequuntur, ac saepe in ipso [solo] uertice religant. Principes et ornatorem habent: ea cura formae, sed innoxia;

38, 1 Suebis *Halm*[1], Sueuis ω, *et sic infra*   4 quamquam] quam β π   8 saepius **X**, saepe **Y**   9 horrentes capilli *Gudeman 1916*   10 retro sequuntur] retrorsum agunt *Haupt*, retorquent *Madvig*   solo *om.* **m Lvr s** (*add.* s[2]), solo, *in mg. uel superscr.* ipso **VdE**   religant **mhs**[2], rei ligant **W**, religatur β, ligant **a s**, ne legant φ, *uide pp. 100 f.*   11 ornatorem (hor- φ) **XNs**[2] φ, ornatiorem **a** *praeter N*, β **s**   innoxia *Muretus*, innoxiae **Xs**[2] **N**Δχ β, inopiae **I** φ, inopiae, *in mg.* innoxiae **pM**, innoxia est *Mützell*

38, 9 apud Suebos . . . sequuntur: The text is not satisfactory. Such a type of expression as *apud Suebos aliquid faciunt* (*Suebi*) is at best inelegant, and according to Gudeman (1916, 250 f.) the entire *Thesaurus* material offers no example of such a usage in the whole field of Latin literature. Again, *sequuntur* is open to suspicion. While it is possible to understand *manu* or *pectine sequuntur*, all parallels seem to be lacking. Gudeman's *horrentes capilli* obviates the difficulty of understanding *Suebi* as the subject of *sequuntur* but leaves the verb without an object. Elsewhere in Tacitus the object of *sequi* is either expressed or clearly implied in the context. Haupt's *retrorsum agunt* is based on Quintilian XI, 3, 160 *Vitiosa enim sunt illa . . . capillos a fronte contra naturam retro agere, ut sit horror ille terribilis*.

10 f. ac saepe . . . religant. Principes: I so punctuate as to make *Suebi* the subject of *religant*, in accordance with the usual interpretation. Nevertheless, it is possible that we should read *religant principes* with a full stop (or semicolon) before *ac*. (I now observe that this is the punctuation proposed by Cluverius I [ch. 16] p. 131.) With the words *in ipso uertice religant* Tacitus may be describing a more ornate form of hairdress peculiar to the *principes*. See note on *ornatorem*.

10 ipso [solo]: The corruption was probably *IPSO > IPSOSO > ipso solo*, *i.e.* dittography followed by "emendation." Those who keep *solo* explain it as intensifying *ipso*, but such emphasis here seems out of place.

11 ornatorem: This reading has the preponderance of manuscript authority over *ornatiorem*, and is, I believe, better suited to the context. Freinsheim once proposed it, but apparently without knowledge that it had manuscript authority. Had Tacitus merely told his readers that the chieftains wore a more ornate coiffure than the commoners, the apology contained in the conclusion of the chapter would hardly have been neces-

neque enim ut ament amenturue, in altitudinem quandam et terrorem, adituri bella, compti ut hostium oculis ornantur.

39. Vetustissimos [seu] nobilissimosque Sueborum Semnones memorant; fides antiquitatis religione firmatur. Stato tem-

---

13 adituri bella *post* amenturue *transp. Acidalius, quae uerba forsitan post* compti *sint ponenda*   13 compti ut] comptius *Lachmann*   bello **W**   ut] et **N**, *del. Halm*[4]   ornantur h *ex sil.*, s² I𝑥, ornantur, *superscr.* armantur **N L**, armantur, *in mg. uel superscr.* ornantur **W pM VdEr**, ornatum v, armantur m △ k ϕ s

39, 1 Vetustissimos seu **Xs²**, seu *seclusi*, Vetustissimos se **a β**, Vetustissimosque ϕ, Vetustissimos **N r al s**, *uide pp. 98 f.*   nobilissimos **mh**   Semnones (*uel* sēno-) hs² △ξ r, Semones, *in mg. uel superscr.* semnones **W N VdE**, semnone π, semones m I k s, Senones (*superscr.* m *L*) **Lv**, semone **ba**   2 Stato **Ws²** σ β b, Statuto, *in mg.* stato **E**, Statuto **m** ξ **a**π, Estiuo **s**, *de cod. h non liquet* (*uide p. 170*)

---

sary. But the assertion that these untutored children of Nature employ the services of hairdressers might well require a specific and elaborate explanation that they are "beautifying" themselves for the eyes of their enemies and not for their mistresses, as did the young dandies of Rome.

Numerous representations (*stelae*, reliefs, bronze statuettes) of German warriors with the hair done in a knot have come down to us from antiquity (see Girke II, 3–5 and the literature there cited). Almost without exception the hair is shown drawn together and knotted just above the right ear, but a bronze statuette in Paris (Bibliothèque Nationale, No. 915) seems admirably to illustrate the hairdress which Tacitus has described in the words *in ipso uertice religant*. (Photographs in Kossina, Tafel XLV, Abb. 443; Girke, Tafel 38a; Schweizer-Sidler, Abb. 3.) This coiffure is elaborate, with the hair twisted into a peak or horn just to the right of the crown of the head. Girke suggests that the peak was formed with the aid of resin and pomade. I do not think it too fanciful to suppose that a hairdresser was employed to effect so elaborate a coiffure.

11 **innoxia**: The *innoxiae* of the MSS., which is hardly acceptable, may best be explained as due to assimilation with the preceding *formae*, though it may be a corruption of *innoxia est* (cf. ch. 6, 10 *galeae* for *galea est*).

13 **adituri bella, compti**: The text would be more intelligible if we read *compti, adituri bella*, making *in altitudinem quandam et terrorem* dependent on *compti*. But, as Professor F. G. Moore has suggested to me, the difficulty may be imputable to the author himself, as the result of his attempt to pile up antitheses to *ament amenturue*: (1) *in altitudinem quandam et terrorem ornantur*, (2) *adituri bella ornantur*, (3) *compti ut hostium oculis ornantur* (*ornantur*).

ut hostium oculis: The majority of editors have condemned *ut*, but hardly with sufficient cause. John in *GG* 1714 understands, *ut par est*: "with hair dressed in a style fit for the eyes of their enemies."

39, 2 **Stato tempore**: The doublets *stato:statuto* were in Hf. (cf. p. 133). Mf. says that *stato tempore* is used of a periodically recurring event, while *statuto tempore* would be used of a point of time agreed upon in some particular instance. Tacitean usage bears out this distinction: *Ann.* XII, 13, 10 *qui* (Hercules) *tempore stato per quietem monet sacerdotes*; *Hist.* IV, 81, 1 f. . . .

pore in siluam auguriis patrum et prisca formidine sacram nominis <eiusdem> eiusdemque sanguinis populi legationibus coëunt caesoque publice homine celebrant barbari ritus horrenda primordia. Est et alia luco reuerentia: nemo nisi uinculo ligatus ingreditur, ut minor et potestatem numinis prae se ferens. Si forte prolapsus est, adtolli et insurgere haud licitum: per humum euoluuntur. Eoque omnis superstitio respicit, tamquam inde initia gentis, ibi regnator omnium deus, cetera subiecta atque parentia. Adicit auctoritatem fortuna Semnonum: centum pagis habitant, magnoque corpore efficitur ut se Sueborum caput credant.

40. Contra Langobardos paucitas nobilitat: plurimis ac ualentissimis nationibus cincti non per obsequium sed proeliis et periclitando tuti sunt.

---

3 patrum W, h *ex sil.*, χ bazRc s, patrium m IpM β 1, patruum NΔ euA, *cf. p. 141* sacram h *ex sil.*, s² Δ χ, sacrum, *in mg. uel superscr.* sacram W N, sacrum (sacrorum *s, in* sacrum *corr.* s²) ω 4 nominis Δ φ, omnis, *in mg. uel superscr.* nominis Wh N, omnes, *in mg. uel superscr.* nominis l' numinis VdE, omnis ms² Iξ, omnes Lk t, numinis vr, nominibusque s eiusdem *suppleui, om.* ω eiusdemque] eiusdem a L s (*corr.* s²) 8 prae se] preesse Ws², pro se I v, pro(ferens) ψ esta Wm, es *om.* Iξ ad colli W 11 atque] ad quod (d quod *in ras.; uide p. 153*) W 12 pagis habitant *Ernesti*, pagis habitantur ω, pagi iis (*potius* is) habitantur *Brotier* 13 corpore m NIχ rk φ s, corpore, *in mg. uel superscr.* tempore W λdE, tempore, *in mg.* corpore pM, tempore, *in mg.* corpore numero h, tempore s² Δ v, *cf. p. 134* seuorum *in* sueuorum *corr.* W

40, 1 Langobardos s², *Pichena* (*sed* Langobardis *iam apud Beroaldum*), largobardos h Vτ s, largabardos m, longobardos (-dis χ) ω 1 nobilitat Xs²NΔ, nobilitas Y 3 et (peri-)] ac mh β

---

statos aestiuis flatibus dies et certa maris opperiebatur; III, 30, 4 *stato in eosdem dies mercatu;* Ann. I, 48, 11 f. *de sententia legati statuunt tempus, quo foedissimum quemque . . . ferro inuadant;* XIII, 44, 11 *statuitur nox.*

4 nominis <eiusdem>: It should be observed that *omnes*, the universally accepted reading, is almost totally lacking in manuscript authority and obviously represents an attempt to emend *omnis*, which is itself, in my judgment, nothing more than a corruption of *nominis* (cf. pp. 133 f.). *Nominis* restored to its rightful place affords a clue for filling in the lacuna indicated by the *-que* of *eiusdemque*. With *nominis eiusdem* cf. 38, 4 *quamquam in commune Suebi uocentur.*

12 pagis habitant: For a possible explanation of the corruption from the active to the passive see p. 104, note 2. I find Brotier's *pagi iis* (better *is*) *habitantur* too harsh to be acceptable, though the emendation is simple palaeographically.

Reudigni deinde et Auiones et Anglii et Varini et Eudoses
et Suardones et Nuithones fluminibus aut siluis muniuntur.
Nec quicquam notabile in singulis, nisi quod in commune
Nerthum, id est Terram matrem, colunt eamque interuenire
rebus hominum, inuehi populis arbitrantur.

Est in insula Oceani castum nemus dicatumque in eo
uehiculum ueste contectum; attingere uni sacerdoti concessum.
Is adesse penetrali deam intellegit uectamque bubus feminis
multa cum ueneratione prosequitur. Laeti tunc dies, festa
loca quaecumque aduentu hospitioque dignatur. Non bella
ineunt, non arma sumunt; clausum omne ferrum; pax et quies
tunc tantum nota, tunc tantum amata, donec idem sacerdos
satiatam conuersatione mortalium deam templo reddat. Mox
uehiculum et uestis et, si credere uelis, numen ipsum secreto
lacu abluitur. Serui ministrant, quos statim idem lacus
haurit. Arcanus hinc terror sanctaque ignorantia, quid sit
illud quod tantum perituri uident.

41. Et haec quidem pars Sueborum in secretiora Germaniae
porrigitur; propior, ut quo modo paulo ante Rhenum, sic nunc
Danuuium sequar, Hermundurorum ciuitas, fida Romanis;
eoque solis Germanorum non in ripa commercium, sed penitus
atque in splendidissima Raetiae prouinciae colonia. Passim

---

5 Suardones h *ex sil.*, ξ r, φ *praeter b*, Suarines, *in mg. uel superscr.*
suardones **W dE**, suarines seu suardones **s**, suarines σ λk **b**, smarines
m, *om.* **v**   nurchones **W**, Vuithones **hs**², muthones **m**, Nurtones
(i *fortas. alt. m.*) **L**, nuitones **r**, mutones **b**, huitones π, Vnithones *Malone, p. 48*   7 necthum **m**, Neithum λ, Nertum
E b, herthum **p** *et sic Rhenanus 1519*, Nehertum ψ, Verthum **a**
7 Terram] deum **W**   9 castrum (*in* castum *corr.* N) **m** σ
9 eo *Rhenanus*, ea ω   15 armata **m r** φ   17 uestis *Andresen*, uestes ω   20 illud] id Iξ φ

41, 1 Sueborum (-uo-) *ed. Vind. 1500 et sic* (-uo-) *u*² *in mg.*,
uerborum ω, Varinorum Δ, neruorum **t**   2 proprior **X N** φ,
propior **VdE**, *uide p. 103*   5 atque] ac **W t**

40, 5 Suardones: On the misplaced variant *suarines* see p. 134. The name is otherwise unknown. Schönfeld unfortunately adopts *Suarines* (*A.P.V. s.v.*).
    9 eo: On the confusion of *o* and *a* see p. 53.

sine custode transeunt; et cum ceteris gentibus arma modo castraque nostra ostendamus, his domos uillasque patefecimus non concupiscentibus. In Hermunduris Albis oritur, flumen inclutum et notum olim, nunc tantum auditur.

42. Iuxta Hermunduros Naristi ac deinde Marcomani et Quadi agunt. Praecipua Marcomanorum gloria uiresque, atque ipsa etiam sedes pulsis olim Bois uirtute parta. Nec Naristi Quadiue degenerant. Eaque Germaniae uelut frons est, quatenus Danuuio peragitur.

Marcomanis Quadisque usque ad nostram memoriam reges mansere ex gente ipsorum, nobile Marobodui et Tudri genus (iam et externos patiuntur), sed uis et potentia regibus ex auctoritate Romana. Raro armis nostris, saepius pecunia iuuantur, nec minus ualent.

43. Retro Marsigni, Cotini, Osi, Buri terga Marcomanorum Quadorumque claudunt. E quibus Marsigni et Buri sermone cultuque Suebos referunt; Cotinos Gallica, Osos Pannonica lingua coarguit non esse Germanos, et quod tributa patiuntur. Partem tributorum Sarmatae, partem Quadi ut alienigenis imponunt. Cotini, quo magis pudeat, et ferrum effodiunt.

---

6 et sine a *praeter* Δ   7 his] hic (*corr. inc. m.*) **W**
42, 1 Naristi (ma- *I*, *in* no- *mut. inc. m. W*) **W** σ λ **bzuA**, narisci (no- s, ma- *a*) ω   2 marcomannorum (-cho- *s*) **W L s**, marcomorum **m**   4 Naristi] *ut supra* (naristi *r s*)   5 peragitur] praetexitur *Rhenanus 1544*, praecingitur *Tagmann, p. 41*
6 Marcomannis (-cho- *s*) **W L s**
43, 1 Cotini *Mf. 1853*, Gotini (-thi- *m* ξ) ω   Osi, Buri] osiburi **m** Δ φ **s**, osiburi, *in mg.* siburi **W**, Osi Buri *ex sil.*, *in mg.* siburi **h**, osiburi, *superscr.* osi Buri **N**, Osi.Burii, *in mg.* siburii **M**, siburi **s**², *cf. p. 135*   Marcomannorum (-cho -*s*) **W L leu s**   3 cultu **X**   Cotinos *Mf.*, Gotinos (-thi- ξ) ω   6 Cotini **m** σ, φ *praeter a, rubr. in mg.* **h**, Gotini (-thi- ξ) ω   effodunt **W**

42, 1 **Naristi**: See *A.P.V. s.v.* Varisti.

5 **peragitur**: "This is, so to speak, the front of Germany as far as it (*the front*) is described (*drawn*) by the Danube." The use of *peragitur* becomes clear, I believe, if the construction is cast into the active form: *Danuuius Germaniae frontem peragit*. *Frontem* is an accusative of the result produced, as is *gyros* in Pliny, *N. H.* x, 59 *eaedem* (**grues**) *mansuefactae lasciuiunt gyrosque quosdam indecoro cursu uel singulae peragunt*. Cf. also *ibid.* IV, 121 *peracto ambitu Europae*. Although numerous "emendations" have been proposed, I have been unable to find any adequate statement of the objections to *peragitur*. It is, however, gratifying to note that most of the more recent editors adhere to the manuscript tradition.

TEXT, CRITICAL APPARATUS, CRITICAL NOTES   319

Omnesque hi populi pauca campestrium, ceterum saltus et uertices montium [iugumque] insederunt. Dirimit enim scinditque Sue*b*iam continuum montium iugum, ultra quod plurimae
10 gentes agunt, ex quibus latissime patet Lugiorum nomen in plures ciuitates diffusum. Valentissimas nominasse sufficiet: Harios, Helueconas, Manimos, Helysios, Nahanarualos. Apud Naha*n*arualos antiquae religionis lucus ostenditur. Praesidet sacerdos muliebri ornatu, sed deos interpretatione Romana
15 Castorem Pollucemque memorant. Ea uis numini, nomen Alcis. Nulla simulacra, nullum.peregrinae superstitionis uestigium; ut fratres tamen, ut iuuenes uenerantur.

Ceterum *H*arii super uires, quibus enumeratos paulo ante populos antecedunt, truce*s* insitae feritati arte ac tempore

---

8 iugumque *secl. Acidalius,* montium iugumque *secl. Reifferscheid, p. 624*   10 Lugiorum Mf. *1853,* legiorum, *in mg. ucl superscr.* vegiorum **WN**, regiorum **h** (*cf. p. 170*), vegiorum **Δs**², leugiorum **I**, Legi̇orum **VdE**, legiorum **p L**, legiorum **m M**χ **vk s**, ligiorum (lignorum ψ) **r** φ   12 Heluaeonas Mf. *1853*   helysios (Ely- ξ z) α ψ, helysios haliosnas q̄ uel alios (*cf. pp. 76 f.*) **W**, Helysios, *superscr.* halisiosnas **V**, helisios (eli- *L*, ęli- *R*, -sos *b*) **m Lk blR s**, Helisios, *superscr.* Heliosnas (*cf. p. 171*) **h**, helisios, *in mg.* halisi̇onas (-ionas *ut uid. E*) **dE**, *sed lect. mg. in E quasi ad* heluetonas (*sic*) *pertinens,* haliosnas **s**² *super* heluecanas (*sic*), Alisionas, *in mg.* helisios **r**, heliciosna **a**, Alisiosnas **v**   13 Nahanarualos **Δ t**, nabanarualos π, nahauernalos **s** (naharwalos **s**²), naharualos ω   13 religionis **h** *ex sil.,* ξ λE al **s**, regionis ω (*et E in mg.*)   18 Harii] alii (aliis *m*) ω, arii **s**, **t** *in mg., et sic rest. Puteolanus*   19 truces *Beroaldus,* trucis ω   feritatis **h**ψ, feritate **m s** (*corr. s*²)

43, 8 [iugumque]: Apparently a repetition from the following line.
  10 Lugiorum: Mf. (487) retracts his former conjecture *Lugiorum* in favor of *Lygiorum,* but the reading of the **X** family points rather to *Lugiorum* (see p. 98).
  12 Helueconas: See *A. P.V. s.v.* Elvecones.
  Helysios: As the name is not found elsewhere, it remains uncertain whether we should write *Helysios* or *Helisios* (cf. p. 243). On the origin of the variant *haliosnas* see pp. 135 f.
  Apud Nahanarualos: Our MSS.

clearly indicate that Hf. here read *naharualos,* but read *nahanarualos* immediately before this (cf. p. 194⁵). Since the name is otherwise unknown, a definite choice between the two spellings seems impossible. I give preference to *Nahanarualos* on the general principle that letters were more easily lost than added in the transmission of a text. Schönfeld, *A.P.V. s.v.* Naharvali, is mistaken in stating that this form has the better manuscript authority, though he may be right in seeing in *Nahanaruali* a corruption due to dittography.

lenocinantur: nigra scuta, tincta corpora; atras ad proelia noctes legunt ipsaque formidine atque umbra feralis exercitus terrorem inferunt, nullo hostium sustinente nouum ac uelut infernum aspectum; nam primi in omnibus proeliis oculi uincuntur.

44. Trans Lugios Gothones regnantur, paulo iam adductius quam ceterae Germanorum gentes, nondum tamen supra libertatem.

Protinus deinde ab Oceano Rugii et Lemonii; omniumque harum gentium insigne rotunda scuta, breues gladii, et erga reges obsequium.

Suionum hinc ciuitates ipso in Oceano praeter uiros armaque classibus ualent. Forma nauium eo differt, quod utrimque prora paratam semper adpulsui frontem agit. Nec uelis ministrantur, nec remos in ordinem lateribus adiungunt: solutum, ut in quibusdam fluminum, et mutabile ut res poscit hinc uel illinc remigium.

44, 1 Lugios *Mf. 1853*, lygios (li- *m p L ɸ*) ω Gotones b1zuA, *Crollius* regnantur N∆, regnant *ex* regnantur *ut uide* W, regnant ω, *cf. p. 151* 4 lemouii Wm σ w V eu, Leiuonii *Karsten*, Levionii *Lundström* 7 ipso Wm σ bzuRAc s, ipsae (ipse) h *ex sil. (cf. pp. 175 f.)*, ξ β ale oceano (occe-) h *ex sil.*, a, oceanum (occe-) ω 8 nauis Wm 10 ministrant *Lipsius*

44, 1 **Gothones:** See *A.P.V. s.v.* Gutones.

4 Lemonii: It is not certain whether Hf. read *Lemonii* or *Lemouii* (cf. p. 151).

7 Oceano: See note on 6, 18, and cf. p. 141.

10 ministrantur . . . adiungunt: The change from the passive to the active in these closely correlated clauses is harsher than usual, since the subject of *ministrantur* is not expressed, but must be supplied from *nauium* in the preceding sentence. Yet I do not see the necessity for adopting Lipsius' *ministrant*. The closest parallel I have noted is ch. 16, 1 f. *Nullas Germanorum populis urbes habitari satis notum est, ne pati quidem (Germanos) inter se iunctas sedes.* Cf. also 16, 14 (hostis) *aperta populatur, abdita autem et defossa aut ignorantur* . . . ; Ann. VI, 44, 5 f. *nihil omissum, quo ambiguos inliceret, prompti firmarentur.* For an abrupt change of subject without change of voice cf. 3, 1 f. *memorant . . . canunt;* 5, 4 f. (terra) *pecorum fecunda, sed* (pecora) *plerumque improcera.* More often, to be sure, when there is a change of voice within a sentence, the subject of the passive verb also serves as the object of the active verb: 6, 11 f. (equi) *docentur, . . .* (equites equos) *agunt;* 18, 17 f. *quae nurus accipiant rursusque ad nepotes referantur;* 29, 5 f. *nam nec tributis contemnuntur nec publicanus atterit.*

Est apud illos et opibus honos, eoque unus imperitat, nullis iam exceptionibus, non precario iure parendi. Nec arma, ut apud ceteros Germanos, in promisco, sed clausa sub custode, et quidem seruo, quia subitos hostium incursus prohibet Oceanus, otiosae porro armatorum manus facile lasciuiunt: enimuero neque nobilem neque ingenuum, ne libertinum quidem armis praeponere regia utilitas est.

45. Trans Suionas aliud mare, pigrum ac prope immotum, quo cingi claudique terrarum orbem hinc fides, quod extremus cadentis iam solis fulgor in ortus edurat adeo clarus ut sidera hebetet; sonum insuper emergentis audiri formasque equorum et radios capitis aspici persuasio adicit. Illuc usque, et fama uera tantum, natura.

---

14 parendi] imperandi *prop. Passow*   15 promisco **WmN**Δ, promiscuo ω, *cf. p. 143*   17 otiosae *Colerus*, ociose *ex* ociosa *ut uid. inc. man.* **W**, ociosa ω

45, 1 Transsuionos (-nes *m*) **Wm**, tn̄suionas s²   Suionas] Sitonas *Meiser* (*uide ad 45, 30 ff.*)   3 in ortu se durat **Wh a s**, in ortu sedurat **m** φ, *cf. p. 114*   4 ebetet et **hs²**, habet et **m**, habet **s**   equorum u², *Colerus*, eorum **m vr** φ **s**, eorum, *in mg.* deorum **W**, deorum, *in mg.* eorum d**E**, deorum hs² α λk   5 usque tantum natura, et fama uera *Döderlein*   et] ut φ, it *Heinsius*, si *Grotius*

---

17 otiosae: I accept the *uulgata*, since the manuscript reading *otiosa manus*, "an idle band," is less forceful than *otiosae manus*, "idle hands," and the singular *manus* does not elsewhere in Tacitus take the plural verb (*Ann.* XIV, 36, 8, *manus* is not itself the subject, but is in apposition to the subject).

45, 5 Illuc . . . natura: This passage is a well known *crux* (see the long list of attempted emendations given by Walther). The text is probably corrupt, though it is intelligible if we are permitted to understand *Illuc usque et famā uerā illuc tantum pertinet natura:* "Up to that point, and by true report thus far only, extends the world" (Furneaux). It is also possible to take *fama uera* (est) as parenthetical. Yet the ellipsis of *illuc* before *tantum* is harsh, for any reader would instinctively feel that *tantum* belongs either with *uera* or *natura*. I do not agree with those who regard *et fama uera* as parenthetical and join *tantum* to *illuc usque* without a connective. Granting that *usque tantum* is Latin, could any writer expect his readers to perform such a feat of mental gymnastics? Grotius' *si*, though adopted by Halm and retained by Andresen, demands this joining of *tantum* to *illuc usque*, and is thereby unacceptable to me.

Natura is commonly taken to mean "the created world," just as it does in *Agr.* 33, 27 *in ipso terrarum ac naturae fine. Rerum natura* is similarly used by Seneca. *Suas.* I, 1 *nec usquam rerum naturam desinere.* Another possibility is suggested by the emendation of Heinsius, adopted by Crollius in the Bipontine edition.

Ergo iam dextro Sue*b*ici maris litore Aestiorum gentes adluuntur, quibus ritus habitusque Sue*b*orum, lingua Britannicae propior. Matrem deum uenerantur. Insigne superstitionis formas aprorum gestant: id pro armis hom*i*numque tutela securum deae cultorem etiam inter hostes praestat. Rarus ferri, frequens fustium usus. Frumenta ceterosque fructus patientius quam pro solita Germanorum inertia laborant. Sed et mare scrutantur, ac soli omnium sucinum, quod ipsi glesum uocant, inter uada atque in ipso litore legunt. Nec quae natura quaeue ratio gignat, ut barbaris, quaesitum compertumue; diu quin etiam inter cetera eiectamenta maris iacebat, donec luxuria nostra dedit nomen. Ipsis in nullo usu: rude legitur, informe perfertur, pretiumque mirantes accipiunt. Sucum tamen arborum esse intell*e*gas, quia terrena quaedam atque etiam uolucria animalia plerumque interlucent, quae implicata humore mox durescente materia cluduntur. Fecundiora igitur nemora lucosque, sicut Orientis secretis, ubi tura balsamaque sudantur, ita Occidentis insulis terrisque inesse crediderim quae uicini solis radiis expressa

---

7 saeuici, *in mg. uel superscr.* sueuici W N λdE, saeuici m I k
8 adluuntur X ΔI dvrk, adlu- *ex* ablu- b, alluuntur Nξ π, abluuntur λE a, adluuntur *ex* adbuuntur *ut uide* s   9 proprior m E bzuAc
10 hominumque *Urlichs*, omniumque ω, omnique W² t, *Lipsius*
15 glaesum *Mf. 1873*   19 profertur (per- *k*) Lτ c s   22 implicate W   23 et sicut *Mähly*   25 quae] quo *ut uid.* m, quam π, quâ *Detschew*   25 radiis X (*h ex sil.*), a *praeter* I, dr a s², radius I, β *praeter* dr, φ (*praeter* a, *om.* Ac), s, *cf. p. 103*

---

illuc usque it fama: uera tantum natura. "To such absurd lengths does popular report travel, but only the phenomena of nature are to be credited." (*I.e.*, we may believe *quo cingi . . . hebetet*, but not *sonum . . . aspici*.) I do not find the correction of *et* to *it* altogether convincing. More probably, I think, some word has been lost before *et: Illuc usque* <***> *et fama: uera tantum natura.*

10 hominumque: Urlichs' simple correction of *omniumque* to *hominumque* seems to me almost certain, in view of the antithesis produced between *hominum* and *deae*. Those who keep the manuscript reading regard *omniumque* (neuter) as an objective genitive with *tutela*.

23 ff. Fecundiora . . . labuntur: An anacoluthon offers the simplest explanation. The author begins with the idea uppermost in his mind, *fecundiora . . . nemora lucosque*, but by the time he has reached his verb (*inesse*) his thoughts have shifted from the source of the substance to the substance itself, and he takes for his subject the implied antecedent of *quae* instead of *nemora lucosque*.

atque liquentia in proximum mare labuntur ac ui tempestatum in aduersa litora exundant. Si naturam sucini admoto igne temptes, in modum taedae accenditur alitque flammam pinguem et olentem; mox ut in picem resinamue lentescit.

30   Suionibus Sitonum gentes continuantur. Cetera similes uno differunt, quod femina dominatur: in tantum non modo a libertate sed etiam a seruitute degenerant.

46. Hic Sue*b*iae fin*i*s. Peucinorum Venethorumque et Fennorum nationes Germanis an Sarmatis adscribam dubito. Quamquam Peucini, quos quidam Bastarnas uocant, sermone,

---

26 ui] in **Wm I RA s** (*corr. s²*)   27 litore **W**   30-32 Suionibus . . . degenerant *in fine cap. 44 ponenda censuit Crollius probantibus Meiser (p. 49) et Mf.* (*11, 7 ff.*)   30 Ceteras *in* -ris *corr. inc. m.* **W**   31 differunt β ξ ae s, differuntur Xσ φ; *cf. p. 104*

46, 1 Sueuiae, *superscr.* sueuae **N V**, Sueuę **Δ**   Peucinorum Iξ τ, Peucinorum, *in mg. uel superscr.* peucurorum **W N λ**, Peucurorum, *superscr.* cini, *rubr. in mg.* Peucini **h**, Peucurorum **Δ**, Prutinorum **s**, peucurorum/ peucinorum **s²**, Prucinorum φ   Venetho rumque **Wh N V**, ψ *praeter R*, **s²**, Venetorumque ω, Venedorumqu *Rhenanus*   3 quidem **Wh v**, quidam *e* quidem *corr. ut vide* **m**

46, 1 **Peucinorum**: See *A.C.S. s.v.* Peuce for the passages in ancient literature in which this name is found. On the variant *Peucurorum* see p. 137.

Venethorumque: See *A.P.V.* 280 f. Schönfeld regards both *Venedi* and *Venethi* as genuine forms.

3 **Quamquam . . . agunt**: Most editors treat this clause as an appendage of *dubito* (with a full stop after *agunt*), which makes our author imply that the Peucini are the most definitely German of the three tribes under discussion. Thereby a meaning is read into our text which is not merely unjustifiable, but is actually refuted by what Tacitus has to say of the Venethi and Fenni, as I shall now attempt to show.

If the Venethi are further removed from the Germans than are the Peucini, they must be more closely akin to the Sarmatians, since the author offers no third point of comparison. But what are the Sarmatian characteristics which Tacitus adduces for the Peucini and Venethi respectively? The Peucini by their physical appearance betray an actual infusion of Sarmatian blood. The Venethi have *borrowed* or *taken over* (*traxerunt*) many Sarmatian habits, of which the author mentions but one, viz. brigandage. The reader may draw his own conclusion as to which is the stronger argument for Sarmatian kinship. (Gudeman seeks to avoid this difficulty inherent in the usual interpretation by reading *et ex moribus*, thereby making Tacitus attribute intermingling of Sarmatian blood to the Venethi as well as to the Peucini.)

Another obstacle in the way of the commonly accepted explanation is found in the pronoun *Hi*. If the author's line of thought is, "the Peucini are essentially Germans; the Venethi are less so, but I am still willing to classify them as such," he should have written *sed hi quoque*, or *et hi tamen* as proposed by Reifferscheid. (Reifferscheid's meaning is

22

cultu, sede ac domiciliis ut Germani agunt (sordes omnium ac

4 ac torpor procerum] at corpora Peucinorum *Mützell*, ac torpor: ora Peucinorum *Halm 1864*, ac torpor: ora procerum *Heraeus*

strangely misunderstood by Mf. 518. Naturally R. did not suppose that *tamen* indicates a contrast between the Venethi and Peucini. It is the unqualified use of the pronoun *Hi* which produces this contrast.) Let us then suppose that our author's meaning is about as follows: "I am quite unable to determine whether the Peucini should be called Germans or Sarmatians. The Venethi have adopted many Sarmatian habits. *These* (*i.e.* the Venethi in contrast with the Peucini), however (in spite of their Sarmatian habits), are to be classed as Germans rather than as Sarmatians." The pronoun *Hi* now assumes its proper force of marking a contrast between the Venethi and Peucini.

Let us now look at Tacitus' discussion of the Fenni. Those who believe that Tacitus pronounces the Peucini to be the most definitely German of the three tribes are forced to the conclusion that he regards the Fenni as the most remote from the Germans and as the most closely akin to the Sarmatians. But what is the evidence of Sarmatian kinship? Certainly the Fenni do not spend their time on horseback and live in wagons, for they have no horses. Do they have the predatory habits of the Sarmatians? Evidently not, for *beatius arbitrantur quam . . . suas alienasque fortunas spe metuque uersare; securi aduersus homines.* . . . Do they, like the Sarmatians, have no fixed abodes? I do not believe that any argument can be drawn from Tacitus' fantastic account of the "dwellings" of the Fenni. Finally, is the relationship of the Fenni to the Sarmatians indicated in general by the same low scale of civilization? Seemingly the answer depends upon which race, German or Sarmatian, is characterized by *sordes* (line 4), for we could hardly wish a better description of *sordes* in its most abject form than is found in Tacitus' account of the life of the Fenni.

The interpretation which seeks to establish a sequence, beginning with the tribe most closely akin to the Germans and ending with the tribe most remote from the Germans, is untenable. Far stronger arguments can be found for assuming that the sequence is exactly the opposite. Yet I prefer to read nothing into our author's words that is not expressed. As I understand the chapter, Tacitus pronounces in favor of the Germanic nationality of the Venethi, but for the Peucini and Fenni he indicates no preference whatever.

4 sordes . . . procerum: The text may be corrupt, but I do not find any of the proposed emendations convincing. The difficulty lies in the fact that it is a moot point whether the words *sordes . . . procerum* are to be understood as a parenthetical insertion in the *quamquam* clause (in expansion of the preceding *cultu*) or should be taken as part of a double apodosis of which *conubiis . . . foedantur* would form the second member. In the former case *sordes . . . procerum* are meant as German characteristics, in the latter case they must be understood as characterizing the Sarmatians. On the whole, I find it easier to take these words with *quamquam*. Additional evidence for laziness of the chieftains as a German characteristic is to be found in the fifteenth chapter. Support for the belief that *sordes* of the masses marks the Germans is sometimes sought in ch. 20, 1 *in omni domo nudi ac sordidi*, and 4 f. *inter eadem pecora, in eadem humo degunt*, but probably the word does not denote actual "filth" so much as "lack of the refinements of civilization" (cf. Baumstark II, 313 f.).

torpor procerum), conubiis mixt*is* nonnihil in Sarmatarum habitum foedantur. Venethi multum ex moribus traxerunt; nam quidquid inter Peucinos Fennosque siluarum ac montium erigitur latrociniis pererrant. Hi tamen inter Germanos potius referuntur, quia et domos figunt et scuta gestant et peditum usu ac pernicitate gaudent: quae omnia diuersa Sarmatis sunt in plaustro equoque uiuentibus.

Fennis mira feritas, foeda paupertas: non arma, non equi, non penates; uictui herba, uestitui pelles, cubile humus: solae in sagittis spes, quas inopia ferri ossibus asperant. Idemque uenatus uiros pariter ac feminas alit; passim enim comitantur partemque praedae petunt. Nec aliud infantibus ferarum imbriumque suffugium quam ut in aliquo ramorum nexu contegantur: huc redeunt iuuenes, hoc senum receptaculum. Sed beatius arbitrantur quam ingemere agris, inlaborare domibus, suas alienasque fortunas spe metuque uersare: securi aduersus homines, securi aduersus deos rem difficillimam adsecuti sunt, ut illis ne uoto quidem opus esset.

Cetera iam fabulosa: Hellusios et Oxionas ora hominum

---

5 mixtis Δt, mistis w, mixtos ω, mixti u² *in mg.*   6 Venethi **Wh** **N V** s², Veneti ω, Venedi *Rhenanus*   et ex moribus *Gudeman 1928*   7 quidquid **mv**, quitquid **W**, quid **b**, qui π, quicquid ω   8 Et hi *Reifferscheid*   9 figunt λ, fingunt ω   10 peditum] pecudum λ, pedum *Lipsius*   11 palustro **W** zuR, c² *in mg.* 13 herba] fera *du Mesnil*   Sola t τ a s   23 oxionas Nχ k, φ *praeter aR* (obsi- z), oxianas **m** a, oxionas, *in mg. uel superscr.* etionas **W** λd**E**, oxionas, *rubr. in mg.* al. etione h, etionas Δ v, Ethionas r, exionas **IM** s, esionas **R**

---

5 mixtis: On a similar confusion between *ti* and *to* in the Hersfeld *Agricola* see p. 56. Yet the *mixtos* of the MSS. may indicate that there is some deeper corruption in this most obscure passage.

9 figunt: The adoption of this reading, a conjecture of λ for *fingunt*, seems unavoidable. The point which the author wishes to make is the permanence or fixity of abode. Cf. *Ann.* XIII, 54, 6 *iamque fixerant domos*.

10 peditum: In view of the preceding *scuta gestant*, I am unconvinced that Lipsius' *pedum* is an improvement over the *peditum* of the MSS.

23 Oxionas: On the variant *Etionas* see p. 137.

uultusque, corpora atque artus ferarum gerere; quod ego ut
incompertum in medium relinquam.

---

24 uultusque et corpora α τ   25 incopertum W   medio
Halm²

Cornelii Taciti de origine & situ Germanorum liber explicit
Wm V, Finis Δχ zuRAc, finis:—/θελοσ I, Τελωσ N d, OPVS
ABSOLVTVM BONONIAE ANNO DN̄I M.CCCCLXIIII AD
PETITIONEM .IO. MARCANOVAE:—M, FINIT L, τεκοσ./
CORNELII TACITI DE ORIGINE ET MORIBVS GERMANO-
RVM LIBER EXPLICIT E, Laus deo clementissimo k, Cornelii
Taciti oratoris Eq. Ro. liber de origine et situ germanorum finitur b,
Explicit cornelii taciti nepotis liber a, FINIS./ Cornelii taciti equitis
.r. libellus de situ germanie finit:— 1, *subscriptio deest* h (?), v e s,
subscriptio cod. r in p. 87, adn. 1, uidenda est

---

25 in medium relinquam: In view of the following well-known quotation from Gellius XVII, 2, 11, I fail to see why the manuscript reading should be questioned: *Nos, inquit* (Q. Claudius Quadrigarius), *in medium relinquemus. Vulgus "in medio" dicit; nam uitium esse istuc putat et, si dicas "in medium ponere," id quoque esse soloecon putant; set probabilius significantiusque sic dici uidebitur, si quis ea uerba non incuriose introspiciat; Graece quoque* θεῖναι εἰς μέσον, *uitium id non est.*

APPENDICES

I

A SURVEY OF THE TEXTUAL HISTORY OF THE GERMANIA

The Earliest Period

During the infancy of typography three independent recensions of the *Germania* were published: (1) the *princeps*, (2) the Nuremberg edition of Creussner, and (3) the Viennese edition of Winterburg.

The Spirensis, 1470 (?)

The *editio princeps*, sometimes called the *Spirensis*, which contains all the works of Tacitus then known (*Annales* XI–XXI [*sic*]; *Germania*, *Dialogus*), is said to have issued from the press of Vindelin of Spire in Venice, *c.* 1470. The text of the *Germania* was drawn from some lost member of the α group, and accordingly this edition has the importance of a manuscript (= w of my apparatus).[1] The text of the *princeps* for the *Germania* alone was repeated three times: Bologna, 1472, and Venice, 1476 and 1481. Of the three repetitions only that of 1481 shows any noteworthy changes, which may have been drawn from other editions.[2] A revision of the

Puteolanus 1475 (?)

editio princeps by Franciscus Puteolanus, with the addition of the *Agricola*, appeared in Milan, *c.* 1475. Although Puteolanus successfully restored the correct readings in a few places,[3] it is not probable that he drew from any second

---

[1] See p. 89.

[2] 9, 3 *sueuorum*, 15, 5 *habent miram diuersitatem*, 26, 6 *labore*, 31, 4 *caeso*, for the *Suenorum*, *habent mira diuersitate*, *laborare*, and *exso* of the *princeps* and two earlier reimpressions. With the exception of *labore*, which appears in the editions of Creussner and of Gensberg, these corrections are first found in the edition of Puteolanus.

[3] 6, 11 *uariare*, 8, 3 *pectorum*, 45, 27 *succini*, for the *uarietate*, *peccatorum*, and *succin* of the *princeps* and its three reimpressions (also cf. note 2). Also 43, 18 *Arii*, and 46, 1 *finis*, for the *alii* and *fines* of ω.

source, either manuscript or printed,[1] and his revision is in no wise thorough-going. The reproduction of this edition made by Philippus Pincius in Venice, 1497, is commonly known as the second edition of Puteolanus, but it is perhaps more accurate to speak of it as the edition of Pincius, even though in the *Germania* there is scarcely a change over the earlier impression.[2]

The second of the three independent recensions is the edition of the *Germania* alone said to come from the press of Fr. Creussner in Nuremberg, c. 1473. The text is drawn from a lost manuscript of the τ branch of the β group, and, like the *princeps*, this edition assumes the importance of a manuscript (= k of my apparatus). The edition said to have issued from the press of Johannes Gensberg or of Johannes Schurener in Rome, 1474, belongs to the same recension, though it is scarcely a copy of the Nuremberg edition, since it has certain readings differing from the latter, but found in some or all manuscripts of the τ branch.[3] Of the two editions that of Gensberg is by far the more faulty.

The third independent recension of our text is to be found in an edition of the *Germania* with the poem of Conrad Celtis, *De Situ et Moribus Germaniae*, and an extract (*de hercinie silue magnitudine*, etc.) from his book, *De Situ et Moribus Norimbergae*, said by Copinger to have issued from the press of J. Winterburg in Vienna, 1500 (= *ed. Vind.*).[4] The text of the *Germania* in this edition has been conflated from a lost manu-

---

[1] This is shown by his emendations, 14, 9 *et ut facilius . . . clarescant*, and 15, 5 *habent miram diuersitatem*, for the *et facilius . . . clarescant* and *habent mira diuersitate* of the *princeps*. In both cases the correct readings could have been restored from the editions of Creussner and Gensberg or from many of the MSS.

[2] I have noticed only 36, 4 *nomina* for *nomine*.

[3] 2, 5 *urbe* Gens. vr, *orbe* kω; 6, 18 *primum* Gens., *primo* k (the variants were in τ); 6, 22 *conscilium* Gens. d, *consilium* k (variants in τ); 11, 4 *incidit* Gens. ω, *inciderit* kE; 15, 7 *uiritim* Gens. ω, *iurium* k; 19, 9 *vocatur* Gens. ω, *vocantur* k; 19, 15 *funere* Gens. dv, *finuere* k; 31, 1 *raro* Gens., *rara* k (variants in τ).

[4] Massmann, 30, dates *1509? 1515?*, and Holder accepts the former date.

script of the β group, presumably λ, the archetype of **VL**, and from Puteolanus' recension of the *princeps*.[1] Were it not marred by numerous stupid blunders, it would be by far the best of the early recensions of our text. It clearly reveals the work of a scholar, and one may wonder if the impression known today is not a poor reprint of an earlier edition, perhaps one made by Conrad Celtis himself.[2] The edition of the *Germania* appearing with the pseudo-Berosus in Paris, 1511, is a reprint of *ed. Vind*.[3]

From 1500 to Rhenanus, 1519

Of these three early recensions, the *princeps* as emended by Puteolanus became the *vulgata*. The *Germania* was published separately in Leipzig, 1502 and 1509, in Erfurt, 1509, and appeared with the rest of the Tacitean works in Venice, 1512. Apparently all these editions depart from the text of Puteolanus only in arbitrary changes made here and there by their respective editors.[4] The edition of Puteolanus was also used in constituting the text of the Vienna edition of 1515,[5] though *ed. Vind.* 1500 seems rather to be the underlying basis. Beroaldus' edition of the works of Tacitus in 1515, famed though it is as being the *princeps* of *Annales* I–VI, is for the other works scarcely more than a reimpression of Puteolanus

[1] See my discussion on pp. 209 ff.

[2] Cf. Massmann, 31.

[3] I have not seen the Paris edition, but Holder's statement (*Mitth.* 46) that it is a copy of *ed. Vind.* is borne out by the readings given by Hess, 1827, and by the fact that both editions offer the same title for the *Germania* and have the poem of Celtis.

[4] Collations of all except the Erfurt edition through ch. 27 by Hess, 1834. I have no first-hand acquaintance with any of these editions except Leipzig, 1509, of which I have photostats. Passow (xiii) says of Leipzig, 1502: . . . *quoties recedit a Puteolano, peccat*. Regarding Venice, 1512, Hess (*l.c.* iv): *Edit. Rivian. Venet. 1512 fol. nullum habet usum criticum, quamvis id contendente Walch, quum e Puteol. ita sit expressa, ut nisi in mendis typogr. ab ea fere discedat.* Massman (33), however, says it has many corrections of the text of Put.

[5] Collation (partial) through ch. 27 by Hess, 1834. Also cf. Passow, xv; Tagmann, 71. Hess attributes to this edition, 2, 18 *nunc* . . . *nunc* (= Put.), where the edition of 1500 reads *nunc* . . . *tunc*. The title also is reminiscent of Put. (= *princeps*) rather than of *ed. Vind.*

(*i.e.* Pincius, 1497)[1]. The edition of Andreas Alciatus, Milan, 1517, is said to be a simple reimpression of that of Beroaldus.[2]

BEATUS RHENANUS

The first real critical revision of the text of the *Germania* was made by Beatus Rhenanus. In May of 1519 there appeared in Basel an anonymous edition of the *Germania* with a commentary, whose text does not differ materially from that of Beroaldus,[3] but whose connection with Rhenanus is shown by three marginal notes.[4] In August of the same year there appeared in Basel an edition of Tacitus' works with the notes of Andreas Alciatus, in which the text of the *Germania* has undergone an extensive revision.[5] The real editor of the *Germania* in this impression was not Alciatus, but Rhenanus, as a comparison with the latter's edition of 1533 shows. At the beginning of Rhenanus' commentary on the *Germania* in his edition of Tacitus published in Basel, 1533, we have a statement from Rhenanus himself to the effect that in 1519 he had collated the text of this work with a printed edition lent him by a physician, Hieronymus Artolphus.[6] This *codex Artolphi*,

[1] In the *Germania* I have noted only the following changes, but my examination (copy in Harvard University library) was not thorough: 5, 11 *perinde*, 27, 5 *& grauem* (typographical blunder), 40, 1 *Langobardis*, 43, 10 *Lygiorum*, 12 *Naharualos . . . Naharualos*, 19 *truces*, where Put. (Pincius) has *proinde, ut grauem, longobardis, legiorum, Nahanarualos . . . Naharualos, trucis.*

[2] Massmann, 36.

[3] Collation by Hess, 1827. I inspected rather hastily a copy in the Harvard University library.

[4] 9, 6 *aduectam*, 28, 14 *Neruii*, 40, 7 *Herthum*, opposite *adiectam, Neruli,* and *Nerthum,* in the text. The edition from the press of Valentin Schumann, Leipzig (undated) is probably only a reimpression (cf. Massmann, 37). Hess, 1834, iv, mentions another impression without place or date.

[5] Collation by Hess, 1827, upon which I am forced to depend for my knowledge of the text of this edition.

[6] Rhenanus, 1533, 421: "Denuo relegi hoc de Germanis opusculum, quod anno 1519 contuleram cum exemplari non scripto, sed impresso tantum. Id tum communicauit mihi Hieronymus Artolphus medicae rei consultus, & profuit mihi locis non paucis. Addidi rursum quaedam ex annotationibus illis collati quondam codicis, de quibus hic statim admonebitur lector. Nec in aliis sententiam meam caelabo."

to which he constantly refers, is readily identified with the Nuremberg edition of 1473 (k).[1] This is the source from which the marginal readings and innovations in the text of the so-called edition of Alciatus (1519) had been made, and which Rhenanus utilized still further in his recension of 1533. To the latter he has also admitted numerous conjectures of his own.[2]

It may be said with truth that no single editor has ever rendered service to the *Germania* comparable with that of Rhenanus. In some fifty readings he successfully restored the text from k, and in only a few did his judgment err in the choice between his two sources. Some of his conjectures have later been confirmed by manuscript evidence, and others still rightfully retain their place in our texts of the *Germania*. Other emendations, to be sure, might better have been omitted,[3] especially since in time they acquired the peculiar odor of sanctity which once attended the "vulgata," and

[1] Cf. the following readings, which he states were in the *codex Artolphi:* 3, 3 *barditum,* 12 *acriniprion,* 11, 9 *nec iniussi,* 12 *tamen,* 13, 4 *uel ipsi uel propinqui,* 15, 7 *acuirium* (ac *iurium* k), 18 16 *renunciant, sic uiuentes sic parientes,* 19, 9 *uocantur,* 37, 1 *situm,* 38, 10 *ipso* om., *religatur,* 40, 4 *Vendigni* (*Veu-* k), 13 *quencunque,* 42, 7 *Trudi.* That it was the Nuremberg edition and not the edition of Gensberg which Rhenanus had is shown by the readings, 3, 12 *acriniprion,* 11, 4 *inciderit,* 19, 9 *uocantur,* where Gens. omits the first with a lacuna, and correctly writes *incidit* and *uocatur.* However, 6, 16, he ascribes to his *codex centum,* which is the reading of Gens., whereas k has *centim.* Rhenanus wrongly attributes to k, 1, 9 *Abnobae,* and 26, 7 *sepiant.* The former is reported for h, and according to Walther *ad loc.* was first published as a conjecture of Hermolaus Barbarus in the margin of the edition of 1497. This must mean the edition of Pincius (Put.²), but the copy which I have before me does not show the marginal reading. *Sepiant* appears to be an emendation of Rhenanus' own.

I see no reason for supposing that Rhenanus drew from any other sources than Puteolanus' recension and the Nuremberg edition, though it may be noted that he has sometimes restored the correct reading where it could not have been drawn from either source, but is found in *ed. Vind.* 1500: 13, 3 *Tum in,* 38, 10 *religant,* 41, 1 *pars Sueuorum,* 44, 7 *ipso in oceano,* 46, 24 *uultusque corpora.*

[2] To judge from Hess' collation, the edition of 1519 (Alciatus) has very few of Rhenanus' conjectures.

[3] 7, 14 *exugere,* 16, 10 *inuitet,* 20, 12 *ii et animum,* 21, 12 *poposceris,* 26, 7 *sepiant,* 38, 7 *Sic in aliis,* 43, 14 *Romani,* 44, 1 *addictius,* 46, 22 *sit.*

which even the enlightenment of modern scholarship has not entirely dispelled.

The edition of Rhenanus, which again appeared with a few changes[1] in Basel, 1544, justly assumed its place as the standard text. The Aldine edition of 1534 is merely a repetition of Rhenanus, 1533, and the *Gryphianae* and other editions of Tacitus up to 1574 are said to offer nothing new in the way of critical *subsidia*.

Lipsius and Pichena

The next epoch in the history of our text may conveniently take its beginning with the edition of Tacitus by Justus Lipsius in 1574, though it should be noted that the services which Lipsius rendered to the *Germania* seem in no way comparable with those which he bestowed upon the major works, and which earned for him the title of *Sospitator Taciti*. The first edition was followed by five others in the editor's lifetime (1581, 1585, 1588, 1589, 1600), and by a final one appearing in 1607 after his death. In the first edition the sole aid that Lipsius used for correcting Rhenanus' text[2] appears to have been the Farnesianus (N), but even from this he did not draw the profit that he might.[3] In fact, he mentions it by

---

[1] 35, 10 *Idque*, 42, 5 *praetexitur*, for *Id* and *pergitur* in the earlier editions.

[2] Probably Lipsius did not have either of the editions appearing under Rhenanus' name (1533, 1544), but some later reimpression. There are a number of readings which he prints (at least in the editions of 1589 and 1607) without comment as to their source, though they are not found in the editions of Rhenanus: 5, 19 *faciliori usui*, 20, 8 *ualidique*, 21, 8 *defecerit* (probably from the Farnesianus), 46, 9 *figunt, pedum*. His earlier editions may tell the origin of these readings. I regret that I have access only to a reprint of the edition of 1589 (Paris, 1599) and to the edition of 1607.

[3] For instance, 11, 9, he proposes *nec ut iussi* as an emendation of his own, and 36, 7, cites (in ed. of 1607) *Tracti* as a conjecture of Pichena, though both readings are found in N.

According to Tagmann (73) Lipsius mentions in the preface *ad lectorem* a Venetian edition of 1494, but this is nowhere cited in his notes on the *Germania*. The identity of this edition seems never to have been established.

name (ed. of 1607) but five times in his notes to the *Germania*.[1]

For his third edition (1585) Lipsius had secured from Fr. Modius [2] additional aids consisting of readings from a codex Bambergensis, containing only the *Germania*, and an ancient *editio Romana* of all the Tacitean works. Though the Bambergensis is frequently cited, the *vetus Romana* is mentioned but three times in his notes to the *Germania*.[3] The codex Bambergensis, if not the Arundel manuscript (a) itself, was at least its twin brother.[4] Since a is the most interpolated of all *Germania* manuscripts, Modius' Bambergensis could hardly be expected to place the text on a very firm foundation. The identity of the Roman edition has never to my knowledge been established. Together with the Bambergensis it is mentioned by Modius, *Novantiquae Lectiones* (Frankfort, 1584), *Epistola* xv (*ad Ianum Lernutium*),[5] who says that it

[1] 3, 3 *barditum*, 7, 14 *exigere*, 8, 9 *Fluriniam*, 13, 5 *hebent*, 40, 1 *nobilitat*. Massmann (6) says that he cites from it six times, and Tagmann (17) says eleven times. Either the citations are more frequent in Lipsius' earlier editions, or Massmann and Tagmann had in mind his references (not always correct) to the *libri scripti* (*i.e.* **N** and Bambergensis).

[2] Tagmann (73) cites the *monitio ad lectorem* of the edition of 1585. In the *monitio* of the edition of 1589 Lipsius again mentions the *editio Romana*, which he calls *plurimum proba*.

[3] 1, 9 *Arbonae*, 7, 14 *exigere* (*exugere* Rhenanus), 44, 1 *adductius* (*addictius* Rhen.). Also this edition and the Bambergensis are meant by the *Quidam libri* which read *cultu*, 31, 13.

[4] A comparison of the readings of the two is made by Wünsch, 1897, 42 ff., who is probably correct in regarding them as distinct MSS. While most of the discrepancies might be accounted for by the assumption that Lipsius, following a practice common enough in his day, cites, not the actual readings of the Bambergensis, but his own emendations made on the basis of these readings, yet such cannot be the case in 23, 6, where he attributes to Bambergensis the reading *uino*, whereas a has *uitiis* with ω.

[5] Reprinted by I. Gruter, *Lampas, siue Fax Artium Liberalium* v (Frankfort, 1607), 36 ff.: "Ex Tacito, quem ad vetuste impressum adeo exemplar, vt manu exarati vicem esse possit, collatum Lipsio nostro . . . occasione data missurus sum, haec, mi Lernute enotabam . . . (*citations from Ann. xv follow*). Romae excusus liber ab hinc annis centum . . . Lib. de moribus German. *Nam ne in pace quidem vultu mitiore mansuescunt.* cusus Romanus & scriptus Bambergensis lib. *cultu mitiore mansuescunt* . . ."

was printed a hundred years before, *i.e.* in 1484 or earlier, but bibliographers seem to know of no Roman edition of Tacitus' works earlier than that of Beroaldus, 1515. Modius cites but one reading, 31, 13 *cultu*, which, so far as I know, is found only in *ed. Vind.* 1500 (*Germania* alone) among the early editions.

Pichena, 1607

Lipsius' last edition (1607) found no mean rival in an edition of Tacitus published by Curtius Pichena in the same year.[1] For the *Annals* and *Histories* Pichena was probably the first editor to consult the Mediceus II and the first after Beroaldus to use the Mediceus I, but for the *Germania* his modest critical *subsidia* consisted in Pincius' repetition (1497) of Puteolanus and in the Bolognese edition of 1472. Nevertheless, he used these helps to excellent advantage, displaying rare critical acumen in rejecting the interpolations of Puteolanus and Rhenanus, and, I am inclined to think, produced a text sounder than that of Lipsius, though it must be granted that he could hardly have done so well had he not been able to profit from the labors of Lipsius.

From Lipsius and Pichena to Brotier, 1771

For well over a hundred and fifty years textual criticism of the *Germania* made but little progress beyond the point reached by Lipsius and Pichena. Even the edition of Iac. Gronovius (Utrecht, 1721), in which the text of the *Annals* and *Histories* is based upon a new collation of the Medicean manuscripts, has nothing new to offer for the *Germania* except a list of selected readings from the Arundelianus (= a), a manuscript whose close affinity to the Bambergensis of Lipsius we have just noted. J. A. Ernesti in his edition (Leipzig, 1752) made use of a collation of the Turicensis (= t), whose text is essentially the same as that of the *editio princeps*.[2] His other critical aids were the *princeps* itself, the impression of 1476, whose dependence on the former he recognizes, the Nuremberg

[1] I have been unable to find Pichena's *Ad C. Taciti Opera Notae*, which appeared a few years before his edition. This work is said to have been published first in Florence without date, and to have been reprinted in Hanau, 1600, and again, with certain additions, in 1604. See E. Jacob, *Oeuvres de Tacite, texte latin . . . avec un commentaire . . .* I (Paris, 1875), xlv.

[2] See pp. 183 ff.

edition, which he identifies with the *codex Artolphi* of Rhenanus, the editions of Pincius (Put.²), and of Beroaldus. It is interesting to note that all these are essentially the very props upon which the text had rested since the time of Rhenanus.

BROTIER TO TROSS

Brotier, 1771

A new epoch, characterized by a continually increasing knowledge of *Germania* manuscripts, is marked by G. Brotier's edition of Tacitus (Paris, 1771), which cites from the four Vaticani, 1518, 1862, 2964, 4498 (IVvΔ), hitherto unknown. However, Brotier offers nothing like complete collations of these manuscripts, and his citations are inaccurate.[1] The

Kapp, 1788

edition of J. Kapp (Leipzig, 1788; 2d ed. by Hess, 1824), prepared from the lecture notes of P. D. Longolius, utilizes a collation of the Hummelianus (h) made by Longolius himself,[2] and the fragmentary Monacensis 947, which passed by inheritance from Longolius to Kapp. Although Longolius' collation of h is far from perfect,[3] the entrance of this important manuscript into the muster marked a distinct advance. As for the second manuscript, it is but a copy of the Nuremberg edition (the *codex Artolphi* of Rhenanus).

Passow, 1817

Müllenhoff (90) says that methodical textual criticism of the *Germania* begins with Passow's edition (Breslau, 1817)—a statement which is true enough if one looks to the intent of the editor, rather than to the results actually obtained. Passow offers nothing new in the way of manuscript evidence,[4]

---

[1] For example, 2, 19 he cites for **IVv** *uocati sunt*, which occurs only in I; 25, 8 *impune est* for the *Vaticani*, though **v** omits *est;* and also reports the following incorrectly: 8, 9 *Alberniam* **V**, 25, 2 *ministeriis suis* **v**, 33, 9 *jam urgentibus* **Vv**.

[2] Selected readings from this MS. had previously been published by Hummel in 1776. The collation of Longolius is still extant in the Munich library. See p. 82.

[3] See pp. 163 ff.

[4] He did examine anew some old editions (Venice, 1497, and Nuremberg, 1473), and brought on for the first time the Vienna edition of 1515, the Paris of 1511, and Leipzig of 1502.

and was even unable to find the edition of Brotier with its readings from the four Vatican manuscripts, but he does make an honest attempt to gather into usable form such testimony of the manuscripts and of the oldest editions as he could discover, and to exclude from the text readings which have no basis other than the critical ingenuity of earlier editors. An examination of his critical notes shows how utterly futile were the shreds of disorganized evidence which he was able to piece together. His critical method, I suspect, led him astray about as often as it set him aright.[1]

New collations

The years immediately following the appearance of Passow's edition are marked by considerable activity in the publication of new collations: of t by Orelli, 1819, and of h by Selling, 1830, now an indispensable source for the restoration of this lost manuscript. Of special merit are the *Variae Lectiones* of Hess, (Helmstädt, 1827, 1828, 1834), for which he had independent collations of s (1828) and of f (1834),[2] and of a large number of early editions—still a valuable work for one who does not have access to all the early editions.

J. Gruber in his edition (Berlin, 1832) adopts the Hummelianus as the leading authority, and is followed by N. Bach (Leipzig, 1834), the latter also having collations of s and M which were lent him by Passow.[3] Gruber appears to have been the first to attempt the grouping of the manuscripts of the *Germania* into a stemma.

Gerlach, 1835

More pretentious than any of its predecessors is Gerlach's edition of the *Germania* (Basel, 1835). Gerlach lists eighteen manuscripts, and had he not mistaken Δ and u for the same manuscript he might have listed nineteen! From the colla-

---

[1] To cite an extreme case, 14, 13, on the basis of early editions alone (with the *princeps* erroneously included among them) he recalls to the text Puteolanus' *epulae et convictus!*

[2] A description of f with selected readings had been published previously by A. Wissowa, 1832 (cf. p. 81).

[3] I can find no confirmation of Mf.'s statement (89) that I. Bekker (1831) received a collation of N for the *Germania* from Niebuhr. Bekker does mention in his preface (xlv) a collation of this MS. for the *Dialogus* sent him by Niebuhr.

tions of Massmann, whose work upon an elaborate critical edition was already under way, he published selected readings of **m, o, l, u, A**, manuscripts which were previously unknown, of **N**, previously used only by Lipsius, of **I, V, v**, which had figured in the apparatus of Brotier, and of **M**, some of whose readings had appeared recently in the edition of Bach. He also had access to **s**, and had received from the English librarian Panizzi a collation of **b**, whose existence is revealed for the first time. According to his critics,[1] Gerlach used his material with extraordinary negligence. To cite one of the more startling examples of his *bévues*, we may note that he assigns **m** to the tenth century, attributing this opinion to Massmann, who, however, indignantly denies the imputation.

Epoch of the Perizonianus

Tross, 1841

The appearance of Ludwig Tross' edition in 1841 marks a new development in the textual history of the *Germania*. Tross had learned from friends in Leyden of the existence of the so-called Perizonianus (**L**), hitherto unknown, and upon examination readily convinced himself that this manuscript far outstripped all others in authority. Accordingly, he edited his text on the basis of **L** alone, departing from its readings only when absolutely necessary. In view of the uncertain foundation upon which the text of the *Germania* rested at that time, and in view of the faultiness and inadequacy of such critical apparatus as existed, it is not surprising that Tross was misled into regarding the interpolations of Pontanus and other Italian humanists which this manuscript contains as offering the genuine tradition, and in accepting at its face value Pontanus' note regarding Enoch of Ascoli as the discoverer of the ultimate archetype of all manuscripts[2]—an archetype of which nothing had been known heretofore.

Even though Tross' enthusiasm for his own discovery may be pardoned, there is less excuse for the absurdity voiced by

---

[1] Massmann, 1841, 690; 1847, 5, note 1; Tagmann, 9, and 12 f., notes 17–18; Mf. 91.

[2] See pp. 351 ff.

H. F. Massmann in his review of Tross' edition published in the same year (1841), for Massmann already had at his disposal most of the collations gathered for his future edition, and should have had far better insight into the relationship of the manuscripts than he showed. In this review Massmann seems even more enthusiastic than Tross, declaring the Perizonianus to be the archetype of all other manuscripts! However, he did do a real service to future investigators when he sought out the correspondence of Poggio which throws light on the Hersfeld codex. While his conclusions from the correspondence were in the main wrong, he at least made a step in the right direction.

Massmann, 1847   In 1847 appeared the edition of Massmann, the result of many years of preparation. In his introduction he lists twenty manuscripts of the *Germania*, for most of which he had complete collations, and some thirty early printed editions (through Lipsius, 1574), with most of which he seems to have had a first-hand acquaintance. In his Italian journey of 1833 he had collated or transcribed the manuscripts A, I, l, N, o, V, v, u, and likewise had his own collations of m, of Mon. 947, and of L. For Δ, M, f, s, he had new collations secured from friends. For only five manuscripts was he forced to depend upon collations which had been used previously: for b, that of Panizzi made for Gerlach; for a, which he thought to be lost, the collation of Voss published by Gronovius; for h, the three collations upon which we are still forced to depend; for the lost Bambergensis the readings cited by Lipsius; for t, the collation published by Orelli.

In a way, Massmann's edition has never been superseded, since for many manuscripts it remains either the sole published source from which the readings may be gleaned, or at any rate the sole convenient one. While his collations are certainly not flawless, they hardly merit the criticism offered by Mf. (91). However, little can be said for his disposition of his material, since he makes no attempt at all to group his manuscripts, employs clumsy sigla, and has filled his critical apparatus with a mass of worthless readings, which should have been relegated to an appendix—if worth printing at all. In his edition Massmann has abandoned his former opinion that L was the archetype of all other manuscripts, but advances another opinion equally grotesque. Although he still recognizes the superiority of L, he makes the astounding statement that almost all the manuscripts, and the earliest printed editions as well, are immediate copies of the common archetype (194).

Almost simultaneously with Massmann's edition appeared R. Tagmann's *De Taciti Germaniae Apparatu Critico* (1847), a work based upon a more insecure foundation, but showing greater insight than that of Massmann. Tagmann cites the same manuscripts as Massmann, with the exception that he repeats Gerlach's error of regarding ∆ and u as the same manuscript. For f, s, and t, he had collations which seem not to have been used in earlier publications, and he was able to use Massmann's collation of L. But for the other manuscripts he was forced to depend upon the readings published by his predecessors, which in the case of the Italian manuscripts and m means the inaccurate excerpts from Massmann's collations published by Gerlach.

Tagmann's is the first serious attempt to bring all known manuscripts into groups and families. He divides the manuscripts into seven *familiae* as follows: (1) s h; (2) N I; (3) Mon. 947 and v; (4) V L; (5) m l A u b; (6) a and Bambergensis; (7) M t f. These seven *familiae* he divides into two *classes: classis I* = *familiae* 1–4; *classis II* = *familiae* 5–7. Among the *familiae* he finds a special affinity between 1 and 2 and between 3 and 4. *Classis II* is derived from *classis I*, and consequently may be disregarded. Although his seven *familiae*, save for the position he assigns to s, h, and m, do offer a sort of beginning of the proper classification of our manuscripts, the real advance made by Tagmann lies in the fact that he removed the extant manuscripts further from the archetype than any before him had done. Not only does he deny that L is the archetype of all other manuscripts, but he also maintains that it was not a direct copy of "Enoch's exemplar." Though he seems nowhere to make a definite statement as to the proper basis for constituting the text of the *Germania*, the obvious conclusion is that *familiae 1-4* should serve as the foundation of the text, but that neither any single manuscript nor a single *familia* can be given preference. In other words, his classification implies the basic principle upon which any attempt to establish the text of the *Germania* must rest: the restoration of the common archetype from *all* the independent lines of tradition.

The following year (1848) K. Nipperdey in his review of Tagmann's work offered a substitute grouping of the manuscripts, which carried with it the doubtful recommendation of greater simplicity. He readily agreed with Tagmann that the *familiae 5-7* might be discarded. He goes further and throws out of the running Mon. 947 on the ground that it offers nothing not found in v, which is in the main true enough; and likewise discards h, for the reason that it has nothing to offer over s—an idea so utterly absurd as to make us wonder how it could ever have been conceived. Having thus disposed of more than half of the manuscripts known to him, Nipperdey then finds that L and V are direct apographs of Enoch's manuscript, and that the remainder (**N I v**) are descendants of a third lost apograph of the parent manuscript. However, the manuscripts of the third group show readings borrowed from L and V, while L and V in their marginal and interlinear readings show contamination from the third group. Such a theory of an interchange of readings among the various lines of tradition may well be the joy of the editor who wishes to display his own powers of divination, but hardly of one who seriously hopes to restore the text of the archetype.

The theory of a leading manuscript, to serve as a prop in all cases of doubt, as voiced by Tross and Massmann, was too convenient a labor-saving device to be discarded immediately. The supremacy of L is accepted as an established fact in the edition of Orelli-Baiter (1848), and again by Haase (1855), through the latter doubts if all manuscripts descend from

Enoch's exemplar (p. lx). Ritter in 1848 modifies Massmann's original opinion regarding L as the parent manuscript only to the extent of excluding V from its many-hued offspring, and in his later edition (1864) he has learned no better. Halm in his first and second editions (1850–51, 1857) regards L as the leading authority, using only the sigla *P* (= L) and *alii codd.* in his critical apparatus. Moriz Haupt in 1855, presumably influenced by the classification of Nipperdey, admitted to his critical apparatus V and I as well as L, but regards the Leidensis as superior to the other two, as does Kritz in 1860.

Reifferscheid and Müllenhoff

The great impulse which sent L toppling from its throne was given by A. Reifferscheid. In his *Quaestiones Suetonianae* (1860) he showed that for the *de Grammaticis et Rhetoribus* V and L were not direct copies of the archetype common to all manuscripts, but of an intervening manuscript, and that of the two V was by far the more trustworthy. Four other manuscripts,[1] O N G I,[2] he deemed worthy of his notice, but despaired of restoring from these a single apograph of the basic archetype—and well he might! At the same time he created the phantom of the "apographum Henochianum," which was not entirely lulled to rest until the discovery of Decembrio's note[3] in 1901 and of the Aesinas in the following year. According to this theory, it was not the old manuscript which Enoch brought back from Germany, but only a copy made by him or at his direction. In Reifferscheid's opinion, the numerous double readings found in our manuscripts had their origin in the fact that here and there Enoch was uncertain about the text of the old exemplar, which was partly illegible through age.

In his *Coniectanea in Taciti Germaniam,* published in 1867,

---

[1] There are in all nineteen MSS. of the *de Grammaticis*, though, to be sure, not all had been discovered in Reifferscheid's time.

[2] O = Ottobonianus 1455; G = Gudianus 93; neither containing the *Germania*.

[3] See pp. 8 ff.

Reifferscheid definitely extended to the *Germania*[1] his views regarding the manuscript tradition of the *de Grammaticis*. He posits a close copy of the "apographum Henochianum" from which were transcribed the manuscripts **V** and **L**. Of these two he believes that **V** must be granted the very highest authority, whereas **L** offers the arbitrary interpolations of Pontanus and also the interpolations of a later corrector. As for the other manuscripts, he finds them even more interpolated than **L**, but thinks that out of their number **N** and **I** are to be employed with caution *for correcting the readings*[2] of **V**. These views are unquestionably preferable to the one which gave the supremacy to **L**, for if the editor's faith is to be pinned to any single manuscript it had better be to a relatively good one like **V** than to an interpolated one such as **L**.

Müllenhoff's *Germania Antiqua*, appearing in 1873, though it contains no discussion of the manuscript relationship, evidently follows along the lines laid down by Reifferscheid, since he bases his text on the manuscripts **VLNI**, but in his choice of readings he probably renounced **V** in favor of **NI** more often than Reifferscheid would have sanctioned. Müllenhoff had new collations of the four manuscripts which he used, and his text quite rightly assumed the importance of the standard critical edition. These same manuscript *subsidia* are accepted by Schweizer-Sidler in the second edition of Orelli-Baiter (1877), and by J. Müller in 1887. Halm in his third edition (1874) fell into line at least to the extent of giving **V** a place beside **L** and casting from his text certain readings peculiar to the latter, while to his fourth edition (1883), which vied with Müllenhoff's as the standard, he admitted all four manuscripts **VLNI**. In fact, the manuscript basis established by Reifferscheid and Müllenhoff is the one upon which editions of the *Germania* have commonly rested ever since, save that in the present century **E** has been added to the chosen few—an addition of doubtful value.

[1] He had his own collations of **V** and **I** for the *Germania*, and had examined **N** for certain readings.

[2] The italics are mine.

SURVEY OF THE TEXTUAL HISTORY 343

As might be expected, Reifferscheid's classification did not immediately find complete acceptance. K. Meiser in his *Kritische Studien* (1873) still maintained that L was the best of the manuscripts, while Holder in editing Holtzmann's *Germanische Alterthümer* (1873) rested his critical treatment of the text upon VLs. Nipperdey's edition, appearing in 1876 after his death, is in accordance with the grouping of manuscripts which he had made almost thirty years before,[1] and Hirschfelder in the fourth edition of Kritz admitted among his aids s as well as VLNI. Finally, there was the theory of Holder, which, if it had been adequately set forth by its propounder, might very soon have led to the truth.

HOLDER'S THEORY OF A "GERMANIC" TRADITION

Holder, 1878

The edition of A. Holder, which appeared in 1878, represents a highly laudable attempt to break away from all previous notions regarding the relationship of our manuscripts. As for the critical *subsidia* and general principles underlying Holder's recension next to nothing can be learned from the edition itself. It contains no preface whatever, and has only the following modest *conspectus codicum*:[2]

H = codex Hummelianus (= h)
γ = archetypus codicum M et S
    M = codex Chiemensis nunc Monacensis lat. 5307 (= m)
    S = codex Comburgensis nunc Stutgartiensis (= s)
α = consentientes A″ et Perizonianus uel A′ et a
    A″ = A et a inter se congruentes
        A = codex Vaticanus 1862 (= V)
        a = editio Viennensis s. a. (1509)[3]
    A′ = archetypus codicum A et Perizoniani (= λ)

Holder offers a very brief statement[4] of his plan in the

---
[1] See Schöll's preface, vol. IV, iv.
[2] The sigla in parentheses to the right are my own additions, to indicate the correspondence with my apparatus.
[3] Probably the edition which I call *cd. Vind.* (see p. 328), and for which I accept Copinger's dating of 1500.
[4] Holder excuses his brevity on the ground that he intends to publish a special book entitled, *Textgeschichte von Tacitus' Germania*. So far as I know, this work never appeared.

announcement of the Teubner publishing house for the year 1878, pp. 45 f., though his edition contains not a single reference thereto. From this notice one is surprised to learn that the edition rests upon a much broader foundation than it professes. The editor had entirely new collations of thirteen manuscripts of the *Germania,* made either by himself or by friends (**m**, Mon. 947, **s**, **V**, **v**, **A**, **L**, **N**, **a**, **b**, **l**, **t**, **f**), and for the lost **h** he mentions four collations to which he had access.[1] A study of his critical apparatus had convinced Holder that many manuscripts previously esteemed were quite worthless, and that he had found an uninterpolated line of tradition which was purely "German." Accordingly, in his recension he had purged the text of all "ultramontane" (*i.e.* Italian) influence, such as he found in the greatly over-estimated Perizonianus. The archetype common to all manuscripts was, according to Holder, an eighth-century minuscule manuscript in Westgothic (Visigothic) script. Even this information is cryptic, but doubtless we may assume with Holder's critic Wünsch that he had in mind two distinct lines of tradition from the Hersfeld codex, one originating on German soil, of which the chief representative was **h** and the lesser satellites **m** and **s**, and a second line (the "apographum Henochianum"?), to which all other manuscripts belong, and which is disfigured by the interpolations of Italian humanists.

Holder's second edition, which appeared in 1882 as No. 1 of the *Germanischer Bücherschatz* of the Mohr publishing house, not only has no preface but is also devoid of a *conspectus codicum* and a critical apparatus. Yet the text contains many changes, generally in favor of **h** (or rather in favor of Wh or Whm). On the inner page of the cover of No. 5 of the *Germanischer Bücherschatz* (= Iordanes, *De Origine Actibusque Getarum,* ed. A. Holder, 1882) the statement is made that the new edition of the *Germania* rests upon further investigations of the editor involving new manuscript evidence. It is safe to assume that Holder had availed himself of the collation of **W**

[1] Regarding the fourth collation see p. 345, note 4.

published by Hümer in 1878, and had recognized this manuscript as belonging to his "Germanic" line of tradition.

The failure of Holder's theories to find approbation must be attributed in part to his suppression of the underlying evidence. So revolutionary a view unaccompanied by the necessary documentation met with a pardonable scepticism on the part of his reviewers.[1] To be sure, E. Bährens (1880) in his review of the first edition lends partial support. He expresses himself as convinced that h was a direct copy of the Hersfeld codex made by a German, and that all other manuscripts (including m) descend from the "apographum Henochianum." He would not, however, attribute so much authority to h as did Holder, but would make impartial use of both lines of tradition for constituting the text.

Wünsch, 1893

A systematic attempt to demolish Holder's views was made by R. Wünsch in his doctoral dissertation in 1893.[2] In its presentation of the material, Wünsch's work is a model of technique, and it would be deserving only of praise had he not attempted to prove too much. The merit of his work consists in the following points: (1) he effects a restoration of h from the three extant collations;[3] (2) he institutes a comparison of s^2 with h and shows that the former did not draw directly from the latter;[4] (3) he shows that h has no independent value;[5] (4) he

[1] J. Gantrelle, 1879; E. Wölfflin, 1879; A. Eussner, 1882; G. Andresen, 1885.

[2] In the meantime (1886) there had appeared Schefczik's treatise, *De Cornelii Taciti Germaniae Apparatu critico*, which has the merit of supplementing Hümer's collation of W. Schefczik's classification of the MSS. is concisely stated in his own words (the letters preceded by the sign of equality are my additions): "Codices qui extant ad duo apographa e libro Enoc Esculani (I) facta referendi sunt, quorum alterum (X) codicibus Bb (= VL) repraesentatur, alterum (Y) autem ita servatum est, ut in uno eius apographo (G) libri W_2H (= Wh), in altero (y) relicui nitantur." The classification is quite untenable, but is preferable to that of Wünsch (see below), since it leaves a position of some importance for Wh.

[3] His report of Longolius' collation contains numerous errors. See my corrections on pp. 165 f.

[4] Holder had accepted the readings of s^2 as amounting to a fourth collation of h (see Wünsch, 24).

[5] Here the issue is slightly confused, as he not only shows that the peculiar readings of h have no value, but at the same time tries to prove the same for

establishes a common archetype for **Wh**; (5) he compares the readings of **m** and **s**, and proves that the two cannot be referred to a common archetype; (6) he discounts the theory of a "Germanic" tradition—a theory which Holder himself could scarcely have maintained after the discovery of **W**, which declares itself to have been written in Rome in 1466.

Had Wünsch ceased in his process of demolition at this point, he might have discovered the truth. The really essential part of Holder's classification yet remains, viz. the division of the manuscripts into two lines of tradition from the Hersfeld codex, one represented by **Wmhs**², and the other, more interpolated, line represented by all other manuscripts, *i.e.* the **X** and **Y** families which I claim to have established. Whether or not one of these lines of tradition is German is not a matter of importance—save for the gratification of a national pride.

Apparently it did not occur to Wünsch to rebuild Holder's fabric, but only to raze it to the ground, and therein he wandered into a maze of error. A feature of Holder's classification was the relationship between **h** and **ms**. Now Wünsch successfully divorced **s** from **m**, but took no account of the perfectly obvious relationship between **m** and **Wh**. In fact, he leaves **m** hanging in the air, placing it among the *codices mixti*—ever a convenient term. Although he established an archetype for **Wh**, he was quite unwilling to attribute any importance to this archetype, and was accordingly forced to find for it an inferior position in his stemma, concluding that it had in some way descended from the archetype of **NI** but at the same time showed contamination from **VL**. In the light of all the manuscript evidence, Wünsch's arguments on this point are thoroughly untenable. In other words, Wünsch brought the textual criticism of the *Germania* back to the point which it had reached with Müllenhoff's edition: two apographs of Hf., **X** = **VL**, and **Y** = ω, with **NI** as the leading representatives of the latter family. But Wünsch appears to have expounded

---

some of the readings of **Wh** or **Whm** (pp. 37–43). In the latter attempt he is for the most part unsuccessful.

his views persuasively, since, save for a warning from Rand [1] that **h** may have its value, and a word from Ihm [2] spoken in favor of **W**, the manuscripts of Holder's "Germanic" tradition have rested in oblivion.

The Present Century

The close of the nineteenth and beginning of the twentieth century were marked by considerable activity in bringing to the attention of *Germania* scholars manuscripts hitherto unknown, in the publication of more accurate collations of other manuscripts, and in further attempts at classification. In 1897 Wünsch published a collation of **p**, formerly unknown, whose close relationship with **M** he recognized, and new collations of the fragment **o**, and of luA through chapter 5, but again resorts to his old and convenient theory of "mixed manuscripts."

In the following year (1898) R. Reitzenstein published a collation of **r** through ch. 13 with other selected readings, whose close relationship to **vo** he demonstrates. He creates **a** (= vro) as a third apograph of Hf. to enter the lists with Wünsch's **X** and **Y**.

Müllenhoff's classification
The fourth volume of Müllenhoff's *Deutsche Altertumskunde* did not appear until 1900, some sixteen years after its author's death. On pages 63–87 (ed. 2) of this work is found a more comprehensive discussion of the relationship of the *Germania* manuscripts than had ever before been offered, though in its essence it is further removed from the facts than Holder's rough and ready classification.

This discussion of Müllenhoff appears to be the result of investigations carried beyond the point he had reached when he published his *Germania Antiqua*, though his studies can hardly

---

[1] E. K. Rand 1905, 325.

[2] M. Ihm, "Zur Überlieferung und Textkritik von Suetons Schrift de Grammaticis et Rhetoribus," *Rheinisches Museum* LXI (1906), shows the importance of **W** for the *de Grammaticis*. Following in his lead, I have attempted to place the text of this work upon a firmer manuscript foundation (Robinson 1922 and 1925). Ihm 1907, 1148, states that in a complete apparatus of the *Germania* **W** cannot be omitted.

have extended through the year 1878, since the author makes no mention of **W**, which was discovered in that year, or of Holders' views.[1]

Reduced to the bare essentials, Mf.'s classification of the *Germania* manuscripts is as follows. He divides them into four classes:[2] (1) Class **B** = **VL**, (2) Class **C** = **NΔI**, (3) Class **D** = **hss**^{2}, (4) Class **E** = **vko** and the Gensberg edition.[3] Classes **B** and **E** descend from two separate apographs of the basic archetype (= Hf.), while **C** and **D** together are to be referred to a third apograph. Apograph **B** had the fewest errors of the three, but apograph **CD** recorded the double readings of the basic exemplar more completely than did the other two. As a basis for establishing the text Mf. would take Class **B** (and V in preference to L), but in general would reject the readings of this class when contradicted by the combined testimony of **CD** (taken as a unit) and of **E**. The other manuscripts, which he divides into two groups, **y** and **z** (= ϕ and ξ respectively of my apparatus), belong to the Class **CD**, **z** showing greater affinity with **C**, and **y** with **D**. Müllenhoff in his attempt to establish Class **E** had of course anticipated Reitzenstein, for the former's **E** is the same as the latter's a (= τ of my apparatus).

This classification represents a distinct advance over that implied by the apparatus of Mf.'s *Germania Antiqua*, in that it demands the use of a larger number of manuscripts for the establishment of the text, brings into consideration **Δ**, of which he had a new collation, and is a move away from the supremacy of **VL**. Yet it is the author's unintentional adherence to **VL** which is responsible for two of the outstanding mistakes of his classification. In the first place, he assumes that the agreement of Class **E** with Class **B** in opposition to **CD** restores the basic archetype (= Hf.), instead of realizing that such an agreement refers both **B** and **E** to a single descendant (= β of

[1] Mf. mentions Holder's edition only in passing (94).

[2] The letters denoting the classes are Mf.'s own, but as usual those indicating MSS. are the ones of my apparatus.

[3] He strangely leaves **m** out of consideration.

my classification) of the basic manuscript. Conversely, this same adherence to Class **B** is responsible for the impossible grouping of **C** and **D** as descendants of a single apograph of the basic manuscript, for he fails to see that the agreement of **C** and **D** in opposition to **BE** offers the genuine tradition.

In 1903 appeared F. F. Abbott's collation of the Toletanus (T), a manuscript which had remained generally unknown,[1] until attention was called to it by Wünsch (1897, 59, note 1). Following the lines laid down by Mf., Abbott readily assigned **T** to the former's Class **E**, but because of the relationship which this class seemed to show with the manuscript **V** he was uncertain whether or not it represented a distinct line of descent from Hf.

In 1905 E. K. Rand published a collation of the Harvard manuscript (e), which had previously been known only through vague references to a codex Middlehillensis. Taking e as representative of its group (= ϕ of my apparatus), he shows that this group is independent of Müllenhoff's Class **B** (= VL) and Class **E** (= τ), and that it has a distinct importance for the text of the *Germania*. He finds that the ϕ group is most closely related to **NI** (= Mf.'s Class C in part), and assigns it provisionally to this class, but displays admirable caution, leaving the path open to future investigators.

The Aesinas C. Annibaldi's eagerly awaited account of the codex Aesinas (E), the fortunate discovery of which in 1902 had effectually put to rout the ghost of the "apographum Henochianum," appeared in 1907.[2] Annibaldi's quite pardonable enthusiasm for his important discovery carried him too far in his claims for the *Germania* part of the manuscript, which he declared to be a direct copy of the Hersfeld codex.[3] This claim was at once questioned by his German reviewers,[4] and was definitely

[1] It is, however, listed by G. Hänel, *Catalogi Librorum Manuscriptorum* . . . (Leipzig, 1830), 993.

[2] This work, which contains merely a collation of the *Germania*, was followed by a diplomatic text in 1910.

[3] He reiterates this opinion in his later work, 1910.

[4] Andresen, Ihm, Wissowa, Wünsch, all in 1907.

disproved by A. Schönemann in his doctoral dissertation in 1910.

Schönemann proves that **E**, with its copy **T**, belongs to the same group as **vrko** and the Gensberg edition, and refers them all to a common archetype **Z**, which is of course the same as Reitzenstein's **α** and Müllenhoff's Class **E**, and, like his predecessors, he makes the error of regarding **Z** as a copy of Hf., instead of seeing that this together with his **X** family (= VL of my apparatus) should be referred to a single fifteenth-century manuscript (= β). As representative of his third apograph of Hf., which he calls **Y**, he admits only the manuscripts **NI**.

So far as I can determine, Schönemann's stemma is the one which is commonly accepted today—a stemma which deliberately ignores some two-thirds of the manuscripts of the *Germania!*[1] For example, Andresen's revision of Halm's text,[2] appearing in 1914, contains the following simple *conspectus codicum:* "*B* = codex Vaticanus 1862, *b* = Leidensis Perizonianus, utriusque consensus = *X*. *C* = Vaticanus 1518, *c* = Neapolitanus IVc.21, utriusque consensus = *Y*. *E* = cod. Aesinus lat. 8." Since Andresen does not accept Annibaldi's view that **E** is a direct copy of Hf.,[3] it must be assumed that he regards this manuscript as the leading representative of the Schönemann's **Z** family. Most of the succeeding editions too, I judge, rest upon the same foundation (E. Wolff, 1915, Gudeman, 1916 and 1928, Schweizer-Sidler, 1923, Reeb, 1930), though Annibaldi in his edition (undated) bases his text chiefly upon **E**, and Valmaggi (1924) regards **E** as a direct copy of Hf., but constitutes his text from the three "families."

[1] In fairness to Schönemann it should be stated that his primary purpose was to establish the **Z** family, and that in his **X** and **Y** families he merely accepted the findings of Reifferscheid, Müllenhoff, and Wünsch.

[2] The edition is based upon the editor's own collations of **VLNI** and of Annibaldi's diplomatic text of **E**.

[3] Cf. Andresen 1910, 1316.

II
ENOCH OF ASCOLI AND THE HERSFELD CODEX

In my work on the manuscript tradition of the *de Grammaticis et Rhetoribus*[1] I set forth what appeared to me cogent reasons for discrediting the usually accepted opinion that the Hersfeld codex was brought to Rome in 1455 by Enoch of Ascoli. I note, however, that some recent editions of the *Germania* still ascribe the discovery to Enoch as though this were an established fact. Since I have found no reason for withdrawing from my position, and since my earlier work may not be readily available to all, I now repeat my discussion with certain changes, which will, I trust, place my arguments in a more convincing light.

The current belief[2] that Enoch of Ascoli brought our archetype from Hersfeld to Rome in 1455 rests chiefly upon two notes of the humanist, Iovianus Pontanus, found in the Leyden manuscript (L) of the *Dialogus, Germania*, and *de Grammaticis et Rhetoribus*.[3] On the verso of the first leaf we read: "Hos libellos Iouianus Pontanus excripsit nuper adinuentos et in lucem relatos ab Enoc Asculano quamquam satis mendosos .M.CCCC.LX martio mense." Again in the margin of f. 47ᵛ, at the beginning of the *de Grammaticis* is found the longer note: "C. Suetonius scripsit de uiris illustribus, cuius exemplum secutus Hieronymus ipse quoque libellum de scriptoribus Christianis edidit. Nuper etiam Bartholomeus Facius familiaris noster de uiris illustribus temporis sui libros composuit. Qui ne hos Suetonii illustres uiros uidere posset mors immatura effecit. Paulo enim post eius mortem in lucem

---

[1] Robinson 1922, 19–24.

[2] Doubt regarding Enoch as the discoverer of the Hersfeld codex was voiced by G. Voigt, *Die Wiederbelebung des classischen Alterthums*³ (Berlin, 1893), I, 255, note 3, II, 202, note 1, and by R. Wünsch 1897, 57 f., though the latter afterwards declared in favor of the prevailing view (1907, 1028).

[3] See p. 84.

redierunt cum multos annos desiderati a doctis hominibus essent. Temporibus enim Nicolai quinti pontificis maximi Enoc Asculanus in Galliam et inde in Germaniam profectus conquirendorum librorum gratia, hos quamquam mendosos et imperfectos ad nos retulit. Cui sic habenda gratia [1] ut male imprecandum est Sicconio Polentano Patauino, qui cum eam partem quae est [2] de oratoribus ac poetis adinuenisset,[3] ita suppressit ut ne unquam in lucem uenire posset. Quam ego cum Patauii perquirerem, tandem reperi eam ab illo fuisse combustam; ipsumque arrogantia ac temeritate impulsum de uitis illustrium scriptorum loquacissime pariter et ineptissime scripsisse. IOV. PONTANVS. VMBER excripsit."

Pontanus' statement that the *Dialogus*, *Germania*, and *de Grammaticis* were brought to Italy by Enoch is discredited, if not actually refuted, by the information regarding Enoch's finds which has been gathered from other sources. Yet if the statement is erroneous, at least it seems probable that there was some basis underlying the error. I hope to show that such a basis may be found in the inventory of his manuscripts which Enoch published.

In the year 1451 Enoch of Ascoli was sent by Pope Nicholas V into the northern countries for the purpose of acquiring Greek and Latin manuscripts.[4] He returned to Rome in the autumn of 1455, only to find that his patron Nicholas V had died in the preceding March. The earliest intimation that we have of the return of Enoch and of his finds is contained in a letter of Panormita written from Naples to Giovanni Aurispa toward the end of 1455:[5] ". . . Veniens uero fac tecum deferas Apicium coquinarium et Caesaris Iter, ut refert

---

[1] The original reading seems to have been *habendae sunt gratiae*, which was changed by a later hand to *habenda est gratia*, and finally to *habenda gratia*.

[2] The words *eam . . . est* have been added above the line, but by the original copyist.

[3] Apparently *est inuenisset* corrected to *adinuenisset*.

[4] See G. Voigt, *Wiederbelebung* II, 199 ff., Sabbadini, *Storia e crit.* 276 ff., and the sources there quoted.

[5] Published by Sabbadini, *Stor. e crit.* 283. Regarding the dating of this letter and of the two mentioned immediately below, see Sabbadini, 287, and Rossi, *op. infra cit.* 138, note 4.

Theodorus[1] tuus, nunc iam meus, inuentos Romamque perductos . . ."

Aurispa's reply to Panormita, written on December 13, 1455, offers further details regarding Enoch's discoveries:[2] "Apitium pauperem coquinarium quem petis uidi et legi; dictiones habet aliquas quae tibi forte placebunt . . . Caesaris Iter prosa oratione est, non uersu. Porphirionem quendam in Oratium hic idem, qui Apitium ad nos perduxit, attulit, qui mihi magis aestimandus uidetur quam quicquam aliud ab ipso adlatum. Sed eum qui codices hos inuenit et Romam perduxit ad uos mittam cum omnibus musis suis. Putat enim si hos libellos regi donauerit aliquid praemii ab isto principe se habiturum, ad quod ego maxime illum exhortatus sum. Vale. Romae idibus decembris."

After the lapse of a year and a half Enoch was still seeking a purchaser for his books, and had not abandoned hope of interesting Alphonso of Aragon, as we learn from a letter of Aurispa to Panormita, written August 28, 1457:[3] ". . . Hisce diebus fuit hic Enochus. Quum eum rogarem ut eorum codicum quos e longinquis partibus attulit mihi copiam faceret, et praecipue Porphirionem super operibus Oratii petebam, respondit se uelle omnia prius Alphonso regi tradere; cui opinioni ego hominem maxime sum exhortatus . . ."

Further light is thrown on the character of the discoveries of Enoch by letters of Carlo de' Medici, spurious son of Cosimo, to his brother Giovanni.[4] In a letter written on March 13, 1456, Carlo states that Enoch had made some new finds, but that they were valuable for their novelty rather than for their utility.[5] Enoch was unwilling to allow anyone to make copies

[1] Teodoro Gaza, who had just moved to the court of Alphonso in Naples.
[2] Published by Sabbadini, *Stor. e crit.* 284 f.
[3] Sabbadini, *Storia e crit.* 285–287.
[4] Vittorio Rossi, "L'indole e gli studi di Giovanni di Cosimo de' Medici," *Rendiconti della Reale Accademia dei Lincei*, Classe di scienze morali, storiche, e filologiche, Serie v, Vol. ii (1893), 38–60, 129–150.
[5] ". . . Egli è vero che m. Enocche ha portato qui certe cose nuove, come vedrete per questo inventario vi mando ed invero da farne più stima per la novità che per la utilità . . ." Rossi, *op. cit.* 131.

of his treasures unless he were rewarded for his toils to the extent of two or three hundred florins by some great patron of letters. Carlo feels that so far as most of Enoch's discoveries are concerned the Latin language would be much better off without them, and states that in the opinion of many learned men who had seen his manuscripts they were, with but four exceptions, utterly worthless![1] The contents of the four which escaped so sweeping a condemnation we learn from another letter of Carlo written to Giovanni on December 10, 1457: "Appicius, *de re quoquinaria*, Profirione *sopra Oratio*, Suetonio *de uiris illustribus, Itinerarium Augusti* (i.e. *Antonini*)."[2] Three of these works are mentioned in the letter of Aurispa quoted above.

Now aside from the two notes of Pontanus which I have previously quoted, I know of no mention in contemporary sources of Enoch's name in connection with the minor works of Tacitus. Since Enoch was very anxious to sell his books for a good round sum, it is most improbable that he would have omitted the Tacitean works from his inventory, if he had really found them. But if he did find them and did list them in his inventory, how can the failure of his contemporaries to mention them be explained? Are we to suppose that the scholars of that time regarded them as less important than Apicius, Porphyrio, *Suetonius, de Viris Illustribus* (whatever this work may have been), and the *Itinerarium Antonini?* Are we to go even further, and suppose that Carlo de' Medici thought the minor works of Tacitus a disgrace to the Latin language? Surely in that case there must have been a sad decline in literary taste during the thirty years which had elapsed since Poggio's eager quest!

[1] "... sì che vedete se volete gettare via tanti danari per cose, che la lingua latina può molto bene fare senza esse, che a dirvi l'oppenione di molti dotti uomini, che gli ànno visti, da questi quattro infuori che sono segnati con questo segno ỹ, tutto il resto non vale una frulla; nè anco questi non sono le sette deche di Livio che mancano . . ." *Ibid.*

[2] Rossi, pp. 134 f. From this same letter we learn that Enoch had died at his home in Ascoli, and that Carlo was negotiating with Stefano de Nardini regarding the purchase, or at least the privilege of copy, of the four works which he wanted.

To be sure, we do know from Carlo de' Medici's account that Enoch brought back a *Suetonius, de Viris Illustribus*. This work is generally regarded as identical with *de Grammaticis et Rhetoribus* of the Hersfeld codex, and it is supposed that herein we have a confirmation of Pontanus' statement concerning Enoch. In my opinion this does not offer such confirmation, but rather provides the kernel of truth around which Pontanus built his fiction. Enoch hoped to find a purchaser in Alphonso, and must have sent a copy of his inventory to the court of Naples, where Pontanus was at that time living. Pontanus, as is shown by his note, knew from a passage in St. Jerome that Suetonius had written a *de Viris Illustribus*, and not unnaturally assumed that this was the work listed in Enoch's inventory. Later, finding a manuscript containing the *de Grammaticis et Rhetoribus* (a mere fragment of the larger *de Viris Illustribus*), he erroneously associated this with the find of Enoch, and quite arbitrarily assumed that the *Dialogus* and *Germania*, which were in the same codex, were also Enoch's discovery.[1] It is significant that the Leyden manuscript, which was either written by Pontanus himself, or is a copy of a manuscript written by him, is the only manuscript of the *de Grammaticis* which offers the title *de Viris Illustribus*. To account for the disappearance of the rest of the *de Viris Illustribus*, Pontanus tells the curious story of its having been burned by Sicco Polenton. Not a shred of evidence has been found to substantiate this tale, and it is, I believe, universally discredited.[2] But if we refuse credence to one part of Pontanus' note, why adhere blindly to the other part?

What are we to think regarding the *Suetonius, de Viris*

---

[1] Note that the Leyden codex does not contain the *Agricola*, and that Pontanus' notes reveal no knowledge of this work.

[2] Polenton could scarcely have had any reason for so atrocious an act, unless it were to conceal what he had pirated from Suetonius in the composition of his own *de Scriptoribus Illustribus*. However, Polenton's work is said to reveal no knowledge of the *de Viris Illustribus*. Cf. F. Ritschl, *Parergon Plautinorum Terentianorumque* I (Berlin, 1845), 628–636; *Sicconis Polentoni Scriptorum Illustrium Latinae Linguae Libri xviii*, ed. B. L. Ullman (= Papers and Monographs of the American Academy in Rome VI, 1928), Introd. xiii.

Illustribus, of Enoch's inventory? Save for my conviction that it was something entirely distinct from the Hersfeld manuscript of the *de Grammaticis*, I cannot say. If Enoch really possessed a manuscript of this important work, all traces have been lost, but the slight impression which the discovery made upon Aurispa and Carlo de' Medici leads me to believe that the name conceals some relatively unimportant work falsely assigned to Suetonius—perhaps the *de Viris Illustribus* of the pseudo-Aurelius Victor.[1]

I grant that there is a striking coincidence in the fact that Decembrio saw the Hersfeld codex in 1455, which was the very year of Enoch's return to Rome, but why should this be more than a coincidence? Decembrio does not say that the manuscript first became known in that year, but that it was *seen* (by himself, no doubt). Naturally, in the light of available evidence it is impossible to prove that Enoch of Ascoli did *not* bring the Hersfeld codex to Rome, but, in my opinion, the probabilities are against the supposition that he did.

[1] This work is ascribed to Suetonius in a MS. of the library of the Duke of Marlborough at Blenheim Park: H. Schenkl, *Bibliotheca Patrum Latinorum Britannica*, No. 4960 (= Wiener Sitzungsberichte, philos.-hist. Kl. CL [1905], v Abh., p. 76). According to C. Roth, *C. Suetoni Tranquilli quae supersunt omnia* (Leipzig, 1858), ciii, the work is also ascribed to Suetonius by Angelus Sabinus in his *Paradoxa in Iuuenalem* (Rome, 1474), and was edited numerous times under the name of Suetonius in the late fifteenth and early sixteenth centuries.

III

ABBREVIATIONS AND LIGATURES IN THE HERSFELD *AGRICOLA* (CODEX AESINAS, FF. 56–63ᵛ, 76ᵛ)

-bus: *b.* (final) is employed about thirty times.

-en: m̄ for *-men:* 60, 2, 12 (ch. 29) *lamenta;* 61, 2, 25 (ch. 32) *incitamenta;* 62, 2, 4 (ch. 34) *dementium;* 63ᵛ, 2, 5 (ch. 39) *nomen;* 20 (ch. 40) *ornamenta;* 76ᵛ, 1, 18 (ch. 45) *tamen.*

-er: t̄ for *-ter:* 60, 2, 13 (ch. 29) *muliebriter;* 62, 1, 21 (ch. 34) *interrogate;* 62ᵛ, 2, 23 (ch. 36) *exterriti;* 63, 1, 16 (ch. 37) *cateruae.*

esse: ēe 56ᵛ, 2, 9 (ch. 15); 58, 1, 16 (ch. 19); 60ᵛ, 2, 27 (ch. 31); 61, 2, 8 (ch. 32); 62, 1, 12 (ch. 33).

esset: ē& 58ᵛ, 1, 21 (ch. 21).

est: ē 62ᵛ, 1, 26 (ch. 36); 76ᵛ, 1, 16 (ch. 45).

-is: nob̄ 62, 1, 6 (ch. 33).

-it: *transuex̄* 57ᵛ, 2, 4 (ch. 17).

-m: There are more than 140 examples of the waved or horizontal line above the vowel to denote the suspension of *m.* This usage is almost always limited to the position at the end of the word, but not to the position at the end of the line. Within the word, besides some five or six instances of the suspension of *m* before *-que,* I have noted: 56, 1, 6 *quã/quam;* 59ᵛ, 2, 24 *prõpti;* 60, 2, 27 *doctico͂ mune;* 60ᵛ, 2, 18 *ābitiosi;* 63, 2, 28 *tãquã;* 63, 1, 25 *circũ/ueniebant;* 76ᵛ, 1, 12 *cõplexuque;* 24 *contẽplatione.*

-n: The suspension of *n* is very rare, being found only in *non* and the prefix *con:* 56ᵛ, 1, 10 *cõtumelias;* 62, 1, 29 *cõtra;* 76ᵛ, 1, 7 *cõstans;* 12 *nõ cõtigit;* 21 *nõ.*[1]

---

[1] Observe that four of the six examples occur on the palimpsest page, where the writing is crowded, and which is said to be the work of a scribe different from that of ff. 56–63.

noster: $\overline{nri}$ 58ᵛ, 1, 15. 59, 1, 25; $\overline{nrorum}$ 62ᵛ, 2, 29; $\overline{nris}$ 60ᵛ, 1, 28.

per: $\bar{p}$ is found over twenty times both for the preposition and the prefix.

prae: $\bar{p}$ is found in the text only on 76ᵛ, 1, 8 $\bar{p}ter$. In the margin, 56, 1, 14 $\bar{p}ceptū$; 60, 1, 21 $\bar{p}bebantur$; 63, 1, 18 $\bar{p}bere$; 63ᵛ, 2, 15 $\bar{p}sens$.[1]

pro: ⟨p⟩ is used twice for the preposition (56ᵛ, 1, 17; 76ᵛ, 1, 6) and four times in compounds (60, 2, 28; 60ᵛ, 2, 27; 62, 1, 12; 63, 1, 16).

quae: 58, 1, 22 (ch. 19) $circumcisisq̄$.

quam: $q̄$ (?) reported in $tanq̄$ 76ᵛ, 1, 7.

-que: q. is found about 130 times.

quod: qd 56ᵛ, 2, 22 (ch. 16).

respublica: $reip̄$ 62, 2, 13; $remp̄$ 56, 1, 11.

romanus: $populi \cdot r \cdot$ 56, 2, 8.

sunt: $\bar{s}$ 62, 2, 6 (ch. 34).

uel: ul with horizontal stroke through the l, 58, 2, 7.

uester: $u\overline{rm}$ 60ᵛ, 1, 15 (ch. 30); $u\overline{ra}$ 62, 1, 20 (ch. 34); $ur\bar{o}s$ 62, 1, 21.

-ur: Indicated by t^2 in the ending *-tur:* 57, 2, 13 (ch. 17) *perhibetur;* 63ᵛ, 1, 30 (ch. 39) *formarentur;* 61ᵛ, 2, 1 (ch. 33) *instituebatur* in mg.

-us: Final *-us* indicated by the apostrophe: *man'* 56ᵛ, 1, 8; *figerem'* 76ᵛ, 1, 13.

æ, ę: æ occurs some five times. The *e-caudata* is rare: I have noted but nine instances.

&: This ligature is frequent both for the conjunction and the verbal ending. I have noted it within the word, 58ᵛ, 1, 1 *qui&ti;* in *quin&iam* 59ᵛ, 2, 10.

ᴎ: There are fifteen instances of this ligature, always in a verbal ending.

ꝯ: This ligature is found for final *-us:* *indecorus* 57, 1, 1; *edoctus* 59ᵛ, 2, 1; *conuinnarius* 62ᵛ, 1, 5; *cohortatus* 62ᵛ, 1, 25; *prius* 63, 2, 6; *anxius* 63ᵛ, 1, 25.

---

[1] Cf. p. 22.

BIBLIOGRAPHY

An asterisk is prefixed to the titles of works with which I do not have a first-hand acquaintance.

Abbreviations

A.C.S.	Holder, Alfred. Alt-celtischer Sprachschatz. Leipzig, 1896—.
A.P.V.	Schönfeld, M. Wörterbuch der altgermanischen Personen- und Völkernamen. Heidelberg, 1911.
C.I.G.	Corpus inscriptionum graecarum. . . . edidit Augustus Boeckhius. Berolini, 1828–1877.
C.I.L.	Corpus inscriptionum latinarum. Berolini, 1862—.
D.A.	Müllenhoff, Deutsche Altertumskunde. *See below.*
G & G	Gerber, A., & Greef, A. Lexicon Taciteum. Lipsiae, 1903.
Hf.	The Hersfeld codex. *See pp. 1–14.*
Mf.	Müllenhoff, Karl. *See below.*
M.G.	Monumenta Germaniae historica. **A.A.** Auctores antiquissimi: Berolini, 1877–1919. **SS.** Scriptores. Hanoverae et Lipsiae, 1826—.
P.-W.	Pauly-Wissowa-Kroll. Real-encyclopädie der classischen Altertumswissenschaft. Neue Bearbeitung. Stuttgart, 1894—.
Thesaurus	Thesaurus linguae latinae. Lipsiae, 1900—.

Abbott, Frank Frost. The Toledo manuscript of the Germania of Tacitus, with notes on a Pliny manuscript. *In* The University of Chicago Decennial Publications VI (1903), 217–258.

Acidalius, Valens. Valentis Acidalii, intercurrentibus & M. Ant. Mureti notae in C. Corn. Taciti opera quae extant. Collecta a Christiano Acidalio fratre. Hanoviae, 1607.

A copy of this work was very generously lent to the library of the University of Cincinnati for my use by the University of Göttingen. The notes of Acidalius are also printed in the variorum *editions of Aubertus and of the Gronovii.*

Alciatus, Andreas. See Tacitus 18.

Aldine edition. Cornelius Tacitus exacta cura recognitus et emendatus . . . M D XXXIIII. *Colophon:* VENETIIS IN AEDIBVS HAEREDVM/ ALDI MANVTII ROMANI,/ ET ANDREAE ASVLA/NI SOCERI,/ M D XXXIIII.

Altenburg, Fr. Wilhelm. C. Cornelii Taciti de situ, moribus et populis Germaniae libellus. Hildburghausen, 1825.

Ammon, Georg. *Review of* Gudeman 3. *In* Berliner philologische Wochenschrift XXXVII (1917), 611–621.

Andresen, Georg. *Citations of* Andresen *given without a date refer to No. 5.*

(1) *Review of Holder's editions of the* Germania. *In* Jahresbericht des philologischen Vereins zu Berlin XI (1885), 370–373.

(2) Zu Tacitus' Germania. *In* Wochenschrift für klassische Philologie XX (1903), 276–278.

(3) *Review of* Annibaldi 1. *In* Deutsche Literaturzeitung XXVIII (1907), 2370 ff.

(4) *Review of* Annibaldi 2. *In* Wochenschrift für klassische Philologie XXVII (1910), 1312–1320.

(5) P. Cornelii Taciti libri qui supersunt. Recognovit Carolus Halm. Editionem quintam curavit Georgius Andresen. Lipsiae. Vol. I (*Ab excessu divi Augusti*), 1913, vol. II (*Historiae, Germania, Agricola, Dialogus*), 1916.

(6) Zu Tacitus. *In* Wochenschrift für klassische Philologie XXXII (1915), 883–886.

(7) *Review of* E. Wolff[3]. *In* Wochenschrift für klassische Philologie XXXIII (1916), 1110–1114, 1133–1139.

(8) Tacitus über das Jahr 1916. *In* Jahresbericht des philologischen Vereins zu Berlin XLIII (1917), 84–114 (84–99, *review of* Gudeman 3).
Annibaldi, Cesare. *Citations of* Annibaldi *given without a date refer to No. 1.*
(1) L'Agricola e la Germania di Cornelio Tacito nel MS. latino n. 8 della biblioteca del Conte G-Balleani in Iesi. Città di Castello, 1907.
(2) La Germania di Cornelio Tacito nel MS. latino n. 8 della biblioteca del Conte G. Balleani in Jesi. Leipzig, 1910.
(3) Cornelii Taciti de origine et situ Germanorum liber. Ad fidem praecipue codicis Aesini recensuit, praefatus est Caesar Annibaldi. Augustae Taurinorum, n.d. (*Corpus scriptorum Latinorum Paravianum.*)
Aubertus, Carolus. C. Cornelii Taciti et C. Velleii Paterculi scripta quae extant . . . Parisiis, 1608.
Bears a preface by Carolus Aubertus.
Bach, Nicholas. Cornelii Taciti operum quae supersunt. Emendavit et scholarum in usum illustravit Nicolaus Bachius. Lipsiae, 1834–1835.
Bährens, Emil. Studien zur Germania des Tacitus. *In* Jahrbücher für classische Philologie CXXI (1880), 265–288.
Baiter, Georg. *See* Orelli 2.
Baumstark, Anton. (1) Ausführliche Erläuterung des allgemeinen Theiles der Germania des Tacitus. Leipzig, 1875. (2) Ausführliche Erläuterung des besondern völkerschaftlichen Theiles der Germania des Tacitus. Leipzig, 1880.
Bekker, Immanuel. Cornelius Tacitus . . . ab Immanuele Bekkero . . . recognitus. Lipsiae, 1831. 2v.
Bernegger, Matthias. *See* Freinshemius.
Bernhardy, Gottfried. *See* Döderlein.
Beroaldus, Philippus. *See* Tacitus 15.
Bleterie, M. l'Abbé de la. Traduction de la vie d'Agricola, et des Moeurs des Germains. Paris, 1776.
Borchardt, Rudolf. Tacitus Deutschland. Deutsch von Rudolf Borchardt. München, 1922.
Brotier, Gabriel. C. Cornelii Taciti opera recognovit, emendavit, explevit, notis . . . illustravit Gabriel Brotier. Parisiis, 1771. 4v. (*Ed. altera, Parisiis, 1776. 7v.*)
Brunot, Ferdinand. Un fragment des histoires de Tacite. Etude sur le De moribus Germanorum. Bar-le-Duc, 1883.

Bywater, Ingram. Miscellanea (Tac. Germ. 16). *In* Journal of Philology XVII (1888), 75–79.

Cellarius, Christophorus. Notitia orbis antiqui. Cantabrigiae, 1703–1706. 2v. (*Also published in* · Leipzig, 1701–1706.) *1, 344* (*lib. 2, c. 8*), *on* Germania 1, 1 *Rhaetisque*.

Cluverius, Philippus. Germaniae antiquae libri tres . . . Lugduni Bat., 1616.

Colerus, Christophorus. *Ad C. Cornelii Taciti scripta spicilegium. Hanoviae, 1603.
  The notes of Colerus are also printed in the variorum *editions of* Gruterus *and* Aubertus.

Cornelius, E. Quo modo Tacitus . . . in hominum memoria versatus sit usque ad renascentes litteras . . . Marpurgi Cattorum, 1888.

Croll, Georg Christian. C. Cornelii Taciti opera ex recensione Georg. Chr. Crollii, ed. sec. auctior et emendatior curante Frid. Christ. Exter. Biponti, 1792. 4v.
  Earlier edition by Crollius (*but without his name*), *Biponti, 1779–1780. 4v.*

Detschew, D. Zu Tacitus' Germania 45. *In* Wochenschrift für klassische Philologie XXXV (1918), 236–237.

Dilthey, Julius Friedrich Karl. C. Cornelii Taciti de situ moribus et populis Germaniae libellus. Vollständing erläutert von I. F. K. Dilthey. Braunschweig, 1823.

Döderlein, Ludwig. C. Cornelii Taciti opera. Emendavit et commentariis instruxit Ludovicus Doederlein. Halis, 1841–1847. 2v. (= *Pars v, Bibliotheca scriptorum Latinorum . . . consilio God. Bernhardy instituta.*)

Eckstein, Friedrich August. *See* Walther.

Ernesti, Johann August. C. Cornelii Taciti opera ex recensione Io. Augusti Ernesti cum notis integris Iusti Lipsii et I. F. Gronovii, quibus et suas adiecit. Lipsiae, 1752. 2v.
  Second edition, containing notes of Nic. Heinsius, Lipsiae, 1772. 2v. Also see Oberlin.

Ernesti, Johann Heinrich Martin. *See* Perizonius.

Eussner, Adam. (1) *Review of* Cornelii Taciti de situ ac populis Germaniae liber, nouvelle édition par J. Gantrelle. *In* Zeitschrift für das Gymnasialwesen XXXI (1877), 485–491.
  (2) *Review of* Holder 4. *In* Blätter für das Gymnasialschulwesen XVIII (1882), 411–412.

Fischer, Hermann. Barditus. *In* Zeitschrift für deutsches Altertum L (1908), 145–148.

Freinshemius, Ioannes. C. Cornelii Taciti opera omnia . . . accurante Matthia Berneggero. Argentorati, 1638.

Contains: Joannis Freinshemii *Expositio locorum Cornelianorum* . . . .

Furneaux, Henry. Cornelii Taciti de Germania. Ed. by Henry Furneaux. Oxford, 1894.

Gantrelle, Joseph. (1) *See* Eussner 1.

(2) *Review of* Holder 3. *In* Revue critique, N.S. VIII (1879), 171–172.

Gerlach, Franz Dorotheus. C. Cornelii Taciti Germania. Ad optimorum codicum fidem emendavit notis criticis . . . instruxit Fr. Dor. Gerlach. Basileae, 1835.

Girke, Georg. Die Tracht der Germanen in der vor- und frühgeschichtlichen Zeit. Leipzig, 1922. 2v. in 1. (= *Mannus-Bibliothek 23–24.*)

Golling, J. Zu Tacitus Germania c. 26. *In* Wiener Studien XXX (1908), 342.

Grat, Félix. Nouvelles recherches sur Tacite. *In* Mélanges d'archéologie et d'histoire de l'Ecole française de Rome XLII (1925), 3–66.

Grimm, Jakob. Geschichte der deutschen Sprache. Vierte Auflage. Leipzig, 1880. (*First edition, 1848.*) *I, p. 433:* Germ. 34, 1 *Dulgubnii.*

Gronovius, Abraham. *See* Gronovius, Iacobus.

Gronovius, Iacobus. C. Cornelii Taciti opera quae extant . . . ex recensione et cum notis Jacobi Gronovii. Trajecti Batavorum, 1721. 2v.

Published after the editor's death by his son Abraham.

Gronovius, Iohannes Fredericus. C. Cornelii Taciti opera quae extant . . . Ioh. Fred. Gronovius recensuit . . . Amstelodami, 1685. 2v.

This work appeared after the editor's death, bearing a preface by his son Jakob.

Grotius, Hugo. C. Corn. Tacitus ex I. Lipsii editione cum notis et emendationibus H. Grotii. Lugduni Bat., 1640. 2v.

The notes of Grotius are reprinted in the variorum *editions of the* Gronovii.

Gruber, Johannes von. Taciti Germania seu de situ, moribus et populis Germaniae libellus. Herausgegeben und . . . erläutert von Johannes von Gruber. Berlin, 1832.

Gruterus, Ianus. *C. Cornelii Taciti opera quae extant ex recognitione Iani Gruteri . . . Francoforti, 1607

The notes of Gruterus are also printed in the variorum *editions of* Aubertus *and the* Gronovii.

Gudeman, Alfred. *Citations of Gudeman given without a date refer to no. 1.*
(1) Zur Germania des Tacitus. *In* Philologus LVIII (1899), 25–44.
(2) P. Cornelii Taciti Dialogus de Oratoribus mit Prolegomena, Text und Adnotatio Critica . . . von Alfred Gudeman. Zweite völlig neubearbeitete Auflage. Leipzig & Berlin, 1914.
(3) P. Cornelii Taciti de Germania. Erklärt von Alfred Gudeman. Berlin, 1916.
(4) Tacitus de vita Iulii Agricolae and de Germania with introd., notes . . . by Alfred Gudeman (revised ed.). Boston, 1928.
(5) *Review of* Tacitus Germania . . . bearbeitet von Hans Philipp, Leipzig, 1926. *In* Philologische Wochenschrift XLVII (1927), 685–692.

Haase, Friedrich. Cornelii Taciti opera. Edidit Fridericus Haase. Lipsiae, 1855. 2v.

Hachtmann, Karl. Zur Germania des Tacitus. *In* Historische Untersuchungen Arnold Schäfer zum fünfundzwanzigjährigen Jubiläum seiner akademischen Wirksamkeit gewidmet . . . Bonn, 1882. Pp. 178–189.

Halm, Karl. (1) C. Cornelii Taciti opera quae supersunt. Ex recognitione Caroli Halmii. Lipsiae, 1850–1851. 2v.
(2) Cornelii Taciti libri qui supersunt. Iterum recognovit Carolus Halm. Lipsiae, 1857. 2v. (*Tertium recog.*, 1874; *quartum recog.*, 1883; *ed. 5, see* Andresen 5.)
(3) Ueber einige controverse Stellen in der Germania des Tacitus. *In* Sitzungsberichte der . . . Akademie der Wissenschaften zu München 1864, II, 1–41.

Hartmann, Felix. Literaturbericht für das Jahr 1917. *In* Glotta XI (1921), 110–133.
On p. 129 are mentioned two conjectures on Germ. 44, 3 Lemonii, *one by* Lundström *in* Svensk hum. tidskrift 1, 27 f., *another by* Karsten *in* Acta soc. Fenn. 45, 2 (1915), 77. *I have had access to neither of these publications.*

Haupt, Moriz. Cornelii Taciti Germania in usum scholarum recognita a Mauricio Hauptio. Berolini, 1855.

Haverfield, Francis John. (1) Tac. Germ. 13. *In* Journal of Philology XXVII (1901), 228.
(2) Tacitus during the late Roman Period and the Middle Ages. *In* Journal of Roman Studies VI (1916), 194–201.

Heinsius, Niklaas. Nicolai Heinsii animadversa (ad Tacitum), *published by Ernesti in his second edition*, 1772 (*cf.* praef., p. xlvi).

Heraeus, Karl. Ueber einige unbeachtet gebliebene Fehler und controverse Stellen im Texte der Germania des Tacitus. *In* Festschrift zur Einweihung des neuen Gymnasialgebäudes, Hamm, 1880. (*Programm.*) Pp. 3–14.

Hertlein, Friedrich. Zu Tac. Germ. 3. *In* Philologus LVII (1898), 656–658.

Hess, Philipp Karl. (1) Variae lectiones in Taciti Germaniam. Helmstadii, 1827. (*Programm*).—Commentatio II, *ibid.*, 1828. —Commentatio III, *ibid.*, 1834.

(2) *See* Kapp.

Hesselmeyer, Ellis. Was ist und was heiszt Dekumatland? *In* Klio XXIV (1930), 1–37.

Hirschfeld, Otto. Der Name Germani bei Tacitus und sein Aufkommen bei den Römern. *In* Beiträge zur alten Geographie, Festschrift für Heinrich Kiepert. Berlin, 1898. Pp. 259–274.

Hirschfelder, Wilhelm. Cornelii Taciti de situ ac populis Germaniae liber Friderici Kritzii . . . annotatione illustratus. Quartam editionem curavit W. Hirschfelder. Berolini, 1878.

Holder, Alfred. (1) *See* Holtzmann.

(2) *Description of No. 3.* *In* Mittheilungen der Verlagsbuchhandlung B. G. Teubner in Leipzig, No. 1, 1878, pp. 45 f.

(3) Cornelii Taciti de origine et situ Germanorum liber. Recensuit Alfred Holder. Lipsiae, 1878.

(4) —— Edidit Alfred Holder. Freiburg i.B. und Tübingen, 1882. (= *No. 1, Germanischer Bücherschatz herausgegeben von Alfred Holder.*)

Holtzmann, Adolf. Germanische Alterthümer, mit Text, Übersetzung und Erklärung von Tacitus Germania, von Adolf Holtzmann. Herausgegeben von Alfred Holder. Leipzig, 1873.

Holub, Johann. *Unter den erhaltenen Handschriften der Germania des Tacitus ist die Stuttgarter Handschrift die beste. Weidenau, 1893–1898. (*Programm.*) *In four parts.*

Hümer, Johann. Über eine Wiener Handschrift zum Dialog und zur Germania des Tacitus, und zu Suetons Fragment de gramm. et rhet. *In* Zeitschrift für die österreichischen Gymnasien XXIX (1878), 801–813.

Ihm, Max. *Review of* Annibaldi 1. *In* Wochenschrift für klassische Philologie XXIV (1907), 1145–1148.

Jäkel, Werner. De Taciti Germaniae atque Agricolae codicibus Aesinate et Toletano. Berlin, 1926. (*Diss.*)

Jessen, Chr. *Review of* Kritz 1860. *In* Zeitschrift für das Gymnasialwesen XVI, 1 (1862), 59–77.

John, Constantin. *Review of* Wolff's third edition. *In* Berliner philologische Wochenschrift XXXVII (1917), 835–843.

Kapp, Johann. Caji Cornelii Taciti de situ moribus et populis Germaniae libellus. Ex recensione et cum selectis observationibus hucusque anecdotis Paulli Danielis Longolii ex MSS. editus a Joanne Kappio. Lipsiae, 1788. (*Ed. altera et emendatior. Textum passim refinxit, varietatem lectionis notasque suas adjecit Philippus Carolus Hess.* Lipsiae et Soraviae, 1824.)

Karle, Jos. Ant. Operateure an einem gesunden Gliede oder die neuesten Erklärer zu Tac. Germ. 13. *In* Philologus XXXVII (1877), 354–356.

Karsten. *See* Hartmann.

Kettner, Gustav. Zu Tacitus Germania cap. XIII, XIV. *In* Zeitschrift für deutsche Philologie XVIII (1886), 129–143.

Kiessling, Gottlieb. C. Cornelii Taciti de situ, moribus et populis Germaniae libellus. Commentariis instruxit Theophilus Kiesslingius. Lipsiae, 1832.

Knoke, Friedrich. Bemerkungen zu dem Sprachgebrauch des Tacitus. Berlin, 1925.

Kossinna, Gustaf. Die deutsche Vorgeschichte . . . . 3. verbesserte Auflage. Leipzig, 1921. (= *Mannus-Bibliothek 9.*)

Kraffert, Hermann. Beiträge zur Kritik und Erklärung lateinischen Autoren. Aurich, 1883.

Kritz, Friedrich. P. Cornelii Taciti Germania. Ex Hauptii recensione et perpetua annotatione illustravit Fridericus Kritzius. Ed. tertia emendata. Berolini, 1869. (*Earlier editions*, 1860, 1864. *Also see* Hirschfelder.)

Lachmann, Karl. *The emendations attributed to Lachmann first appeared, so far as I have been able to determine, in the edition of* Haupt.

Landi, Carlo. Urgentibus imperii fatis (nota Tacitiana). *In* Scritti storici in onore di Camillo Manfroni. Padua, 1925. Pp. 443–453.

Lehnerdt, Max. Enoche von Ascoli und die Germania des Tacitus. *In* Hermes XXXIII (1898), 499–505.

Leibnitz, Gottfried Wilhelm von. *Scriptores rerum Brunsvicensium . . . cura Goth. Guil. Leibnitii. Hanoverae, 1707–1711. 3v. (I, p. 9, n. f: Germania 2, 12 a uicto. This reference is taken from O. Hirschfeld, p. 264, note 2.)

Lipsius, Iustus. C. Cornelii Taciti opera quae exstant. Iustus Lipsius postremum recensuit. . . . Accessit C. Velleius Paterculus cum eiusdem Lipsi auctioribus notis. Antverpiae, 1607. (*Earlier editions by Lipsius:* 1574, 1581, 1585, 1588, 1589, 1600.)

Longolius, Paul Daniel. (1) *Collation of the codex Hummelianus entered in a copy of Melchior Lotter's edition of the* Germania. See *p. 82.*

(2) *See* Kapp.

(3) *See* Perizonius.

Lundström. *See* Hartmann.

Madvig, Johann Nicolai. Adversaria critica ad scriptores Graecos et Latinos. Hauniae, 1871–1884. 3v. (*Vol. II = Adversaria critica ad scriptores Latinos.*)

Mähly, J. Tacitus Germania von A. Baumstark (*review*). *In* Zeitschrift für deutsche Philologie VIII (1877), 248–252.

Malone, Kemp. The Votaries of Nerthus. *In* Namn och bygd, tidskrift för nordisk ortnamnsforskning XXII (1934), 26–51.

Massmann, Hans Ferdinand. *Citations of Massmann given without a date refer to No. 2.*

(1) *Review of Tross' edition. In* Jahrbücher für wissenschaftliche Kritik, Jahrgang 1841, zweiter Band (Nov. 1841), 689–717.

(2) Germania des C. Cornelius Tacitus. Mit den Lesarten sämmtlicher Handschriften und geschichtlichen Untersuchungen über diese und das Buch selbst. Quedlinburg und Leipzig, 1847. (*Another title in Latin.*)

Meiser, Karl. Kritische Studien zum Dialogus und zur Germania des Tacitus. Eichstädt, 1871. (*Programm.*)

Mesnil, Adolf du. Erklärende Beiträge zu lateinischen Schulschriftstellern. Frankfurt a. O., 1896. (*Programm.*)

Michaelis, Adolf. Cornelii Taciti dialogus de oratoribus. Ad codices denuo conlatos recognovit Adolfus Michaelis. Lipsiae, 1868.

Mitscherlich, Christoph Wilhelm. Observationes ad Taciti Ann. III, 55, Germ. 5 . . . Gottingae, 1841. (*Programm.*)

Möller, Hermann. Zu cap. 28 der Germania. *In* Zeitschrift für deutsches Altertum und deutsche Litteratur XXXVIII (1894), 22–27.

Mosler, N. Cornelius Tacitus über die Weltstellung von Germanien . . . nach der Lesart aller Handschriften, ins besondere der Münchener, Stuttgarter und Florentiner . . . Uebersetzt und erklärt von Dr. N. Mosler. Leipzig, 1862.

Persson, P. Kritisch-exegetische Bemerkungen zu den kleinen Schriften des Tacitus. (= Skrifter utgivna av K. humanistiska vetenskaps-samfundet i Uppsala, 24, 4. Uppsala, 1927.)

Philipp, Ed. (1) Zur Tacitushandschrift cod. Vindob. II. *In* Wiener Studien XI (1889), 288–290.

(2) Über die Mailänder und die Venediger Handschrift zum Dialog des Tacitus. *Ibid.* XXVI (1904), 290–308.

Pichena, Curtius. C. Cornelii Taciti opera quae extant. Iuxta veterrimos manuscriptos emendata, notisque auctioribus illustrata, per Curtium Pichenam. Francofurti, 1607.

Pincius, Philippus. *See* Tacitus 8.

Puteolanus, Franciscus. *See* Tacitus 5 *and* 8.

Ramorino, Felice. Cornelio Tacito nella storia della coltura. Seconda edizione corretta. Milano, 1898.

Rand, Edward Kennard. A Harvard manuscript of Ovid, Palladius, and Tacitus. *In* American Journal of Philology XXVI (1905), 291–329.

Reeb, Wilhelm. Tacitus Germania, mit Beiträgen von A. Dopsch, H. Reis, K. Schumacher, unter Mitarbeit von H. Klenk, herausgegeben und erläutert von Wilhelm Reeb. Leipzig und Berlin, 1930.

Reifferscheid, August. (1) Suetoni Tranquilli praeter Caesarum libros reliquiae. Edidit Augustus Reifferscheid. Lipsiae, 1860. *Pp. 361–478:* Quaestiones Suetonianae.

(2) Coniectanea in Taciti Germaniam. *In* Symbola philologorum Bonnensium in honorem Friderici Ritschelii collecta. Lipsiae, 1864–1867. Pp. 623–628.

Reitzenstein, Richard. (1) Zur Textgeschichte der Germania. *In* Philologus LVII (1898), 307–317.

(2) Philologische Kleinigkeiten. 2. Das deutsche Heldenlied bei Tacitus. *In* Hermes XLVIII (1913), 268–272.

(3) Bemerkungen zu den kleinen Schriften des Tacitus. *In* Nachrichten der königlichen Gesellschaft der Wissenschaften zu Göttingen, phil.-hist. Kl., 1914, pp. 173–276.

Rhenanus, Beatus. (1) *See* Tacitus 17.

(2) *See* Tacitus 18.

(3) P. Cornelii Taciti annalium ... libri sedecim qui supersunt ... recogniti ... per Beatum Rhenanum ... libellus de Germanorum populis, dialogus de oratoribus, denique vita Iulii Agricolae .... Basiliae, 1533.

(4) *A reimpression of the preceding, with a few changes in the text,* Basiliae, 1544.

Riese, Alexander. (1) Zu Tacitus' Germania cap. 29. *In* Germania: Korrespondenzblatt der römisch-germanischen Kommission des deutschen archäologischen Instituts III (1919), 82–83.
(2) Bataver und Mattiaker. *Ibid.* IV, 60–62.
Ritter, Franz. Cornelii Taciti opera. Ad codices antiquos exacta ... edidit Franciscus Ritter. Cantabrigiae, 1848. 4v. (Second ed. in 1 vol., Lipsiae, 1864.)
Robinson, Rodney Potter. (1) The inventory of Niccolò Niccoli. *In* Classical Philology XVI (1921), 251–255.
(2) De fragmenti Suetoniani de grammaticis et rhetoribus codicum nexu et fide. Urbana, 1922. (= *University of Illinois studies in language and literature VI*, No. 4 [Nov. 1920].)
(3) C. Suetoni Tranquilli de grammaticis et rhetoribus. Edidit, apparatu et commentario criticis instruxit Rodney Potter Robinson. Paris, 1925.
(4) *Review of* Gudeman 4. *In* Classical Weekly XXVI (1932–1933), 58–62.
Rostagno, Enrico. *Review of* Annibaldi 2. *In* Atene e Roma XV (1912), 78–84.
Ryckius, Theodorus. C. Cornelii Taciti opera quae extant ex recensione et cum animadversionibus Theodori Ryckii. Lugduni Bat., 1687.
Schefczik, Heinrich. De Cornelii Taciti Germaniae apparatu critico. Troppau, 1886. (*Programm.*)
Scheuer, Friedrich. De Tacitei de oratoribus dialogi codicum nexu et fide. *In* Breslauer philologische Abhandlungen VI, 1 (1891).
Schmidt, Ludwig. *Review of* Reeb-Klenk. *In* Philologische Wochenschrift LI (1931), 838–840.
Schneider, H. Zu Tacitus Germania VI, 6. *In* Blätter für das Gymnasial-schulwesen XXXVI (1900), 238–256.
Schönemann, Arthur. De Taciti Germaniae codicibus capita duo. Halis Saxonum, 1910. (*Diss.*)
Schultze, W. Principat, Comitat, Nobilität im 13. Capitel der Germania des Tacitus. *In* Deutsche Zeitschrift für Geschichtswissenschaft, N. F. II (1897–1898), 1–15.
Schütz, Hermann. Zu Tacitus Germania. *In* Neue Jahrbücher für Philologie und Pädagogik CXIX (1879), 273–288.
Schweizer-Sidler, Heinrich. Tacitus' Germania erläutert von Heinrich Schweizer-Sidler, erneuert von Eduard Schwyzer. Achte Auflage (dritte der Neubearbeitung). Halae a.d. S., 1923. (*First ed.*, 1871. *Also see* Orelli.)

Selling, Christian Fried. Georg Christoph. Observationes criticae in C. Cornelii Taciti Germaniam. Augustae Vindelicorum, 1830. (*Programm.*)

Sepp, Bernhard. (1) Bemerkungen zur Germania des Tacitus. *In* Blätter für das Gymnasial-schulwesen xxvIII (1892) 169–175.

(2) Der codex Pontani in Leyden. *In* Philologus LXII (1903), 292–305.

Sievers, Eduard. Germaniae vocabulum. *In* Beiträge zur Geschichte der deutschen Sprache und Literatur XLIX (1925), 429–433.

Sternkopf, Wilhelm. Zu Tacitus' Germania c. 30. *In* Philologische Wochenschrift XLII (1922), 237–239.

Strache, Hans. Kritische und exegetische Beiträge zur Germania des Tacitus. *In* Wochenschrift für klassische Philologie XXXIV (1917), 875–880; XXXVI (1919), 67–71.

Sturm, Johann Andreas. In Taciti minorum librorum aliquot locos animadversiones criticae et exegeticae. Particula prior. Köln, 1879. (*Programm.*)

Tacitus, P. Cornelius. *Citations from the works of Tacitus, other than the* Germania, *are made from the edition of* Halm-Andresen (*see* Andresen 5).

Editions of Tacitus later than the year 1519 are listed under their respective editors: Altenburg, Andresen, Annibaldi, Bach, Bekker, Borchardt, de la Bleterie, Brotier, Cluverius, Colerus, Croll, Dilthey, Döderlein, Ernesti, Freinshemius, Furneaux, Gerlach, Gronovius, Grotius, Gruber, Gruterus, Gudeman, Haase, Halm, Haupt, Hirschfelder, Holder, Holtzmann, Kapp, Kiessling, Kritz, Lipsius, Massmann, Mosler, Müllenhoff, Müller, Nipperdey, Oberlin, Orelli, Passow, Pichena, Reeb, Rhenanus, Ritter, Ryckius, Schweizer-Sidler, Teubert, Tross, Valmaggi, Walch, Walther, Weishaupt, Wolff.

Editions of Tacitus through the year 1519 are listed below in chronological order.[1]

---

[1] In the descriptions of these early printed editions reference is made to the following bibliographical works: L. Hain, *Repertorium bibliographicum*, Stuttgartiae, 1836–1838 (reprinted, Berlin, 1925); W. A. Copinger, *Supplement to Hain's Repertorium bibliographicum*, with an index, *The printers and publishers of the XV century*, by K. Burger, London, 1895–1902 (reprinted, Berlin, 1926); R. Proctor, *An index to the early printed books in the British Museum*, London, 1896——; M. Pellechet, *Catalogue général des incunables des bibliothèques publiques de France* I–III, Paris, 1897–1909; G. W. Panzer, *Annales typographici* . . ., Norimbergae, 1793–1803; F. L. A. Schweiger, *Handbuch der classischen Bibli-*

(1) *The editio princeps.* [*Venetiis, Vindelinus*] *de Spira* [*c. 1470*]. Begins without title: ( )AM Valerium Asiaticum . . . Cornelij Taciti illustrissimi historici de situ moribus & populis/ Germanię libellus aureus . . . Cornelii Taciti equitis Romani dialogus de oratoribus claris . . . Finis Deo laus/ Cęsareos mores scribit Cornelius. esto/ Iste tibi codex: historię pater est./ Insigni quem laude feret gens postera: pressit/ Spira premens: artis gloria prima suę.

Hain-Copinger, 15218; Proctor, 4061. I have photostats of the Germania *made from a copy in the British Museum* (IB. 19592).

(2) *Bononiae* [*Balthasar Azzoguidi*], *1472.* [*F. 1ʳ*]: DIODORI SICVLI HISTORIARVM PRISCARVM A POGGIO IN LA/TINVM TRADVCTI LIBER PRIMVS INCIPIT. IN QVO HEC CON/TINENTVR TOTIVS OPERIS PROHE-MIVM? . . . [*F. 93ʳ*]: BONONIAE IMPRESSVM. MCCCC72 . . . [*F. 95ʳ*]: CORNELII TACITI ILLVSTRISSIMI HI-STORICI DE SITV MO/RIBVS ET POPVLIS GERMA-NIAE LIBELLVS AVREVS.

Pellechet, 4266; Hain, 6188. I have collated a copy in the Bibliothèque Nationale (Rés. J. 66).

(3) [*Norimbergae, Frid. Creussner, c. 1473.*] [*F. 1ʳ*]: Cai. Cornelij Taciti. Equitis Ro. Germania incipit. [*F. 11ʳ*]: Laus deo clementissimo.

Hain-Copinger, 15224; Proctor, 2173. I have collated a copy in the National Library of Vienna (6. F. 22).

(4) [*Romae, Iohannes Gensberg or Iohannes Schurener, c. 1474.*] [*F. 1ʳ*]: CAI. CORNELII. TACITI. EQVITIS RO. GER-MANIA. INCIPIT. [*F. 16ʳ*]: Deo Gratias.

Hain-Copinger, 15223; Proctor, 3516. I have collated a copy in the National Library of Vienna (26. H. 29).

(5) *Edition of Franciscus Puteolanus.* [*Mediolani, Antonius Zarotus ?, c. 1475.*] [*F. 1ʳ*]: Franciscus Puteolanus Iacobo Antiquario ducali Secretario. Sal. . . . [*F. 2ʳ*]: CORNELII TACITI HISTORIAE AVGVSTAE. LI. XI./ ACTIONVM DIVRNALIVM. [*F. 151ʳ*]: CORNELII TACITI ILLV-

---

ographie, Leipzig, 1830–1834. In the descriptions which I have taken wholly or in part from Massmann's preface (11, 12, 14, 15, 16, 18), I have adopted certain manuscript corrections entered in the copy of Massmann's edition belonging to the library of the University of Cincinnati, which are clearly the work of a scholar (Prof. A. Holder, I suspect) who had access to the editions in question.

STRISSIMI HISTORICI DE/ SITV MORIBVS ET POPV-
LIS GERMANIAE LIBEL/LVS AVREVS. [*F. 161ʳ*]:
CORNELII TACITI AEQVITIS ROMANI DIALOGVS/ AN
SVI SAECVLI ORATORES ANTIQVIORIBVS/ ET QVARE
CONCEDANT. [*F. 177ʳ*] *with a distinct register:* IVLII
AGRICOLAE VITA PER CORNELIVM TACITū/ EIVS
GENERVM CASTISSIME COMPOSITA.

Hain-Copinger, 15219; Proctor, 5838. *I have photostats of the* Germania *made from a copy in the British Museum* (167. c. 10).

(6) *Venetiis, Andreas de Paltascichis de Catharo, 1476. Titles as in No. 2. Colophon* [*f. 128ʳ*]: . . . Impressi/ Venetiis per Andreā Iacobi Katharēsem Andrea Vendramino Duce/ fortunatissimo./ .Mccccclxxvi. Pridie Kal. febr./FINIS.

Pellechet, 4267; Hain-Copinger, 6189. I have collated a copy in the Bibliothèque Nationale (Rés. J. 72).

(7) *Venetiis, Thomas de Blavis, 1481. Titles as in No. 2.* [*F. 121ʳ*]: Ex aedibus solitae habitationis Nono. ka. Decembres. M. CCCCLxxxi. *Colophon* [*f. 122ʳ*]: . . . Impressū/ fuit per Thomam Alexandrinum huius artis peritissimum Venetiis Re/gnante Ioanne Mocenico duce felicissimo. Anno salutis millessimo qua/dringentesimo octogesimo primo: die uigesima quinta Nouembris.

Pellechet, 4268; Hain-Copinger, 6190; Proctor, 4754. I have collated a copy in the Bibliothèque Nationale (Rés. J. 70).

(8) *Venetiis, Philippus Pincius, 1497.* [*F. 1ʳ*]: *Cornelij Taciti/ Historiae Au/gustae.* [*F. 2ʳ*]: Franciscus Puteolanus Iacobo Antiquario ducali Secretario. Sal. [*F. 3ʳ*]: LIBER/ CORNELII TACITI HISTORIE AVGVSTE. LI. XI. ACTIONVM/ DIVRNALIVM. *Other titles as in No. 5 with distinct register for the Agricola. Colophon* [*f. 106ʳ*] *after the Dialogus:* . . . Venetijs fideliter Impresi ac diligenter/ emendati per Philippū pinci sumptibus nobilis viri dñi Benedicti fontana. Anno dñi/ Mccccxcvij. die. xxij. Marcij. Imperante sapientissimo dño Augustino Barbadico pru/dentissimi ac Inuictissimi Senatus Venetiarum duce serenissimo. *Colophon* [*f. 113ʳ*] *after the Agricola:* FINIS/ Venetijs per Philippum pinci: sumptibus dñi Benedicti fontana. Anno dñi Mccccxcvij/ die. xxij. martij.

Hain-Copinger, 15222; Proctor, 5315. I have used a copy belonging to the library of the University of Cincinnati.

(9) [*Vindobonae, Johann Winterburg, c. 1500.*] [*F. 1ʳ*]:

¶Cornelij Taciti. De origine 7/ situ Germanorum liber incipit. [*F. 9ʳ*]: ¶C.C. de situ 7 moribus Germanie additōes/ Fabula demogorgonis de creatōne mundi praefatio. [*F. 12ᵛ*]: ¶Ex libro C.C. de situ 7 moribus Norimberge de hercinie silue magnitudine 7 de eius in Europa definitōe 7 populis incolis. [*F. 14ʳ*]: ¶Finis.

Hain, 15225; Copinger, 5696; Proctor, 9484. I have examined a copy in the National Library of Vienna (2. H. 107), *and also have photostats of a copy in the Bibliothèque Nationale* (Rés. J. 3218).

(10) *Lipsiae, Wolfgang Stöckl, 1502.* *Cornelij Taciti Illustrissimi hi = /storici de Situ, Moribus/ et populis Germanie Li = /bellus aureus. *Colophon:* Impressum est hoc Cor. Taciti aureum/ opusculum Lips in edibus Vuolfgangi/ Monacensis. Anno domini .M. D. 11.

Massmann, pp. 28 f., No. 9; Panzer ιx, p. 481, No. 55.

(11) *Lipsiae, Melchior Lotter, 1509. Edition of Johannes Rhagius.* Cornelij Taciti Il= /lustrissimi hystorici de situ mori= /bus. et populis Germanie/ Aureus libellus. *Colophon:* Impressum est hoc Cor. Taciti aureū opusculū/ Lips in edibus Melchior Lotters. Anno/ domini .M. D. Nono Vltimo/ die Decembris.

Massmann, pp. 29 f., No. 10. I have photostats (text only) made from a copy in the Munich Library.

(12) *Erfordiae, Johann Canapp, 1509.* *Cornelij Taciti: Equi/tis Rhomani: Illu/strissimi Historici: de situ: moribus et popu/lis Germanie Libel/lus Aureus. *Colophon* (*after* Philippi Beroaldi Endecasyllabum Ad Germaniam *and* L. Hieronimi Magistri Canonici regula/ris in laudem Libri Octostichon): Excusum Erphordię: Aeneis/ Ioannis Canappi literis. Anno dñi .M. D. IX.

Massmann, p. 30, No. 11.

(13) [*Parisiis, G. de Marnef*], *1511.* *Berosus Babilonicus, de his quae praecesserunt inundationem terrarum. Item Myrsilus, de origine Turrhenorum. Cato in fragmentis. Archilochus in epitheto de temporibus. Metasthenes, de iudicio temporum. . . . Cornelii Taciti de origine et situ Germanorum opusculum. C.C. de situ et moribus Germanorum. [*Edidit Joannes Annius Viterbensis*]—[*Parisiis, G. de Marnef*], anno Domini 1511.

This description is taken from the Catalogue des livres imprimés de la Bibliothèque Nationale, *s.v.* Berosus.

(14) *Venetiis, I. Rubeus, 1512.* Bears a preface by *Ioannes Rivius*. *Cornelii Taciti historici gravissimi disertissimique fragmenta accurate recognita ac nova censura castigata. *Colophon:* Impressum Venetiis per Ioann. Rubeum Vercellensem Anno Domini .MCCCCCXII. Die XX. mensis Julii.

Panzer VIII, *p. 409, No. 597; Massmann, p. 32, No. 14; Schweiger* II, *2, pp. 997 f.*

(15) *Romae, Stephanus Guillereti de Lotharingia, 1515.* Edition of Philippus Beroaldus the younger. P. CORNELII TACITI LIBRI/ QVINQVE NOVITER IN/VENTI ATQVE CVM/ RELIQVIS EIVS/ OPERIBVS/ EDITI. *F. 73ʳ (after* Ann. v [VI]): PHI. BEROALDVS LECTORI . . . *Beginning with f. 75ʳ: Puteolanus' preface addressed to Iacobus Antiquarius followed by the remaining books of the* Annals *and* Histories, *with the titles as in the edition of Puteolanus. Then:* P. CORNELII TACITI HISTORICI DE/ SITV MORIBVS ET POPVLIS GER/MANIÆ LIBELLVS. *The* Germania *is followed by the* Dialogus *with title as in edition of Puteolanus. Colophon after the* Dialogus: . . . Romę/ impressi per Magistrum Stephanum Guillereti de Lothoringia Tullen. dioc./ Anno. M. D. XV. Kl' Martii Leonis .X. Pont. Max. anno secūdo. *Finally, the* Agricola *with title and separate register as in the edition of Puteolanus.*

Massmann, pp. 33 f., No. 15. I have made a partial collation of the Germania *from a copy in the library of Harvard University.*

(16) *Vienna, Joannes Singrenius, 1515.* *Cornelij Taciti veridici Historici: de/ situ Germanie z incolarū: vt secla/ olim ferebāt: moribus libel= /lus lectu dignissimus./ Conradi Celtis Protucij: Poete/ fragmēta quedā: de ijsdem, scitu admodum vtilia./ Omnibus diligēter reuisis/ et castigatis. *Colophon:* Impressum est hoc opusculum acurata diligentia/ Ioannis Singrenij Calcographi: Vienne/ Pannonie Mense Januario. Auuo. τ c̄ Decimiquinti.

Massmann, p. 35, No. 16; Panzer IX, *p. 24 (No. 129).*

(17) *Basileae, Ioannes Frobenius, May, 1519.* [*Edited by Beatus Rhenanus.*] *Title page:* P. COR= /NELII TACITI, DE / moribus & popu-/lis Germaniæ,/ libellus./ Cum commentariolo uetera/ Germaniae populorū uo-/cabula paucis explicāte. *Page 3:* P. CORNE-/LII TACITI HISTORI-/ci de situ, moribus & po/pulis Germaniæ,/ libellus. *Text of* Germania *ends, p. 42:* FINIS. *Page 43 (numbered* 34!): IOANNES FROBENIVS/ ZINGLIO SVO S.D. . . . *Page 45:*

Commentariolus, Vetusta Germaniae populorum uocabula paucis explicans, & obiter alia quaedam. *Page 98, colophon:* BASILEAE APVD IOANNEM FRO/BENIVM MENSE MAIO,/ ANNO M.D. XIX.

I have examined a copy in the library of Harvard University.

(18) *Basileae, Ioannes Frobenius, August, 1519.* A new recension of the Germania [by Beatus Rhenanus]. The text of the other works is said to be a reimpression of an edition by Andreas Alciatus, Mediolani, ex officina Alex. Minutiani, 1517. *Title page:* P. Cornelii Taciti. Eq. Ro. Historia Augusta actionum diurnalium: additis quinque libris nouiter inuentis, cum Andreae Alciati annotationibus: De situ, moribus et populis Germaniae libellus . . . Dialogus . . . Cn. Julii Agricolae uita . . . Apud inclutam Basileam, ex Officina Io. Frobenii. *Colophon:* BASILEAE APVD IOANNEM/ FROBENIVM MENSE AV-/GVSTO ANNO .M.D. XIX.

Panzer vi, p. 213, No. 290; Schweiger ii, 2, p. 998; Massmann, pp. 36 f., No. 20.

Tagmann, Robert. De Taciti Germaniae apparatu critico. Vratislaviae, 1847.

Teubert, Chr. Fr. C. Cornelii Taciti Germania, curante Chr. Fr. Teubert. Lipsiae, 1826.

Thomas, Georg Martin. (1) *Emendations used by Halm. Cf.* Halm¹ i, p. iii.

(2) Über einen Codex Venetus zum Dialogus und zur Germania des Tacitus. *In* Münchener gelehrte Anzeigen xxxvi (1853), 9–23.

Tross, Ludwig. *Citations of* Tross *given without a date refer to No. 2.*

(1) Observationes criticae. Hammone, 1828. (*Programm.*)

(2) C. Cornelii Taciti de origine, situ, moribus ac populis Germanorum libellus. Ad fidem codicis Perizoniani, numquam adhuc collati, edidit et notas adiecit Ludovicus Tross.— Accesserunt Dialogus de oratoribus et Suetonii de viris illustribus libellus, ad eundem codicem accurate expressi. Hammone, 1841.

Urlichs, Ludwig. Kritische Bemerkungen zu dem ältern Plinius und zu Tacitus. *In* Rheinisches Museum xxxi (1876), 493–529.

Valmaggi, Luigi. (1) Appunti (Germ. 3, 5). *In* Bolletino di filologia classica xxvii (1920–1921), 13 f.

(2) Aut copulativo (Germ. 19). *Ibid.* xxx (1923–1924), 85 f.

(3) Tacito, Germania. Commentata da Luigi Valmaggi. Torino, 1924.

Voss, P. Kritiske bemerkninger til Tacitus. *In* Tidskrift for philologi og paedagogik VII (1866–1867), 101–113.

Wackernagel, Wilhelm. *Die germanischen Personennamen. *In* Schweizerisches Museum für historische Wissenschaft I (1837), 109. *Cf.* N.S., Suum cuique, *in* Neue Jahrbücher für Philologie und Pädagogik LXXXVII (1863), 72.

Waitz, Georg. Die Verfassung des deutschen Volkes in ältester Zeit. Dritte Auflage. Berlin, 1880. (= Deutsche Verfassungsgeschichte, erster Band.)

Walch, Georg Ludwig. (1) Emendationes Livianae. Berlin, 1815. (*Pp. 125, 273, on* Germ. 35, exercitus.)

(2) Tacitus Germania. Urschrift, Übersetzung . . . von G. L. Walch. Berolini, 1829.

Walter, Friedrich. Kritische Beiträge zu Tacitus. *In* Blätter für das Gymnasial-schulwesen XXI (1885), 512–514.

(2) Studien zu Tacitus and Curtius. München, 1887. (*Programm.*)

Walter, Fritz. Zu Tacitus und Apuleius. *In* Philologische Wochenschrift XLI (1921), 22–24.

Walther, Heinrich. C. Cornelii Taciti opera. Recensuit et commentarios suos adiecit Henricus Walther. Halis Saxonum, 1831–1833. (*Vol. IV*, Germ., Agr., Dial., *with preface by* F. A. Eckstein.)

Weidner, Andreas. Zu Tacitus Germania. *In* Philologus XLI (1882), 367–369.

Weishaupt, M. C. Cornelius Tacitus de Germania. Recognovit, isagoge instruxit, commentario illustravit, et lectionis varietatem . . . adjecit M. Weishaupt. Solodori, 1844.

Whatmough, Joshua. The Osi of Tacitus . . . Germanic or Illyrian? *In* Harvard Studies in Classical Philology XLII (1931), 139–155.

Wiedemann, Theodor. Ueber eine Quelle von Tacitus Germania. *In* Forschungen zur deutschen Geschichte IV (1864), 171–194.

Wiessner, Alfred. Zu Principat und Gefolgschaft in der altgermanischen Verfassung. *In* Deutsche Zeitschrift für Geschichtswissenschaft XII (1894–1895), 2, 312–339.

Wissowa, Georg. (1) Zur Beurteilung der Leidener Germaniahandschrift. *In* Festschrift zum 25 jährigen Stiftungsfest des historisch-philologischen Vereines der Universität München. München, 1905. Pp. 1–13.

(2) Taciti Dialogus de oratoribus et Germania. Suetonii de viris illustribus fragmentum. Codex Leidensis Perizonianus phototypice editus. Praefatus est Georgius Wissowa. Lugduni Bat., 1907. (= Codices Graeci et Latini photographice depicti duce Scatone de Vries, Suppl. IV.)

(3) περικειρομένη bei Tacitus. *In* Hermes LI (1916), 318–319.

Wolff, Eduard. Tacitus' Germania für den Schulgebrauch erklärt von Eduard Wolff. Dritte, verbesserte Auflage. Leipzig & Berlin, 1915. (*Earlier editions*, 1896, 1907.)

Wölfflin, Eduard. (1) (Jahresbericht) Tacitus. Ausgaben und Erläuterungen. Zweiter Artikel (*cf.* Philologus XXV, 92). *In* Philologus XXVI (1867), 92–166. (*P. 132*, Germ. 33, ingruentibus.)

(2) Jahresbericht über Tacitus (1876) 1877–1880. *In* Jahresbericht über die Fortschritte der klassischen Altertumswissenschaft XVIII (1879), 215–260. (*Review of* Holder 3, *pp. 239 f.*)

Wünsch, Richard. *Citations of* Wünsch *without a date refer to No. 1.*

(1) De Taciti Germaniae codicibus Germanicis. Marpurgi Chattorum, 1893. (*Diss.*).

(2) Zur Textgeschichte der Germania. *In* Hermes XXXII (1897), 42–59.

(3) *Review of* Annibaldi 1. *In* Berliner philologische Wochenschrift XXVII (1907), 1025–1030.

Zöchbauer, Franz. Zur Germania des Tacitus. *In* Zeitschrift für den österreichischen Gymnasien XLVIII (1897), 705–714.

INDEX

References are to pages, and include introduction, critical notes, appendices, and proper names occurring in the text of the *Germania* (heavy type).

a = ἀπό: 275.
abbreviations, in codex Aesinas: 20–24; in Hersfeld *Agricola:* 357 f.; in archetype of Hersfeld codex: 52 f.; in remote ancestor of Hersfeld codex; 74, in *Germania* manuscripts: 96, 104², 106, 110–113, 117 f., 119, 121, 132, 140², 150, 153, 158 f., 197 f., 201, 204², 222, 233 f., 313, 316; in continental minuscule: 66; in Insular minuscule: 66; in Raetian minuscule: 72; in manuscripts of the sixth century or earlier: 62 f.; in Veronese minuscule: 72⁴; in codex Mediceus I: 66 f.; obsolete: 62.
ablative absolute, equivalent to independent clause: 305; with *et ipse:* 103.
ablative singular of i-stems: 241 f.
Abnoba: 272.
accent mark: 115.
accusative plural of i-stems: 241 f.
ad = apud: 297.
adcisis crinibus: 295.
addere = dare: 274.
adnuis for *annuis:* 256.
adque for *atque:* 153, 251.
aduersus: 272.
adulescentulus contrasted with *iuuenis:* 290.
adultera: 295.
Aeneas: 273.
Aeneas Silvius (Pope Pius II), manuscript of miscellaneous works of: 85; manuscripts of dedicatory poem in honor of: 80, 84, 86, 89.
Aesinas, the codex, discovery of: 14 f., 349 f.; description of: 15–17; date and provenience of older portions: 24–30; hands in older portions: 20–24; some leaves of, identified with the Hersfeld codex: 17 f.; importance of, for the textual study of the *Germania:* 30 f., 45; *Germania* in: 206–208; v. Hersfeld codex.
Aestii: 322.
Africa: 273.
Agricola, the, discovery of: 3, 7, 8;

Hersfeld manuscript of, v. Hersfeld codex; extant manuscripts of: 31⁴, 81, 87; passages discussed, 1, 3: 10 f.; 14, 4: 32, 35, 54; 14, 8: 33, 42, 48; 15, 8: 33, 42, 50, 75²; 16, 1: 33, 35, 40 f., 50, 54, 55; 16, 5: 48; 16, 7: 48; 16, 10: 33, 48, 75²; 16, 11: 33, 39, 54; 16, 22: 33, 37, 40, 41, 55; 17, 10: 49; 18, 4: 52; 19, 6: 33, 39, 44, 53; 19, 13: 33, 39 f., 43, 47, 48, 50; 20, 2: 50; 20, 8: 54; 21, 11: 33, 37 f.; 22, 2: 33, 42, 48; 22, 5: 33, 37 f., 75²; 22, 8: 33, 49, 50; 23, 2: 53; 24, 6: 33, 39, 44, 53, 57; 24, 10: 75⁴; 24, 12: 33, 42, 239; 25, 3: 33, 37 and note 7; 25, 5: 33, 39, 56; 25, 7: 33, 39, 44, 56, 57; 25, 14: 40; 25, 16: 33, 39, 44, 54, 57; 25, 17: 33, 39, 44, 53; 26, 8: 31; 28, 4: 33, 49; 28, 7: 33, 42; 29, 4: 33, 41, 53, 56; 29, 14: 33, 36; 30, 2 f.: 49, 53, 74; 30, 8: 33, 50; 30, 11: 33, 39, 56; 32, 13: 48, 75; 32, 19: 33, 39, 49, 74; 32, 22: 33, 42, 48, 51, 54, 55; 33, 3: 33, 42, 50, 51; 33, 4: 34, 43, 48, 51; 34, 7: 34, 37, 41, 76; 34, 9: 34, 38², 43, 48, 51; 34, 16: 34, 42, 48; 35, 9: 52; 35, 14: 34, 37 f.; 36, 11: 34, 36 f., 39, 41, 43, 48, 54, 57; 36, 17 f.: 34, 44, 47; 36, 18: 52, 53, 55; 37, 12: 34, 35, 127; 37, 19: 34, 42, 48, 51; 38, 13: 34, 42, 50; 38, 18: 34, 35, 55 and note 2; 38, 19: 34, 42, 53, 59, 75²; 39, 2: 34, 35, 42; 39, 5: 53, 57, 59; 39, 13: 34, 37; 45, 20: 34, 45, 55, 57; 45, 21: 34, 39, 45, 47, 54, 57, 131; 45, 24: 34, 37, 38, 45; 46, 6: 34, 44 f., 48; 46, 21: 10 f.
Agrippinenses: 303.
Albis: 318.
†*Albriniam:* 105 f., 284.
Alci (?): 319.
Alcuin: 28, 29.
Alpes: 272.
Alphonso V of Aragon: 353, 355.
Ammianus Marcellinus, manuscripts of: 4, 7, 27 f., 61, 65.
anacoluthon: 322.

380

anastrophe of *ut* and *nc:* 282.
Andreas, Ioannes, *Novella* and *Additiones:* 2.
Anglii: 317.
Anglo-Saxon minuscule: 64 f.
Angriuarii: 308, 309.
Annales, the, codex Mediceus I of: 26, 66–69, 71 f., 73, 143[1], 334; codex Mediceus II of: 73, 143[1], 334; fifteenth-century manuscripts of: 81, 85, 88; manuscript of, in Fulda in ninth century: 1[1].
Annales Fuldenses: 1[1].
antithesis: 279, 306, 315, 322.
Apicius, manuscripts of: 79[1], 84, 352 f., 354.
Arauisci: 303 *bis.*
Arbon: 105.
Aretino, Francesco: manuscripts of Latin translation of *Letters* of pseudo-Diogenes: 79, 84, 86, 89; *id.* of *Letters* of pseudo-Phalaris: 86, 89.
Arsaces: 312.
Asciburgium: 277.
Asia: 273.
['Ασκιπύργιον]: 277.
assimilation as source of corruption in manuscripts: 49, 315.
asymmetry in Tacitus: 276, 297.
asyndeton: 286 f., 302.
Auiones: 317.
Aurelius, v. Scaurus.
Aurelius Victor, pseudo-, *de Viris Illustribus:* 356.
Aurinia: 284.
Aurispa, Giovanni: 352 f.
auspices among the Germans: 286 f.
aut, for *et* or *ac:* 279; connecting singular subjects of plural verb: 289.

barditus: 276.
barritus: 276.
Bastarnae: 323.
Batauii: 304 *bis.*
beard, allowed to grow as badge of ignominy: 307.
Beccadelli, v. Panormita.
beer: 299.
Beneventan minuscule: 63 f.
Benevenutus de Imola, *Epitome,* manuscript of: 87.
†*bistonem:* 96.
Blondus, Flavius, manuscript of: 89.
Boihaemum: 302.
Boii: 302, 318.
Bonifatius, Abbot of Fulda: 64.
Bracciolini, v. Poggio.

Brandt, Sebastian, *Epithalamium,* manuscript of: 88.
Britannica (*lingua*): 322.
Bructeri: 308 *bis.*
Brutus, pseudo-, manuscript of Latin translation of *Letters:* 86.
Buri: 318 *bis.*

Caecilius Metellus (C.): 312.
Caepio, v. Seruilius.
caerulus: 278.
Caesar (Augustus): 313; **C. Caesar** (Caligula): 313; v. Iulius.
Caesar, C. Iulius: 307.
Campanus, Io. Ant., *de Laudibus Scientiarum,* manuscript of: 87.
Candidus, v. Decembrio.
capital letters: 19 and note 2, 23, 24, 26, 73, 268, 305.
Carbo, v. Papirius.
Carolingian minuscule: 63; in codex Aesinas: 15–24.
Cassius (Longinus, L.): 313.
Castor: 319.
cavalry manœuvres: 281 f.
Censorinus, *de Die Natali,* manuscript of: 81.
centeni: 281 (cf. 289).
Cento Probae, manuscript of: 80.
Chamaui: 308, 309.
Chasuarii: 309.
Chatti: 304, 305 *bis,* 306 *bis,* 307, 308 *bis,* 311 *bis,* 312, 314.
Chauci: 310, 311 *bis.*
Cherusci: 311, 312 *bis.*
Cicero, manuscripts of: 4, 6, 7 f., 25, 62, 78[1].
Cimbri: 312 *bis.*
Ciuilis, Iulius: 307.
claudere, cludere: 238 f.
climate, influence of, on temperament: 304 f.
color purus: 293.
concentus: 276.
comitatus: 289 f.
conditor gentis: 273.
conflation, of text: 35; of variants: 129, 135 f., 194 and note 4; v. contamination.
confusion, of letters, in Hersfeld *Agricola:* 51–60; in *Germania* manuscripts: 98, 102, 107, 109, 110, 111, 125, 127, 132, 134, 136 f., 151 f., 159, 197 f., 222, 285, 325; in codex Mediceus I: 67 f., 71 f.; in codex Mediceus II: 73; of words, in Hersfeld *Agricola:* 49; in *Germania*

manuscripts: 127–129; v. phonetic confusion.
coniuncto orbe: 281 f.
conjectural emendation, in Hersfeld codex: 36–38; in minor Tacitean works: 52 and note 3: in *Germania* manuscripts: 121, 173, 206, 221, 232; v. correction, interpolation.
consonants, confusion of: 245–255.
consulere, used impersonally in the passive: 285 f.
contamination, in *Germania* manuscripts: 91 f., 122, 144, 149, 150, 176 f., 186 f., 190, 208; v. conflation.
contradiction, in *Germania*: 279, 303, 309; of Tacitus with Caesar: 291.
Corbie ab-script: 69[1].
corrections, in Hersfeld codex: 31 f., 35–40, 47[1], 57 f.; in *Germania* manuscripts: 103, 114, 121, 131, 140 f., 144, 146, 156, 180, 182 f., 184 f., 187, 194, 197, 202, 205, 221 f., 313, 314; v. contamination, interpolation.
correctors, in Hersfeld codex: 31 f.; fifteenth-century in Hersfeld *Germania*: 103, 150 f.
corruptions, sources of, in Hersfeld codex: 45–56; in majuscule manuscripts of Vergil: 58 ff.; in codex Mediceus I: 67 f.; in codex Mediceus II: 73; in eighth- and ninth-century manuscripts: 62 f.; common to all manuscripts of the *Germania*: 90; perpetuated as variants: 35–40, 74 f.; same corruptions occurring independently in different manuscripts: 93, 121, 140, 142, 145, 149, 152, 156, 159–162, 174 f., 192 f., 197, 205; secondary stages of: 48, 50, 97, 131, 157 f.; v. abbreviations, confusion, doublets, orthography, and, in general, Hersfeld codex, manuscripts of the *Germania*.
Corvey, monastery of: 66.
Cotini: 318 *ter*.
Crassus (M. Licinius): 312.
cursive script, elements of, in codex Aesinas with parallels from other manuscripts: 20, 21, 25, 29; majuscule in transmission of text of Tacitus: 59, 60[2], 73.

Daci: 272.
Danuuius: 272 *bis*, 305, 317, 318.
dative for genitive: 293.
Decembrio, Pier Candido, note of, regarding the Hersfeld codex: 8–14, 17, 20; *Epitome*, manuscript of: 87.

decumathes agri: 305.
deletion in Hersfeld codex: 32; symbols of: 32[1], 39, 41[1].
describere: 300.
Dialogus, the, discovery of: 3, 7, 9; inscription of: 10, 12; subscription of: 12; lacuna in ch. 35: 13 f., 76, 153; manuscripts of: 10, 11, 13[6], 81 *bis*, 83, 84, 85 *bis*, 88 *bis*, 89, 153, 190[1,5], 206[2].
Dictys Cretensis: *Bellum Troianum*, in codex Aesinas: 15 f., 18 f., 20, 26[5,8] 31[5].
dignatio principis: 289 f.
Diogenes, pseudo-, manuscripts of Latin translation of *Letters*: 79 and note, 84, 86, 89.
dittography: 48, 285, 314; v. repetition.
Diuus Iulius: 302, 313.
Domitian: 313.
doublets, in Hersfeld *Agricola*, tabulation of: 32–34; origins of: 34–40, 50 f.; relative antiquity of: 40–45; creation of, by scribe or corrector: 38 f.; in *Germania* manuscripts: 75, 96–99, 119 f., 121–141, 144, 153 f., 173, 182, 194, 206[2], 222 f., 224, 232, 235, 282, 285, 298; approximate number of, in Hersfeld *Germania*: 137[1]; v. variants.
Drusus: 313; **Drusus Germanicus**: 309.
†*dulcubuni*: 131.
Dulgubini: 309.
durare: 306.

ebrietas: 299.
ebriositas: 299.
Einhart: 1[1], 28.
ellipsis: 274, 286 f., 321.
emendation, v. corrections, interpolation.
enclitics, separation of: 261 f.
Enoch of Ascoli: 8[1], 340, 341, 345, 351–356.
Ephrem Syrus, *Sermo in Ioseph*, manuscript of: 27.
errors, v. corruptions.
est audiri: 283.
et, meaning "even": 276.
et iam for *etiam*: 147, 262.
etiam for *sed*: 287.
et ipse with ablative absolute: 103.
ethnographic literature, Greek, phraseology of, followed in *Germania*: 278, 293, 299.
†*ctionas*: 137.
Eudoses: 317.

exigere ab aliqua re: 291.

Facius, Bartholomeus: 351.
fecundus in: 279.
Fenni: 323, 325 *bis.*
figere domos: 325.
Florus, *Epitome,* manuscript of: 87.
folia: 13.
Fosi: 312.
French minuscule in codex Aesinas: 26, 28, 29.
Frisi: 309 *bis,* 311.
Frontinus, *de Aquaeductu,* manuscripts of: 2, 3, 6, 27[4], 80.
Fulda, monastery of: 1[1], 25, 27–29, 61, 64–66, 73; scripts of: 29, 65; library catalogue of: 29; chartulary of: 65[3].

Galli: 272, 275, 302 *bis,* 303, 305.
Gallia: 313; **Galliae:** 279, 302, 312, 313.
Gallica, *gens:* 302; *lingua:* 318.
Gambriuii: 274.
Gaza, Teodoro: 353.
genitive, in *-ii:* 242; plural in *-ium:* 126, 244; objective: 322.
gens: 275.
German, scribe in codex Mediceus I: 26; scriptoria, v. Fulda, Hersfeld, Lorsch, Raetian minuscule.
Germani: 271, 272, 275, 276, 292, 302, 303 *bis,* 305, 306, 312, 313, 314, 317, 318, 320, 321, 322, 323, 324, 325.
Germania: 272, 273, 274, 277 *ter,* 279, 302 *bis,* 303, 305 *bis,* 312 *bis,* 314, 317, 318.
Germania, the, discovery of: 3, 7, 8; inscription of 10 f., 202, 267[3], 271; extant manuscripts of (v. manuscripts of the *Germania* for analysis): 79–268; lost manuscripts of: 79[1], 91 f., 148 f., 157 f., 162 ff., 173, 177, 180, 183, 187, 190, 201, 203, 208, 211, 225, 228, 233, 327, 328; editions of: 79[1], 83, 89, 202, 209–211, 327–350, bibliography; survey of textual criticism of, since the invention of printing: 327–350.
Germanica origo: 303.
Germanicus: 313; v. Drusus Germanicus.
Germanicus: 309 f.
Giasone del Maino, *Epithalamium,* manuscript of: 88.
glosses: 35, 127, 149, 235; v. marginal entries.
Gothones: 320.
Gozbert, Abbot of Hersfeld: 26.

Graecae litterae: 277.
graphical errors, defined: 51; v. confusion of letters, abbreviations.
Grimald, Abbot of St. Gall: 27.
Guarino of Verona: 2 f., 12.
Guarnieri, Stefano: 15, 18.

Haemste, Hugo: 89.
hair, kept long as mark of disgrace, or as perpetual vow: 307.
hairdress among the Germans: 314 f.
half-uncial script: 61–63.
†*haliosnas:* 135 f.
Harii: 319 *bis.*
haud minus facile: 299.
haud proinde: 279 f.
Hellusii: 325.
Heluecones: 319.
Heluetii: 302.
Helysii: 319.
Hercules: 276, 284, 309, 310; Herculis columnae: 309.
Hercynius saltus: 305 *bis;* **Hercynia silua:** 302.
Herminones: 273.
Hermunduri: 317, 318 *bis.*
†*herquinius:* 97 f.
Hersfeld, monastery and library of: 1, 6, 26–28; anonymous monk of: 2–5, 7, 12.
Hersfeld codex, the, of minor Tacitean works and Suetonius, *de Grammaticis et Rhetoribus,* correspondence concerning: 1–5; described in *Commentarium* of Niccolò Niccoli: 5 f.; brought to Rome: 8; described in note of Decembrio: 8 f.; comparison of descriptions by Niccolò and Decembrio: 10–14; fragment of, preserved in codex Aesinas (*q.v.*): 15–20; separation of *Agricola* from rest of the manuscript: 206[2]; restoration of gatherings: 18 f.; dating of: 24–28; script of: 21, 22–24, 26, 145; script of, compared with other manuscripts: 24–27, 29; provenience of: 24–30; correctors in: 31 f.; doublets in, v. doublets; sources of corruption in: 45–56, 236–260; errors in, compared with those of codex Mediceus I: 68; errors made in transcription distinguished from earlier errors: 57–60; archetype of, in minuscule script: 57–60; date of archetype: 61–63; investigation as to character of minuscule script in archetype: 60–73; more remote ancestry of: 35, 60, 73–78; v. abbreviations, capital letters, enclitics,

manuscripts of the *Germania*, orthography, paragraphing, prefixes, punctuation, reference-symbols, *scriptura continua*, stichometry.
hiatus: 277.
hic, in vivid descriptions: 276; to mark a contrast: 323 f.
Hieronymus, Sanctus: 351.
Hinderbach, Johann: 89, 156 f.
Hispaniae: 312.
Historiae, the, manuscripts of: 73, 81, 85, 88, 143[1], 334.
Hrabanus Maurus: 27, 28, 29.
Hyginus, *de Astris*, manuscript of: 86.
hypallage: 281.

imperii fata: 308 f.
indicative with *si* = ἐάν: 286.
indulgere: 299.
infinitive, historical or descriptive: 283.
Ingaeuones: 273.
inscientia for *inscitia*: 10, 12.
Insular minuscule: 21, 29, 63, 64–67.
interpolation, in Hersfeld *Agricola*: 31, 37 f., 50; in *Germania* manuscripts: 103, 105 f., 108, 112, 119, 121, 123, 126, 133 f., 136 f., 146, 151, 155, 172 f., 192 f., 222, 228, 233, 316; v. corrections.
inuento nomine: 275.
Iosephus, *de Bello Iudaico*, manuscript of: 85.
-is, final, becoming *e*: 239.
Isis: 284.
Istaeuones: 273.
Italia: 273, 313.
Itinerarium Antonini: 352 f.
Iulius, Diuus: 302, 313.
iuuenis, contrasted with *adulescentulus*: 289 f.

lucus: 293.
Laërtes: 277.
Lamola, Giovanni: 2[2].
Lampert of Hersfeld: 26.
Langobardi: 316.
Lemonii: 320.
liburna: 285.
ligatures, in codex Aesinas: 20–23; in Hersfeld *Agricola*: 75 f., 358; in Raetian minuscule: 72.
lineamenta colorum: 292 f.
Liuius, manuscript of: 4, 7 f.
Lorsch, manuscript from: 66[2].
Lucianus, manuscript of Latin translations from: 80.
Lugii: 319, 320.
Luigi da Spoleto: 6.

Lupus of Ferrières: 24 f., 29.

majuscule script: 58 f., 60, 68, 71, 73: v. capital letters.
Mallius, Cn.: 313.
Manilius IV, 595 ff. discussed: 310.
Manimi: 319.
Mannus: 273 *bis*.
manuscripts of the *Germania*, description of: 79–90; division of, into X and Y families: 91–93; division of Y family into groups αβφs: 91–93; readings of X contrasted with those of Y: 93–101; partial agreement with X of all groups of Y: 101–104; agreement of Xs against αβφ: 104–108; agreement of Xφ against αβs: 108–109; agreement of Xα against βφs: 109–110; agreement of Xβ against αφs: 110–112; agreement of Xφs against αβ: 112–114; agreement of Xαφ against βs: 114–115; agreement of Xαs against βφ: 115–116; agreement of Xβs against αφ: 116–117; agreement of Xβφ against αs: 118; agreement of Xαβ against φs: 118–119; conclusions: 119–121; line of demarcation between X and Y families broken because of doublets in Hersfeld codex: 121–137; because of other possible reasons: 138–141; probable number of doublets in Hersfeld codex: 137[1]; agreement of Wm against hY: 141–144; agreement of Wh against mY: 144–146; agreement of hm against WY: 146; agreement of Ws[2] against mhY: 146–147; agreement of ms[2] against WhY: 147–148; agreement of hs[2] against WmY: 148–149; relationship of h and s[2]: 148 f.; sources of s[2]: 148 f.; agreement of Wσ against mhY: 150–151; agreement of mσ against WhY: 152; relationship of σ and m: 152; codex W: 153–157; excellence of W: 153–155; W a direct copy of X: 155; stichometry of X as indicated by omissions in W: 155; W not the ancestor of hm: 155; agreement of W with scattered members of the Y family: 155 f.; second hand in W: 156 f.; codex m: 157–162; m not a direct copy of X: 157 f.; possible reminiscences of *scriptura continua* in m: 159, 260 f.; agreement of m with isolated manuscripts of the Y family: 159–162; relationship of m to s: 162; codex h: 162–177; restoration of h from extant collations: 162–

172; technical procedure of Longolius in making his collation: 163–165; correction of errors in Wünsch's report of Longolius' collation: 165–166; tabulation of discrepancies between collations of Longolius and Selling with restoration of readings of h: 166–171; statement of procedure in reporting readings of h: 171 f.; errors in h: 172 f.; h perhaps not a direct copy of X: 173; second hand in h: 173 f.; agreement of h with manuscripts of the Y family: 174 f.; possible contamination between h and α: 175–177; the α group: 177–190; difficulty of restoring α because of contamination: 177; tabulation of readings of α: 177–180; the ξ branch: 180–182; peculiar readings of α and ξ of little importance: 182 f.; the χ branch: 183–186; corrections and interpolations in t: 184 f.; f a copy of w: 185 f.; contamination in pM from τ: 186 f.; the σ branch: 187–190; contamination of σ from X: 91 f., 93, 187; tabulation of readings of σ: 188 f.; peculiar readings of σ of no importance: 189 f.; the β group: 190–211; tabulation of readings of β: 191–193; merit of β: 193 f.; relationship of V and L: 194–203; archetype of VL not a direct copy of Hersfeld codex: 201 f.; worth of V and L: 202 f.; the τ branch: 203–209; tabulation of readings of τ: 203–205; peculiar readings of τ of no merit: 205; T a copy of E: 206–208; importance of E and d in preserving doublets: 206[2]; refutation of Annibaldi's belief that E was a direct copy of the Hersfeld codex: 206[2]; relationship of r and o: 208 f.; contamination in r from φ: 208; codex Monacensis 947 a copy of k: 209; relationship of Vienna edition of 1500 to β groups: 209–211; the φ group: 211–233; tabulation of readings of φ: 212–221; character of errors in φ: 221 f.; importance of φ group: 222 f.; the manuscripts ba: 223 f.; the π branch: 225–228; the manuscript l: 228; the ψ branch: 229–232; the manuscripts e, u, and z: 232; relationship of Ac: 233; the manuscript s: 233–235; twofold character of readings in s: 233 f.; true character of s: 235; orthography: 235–260; vowels: 236–245; consonants: 245–255; prefixes: 255–260; traces of *scriptura continua:* 260–262; punctuation: 262–264; paragraphing: 264–268; capitalization: 268.

Marcomani: 318 *quater.*
marginal entries: 21, 34 f., 149, 156, 164, 187, 298; v. doublets.
Marius, C.: 313.
Maroboduus: 318.
marriage: 295 f.
Mars: 284.
Marsi: 274.
Marsigni: 318 *bis.*
Maschius, Ranerius: 87.
Mater deum: 322.
Mattiaci: 304.
de' Medici, Carlo and Giovanni: 353 f.
Meigenhart: 1[1].
Mela, v. Pomponius.
memorant: 99[3].
Mercurius: 284.
meretrix: 295.
Merovingian minuscule: 63 f.
Metellus, v. Caecilius.
minuscule script, in archetype of Hersfeld codex: 58 f.; v. Beneventan, Carolingian, Corbie ab-script, French, half-uncial, Insular, Merovingian, north-Italian, Raetian, Visigothic.
Mirabilia Vrbis, manuscript of: 86.
Moenus: 302.
de Mure, Conrad, *Fabularius,* manuscript of: 88.

Nahanaruali: 319 *bis.*
nam, marking transition to new idea: 307.
Naristi: 318 *bis.*
natio: 275.
natura: 321 f.
Nemetes: 303.
neque, connecting singular subjects of plural verb: 289.
Nero: 313.
Nerthus: 317.
Neruii: 303.
Niccoli, Niccolò, letters to from Poggio: 2–5; *Commentarium* of: 9–14, 27[4], 30[1].
Nicholas V, Pope, v. Parentucelli.
nisi si: 272 f.
nomen: 311 f.
Noricum: 279.
north-Italian minuscule: 69.
Nuithones: 317.
Numagen, Petrus: 88.

Nypsus, M. Iunius, *de Mensuris*, manuscript of: 81.

ob metum: 275.
Occidens: 322.
Oceanus: 272 *ter*, 273, 277, 293, 309 *ter*, 312, 317, 320 *bis*, 321.
omission, in Hersfeld *Agricola:* 47 f., 52[4]; in antecedent of Hersfeld codex: 74; in *Germania* manuscripts: 123, 127-129, 132 ff., 137, 159, 302, 306 f., 316, 322.
opiniones = opinio: 277.
orbis: 281.
Oriens: 313, 322.
origo gentis: 273.
ornator: 109, 314.
de Orthographia et Figuris, manuscript of: 86.
orthographical, revision of text in antiquity: 251[3], 256; variants: 37 f., 97 f., 123.
orthography, in Hersfeld *Agricola:* 32; in Germania manuscripts: 82, 100, 108, 110, 112, 122, 124, 143, 145, 147, 154, 158, 162, 202, 224, 235[4]; in Hersfeld *Agricola* and *Germania* manuscripts compared: 235-260; in oldest Latin manuscripts: 32; of tribal names: 273, 304.
Osi: 303 *bis*, 318 *bis*.
otiosae manus: 321.
Oxiones: 325.

Pacorus: 313.
pagella: 13 f.
pagina: 13 f.
Pannonia: 279, 303.
Pannonica (*lingua*): 318.
Pannonii: 272.
Panormita (Antonio Beccadelli): 2, 7, 12, 20, 352 f.
Papirius Carbo (Cn.): 312, 313.
paragraphs, division of text into: 82, 194, 202, 264-268.
parare: 306.
παρενθήκη: 276.
parenthetical insertions: 274, 321, 323 f.
Parentucelli, Tomasso (Pope Nicholas V): 6 and note 2, 352.
parere: 294.
Parthi: 293, 312.
Paulus Diaconus, *Historia Miscella*, manuscript of: 27.
peditum pernicitas: 325.
peragere frontem: 318.
περικειρομένη: 295.
perinde: 143, 279.

Persius, manuscript of anonymous commentary on: 83.
Petrus Lombardus, *Compendium*, manuscript of: 85.
Peucini: 323 *bis*, 325.
†*peucurorum:* 137.
Phalaris, pseudo-, manuscript of Latin translation of *Letters:* 86.
phonetic confusion: 32, 51, 53 and note 4, 96 f., 100 f., 102, 106[2], 107, 117, 122, 124, 129 ff., 135, 145, 147, 285, 294, 311, 313, v. orthography.
Plinius, *Epistulae*, manuscript of: 87; pseudo-, *de Viris Illustribus*, manuscript of: 81.
plural verb with singular subjects connected by *aut, neque,* or *uel:* 289.
plures = complures: 272.
plurimum = plurimorum: 311.
Poeni: 312.
Poggio Bracciolini, correspondence regarding the Hersfeld codex: 2-5.
Polenton, Sicco: 352, 355.
Pollux: 319.
Pomponius Laetus: 39[1].
Pomponius Mela, manuscripts of: 80 *bis*, 86; I, 56, III, 1, discussed: 310 f.
de Ponderibus, manuscript of: 81.
Pontanus, Iovianus: 84, 200, 203, 351 f., 355.
Ponticum mare: 272.
Porphyrio, *in Horatium*, manuscripts of: 83, 353 f., 354.
praestare aliquid in aliqua re: 308.
praetractare: 150 f., 287.
prefixes, orthography of: 255-260; separation of: 157, 261 f.
de Primis Italiae Regibus, manuscript of: 85.
primum = primo: 282.
principes: 286 f., 289 f., 314 f.
probatio ciuitatis: 289 f.
proceres: 324 f.
proinde = perinde: 279.
promiscus: 143[1].
proper names, in Hersfeld *Agricola:* 34, 268; genitive of in *-ii:* 242.
propior a: 143.
prosthetic *i:* 107, 244.
prostitution: 295.
Pruteni: 119.
Ptolemaeus, *Geographia*, manuscript of: 80.
punctuation: 82, 262-264, 298 f., 305 f.

Quadi: 318 *quinquies*.
quaternion-signature in ancestor of Hersfeld codex: 76 f.
-que written *que:* 261 f.

quire-signatures in oldest Latin manuscripts: 77[2].
quoque: 280.

Raeti: 272.
Raetia: 277, 317.
Raetian minuscule: 69–73.
Raeticae Alpes: 272.
redundance: 278.
redire: 310 f.
reference-symbols: 43–45, 60.
relinquere in medium: 326.
Remmius Palaemon: 299.
repetition, errors due to in Hersfeld *Agricola:* 48, 75; in *Germania* manuscripts: 107 f., 113 f., 143[7], 297, 308, 313, 319
Reudigni: 317.
Rhenus: 272 *bis*, 274, 277, 302, 303, 304 *ter*, 305, 308, 309, 317.
ring, iron, as badge of ignominy: 307.
Rinuccio da Castiglione, Latin translation of *Letters* of pseudo-Brutus, manuscript of: 86.
Romani: 317.
Romanus: 303, 304 *bis*, 306, 308, 309, 313, 318, 319.
Romanus: abbreviation of: 113.
Romulus: 273.
Rudolph of Fulda, *Translatio Sancti Alexandri:* 1[1], 278, 285–287.
Rufinus, Q. Aradius, *Letter* of Septimius to: 15.
Rufus, de Prouinciis: manuscript of: 80 f.
Rufus, Sex., *Breuiarium*, manuscript of: 87.
Rugii: 320.

sacerdotes: 286 f.
Sallustius, *Catilina* and *Iugurtha*, manuscript of: 80.
Samnis: 312.
Sarmatae: 272, 293, 318, 323, 325 *bis*.
Saxons: 307.
Scaurus Aurelius: 313.
scriptura continua: 24, 31, 46 f., 52, 63, 114, 135, 147, 159, 260 f.
Semnones: 315, 316.
Seneca, *Apocolocyntosis*, manuscript of: 81.
sequi manu uel pectine: 314.
Septimius, *Letter* to Q. Aradius Rufinus: 15.
seruatur = cauetur: 301.
Seruilius Caepio: 313.
signare memoriam: 302 f.
significare: 303.
siquidem, postpositive: 305.

Sitones: 323.
slaves: 300.
sordes: 324.
spectaculum: 308 f.
Speculum (Guillaume Durand): 2.
stato tempore, distinguished from *statuto tempore:* 315.
stemma codicum: plate at end of volume.
Stephanus, Iohannes, Latin translation of philosophical sayings, manuscript of: 86.
stichometry, in Hersfeld codex: 78[2]; in ancestor of Hersfeld codex: 74–78; in *Germania* manuscripts: 155, 158, 205, 224[1], 233[1].
Suardones: 317.
†*suarines:* 134.
subject of verb changing in closely correlated clauses: 279, 320.
subjunctive, in relative clauses of fact: 277; potential: 296.
substitution of words: 50.
Suebi: 274, 284, 314 *sexies*, 315, 316, 317, 318, 322.
Suebia: 319, 323.
Suebicum mare: 322.
Suetonius, *de Viris Illustribus:* 351 f., (pseudo-) 354 ff.; *de Grammaticis et Rhetoribus*, discovery of: 3, 7, 9; manuscripts of: 81, 83, 85 *bis*, 88, 89, 153, 190, 206[2]; passages cited, inscription: 3, 7, 9; 1, 1: 11 f.; 4, 3: 38[2], 54; 10: 37; 13: 37; 14, 2: 58[3]; 22: 35[1]; 24, 2: 56.
Suiones: 320, 321, 323.

Tacitus, Cornelius: 271.
Tacitus, knowledge of, in antiquity and the Middle Ages: 1[1]; sources: 278, 293, 299, 303; works, v. under separate titles.
tamquam, restrictive: 278; repeated: 296.
temere: 285.
Tencteri: 308, *quater*, 314.
tenent: corruption of *temere*(?): 285.
Terra Mater: 317.
Tiberius: 309 f.
Tours, Abbey of St. Martin: 28 f.; script of: 25 f.
Traianus: 312.
Tractates on the Holy Land, manuscript of: 85.
Transrhenani: 275.
Traversari, Ambrogio: 5.
Treueri: 303.
Triboci: 303.
Tuder (or **Tudrus?**): 318.

Tuisto: 273.
Tungri: 275.

Vbii: 303.
Vlixes: 277 *bis*.
"ultimate" group of manuscripts: 92, 201 f.
uncial script: 19[3], 26, 48[5], 73.
uniuersi = *toti*: 301.
Vsipi: 308.
ut = *ut par est*: 315.

Vandilii: 274.
Vangiones: 303.
variants, marginal, misplaced: 41, 42, 75, 98 f., 134, 135 f., 235; orthographical: 37 f., 97 f.; unexpected appearance of: 135, 136; v. doublets.
-*ue*: 278 f.
uel, connecting singular subjects of plural verb: 289.

Veleda: 284.
Venethi: 323, 325.
Ventidius (Bassus): 313.
Vergilius, majuscule manuscripts of: 58 f.; *Geor.* III, 351, discussed: 310.
Vespasianus: 284.
uicus: 301.
Visigothic minuscule: 63 f.
uocati sint distinguished from *uocati fuerint*: 275.
vowels, confusion of: 236–245.
vows, perpetual: 307.

Wimpheling, Jacob, *Distichum*, manuscript of: 88.
wine: 299.
Winithar, script of: 71[7,9], 72 and note 6.
word-separation, v. *scriptura continua*.